TO THE VICTOR GO THE MYTHS & MONUMENTS

© Copyright 2016 by Arthur R. Thompson
All rights reserved

Published by American Opinion Foundation Publishing
750 N. Hickory Farm Lane
Appleton, WI 54914

Cover Design by Joseph W. Kelly

Library of Congress Catalog Card Number: 2016939793

Hard Cover:
ISBN 978-1-936698-01-1

Hard Cover, Deluxe, Special Edition:
ISBN 978-1-936698-02-8

Paperback:
ISBN 978-1-936698-03-5

Printed and Manufactured in the United States of America

TO THE VICTOR GO THE MYTHS & MONUMENTS

The History of the First 100 Years of the War Against God and the Constitution, 1776 - 1876, and Its Modern Impact

by
Arthur R. Thompson

The most effective way to destroy people is to deny and obliterate their own understanding of their history.
— *George Orwell, author of 1984 and Animal Farm*

To be ignorant of what occurred before you were born is to remain always a child.
— *Cicero*

Table of Contents

A Message From the Author..ix
Introduction..xix
Chapter 1, Background..1
Chapter 2, Control of History and Thought..............................39
Chapter 3, Subversion and Treason in the Early Years............57
Chapter 4, The Jefferson Years..101
Chapter 5, War and Jackson..109
Chapter 6, The Rise of "Two" Conspiracies............................117
Chapter 7, Communes...149
Chapter 8, 1830 — 1865: An Overview...................................163
Chapter 9, The Use of Many Fronts.......................................179
Chapter 10, Neo-Radicals..215
Chapter 11, Republican Party Origins...................................235
Chapter 12, Slavery...257
Chapter 13, War..305
Chapter 14, Assassination..369
Chapter 15, Reconstruction..389
Chapter 16, Postwar Leftists...397
Chapter 17, Post Mortem..423
Chapter 19, The Future, Where Do We Go From Here?.........447
Appendix One:...457
Appendix Two:...459
Bibliography...463

About The Author

Arthur R. Thompson was born in Seattle, Washington, in 1938. He attended the University of Washington, the Washington Military Academy, and several art and design schools. Eventually, he served as an officer in the Select Reserve Force of the Army and National Guard. He worked for Boeing for several years, then published an intelligence newsletter after he worked in tandem with the Police Intelligence Squad in his metropolitan area, where he helped stop planned riots in the inner cities by communist groups. He helped the police infiltrate area communist organizations and learned their strategies and tactics.

From 1982 until 1995, he created and led small manufacturing businesses, which took him all over the United States and Western Europe. He also went to Europe on a political fact-finding tour for The John Birch Society in 1989, at which time he witnessed the Berlin Wall coming down and became acquainted with many businessmen, academics, and members of the German Cabinet and the European Community, which became the European Union.

Mr. Thompson has also served on his small town's city council, was the chairman of his local Chamber of Commerce, worked as an official and an elector for the Republican Party, and was a local leader in the State of Washington for the Christian Coalition.

Most of the research for this volume was done in the period when he traveled the United States for his businesses, visiting libraries all over the country.

Before and after his years in manufacturing, he served on the staff of The John Birch Society, and he has been the organization's CEO since 2005. He is also the author of International Merger by Foreign Entanglements (2014). His children reside in the Pacific Northwest, while he resides in Appleton, Wisconsin, with his wife, Joanne.

Other works by the author:
The Soviet of Washington, 1969
The Terror Triangle, 2011
International Merger by Foreign Entanglements, 2014

In order to release this work as soon as possible, the author decided not to wait for a year to have it read like a flowing novel. It reads more like a book of facts.

The facts are not footnoted. In this day and age, if in doubt or you desire more elaboration, you can surf the Internet to discover 95% of the facts for yourself. Plus, *the author wants the doubting reader to look into matters for himself and to fully explore history*. Being skeptical is a good beginning.

This is more of a narrative than a book. It will be repetitive from time to time to remind the reader of the background of certain personalities who were involved in various movements over a period of decades.

This book is dedicated to everyone, just so I do not leave anyone out; however, I want to make a special dedication to my wife, Joanne, who was instrumental in making sure that I finished the project. If you are inclined to thank anyone for the book, should you desire to do so after reading it, she is the one to thank.

A special thank you goes to George and Nancy Wallace of Oklahoma and the Curry Family Foundation who made this project possible.

Please read the following "Message" and "Introduction" before tackling the body of this tome for a complete understanding of the historical context — and to recognize where the author stands. *It is wise to understand the thinking of an author before reading his chronicle of history*.

A Message From the Author

The only difference between reality and fiction is that fiction needs to be credible.

— Mark Twain

History has always been alive to me. I have never read history without mentally placing myself at the events. Consequently, I love reading history and it can be much better than a novel since it really happened; it is not fantasy.

Or, so I thought.

By junior high school (middle school to the younger set) I realized history books do not always contain the entire story, and this can happen due to space constraints, or the ignorance of the author of certain related facts.

Then after reading several books on the same subject I began to see that the facts sometimes were contradictory; one author would say one thing, someone else another.

From this point, it was not a huge leap to realize that "history" may be distorted by an author to serve the author's bias, or agenda, by deliberate omission to hide facts, even to the point of creating "fact." After a time, I grew to realize that the author may be serving a larger agenda. And, if many authors were doing the same, it became obvious that it was an organized agenda, not just one's individual agenda.

This problem shows up particularly when reviewing history books intended as texts for schools, as opposed to those written for reading outside the field of structured education. Books written and published by small, independent publishing houses that are not connected to establishment-influenced firms tend to be less of a problem relative to an organized worldview, but can be a problem due to bias.

A major difficulty with the ability to make decisions is having all the facts. Even the most logical thinker can reach the wrong conclusion if he does not have sufficient knowledge of all the facts dealing with that decision.

Political decisions are made by the American people, since we are a free country, and what decisions we make can be manifested at the polls and affect our entire country. If the people do not have all of the facts, what then? This work attempts to bring many realities home to the reader to enable him to begin to see what has been happening for some time and to realize that the process has been accelerating during his lifetime.

The forces at play two hundred years ago are the same that are involved today. We attempt to show this throughout the narrative and how the same tactics are in use today.

History is the tale of individuals and peoples. Everything human is driven physically by God and nature, but almost always by people. This is irrefutable fact. The point is that *people* think up, organize, and finance the issues, movements, agenda, plans, wars, etc. And the people responsible usually want the credit for doing so.

Unless it is for evil.

Evil men do not proclaim their intentions unless it is for the purpose of coercion or intimidation: terror, in other words. Often they will project a benevolent side to their terror. Even "Scar Face" Al Capone put up soup kitchens and other charities in Chicago to win the favor of the people and make it look as if he were really a benevolent person. All the while his Mafia committed murder, extortion, and a multitude of other crimes against these same people.

Malevolent politicians do the same.

There is nothing more evil than the lust for power. It goes well beyond the lust for money, sex, food, or any other lust — if for no other reason than the fact that with power all other lusts can be satisfied. Money is only useful up to a point, which we will demonstrate further on.

Adolf Hitler was not rich, nor were Mao Zedong, Josef Stalin, Napoleon, etc. They had all they wanted by first gaining power. Then they became uber rich, not only monetarily but in what money could not buy, but power could.

And that is what this book is all about: The early years of our country and how certain individuals, organized individuals, have tried to gain power. In turn, their organizations have served a higher power. There has been a master plan, with master planners, but they have not always agreed among themselves on strategy, leaders, timing, etc. They will almost always use any amoral means to accumulate their power — that is the one thing they do agree on — unless the risk of failure or exposure is too high — that is the only "morality" they see.

One must understand that just because radical, even moderate organizations may seem to be independent of one another does not mean that they are not controlled by a central source. It is much like a hand — the fingers can operate independently, but everything they do is in support of the hand. And, the fingers cannot operate without the support of the hand.

Likewise, just as with organizations controlled by the central source, not all of the fingers have the purpose and strength of other fingers of a hand. Certainly, the little finger does not have the attributes of the thumb, but no one thinks that the hand would be better off without it. The little finger serves as an example of the conservative organizations controlled by the central source and has the appearance of opposition to the rest of the hand. It augments the entire movement but is weaker than the other fingers, which represent important aspects that propel the Insider agenda forward.

In addition, the study of organizations that are of a social and/or political nature show that many of them have interlocking directorates, or at least a few key personnel who have links to other organizations. This ties them together into a generally common agenda. This is the aspect that most people cannot see, and is something that will become quite noticeable as you read through this work.

It was true in 1790, 1850, and it is true today. Any research into current political organizations will rapidly demonstrate an interlocking relationship by the personnel who serve in key positions or on their boards. In many cases, they belong to the same umbrella organizations, taking their direction from these. Without this research, most people never see the interrelationships and therefore the common thread that governs their actions.

A key to understanding political initiatives, regardless of the seeming impetus or diverse opinions involved, is to look at the results. The results are what was intended in the first place and provide the clues for who or what was behind the initiative to begin with. Linked to this is having enough experience to recognize the probable outcome by knowing the people involved and their history.

Some say that in order to know what is going on we should "follow the money." In so doing they recognize that the money source wants something for their funding. If the same entity or person is financing a multitude of people and/or organizations, then it is obvious that they probably want more out of the results than simple philanthropy. Also, if the same person or group finances a diverse number of politicians or organizations, it is highly likely that they want at least some of the same results from each entity they support.

A Message From the Author

People can understand this. Some never understand that control can be wielded by other means: coercion, blackmail, but especially the ability to deliver power to someone who lusts after it.

Often, it is simply the ability to deliver a better position, remuneration, or notoriety that will get a person to do another's bidding: a chair at a university, a seat on the board of directors, a platinum recording, a starring role, a political election — whatever it takes to enlist the individual into the agenda. The individual may not even realize the evil intended at the end of the road.

Most of the time the individuals will either be unaware of the ultimate outcome or have an education that will not allow them to see the big picture and be unable to connect the dots. Regrettably, almost all modern education does not teach a person how to think, but what to think; it goes well beyond political correctness.

One of the most dangerous of "what to think" is the idea that there are no conspiracies in politics. The history of man is composed of conspiracies to gain power; remember, men make things happen. This is no longer taught in the vast majority of public and private schools today. It was taught at the beginning of our country.

In fact, what is taught is that a belief in conspiracies is shallow thinking, and perhaps even paranoia. In 1776, it was taught as fact.

Morality is no longer taught with a Judeo-Christian base. On one hand, history is no longer seen from a viewpoint of groups of people making things happen, and on the other, the student is not armed with a morally based view that instills honor, integrity, and these types of heroes as role models. The history of true American heroes has been lost, as well as a pride of country and examples for the student to follow. These things have been replaced with political correctness and false heroes from the Left.

When two or more people plan in secret to effect an evil purpose, it is the definition of a conspiracy, whether you like the word or not.

Another way of demonstrating how a conspiracy works is like a Punch and Judy show. It is the same person operating both Punch and Judy behind the curtain. They are always fighting one another for the amusement of the audience, but the puppet master is always in control. The difference in real life is that the puppet master is directing real people and he cannot always control their actions since they have strong ambitions.

Another problem the puppet master has is that in real life the puppet may develop or redevelop a conscience.

You will see in this work how seemingly diverse organizations and individuals work toward the same ends even when they profess to be on opposite sides of an issue — just like Punch and Judy.

There is also the matter of using several different tactics. Just as an invading force uses different weaponry to serve different purposes, they all have the same goal of a successful invasion. And, they coordinate the use of those weapons to attain their goal. Each may launch from a different location, land at a different site, fire at a different target, but all with the same strategic end in mind.

This is also the case with the accumulation of power. The use of different issues and organizations may seem unrelated to the casual observer, when in fact they serve a master plan and are under a central control. This may even be hidden, and quite often is, from the general membership of the organizations in play. Lenin, the Russian communist leader, said that communism must be built by non-communist hands — dupes in other words. This has always been a tactic of anyone seeking power, to use the unsuspecting or simply the ignorant, to do their work for them.

Certainly this tactic is understood in warfare, where a commander uses different feints and ruses to get the enemy to react in a way that gives the commander the edge in battle. Or, his intelligence arm will use false flags and counterintelligence to hide the real objective, or simply to delay the engagement by his enemy's troops until it is too late. And, the "grunt" may not know the larger purpose of his unit's action and how he fits into the general battle strategy.

Probably the best known use of such tactics was played out with the invasion of Normandy on D-Day, 1944. Once the Germans woke up to the fact that they had delayed making important decisions based on false flags and ruses, the invasion was established.

Regrettably, the same is true of political movements that have in mind an accumulation of power over the people. And, one of the biggest hurdles most people have in combating an accumulation of power is that they usually do not see it until it is too late to do much about it — or *feel* that they cannot do much about it. Those who mean to rule go to great lengths to hide the fact that they are indeed evil — and vulnerable.

The two exceptions, where the accumulation of power was recognized widely in the United States, were at the beginning of the War for Independence and then again in the mid-20th century. There were organized efforts to bring out the fact that evil men intended to impose a draconian rule. Enough people recognized this in 18th-century America to bring about independence, but not enough people to completely stop it in the 20th century. The battle continues, and more are becoming aware.

As a result, more false flags and ruses are being played out against the American people than at any previous time in our history.

Power cannot be generated without many willing hands. It is not necessary that all understand the end in mind relative to how the power will be put to use. Indeed, most people who help others accumulate power end up regretting what they have done. In many cases, these people are the first to be eliminated once power is consolidated, since these are the people who have the potential to take out the newly installed dictatorship because they were involved in bringing it about in the first place.

The Reign of Terror in revolutionary France was as much about the elimination of competitors to a select group of revolutionaries under Maximilien Robespierre's leadership as it was the elimination of royalty and the clergy. The Night of the Long Knives in Germany was Hitler's way of eliminating the Nazi Brown Shirt leadership when they indicated that they would compete for power. Stalin's war on terrorists from the late 1920s into the 1930s was actually a tactic to eliminate his competition — there were no "terrorists." In more recent years, Saddam Hussein of Iraq didn't waste any time at all: he eliminated the inner core of the Ba'ath Party after they had helped him come to power in the first week.

In all of these cases, the competitors were the people who helped Robespierre's, Hitler's, Stalin's, and Saddam's inner circles come to power.

The organizations and people working for power here in America have existed for many generations. Their work has continued on through their children, protégés, and evolving movements. Some of these movements have not disappeared or morphed from their primary aims and structure over many generations. One obvious example would be the socialist movement and its end result, communism.

The movements that existed in the early 1800s — aside from religious sects — were socialism, the assault on Masonry, temperance, women's rights, health, the occult, abolition, Manifest Destiny, atheism, and the attack on property rights in general. In all of these, they had interlocking leadership.

By no means are these movements the only examples, for all types of issues, means, and organization have been used to accumulate power.

And this is the story you are about to read.

A Message From the Author

It is an unbelievable story because it flies in the face of everything you have been taught and learned in school — *any school.*

The reason for this is that one of the first seats of influence a conspiracy captures — and that is what we are dealing with here — is the information centers: publishing, libraries, media, academia, and so forth. Never forget this. The current exception, so far, is the Internet, albeit they are working diligently to control that as well using several tactics to do so, government control being only one of them.

Developments such as the initiative to make the Internet international are very dangerous to the future of information and free access to it. Yet the reasons given are to free up the Internet from American control. All international organizations are run by socialists or those who desire a one-world government. There are glaring examples already of facts that are twisted, omitted, and/or obfuscated on the Internet when it comes to historical personalities. If an international control were to be established, that control would be socialist at best since the majority of the countries that would be involved in this type of control are socialist.

It would set up a system of censorship far beyond what Americans, both liberal and conservatives, can even imagine today. It is hard to ferret out the facts in history today. It would make it nearly impossible tomorrow.

It would make the process of the *memory hole* in George Orwell's *1984* a reality — a centralized means to control education and thought based on facts that either no longer exist or have been changed to fit the internationalist agenda.

One way or another, this initiative would initially be sold under the United Nations auspices. What if a member of the Chinese communist government was put in charge, or a Russian, Iranian, Pakistani, radical Muslim, etc., or a committee stacked with such individuals? All in the name of fairness, balance, and diversity you understand. The initial stages of control by the UN might be hidden in the media reports trying to get support for such an initiative.

This being said, we are also aware of American-based attempts to limit the information highway, both in access and information.

We have also witnessed the purging of information as the result of too much exposure of a problem. The purging is done to prevent further exposure of what is behind various personalities or organizations. Most of the time it's done by the organizations themselves on their own websites, hiding information that would lead to the failure of their mission. Some information sites have eliminated facts that were well known at one time but suddenly seemed to vanish.

Another thing never to forget is that they will do all they can to capture the intellectual centers of their opposition. In many cases they will not be overt in changing what is disseminated, only creating a neutralizing effect on the followers of their opposition, to influence these people to do nothing, or something ineffective, preventing their success. This is generally manifested in false solutions.

You will see how a small group of intellectuals in New England and New York changed the conscience of America from a Judeo-Christian outlook to a Rational-based conscience, utilizing issues that were a problem for Christians, such as slavery, drunkenness, etc., and propelling our country toward war and empire.

Since the onset of our country, there has been a major initiative to start newspapers and magazines by what we would call the Left today. In the beginning the number of outlets was small, but over the years it has grown into a sizable number of like-minded people providing "news" to the public.

Over the entire history of this country we have seen an increasing consolidation of news sources toward putting them into the hands of one corporation or individual. It has not yet reached this level, but it has reached the point of liked-minded corporate heads controlling 90 percent or more of the news sources.

Today, a variety of news outlets are used to make it look diverse, but the central theme is never allowed to deviate from a narrow view or interpretation of the news. Even if it is "fair and balanced," half of the balance serves the Left.

On an international scale, this control of news is channeled through a few news services that supply copy or video for all the other outlets.

In other words, it does not take much today to ensure that the average citizen only hears what a few want them to hear and in a manner that does not threaten their agenda, except for the Internet — for now.

The well-known names that have been presenting the news to the people over the past few decades by and large belong to the same organizations that promote a world power structure, such as the Council on Foreign Relations (CFR) in the United States and related organizations in other countries.

One major change in the reporting of the news over several decades has been a steady move away from reporting to commentary, giving the view of the reporter (or owner) rather than strictly the news. Rarely does a lead story start with facts. It starts with some idea to tug at the heart of the reader as a setup for the bias of the writer or news service within the remainder of the story.

When you peruse our bibliography, you will discover that in many instances the references are printed by establishment publishing houses. There is not a single book that tells the entire story. Each book has a fact or series of facts contained in its pages which may not be in other books. Taking all the facts together and presenting them in a logical manner and in relationship to a larger picture, portrays a very different landscape than the view of "history" in our schools.

I am not an historian. I have just read a lot of books, the enclosed bibliography being only a portion, and spent a lot of time in library archives, coupled with a great deal of experience with "up close and personal" research of leftist organizations. What I am expert at is knowing the value of organization and that no major historical event happens by chance, that someone planned it that way. This gives one a completely different outlook when reading history. It leads to the right questions to ask. You cannot find the right answers unless you know the right questions. This is very true of the Internet. Most of the information is contained in the "cloud," but you have to know what you are looking for, or at least have some hint of it.

How can I recognize the value and results of organization? Simply because I have been active in organizations that make things happen in opposition to those you will be reading about and their agenda. Organization coupled with information is the key. The enemies of our country use it very well and fear anyone who does so in opposition — except our enemies use *dis*information.

At this point it is wise to quote Abraham Lincoln from his "House Divided" speech on June 16, 1858. As you will see further into this tome, he probably understood the concept better than most:

> (W)hen we see a lot of framed timbers, different portions of which we know have been gotten out at different times and places and by different workmen — Stephen, Franklin, Roger and James, for instance — and when we see these timbers joined together, and see they exactly make the frame of a house or mill, all the tenons and mortices exactly fitting, and all the length and proportions of the different pieces exactly adapted to their respective places, and not a single piece too many or too few — not omitting even scaffolding — or, if a single piece be lacking, we can see the place in the frame exactly fitted and prepared to yet bring such a piece in — in such a case, we find it impossible to not believe that Stephen and Franklin and Roger and James all understood

one another from the beginning, and all worked upon a common plan or draft drawn up before the first lick was struck.

The same concept has existed throughout history and prevails even today in initiatives to move the United States toward a socialist nation, yet the media and academia do all they can to sway people away from believing or understanding it. By not understanding it, that it is planned, and who is doing the planning and implementation, they cannot defeat it.

People make things happen. *Organized* people really make things happen. Collectivists organize, they group together. Individualists eschew grouping together, even to save themselves. That is why individualism has been losing at this point in our history.

One of the things which became very apparent to me in the process of putting this work together was that by and large the information centers for American history are in New York and London. Most establishment publishing houses have offices in one or both locations. It is very interesting to observe that many of the American histories are actually published by institutions such as Oxford, or affiliated with Oxford. In other words, there is a decidedly English bent to them — and a centralization of control over American "history."

This is a result of a long-standing British influence on the United States, since she was after all the major influence on our country, which did not entirely dissipate after the War for Independence. The English investors in America were not asked or forced to divest themselves of their American investments. English investment continued after the war. A little over a century later, this influence received a boost as a result of the secret society Cecil Rhodes' helped found and finance, which led to the Royal Institute of International Affairs (RIIA), or Chatham House, and her sister organization in America, the Council on Foreign Relations.

What you will read will be quite different than what was taught us in our schools. Some of it will make you mad at the author, but read on. As the narrative grows, the more you will see that we missed something in school, something important. In many cases, we will supply you with information that will augment your outlook as to events and personalities in history. Do not reject or embrace it all. Use the information to supplement what you already know and apply it to your overall opinion of the person rather than simply think at any juncture in the narrative whether the person was good or bad.

Some historical personalities did things out of ignorance and some later repented of earlier deeds, either out of ignorance or having developed a conscience.

No one likes to lose heroes, or have their heroes attacked. This book will cause you a great deal of anguish in this regard. Try to remember that it is not the messenger that you have to be angry with; it is those who have kept the information from you all this time, and/or given you *their* heroes instead of the real heroes of freedom, to the point of vilifying the real heroes. A prime example of a real hero vilified would be George Washington.

Remember that the men who founded this country were great; likewise, they were fallible. Some went through periods when their character could have been better, then saw the error of their ways, and became great again. Some did not. A fine example of great, fallible, and then returning to his former self would be Thomas Jefferson.

There are many figures that have played major roles in trying to move our country away from our Constitution toward an accumulation of power of whom you have never heard. Likewise, the converse is true of men who did all they could to keep our country free, never receiving the credit they deserve.

In some instances, if the patriot was well known, the Conspiracy smeared them into ineffectiveness, and continues to do so to this day.

This tactic is used even in the present, both of current personages as well as historical figures who have been gone for centuries, such as George Washington, the idea being that if Washington is diminished in your eyes you will be less inclined to listen to the advice he gave about our government and the forces arrayed against our country. This has always been one of the main objectives of the smear. In the case of Washington, it has been a very subtle process.

The involvement of early Americans in anti-God movements will be shocking to those who have never realized that such a movement was active in the United States until recent history. It actually goes back to the very beginning of our country.

A great deal of effort has gone into the elimination of facts that pertain to the influence of those who mean to rule us, particularly in the United States. Reading about conspirators in Europe is relatively easy. Doing the same about America is very difficult.

This is because the importance of the United States and our citizens in the general scheme of world politics is so important that an extensive effort has been made over the years to deprive Americans of information that is vital to not only our survival as a free state, but as a result, the freedom of the entire globe.

Another reason is that we still have a relatively free country and if the American people understood what was going on, they could put a stop to it. This is not the case in other countries where the people have even less influence on their government; therefore, hiding the truth about certain aspects of their history is not as important as it is in the United States.

Since 1958, with the advent of a concerted, grassroots-implemented education about such matters, it has been more difficult for the historical record to be suppressed. Recently we have seen an influx of new books which tell part of the story, and some authors who are now admitting that the primary conspiratorial wellspring in Europe, the Illuminati, did not die when our history books said it did. Therefore admitting, the average reader then assumes the remainder of the book is accurate, even when it propagates the myth of the ineffectiveness of the Illuminati.

The idea now is to hide from interested Americans reading such matters that there is any American connection to early Illuminists and the direct influence of these men on American organizations and personages. For instance, if there is a denial that Mirabeau or Filippo Michele Buonarroti were Illuminati members, or *were working for them*, then any direct line from the Illuminati and those they influenced is broken. Yet the direct influence of these men is important to know, as well as the source of their passion.

These men are only two examples of many.

Let us express the situation in another way: Since 1958, a concerted effort has been made to expose and oppose the enemies of our country and their history. As more of this information has been made available, there has been an effort to agree up to a point about such organizations as the Illuminati, but in the process hide the fact or discourage anyone from looking into the connection from the Illuminati into modern times.

History is the chronicle of people. People make things happen. Expose evil people and you will find that you are their instant target — especially if you find a way to go around the media to reach the opinion molders.

We will not delve into the facts pertaining to the money powers. Too much emphasis has been placed in this quarter regarding their influence in history. It is well documented; indeed, over documented — there is no need to add to it. The money powers have not always been behind history to the extent many authors would have you believe. We will explain along the way. And, too often the "history" is slanted to put a racial aspect to it in order to help further divide and conquer the Conspiracy's opposition.

This book may not find its way very far into the American psyche. It is admittedly weak in some areas and this is due to the tremendous amount of work necessary to ferret out the facts; in some instances the facts are lost to us. The hope is that it will serve as a means to stimulate others to seek out the truth, and from their vantage point, publish more.

INTRODUCTION

This work is not intended to look at all considerations surrounding historical events or the personalities involved. Rather it is to bring forward relatively unknown facts to supplement the reader's knowledge, thereby providing a greater insight toward understanding the historical pressures that have influenced American society and politics.

We will not delve into battles in war or explore the political parties in depth with the exception of the two major parties. They are not that important except to understand their origins. This is one of the dirty little secrets of politics. It is not the parties that make votes. *Parties only gather votes* that are available to them. This is why they take polls, go out of their way to develop platforms based on the polls in order to appeal to the voter, and rarely engage in political education.

Political parties simply gather the votes available as a result of the majority of the electorate's education, experience, and self-interest. These are what "make" votes, yet few outside of the socialist movement understand this most basic fact. What a voter believes in and what he wants is the result of movements that involve the education, or what may be labeled education, of the people.

The person who educates will always have more influence on society than the person who gathers the results. And, the people who organize to bring about change will always win if they are better organized than their opposition. If both education and action are accomplished within the same organization, their influence will extend well beyond their numbers — with or *without* the help of the media.

It has been said that war is the violent extension of politics. This is true. In the scheme of understanding events, the politics surrounding a war are more important than the battles, but the citizens' eyes are kept on the battles rather than the politics.

Likewise, political parties are the *extension* of political movements and small, influential groups. These are the important things to study and are the area we will be exploring. In many instances, political action if engaged in by the leaders of any movement will usually diminish the effectiveness of the movement, even while it may elevate the influence of those people. In other words, the leaders concentrate on their own political elevation rather than spending the time on promoting the movement exclusively, thereby denying the movement needed leadership and impetus unless they remain very active in the group, using their new position as a "bully platform." The Left does this; in the conservative movement it can happen but it is rare.

A corollary is that the Left put their energy and money behind their agenda. The average conservative, especially the businessman, does not, and in most cases distains to do so for a variety of reasons. This is one of the basic reasons the Left has advanced and conservatism only flourishes when an organization is formed to promote constitutional principles and lasts as long as the organization can sustain itself.

A related problem is that the Left is composed of collectivists. That is what they do: collectivize. They form organizations and work together — it is their nature. On the other hand, individualists rarely work together for long politically, they are after all individualists, and when they do it is like herding cats, each wanting to do it their way with their ideas. This gives the collectivist an advantage. However, this condition, in certain ways, has been changing gradually over time.

There will be times you will doubt what is portrayed. Read on, for the picture will come into focus with additional facts. In many instances, the scope of the information is actually worse and to describe it would mean a volume so large that no one would bother to pick it up and read. After all, we are talking about a hundred years of history, and out of necessity, spanning two continents.

The number of people who engaged in founding this country and what they laid on the line to do so is truly inspiring. Yet history lessons today gloss over their sacrifice and in some cases make the Founders look like a bunch of slave-holding elitists, only interested in their own well-being and business. It would have been impossible to enlist the citizen soldiers — who were volunteer militia laying their lives on the line — into the fight during the War for Independence had that been the case.

Some books are so vindictive toward patriots such as Alexander Hamilton and John Hancock that the student should muse as to why they had any support at all among the people in their day if the charges against them are accurate. This vindictiveness even carries over into the modern conservative and so-called conspiracy-type of historical genre, due to skewed historical facts, and the fact that Hamilton did a number of things in reaction to a conspiracy that wanted to destroy the structure laid down by our Founders, and they have never forgiven him of it.

In some cases, it was an overreaction, but the fear was real. Rarely are the actions of Hamilton seen through the lens of his concern for the Illuminati threat to America.

Hamilton and Jefferson were on opposing sides after the War for Independence. Jefferson is looked upon today as a libertarian and Hamilton as a man who was opposed to the freedom of the people. Yet it was Jefferson who, while supporting colonization, held slaves and did not even free them in his death, while Hamilton worked for the abolition of slavery.

Much of the attack against Hamilton lingers today with a predisposition to interpret his words in the extreme. Most if not all of the modern libertarian view of Hamilton comes to us via the Jacobin propaganda mill. It is true that Hamilton referred to wanting a monarchy, but he meant it in the sense of an executive branch, not a king. The terms were not yet fully defined as we see them today.

A letter supposedly written by Hamilton, later proven to be a forgery, invited the second son of King George III, Frederick, Duke of York, to become king of the United States. These sorts of tactics were widespread in the beginning of our country against Jacobin enemies, with lingering consequences up to today. As you read further along, you will see other examples of the same techniques used against all enemies of the Conspiracy.

Think about this last example logically for a moment. What power did Hamilton have to offer anyone such a position even if he wanted to? Would he have been able to convince the majority of Americans to go along with the idea if he had? It was all too illogical, yet many Americans fell for the forgery and continue to believe such examples even today, all planted by not only the enemies of Hamilton, but of the American system.

One student history book viewed by this author even claimed that John Hancock was transported everywhere in a sedan carried by servants and as he was borne through the streets he would throw coins out of his window to curry favor, an obvious attempt to diminish Hancock's character in the mind of the reader.

There have been school history books that have more to say about famous movie stars than George Washington, whose image left in students' minds is that he wore wooden false teeth — and oh, by the way, he was the first president of the United States.

Such revelations about our first presidents are not unusual, and students do not have a complete picture of our Founders. A professor in a Midwest university told this author one year that the majority of his freshman class knew that Thomas Jefferson was a slave-holder, but only three knew that he was a president of the United States.

Worse, modern studies on the Constitution are so skewed as to make the original intent nonexistent in students' minds. As an example, the Bill of Rights widely taught in many schools in the 1970s were put forth in such a manner as to give an entirely different idea of what they are, though they were presented as the actual Bill of Rights. Quoting just two:

Amendment II: The people have the right to keep and bear arms, but Congress may regulate private weapons.

Amendment IV: People or their houses or other belongings cannot be searched or seized without good cause.

This false image of the Bill of Rights continues as of this writing in recommended books on the Constitution by what is known as Common Core (CC). In the CC-recommended book for schools *United States History*: *Preparing for advanced Placement Examination*, the Second Amendment is written thus: "The people have the right to keep and bear arms in a militia."

Consult your copy of the Bill of Rights and see what it really says and how the above versions can mislead the student. For instance, the Second Amendment does not give Congress the right to regulate private weapons. This has become a practice assumed by Congress and often upheld by the courts in direct violation of the Second Amendment.

The CC-recommended book writes that the First Amendment reads, "Congress *may* make no laws...." The actual Amendment states, "Congress *shall* make no laws...." It may seem to be a subtle difference, but there is a difference between *may* and *shall*. And, the amendment is not stated as it is in the actual Bill of Rights.

Subtle changes and not so subtle ones — they add up to dumbing down the student as to the real meaning and purpose of the Constitution.

The danger of this is that in the case of the Second Amendment, forty years of teaching students the incorrect version has had its effect on the people of America as these students reach adulthood and start to vote. They fall for the rhetoric of leftist politicians who clamor for the disarmament of the citizen as a means to curtail crime. They have no sense for the original intent of the Constitution or the fact that statistically more guns have always led to less crime.

For instance, every able-bodied male in Switzerland has a fully automatic assault weapon in his home as part of being enrolled in the reserve defense force. As a result, burglary is almost nonexistent, at least not when the man is at home. Also, relative to intentional murder, Switzerland is listed as 200 in the list of the nations of the world of killings per 100,000 people. Anti-gun advocates would have everyone believe that more guns leads to more crime, when crime is connected to morality, not weapons.

Anti-communists from the 1790s to present are made to appear to be just a little crazy or just plain dangerous, such as Alexander Hamilton and Joseph McCarthy. No one ever thinks about why McCarthy was elected and re-elected as a U.S. Senator if he was as bad as he was, and still is, depicted in the media and history books — *especially* if the media was against him. Or, why Washington chose Hamilton as his secretary of the Treasury.

On the other hand, many statues and monuments of individuals dot the American landscape who should no more be honored than some of the worse villains of history, but then, *to the victor go the myths and monuments*. The victors almost always write history, obfuscating that which makes them look bad, while accentuating or inventing things that make the vanquished look bad.

In the case of the American Civil War, the above is the case for both sides of the conflict. Both have rewritten history and set up monuments to some of those best forgotten. Worse, there is too much concentration on the battles and not on the politics and the influences on these events. What the average student has been taught of the personages and events up to and including the war, except for the battles, is mythology.

This book is intended to give an overview of who and what has been behind the type of education we have received, by revealing the forces at work in the United States since our onset. It will not discuss all aspects of American history, and we are sure that in the course of time even more valuable information will be revealed that enhances the story. In fact, we hope that this work will encourage others to look closer at events through history and bring more information forward to the American people.

We will concentrate more on the Northern aspects of this U.S. history rather than the Southern, simply because it was the Northern influence that won out and still dominates our thinking today.

The whole idea of a master conspiracy at work in America is constantly pooh-poohed. The idea is to make the reader imagine that if you do believe in such a conspiracy, you are somehow an idiot. After all, goes one argument, such secret societies are ineffectual; otherwise you would have heard more about them. The fact that they are secret seems to elude them.

It would seem quite logical that if a society is secret and does everything it can to remain so, that information on and about it would be in short supply.

These themes or some variant have been used ever since the Illuminati and related organizations were exposed.

An example of this idea is contained in a book that outlines one of the biggest secret societies that existed in America: the Brotherhood of the Union, or Continental Brotherhood, even known as the Brotherhood of America. The book is *A Secret Society History of the Civil War*. It describes the Federalist fear of secret societies during the Washington-Adams era and then states:

> Although *no evidence existed for the Federalist paranoia*, some Illuminatists, Martinists, or Mesmerists made it to the United States. (Emphasis added.)

The author then goes on to mention a long list of secret movements and communist leaders that were active or became active in America up to 1820. We will describe later how they were not "ineffectual" and lacking in influence.

An example of this type of anti-conspiratorial genre after the Civil War was contained within a small book titled *The Political Conspiracies Preceding the Rebellion*, published in 1882 and authored by Thomas M. Anderson, the nephew of Robert Anderson of Ft. Sumter fame. While the title uses the word *conspiracy*, the very first words in the book are designed to make the reader think that conspiracies only existed in the South and they were simply of a sort that seized federal forts and arsenals.

> I purpose in this monograph to give an account of the political conspiracies immediately preceding the Rebellion of 1861 against the authority of the National Government of the United States of America.
>
> It would be absurd to assume that one of the greatest civil wars of modern times was the result of conspiracies.

INTRODUCTION

> The causes which led to it were far too deep and strong to be controlled by the machinations of politicians.
>
> Nevertheless the outbreak of the Rebellion was preceded by a number of conspiracies the object of which, so far as the Southern leaders were concerned, was to gain certain advantages by cunning and *finesse* before they resorted to the arbitrament of war.

Note that he used the term *national government* rather than *federal*; there is a big difference in these two forms of government. One is a federation of states, the other a central government. Note also that he pointed to Southern conspiracies, not specifically to Northern ones. This was a common failing in the North. They could see it in the South but not right next door.

The student of history is sometimes allowed to believe in small, inconsequential conspiracies, but not one that combines them all into a master conspiracy. It is not "intellectually sound" to think in terms of a large conspiracy and so the student, even if he believes otherwise, will remain silent so as not to make himself out to appear paranoid and a shallow thinker to others.

It is illogical to believe that so many secret societies could have the same identical goals and practices without some connection. We will show that there is a connection.

There will be times that you will become depressed with the dark side of American history. We dwell on these facts simply because they have been lost from the record. Remember during these times that there were also great men who gave us or preserved our heritage, and we need to remember and honor them.

It is important to know the history of the revolutionary forces aimed at overturning the independence of the American people and our Constitution in order to understand what is going on today. As the Senate of the State of New York stated in 1920 in their report *Revolutionary Radicalism*, which documented American communism, it was impossible to understand what is happening today without going back to 1848. We would only disagree as to the date. One needs to go back to at least the 1750s in Europe.

It is always a difficult thing to realize that the education you received in school was deficient in history, and once you realize this, where do you go to remedy the problem? Many of you are now thinking that it was different in your school, and you received a good historical perspective as well as the facts.

This author knows of no program in America that teaches the facts of American history in such a manner as to bring a true perspective forward of the adverse influences on American society and government by those who desire power. This is not just in government schools; it includes private, religious, and home schooling since they are adversely influenced by what printed "history" is available.

> A conspiracy is nothing but a secret agreement of a number of men for the pursuance of policies which they dare not admit in public.
>
> — Mark Twain

The idea of conspiracies at work was a universal idea when our country began, and there were Founders of our country who were quite concerned about them. In fact, at one point in our early history, John Jay was the head of the New York Committee for Detecting and Defeating Conspiracies. Not investigating — detecting! The idea of an investigation naturally follows detection, but they were aware of the fact that conspiracies exist and that everything that happens is done because someone wants it that way, and they set about to detect them as it related to the welfare of our American cause.

The American War for Independence was rife with conspiracies on both sides — forming them, detecting them, and establishing counter-intelligence to thwart them. They understood that conspiracy was the natural sidebar to any conflict, either political or bellicose. Included within this genre were the governments of France and Spain, also weighing in on the defeat of the British.

A book should be written about this aspect of the war because all of these governments were involved in conspiracy, and a second look needs to be taken as to how these governments dealt with the United States through this tactic throughout the first one hundred years of our existence. This author knows of no definitive study of this method of foreign intrigue in regard to these countries and the political movements within the United States after the War of 1812.

Probably the most definitive novel as to what the future will look like if liberty dies in the United States is the novel *1984* by George Orwell. It has the world divided into three regions ruled by an Inner Party. Early on the socialist leaders realized that the three countries which would come to dominate the world would be the United States, Russia, and quite possibly China.

This was the opinion of the Italian disciple of Pierre-Joseph Proudhon, Giuseppe Ferrari. He feared that large states would lead to the destruction of European dominance in favor of the U.S., Russia, and eventually China.

The book *The New Rome; or, The United States of the World*, published in 1853 by two German revolutionary immigrants to America, Charles Göpp and Theodor Pösche, foretold that Europe would be eclipsed by the two great powers on either side, Russia and the United States, and that the great battle for the world in the future would be fought in the air. It advocated an American world republic and its annexation of Europe. The book was dedicated to President Franklin Pierce.

Likewise, Karl Marx looked to America and Russia as the countries "on the come" — that they would be the new powers in the world.

It was obvious to the powers-that-wanted-to-be that great pains needed to be taken to subvert and take over these nations. Of the three, Russia was dealt the death blow first in 1917. China fell thirty years later. In both cases, Americans in and out of government played key roles in bringing these sad events about, especially China.

It is interesting that the best ally of the North during the Civil War was Russia, the czar sending two fleets into U.S. waters to help the North protect New York harbor in September 1863, and then San Francisco Bay. They remained there on "leave," sailing off in April 1864.

The blockade of the South by the Northern navy initially left the Northern ports unprotected and vulnerable to the sea raiders that had been built in Europe for the Confederacy. The *Alabama*, the *Florida*, and the *Shenandoah* were top-of-the-line warships with the latest technology of the time. They were primarily tasked to ravage Northern merchant vessels, which they did to such an extent that they were hard-pressed by the end of the war to find any American merchant vessels left to sink.

By March 1864, the Confederate raiders had swept the oceans so thoroughly of American ships that the commander of the Confederate *Tuscaloosa* reported that out of 100 ships seen by him in the North Atlantic, only one was of American origin.

American shipping did not recover its maritime competitiveness against England until World War I.

After the battle of Antietam, lost by the South, the Confederate ships under construction in England were seized by the British government.

There was one incident when two Confederate cruisers, *Alabama* and *Sumter*, showed up off San Francisco, and the Russian Rear Admiral Andrei Alexandrovich Popov ordered his six vessels to "put on steam and clear for action" against the Confederate vessels. The Confederates sailed off before any action took place.

Introduction

The Russian government then admonished Popov that it was not the intent to "involve our government in a situation which it is trying to keep out of." Then why anchor for so long where there was the possibility of trouble that could involve the fleets in some capacity?

There were quotes from people who stated that, based on the information they had from Lincoln and Admiral David Farragut, the Russian fleet most certainly would have assisted the United States should the ports in which the Russian fleets were anchored have been attacked.

There was more to the benevolence of the czar than simply wishing to help the Union. At the time, due to the politics of Europe, it was convenient to place his fleets into American waters rather than risk them coming into conflict with English and French navies. However, it appears that the intent was also to help protect American waters, and there was even talk of an American-Russian alliance. But again, due to the politics of Europe at the time, Russia could not afford direct involvement due to neutrality laws. Nonetheless, the Russians were treated as allies, wined and dined, and speeches were given by local officials, leaders, and prominent citizens, which demonstrated that the Northern citizens considered them *war* allies.

Apparently the fleet that arrived in San Francisco had sealed orders. These orders were to be opened the moment the U.S. became involved in a war with any European nation.

An interesting vignette regarding the Russian fleets comes from *The United States, II, From the Civil War* by David Saville Muzzey, 1924, on page 47f:

In the recently published "Letters of Franklin K. Lane" (1922) there is a most interesting Manuscript note, dated December 29, 1911, recording a conversation with Mr. Charles Glover, president of Riggs National Bank, who remembered as a boy handling two warrants upon the United States Treasury for the payment of $1,400,000 and $5,800,000 respectively for Russia. The existence of these two warrants was explained later to Mr. Glover by Senator Dawes. The first represented the price for which Russia had offered us Alaska before the Civil War. During the war Seward had invited Russia to make her friendly naval demonstration, secretly agreeing to pay the expenses of it out of "contingent funds." Those expenses amounted to $5,800,000, and they were paid by adding this sum to the original purchase price of $1,400,000. Therefore, although we paid Russia $7,200,000, less than a fifth of the sum was all she actually asked for "one of the richest portions of the earth in mineral deposits."

The Dictionary of American History said the Senate gave its advice and consent to the purchase of Alaska "out of gratitude for Russia's having sent its fleet to American waters in 1863, supposedly as a demonstration against England and France, which were sympathetic to the Confederacy."

By the end of the war, the North had built up their fleet so that no Northern port was threatened. The U.S. Navy started with 42 vessels and had 650 by war's end.

Without a good perspective on history, the average citizen is handicapped and it is difficult for him to make informed decisions and look to honest political leadership.

One problem that has plagued most Americans is the inability of being able to marry the government's domestic policy with its foreign policy. Generally speaking, some people tend to want more socialism but decry an imperialistic foreign policy; others decry the domestic march toward socialism and embrace the foreign policy of promoting democracy, or even enforcing democracy in other countries.

The problem is that they are one and the same because the same people in government implement both policies at the same time. They are initiatives toward one policy: world government with a government-controlled economy. We will explain the problem with promoting democracy in other countries further on.

Think about it for a moment. Will a government that is marching us toward socialism domestically do something different overseas? Will a government that is bent on eliminating God, prayer, and the Ten Commandments from American public life desire to do the opposite overseas?

It defies logic to think that American politicians want to impose socialism on America but want freedom everywhere else.

Let us make the point that power is often the motivation of political leaders, particularly those behind the scenes who wield great influence but are relatively unknown to the public. If not power, then self-aggrandizement, and those who do want power can manipulate the latter type of politician for their own ends.

Since the average American sees growth in government and believes that it is simply a march toward socialism, yet are not aware of a true perspective of history itself, they cannot appreciate what is really happening. False leaders can come from all walks of life, and this fact can sometimes confuse Americans who think that it is all about socialism — the desire for some form of economic equality for the masses. It has nothing to do with this idea at all, other than to serve as a smoke screen for what the endgame really is: Power.

We will explain later why it is not the money-power that is the endgame.

Since two can play this game, the two sides of politics — socialism and liberty — can be manipulated into solutions that give power to those they believe they are opposing.

It is not unusual for the constitutionalist to become confused by people who have left the radical movement. Too often, they bring over their prejudices, even their socialist ideas watered down to acceptability. This had been a problem in the 20th century with those who left the communist movement, or its fronts, as well as defectors in the Cold War from the KGB of Russia. One can never be absolutely sure of their motivation or dedication to constitutional *principles*.

They may have been tasked specifically to defect and infiltrate the organization and the thinking of their opponents to throw them off track or neutralize their efforts. In some instances, the honest Russian defectors from the USSR were murdered to silence their revelations. And the average American never heard of them or their sacrifice for freedom and the American people. Some remain in hiding today under aliases to prevent reprisal from the Russian FSB.

A case in point which did gain some notoriety was Alexander Litvinenko, who revealed that Ayman al Zawahiri, the second in command of the terrorist organization al Qaeda who became the head of the organization on the death of Osama bin Laden, was a trained Russian asset of the FSB/KGB. For Litvinenko's revelations and his potential for revealing even more of Russia's long range plans, he was poisoned with a radioactive substance in Britain by Russian agents and died a slow, excruciating death.

The neoconservatives and mass media that help support the idea of a War on Terror and Homeland Security ignored his revelations.

The problem of believability and trust was the same in the 19th century with individuals such as Orestes Augustus Brownson and Heinrich Börnstein. Their revelations were helpful, but their later activities appeared to help the radical agenda move forward, albeit slower, particularly with Börnstein although many Catholics complained to the Pope about the Catholic convert Brownson, that he was liberalizing Catholicism. After a report of Cardinal Johann Baptist Franzelin, who scrutinized the complaints, Brownson was ordered "to be more moderate in his views."

The same is true of men in England. Benjamin Disraeli, who became an on again, off again prime minister, started out as a Radical. He helped form the Young England group within Parliament in the early

Introduction

1840s then became a member of the conservative party. As he became more prominent in Parliament he again supported the Radical agenda.

He said two things that set the stage for what we are going to be talking about in this book:

> For you see, the world is governed by very different personages from what is imagined by those who are not behind the scenes.
> — *Coningsby: Or The New Generation*

And,

> The governments of the present day have to deal not merely with other governments, with emperors, kings, and ministers, but also with the secret societies which have everywhere their unscrupulous agents, and can at the last moment upset all the governments' plans.
> — Speech at Aylesbury, Great Britain, September 10, 1870

Another problem Americans have had is that they cannot see through men who profess to be Christians selling them something that is anti-Christ. All throughout the history of America, including the present day, men will stand and profess Christianity and in the next instant promote some aspect of international socialism. It is usually subtle, a small step, but ultimately leads to the New World Order, the professed goal of international socialism.

A modern example was a prominent governor who courted the pro-life movement at the same time he engaged in activities that would have led to the merger of North America into one nation, which would destroy the Constitution and independence of the American people. Likewise, he was known to have attended a Bilderberg meeting of internationalists who want more U.S. involvement and entanglements leading to a total subjugation of America to the United Nations.

In the end, the UN would dictate to the American people about such issues as abortion, euthanasia, property rights, etc., if we become subjugated to the UN, since after all, we would be one vote in a sea of over 150 socialist votes. So, a politician can make it appear that he is conservative to gain support, especially a social conservative, and still promote the New World Order, which in the long run would negate everything he professes to be for or against — and, too many do this with intent.

The idea is to gain the support of Christian conservatives by supporting the social issues while they mislead the movement into a subtle support of the agenda of the internationalists. When a citizen is aware of the charade, it becomes difficult to convince people of the tactic. "After all, he is a moral man! He can't be what you say he is."

Another modern example is Christian denominations honoring the life of Nelson Mandela of South Africa, a communist terrorist leader. After his death, the South African Communist Party admitted that Mandela had always been a leader on the Central Committee of the Party, even as president of South Africa. Due to the ignorance of the goals and tactics of the communists, Christians honor people they do not realize are their enemies, as we shall see more of in this tome.

One of the main goals of the Conspiracy is to gain control of the publishing and media arms of its opposition. In this manner, they can appear to be supporting the main premises, philosophy, and/or religious base but use this tactic *to prevent a correct solution from being applied* that will in the long run mean the defeat of their opposition.

Early on, the Conspiracy captured a major American Christian sect and used it to influence other Christians. This tactic continues today and while the books, magazines, and media output appear to be Christian based on the general ignorance of history, the real roots of the problems, or constitutional principles, they are able to present false solutions to the brethren that will fail. The same holds true of the Jewish faith.

And all the while they give the appearance of being brothers.

Except for examples here and there, we will not be exposing the Christian sects that have been co-opted since we wish to inform all Americans as to the problems that exist with history and not shut off people who may be part of a church that they would not understand has been co-opted by the Conspiracy. They would not believe it or appreciate the exposure. By understanding history, they will be able to reach a conclusion themselves about any church and its position relative to fighting the evil forces that mean to rule us. We wish this to be the criteria for evaluating all modern movements.

The New World Order is a term that is used to portray the end goal of the Conspiracy. Constitutionalists did not invent this term, rather it is used by the minions of the Conspiracy themselves as their objective. A presentation lasting an hour could be shown of the people and publications on the Left and American establishment politicians who use the term, from Karl Marx to Fidel Castro, Mikhail Gorbachev, Adolph Hitler, Joseph Biden, Richard Nixon, Henry Kissinger, George H. W. Bush, and scores more. These illustrations can be readily verified online.

Let us use just one of the instances that has been used to signify the end goal:

> The revolutionary movement which began in 1789 in the Cercle Social, which in the middle of its course has as its chief representatives Leclerc and Roux, and which finally with Babeuf's conspiracy was temporarily defeated, gave rise to the communist idea which Babeuf's friend Buonarroti re-introduced in France after the Revolution of 1830. This idea, consistently developed, is the idea of the new world order.
>
> — Karl Marx and Frederick Engels, *The Holy Family*, 1844

Note that Marx and Engels referred to the new world order as the *communist* idea. As you will come to see, the Cercle Social organization had a great deal of influence in the changes of American society.

This quote will take on more significance as you read further as to the antecedents of the modern communist movement and its direct tie to the Illuminati.

One wonders if some scholars try to deliberately mislead the student of history or if they are simply passing on their own ignorance of facts. There are those who state that the first use of the phrase the New World Order came from the founder of the Baha'i Faith in the early 1860s. As you can see above, this cannot be the case.

Believing this, it takes away the question as to why the Great Seal of the United States would have the Latin phrase *Novus Ordo Seclorum* on its reverse, placed there well after the founding of the country. This has been translated as the New Order of the Ages, but many Latin scholars say that the better translation is the New World Order. The more one researches why and how we even have a reverse to our Seal, let alone the progression of the design over the years and who was responsible for it, the more confused one can get.

The point is, the more you obfuscate such matters, the more you leave Americans in the dark about the influence of the Illuminati on our country from the onset.

The term *New World Order* actually has two meanings. Most believe it to designate a world government, and they are correct. However, it is also used to designate the Order which will run that government — the organization behind the scenes comprised of what Orwell called the Inner Party in his novel *1984*.

Socialism/communism is only used to enlist the masses into a cause of which they have little appreciation or understanding.

A well-recognized name in American history, Horace Greeley, publisher of *The New York Tribune*, is best known for his advice: "Go West young man. Go West." He was an energetic socialist leader in his day. He stated in 1850,

> We believe that Government, like every other intelligent agency, is bound to do good to the extent of its ability — that it ought actively to promote and increase the general well being — that it should encourage and foster Industry, Science, Invention, Intellectual, Social and Physical Progress ... Such is our idea of the sphere of Government.

This has been the siren song of all socialists since the beginning of our country. What many do not stop and think about is that first government must take away wealth, property, even control from the individual in order to accomplish the above. In the process, that alone gives the government inordinate power.

Once the government starts down this path, if one extends the lines, it becomes obvious that government will decide what industry is, what science is, whether an invention should be pursued or utilized, what true intellectual pursuits are, and how we are to be organized socially. For those of you old enough to remember, how can you forget the pictures of youth under totalitarian Germany and Russia engaged in mass synchronized physical exercise formations, fulfilling "physical progress"?

The latter is the most benign idea of physical progress: the building of sound bodies. Hitler went to the extreme and tried to focus physical progress in the Aryan race, eliminating as many Jews, Gypsies, and Slavs as he could. The Lebensborn program was set up by Heinrich Himmler, the leader of the notorious Schutzstaffel, or SS, to help unwed mothers of pure Nordic blood, and it likewise encouraged helping young women who had become pregnant by SS officers. Thirty-five Lebensborn hospital facilities were set up in Germany and the occupied countries. The plan was to have Germans adopt these Aryan children.

In a word, what we are talking about relative to government involvement in all of the above is totalitarianism, and whoever controls the government controls these aforementioned endeavors.

The other means for those who want power and want to wrest it from the people rests in the idea of the destruction of the fabric of society through solving crises with the solutions designed to increase the power of the state. This can be manipulated at the same time as the above outline of Greeley's as a means to accelerate the overall process.

Part of the process of breaking down the social order and silencing opposition is to use tolerance as a tactic, not a goal. Tolerance is something to be demanded as long as the philosophic party is not tolerated; but as soon as the philosophers gain secret power, tolerance is an obstacle to be used as a means to stamp out their enemies.

Complete tolerance means intolerance imposed by government toward morality, forcing moral people to put up with immorality in public life, business, and education — even in their churches. It is already a crime punishable by imprisonment in countries such as Canada and Sweden to preach that homosexuality is a sin, even from the pulpit. The Canadian Supreme Court has upheld their laws against "hate speech," which restricts anti-gay rhetoric. The same has applied to pro-life demonstrators on or near college campuses in Canada.

Tolerance means allowing anything. It is an intellectual argument against upholding private and especially public morality. It is the social revolution as described by Karl Marx.

There is a clear and present danger when the intellectual life of a nation falls into the hands of its enemies.

Tolerance is used as the siren song for breaking down public morality. The breakdown of civic morality is essential for the creation of a totalitarian regime. The people will not stand for the actions of a dictatorship if they are moral in their civil and personal life.

The political observer will notice that the liberal-socialist has a double standard, and will tolerate anything except those things about which they disagree, usually in the name of tolerance.

Early on, the revolutionary forces in our midst did all they could to effect morals. Richard Henry Lee, a signer of the Declaration of Independence, stated in a letter to James Madison on November 26, 1784:

> Refiners may weave reason into as fine a web as they please, but the experience of all time shows religion to be the guardian of morals; and he must be a very inattentive observer in our country who does not see that avarice is accomplishing the destruction of religion for want of the legal obligation to contribute something to its support.
> — *Memoirs of the Life of Richard Henry Lee, and His Correspondence*

You will see further on why Lee was so concerned at that time.

Once the masses help break down the old social order, or acquiesce to a breakdown, the organization behind the scenes wrests total power in the midst of the chaos. It has happened over and over again in history and has been given the appearance by establishment historians as some sort of cycle of man and civilization to mask the fact that organization was behind it.

So the radical activist, the moderate financier, the hard-nosed industrialist — whoever — can advocate communism or back it, and since the average American does not understand the endgame, it is difficult for them to connect the dots between the rabble in the streets and the master organization composed today of the rich and/or powerful.

The breakdown of the old social order has an element to it that is far more sinister than the simple idea of changing the people in government or the system itself. It goes back to what Alexis de Tocqueville had to say about America after his extensive trip here in 1830 in his book *Democracy in America*:

> Moreover, almost all the sects of the United States are comprised within the great unity of Christianity, and Christian morality is everywhere the same. In the United States the sovereign authority is religious, and consequently hypocrisy must be common, but there is no country in the whole world in which the Christian religion retains a greater influence over the souls of men than in America, and there can be no greater proof if its utility, and of its conformity to human nature, than that its influence is most powerfully felt over the most enlightened and free nation of the earth.
>
> The Americans combine the notions of Christianity and of liberty so intimately in their minds, that it is impossible to make them conceive the one without the other, and with them this conviction does not spring from that barren traditionary faith which seems to vegetate in the soul rather than to live.
>
> There are certain populations in Europe whose unbelief is only equaled by their ignorance and

INDUSTRIALISTS WHO FINANCED SOCIALIST AND TERRORIST CAUSES:

Robert Owen. Scottish industrialist who promoted communism in Europe and the Americas.

Frederick Engels. Industrialist. With Marx, the front men for communism.

Gerrit Smith. Supporter of John Brown's terrorism and one of the men who posted bail for Jefferson Davis with Cornelius Vanderbilt and Horace Greeley.

Andrew Carnegie. Steel magnate. British Chartist.

Cornelius Vanderbilt. Sugar daddy to Victoria Woodhull and Tennessee Claflin, leaders of Section 12 of the Communist International. Posted bail for Jefferson Davis with Horace Greeley and Gerrit Smith.

their debasement, while in America one of the freest and most enlightened nations in the world fulfills all the outward duties of religion with fervor.

> Upon my arrival in the United States, the religious aspect of the country was the first thing that struck my attention; and the longer I stayed there, the more did I perceive the great political consequences resulting from the state of things, to which I was unaccustomed. In France, I had almost always seen the spirit of religion and the spirit of freedom pursuing courses diametrically opposed to each other, but in America I found that they were intimately united, and that they reigned in common over the same country.

While De Tocqueville's observations were sound on one level, his association with many of the politicians of the day amongst the American Democrats clouded his vision as to what our country really was: a Republic, not a Democracy. Also, he is widely quoted regarding the fact that America was a moral country and that if she lost this morality she would cease to be great. The problem with this statement is that morality is whatever the reader deems it to be, even though many have used the quote to promote scriptural morality. The extensive quote above is far more to the point and it demonstrates what the enemies of freedom need to do to change our system and have been doing for a long time: removing morality from public life by diminishing the role of religion in support of Constitutional government.

The point is that the attack on the American system is in reality an attack on the Judeo-Christian basis of our government. The old social order must be destroyed; the foundation must be destroyed for the enemies of freedom to prevail. While there were and are many who take a stand against the more radical in our society, and this may cloud one's judgment as to whether or not they are true friends of liberty, the final analysis must be if they are supporting the Judeo-Christian rock that formed the foundation of our system.

Based on the writings of the early socialists and communists, they follow the aims of the Illuminati when it comes to religion: they want to remove it, destroy it, and substitute it with the state. This is not only within the works of the Illuminati but *throughout* the history of socialism in all its forms, regardless of what they call themselves. It is also a problem in the modern world, based on the experience of this author having been involved in infiltrating communist and socialist organizations.

A moral and responsible people are difficult to subvert to thereby establish a dictatorship over.

One of the mistakes that some historians have made is that the above philosophy has to do with self-worship. This is only the first step toward eliminating religion to be substituted by the state. Abbe Augustin Barruel, in his tome *Memoirs Illustrating the History of Jacobinism*, said,

> For Dietrich, Condorcet, Babeuf and other recent adepts of Weishaupt, there need be no moderator except the man-king, who has nowhere anyone but himself for a master.

The adepts have learned to present a false face to the public while holding beliefs the public would reject. Just as they have the façade of benevolence when it comes to why they want certain legislation, many present a façade of religious belief to hide their true intent.

Adam Weishaupt, the founder of the Illuminati, said this about using subterfuge:

> A cover is always necessary. In concealment lies a great part of our strength. Hence, we must always hide ourselves under the name of another society.
> — *Illuminati Manifesto for World Revolution*

Introduction

The close collaborator of Karl Marx was Frederick Engels, an *industrialist*. They wrote *The Communist Manifesto* together for the League of the Just, who had merged with Marx's much smaller Communist Correspondence Committee in June 1847, changing their name to the Communist League, and adopted an overt side, an open movement on top of being a secret society. They never stopped their covert activities, and this is what made the communists so proficient in Cold War espionage in the 20th century, enabling them to make up for the deficiencies in their system that stifled progress and industry.

Another example of an industrialist who advocated communism was Robert Owen, famous for founding communes and his influence on many prominent Americans. Perhaps no other businessman of his age had more influence on the communist movement. He also tried to establish it in Mexico in the late 1820s, and even as an elderly man he was in Paris during the revolution of 1848 to help Louis Blanc and others in establishing the direction of political socialism.

During the presidency of James Monroe, Owen spoke in the Hall of Representatives just after he had purchased the small community "Harmony" to expound on his ideas of socialism. In attendance were the president, President-Elect John Quincy Adams, House Speaker Henry Clay, and numerous representatives senators, Supreme Court justices, and Cabinet members. This represented the type of curiosity or support for the movement at the time.

Owen also influenced the Frenchman Etienne Cabet, who introduced two communes to America. Cabet was the link between the secret Jacobins and the working-class movement. Cabet was a member of the Paris Carbonari Society.

Later, a good example of an industrial socialist would be Andrew Carnegie, one of Carl Schurz' pallbearers. To quote Carnegie,

> I was brought up among Chartists and Republicans. Our family is distinguished for having an uncle in jail for holding a prohibited meeting in Chartist times. My childhood's desire was to get to be a man and kill a king.
> — *The Life of Andrew Carnegie*, Burton J. Henrick

Carnegie puts it this way after only hinting at his family involvement in Chartism:

> As a child I could have slain a king, duke, or lord, and considered their deaths a service to the state and hence an heroic act.
> — *Autobiography of Andrew Carnegie*

Carnegie's father was a leader in the Chartist movement and a friend of Cobbett, writing for his *Political Register*. He moved to America in 1848.

Carnegie, like all true socialists, had no religion as it is understood by the average American. He was an admitted free-thinker and rationalist. His family were Chartist leaders in Scotland and Swedenborgians. Carnegie likewise was a Swedenborgian as a youth in America.

Carnegie's mother was a follower of William E. Channing the Unitarian and Transcendentalist. Carnegie came to know Edwin Stanton in Pittsburgh in 1847 while a messenger, then telegrapher for the railroad office. He through his obvious intelligence was hired by a railroad owner and became active in railroad management. He later managed the telegraph lines for the Union into Washington during the Civil War.

Perhaps Carnegie had something more in mind when he financed the establishment of libraries across the country than simply providing books for those who could not afford them. Control what people read and you control how they think.

The Chartists were the communist revolutionaries of England, as much as they try to hide this today. The Chartist newspaper, the *Red Republican*, published *The Communist Manifesto* on its front page in November 1850. The newspaper was published by George Julian Harney, who had become an associate of Marx and Engels for a time, but like most socialist leaders they had their differences as to who would be leader. He founded the International Democratic Association in 1845, an organization of communists, and that is when he had a falling out with Marx and Co.

Harney was a supporter of the Union and moved to the United States in 1863, where he went to work as a clerk in the Massachusetts State House, the government seat, for 14 years. After retirement, he returned to England.

As you will see, Harney joined a long list of communist leaders who had no problem finding work immediately in American government, academia, and/or publishing when they moved here.

Although Frederick Engels had met Marx in Germany, it was his relationship with the Chartists and Owenites in England that cemented his revolutionary zeal.

Another example would be J. P. Morgan. He attended the University of Göttingen, Germany, in the 1850s for a couple of years, at which time he enjoyed membership in the student clubs but shied away from the dueling matches that tended to scar one's face. The significance of such clubs will become more apparent as you read further. Göttingen was a center of Hegelian activism and had been the last refuge of Weishaupt. Among the German literati, Göttingen was referred to as the German Athens and had a history of student secret societies.

Professors Ludwig Timotheus Spittler, Christoff Meiners, and Johann Feder at Göttingen *were known members* of the Illuminati. Keep in mind that universities in those days were not the vast institutions of today and were quite small based on today's standards. This number of identified Illuminists was significant, and the fact that they were at Göttingen displayed a penchant among the faculty for Illuminist teaching and their susceptibility to Illuminist organization.

Morgan's father made a fortune running the blockade during the civil war. Morgan himself made a small fortune buying government surplus rifles, re-boring them and selling them back to General John C. Fremont for six times what the government originally paid for them.

His maternal grandfather, Rev. John Pierpont, was a fiery abolitionist and friend of William Lloyd Garrison and Henry Ward Beecher, and was a Spiritualist.

Such men had an ambition that went beyond the façade of communism, namely how socialism or communism could be used to accumulate power in the hands of the state — and they meant to be the head of state, or rather, the power behind the state.

A modern example would be:

> Some even believe we are part of a secret cabal working against the best interests of the United States, characterizing my family and me as "internationalists" and of conspiring with others around the world to build a more integrated global political and economic structure — one world, if you will. If that's the charge, I stand guilty, and I am proud of it.
> — David Rockefeller, *Memoirs*, 2002

Rockefeller was for 15 years the chairman of the board of the Council on Foreign Relations.

Introduction

It is not money power; it is state power that is desired. It is far more powerful. Hitler, Stalin, Mao were poor. They didn't need money, for once they wrested power into their parties, they not only did not lack for any material thing, but they controlled everything within their grasp. This is why some rich individuals support communism, since money only buys so much power and it will not buy a moral person or a moral people.

Let us include an example of the power of total government vs. the power of money: Imagine yourself in a public place when a Rockefeller walked in and told you to shoot your companion. You would immediately get on your cell phone and dial 911, telling the operator that there was a madman there, to come and get him. Rockefeller would be placed under arrest and taken down to the courthouse. No, he would not stay there very long since he has influence and retains a lot of lawyers. But the point is that you would not have done what he asked no matter how much money he had — or offered you.

Now imagine yourself in a house in communist China in 1950. Mao walks in and tells you to shoot your companion. Under these circumstances you would know that you had two choices: either your companion or you would die, probably both if you refused. The power of total government is far greater than money. Money will only work on the immoral and unethical.

Let us also refer to another example to show there is more behind communism than meets the eye. Quoting from the opening of the book *The Naked Capitalist*, by W. Cleon Skousen, former FBI official and chief of police of Salt Lake City:

> "I think the Communist conspiracy is merely a branch of a much bigger conspiracy!"
>
> The above statement was made to this reviewer several years ago by Dr. Bella Dodd, a former member of the National Committee of the U.S. Communist Party.
>
> Dr. Dodd said she first became aware of some mysterious super-leadership right after World War II when the U.S. Communist Party had difficulty getting instructions from Moscow on several vital matters requiring immediate attention. The American Communist hierarchy was told that any time they had an emergency of this kind they should contact any one of three designated persons at the Waldorf Towers. Dr. Dodd noted that whenever the Party obtained instructions from any of these three men, Moscow always ratified them.
>
> What puzzled Dr. Dodd was the fact that not one of these three contacts was a Russian. Nor were any of them Communists. In fact, all three were extremely wealthy American capitalists!
>
> Dr. Dodd said, "I would certainly like to find out who is really running things."

And,

> There is a power somewhere so organized, so subtle, so watchful, so interlocked, so complete, so pervasive that they better not speak above their breath when they speak in condemnation of it.
> — Woodrow Wilson, *The New Freedom*, 1913

Some history teachers may not be aware of the above, but are aware of some of the true history of the United States. Due to a variety of forms of political correctness and academic realpolitik they do not teach it. This is true in government schools, private schools, and in the history curriculum of home schooling. It is easier to go along with the system than it is to make waves, but exceptions do exist.

This author was once asked to speak to a public-school history class about the dangers of communism.

The teacher said that he did not use the history book that the school provided but taught the students real history. He was mistaken, as I learned; however, while he taught more history he lacked the knowledge to teach it to the level as we have expressed that it needs to be done.

It is hard to estimate how often students have expressed that they found history boring. Real history is very exciting. It has been deliberately sterilized to the point of boredom to turn the average citizen away from any real interest in history or politics, thus they will not have the ability to understand what is required to preserve liberty. And, they see no value in studying history because they are not taught that history is human experience and that to understand it will prepare one for responsible citizenship. Even if they did, the school history books today will not prepare anyone for good citizenship.

There seems to be an opinion that exists that history is irrelevant, that we only need to know events and personalities of the last decade or two. Such an attitude will ultimately lead to ignorance, followed by the loss of liberty. You cannot find your way home if you do not understand where you came from. In other words, you cannot work for a correct solution if you do not understand the history of these United States, the individuals who established them, and the foundation on which they established them.

Throw in the mix that history just doesn't make sense to some and so they have no interest in it, and you have a population that has no historical perspective or the knowledge with which to stop the forces that mean to enslave us.

Without the true facts of our history it is impossible to fully understand what has been happening to America that has led to the situation we are in today and, therefore, its solution. Regrettably, this is also true of those who consider themselves constitutionalists.

In addition is the lack of respect for our Constitution. As the years have gone by, the Constitution has taken less and less of a role in school curricula, so fewer citizens pay much attention to it. This is manifested in the body politic, with the citizen thinking that it is acceptable to disregard the Constitution for an emergency and enabling the federal government to help out people in need, which always leads to more power being accumulated into the hands of the state. For in order for government to help someone, it first has to take it away from someone else.

The worse situation is the total disregard for the oath to the Constitution by nearly every citizen who takes the oath: police officers, military personnel, civil servants, and elected officials. Most haven't even read the Constitution to even know that is the case, and what it is that they have sworn to uphold and protect.

Generally speaking, in a free society no document that sets the law for a free peoples' government can work unless the people are moral. That fact seems to be one of the great secrets of our age. There are those who are trying to bring this fact back into American life, and great pains have been taken to do so. This was the greatest vice of the Age of Reason: to change a moral society into an amoral society, not linked to Truth as defined in a Judeo-Christian sense but in what is "good" for the people, a collective morality set by the state in the name of the people, called Reason.

This was the difference that de Tocqueville saw between American liberty and European advocates of democracy. While he abhorred socialism and appreciated the religious basis of America, he did not abhor the lack of a religious basis among the Europeans since he was enthralled by the Philanthropists in his youth, a religion invented to replace Christianity as part of the influence of the Illuminati strategy.

Liberty is a great thing, but it must be tempered with morality or it becomes license.

Today, one cannot imagine the opinions and divisions that separated the men who formed this country after the War for Independence. The desire for independence and liberty united them, but even during the war there were vast differences of opinion and ambition. We give you two examples:

Introduction

Rev. Timothy Dwight, president of Yale College, when speaking of the possible election of Thomas Jefferson to the presidency, stated,

> … the Bible would be cast into a bonfire, our holy worship changed into a dance of Jacobin phrensy, our wives and daughters dishonored, and our sons converted into the disciples of Voltaire and the dragoons of Marat.
> — *Six Frigates: The Epic History of the Founding of the U.S. Navy*

This opinion was the result of the Jacobin agitation and immorality advocated and exhibited by their adherents on the minds of the religious leaders at the time. They feared for the future of the country with certain men in authority who cooperated with Jacobins, including Jefferson at the time.

Even later in our history, as a second example, when historians came anywhere near telling the truth about these years, such passages as what appeared in McMaster's *History of the United States*, Vol. I, 1884 would be printed, but with little background or elaboration:

> We doubt whether any name in our Revolutionary history, not excepting that of Benedict Arnold, is quite so odious as that of Thomas Paine. Arnold was a traitor, Paine was an infidel … Since the day when the Age of Reason came forth from the press the number of infidels has increased much more rapidly that it did before *that book* was written.

Morality means more than simple "Thou shalt not's." It also means "Thou shalt." More importantly, it means that in a government "of the people," the people cannot ask the government to do things that they individually are morally bound not to do, such as taking from one to give to another just because they have come together and formed a government. They cannot give a "right" to that government that they themselves do not possess.

The number of people involved does not change the morality of a thing.

The things that government can do are specifically stated in the Constitution — likewise, what they cannot do; "they" because no matter how you slice it, government is made up of people. Government is not some sterile entity; it is comprised of people, who either do the right thing or the wrong. These people should never have immunity from the consequences when they do the wrong thing simply because they are part of the government. Indeed, they should feel the consequences even more than the average citizen or the government will get out of hand, as history has shown.

Our Constitution not only limits the government, it is designed to protect our God-given rights. *After securing our independence*, the latter is its primary function. Yet the student today is not informed that his rights come from God as it firmly states in the Declaration of Independence. Since God is no longer in the classroom as He once was, the American system cannot be taught to students to give them a complete understanding.

Interestingly, the neoconservative movement, while professing an understanding and appreciation of the Constitution, never seems to be able to mention the fact that the first duty of the Constitution is to protect our independence. Without independence, the Constitution and our system cannot work, since we will be beholden to another entity.

It is amazing how many constitutional study programs for adults are held without ever mentioning this basic fact. The more organizations that promote the Constitution are connected to the neocon movement, the less inclined they are to emphasize the need to retain our independence, since neocons are essentially internationalists, which will become obvious as you read further.

Today, the Declaration only comes out as a decoration on the Fourth of July, while the Constitution is largely ignored by all; both major political parties advocate and Congress passes unconstitutional acts while engaging in agreements that ensnare us in foreign entanglements, limiting among other things the independence of the American people. Worse, they stand by while the executive branch of government practices a type of oligarchy that flies in the face of the Constitution. Under the Constitution, Congress has the overriding authority over both the executive and judicial branches — if they will exercise it.[1]

One of the increasing problems is the delegation or ceding of congressional mandates, as stated in the *Constitution*, over to the executive. This has been an ongoing problem since the Civil War. Such modern delegation includes "fast track" trade negotiation and the formulation of the budget. These are congressional prerogatives, not executive responsibilities. Such actions throw the balance of power between the three branches of government off track and destroy the very fundamental division of powers that will lead ultimately to total executive power unless checked.

Keep in mind that the Congress is supposed to "set the dials" on what the executive branch is to implement, and the extent of that implementation, not the other way around. The practice today is more of the executive branch telling the Congress what it wants.

The executive is to manage what the Constitution mandates and what Congress has passed, and represent the American people on the international stage, not assume power to the level of potentate. The executive was also to veto any unconstitutional or ill-advised acts passed by Congress.

While it is true that a certain amount of congressional laziness enters into it, because most people do not understand conspiracy, they cannot fully understand why Congress allows the executive branch the powers that they do. It is not a "party" problem where most people point the finger of blame at the opposite party. As you will see, there are organizations that work behind the scenes within both political parties.

The problem with advocating any unconstitutional act is that the Constitution is a whole; abrogate any part of it and the whole will suffer and ultimately die. In that it is similar to cancer, spreading throughout the entire structure.

The Democrats generally advocate laws that take from one to give to another, all in the name of providing services to one segment of society or another, citing some adverse human condition as the reason. The Republicans have a history of advocating laws that destroy the power of Congress to maintain independence, and at the same time, the independence of the American people, such as pacts which pose as free trade agreements but in reality are regional government treaties under the United Nations having little to do with trade other than the title. They are in fact unions, tying countries together by economically integrating them.

Both parties place the war power in the hands of the United Nations by ignoring the need for a congressional declaration of war, instead passing resolutions confirming United Nations resolutions to engage in war. This has been the case in *every* conflict since World War II.

The problem has progressed down the road away from the Constitution so much that President Barack Obama came to believe he has the sole power to go to war, with or without the Congress. This condition is a totally imperialistic attitude befitting a king or emperor, and demonstrates that the Congress may go the

---

1   We recommend, and will again, the book *International Merger by Foreign Entanglements*, by Arthur R. Thompson. It explains in plain language the problems of ignoring the words of Washington and Jefferson about our involvement in foreign entanglements. www.ShopJBS.com.

route of the Roman Senate and simply be a showpiece, unless steps are taken to halt the process.

Another example was Obama's edict relative to amnesty for five million illegal immigrants. He did not have that power, but took upon himself rewarding, once again, those who have violated our laws. The condition was created by the federal government not enforcing federal law and preventing the states from doing so, and *then in the name of the problem they created*, they assumed powers not in the Constitution.

Further, both parties support government intrusion on the Bill of Rights in the name of eliminating terror, such as the Fourth Amendment. (The Constitution applies everywhere *but* airports, transportation hubs, government office buildings, etc?)

And when it comes to the United Nations, at the top both parties support it and allow it to dictate both domestic as well as foreign policy, no matter how much their rhetoric says otherwise or the show business performed at the UN by U.S. envoys.

One of the main principles of our government, indeed the primary principle, is the establishment and preservation of our independence as Americans. This was once taught in our schools as the first thing we learned. Today this concept is nearly absent in the schools, including private education. One cannot underestimate the need for Americans to think as an independent people. This does not mean we cannot interact with others, trade with them, appreciate their cultures, etc. It is always good for people to understand and appreciate each other. But when it is used to break down the idea of American independence and our wonderful experiment of liberty, then it becomes a problem.

The history of those who seek power is a war against the United States Constitution. On occasion it has been so bad that the disregard for it has been publically flaunted. For instance, William Lloyd Garrison, the radical abolitionist, openly burned the Constitution on the streets of Boston in 1854 and worked to destroy it — in the name of abolishing slavery, of course! But he wanted it gone completely, not to be just something that could be corrected by an amendment.

In addition to historical and constitutional studies, or lack thereof, a look at the English and grammar texts used in schools before the Civil War is a revealing narrative of what was taught: a much higher level of competence and morality. It was rare text that did not use Scripture and moral lessons in a steady barrage to teach good citizenship and morals as well as proper reading and language skills.

God was included in the lessons, for if not, the teacher could not teach the American system of government correctly. Our rights come from the Creator, declares the Declaration of Independence. If God is left out of the classroom, how can one teach the basic fundamentals of our founding documents and American system of government?

Compare these older texts to those in use today, and the differences in competence and morality at each grade level is striking. Some *primers* in use in the 1850s would be considered high-school texts today. Today God is absent. In fact, any reference to the Judeo-Christian God has become unlawful in government schools. Before the federal Department of Education this was not the case.

You might ask the question: What made something unconstitutional after 225 years of use? Conversely, what made something constitutional after being against the law for 225 years?

What changed was society, not the law.

As we will document, the organizations that have influenced our country for over 230 years have had two basic ends in mind: to change us into a socialist one world system, and to proclaim that God is dead. Surprisingly, there was no contravening *organization* until 1958.

No totalitarian government can allow their people to have a loyalty to anything greater than the government — not family, not business, particularly not a religion — unless the religion is controlled by the state. Every aspect of a totalitarian state in modern times does all it can to separate the people from all these ties through a plethora of programs.

A free people and their government encourage the opposite: a reliance on God. It is the helm of the ship of a free state and serves to make any civilization's people self-ruling.

Recall that the Roman government had a war against the Jews and Christians simply because they had a loyalty to something higher than the state and would not acknowledge the emperor as god.

To achieve power one must tear down the old social order, a belief in God, respect for one's neighbor's rights and property, and the bond of family. As Marx and Engels stated at the conclusion of *The Communist Manifesto*, after stating support for all democratic parties, unions, and the attack on property:

> They (the communists) openly declare that their ends can be attained only by the forcible overthrow of all existing social conditions.

They then demonstrate that it is to be a world movement, and a world government:

> Let the ruling classes tremble at a communist revolution.
>   The proletarians have nothing to lose but their chains. They have a world to win.
>   Workingmen of all countries, unite!

As we shall see, the basic goal of the communist is not that much different than that of Voltaire and is completely in accord with the goals of the Illuminati, an organization that followed Voltaire's outline and was formed in Germany a year after the onset of the American War for Independence and the same year that independence was declared.

A totalitarian state cannot allow the people to have a quality education or important facts any more than it can allow a loyalty to God. In both Nazi and communist states, God was eliminated from the classroom and the Leader's picture was the replacement. Regarding proper education, the Gestapo, the Nazi government's secret police, for instance, in German-occupied territories during World War II confiscated works pertaining to Illuminism and secret societies, making sure that such references could not be cited in future histories.

The same is true of Hitler's records in Vienna, Austria, confiscated by the Gestapo at the moment of the Anschluss. There are many facts that are known but remain suppressed that give a much clearer picture of Hitler and his motivations. His police record in Vienna would have probably tarnished the Nazi movement's masculine image forever.

Modern society is not that much different than ancient Rome when it comes to placing the head of state in a position of power and adulation. It is, after all, human nature and the reason the Constitution was written the way it was.

Ignorance of basic principles and how seemingly innocent initiatives can be used to manipulate the citizenry, even rob the citizens of their rights and/or possessions, is not new to America. It has been a problem from the onset of our birth as a country.

During the War for Independence it was not well recognized by the average citizen that paper money was a detriment to the well being of a nation. The American Continental Congress adopted paper money they called a "Continental" out of necessity and ignorance as to the consequences of doing so.

The extension of credit to our fledgling country by Royal France only facilitated this error. Without paper money, the initial stages of the war may have been unsuccessful. But the price that was paid later in human and commercial misery hurt the overall well being of the country. However, the freedom from government that was enjoyed by the people as a result of the war allowed the economy to rebound and grow rapidly, erasing this tragic memory from the people.

Quoting from *The French and American Revolutions Compared*, by Friedrich Gentz, 1800, as translated by John Quincy Adams:

> When the American revolution was concluded, the country proceeded with rapid steps to a new, a happy, and a flourishing constitution. Not but that the revolution had left behind it many great and essential ravages: the ties of public order, had, in a long and bloody contest, been on all sides more or less relaxed; peaceful industry had suffered many a violent interruption; the relations of property, the culture of the soil, the internal and foreign trade, the public and private credit, had all considerably suffered by the revolutionary storms, by the insecurity of the external relations, and especially by the devastations of paper money. Even the morals and the character of the people, had essentially, and not in every respect advantageously affected by the revolution.

On the other hand, the French revolutionaries who later also instituted paper money, fully recognized its problems, especially from the example of the American Continental system, and the French revolutionaries not only used it to rob its citizens but to destroy the ability of its citizens to be independent of the state because they were required by punitive laws to only use the state's paper.

The French Revolution produced the first hyperinflation in the Western world. It was one of the primary reasons for the dictatorship that followed. There was not another country that used this tactic until after 1900. Only with the use of the government printing presses can hyperinflation occur.

Paper money has always been used by the state as a hidden form of taxation by simply running the presses. The increase of paper in relationship to goods will drive the "price" of the goods up — it takes more paper to buy a commodity. When the money comes off the press, it has the same acceptability as the current market value. However, as the marketplace is inundated by more paper, and the money circulates out further and further away from government, the goods and services in relationship to that paper cost more — rather, require more paper money. If a plate costs X in the store, doubling the money supply without doubling the number of plates will make the cost of the plate 2X. The plate's value has not changed, only the number of paper dollars in relationship to it.

The process is so insidious that it is not the government that gets the blame for the increase in prices, it is the merchant. It results in the idea of the increase in wages and prices being inflation when it is really the government and its printing presses. The increase in wages and prices is the result of inflation.[2]

The government has reaped the benefit of the new money because it has been spent before the negative effect of the new money has been felt. Likewise, those closest to the government will have more benefit than those the furthest removed. The ones who suffer the most from inflation are the elderly on fixed incomes and/or investments.

Draconian government always lies to the people. Since the government is to blame for inflation, they will use government-produced statistics to convince people that it is not as bad as it really is. In today's world, the government falsifies inflationary figures to deny the elderly increases in their Social Security.

---

2 The increases can also be caused by government through the process of regulation of industry and agriculture.

This is because Social Security raises are attached by law to the inflationary statistics as the basis for annual increases.

The elderly, retired citizens are placed in a position where they are convinced that they need more government because they find themselves in a predicament. Their money has essentially been devalued and they, due to their circumstances, cannot work to stay alive, except at the subsistence level or just above it. They become fearful of what lies ahead and look for help, and the government supplies it at first, turning the elderly into a voting bloc.

Likewise, if the government says that inflation is down, regardless of contrary evidence in the marketplace, it also is used as an excuse to keep interest payments down. This helps the government when paying the interest on government debt. It penalizes the elderly, who have to live on investments tied to the interest rate.

If morality decreases, the young will find excuses not to be directly inconvenienced by the need to take care of the elderly, pawn it off to the state, and ultimately complain that their taxes have become burdensome, resulting in pressure to eliminate what have become useless eaters. Fantastic? This process was well on its way in Nazi Germany, and euthanasia is still practiced there today, as it is in many other European countries.

The elimination of the elderly serves three purposes as far as the government is concerned. One, state-sponsored services such as healthcare are less of a burden to the state. Two, by confiscating of property through the use of estate taxes the government receives eases the burden of deficits. Three, the older people, who can advise the younger generation, who remember history and have a better all-round education and who can possibly contradict the government positions and statistics, are eliminated from society.

Stable societies have always revered the elderly and looked to them for advice and the truth of history as they lived it. Modern society reveres youth and looks to government.

Euthanasia is a win-win for government. It is amazing how many conservatives in Congress never mention Section 1553 in Obamacare, the Affordable Care Act, relative to euthanasia. The language is convoluted, but the intelligent can read the meaning, and the meaning is that government will give grant monies to institutions that practice euthanasia.

We note that young Americans complained bitterly that they were being forced to pay for the elderly in regard to Obamacare. It is a reflection of two evils: government health care and forcing everyone to pay regardless of their circumstances — and the conditions that lead to the attitude outlined above.

Along with the elimination of the more elderly citizens, the memories of the old, tried and true ways, events, and history die with them, making it increasingly easier for the state to lie to its younger citizens and obfuscate history and the principles of good government.

Before we get too far removed from the subject of inflation, we must note that hyperinflation, such as occurred in Germany in the 1920s, always leads to a dictatorship. The disorder that occurs in the economic life of the country, the destruction of the wealth of all classes, etc., brings about the condition whereby government starts to intervene totally into the lives of the citizens and all aspects of the economy and business.

And, it was created by government to do precisely that. The conditions that produce hyperinflation are produced not out of ignorance, but by design. People in government know the results of their actions, what will happen if they outspend the growth in GDP. It is not stupidity.

As we shall see, inflation has been one of the issues supported by communist movements, and several political movements in the United States advocated its use during the 1800s. It is one of the means to help break down society by the ramifications of inflated currency on the economy and well-being of the people. It can be done slowly, or quickly by hyperinflation.

In speaking of the communist movement, J. Edgar Hoover, Director of the FBI had this to say:

Yet the individual is handicapped by coming face-to-face with a conspiracy so monstrous he cannot believe it exists. The American mind simply has not come to a realization of the evil which has been introduced into our midst. It rejects even the assumption that human creatures could espouse a philosophy which must ultimately destroy all that is good and decent.

— *Elks Magazine*, October 1956

Much of what you will read in this volume will be so alien to what you have learned over the years that it will be hard to believe at first.

This is particularly true since the official histories have produced a number of heroes for you whose reputation will be destroyed in these pages. No one likes their heroes criticized, and everyone has heroes. What most do not realize today is that their heroes have been made for them by the media. The same is true in the history books. Likewise, you will learn about men and women who were very important in the political processes that have been expunged from history.

Again, there is a clear and present danger when the intellectual life of a nation falls into the hands of its enemies.

Many of the situations that will be exposed will be just common sense once you look at them in a different light. Some things will produce a complete paradigm shift in your thinking. It will not be a boring read.

NOTE

Due to the history and time frame of the following chronicle, *many words will be used that were common for their age*. In this politically correct atmosphere that we live in, some may feel offended. There is no sentiment by the author to disparage any religion, race, or in any way to support the subjugation of any people through slavery or totalitarian government. Quotes will not be altered simply to conform to modern sensibilities, and in the body of the text it is much easier to use the vernacular of the time; it helps set the mood of the day.

The author is not 100 percent Caucasian and has no feelings one way or the other about race. He always judges people as individuals, not as racial groups. When it comes to what some wish to be called, for instance, the black movement has changed the vernacular in reference to what they want to be called four times in this author's life. Negro is a race; black is a color. There are many black races that are not Negro. Let us be specific.

There will be times that it may appear that the narrative is opposed to a good cause, and this is simply not the case. Keep in mind that those who want power support good causes for their own ends and have no desire to actually fulfill their promises to the causes they, on the surface, support.

We will jump around from time to time. There will be instances that will help you understand the earlier history if we give you the later history first. Sometimes people reveal themselves completely at a later date and involvement; and, it would have been better to understand their motivations earlier. We will alter the chronological order from time to time as we deal with any one issue or situation to help build your understanding of the motivation of the people involved. These will be obvious.

1

Background

In politics, nothing happens by accident. If it happens, you can bet it was planned that way.
— A quote purportedly of President Franklin Delano Roosevelt

Whether Roosevelt actually said this or not, it is close enough to the truth that many people have used it over the years to demonstrate that the people involved are more important than the events of history; after all, it is people who make the events of history or there is no history.

The problem with modern established historians is that they almost always write in such a manner as to eliminate any thought of conspiracy relative to historical events. If mentioned, then the conspiracy is made to appear as an isolated incident or of little long-range consequence.

Even more important than individuals, the influence of organizations on history, particularly secret or semi-secret societies, is not well understood among Americans today. It once was.

No one man can rule a totalitarian state, especially in a complex society. If he does, it will only be until he sleeps and is murdered by the second in command to make room for him. Actually, it is an oligarchy that rules and they put up a mouthpiece the people think is the ruler. Kings have their earls and their viscounts and on down to the knights. Hitler had his Nazi Party Gauleiters and Stalin his communist commissars, and so forth.

It is amazing that Americans can fall for the idea that a Hitler, Stalin, Castro, and myriad despotic bullies could pull themselves up by the bootstraps so that they could bully millions. They had organization behind them — every one. This includes such modern Americans as Obama. We are to believe that he rose to being president while never holding down a real job, being a community organizer (working under others), then running for office, never to stop until he came to the Oval Office — and he did it all by himself. A quick study online will tell the researcher who and what has been behind Obama since his formative years.

It is the inner party within the political movements that rule, and they by a very small coterie of insiders within a political society. They always try to control "history." As George Orwell put it in his novel *1984*, the Inner Party motto was: "He who controls the past, controls the future."

It is paramount that those who mean to rule keep the people in ignorance of not only the past, but the future. The populace must remain unaware of those events and processes that may influence the future and be adverse to the goals of the rulers.

The same is true in the reverse: How do you know how to find your way home if you do not know where you started from? One cannot understand how to restore constitutional government, for instance, unless he understands real history and the foundations of the Constitution.

Conspiracies, again, will always try to control what history their targeted people are allowed to learn.

> A people without a heritage are easily persuaded.
>
> — Karl Marx

Occasionally, good people will understand as well.

> The future is always built out of the materials of the past.
>
> — Booker T. Washington

When studying the influence of modern political societies many students start with the Illuminati. It is difficult not to.

A quote that illustrates this is from no less a personage than Winston Churchill, the famous war-time prime minister of Great Britain. While his motivation may be questioned writing "Zionism versus Bolshevism," in the *Illustrated Sunday Herald* in February, 1920, nonetheless it is illustrative of the fact that many people have known of the Illuminati and have referred to them as the genesis of modern day totalitarians:

> From the days of Spartacus-Weishaupt (who founded the secret order of the Illuminati on May 1, 1776) to those of Karl Marx ... , this world wide conspiracy for the overthrow of civilization and for the reconstruction of society on the basis of arrested development, of envious malevolence, and impossible equality, has been steadily growing. It played a definitely recognizable role in the tragedy of the French Revolution. *It has been the mainspring of every subversive movement during the nineteenth century....* (Emphasis added)

While the Illuminati weighed heavily on such events as the French Revolution and subsequent upheavals, the Illuminati was a child of several secret and semi-secret initiatives that were entangled in what is known as the Age of Reason, which is sold to the student of today as the Great Enlightenment, something that opened the door to liberty for the common man. While there were great writings of the age, there were also great deceptions as well. One example would be the book *Age of Reason* by Thomas Paine, a direct product of the age.

The title page of the first edition of the *Age of Reason*, Part Three, stated that it included "An Examination of the Passages in the New Testament quoted from the Old, And Called Prophecies, Concerning Jesus Christ. To Which Is Prefixed An Essay On Dreams, Also, An Appendix, Containing The Contradictory Doctrines between Matthew and Mark." The title itself begins the process of doubt and a clue of the author's motivation.

The student of today looks to the figures of the age such as Voltaire rather than studying how the founding fathers of America took the best of the wisdom of all ages and gave us the wonderful system that we have; a system that has had the greatest influence on earth, both for good and ill, but overwhelmingly good.

There is scant difference between the goals of the French and German philosophers of the Age of Reason and the Illuminati. If one studies the goals of Voltaire, for instance, those of the Illuminati are strikingly similar.

Voltaire, for the purpose of wiping out Christianity, associated with Frederick II, King of Prussia; Jean le Rond D'Alembert; and Denis Diderot, principal compilers of the *Encyclopedie*. He and they formed a systematic design to destroy Christianity and inject atheism in its place.

The principal parts of their aims were:
1. Compilation of the *Encyclopedie* with the rendering of Christianity as absurd and ridiculous and the minds of the reader steeled against conviction and duty.
2. Overthrow of religious orders in Catholic countries as a step toward overthrow of all religion in those countries.
3. Establishment of a sect of philosophists as the core of the movement.
4. Elevation of themselves to positions of influence and power.
5. Fabrication of books of all sorts against Christianity, especially such as create doubt and generate contempt and derision.
6. Formation of a secret academy, with Voltaire as president, in which books were formed, altered, forged, and imputed as posthumous to deceased writers of reputation.

They also attacked morality, government, and tradition. The *Encyclopedie* was published in 1751 and the first edition featured a winged Lucifer on the title page.

Thomas Jefferson wanted the *Encyclopedie* to be spread throughout America. He and Madison had copies. Jefferson recruited Benjamin Franklin, Madison, and Monroe as subscribers. The Marquis de Lafayette was a subscriber as well.

The banning of the publication in France in 1759 led to problems so acute that Voltaire finally deserted Diderot around 1772.

The sixth step above also included the use of forged documents and letters to discredit their enemies. The Illuminati made this practice an art. By the time of the formation of the United States such practices had become common against Illuminist enemies, including the Washington and Adams administrations.

As an example, letters were circulated purportedly written by Washington to convince Americans that he was pro-British as president, as a means to turn the people against the administration. They were forgeries.

The goals of the Illuminati were:
1. The destruction of Christianity.
2. The destruction of nations as such in favor of universal internationalism.
3. The discouragement of patriotism and substitution of the cry for universal brotherhood.
4. The abolition of family ties and marriage by means of systematic corruption.
5. The suppression of the rights of inheritance and property.

The aims of the Illuminati based on the stated goals, as well as the practice of their followers, could be delineated as: The overthrow of all government, the destruction of all religion, the abolition of private property, the death of individualism and family, the deification of sensuality, the repudiation of marriage, the state control of children, and the establishment of a world government.

A report by the California Senate pointed to the Illuminati as the seed of communism:

So-called modern Communism is apparently the same hypocritical and deadly world conspiracy to destroy civilization that was founded by the secret order of The Illuminati in Bavaria on May 1, 1776 and that raised its whorey head in our colonies here at the critical period before the adoption of our Federal Constitution.

— *Report of the California State Investigating Committee on Education*, 1953

Did you learn this basic fact when you went to school — any school?

The socialists/communists that the Illuminati spawned all have the abolition of private property as a hallmark of their agenda. Louis Blanc, the French socialist, said: "Property, then, is the great scourge of society; it is the veritable public crime."

Contrast this with John Adams:

> The moment the idea is admitted into society that property is not as sacred as the laws of God … anarchy and tyranny commence. *Property must be secured or liberty cannot exist.*
> — *The State and Freedom of Contract*

Or, James Madison in his essay "Property":

> Government is instituted to protect property of every sort.... This being the end of government, that is *not* a just government, … nor is property secure under it, where the property which a man has … is violated by arbitrary seizures of one class of citizens for the service of the rest.

The Illuminati were at first forbidden by Weishaupt to recruit women, Jews, pagans, monks, and members of other secret organizations unless the organization was targeted for infiltration, with a few exceptions. He preferred men who were between the ages of 18 and 30. These rules were later amended, especially in regard to Jews, who were generally excluded until after the 1820s.

The practice of excluding Jews in America from secret or semi-secret groups of elitists continued well into the 20th century in the North. This was not true in the South before the Civil War.

The Illuminati followed the pattern set by Voltaire, particularly the ideas embodied in his step six. Out of this came the communists, a two-century old organization which was originally a secret society before becoming an overt political party. Just before the formation of the Second International, in 1888, Engels wrote a preface to *The Communist Manifesto* for the English edition in Britain. In it, he revealed the fact that "the Communist League … unavoidably a *secret society*." (Emphasis added.) The Communist League was the covert organization that formed the open communist party and remained in control behind the scenes. Prior to this time, the secret organization was called the League of Outlaws, the League of the Just, and then the Communist League.[3]

An open political party can be met head on. A secret society is difficult to fight since they are invisible; and as such can deny their existence to the general public.

A person can deny that he is a member of the Communist Party under oath yet work for communism his entire life. The investigators ask the wrong question, since they only think that a person can belong to a surface political party, not a secret society behind it. Over the history of the communist movement in the 20th century, many people were working for the movement, in deep cover, without membership in the overt party. One such example was Ralph Bunche, who served as our ambassador to the United Nations a few years after World War II.

Engels tried to make it seem as if the secret society of communists had dissolved after a trial of its central committee in Köln, Germany; however, as we shall see, there remained a secret leadership behind the scenes.

---

3   It is interesting that in the introduction for the 1872 edition of *The Communist Manifesto*, Engels wrote that the League of the Just was a secret one. In the 1888 edition, he referred to them as a secret society.

European Revolutionaries Who Had A Profound Influence On American Society:

Philippe Bounarroti. Illuminati. Friend of Robespierre. Carbonari leader.

Gracchus Babeuf. The Illuminati member to whom Marx and Engels traced communism.

Louis Auguste Blanqui. Carbonari friend of Bounarroti. Head of the Paris Commune. Communism and fascism can be traced to his influence.

Giuseppe Mazzini. Born to a Jacobin father. Leader of the Carbonari.

Comte de Mirabeau. Illuminati pornographer. Associate of Benjamin Franklin. Atheist.

Nicholas Bonneville. Illuminati. Founder of the Cercle Social. Intimate of Thomas Paine. Father of Benjamin Bonneville.

A Theological Dictionary by Charles Buck, published in 1818, had this to say about the Illuminati:

> But the "real object," we are assured by Professor Robison and Abbe Barruel "was, by clandestine arts, to overturn every government and every religion; to bring the sciences of civil life into contempt; and to reduce mankind to that imaginary state of nature, when they lived independent to each other on the spontaneous productions of the earth."
>
> But it would far exceed the limits to which this work is restricted, to give even an outline of the nature and constitution of this extraordinary society; of its secrets and mysteries; of the deep dissimulation, consummate hypocrisy, and shocking impiety of its founder and his associates ... in concealing their real objects, and their incredible industry and astonishing exertions in making coverts; of the absolute despotism and complete system of *espionnage* established throughout the order ... with their various subtle methods of insinuating into all characters and companies; of the blind obedience exacted of their Novices, and the absolute power of life and death assumed by the order ... and of the pretended morality, real blasphemies, and absolute atheism, of the founder and his tried friends.

We are further told that the popular belief is that the Order had been suppressed by the Bavarian government in 1786:

> ... but revived immediately after, under a different name, and in a different form, all over Germany. It was again detected and seemingly broken up; but it had by this time taken so deep root, that it still subsists without being detected, we are told, into all the countries of Europe.

More "scholarly" works admit that the Illuminati existed up to 1800, but try all they can to not only convince the reader that there is no proof of its existence after this time, but deny historians who claim that certain individuals were members, such as Buonarroti and Mirabeau.

Yet evidence persists that the latter arguments cannot be true. It was Mirabeau, after all, who invited the Illuminist leader Christian Bode to bring the program of Illuminism to France. Talleyrand worked with Mirabeau to convince Bode. It was Mirabeau who was the public figure of the Illuminati in France. He wrote with Illuminists, hired Illuminists, and sloganeered Illuminist thought and action.

Talleyrand, one of the most important luminaries of eclectic Masonry, and an Illuminist himself, was instrumental with other Illuminists in the rise of Napoleon I from 1797 to 1799.

Mirabeau is said by some to have been initiated into Illuminism at Brunswick. According to Howard Mumford Jones in *America And French Culture, 1750-1848*, Mirabeau was initiated as an Illuminati by Bode in Berlin. Regardless, the evidence is overwhelming that Mirabeau was a member of the Illuminati.

One can find reference in the scholarly book *Illuminati Manifesto of World Revolution*, by Marco di Luchetti, to a list of members of the Illuminati which was submitted to the Austrian government in Vienna by the government of Bavaria, individuals of high station. This was done to alert the government of people whom they may have dealings with of an international nature. On this list were included the names of Mirabeau, Jacques Pierre Brissot, Lafayette, and Thomas Paine.

This list is made reference to by several scholars, yet seems to have been ignored by many American so-called experts on the Illuminati since it contains such names as the aforementioned. If these people were Illuminists, then it leads to a much more serious problem as it relates to the United States, as we shall see. There were a few names of harmless Masons on this list, but there is no evidence that Paine was a Mason.

In 1788, Mirabeau made no secret of his allegiance to the Illuminati in his work *On The Prussian Monarchy*.

After returning to Paris, Mirabeau, Nicholas Bonneville, and Bode introduced Illuminism to the lodge of Les Amis Réunis. However, the credit of disseminating Illuminism throughout France overall was given to Bode and Christian Wilhelm von dem Bussche. They were only a few of many who actually disseminated Illuminism all over France.

If one claims that Mirabeau and Buonarroti were not Illuminists, then it is difficult to trace the continuation of Illuminism *directly* to some organizations after 1800. The same can be said of Brissot and Bonneville; however, in the case of these two men, there is less denial of their membership as there is a downplaying of their importance, *particularly as it relates to America*.

This seems to be the point of it all: Deny the existence of the Illuminati at any and all junctures in time. When they are exposed, deny that they are anything but a misunderstood group of insightful men who wanted to change the world into a paradise of enlightenment. And, above all, downplay the influence on the United States.

For instance, *The German Museum, or Monthly Repository of the Literature of Germany*, published in London in 1800, had this to say about the Illuminati:

> The society declares therein, for the satisfaction and security of its members, and in order to prevent all unfounded suspicions and doubts, that they do not mean to propagate principles, or to countenance actions detrimental to the state, the church, or morality, and that all their endeavours would exclusively concentrate to render the improvement of the moral character interesting and important to man....

It goes on to promote the Illuminati as persecuted men who only had the best interests of mankind at heart. Note that this was 1800, supposedly *after* the Illuminati ceased to exist.

There are even books which tell a great deal of the Illuminati but try to make the point that Weishaupt is misunderstood and really wanted less government, not more — it was the other members that wanted mayhem and statism.

The work of Mirabeau is far more interesting and may indicate that there was not only a connection to the Illuminati but perhaps another impetus behind both the Illuminati and Mirabeau.

In the same year that the Declaration of Independence was issued in America in contrast to the foundation of the Illuminati in Europe, Mirabeau penned a program under the name of Arcesilaus which served as the basis for a plan similar to the Illuminati but more gradual in its implementation. Something that would be referred to today as the Gramscian approach: infiltration and patient gradualism.

Mirabeau, Weishaupt, and Bonneville all stated that their goals would be accomplished by incremental steps, not overt revolution per se. Bonneville put it this way: "secured little by little, universally, innumerable steps that must be taken on our ladder."

Mirabeau's plan was full of glittering generalities and virtuous-sounding language; however, there were more subtle and sinister references to the "enlightened" members of his association and that religion was superstition. He stated that the association must graft itself into Masonry and use it unknowingly by its general brotherhood.

The association would have two degrees: The first would believe they are working for the good of humanity. The second would be interested in international power. Since it only outlined two degrees while most secret societies have at least three, one has to speculate what was not committed to paper.

Mirabeau said that the organization, if exposed, would submerge to resurface later under another name. This was also the instruction of the Illuminati in its Regent Degree: "For this reason we should *always conceal ourselves under the name of some other association.*"

Weishaupt put it this way to his Illuminati cohorts:

> Conceal the very fact of our existence from the profane. If they discover us, conceal our real objective by profession of benevolence. If our real objective is perceived, pretend to disband and relinquish the whole thing, but assume another name and put forth new agents.
> — *Illuminati Manifesto for World Revolution*

Perhaps one of the most glaring examples of passing off the Illuminati as a passing note in history is in the *Story of Civilization* series by Will and Ariel Durant, the volume *Rousseau and Revolution* once one of the most widely read history series in 20th century America.

The massive tome on the title's subject mentions the Illuminati in three sentences. The third sentence says, "In 1784 Karl Theodor, the elector of Bavaria, outlawed all secret societies, and the Order of the Illuminati suffered an early death." Not only is the significance of the Order ignored, the fact is ignored that the elector of Bavaria *specifically* outlawed the Illuminati, not just in 1784, but four times again.

When you read it and understand the significance and power of the Order, it is almost as if the authors are saying, "Well, we got that out of the way, now let's move on." Yet, *in the period of revolution that is the subject of the volume, the Illuminati was the impetus and leadership on the Continent.*

Even the Russian communist leader Leon Trotsky recognized that the Illuminati were the root of revolution. In *My Life*, he says that,

> In the eighteenth century, freemasonry became expressive of a militant policy of enlightenment, as in the case of the Illuminati, who were the forerunners of revolution; on its left, it *culminated* in the Carbonari. (Emphasis added.)

It is unfortunate that he did not identify the right-wing descendant of the Illuminati.

The Illuminati recruited between two and three thousand members. Only 1,200 have been identified based on existing documents. Many documents of the Order were hidden or destroyed by Illuminati members, and much later by the Gestapo.

When one insists that the evidence portrays the continuance of the Illuminati, another argument is that it is due to the books of Abbe' Barruel and others who fantasized so much about the Illuminati in their exposures that others read their books and used them as texts on setting up their own conspiracies!

It is not unlike the claim that The John Birch Society produced more communism because they were exposing the Communist Conspiracy. It is twisted logic used to confound the reader. In the 1900s it was known as anti-anti-communism, and usually came off the communist press: The tar-brushing of true anti-communists to make them look paranoid in order to have the people ignore their warnings.

The technique was perfected in the period of 1789 to 1805, particularly in America. The most effective people trying to expose the Illuminati and its importation into the United States were treated as if they were paranoid at best, probably mad, and posed a worse threat to liberty than the fantasy they were trying to expose. This was a continuing theme put forward by all parties supportive of organizations and initiatives of Illuminism. It continues today.

It was not simply that this was a theme used *when the subject came up* in early America. It was injected into the political discussions and writings as a matter of course to keep the thought in the front of people until it was ingrained in them that any speeches, writings, or conversation about the Illuminati Conspiracy was the figment of the wild imagination of conspiracy theorists to promote the theorists' agenda against liberty-minded democrats.

In other words, it was a systematic campaign to implant a predisposition to reject anyone or anything that tried to expose what the Illuminati and its minions were doing. The same pattern has been used over the last two centuries to do likewise to anyone trying to expose the progeny of the Illuminati.

This same technique was used to create a predisposition in the minds of Americans toward any writings of our Founders who were in government or a position attempting to steer the fledgling country on a correct course. In this manner, they were able to have many people believe these men had different or hidden motives behind their actions. The result of this propaganda lingers today. This was done to Washington, Adams, and Hamilton particularly since they were in a position to effectively and physically oppose Illuminist initiatives.

Voltaire was involved in a secret academy whose prime purpose was the destruction of Christianity. The following quote from one of Voltaire's letters to D'Alembert is revealing:

> Let the Philosophers unite in *a brotherhood like the Freemasons*, let them assemble and support each other; let them be faithful to the association. Then I would suffer myself to be burnt for them. This SECRET ACADEMY will be far superior to that of Athens, and to all of those in Paris. But every one thinks only for himself, and forgets that his most sacred duty is to *crush the wretch*.

By wretch, Catholics believe that he was referring to the Catholic Church. That was to be the first step. In reality, he wanted to eliminate the Christ and Christianity. One only need read the volume *Memoirs*, illustrating the antichristian conspiracy by Abbe Barruel available online.

This quote also indicates that the secret association had problems with the ambitions of its own members with "every one thinks only for himself," and they do not always work for the association's goal, placing themselves first. This was and will always be a problem for such organizations.

The writings of such groups as the Encyclopedists were banned by the Royal French government, not because they threatened the royal house but because they were a deception and device aimed at Christianity and the social order of the day to replace them with something else. That something else was to be a new social order run by a few who had an ambition to rule the people, more than it was to get rid of the existing rulers.

While the average student believes that encyclopedias in general are short, noteworthy references, they are also a method of channeling the thinking of the student by the authors across a broad spectrum of information. Good teachers in the past discouraged students to use them as references, asking that they go to better sources for information for essays and papers.

Just as the group around Voltaire used this means to sway people, so did the Americans George Ripley and Charles A. Dana with their *New American Cyclopedia*. These two men were leaders in the communist movement in its early years and editors of notable newspapers. Karl Marx contributed extensively to its content and Adam Gurowski, the Carbonari radical, served on its editorial staff. This work evolved into *The American Cyclopedia* in 1873.

Today, encyclopedias are phasing out due to the Internet, and more information presenting two or three sides to a situation is presented. The socialists can no longer control the information services completely as long as the Internet remains uncontrolled by governments or a small group.

You cannot draw a line of separation between the Illuminati and the personages involved such as the Encyclopedists, Voltaire, and Mirabeau. Their work, activities, and allies overlapped to a great extent.

The Illuminati was founded by Adam Weishaupt, a professor at Ingolstadt University in Germany. At the time, he was not a Mason. He joined the Masonic Grand Orient in Munich in 1777, a year after he founded the Illuminati. He believed that Masonic books were too accessible to the general public to make them worthwhile.

Weishaupt did what other conspirators did in the age: attempted to graft their conspiracies into an existing secret society, regardless of that organization's purpose and constitution. In other words, piggy-back on something that already existed.

Weishaupt was to the secret societies of the day as Lenin was to the communist movement over a hundred years later. They both gave *organization* to the secret movements beyond anything that their contemporaries could achieve. Ideas are one thing, putting feet under them another.

In regard to point six of the aims of Voltaire, radical Americans in the future adopted this idea, at least to the extent of wanting to rewrite history.

One of the key men in the Carbonari Young America movement in the United States was John O'Sullivan, editor of *The United States Magazine and Democratic Review*, or simply *The Democratic Review*. He said in 1837,

> All history has to be re-written; political science and the whole scope of all moral truth has to be reconsidered and illustrated in the light of the democratic principle. All old subjects of thought and all new questions arising, connected more or less directly with human existence, have to be taken up again and re-examined.
>
> — *John O'Sullivan and His Times*

The same year, Ralph Waldo Emerson, in his Phi Beta Kappa Society oration at Harvard in 1837, titled "The American Scholar," said,

> Each age, it is found, must write its own books. Or rather, each generation for the next succeeding. The books of an older period will not fit this.

The thought is to change history and philosophy from the old to a new, but rarely a publically defined "new."

The problem that most people have is that they do not understand the value of organization or are not inclined to suffer the hardships of forming and sustaining it. They will usually remain at the philosophical level or engage in the political aspects of a movement. It is organization and not the latter two that gets the job done, provided it is organized effectively.

By organization, we mean members organized for action, not simply a membership list. They have an agenda, produce the tools to implement it, train leaders, form a structure from the top down to the local areas of their territory, and are concerted in their activity. It is work, and a lot of it is frustrating work. It takes a great deal of dedication to a cause, or an overwhelming ambition to achieve their goals and to sustain the organization indefinitely.

It was relatively easy for conspirators to capture control of the intellectual life of any country since they were organized and coordinated; the rest of the intellectual field was not. Not only was it not organized, it was fragmented simply due to the fact that it was free and had a diverse discourse with no goal in mind other than the individual's desire to promote his particular views or position, not the agenda of an organization.

Organization will always overcome disorganization. Superior organization will always overcome inferior organization. Truth, honor, and the American way will only be held up by organizing them to be held up — on a national scale, not locally fragmented in aim or purpose — with a concerted direction.

While organization will always win over disorganization, there comes a time, if organization is successful, that a "tipping point" is arrived at where the disinformation or evil philosophy will move forward of its own accord by the weight of the work done by organization of injecting these thoughts into the public psyche. In other words, the ideas of the organization have permeated the population to such an extent that the organization no longer needs to be directly involved. It is like a wagon at the top of a rounded hill. It is motionless because there is no slope at the top. Willing hands push it to the lip of the hill and propel it into motion. Once it reaches a certain point, the wagon rolls by itself — with the same disastrous results if done by and for an evil purpose.

A lie widely disseminated will do likewise, becoming truth in the minds of the people once it reaches the tipping point of public acceptance. Conspirators in the past have understood this. Joseph Goebbels, propaganda minister of Nazi Germany, repeated lies over and over again until they became fact in the public mind. It did not matter that they were lies because no dissent was allowed to help convince the German people otherwise.

The same general condition has been repeated over and over again in the history of the American people through newspapers, books, and finally the media, whom conspirators or likeminded academics have influenced. There are many examples, but perhaps the most egregious as well as recent is the idea of global cooling, warming, or climate change — depending on what recent decade you are looking at, and it changes depending on the latest storm or heatwave — as a result of human intervention. The facts of the matter rarely see the light of day and the propaganda is used to move the American people into allowing a state of control by government over all aspects of life.

There are several volumes available which record the history of the Illuminati. Some of the modern ones are a bit bizarre and one must be careful in this study. This is particularly true of the Internet. Generally speaking, ninety percent of the information about the Illuminati online is built on the idea that the Illuminati still exist, but openly. Various lists are purported to reveal the current membership. It is highly doubtful that these lists and organizations are true Illuminati in the sense of the Bavarian antecedent.

It has been difficult for the Illuminati to be completely expunged from history, so their minions have produced a smoke screen and there are three things which can cloud one's study of the organization: One, the idea that everything that has happened since the Illuminati's founding is attributable to it. This is used to obfuscate history among those who see everything as a conspiracy and therefore render them ineffective in educating their fellow citizens. It is true that people make things happen, but it is not necessarily true that they are conspirators. Two, the idea that the Illuminati were not as influential as they really were. This technique is for the more sophisticated student, to dissuade him from looking further. The reality lies somewhere between these two opposites. It has been the accumulative effect of Illuminist activity, a tipping point that has been the problem. Lastly, the idea that the Illuminati disappeared after its initial exposure by the Bavarian government. This is simply not true.

Modern examples of the premature demise of the Illuminati abound. In 2011, *U.S. News & World Report* issued a "Collector's Edition" titled, *Mysteries of History, Secret Societies*. In it, they went through a large list of secret societies, including the Illuminati. The magazine article on the Illuminati contained all three of the above clouding reasons to ignore the organization in history:

> There are other instances, however, where the myths have far outdistanced the reality. The most famous example is the Bavarian Illuminati, an 18th-century political club that existed from 1776 till it entirely disappeared after 1785, when an edict by the Bavarian government forced it to disband for supposed subversive activities. Most historians contend that it posed no active threat; that its members were merely spouting the radical ideas which pervaded European salons at the time. Nonetheless, fear of the Illuminati was irrevocably instilled — and, more than two centuries later, its specter still haunts conspiracy theorists. Not long after its demise, in the early days of the American Republic, public sentiments were inflamed by a book by Scottish scientist John Robison titled *Proofs of a Conspiracy Against All the Religions and Governments of Europe, Carried On in the Secret Meetings of Free Masons, Illuminati, and Reading Societies*, which claimed not only that the Illuminati had masterminded the French Revolution, but also that it had infiltrated Continental Freemasonic lodges and was threatening the stability of Europe. Americans feared that the group's radical ideas would soon cross the Atlantic. Of course, it never happened.

You can now rest easy according to modern establishment "there is no conspiracy" theorists.

If one gets by the idea that the Illuminati did not die when reported and wasn't what the pundits said it was, then he is propagandized with the idea that what happened stayed in Europe and never crossed the ocean to America. We will demonstrate that it did — overwhelmingly.

The Internet is rampant with falsehoods about the Illuminati, ranging from every problem is due to the Illuminati, to apologies for the organization. Even the date and place of Weishaupt's death is all over the map, from 1811 to 1830, from Gotha to Göttingen.

The fact is that the Bavarian government had to issue a total of three edicts aimed at the Illuminati over a period of two years after its initial exposure, from June 1784 to August 1785. In the latter edict, it refers to the fact that in spite of its earlier edicts against the Order, they still were recruiting and holding meetings, and again repeated the warning of the death penalty for recruiters into the Illuminati.

Many references to the Order claim its death, especially in Bavaria, in 1787, the year the last Bavarian raid was made on a home of an Illuminist when they discovered that the Order was still operating. Yet, the Prussian king, Frederick William II, was reporting the existence of the Order to others as late as October of 1789.

The Bavarian government was adamant in its fear for the future if the Illuminati were not stopped. An excerpt from one edict against the Order stated:

> As more time passes it is further realized how harmful and dangerous the Order of the Illuminati will be for the State and religion, if allowed to flourish here and beyond. It is impossible

to predict the deplorable effects that would result for posterity if we stand back, if not handled very seriously while there is still time to forcefully eradicate a disease which is far more daunting than the plague itself.

— *Perfectibilists*

These edicts and supporting documentation were sent by Bavarian authorities to virtually every other ruler of the German Confederation and principalities. By and large they were ignored, for by that time too many members of the German royal families and/or their advisors were already members. The fact that many of royal birth, both in Germany and France, were members indicates that the elimination of all royalty was not the goal.

The Order simply went further underground, later to resurface with new names and images such as, but not limited to, reading societies, Jacobin clubs, and in Germany, the German Union.

In 1790, the Bavarian government issued another edict, the fourth, against the Illuminati. In this edict it refers to the fact that in spite of the earlier three edicts against the Order, they still recruit and hold meetings, and it repeats the warning of the death penalty for Illuminati recruiters. The last edict came in 1794.

After making a stand against the Illuminati, Bavaria finally fell under their spell in 1799 by the influence of the Illuminist Maximillian Josef Montgelas. He was a Francophile, although Bavarian, who helped lead the kingdom while under Napoleon's "protection," and before the Illuminists deserted Napoleon entirely.

It is estimated that 430 reading societies were founded in the German-speaking areas of Europe from 1760 to 1800. These societies used their resources to gather books and purchase expensive volumes and magazine subscriptions. Those who controlled these societies had control of the reading material as well as the discussion of them. It became a perfect environment to instill radical views.

The importance of the Illuminati taking over the publishing, reading societies, *et al.* by the German Union and other entities cannot be overstated. Adam Weishaupt expressed it this way, as reported in John Robison's *Proofs of a Conspiracy*:

> By establishing reading societies, and subscription libraries, and taking these under our direction, and supplying them through our labours, we may turn the public mind which way we will.

The German Union used the degrees of the Illuminati as an extension of the Order. They faltered, but the reading clubs continued on.

The Illuminati influence spread too rapidly to have been an organization that was founded in a vacuum. There had to have been other networks that helped drive the work of the Illuminati. These obviously were of the aforementioned Enlightenment, but had to have had a more central source of direction.

Some claim it was the Rosicrucians, yet *modern* Rosicrucians claim they *sprang out* of the Illuminati. And, it is claimed that Weishaupt was a Rosicrucian. In addition, it becomes confusing because the Rosicrucians were the first secret organization to combat the Illuminati. Since the Illuminati had a superior organization, in the long run they may have infiltrated the Rosicrucians. Rosicrucian writings do refer to the Illuminati in their degrees, that a Rosicrucian could attain a certain degree that is referred to as "Illuminati".

Secret organizations may have the same goals but be at odds with each other, or even enemies, because each of them wants to rule, just as the Nazis fought the communists. Their end goals were essentially identical but the ambition to rule overrode any commonality. These differences were used by the

CHART ONE
Rosicrucians influence on America, based on Rosicrucian-published histories.

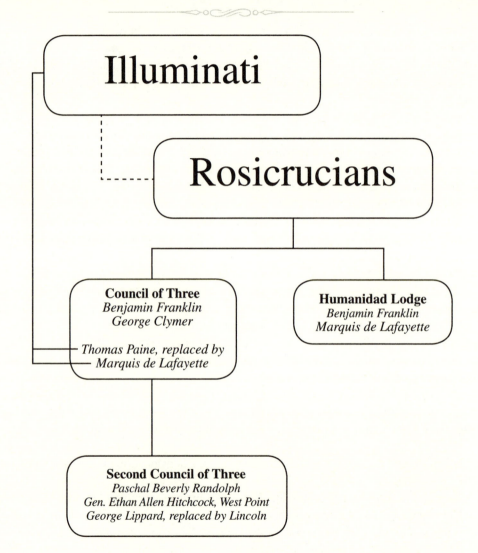

Rosicrucian Council of Three:
Late 1700s' Council:

Benjamin Franklin. An American Founder. In Europe cavorted with and worked in occult circles with many Illuminati.

George Clymer. An American founder. Pennsylvanian politician and businessman. Signed both the Declaration of Independence and Constitution.

Thomas Paine. American revolutionary pamphleteer. Member of the Illuminati and anti-Christian. Replaced on the Council by Lafayette.

Marquis de Lafayette. Illuminati and Carbonari conspirator.

ROSICRUCIAN COUNCIL OF THREE:
Revitalized 1850s' Council:

George Lippard. Rosicrucian leader and author revitalized the Council of Three. Founded the Brotherhood of the Union. Replaced on the Council by Lincoln.

Abraham Lincoln, President

Paschal Beverly Randolph. Rosicrucian leader and friend of Lincoln.

Gen. Ethan Allen Hitchcock. Commandant of West Point. Rosicrucian leader, Swedenborgian, military advisor and friend of Lincoln.

pinnacle of the Conspiracy to manipulate them into conflicts that benefited the long-range goals of the Conspiracy, such as World War II.

Of all secret societies, the Rosicrucians have been the most elusive to pin down. There is much written about them that is deliberately fabricated to throw people off the track. One does not know if *their* claim of Lincoln's membership is true, for instance. He is claimed, as well as Jefferson, Franklin, Giuseppe Mazzini, and Albert Pike, whom they say attained the Order of the Rose from England.

The head of the Rosicrucians in his writings in the early 20th century claims that Lincoln was chosen by the Supreme Council as the "anointed one" to carry further the work of what they called "freedom." They further claim that earlier there existed a Council of Three composed of Benjamin Franklin, George Clymer, and Thomas Paine, then Paine was replaced by Lafayette. Franklin and Lafayette both belonged to the Humanidad Lodge, which allegedly was a Rosicrucian entity. It is rare that anyone refutes these two facts: their membership and that it was a Rosicrucian entity. Claims of Franklin, Lafayette, and Paine as leaders in their order are persistent throughout all three modern sects who claim to be the true Rosicrucians.

According to the Rosicrucians, the Council of Three was revitalized in 1842 by George Lippard. It is said by the Rosicrucians themselves that this council consisted of Dr. Paschal Beverly Randolph, Gen. Ethan Allen Hitchcock, and Lincoln. This is a recurring "fact" in most Rosicrucian published sources.

These sources also state that Gen. Hitchcock introduced Lippard and Randolph to Lincoln. In all of Randolph's biographies it is stated that he became such a good friend of Lincoln's that he was on board the train taking the corpse of Lincoln from Washington, D.C., to Springfield, Illinios, but was asked to detrain because some of the other personages objected to a man of color being aboard. Randolph was of mixed blood.

Hitchcock served in many positions in the army, including a stint as Commandant of West Point, and finally serving as chairman of the War Board under Secretary Stanton during the Civil War.

There were rival Rosicrucian organizations due to the splitting off of groups within the original cabal, particularly around the late 1880s into the early 1900s, with the rivalry being intense.

What is known is that the world headquarters of the Rosicrucians was moved to America in 1848 and they stood for a parliament of the world. They are only one of *many* key conspiratorial organizations that moved their headquarters to America just before or after the Civil War.

Go into any old library that has books printed *by the Rosicrucians* about their history and they will state that George Lippard, Lincoln, Dr. P. B. Randolph, F. B. Dowd, Franklin, Jefferson, Paine, Lafayette, Napoleon III, Charles Mackey, John Healey, Dr. James R. Phelps, George Clymer, Goethe, Mazzini, Albert Pike, and Gen. Ethan Allen Hitchcock were members. Who knows for sure? Are they trying to elevate themselves by mentioning these people as initiates, or are they telling the truth?

When secret societies reveal themselves, how much is true? We have no doubt that when Masonic authors claim someone is a member of the Masons there is no reason to doubt their word. Is this true of Rosicrucian leaders who write about their history, or is it a means to throw names around to entice the gullible to seek initiation?

Of the above list of Rosicrucians, what is known is that Hitchcock was a Swedenborgian and the author of Swedenborgian books, including *Christ the Spirit,* in which he attempted to show that Scriptures were symbolic books written by members of a Jewish secret society. He was a warm personal friend of Lincoln as well as a military advisor. He appears to have been a Rosicrucian, since he is listed as such by every leader of that society in every book written about the Order.

Hitchcock was the Commandant of Cadets at West Point from 1829 to 1833. How much influence he had on the cadets towards enlisting in secret societies is not known. To believe that he had no influence in this regard goes beyond common sense. Conspirators have always used institutions of higher learning to recruit into their ranks.

A modern television movie produced in 1970, starring Glenn Ford, called *The Brotherhood of the Bell*, is a good analogy of this technique.

Returning to the Illuminati, Weishaupt put together an organization that used the pattern of previous historical and contemporary conspiracies and secret societies. He had access to a large number of texts on secret societies and occult groups. He was attracted to these books of a forbidden nature in Baron Johann Adam von Ickstatt's library. The baron was a professor and rector of the University of Ingolstadt, and had adopted Weishaupt after his father had died.

There were several secret and violent societies in existence at the time which could have served as a basis for the Illuminati, at least a basis for recruiting into the Illuminati.

There has been speculation as to what organization was behind the Illuminati, but it has been difficult to say with any degree of certainty. However, those who have had experience with organizing know that rapid growth of a new organization is not as much due to the organizers per se as it is that it has been founded on an existing movement.

It does not necessarily mean that the existing unit is responsible. It could be that it was co-opted by Illuminati members who were better at convincing people that there was something better to belong to.

It was not the Masonic orders, as some believe, since it was after its founding when the Illuminati attempted to take over Masonry. There were other organizations that tried to use the Masonic orders, with varying success. Or, they invented Masonic orders to help propagate their ideas as something ancient, secret, and beneficial.

The first degrees of the Illuminati served as tests for the higher degrees. Initiates were only allowed to advance as they demonstrated their amorality. The highest degrees were reserved for those whose station and reputation could best serve the Order.

The French wing of the Illuminati formed a Secret Committee of United Friends. They renounced all allegiances to God, family, and country save that to the Order.

The Illuminati was so successful that they were able to take over Grand Orient Masonry on the Continent, but not the larger Scottish or York Rites. Not every lodge was a pushover for the Illuminati. A lodge in Berlin declared war on them and called them "a masonic sect that undermines the Christian religion and turns Freemasonry into a political system." Nonetheless, by 1788, every lodge under the Grand Orient, about 629, was said to have been indoctrinated with the system of Weishaupt. Grand Orient Masonry still remains a problem today, not only in general, but for the rest of Masonry as well.

There were continued attempts, with some degree of success and failure, to use the Scottish and York Rites on into the future, and this played a major role in the 1820s in American history.

For example, the 33° was grafted on in a ploy to influence Masonry rather than being a part of the original rites, which only structured three degrees, and certainly one of the Commanders of the American Southern Jurisdiction of this Order, Albert Pike, was a master in the Conspiracy, if not an Insider. The Italian wing of this degree has as its motto, "I destroy in order to build," according to the former head of the Smithsonian, James H. Billington, in his tome *Fire in the Minds of Men*.

Delmar Duane Darrah, 33°, in his book *The History and Evolution of Freemasonry*, describes what they believe in the higher, grafted, on degrees:

In the evolution of man, we have passed from the individual to the family, to the community, to the state and interstate alliance, and in due time will pass to a united group of nations; the dream of Freemasonry; the fulfillment of God's plan; in the parliament of man; the federation of the world.

According to Scripture, God's plan is in the story of the Tower of Babel: the dispersal of man due to man's disobedience to God, not a world government. It is interesting that the promoters of the European Union in the 1990s used the depiction of rebuilding the Tower of Babel on one of their posters and plastered it all over Europe in all of the languages of the various countries to show that what they were doing was rebuilding the tower through the EU and reuniting man.

This fact will take on a significance that will astonish the reader once you see what lies ahead in the story.

God did not want a federation of man, which is why he dispersed them, for He knew that such a federation would at some point try to supplant God with government; and in any case, the larger the government, the more likely it would become corrupt and separated from the best interests of the people. Power corrupts.

Much of what we know of this 33° comes to us in well-edited form by the degree leadership, since the early records of the Southern Jurisdiction of the 33° in Charleston were destroyed during the Civil War. A volume published by them does exist, which gives a brief synopsis of their history from 1801-1861.

On the frontispiece is a painting of the original founders of the "Mother Supreme Council." As you shall see, often the number of men who started secret societies was five. The history of the 33° says eleven started it, but the painting only shows five.

Whether this number of men starting so many secret societies is a human representation of the points on a pentagram we do not know, but it is interesting that the pentagram plays a large role in the symbolism of secret societies.

However, much has been written about Masonry being the Conspiracy, which has turned the average Mason away from fighting the Conspiracy due to the distortion and the holding of all Masonry responsible. The true Mason knows that he is not part of any conspiracy so rejects any thought that the Conspiracy could contain all or any part of Masonry. Since Masons tend to be of the middle class, an important portion of society in general is thus segregated from fighting something that poses a danger to its own vows and class, in addition to the well-being of liberty.

As most know, many of the Founders of our country were Masons, such as George Washington and James Madison. Had Washington been part of the problem, he would not have done the things he did in his life, or been an adversary of the Illuminati and Jacobins.

The Masonic background of many of our Founders has been used as a means to diminish the worth of these men among certain segments of American society. On the other hand, the backgrounds of men who cooperated with serious European conspirators and enemies of Christ are either extolled or forgotten, depending on their influence on the historical record.

The majority of the Grand Lodges at the time of the inception of the 33° and for several decades did not recognize it as regular Freemasonry.

While Masonry tends to be a national organization in foreign nations, it is not the case in America. Blue Lodge jurisdiction does not cross state lines, thus it is less likely to be used as a centralized entity to destroy America: 1. It is decentralized and not monolithic across state lines. 2. The ability to use it by corrupting it is hampered by its self-governing limitation; in other words, the structure helps stem the growth of power within it. At one time, Washington was offered the leadership of all American lodges, but he refused. Keep in mind that the country was a lot smaller at that time. The last serious attempt to nationalize American Masonry was made in the 1850 by the organizer of the women's auxiliary Eastern Star, Robert Morse. It failed.

There are over 200 independent and sovereign Masonic jurisdictions around the world. Most of them tend to be national rather than split among local political boundaries, as is the case in the United States.

What is also different about American Masonry is the divergence of the number of orders; it is not just one order as it has tended to be in other countries over the centuries.

The refusal of Washington to lead a nationalized Masonry was part of his character. His life is an example of giving up power when he had it, from commander in chief of the army to president. And, he eschewed any attempt to make him a king. Yet modern histories tend to make Washington out to be a very ambitious man who wanted power. This is part of the campaign against Washington, to diminish him in the eyes of the student so that they will not listen to his advice for the future direction of the country in such documents as his Farewell Address.

A cross section of Masonry has included the diabolical as well as men of loyalty and honor: Charles A. Lindbergh, Jr.; Gen. Douglas MacArthur; Meriwether Lewis; and thousands more.

Interestingly, there is no actual evidence that Jefferson ever belonged to the Masons. It is true that he attended some public Masonic ceremonies, such as laying the foundation for a major building, but so did a lot of non-Masons in those days, just as people attend the ground-breaking for a new development but are not part of the contracting company or the financier or the architect or the owner of the project.

Jefferson did attend meetings of the Lodge of the Nine Muses or Sisters in Paris when he was our ambassador there. This lodge was one of the linchpins of the Conspiracy in France. Whether he was actually a member as was Franklin is not known, since the records were confiscated by the Gestapo.

It is interesting that Washington, the enemy of the Illuminati, was a Mason. Jefferson, who was a friend of the Illuminati for a time, as we shall demonstrate, apparently was not a Mason. Lodges do not usually allow non-members to attend lodge meetings; however, the Nine Sisters held occasional events by invitation.

This author has an aversion to belonging to anything that keeps secrets from the public, no matter how good these secrets may be. Especially if they are good — why keep them from the public if they are beneficial? One must remember that a conspiracy keeps itself hidden as much as possible. Too much is known of Masonry for it to be the Conspiracy. After all, why advertise where the meetings are, and on what date, at the edge of town on a billboard along with the other organizations residing in that hamlet? Or, wear a ring, display the emblem on a car, or march in a parade, allowing the whole town to see who you are?

You may even go online to find a website that lists 10,000 members of the Masonic order — so much for a really secret membership.

It is true that Masonry has its secrets, but any enterprising citizen with a little time on his hands can find out what these secrets are.

Finally, every dictatorship, from the Jacobins in revolutionary France to Hitler and Benito Mussolini and on, outlaws Masonry unless it forces it to come under government leadership; this happened under Napoleon III, but this is rare. Napoleon ordered the Masons dissolved but reinstituted them under the leadership of his nephew Prince Lucien Murat as Grand Master in 1851.

What is also not well known is that one of the most famous volumes written to expose the conspiracy of the Illuminati, *Proofs of a Conspiracy*, was written by a Mason as a warning primarily to his Brothers that they were under attack from this organization and to beware of it.

One may have differences with certain aspects of Masonic principles and beliefs, certainly in the area of religious precepts and particularly the Grand Orient. But religious differences do not always equate to subversion of liberty, at least not in the Western world.

In the United States, the most famous anti-Illuminist who was a private citizen was Rev. Jedidiah Morse, the father of the famous inventor of the Morse code. While not a Mason himself, he was invited to Masonic conventions to address the assembled on the dangers of the Illuminati. He stated in *A Sermon to the Grand Lodge of Freemasons* in 1798 that men needed to be judged by their fruits, and by the fruits of those assembled, the Masonic convention, he judged them favorably — but warned them to beware of corruption.

There can be little doubt that the Grand Orient over the 19th century particularly was involved in Illuminist conspiracy. The elimination of Masonry on the Continent by onerous regimes was in line with the attitude of eliminating competition for power once the power transferred to the main conspirators. They do not like competition.

The center of the Conspiracy is elsewhere; however, many of the key conspirators over the years have joined Masonry, usually the Grand Orient.

One must make the distinction of whether subversive activities are performed by Masonry or by individuals who happen to be Masons.

Good people must realize that when it comes to their common good, organizations that have differences today will suffer together under the yoke of communism if they do not work together to stand against the threat while they have the chance.

William Z. Foster, the head of the U.S. Communist Party, had this to say in his book *Toward a Soviet America* in 1932:

> … all the capitalist parties … will be liquidated, the Communist party functioning alone as the Party of the toiling masses. Likewise, will be dissolved all other organizations that are political props of the bourgeois rule, including chambers of commerce, employer's associations, rotary clubs, American Legion, Y.M.C.A., and such fraternal orders as the Masons, Odd Fellows, Elks, Knights of Columbus, etc.

While the communists persecute Freemasonry in communist countries, they also exploit it in free countries. The KGB had training bases in Russia for agents to learn how to exploit Masonry and religious groups just as did the Illuminati. We assume the Russian FSB has continued this practice as they have other KGB initiatives.

Concentrating on the Masons misses the mark, and much is done to focus people on this and other erroneous targets. This problem also persists by focusing on the Council on Foreign Relations, the Trilateral Commission, Bilderbergers, or similar organizations as the center of the Conspiracy, when they are only outer rings of conspiracy influence, albeit very important ones.

The year 1776 was pivotal for the history of mankind. Within two months of each other, the Order of the Illuminati was founded on May 1st and American Independence declared on July 4th. One would wreak havoc on mankind, while the other would bring more benefits to the world than any other human factor. For a religious person, one would think that two opposing spiritual forces were at work. And, subsequent events over the years reinforces this thought.

Keep in mind that Lexington, Concord, and Bunker Hill all happened in 1775, the year before the Declaration. This was the year of the birth of liberty. One year later, they affirmed it. The birth of the evil of the Illuminati was also a year after the birth of resistance to tyranny. It became the opposition to liberty by becoming the faux organization for liberation, just as modern organizations claim to be working for freedom while led by the socialists.

Just as Americans celebrate July 4th, the protégés of the Illuminati do likewise on May 1st, yet not one in a thousand members in these modern organizations understand why they march in May Day parades. If any explanation is forthcoming, it is that the celebration is a leftover from the pagan rituals in ancient Europe — lots of people celebrate May Day is the excuse.

1776 was also the year that the atheist Mirabeau penned his plan for subverting Christianity and the old social order, which would fold into the Illuminati organization in France and elsewhere.

During our War for Independence, there were key individuals who were under Illuminist influence who played major roles in the war, either philosophically or militarily. Several Illuminati societies are on record as being formed in America earlier than 1785.

Depending on whose documentation and research you believe, the first Illuminati lodge was either the Lodge of the Order (or Wisdom) in Virginia, supposedly the 2660th Grand Orient Lodge, or the Grand Orient Lodge of New York, which was founded four years before the end of the war.

They were sister lodges and corresponded with the Grand Orient Lodges in France. There were at least 14 lodges founded from these lodges, with probably 16 lodges established by 1799 around the country. Some sources claim 39 lodges.

These lodges were considered to be imposters by the Freemasons in America at the time.

There were some chroniclers of the Illuminati who believed that the Conspiracy went from Germany to America and then back to France from here through the French who helped us during the War for Independence. There has been no definitive documentation for this belief.

Between 1790 and 1800, the membership included clergymen in New England. You might wish to keep this in mind as we progress through the chronicle of the involvement of New England clergy in a wide variety of socialist causes in the early 1800s.

This was not new to the Conspiracy. Many Illuminated lodges existed in Europe comprised of clergy who were just as opposed to Christianity as the other Illuminists.

The Lodge of Wisdom had a membership of over 100 members. If similar lodges had a corresponding number, there may have been approximately 1600 Illuminists in America by 1799, if you use the smaller number of lodges in existence. Most of these members were foreigners, and of these mostly Frenchmen. A minority were American. As Jedidiah Morse expressed the problem:

> Nay there is too much reason to fear that the many thousands of Frenchmen who are scattered through the United States, particularly southward of New England, are combined and organized (with other foreigners), and some disaffected and directed by their masters in France, and that they are in concert, systematically conducting the plan of revolutionizing this country.
> — *Present Dangers*, 1799, Page 46

Illuminists petitioned John Adams when he was president to settle a colony in America. He rebuffed them.

Illuminists played key roles in bringing in France on our side of the War for Independence against England when the French king was initially opposed to doing so. They hoped to build a base here from which to conquer and then control the world. This was, of course, before they revolutionized France, which presented another element to their plans.

As we go through the French Illuminist influence on the United States, keep in mind the fact that the influence of German Illuminism was already here, according to the testimony of Illuminists in the Bavarian government's investigations. This influence was more covert, has never been documented, and predated the Grand Orient lodges.

The most striking early success by Illuminati agents was the French Revolution. By no means was the Illuminati acting alone, but without their influence it is doubtful the revolution would have occurred, at least at the moment in time that it did, and it certainly would not have taken the incredibly violent turn that it did. Since the Illuminati had a superior organization, they played the dominant role.

Most people do not realize the influence a few can have if they are organized and have solid leadership and direction. Some who try to diminish the influence of the Illuminati in the mind of the reader claim that there were no more than 27 members of the Illuminati that were involved in the French Revolution, the rest were dupes. Since Paris was the center of a centralized royal government, they only had to basically operate in Paris and after gaining control, radiate their terror out from there to the rest of France.

Twenty-seven people strategically placed within the revolutionary organizations, working in concert behind the scenes, would be all that was necessary. However, this number is based on the known members and does not include those that many today try to claim were not members, even though everything they did was in support of the Illuminati.

This being said, there were many initiatives to bring Illuminati influence to bear on France. It was the practice of the Illuminati to form auxiliary organizations to further the work and provide a layer of deniability that what activity was seen was part of the Order. A rather extensive list of individuals who were members of the Illuminati and organizations fit this pattern. These are a few:

- Filippo Buonarroti formed the Sublime Perfect Masters somewhat later, but it was the first "political" secret society in the 19th century. Buonarroti, an Illuminist, served under Robespierre, becoming his friend in 1793.
- The Asiatic Brethren was formed by members of the Illuminati, but at the time was not recognized as Illuminist and so escaped much of the reaction against the Order.
- Franz Anton Mesmer formed about 20 Harmony lodges throughout France headquartered in Paris.
- Bode recruited the Marquis de Savalette de Langes, the head of the Paris Amis Reunis Lodge, into the Order in August 1787, and members of this lodge were the leaders of all of the movements of the revolutions of 1789 and 1792.
- Alessandro Cagliostro founded Egyptian Rite lodges all over France.
- Bonneville's Cercle Social did likewise across France and back into Germany, and in America.

There were other lesser known Illuminists who also formed lodges throughout France.

One of the key attributes of such organization was the layer of influence each member was to attain. The aim was to impact as many people as possible. Some would only have direct influence on another, but some, due to their efforts, could have a wide band of control, particularly if they were able to rise to the leadership of other organizations or sects.

The impact of these auxiliary organizations in and of themselves was powerful, but what gave them even more power was the centralization of the concerted action they represented, and that centralization and direction came from the Illuminati.

Most honest historians who discount the effect of organization generally do not understand how it works if done correctly. They have never been involved in that type of organization.

There are many modern examples of a few communists, working together in secret, having a great effect on the issue, organization, or movement they targeted. A mid-20th century example would be the American Alger Hiss, a Soviet agent, the men in his coterie, and their total control along with Soviet Russian communists in the founding of the United Nations. Alger Hiss, while working for the U.S. State Department, became the interim Secretary-General of the UN until a man was elected from the General Assembly.

Perhaps the best, most-recent example of central organization and how it works was the upheavals just after the Ferguson, Missouri killing of a black man by a policeman in late 2014. There were immediately widespread demonstrations all over the United States. They used the same slogans, demanded the same goals, etc. There were several organizations involved, all financed by Soros foundations and institutes. They all pointed to the writings of each other, the websites, etc., as if being an echo chamber, making it look as if the demonstrations were spontaneous expressions of rage by minority communities, when in fact they were in concert and supported financially, even down to the payment for buses to bring in demonstrators from out of town.

To the average citizen, all seemed to be disorganized and spontaneous.

Organization is very important, for both sides. The Illuminati knew how to organize. Individualists did not until 1958.

The Illuminati had tremendous influence by the stations they held in French society. This influence flowed out and down throughout a very wide swath. They did not recruit the average man on the street. They recruited people of influence or people they could see would become influential, such as the sons of prominent men.

Finally, no better example could be used of how the Illuminati wielded their influence than by looking at the Cercle Social under the leadership of Nicholas Bonneville. There were several layers of influence that flowed out and down from the inner core. The inner core was actually the Cercle themselves. They organized the Universal Confederation of the Friends of Truth, which had a membership of about 6,000 in Paris. This organization was also called the Society of the Friends of Truth.

At the widest level or circle of influence was their public journal, *Bouche de Fer* (*Mouth of Iron*). This reached out to several thousands of people. In the end, personal as well as organizational influence took the lead in a handful of people having tremendous influence for revolution.

The Cercle was the most influential of the Conspiracy's fronts but lost control of the revolution to Robespierre for a time.

Early on, when the Illuminati were under attack, it was decided by the then leader, Bode, to call Illuminati the Philalèthes, or Philadelphes. In this manner, they were able to throw people off with further deniability as to their real purposes. Likewise, it made it appear as if they were French to the uninitiated, rather than German in origin.

Louis Blanc and associates of Louis Auguste Blanqui were involved and had cross-ties with the Philadelphians or La Commune Revolutionnaire.

Working in France with an organization of German origin needed a little exterior paint to make them look Francophile; Frenchmen could then be more comfortable working with them in the lower degrees. It is only one example of this conspiracy using whatever façade was necessary to carry their work forward: religion, class, race, nationality, etc.

This nationalist appearance by an international organization later evolved into a situation that did become nationalistic in character and worked against the Illuminists for a time in France.

The French revolutionaries were enamored of Philadelphia as a symbol of liberty. They used the term as a code or motto at several turns. It would also lead many to remove to Philadelphia as a result. This became a problem for American liberty later.

Buonarroti also revived the organization called the Philadelphes after his Sublime Perfect Masters infiltrated the organization. The members of this group helped form the International Workers Association (IWA), the First International. No less than one-third of the governing board of the IWA were members, but by the end of 1856, Marx and his followers were in control. This Rite was implanted into America no later than 1856.

Most students are led to believe that only French royalty was led to the guillotine, but thousands of priests and nuns were slaughtered as well in an attempt to eradicate Christianity by first decimating the Catholic leadership. Likewise, some royalty belonged to the Illuminati, and an occasional member gave his life up to the guillotine for the cause, but this was usually a result of inner rivalry amongst the conspirators.

At the Jacobin Club, Adrien-Marie Legendre proposed a much more expeditious measure for getting rid of the priests. He said,

> "At Brest boats are found which are called Marie-Salopes, so constructed that, on being loaded with dirt, they go out of the harbor themselves. Let us have a similar arrangement for priests; but, instead of sending them out of the harbor, let us send them out to sea, and, if necessary, let them go down."
>
> — *Journal de Amis de la Constitution*, Number 194, May 15, 1792

The guillotine also welcomed citizens who had the capability of organizing resistance against revolutionary leadership. In one case, in the French Vendee district, the revolutionary leaders used the army rather than the guillotine to completely wipe out the opposition to revolutionary edicts against the Catholic Church and military conscription — men, women, and children; the death toll was in excess of 100,000, with estimates as high as 300,000.

Keep in mind, this was the French army that killed French civilians simply because they objected on religious grounds to what the French government had become and was doing to their church. Hitler and Stalin learned the lesson well.

In Vendee today, a shrine exists with the many bones of common men, women, and children slaughtered for defying the Conspiracy.

As a result of the Grand Orient lodges established in French-settled areas such as Charleston, New Orleans, New York, Philadelphia, and Virginia; the Gallo-American Society of Brissot; and colonizing of Illuminati units in America, there was a great direct and indirect influence on American politics. The depositions of two defecting Illuminati in Bavaria in 1785 revealed that lodges had been established earlier in America. It was suspected that Illuminist lodges existed in America, and certainly Jedidiah Morse and others tried as best they could to document this, but this confession made it certain.

Keep in mind that the testimony above said Illuminati circles were established before 1785. The

Lodge of Wisdom, however, was not established until 1786, and other French-inspired Illuminati lodges came out of this effort. In other words, there were other German- inspired lodges established first.

This is what led to some saying that Illuminism came to America first and was then exported back to France based on the relationships developed during the War for Independence. If this happened, it paled in comparison to the efforts outlined above.

After Illuminists infiltrated our systems of high learning, such as Harvard and Yale, they started to recruit into their schemes the young, bright students that they instructed. On the Yale campus, for instance, Skull and Bones was established, also known as the Order. It was founded in 1832 primarily by Gen. William Huntington Russell and Alphonso Taft as chapter 322 of a German secret society, although others were involved.

Documentation of the establishment of the Order — and its affiliated fraternities later — always identifies the student founders but never takes into consideration that the college officials had to agree to their establishment and connection to the university just as they do any other campus organization. Therefore, the influence within the faculty was already in place.

Speculation is that the Order was the Illuminati, but no absolute proof has been found that it was. It certainly became an archetype of the Illuminati. Since Russell studied at the University of Berlin, and Skull and Bones became known as the Brotherhood of Death, it is likely that it was out of the Totenbund, itself a descendant of the Illuminati. It was Russell who brought the Order to Yale and partnered with Taft to get it started.

A telling clue of their origin, even though circumstantial, is the use of the term "the Order," just as the Illuminati was known.

The best study of the Order is *America's Secret Establishment*, by Antony Sutton, former professor at Stanford University's Hoover Institution. It details many areas of financial and establishment educational institutions run by members of the Order.

Research for this volume has demonstrated that members of the Order permeated a broad spectrum of society. Our purpose is not to document this organization other than how it fits the narrative, since the work has already been done by Antony Sutton. Members were and are involved in academia, the diplomatic service, the Treasury, Defense, and State Departments, the Attorney General's Office, religious institutions, state legislatures, state constitutional conventions, the Congress, etc. To fully grasp the problem of the Order, one needs to read Sutton's tome, which will give a better picture of the documentation of personalities in this work.

Georg Wilhelm Frederich Hegel was an important precursor to Marxism and had been directly influenced by Illuminati, if not one of them. The records of who were actual members are not complete by half. Russell became steeped in the philosophy of Hegel and remained interested in the Hegelian Dialectic all of his life.

Over the years, the control over Yale after 1862 by members of Skull and Bones has been remarkable. Members of the Order encouraged the formation of secret societies on other campuses as they gained influence. In the early years an inordinate number became instructors of higher learning in educational institutions. Andrew Dickson White of the Order was the first president of Cornell, and he encouraged the formation of a secret society on that campus.

He announced that Cornell would be "an asylum for *Science* — where truth shall be sought for truth's sake, not stretched out or cut exactly to fit Revealed Religion." (Emphasis in the original.)

Another early Cornell leader who was a member of the Order was the trustee Francis Miles Finch.

He was appointed by President Ulysses S. Grant as the collector of internal revenue for the 26th District of New York. Later he became the dean of the law school at Cornell in 1891.

Perhaps the most influential man who promoted the Order in academia was Daniel Coit Gilman. Not only was he a Skull and Bones man, but other members of his family were as well. He was the first president of Johns Hopkins, the University of California, and the Carnegie Institution. He had studied under Hegelians in Germany and wanted to influence Americans through the churches, schools, politics, and literature.

He was the first president of the American Historical Association and served on the Smithsonian Board of Regents. He was renowned for his expertise in education, yet one of his daughters, Elisabeth, became a social activist in the Socialist Party, running on their ticket several times.

Gilman trained John Dewey at Hopkins. Dewey went on to become the recognized leader of American education within liberal circles. Gilman appointed other members of the Order and Hegelian-trained people into prominent chairs at the institutions he controlled, especially Hopkins.

Gilman is only one example of a person rising to prominence that used his position to propagate the Order's agenda by the infiltration of like-minded people to positions of influence and power. Another example would be F. W. Fisk, who became the president of the Chicago Theological Seminary. It would not just be secular education that would come under their purview.

The banking profession is rife with the Order. There are a number of websites that have extensive lists of people who have come through Skull and Bones and their influence was and is staggering.

Since the Order recruited students, it could not be part of the inner core, but a first step toward something else. Many prominent men have come out of its ranks, but more have disappeared from history after leaving the campus as well, never becoming prominent or important enough to be publically noticed.

The son of co-founder Alphonso Taft, a Skull and Bones man himself, was William Howard Taft, a Republican, who became president, chief justice of the Supreme Court, and founder of the National Chamber of Commerce. The more famous modern generational Order members in the 20th century were the Bush family — Prescott, George Sr., and George Jr..

Taft, as president, appointed another member of the Order as his Secretary of Treasury, Franklin MacVeagh.

As stated, Russell brought Skull and Bones to Yale University from Germany, where he had been in 1831-32. He later served in the Connecticut State Legislature in the mid-1840s. He founded the Collegiate and Commercial Institute in New Haven. At this institution, he trained the students in military drill *in anticipation of a civil war, many years prior to the war*. In this, he was an American reflection of the German Turner units.

It is not too much of a stretch to ask whether the work of Russell in this regard was a direct reflection of his close association with organizations in Germany that spawned the Turnverein. We will show that one of the main goals of the Turner organizations in America was the formation of a militia trained for the future civil war ten years before the war broke out. The idea of a civil war was on the mind of the communist leadership within the Turners, and they prepared for it just as they had prepared in advance for the communist revolution of 1848 in Europe.

Russell grew close to John Brown and was involved in supporting his efforts in the Kansas conflict in the 1850s. He is rarely mentioned in this regard, and most of the focus on who backed Brown's efforts is on the so-called Secret Six. Yet, it was Russell who became one of the trustees of Brown's will.

Many of Russell's students became drill masters at the beginning of the war. He was made a general in the Connecticut National Guard from 1862 to 1870 by the Legislature.

Members of the Order worked both sides of the Civil War. William Barry, who came through Skull and Bones in 1841, presided over the Mississippi secession convention as the leader of the state Legislature and served in the provisional Confederate Congress until 1862, when he joined the army. Another member of the Order served as the chairman of the secession convention in Louisiana, John Perkins, Jr. He also served in the Confederate Senate. Remember this as we discuss the fact that the conspiracy worked both sides to promote a war.

Part of a network of similar "fraternities" was Scroll and Key, founded also at Yale in 1842. It too appeared to be a chapter of the Order, although that is not its reputation. Very famous people have come out of Scroll and Key, and they tend to be quite liberal in their politics. Another was Wolf's Head, founded in 1883. Each was established out of the controversy of the earlier secret societies. As one fell into disrepute, another society was formed.

Modern conspiracy buffs concentrate on Skull and Bones but neglect the two other organizations. Many of the men who have promoted socialist movements have come out of these two societies. For instance, Robert Hutchins, the promoter of the Great Books program, worked with Socialist Party leaders. He came through Wolf's Head.

The establishment of these newer secret societies matched the tactic, a variation, of forming new organizations out of the old to mask the fact that the old still existed — at least the leadership of the exposed organization.

These campus secret fraternities were very useful in fulfilling an important tactic promoted by the Illuminati. This tactic is to not only enlist the brightest students but to target the progeny of their enemies, making their sons into minions. In this way, the younger can coast on the reputation of the elder among the Illuminists' opposition, subverting much of the father's organization and effectiveness as trusted friends.

In addition, they capture the financial base of their enemy upon his death by having enlisted the heir into their cause.

An example of this would have been Timothy Dwight V. The older Dwight was a fighter against the Illuminati and its influences. The younger Dwight became a member of the Order, studied in Germany under Hegelians, and later served on the American committee for the revision of the English version of the Bible from 1878 to 1885. He became the president of Yale in 1886.

An earlier exclusive club was established at Harvard in 1791. This would have been six years after members of the Illuminati said that circles had been established in America. The club is the Porcellian Club and has the earmarks of being a recruiting ground rather than a secret society for the Conspiracy; however, more research must be made into its influence, particularly today in the Microsoft Corporation and the House of Morgan.

Part of the problem researching the Club is that various dates have been given as to its founding, but the Club itself states it was founded in 1791.

Several members went on to great heights in American life and society, while others simply disappeared from notice, just as early members of Skull and Bones. A short list you would find of interest would be Theodore Roosevelt, Edward Everett, Oliver Wendell Holmes, Sr. and Jr., James Russell Lowell, Wendell Phillips, student leader of the Club, Charles Sumner, and a few who seemed to have been named later in life as honorary members such as a Major General George Gordon Meade, victor at Gettysburg, and August Belmont.

Just as other clubs were later formed at Yale, many other elitist clubs were formed at Harvard years after the Porcellian Club, usually due to the disappointment at having been passed over by Porcellian which had a limit on the number tapped. However, these clubs grew as Harvard enrollment grew. In the early 1800s, the classes were below two hundred students. Enrollment today is over 20,000.

Hegel had a great influence on German intellectual circles, and thus on Americans who studied there. As a youth, Hegel came to consider that Christianity was a moral error. He never changed that opinion. Hegelians believed that the state is almighty and seen as the march of God on earth. Hegel was directly influenced by members of the Illuminati.

At first, Hegel identified with the Jacobins, and was then a Girondist. Girondists were the original Jacobin and Cercle Social members who lost control to the Robespierre faction in France. Indeed, the core of the Girondists were leaders in the Cercle. His roommates, Friedrich Hölderin and Friedrich Wilhelm Joseph Schelling, became important thinkers in the development of German Idealism. Later, Schelling would fall out with Hegel and Hölderin would become hopelessly insane.

Hegelian philosophy greatly influenced German thought. One of the most important aspects of his philosophy was the theory of thesis and antithesis leading to the synthesis: the Hegelian Dialectic. This essentially is an amoral tool used by conspiratorial forces to endorse compromise as a convoluted philosophical thought rather than simply stating up front that it is the tactic of getting people to give up their principles and gradually moving them in the direction you wanted them to move in the first place — a step at a time — all in the name of a "scientific" social theory rather than calling it what it is: compromise.

Hegelian teaching, therefore, was designed to lessen one's faith in Christianity while outlining the means to get people to compromise their beliefs in the name of intellectual pursuits and rationalization. This teaching among students studying philosophy and related sociology spread this false doctrine, radiating out into more and more educational institutions as sound doctrine. By so doing, it spread the influence in intelligentsia among those who may or may not have been part of an organized conspiracy, in turn doing the Conspiracy's work for them.

To overcome Hegelian philosophy one would need a strong moral base and just plain common sense based on logic, two things that modern education rarely teaches.

Philip Schaff, a German Hegelian, was a professor of sacred literature at Union Theological Seminary in New York City. He had been arrested for heresy, but the charges were dropped. He was president of the American Bible revision committee organized in 1871 and worked in close cooperation with English revisionists. In this he preceded Timothy Dwight V.

It isn't what Scripture says; it is how it is translated. It becomes very important for students to understand Greek to be able to read the original texts of the New Testament, as well as those of the Greek philosophers, not the possible bias of the translator. Of course, it also helps to know Hebrew for the Old Testament.

Much of the lack of education regarding these two languages can be overcome by the use of extensive concordances, but not entirely since a word may be known by the nuance of its use with other words.

A later revolutionary, Alexander Herzen, who would link up with Mikhail Bakunin, the Russian revolutionary, was close to Mazzini. He said, "Hegel is the new Christ bringing the word of truth to men...." He said of Carl Schurz that he was the best of all German immigrants to America. He also was a follower of the socialist Charles Fourier.

While it is not an example of a son joining the other side, it certainly is an example of the son not being the father when it came to understanding the Conspiracy. Rev. Morse was an American opponent of the Illuminati from the very beginning; his son Samuel Morse, while also an opponent of conspiracy, believed that it was the Catholic Church. By so believing, he was neutralized away from fighting the true source of the Conspiracy and at the same time served them by attacking what the Conspiracy wanted eliminated.

In the beginning, the Catholic Church was a bulwark against Illuminism. The Catholic Church of today is not the same as it was 200 years ago, or 100 years ago when it comes to opposing Illuminism.

The modern example of the same initiative would be targeting the sons of prominent members of The John Birch Society who fought all of their lives for constitutional government. There are instances of members of the Society who had children who went on to be more prominent than their fathers and used their positions to neutralize the influence of constitutional organizations within the so-called conservative movement. And, they disparaged the JBS at every opportunity. One became a governor, another vice-president, and another a wealthy financier of neo-conservative causes. Finally, one published a book attacking the Society as well as her parents. She realized that tolerance was needed when her two sons joined the gay community.

In almost every case, the sons and daughters were changed by their education at major universities.

Not all campus secret societies are a danger to liberty, and many such societies proliferate on the more prestigious campuses. The sheer number helps provide camouflage for the ones which are conspiratorial.

Some started as secret societies, or at least kept their membership or mission secret. One such was the Phi Beta Kappa fraternity at Harvard. John Quincy Adams was involved in eliminating the secret aspect of this fraternity from its constitution.

The first recorded secret society in America on a campus was at William and Mary, the F.H.C. Society. It was founded in 1750 and the name is based on the Latin phrase "Fraternitas, Humanitas, et Cognito," or, Brotherhood, Humaneness, and Knowledge. Its most illustrious member was Thomas Jefferson.

One of the biggest mistakes made by those who recognize that a conspiracy exists to enslave the world is that it stems from the money power. The Conspiracy built the money power, not the other way around. It is the case with every aspect of the economic and academic world — even the arts. The Conspiracy uses their people to build the reputation and influence of their minions so they are able to influence the education, economic systems, and industry of any country, and ultimately, the world. In America, they helped build the Rockefellers and Carnegies just as much as these men helped themselves. In turn, these minions used their money and influence to further subvert their countries.

As we shall explain later, the goal is to subvert society first as a prelude to revolution in government. This includes the elimination of any idea of God across all sectors of society. Thus there are many facets of society they have to control, and they attempt to build up the leadership of those sectors in order to lead others into false doctrine or illogical thinking, at the same time doing all they can to change the people from following age-old principles to following Illuminist philosophy.

Two of the individuals who were influenced by the Enlightenment and — if not under Illuminati influence at the time of the War for Independence, came under it soon after the war — were Thomas Paine and Lafayette.

If Thomas Paine had stopped writing after *Common Sense* he would have made an important contribution to mankind, but even within *Common Sense* were the seeds of something other than God-given, individual rights. Increasingly, every major thing he wrote after this served another master than Liberty, but was made to appear as if it was in defense of liberty. Not everything Paine said was in error, obviously, otherwise he would not have had people listen to him at all. For instance he said, "money is money and paper is paper, and all the inventions of man cannot make it otherwise." When he was speaking of money he meant precious and semi-precious metals — sound economics.

His famous *Rights of Man*, however, did not advocate the rights of the individual but the rights of man as a whole, as a people, as a nation. In the second part, Paine sketched the outline of the modern welfare state: a graduated income tax to pay for government schools, old age pensions, public housing, and help for the needy. This is the primary reason collectivists always refer to this work of Paine and Paine himself. It is a primer for communism, the collective rather than the individual.

By 1797, Paine was calling for an inheritance tax.

When he left the United States for England, his protector in London was the protégé of the Illuminist Mirabeau, Etienne Dumont. After this association he moved to France, and shortly thereafter lived with the communist Nicholas Bonneville and his wife, Margaret, from 1797 to 1802. Bonneville had become an Illuminist by Weishaupt's associate Christian Bode in 1787.

It is difficult to believe that Paine, under the influence of and then living with an Illuminist for years, did not become one himself. There are historians who claim Paine was an Illuminist in England prior to moving to France, and that he had started several illuminated lodges that were in existence when Robison wrote his *Proofs of a Conspiracy* in 1797. Then there is the listing of his name on the roster of Illuminati furnished to Vienna by the Bavarian government by Count Graf Lehrbach, who lists him as being from England, before he moved to France.

Paine was also listed as a member of a German lodge, the same as Bonneville, under the Duke Ernst of Gotha as Grand Master — the same duke who served as Weishaupt's protector after he left Bavaria.

There were at least eight Illuminated lodges in England by the time Robison wrote his *Proofs of a Conspiracy*. There were many concerns the British Parliament had about not only the Illuminati, but other secret societies of the day, which we now know were adjuncts of the Order. Cagliostro moved to England for a time, joining the London Theosophical Society, and worked to form Illuminated lodges. Franz von Baader and Xaver Zwack did as well. The concern was so great that Parliament passed the *Unlawful Societies Act of 1799*. It excluded Masonry from the law.

This was done, just as were the Alien and Sedition Acts in America, to curtail the agitation, espionage, and subversion of the Illuminist organizations.

We should define what we mean by Illuminated lodges. Many lodges and small groups are started or led by Illuminati and they propagated illuminist ideas and control, but not all members were illuminati, had they been the Order would have consisted of tens of thousands. By assuming leadership roles, the hard-core Illuminist controlled lodges, organizations, and movements influenced the thinking, thereby the political direction, of hundreds of thousands.

Keep in mind that Bonneville, according to many historians and it appears to be true, was the most important member of the Illuminati in France at the time Paine moved in with him. Much of the modern communist movement can be traced directly to Bonneville and his Cercle Social.

For a time, the Marquis de Savalette de Langes, the consecrator of the Lodge of Les Amis Réunis (The United Friends), was an aide-de-camp to Lafayette. He was an Illuminist who had, through his position earlier as the Keeper of the Royal Treasury of France and the initiation of many financiers into Les Amis Réunis, a great deal of influence on banking in Western Europe, particularly France.

The origins of the Cercle Social came out of the Contrat Social lodge. The key membership of both the Cercle and the Contrat overlapped. Bonneville, the leader of the Cercle, was a member of both, as were the Marquis de Condorcet, and Abbe Claude Fauchet, a co-founder. The Log Contrat Social was led by Dr. Boileau, who matched the rites to the rites of the Berlin Illuminati.

Lafayette claimed to have been initiated into Masonry at the Log Contrat Social of Paris before he came to America. So by his words, he was already involved in Illuminism while serving under Washington. How many Americans did he influence into the Order? It also demonstrates that enemies of the Illuminati such as Washington and Hamilton could be fooled by them as long as there was any common goal or seemingly common goal. This problem persists today in Republican and conservative ranks.

The Theophilanthropic movement was meant to replace Christianity. It is traceable to the deistic society of David Williams and Benjamin Franklin in London in the 1770s. It included many members of the Paris lodge of the *Neuf Soeurs*, or Nine Sisters, sometimes referred to as the Nine Muses: Franklin, Paine, John Paul Jones, people associated with Illuminism, and Dupont de Nemours who was a Theophilantropist.

Later, Dupont, residing in the United States, would be used by Jefferson to *initiate* the purchase of the Northwest Territory from Napoleon.

Franklin had a reputation of having dabbled in the occult and been a ladies man while in France. Years before, he kept company with subversive Englishmen and participated with those who dabbled in Satanism and immoral practices in the Hell Fire Club. By 1777, Franklin was one of the most prominent Masons in the world. Nearly every Grand Orient lodge in France enrolled him as a member.

Paine and five families in Paris formed the First Church of Theophilanthropy in 1797. The movement grew to 18 "churches" in Paris alone. It was banned by Napoleon but lived on in America in the deist clubs that surrounded Paine and Elihu Palmer. Movements of this "church" sprang up in New York, Newburgh, and Philadelphia. Under the umbrella of deism and Theophilanthropy, a network of societies, clubs, journals, and newspapers also came into existence. According to the *Dictionary of American History*, deistic societies in the U.S. were linked to the Illuminati and the French Revolutionary Cult of Reason by 1800. Others claim a much earlier date.

The presses of Paine's friend Bonneville published their writings.

Paine, never a citizen of France, was elected as a delegate to the revolutionary French Convention in Paris to help promote the revolution abroad. As was the way with Robespierre, any rival was imprisoned, and Paine was no exception. No one seems to understand just how Paine escaped the guillotine.

Once freed, as circumstances changed, Paine decided to return to the United States, and Bonneville asked him to take his wife and three children to America, which Paine did. Bonneville feared he would be arrested and possibly executed.

Bonneville's interaction with foreigners, including Americans, and the fact that he was building his own organization, made him suspect. And, he was a rival to other revolutionaries, which was and always has been a problem within their leadership. The French Revolution had become nationalistic in character and distrusted the internationalists after a time, particularly under Napoleon, who imprisoned Bonneville.

The whole idea of "nationalism" came out of revolutionary France. The idea is so prominent today that it is hard for people to accept this fact.

Prior to nationalism, tribe or race was the main factor in unifying people. Even within Europe, many people existed who were detached from other Europeans due to differences in language, race, sect, etc. While an outsider would consider all Europeans to be of one race, Europeans have never thought so, with decidedly different customs, language, and racial categories such as Anglo-Saxon, Norse, Lapp, Lett, Teutonic, Slavic, Serbian, Croatian, etc. Often these differences existed within the same country, and that was the case in France.

Nationalism was used to tie the diverse peoples together within a national boundary, to put their country before their minority. Nationalism was also used once Germany became a country.

Nationalism was a program of the Conspiracy agenda. It was a stepping-stone toward building the New World Order (NWO): first consolidate a country from a federation or confederation into nationalism, then regionalism, finally the NWO. This aspect will come out more as we discuss the two major arms of the Conspiracy in America after 1800.

Nationalism became the alternative to internationalism — a false solution because it was literally one step backwards from the two steps forward into world government from what they had advocated. True, the French government was national, but it was embodied in a personality: the king. Once the king was gone, the government after the Reign of Terror — initially an internationally-based movement — established a nationalist fervor.

There has always been a fight among those who want internationalism as opposed to nationalism, for several reasons. Some conspirators wanted nationalism, to be ruled by them, rather than to be only a small part of the larger internationalism. Some wanted this as an interim step toward internationalism or simply as an *appearance* of an alternative for the people to support in opposition to internationalism.

"All roads lead to Rome," as the saying goes when it comes to support for either idea. Those who used nationalism as a first step toward an attempted internationalism ruled by them were Napoleon, Hitler, and Mussolini. Those who have attempted to use regionalism as the first step, then internationalism, have been Stalin and modern organizations and personalities promoting a national government in the United States, to be followed by regionalism, and finally a New World Order under the United Nations.

This is not to say that Napoleon and Hitler, especially, did not evolve into regionalism after conquering certain portions of Europe. Hitler tried to form the European Economy Community under Albert Speer, his economic minister, something that was later accomplished under the international socialists, becoming the European Union.

Rivalries have existed within the Conspiracy that have led to war when arguments have arisen as to who should rule and which is the best method for achieving the end goal of world government: nationalism, regionalism, or internationalism. These all lead to the same end of oppressive government due to the accumulation of power, and power corrupts.

The biggest difference between the two roads to world power is that nationalism to internationalism is usually accomplished by a war of aggression. Nationalism to regionalism to internationalism is usually accomplished by a massive ruse where people do not catch on to what is going on until after they have accepted the conditions that lead to international control.

Hitler tried the nationalist route, as most other men of the preceding centuries had done in Europe. They all failed. The international socialists have been using regionalism to build a European State, the European Union, a step at a time. They are succeeding.

By using nationalism, the Conspiracy was able to pull most of France into their plans. The people, even those who supported the revolution, had grown weary of the carnage. The glory of France as a nation became the motivator, rather than internationalism.

The Conspiracy turned on Napoleon once he got to the point of believing that he could rule the world, leaving his mentors behind. The same happened to Hitler.

France, like most countries of Europe, was composed of divergent peoples who spoke different languages or dialects, had racial differences, etc. Even today there are small areas in Europe that do not speak the official language of their country on a daily basis. Getting people to think as nationalists rather than putting their tribe or section first was an important step on the path toward a New World Order. It separated the people from their local government as a result.

The film *Triumph des Willens* (*The Triumph of the Will*) by Leni Riefenstahl was used by the Nazis to build nationalism and the feeling of personal unity in the average German, since Germany had been a federation of many states and was never a "national" country. Otto Bismarck had pulled most of the confederation together into the modern German state in 1870, but not all of the German-speaking ethnic Germans had ever actually been a part of the country called Germany. Hitler's attempt to pull them all together was one of the reasons the German people supported him initially. German pride got in the way of common sense.

The film *The Triumph of the Will* should be seen on YouTube by those interested in learning the techniques of propaganda in use today by conspirators perfected by Riefenstahl. It is a lesson in how a nation and its people can be sucked up into evil and enjoy it until the end when it all crashes around their heads.

Once installed by the conspirators as the leader of France, Napoleon set out to make the revolution suit *his* ambitions. This is what ultimately defeated him. What most do not know is that the Conspiracy helped him defeat his enemies from within their countries as much as he defeated them on the battlefield, particularly in Germany. There were several areas where the Illuminati conspired with the French army to become part of Greater France, before and during Napoleon's initial conquests. That assistance stopped once he tried to be the master of all on his own. The Conspiracy turned against him, and, as they say, he met his Waterloo.

This is also one of the great secrets of World War II. The so-called Fifth Column helped Hitler's forces advance across Europe until he attacked one of the Conspiracy's Insiders, Stalin. Once he did that, the forces of the German war machine suffered defeat since they could no longer rely on the communists, for instance, within such countries as France and especially the United States to help them.

The communists helped keep America out of the war until Hitler attacked Russia, and then the party-line changed from peace to war even before Pearl Harbor.

At the beginning of World War II, it was not unusual for French forces to be surrendered to the advancing German army by French communist officers while the Hitler-Stalin Pact was intact.

It is rather ironic that French forces fighting the Germans were surrendered, when over a century earlier it was the other way around. The French revolutionary army used secret societies in the countries they were going to invade to stir up revolution in those countries to weaken the resistance to the French forces, including the German countries. Once Napoleon took control and deserted the Conspiracy, secret societies segued into resisting the French in the French-occupied countries.

The term, *the Fifth Column*, came about during the Spanish Civil War when Gen. Francisco Franco, having four columns converging on a city, said he would also use a "fifth column" of his supporters inside the city among its citizens.

There is a now-obscure Hollywood production based on the theme of French units being surrendered by communists to German forces that used to air on television in the 1950s, but today the movie and its theme are almost lost from history since they do not fit the denial of conspiracy in the scheme of things.

In late 1790 Bonneville set up an organization called the Cercle Social, or Social Circles, which was to be an inner party. In turn they organized the Universal Confederation of the Friends of Truth as a mainstay of many front groups, a substantial influence. They were occult and anti-Christian. Karl Marx and Frederick Engels considered the Circles to be the antecedents of the communist movement, since the leaders advocated many of the programs widely held by communists today, such as agrarian reform, no inheritance, etc. In addition, one can trace the leadership out of the Cercle Social from one phase to the next into the leadership of the parentage of communism in less than fifty years. The initial members of the Circle were Illuminists.

Billington, in his tome *Fire in the Minds of Men,* states "Bonneville was … the decisive channel of Illuminist influence" in France.

The Cercle Social was to be the fourth branch of government to oversee the other three functions: executive, judicial, and legislative. They were to be the Inner Party as outlined later in George Orwell's *1984*. It advocated a world revolution and government and a universal world language: French.

The Cercle Social was an imitation of certain aspects of the German Union and Freemasonry, but had no affiliation with Freemasonry. Members included Brissot, Condorcet, Paine, Anacharsis Cloots, Gracchus Babeuf, and others.

The use of the term *circle* came directly from Weishaupt, who used the term extensively in one form or another, and a dot within a small circle was the codified symbol of the Illuminati in correspondence. The clergy within its ranks apparently advocated land reform and the organization was the first to advocate women's rights. They were some of the first to advocate a social welfare program based on a progressive tax system.

The progression of the Conspiracy from the Illuminati may be traced by the people involved, the organizations they formed, the use of terms, and even the names of the papers they started. Bonneville printed *Le Tribun du Peuple* (*The People's Tribune*). After the formation of the Cercle, he published *La Bouche de Fer* (*The Mouth of Iron*). Nearly every paper established after this, over a substantial amount of time which used *tribune* or *iron* in its title or masthead, derived their philosophy or organization directly from Bonneville's Cercle Social.

Bonneville considered himself to be the philosophical heir of Adam Weishaupt. He was not the only one.

Out of this organization came two leaders who formed the Conspiracy of Equals: Babeuf and Buonarroti. In the process, they also launched a radical newspaper called *Tribun du Peuple*. From here can be traced the foundations of communism and Nazism.

Bonneville expressed the ideas to be known later as Hegelian that the voice of the people is the voice of God. He declared, "Man is God!" Even so, clergymen were part of their ranks, subverting Christianity from within. Indeed, a leader within the Cercle was Abbé Claude Fauchété who was himself a clergyman.

A major idea in the history of completely overturning the old social order was to foster changes in the definitions of words. Bonneville thought that one could influence people by remaking certain words socially acceptable or unacceptable — the precursor of political correctness.

His followers sponsored changes in the French vocabulary as the means of ushering in a new age. They used words with a new meaning or different meaning, even the opposite meaning that had preceded. Members of the Cercle even wrote a new dictionary to foster this idea. Bonneville was credited with introducing the word "citizen" used during the revolution rather than the standard polite title "Monsieur," as it was too aristocratic.

The major goal of the Cercle was to initiate a world revolution that would bring about mandatory atheism. They would use Masonry around the world as their tool to help them achieve this end, eliminating God and promoting one worldwide language. Bonneville even used the lesson of the Tower of Babel in reverse as his example.

After Bonneville's wife and children came to the U.S., Paine was able to get Bonneville's son, Benjamin, appointed to West Point; he became renowned throughout the United States as an explorer for the U.S. Army. He was appointed to the Point and then promoted as an American hero as a result of his exploratory expedition, even though he was a son of a notorious communist and under the watch of a man who had lost his reputation, at the time, among most of the American people as an Illuminist.

Bonneville's expedition in the West was financed by John Jacob Astor, the rival of the Hudson Bay

Company in the fur trade. Washington Irving, who knew Nicholas Bonneville in New York and was impressed by him, met Benjamin and together they worked out an arrangement that enabled Irving to write and publish Benjamin's adventures.

Many famous landmarks and government sites are named after him: Lake Bonneville, Bonneville Salt Flats, Bonneville Power Administration, Bonneville Dam, etc.

Benjamin Bonneville served as Lafayette's aide on his triumphant return visit to the United States. He then returned to France with Lafayette as his guest for some time. During the Civil War he was brevetted a brigadier general.

His father was one of the most important communists in history. The reason many Americans have not heard of his father is probably due to the fact of his influence on America and the need to hide this impact. You can trace the influence of the Illuminati from Bode to Bonneville to Paine, and Bonneville to Babeuf to Horace Greeley, and subsequently to both Paine and Greeley's associates.

The same can be said of the communist movement. It may well be that this is a second reason Bonneville is not well known among the average student. For to know Bonneville is to realize that the thread of the Conspiracy is woven in history from that period into modern times.

The hypothesis of a Conspiracy does not rise to the level of theory; it rises to the level of fact — a fact that is suppressed.

In addition to the work of Bonneville, you can trace a direct line from the Illuminati to the French Revolution to the communist League of the Just by the person of Filippo Michele Buonarroti. He was greatly influenced by Jean-Jacques Rousseau. He joined the Illuminati in Florence in 1786 and was befriended by the leader of the Reign of Terror, Robespierre, later in Paris.

Buonarroti also was a leader in the Carbonari. He was only one example of interlocking several surface organizations into Illuminist control by key personnel. Again, you may also trace the communist movement from the Cercle Social of Bonneville, Babeuf, Buonarroti, Theodore Schuster, Marx, and Engels.

Bonneville was in correspondence with a branch of his Social Circle organization in Philadelphia, and a Circle of Free Brothers may have existed there in 1790 from their beginning. While the Social Circles may have faded out, the focal point for communist conspiracies was the Bonneville influence. Babeuf, connected with Bonneville, built his communist Conspiracy of Equals around his journal *The Tribune of the People*.

Bonneville came here in 1815 because he was in trouble with the Napoleon government. Little is known of what he did while he resided in the United States other than open up a school for young ladies in New York. He finally returned to France in 1819 in obscurity.

One would like to know the identity of these ladies and how they may have influenced their husbands later. We are not aware of any documentation detailing the enrollment of these ladies — or the parents who would have had them attend Bonneville's school.

Too many historians overlook or downplay Bonneville's importance to the Conspiracy. It may well be that it is due to his direct linkage from the Illuminati leader Bode through Bonneville into America through Paine, Joel Barlow, and Palmer. By the study of Bonneville, it would become clear that Illuminati influence came to America and flourished early on. There have been many instances of deliberate obfuscation of facts by so-called responsible historians to throw Americans "off the scent" when it comes to this influence embedding itself into American society.

The first wave of Illuminism came to America directly from Germany. The second wave came through France. The third wave came again from Germany, through American students who studied in Germany.

The significance of the third wave of Illuminism into the U.S. is that it became essentially an American wing of Illuminism as opposed to an alien majority within the American movement, as was the case in the 1780s and into the 1790s. The first waves were essentially alien, from Germany and especially France, albeit they caught many Americans up in their nets. The third wave came from Americans returning from Europe who were caught up in the European revolutionary movements and/or influenced by their studies at European universities, especially Germany.

Paine and his friend Joel Barlow served as links between the American and French revolutionaries, and Barlow had been made a citizen of revolutionary France.

Benjamin Franklin was the man who urged the young Paine to immigrate to America in the first place and gave letters of introduction to Paine, enabling him to find friends and employment in America. Later, along with Paine, Franklin was involved in many of the same circles of the French organizations that were trying to replace Christianity, such as the Theophilanthropists. It would not be the only time that Franklin would sponsor a person who would play a major role in the Conspiracy in America.

After Paine's return to America from France, many people shunned him since he had taken on the Illuminist worldview of Christ and Christianity, being very vocal about it. He believed, "The world is my country.... To do good is my religion." It was one thing to advocate Republicanism, another to be openly anti-Christian. He also had abandoned the American dream of liberty. While in London, on November 4, 1791, Paine gave a toast to the "Revolution of the World." He had become an internationalist.

Even though Paine had by this time become a pariah to most, the State of New York under the influence of George Clinton presented him with a farm. Late in life, he was known to be frequently intoxicated. In his last days, he was moved to the home of William A. Thompson, once a law partner of Aaron Burr. Thompson's wife was a niece of Elihu Palmer.

After Paine's death, an English Chartist revolutionary, William Cobbett, living in America for a time, dug up his bones, took them back to England and placed them under his bed, or in the attic, depending on which source you believe.

Paine's bones disappeared after the Englishman's death, but many claim to own various parts. For this to be true, one has to ask the question, how? What sort of person or organization would want a bone of Paine and for what purpose? How did they know where to get one and what kind of organization was involved in disseminating the bones?

Cobbett was also an admirer of Andrew Jackson and wrote a biography of his life.

New York was the scene of what friends Paine had in his last days. At the time, Illuminist influence was strong in New York. One of his admirers, and in agreement with Paine's religious views against Christianity, was John Pintard. He became one of the founders of the Tammany Society, which became a power in NY politics.

Paine's influence on men like Barlow during his life, and Parker Godwin after, cannot be overestimated.

Parke Godwin became an assistant to William Cullen Bryant of the *New York Evening Post* in the 1840s. Godwin was a socialist and was a vice president of the American Union of Associations, building Fourier-style socialist communes. He was the editor of the Brook Farm commune's organ the *Harbinger*. In the 1850s, he was with *Putnam's*. In 1860 he was a speaker for the Republican Party, and during the Civil War became an early member of the Union League Club of New York.

Charles Fourier was the originator of a style of socialism that promoted communes he called *phalanxes*, which he wanted to be the bedrock of a World Congress of Phalanxes. He was anti-Semitic and defended homosexuality among men and women. Fourier was very influential on Emerson, Henry D. Thoreau, Marx, and Engels (although Marx and Engels rejected the idea of communes). Fourier rejected just about everyone and everything associated with socialism and communism unless they were his disciples, and even many of them. He influenced the early members of the Carbonari and the Illuminists during the period of the 1810s. His chief disciple was Victor Considerant, and in America it was Albert Brisbane.

Barlow was with Paine in Paris. He had been a Congregationalist minister and a chaplain with a brigade during the War for Independence. While in France, he tried to get elected as a member of the France Assembly but was defeated. Later, he became a wealthy merchant, land speculator, and poet. He was appointed our consul to Algiers in 1795 and returned to America in 1805. In 1811, on the verge of war with France, he was appointed our minister to France under Napoleon.

Prominent men such as DeWitt Clinton, governor of New York and friend of Lafayette, and Albert Gallatin, U.S. Treasury Secretary, remained staunch friends of Paine.

Once the French Revolution was in place, Illuminist influence on America grew and played the major role in splitting our country into two basic factions, which became the early political parties: the Federalist and Republican, which the latter changed its name to Democrat.

Loyalty to the Conspiracy and its goals was the hallmark of the Republican Jacobin members, regardless of their station, responsibility, or background. In fact, they prided themselves on using the trust of others to in turn violate that trust in favor of the greater loyalty of their cause.

An example was Brissot, a member of the Illuminati who attacked the French royal government on a trip to America while in the pay of the French royal government. He spread the Gallo-American Society throughout the colonies, and when the revolution in France broke out his disciples in America began to call themselves Jacobins.

Likewise, his agents within the royal French government helped bring down the government from within.

The underlying reason that Illuminist influence in America did not result in a revolution similar to France was the morality that ran through the entire structure of American society and local governments, even though the morality level had suffered as a result of the War for Independence. Another reason was that the governments of America were not centralized as they were in France, so taking over one area did not mean they had control over another. What central government there was, the federal government, was run by Washington and Adams. Since neither of these two men had any respect for the Illuminati, they came under immediate attack.

And, while the Enlightenment had its adverse effect on certain Americans just as it had its effect for liberty, Illuminist influence was not yet strong enough to win over America; however, the direct descendents of the Illuminati would be responsible for the formation of both our modern, major political parties: the Republicans who adopted the name Democrats in the 1780s, and the Republicans (again) in the 1850s.

From this time on, the Illuminati, its front groups, and/or successors, have been an important part of American history. The pursuit of their aims, along with the rhetoric of the Illuminists, is too persistent through the years for there not to be a connection. Also, the direct ties to the Illuminati through many individuals that were either influential Americans or immigrants to America are too numerous to deny.

2

CONTROL OF HISTORY AND THOUGHT

The reasons that a conspiracy remains unknown to the majority of Americans are:

One, the America people are so trusting of their political leaders, judging others by themselves. In other words, they are honest and forthright, so they believe others to be the same — until proven otherwise. They just cannot believe that some people can be devious or want the kind of power witnessed in other countries. "This is America, things like that don't happen here," is the thought.

People tend to listen to the rhetoric rather than look at the actions of leaders. As long as the leaders are saying enough of the right things or what the audience wants to hear, the people largely ignore what then is done in their name.

The information withheld from the general population diminishes the ability of the average American to notice that even more information is withheld — they lack the knowledge or experience to realize that certain facts may not be presented, in order to paint a very different picture of what is going on. For instance, if the listener does not remember that government power is supposed to be divided between the three branches, he may not realize that a president, for instance, is talking about usurping the power of the other two branches when he says he will simply do what he wants without Congress or the Supreme Court. A segment of society will trust what the president is saying simply due to the trust factor of all Americans toward their politicians and the ignorance factor of how our government is structured to work.

While this may seem to be an extreme statement, what has been happening increasingly since the year 2000 is precisely the pattern illustrated above.

An example of how ignorance combined with the trust factor can be used to move the agenda of the Conspiracy forward is the issue of immigration reform: the average American may understand the problem, but what about the millions of aliens watching television who have a vested interest in amnesty? They do not understand our system. If a president says he wants to give them amnesty but Congress impedes the process they can be whipped up in our communities to be destructive of our system, due to their ignorance and self-interest.

This tension and possible subsequent violence could be fanned by the community organizations under the control of the minions of the Conspiracy until the situation would look impossible. The media would fill the television screens of scenes of isolated violence to make it look even worse than it is. And all the while it would be presented as a spontaneous uprising of people who simply want their "rights."

The agitation manifested in the streets over the issue could then be used to actually give more power to the president, and the majority of the people would welcome this since it would stop the problem of unrest in the communities around the country — anything to restore law and order.

Such tactics have been used before. And, whether it will happen with this particular issue, there are certain conditions that may facilitate their use in the future if violence in the streets is what the Conspiracy wants.[4]

A second reason is that over the decades the minions of this Conspiracy have done all they can to control the information and education that the average American receives and the history deposited in libraries.

As we will demonstrate, over the 19th century they gradually gained working control over the information the public received through the newspapers, especially the history deposited in historical associations and major publishing houses. The Insiders have started — or gained — effective control of what we call the media today, so that when the average citizen reads or sees the news, it is sanitized from any hint of what is really going on. Television, for instance, purges any employee or commentator who begins to get too close to exposing even the outer rings of the Conspiracy. They will allow certain conservative issues, but not those that get too close to actually informing the viewers of the reality of moving the U.S. into a New World Order.

In the 2010s for instance, once it became obvious to several political pundits and conservative commentators on national television that something organized, behind the scenes, was affecting national and world events, they independently started to research and then address the issue. In addition, they became more constitutionally oriented. In other words, as they became more familiar with the facts, they experienced a paradigm shift. Once this happened, their contracts were not renewed. There were a couple of exceptions where personalities came back on the air, but their presentations were not the same as before.

This was on television. The same process had been going on in radio since ± 2000. In fact, many radio stations that specialized in "talk radio" of a conservative nature were bought out and the format changed. The numbers are not known, but it was substantial. Local or regional radio is a very tough business. They always struggle and when a buyer comes along and the price is right, most will sell out.

There have been instances where radio stations have been good at reporting the news independently, but if they got too close to the truth relative to what was really happening in their communities, community action groups united against them and petitioned the Federal Communications Commission not to renew the station's license to operate — all in the name of serving the community with political correctness. Most, if not all, caved in. And, the general public had no idea what was going on to control the stations since most of the action against the stations was behind the scenes.

As an example of the information given to the American people by a major news magazine, *Time* serves as a case in point. *Time* has international editions as well as the edition seen in the United States, all produced with the same date. It is not unusual for *Time* to feature a serious lead article on current events on the cover of their magazine in all of their editions except the United States. The lead article in the latter is instead fluff about some social or political-correctness issue.

Another example of taking people's eyes off the real story was the debate over whether Obama should have called the terrorists in the Middle East *Islamic* terrorists, that unless you identify the enemy by name you cannot defeat them. That is simply balderdash. Would it have mattered whether we called the Nazis *Nazis* or *German extremists* in order to defeat them?

While everyone was in a tither over this mote, the big story of who trained and armed the terrorists, who kept financing them, etc., went unreported.

---

4   Unrest that might emanate out of the Hispanic community would take a horrible toll on America. Most Americans are not aware of the horrific violence that has been taking place south of the border. This violence could soon invade our country, as we are being invaded by millions, not just looking for jobs, but fleeing the violence. We do not wish to describe what has been happening. Let us just say that the stories out of the Middle East about atrocities there are nothing compared to Mexico. WARNING: If you should wish to try to prove or disprove this last statement, do not search online for beheadings and such in Mexico unless you are prepared to be scarred for life by what you will see.

One key aspect of American liberty needs to be noticed since it is rarely mentioned on national television or radio: independence. In order for us to have liberty and the Constitution enforced as written, the American people must maintain their independence. If we do not, the government will do what an outside entity will tell it what to do, whether or not it is an invader or the entanglement and subsequent merger of our system into an international government.

It is very telling that major conservative stations and personalities *never mention* the need to retain our independence and instead work to involve us in foreign entanglements that lead to an international system, all with some excuse or other that we need to be involved in the global economy, NATO, or some other military alliance or adventure.

In addition, it is very interesting to note that the conservatives remaining on national TV and radio almost to a person are pushing a constitutional convention to add amendments to the Constitution. It is all too uniform among these "independent" pundits.

The history of the Civil War and related aspects are controlled through a system of "experts" who pronounce their imprimatur on books written and published, particularly the sub-genre of the history of Lincoln. In this manner, only the politically correct receive reviews in the usual places. Never mentioning a book condemns it to obscurity. And through obscurity, few read it and it rarely finds a place in the system of libraries, never becomes "mainstream" in the American psyche, and is lost down the memory hole.[5]

An example of this is in the reputation of George Armstrong Custer. The prevailing opinion is that he was a blowhard who stumbled into a lot of Indians and got his command killed. Yet there are small obscure volumes here and there written by those who served under him that paint a very different picture of the general. Regardless of one's opinion regarding Custer, the fact is that any book that represents Custer as something other than the politically correct version is ignored.

Perhaps the reason for this is that even though Custer was as cruel as many other Union generals, he was one of the Civil War generals who wanted the country to return to the Constitution and was very concerned about the corruption involving Indian affairs in the federal government. He has never been forgiven for these opinions.

You might ask yourself how it is that certain books that sell in the tens of thousands get on the bestseller lists when books that circulate in the hundreds of thousands or millions are never mentioned. Books such as *None Dare Call It Treason* and *None Dare Call It Conspiracy* that sold six to twelve million each in the 1960s and 1970s were ignored by book reviewers and book sections in the major newspapers.

In Europe, the process of controlling history has paralleled that in America. This process was accelerated by the Gestapo in German-held territories during World War II with the confiscation of works on the Illuminati and secret societies, since there is substantial evidence that the Thule Society, the parent of Nazism, was a direct descendent. Even so, it is easier to study the history of the Conspiracy in Europe than it is in America.

A Third reason that a conspiracy remains unknown to most Americans is that, when responsible people start to expose the Conspiracy, the Conspiracy spreads false conspiracy theories that are so bizarre that it makes those spreading them seem irresponsible, because, after all, "there is no conspiracy," and when they see these fantastic theory-promoting people in operation it simply reinforces this idea. Those

---

5   A problem with the control of the history of Lincoln, and especially his assassination, is that the picture of the people and reasons behind his assassination has been made so muddled with various conspiracy theories that the real picture, even if contained within the pages of some history, is lost. There are simply too many supposed historians who have a theory of who and what was behind the assassination so that, other than Booth pulling the trigger, there is no certainty. We will deal with this subject further on.

who responsibly tell the story of the Conspiracy and understand the bizarre nature of these stories, but do not use them, still suffer from their propagation because the reputation of the bizarre rubs off on them as well. It is meant to.

It can be done simply by having a small number of people promote the idea that certain organizations that are fronts of the Conspiracy are actually controlled by the Jews — that it is a Jewish conspiracy. Just as blaming Masons turns off American Masons, this immediately turns off the Jewish community and stops them from joining in any anti-conspiratorial battle. Not only that, Jewish people have a tendency to help those who appear to be the detractors of such anti-conspirators, giving the detractors more influence because they appear to be on the side of the Jewish community.

It has become standard to identify as anti-Semites all those who profess these same organizations are part of the problem, even if they do not believe or state that these organizations are run by Jews.

For example, say that XYZ Council is a problem. The anti-Semite says that the XYZ Council is not only a problem, it is run by Jews. Another person could say that XYZ is a problem and those that heard this from the anti-Semite first automatically believe the second person is also anti-Semitic, when they are not.

This, more than anything else, is the reason most anti-Semitic organizations exist today: to throw enough mud around to prevent the success of good people trying to educate their fellow citizens about a conspiracy; to take the focus off the real problem and dump it on innocent people; and, to build anti-Semitism among people who only want to stop the problems they see manifested in their country, if they believe the lie.

Jews almost always suffer under the boot of conspiratorial success.

Perhaps the most notable writer on conspiracies with the greatest number of books circulated on the subject in her time was Nesta Webster, just after the turn of the 20th century. She fell into the trap of believing in a Jewish Conspiracy for a time until her research told her that it was not correct, that the conspiracy used Jews as agents out front during the Napoleonic period to put the heat on them rather than as the true source of revolution. She later published a clarification of this mistaken view in her late edition of *World Revolution*.

The tactic of the Illuminati also using Jewish names as aliases, particularly in the heyday of the Asiatic Brethren, even though they were not Jewish, played a role in this charade. Jews were not allowed as anything other than low-level agents of the Conspiracy until forty years after the founding of the Illuminati. They were considered too close-knit to their faith and race to be trusted by the Insiders to be members of the inner circle. There was a layer of anti-Semitism based on racism that ran through many of the conspirators, in addition to their distrust of other people who were religiously oriented: the Jews were both a race and a religion.

Many secret societies, such as the Asiatic Brethren, had Jewish members, but they were forced to violate their Jewish kosher diet and rituals. In other words, they were forced to give up their Judaism before they could be entrusted with higher orders. It was as if a Christian were to reject Christ, or a Muslim were required to reject Mohammed before being accepted into the higher orders, and many of these did.

After years of persecution, protecting their faith and conspiratorial influence on them, the Jews have tended to become paranoid, thinking that the whole world is against them. This causes them to react accordingly at any perceived slight; they have become "thin-skinned," and this reaction in itself breeds anti-Semitism, since Gentiles cannot seem to understand the reaction and get offended over it. This condition works well for the conspiratorial tactic of "divide and conquer."

Just as what happened to the Masons, totalitarian states in Europe almost always persecuted the Jews, even unto death. If it were a Jewish conspiracy one would think that the Jews would benefit, not suffer.

The Conspiracy has gone to great lengths by producing false flags and literature to throw people off the track and to get them involved in looking in the wrong direction for their leadership. One such nefarious work is the *Protocols of the Elders of Zion*, which has been used widely to "prove" that the Jews are the Conspiracy. The document's source is false, and any online search has a great deal of information of this fact.

As we will relate further on, the leaders of the communist movement were for the most part racists as well as atheists. Marx, even though born into a Jewish family, grew to hate Jews long before anyone had ever heard of him. He would never have followed a Jewish leadership, period. We will detail this, as we said, further on.

Are Jews and Masons involved? Yes, but so are Christians, Muslims, Germans, English, Russians, and Chinese — and Americans of all stripes. In the early years of radicalism in America, when conspiratorial and secret societies started, Jewish involvement was almost nil and those who were involved were atheists.

The Insiders are not from one race or religion. If they were, the second-tier minions would not follow them since it would be obvious that they could never attain Insider status. This does not mean that prejudice does not flourish within their ranks, it certainly does. But each one thinks that they can and will be "The Leader" or they would find some other path to power.

The Asiatic Brethren opened up membership for men of the Jewish religion in Illuminist and Rosicrucian-influenced circles — it was ahead of its time in this regard. The Rosicrucians as well as the Illuminati did not allow Jews to be initiated, with very few exceptions, until the period of the Napoleonic conquest. Even this allowance did not extend to the strictly German lodges, and was rescinded after Napoleon was defeated. However, those who were admitted had to renounce their religious beliefs and traditions. While there may have been a rivalry between the Rosicrucians and Illuminati, it appeared to be a mixed influence in the Brethren.

The Asiatic Brethren not only opened up membership to those of the Jewish faith, they were instrumental in recruiting Turks, Persians and Armenians. It extended further east and began to adopt Hindu doctrine and symbols in an attempt to recruit into India. It promoted reincarnation and adopted the swastika as their sign of recognition.

Many of their leaders adopted Jewish aliases, whether they were Jewish or not.

There is some evidence of Rothschild involvement, but this was long after the founding of the Illuminati. Sigmund Geisenheimer was the head clerk in the Rothschilds' banking house. He belonged to an Illuminated lodge in Mainz. He founded the Judenloge, for which the local rabbi excommunicated him, demonstrating that the real Jews did not want to have anything to do with Illuminism.

Salomon Mayer von Rothschild joined this lodge for a short time before moving to Vienna.

That the Rothschilds have had a great amount of influence, there can be no doubt, but they are blamed for more than they succeeded in doing to control world events. Missing from the idea of the world financial manipulations early on have been banking families in England, Germany, and America who were not Jewish and in fact were prejudiced against the Jews. By focusing only on the Rothschilds, two things have been distorted: the fact that other financiers have been involved, and the promotion of anti-Semitism, since the idea of a Rothschild conspiracy makes it a Jewish one, serving the "divide and conquer" tactic.

Asiatic Brethren lodges spread all over Europe. Their connection to the Illuminati was not publically known, so they avoided the stigmatism and persecution that was leveled against the Illuminati at the time.

The importance of this group has also produced the fiction of its early demise and lack of any real importance among historians, yet the future King of Prussia, Frederick William, joined the group. He was by no means the only man of stature who did. Later, an American connection to the royal house of Prussia came through Thomas Anthony Thacher, a Skull and Bonesman, who taught the crown prince and his cousin, Prince Frederick Charles. Other connections to the United States came from the membership of Paschal B. Randolph, who joined the Brethren and carried the order to America.

Semantics also plays a role.
The use of language to distort meaning or the thought process has been developed to a science. This process started early on, particularly by the Cercle Social.

All of life is relationships. Communication is an important aspect of developing relationships, which makes the same definition of words by two parties very important. By controlling the definition of words, you can draw people together or cause them to grow apart.

Thus, the story of the Tower of Babel — confounding the languages automatically separated the people.

One can even use the same words and be speaking to two different audiences at the same time. If the initiated understand that the meaning is something other than what the larger audience thinks it is, the results can be manipulated.

For instance, if you say the word Chicago, it means whatever the thought processes are for the individual hearing it. It may mean O'Hare Airport to a traveler, it may mean a rock band, it may conjure up images of political corruption or crime, or it may mean police repression (as it did to a particular generation of youth as a result of a Democrat Party convention held there and the suppression of demonstrations connected with it). "Chicago" is only a sample of the thought process connected to a word and how it can have a fluid meaning.

As examples, two modern movies reached a double audience: *Patton* and *MacArthur*. Those who admire the two generals can be sitting right next to younger or less knowledgeable people, and both would get two different messages. The admirer of these men has no idea that the other person can be conditioned to be against the generals by the movie, since the admirer has a lot more information that swirls around in his head as he is reminded of events that the younger citizen has no knowledge of, or insufficient knowledge.

By the 20th century the Conspiracy had nearly total control of the semantic war. Developments after December 1958, however, caused the beginning of a reversal of this influence on how we think.

Another example of the problem with the definition of words is the use of the term *democracy*. To the average citizen, it is the American system of freedom. To a constitutional scholar it means exactly the opposite, since the Constitution states we are a republic and he knows the difference.

In regard to the definition of democracy, it changed gradually over the decades either by direct management or intellectual influence. The exception today to this influence is the Internet. Here too, a systematic consolidation of control has begun, both by government and the major corporations that supply Internet services. However, it has been difficult for them to keep up with the innovations of enterprising inventors with new ways and means of communication every year and the mass of information that is accumulated in the system every second of every day. What usually happens is that the innovator is bought out at an exorbitant price and the service is absorbed into the larger system and control.

Likewise, the entire library system in this country is controlled by a "centralizing" of which books should be stocked, and if something creeps into the library that is a detriment to this Conspiracy, it disappears. In researching this work, this author has experienced first hand many times over the years the "disappearance" of certain volumes not only from library shelves available to the public, but even within the rare book archives not generally accessible to public view and under very good security. These archived volumes usually are those of a nature of exposing secret societies or communist movements' influence in American history prior to 1900.

In some instances, the libraries had no idea that these volumes were missing, since no one knew of their existence and therefore asked for them, which would have alerted the librarian.

Once you have control of the major publishing houses and book reviews, it then becomes only a matter of convincing local libraries to have annual old book sales to gradually get rid of history and replace it with mythology. Out with the old and in with the new. Libraries usually stock books reviewed by major reviewers such as *The New York Times*. Rarely do they purchase a book from an independent publisher that is not reviewed. In addition, no one ever stops to think of just who the people are who get elected or appointed to library boards.[6]

And that is what American history is today: mythology. So many pertinent facts are no longer well known, or known at all, that have a direct bearing on how Americans think, or how they understand what has been happening to their country since the very beginning and, more importantly, what is happening today.

The only means by which one can overcome this deficiency is to spend countless hours in libraries, archives, and antique bookstores across America. One book may not have expunged a fact, then another. One library or used bookstore may yet have a book or document that is no longer available anywhere else. Putting these facts together over time builds a picture puzzle far different than the picture given us in history classes in school.

This deficiency weighs heavily on the history lessons in private and home schooling as well, preventing a clear picture of what Americanism is all about. In many ways, the private schools are victimized by some of the publishers from whom they purchase texts.

The problem is that whether you use the libraries, old books, or the Internet, you first have to know the right questions to ask.

Look at the results of an action, then work backwards to find out what caused it — who caused it, and why.

The ignorance level of Americans relative to history or the basic law of the land, the Constitution, is so acute that when one states the truth, citizens may not only disbelieve the messenger, but ridicule him.

It is true that more and more books are being published outside of the mainstream, and some organizations are doing what they can to educate their fellow citizens, such as The John Birch Society, but the lost history is so overwhelming that no one volume can tell the story. This volume is an attempt to do an overview of this problem.

Control Education

No better example from the early years of gaining control of American history can be given than that of historian George Bancroft. George Bancroft, known as the father of American history, became a disciple of German Hegelians, spending years in their study in Germany. Hegel had great influence on such men as Karl Marx, although Marx disagreed on certain aspects of Hegelian thought. The Hegelian influence, along with other German Illuminist influence, was the beginning of control over history and education in America.

---

6 An excellent study of this tactic is John T. Flynn's *While You Slept, Our Tragedy in Asia and Who Made It*, the Devin-Adair Company, New York, 1958. See Chapter VIII, A Pool of Poison.

Some trace the control of government education back to John Dewey. Better students trace it to Horace Mann. In reality it was those plus others — including Edward Everett, George Bancroft and their friends under the influence of Hegelian Germans — coupled with the so-called Transcendentalists. They shaped the study of history in our schools. Johann Heinrich Pestalozzi, a Swiss Illuminist, also had influence in American education very early on through Bancroft and the Transcendentalists.

The control of education has always been vital to those who mean to rule. Illuminati instruction in their degrees stated, "The Perfect will therefore spare no pains to gain possession of the Schools which lie within his district, and also of their teachers."

The Degree of Regent stated: "You must also gain over to the Order the common people. *The great plan for succeeding in this is to influence the schools.*"

Louis Auguste Blanqui viewed education as "the force that governs the world" and "the only real revolutionary agent."

Blanqui, a member of the Carbonari, participated in many street battles and was a friend of the Illuminist Buonarroti. Blanqui initiated an uprising in Paris in May 1839 in which the forerunner of the Communist League, the League of the Just, participated. During the brutal Paris Commune, he was elected the commune's president. Benito Mussolini's fascist newspaper, *Il Popolo d'Italia*, carried a quotation by Blanqui on its mast: "He who has iron, has bread."

Early in our history, men associated with the American Illuminati, such as DeWitt Clinton, became leaders in the public school movement. In New York City, a Public School Society was formed to provide an education for children of parents who did not participate in any religious society which provided schools for their children.

Clinton served as the first president of the society from 1805 to 1828. While there were men associated with the organization who had the best intentions, the board of trustees did have its contingent of Illuminist- and/or Jacobin-connected men, such as Peter Cooper and Samuel Osgood. Its trustees over the years included men who were prominent in New York, and again, while they had the best of intentions, the schools gradually went the route the radicals wanted.

Clinton was also a regent of the University of New York from 1808 to 1825, and organized the Historical Society of New York in 1804 and served as its president. He became the Grand Master of the Knights Templar from 1816-1828.

Years later, John O'Sullivan, whom we will address further on, was the political enemy of the Public School Society, though this opposition looked a great deal like controlled opposition emanating from the same fountainhead.

George Bancroft started the preparatory Round Hill School in 1823, primarily for students seeking admission to Harvard. He did this in league with Dr. J.G. Cogswell after they had spent a good deal of time in Germany studying and keeping company with various Hegelians and Illuminati. Cogswell studied for two years at Göttingen starting in 1816, and kept company with George Ticknor and Edward Everett.

While studying in Germany, Bancroft took the time to seek out notable men who were Illuminists, promoters of education to raise up people for the State, Carbonari, and Occultists such as Goethe, Humboldt, Hegel, Schleiermacher, Cousin, Constant, and others. It was obvious that Bancroft had an agenda much different than other American educators.

Round Hill was a boarding school which embraced the enlightenment but retained some of the aspects of Puritan beliefs. Harvard put up much of the money necessary to start the school. It was based on the teachings of Rousseau, Philip Emanuel von Fellenberg and the Illuminist Johann Heinrich Pestalozzi.

CHART TWO
Illuminati influence through two institutions on American goverment and society.

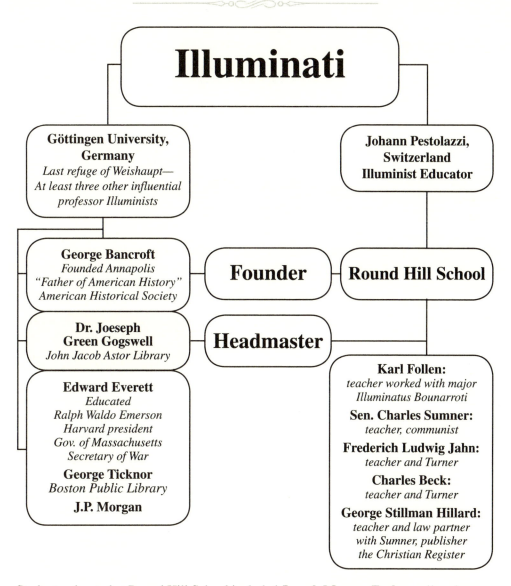

Students educated at Round Hill School included **Joseph Murray Forbes**, railroad magnate; **Henry Whitney Bellows**, leader of the National Conference of Unitarian Churches, Union League, and U.S. Sanitary Commission; **William Ellery Channing**; **Gen. Philip Kearny**; and **George Gibbs**, also a leader in the Union League of New York.

CHART THREE
Illuminati influence on American literature and intellectual circles.

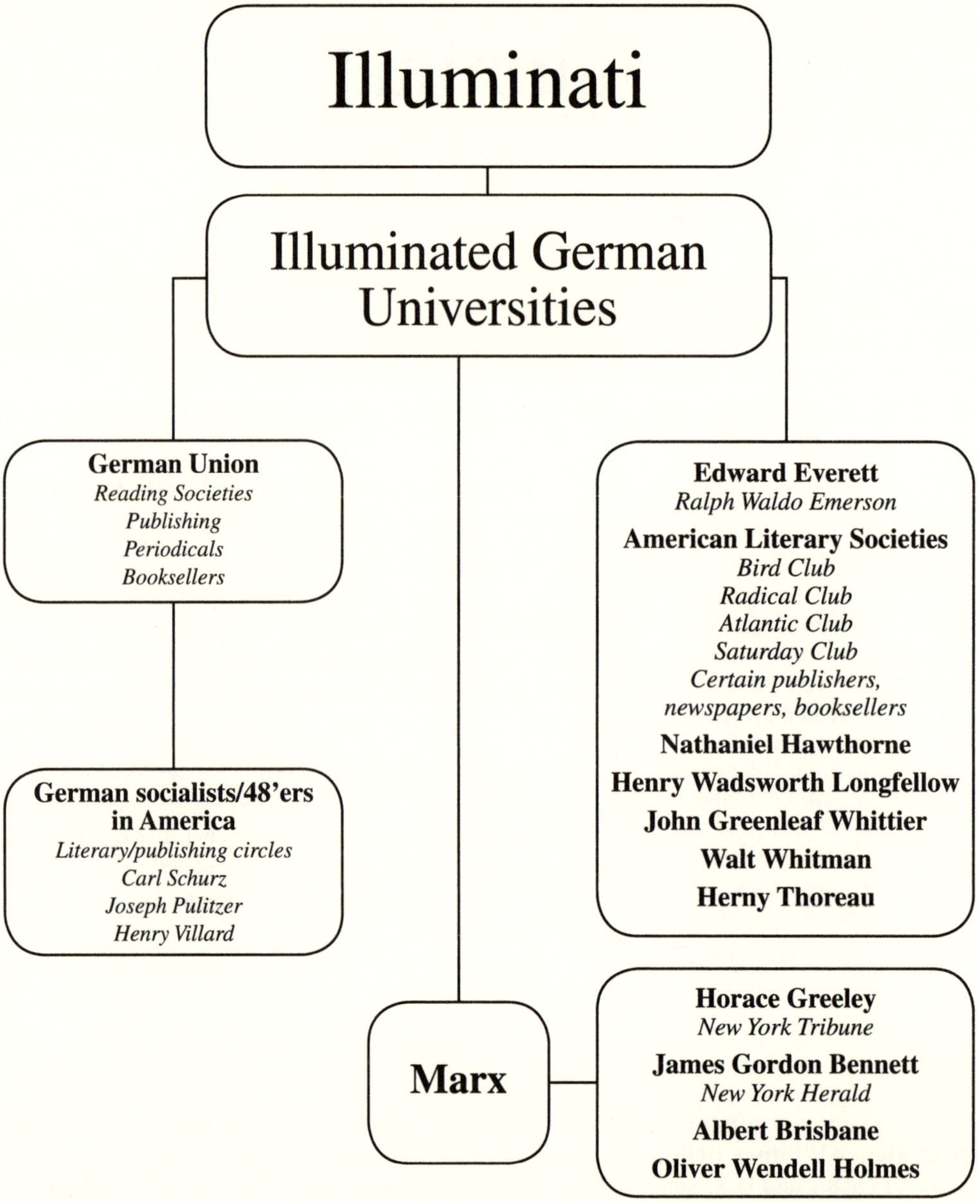

Illuminati

Illuminated German Universities

German Union
Reading Societies
Publishing
Periodicals
Booksellers

Edward Everett
Ralph Waldo Emerson
American Literary Societies
Bird Club
Radical Club
Atlantic Club
Saturday Club
Certain publishers,
newspapers, booksellers
Nathaniel Hawthorne
Henry Wadsworth Longfellow
John Greenleaf Whittier
Walt Whitman
Herny Thoreau

German socialists/48'ers in America
Literary/publishing circles
Carl Schurz
Joseph Pulitzer
Henry Villard

Marx

Horace Greeley
New York Tribune
James Gordon Bennett
New York Herald
Albert Brisbane
Oliver Wendell Holmes

When the conspirator Karl Follen first arrived in the United States, he became a teacher at Round Hill along with his friend Charles Beck, who came over on the same ship with him. Beck had to leave Germany since his revolutionary sentiments threatened his liberty.

Beck was a pupil of Frederich Ludwig Jahn, who had founded the Turner organization, a direct descendant of the Illuminist network, which we will elaborate on later. Whether or not Beck established the secret-society aspect of the Turner group at Round Hill is not known. He did translate Jahn's book *Deutsche Turnkunst* into English. He remained longer at the school than Follen and then went on to establish his own school. He served in the Massachusetts Legislature for two years and became active in the U.S. Sanitary Commission, founded by their student Henry Whitney Bellows.

George Stillman Hillard taught at Round Hill for a time. He would go on to be an editor with George Ripley of the *Christian Register* and an associate of the Charles Sumner, who also taught at the school. Sumner became a Radical Republican and advocated a world government and court, and would ultimately join the communist First International.

Many students who came through Round Hill went on to great heights in public life:

- Joseph K. Barnes, the chief medical officer of the U.S. Army, who was present at Lincoln's death bed and attended both the wounded William Henry Seward and President James Garfield.
- John Murray Forbes, the railroad magnate, would later help provide money to arm Kansas members of the American Anti-Slavery Society. He was an elector for Lincoln, and became a confidential agent for Secretary of the Navy Gideon Welles in Paris during the war. He was an intimate friend of Ralph Waldo Emerson.
- Henry Whitney Bellows was a Unitarian preacher who became the president of the United States Sanitary Commission and formed the National Conference of Unitarian Churches. He was an admirer of Theodore Parker, and one of his parishioners was William Cullen Bryant.
- William Ellery Channing was educated by Charles Sumner at Round Hill. Later, he was very active in socialist circles. He was very close to the wife of Karl Follen, Elizabeth.
- Union Gen. Philip Kearny, who served with the French and earned the French Legion of Honor twice, the only foreigner to ever do so, was sent to Round Hill in his youth by his father, since his studies were not going well in the school he was enrolled in at the time.

Cogswell ultimately took over the school, and later became the supervisor of the John Jacob Astor Library in New York City.

George Bancroft was a member of the Transcendentalists, the spiritual group that had a great deal to do with selling a spiritual substitute for Christianity along with the seemingly intellectual side of socialism. Orestes Brownson, who left the Transcendentalists in 1843, claimed the group was actually followers of Fourierism and Owenite communism. The evidence supports this.

Bancroft's friends in Germany included many individuals who were of the liberal school of leftists such as Friedrich Schleiermacher and Wilhelm von Humboldt, who was involved in the Tugendbund, a direct descendent of the Illuminati, before he gained his reputation. Bancroft earned his doctorate at Göttingen, in addition to studying at Heidelberg and Berlin.

Bancroft became active in American politics, and his first appointment was to the Collector of Customs of Boston by Martin Van Buren. His appointees under him were Nathaniel Hawthorne and Orestes Brownson, both before they supposedly fell out with the socialist movement. Bancroft became the Secretary of the Navy under James K. Polk and established the Naval Academy at Annapolis without the consent of Congress. The academy was a good idea, but the manner in which it was established set a precedent for the lack of government oversight from then on.

Active in the movement which led to the Naval Academy was William Chauvenet, a member of the Order, Skull and Bones, and he was the most prominent of the initial academic staff. Another member of the Order, Charles F. Johnson, later taught mathematics. Bancroft then became acting Secretary of War for one month. During this brief period he was very instrumental in helping forge an American empire. He then became ambassador to Great Britain, Russia, and Germany.

Bancroft's *History of the United States* was heavily criticized when published, but he came through the fray with the help of like-minded friends. It was revised and added to over several years. He went on to be an early member of the Union League Club of New York and the head of the American Historical Association in 1886. The Union League was originally called the National League and favored nationalization over state sovereignty. Bancroft also served as the president of the American Geographical Society.

To give you an example of the type of history these men would print, Bancroft's *History of the United States*, Volume 6, page 450 stated:

> The people of the States demanded a federal convention to form the Constitution ... the Federal Congress offered that Constitution severally to the people of each State, and by their united voice ... it was made the binding form of government.

This is not what happened, and anyone who has studied the event knows it. The convention was called to amend the Articles of Confederation, not write a completely new form of government. As the historian David Saville Muzzey said, "Every clause in this passage is erroneous."

This is not atypical of what is contained in history books, and for the young student it produces a mind-set they will never get out of for the rest of their lives. It is close enough to the truth to get away with it, but it is not the whole truth. The subtle alterations of the truth can affect students' thinking about politics forever.

The first president of the American Historical Association was Andrew Dickson White, the Order. The association would go on to establish the manner in which history was to be taught in American high schools. White amassed collections of books on the Reformation, witchcraft, and the French Revolution. He would serve as our minister to Germany and Russia, and lead the American delegation to The Hague Peace Conference.

Bancroft, White, and their associates had an influence on published history which played a role in the initial "dumbing down" of American students. By the late 1800s, they came to dominate "history."

Due to the influence of Hegel and Johann Friedrich Herbart, American educators who studied in Germany ultimately dominated the education colleges in the United States. Herbart was a disciple of Pestalozzi, and was one of two of Pestalozzi's successors who carried his legacy far beyond the reach of other men. The second was Friedrich Fröbel, a man we will discuss later.

Another layer of Illuminist influence came through Wilhelm Wundt, the German founder of experimental psychology. His grandfather was Karl Wundt, a known member of the Illuminati. While it may be argued that the grandson was not necessarily the grandfather, nonetheless the influence of the Illuminists remained embedded in German higher education in many universities. In addition, the younger Wundt was a disciple of Herbart and Hegel, and applied their principles into the field of education in both technique and philosophy.

There is sufficient documentation available for the enterprising student to find online for the background and influence of the above-mentioned Germans on American education.

It is well documented that three men of the Order studied under the younger Wundt, and we will not dwell on the subject herein since it is very easy to access the information online and in several available books. That being said, if the younger Wundt did follow in his grandfather's steps, it says a great deal about American education since Daniel Coit Gilman, Timothy Dwight, and Andrew Dickson White all studied under Wundt, went on to lead several prestigious colleges, and had a tremendous influence on American education. They brought a simmering movement in American education to a boil by the late 1800s.

History Manipulated, Not Cyclical
The main battleground between the two forces, liberty and Illuminism, has been in the United States, since ultimately the key to world control would be America. The potential growth of the U.S. was obvious to all, and that at some point America could be a major, if not the primary Western country, *ergo* the world. From the days of Washington and Adams, the Conspiracy has done all it can to disguise itself, both through denial that there is a conspiracy, and by using their slowly gained influence to dumb down and to numb Americans' thinking processes as part of their efforts to control our citizens.

America would be the freest country on earth, allowing the Conspiracy to operate at will, as long as their organization and their true objectives were not exposed to the American people. Americans believe in freedom of speech, assembly, etc., and this would be used to build the might of the Illuminists to attack the remainder of the world; in other words:

Freedom would be used against itself in a sea of ignorance.

It has been said that only a moral and religious people can succeed at self-rule. The caveat is that they must also have an understanding relative to the principles of freedom and the wiles of those who mean to destroy it.

One of the teachings in modern history is that civilizations are cyclical in nature, that they rise and fall in a particular pattern.

This has been an idea planted in our minds to make what has been happening to our country seem inevitable and unstoppable. There is no cycle of history. What has been happening over human history is that there have always been the few that want to rule the many, a grab for power. The few have learned that there are certain methods for accomplishing this, and if done in secret it appears that it all happens quite by accident or as some result of history.

The deterioration of a civilization is not cyclical. There are countless civilizations that existed without deterioration until conquered from the outside, disappeared due to changes in their environment, or were inundated by catastrophic events. Our eyes are allowed to only concentrate on those civilizations that lend to the argument of a cycle of deterioration.

Rome is used as the prime example to make the point that civilizations deteriorate and that the United States is on the same path as ancient Rome. What is not told, at least with any significance, is that the few who wanted to rule the Roman Empire were involved in the secret Mithraic cult and had a great deal to do with the expansion of government and the moral deterioration to thereby gain complete control over the Roman people.

American Intellectual Conspirators:

Edward Everett. First American to receive a doctorate from Göttingen University in Germany where Adam Weishaupt and other Illuminati were professors. Delivered the main address at the Gettysburg dedication. Porcellian Club of Harvard.

Ralph Waldo Emerson. Educated by Edward Everett. Became the leader of the death of God movement.

George Bancroft. Educated at Göttingen University, Germany where Adam Weishaupt and other Illuminati were professors. Founder of Harvard's Round Hill School. Secretary of the Navy. President of the American Historical Society.

Joseph Green Cogswell. Educator at Round Hill School. Porcellian Club of Harvard.

There have been very few things written about the cult. There have been programs on HBO and the History Channel that have mentioned Mithraism, but they have not done a comprehensive job of getting the significance across to the viewer.[7]

It is evil men using the same techniques that produce the "cycle," not a natural product of man. The natural man wants to enjoy life and family, and to be left alone to do so.

It is not that history repeats itself; it is the misapplication of human nature by a few who desire to rule. If they come to power, the only thing that alters that is the collapse of totalitarianism, either through its inability to sustain itself, or through an overwhelming revival of civic morality among the people. Conspirators throughout time have learned to harness human nature; this is what creates the illusion of a cycle. *It is not a natural, inevitable cycle if it is deliberate.*

One of the most important psychological tools used by the conspiracy has been the idea of inevitability. Not only are "cycles" and wheels of the progress of civilization used to promote the idea of inevitability, they also provide the means of writing books that are very good in identifying problems in society and politics, but at the same time making it appear that there is no solution, the problems are just too great, and making anyone who is concerned, despondent and sapped of any desire to get involved in a losing fight to save America. If one thinks that there is no hope, then why spend the time and energy in fighting the "inevitable?"

It is a seductive argument that reinforces the natural desire to be left alone to pursue one's own aspirations — to build his family, business or career — and to simply engage in activities that enhance both. He does not want to have to take the time to defend hearth and family unless he absolutely is compelled to do so. Short of the impetus of an invasion, it takes a great deal of understanding to motivate someone to get involved in fighting something that most people cannot see. If they cannot see it, they don't see the need to fight it.

There have been many authors and so-called experts who have grown in reputation during the latter part of the 20th century who have exposed the problem but done little to remedy it. Many have written about or commented on the issues without actually becoming involved in forming an effective organization — oftentimes their efforts go no further than making a phone call, or being a paid speaker or author. In almost every case, they have led to more demoralization of those who have awakened to the problems that have beset our country.

They feed on the idea that by their broadcasting of the problem, somehow the viewer, reader, or listener does not need to get involved. They are made to feel involved by buying books, listening every day, or talking to peers at work about what they have heard. And somehow doing this, along with millions of others, will solve the problem. But it is not effective organization — it is talk.

Grasping for power must be done in secret, for the lust for power is a very dangerous game, both from the standpoint of the targeted peoples finding out and doing something about it, and the fact that when there are those who come together to grab power, they each want that power, compete for it, and even kill each other for it.

A modern overt example is the secret criminal society La Cosa Nostra or Mafia. 20th- century America was replete with murders of Mafia leaders by other leaders for control and power over the underworld, which in turn has been known to control local and state politics.

It is interesting to note that people can believe that the Mafia can control local and state politics, but reject the idea of any other conspiracy that wants to do so.

---

[7] One of the best short articles on the subject is at www.thenewamerican.com. Search for "Mithraic Mysteries and the Cult of Empire," by Charles Scaliger.

The classic example of killing their own is in the aftermath of a successful consolidation of political power. From Rome to revolutionary France, any competition to the leadership was eliminated, even if they had worked together to consolidate power — *especially if they had worked together to consolidate power*. These are usually the people who initially pose the greatest danger to those at the top in the scramble for and consolidation of power.

Robespierre had Georges Danton eliminated, along with anyone else who might challenge his control, until he too was eliminated from power. Stalin did likewise in his great purge, as did Hitler in his Night of the Long Knives against the Brown Shirt leadership, who had helped him come to power, including his mentor, the homosexual predator Ernst Roehm.

Working with power-hungry megalomaniacs is a precarious profession.

A modern wag has expressed it this way: The trouble with fighting the Conspiracy is that we are dealing with criminals. The trouble the Conspiracy has is that they have to deal with criminals. There is no honor among thieves.

In the end it all falls apart because total power for the few ultimately implodes. It sucks the life out of any country or civilization to the point that it becomes unsustainable, unless sustained economically from the outside. It will collapse into a dark age or be conquered from without. But the point is that these things will not happen without the manipulations of those who care more for their own lust for power than due to any natural "cycle."[8]

A close study of history from the standpoint of who and how something happened in history, rather than just noting the events, demonstrates the fact that, as was noted before, nothing happens in politics that wasn't planned that way.

The "cycle" theory is promoted by these conspirators to prevent those who are concerned about their plight from doing anything about it, since after all, it is inevitable!

The whole idea of inevitability in the collapse of civilization by natural deterioration has become so pervasive that it is propagated over and over again by hundreds of well-meaning authors. The control of any civilization's thought processes can alter their future. As we have seen, illuminated organizations have done this in various countries and it has been their intent: the coordinated few controlling the many, thereby their "history."

Do you realize sufficiently what it means to rule — to rule in a secret society? Not only over the lesser or more important of the populace, but over the best of men, over all ranks, nations, and religions, to rule without external force, to unite them indissolubly, to breathe one spirit and soul into them, men distributed over all parts of the world?... And finally, do you know what secret societies are? What a place they occupy in the great kingdom of the world's events? Do you think they are unimportant, transitory appearances?

— Adam Weishaupt, founder of the Illuminati
Nachtrag von weiterein Originalschriften

---

8   Communist Russia and China have always been sustained by the American taxpayer or consumer. Any enterprising student may look online for the economic help, trade, and integration by major American businesses into these two economies, even under the USSR. The World Bank, IMF, and the Export-Import Bank are good places to start. The second step is to explore the major American industrial companies and their integration into these two countries' industry. Also, the works of Dr. Antony Sutton show the collusion between American industrialists and communist Russia. The resultant economic integration due to the so-called trade policies that have helped build Chinese and Russian industry has placed America in a dangerous position in any future prolonged world war. Time spent looking at this subject online will open up a whole new vista supporting the fact that American military equipment is now reliant on 80% foreign components.

The Conspiracy actually fears the people waking up, and a great deal of time and effort is expended by conspirators in neutralizing their opposition. The idea of a cycle or inevitability is only one method. Two of the Conspiracy's paramount tenets for neutralizing their opposition are: Convince people that a conspiracy does not exist; and, assume the leadership of your own opposition — where none exists, create it. By this method, you have complete control.

This technique is also used to create the illusion of "opposing" sides in major issues. Sometimes, the issue created and the divide produced are of such a severity that they can result in war or civil war. While this may seem to be counterproductive, it is used to manipulate the population involved. It is the population that suffers, not those behind the scenes.

By controlling both sides of an argument, it matters little who "wins." Those who control the argument win.

Part of this process involves tolerance as a tactic. It is never to be a goal, even though it is made to appear to be a goal. Tolerance is something to be demanded as long as the philosophic party is not tolerated; but as soon as the philosophers gain secret power, since tolerance is an obstacle to stamping out their enemies, tolerance then becomes political correctness, and anything outside of this correctness is intolerable.

Tolerance is the process of changing one set of standards for another.

While there is a clear and present danger when the intellectual life of a nation falls into the hands of its enemies, it is compounded when they control the opposites, dominating the nature of the outcome.

A modern adaptation of controlling the argument is the political debates aired on national television. The art has reached such professionalism that few can detect that certain candidates are not allowed the same amount of time as others and are even debated by the moderator. The candidate blessed by the Insiders is allowed to win the debate. Sometimes it may be more than one candidate. The main idea is to eliminate the candidates that are undesirable by the mass media.

By the way, debates are usually lessons in frustration. In order to really develop an idea and have it stick in the mind of the listeners, adequate time must be given the speaker to develop sufficient background for an issue. Debates rarely allow the constitutionalist enough time to present a case. Also, the other side usually will interrupt, while the constitutionalist will not out of politeness. This will always cause the listener to lose his concentration on the constitutional argument.

In Germany, reading clubs became the means not only to inject Illuminism into German intellectual life, but to take control of all means of publishing and distribution of books, magazines, and the reviews of same; and to produce a coordinated attack against conservative thought and publishing. It was replicated in America, as we shall see, and it is the slow method of instilling change.

The quick way to change society is war, and this at the same time is the best method for consolidating power within a country. Not from the outside, but on the inside, with changes from the top down that increase government control inside the country, all done in the name of the war effort. Patriotic citizens will do almost anything in the name of the war effort, even allowing chains to be placed on them if it will help win the war.

Nazi Germany is a prime example. What the Nazis did by the end of the war to their own people would not have been tolerated at the beginning of the war. The Nazis created crisis after crisis, building up and leading to war. Their entire *modus operandi* of building government control began with the Reichstag fire, then the crises of re-occupying territory stripped from Germany at the end of World War I (even their invasion of Poland that started WWII had this element of re-occupation — as far as the German citizens were concerned, Western Poland was Prussia and a part of the German Empire they lost due to the Versailles Treaty).

The first use of war to control the citizens by the modern conspirators was the French National Convention of 1792 subsequent. In the name of the war effort against such enemies as Austria, the government called for emergency measures and denied the people and government rivals any semblance of constitutional democracy, culminating in the Reign of Terror. This was used to eliminate all rivals to Robespierre and his henchman Antoine Saint-Just.

The pattern for much or all of this use of war can be found in a novel by George Orwell, *1984*. Orwell also outlines the fabric of the world government so desired by this conspiracy within the pages of his novel. In fact, the novel's anti-hero, Winston, worked in a government office whose prime responsibility was purging the country of any information or history that would be detrimental to the latest party line issued by the Inner Party.

Anything that was stored that contradicted the new party line was systematically destroyed. The old history, news — whatever — that was in the way of the "new truth" subsequently had to be eliminated because at some point in the future someone might stumble onto the real truth and use it against the Inner Party.

Government has never had this ability, although the Internet may make it possible should it come under Insider control.

Orwell also pointed out that the Winston's of the world thought that they belonged to the ruling party, when in fact there was a secret Inner Party that ruled the world. This was the tactic outlined by Engels when he said that while they formed an open communist party, they retained the secret society of the Just under a different name.

In *1984*, the Insiders had separated the world into three parts, each warring against the other in order to better control their peoples in the name of patriotism and the war effort. But at the top of the three parts, they were working together.

As a man who had extensive relationships with socialist and communist leaders, Eric Arthur Blair, aka "George Orwell," knew the future they had in mind. He worked with both, but in the end he made sure that he was buried in consecrated ground in a church graveyard.

Simply knowing that the deterioration of countries comes from a few who want power — and who once they attain that power destroy civilization — is a very hopeful thing to realize. It means that the process can be not only defeated but reversed by the process of eliminating conspirators from gaining power in the first place, by identifying who they are and what they hope to gain.

The goal of these conspirators has always been a world parliament controlled by them, not dissimilar to the *Star Wars* movie plot.

There are two roads to this goal — doing it all at once, or doing it in the manner outlined in *1984*; in other words regionalism, a steady consolidation of governments. These conspirators call their goal a *New World Order*.

3
SUBVERSION AND TREASON IN THE EARLY YEARS

After American independence was wrested from England, there was contention over several matters early on in the former colonies, varied in number and intensity. On a country-wide scale there were obvious problems with the Articles of Confederation, which led to a convention to amend the Articles. Instead, the delegates decided to hold what became known as the Constitutional Convention, not only producing a completely new document, but a new form of government. This was in violation of their instructions. A fierce public debate ensued over this newly crafted Constitution, particularly since the delegates had not done what was asked of them: simply to amend the Articles.

The convention was held in secret, and the famous question to Benjamin Franklin on his leaving the convention and his reply illustrate this secrecy. A group of citizens had gathered outside of Constitution Hall and one woman asked the question: "Well, Doctor, what have we got, a republic or a monarchy?" "A Republic, Ma'am, if you can keep it," replied Franklin.

Luckily, the convention was manned by brilliant men who understood history and the principles of good government and human nature, and gave us a codified rule of law that has become the oldest constitution in use — over two hundred years.

Likewise, the Confederate Constitutional Convention more than 70 years later was held in secret. Even a proposal to have a stenographer record the proceedings was rejected, and reports of the actions and words of the participants are less than complete.

The precedence of secret enclaves to write or amend the country's law is a strong argument against a modern constitutional convention, or convention of the states, *especially at a time when the delegates would probably not have the historical and principled background as did the men in the preceding conventions, and when our entire political system is inundated with the protégés of Illuminism.*

Many Americans advocate a convention as a means to amend the Constitution in order to present solutions to the growing power of government and/or its lack of fiscal responsibility, but a convention is not necessary to do so. The Constitution has been amended several times without a convention.

If two-thirds of the states petition the Congress to convene a convention and one is called, the debate rages as to whether the Congress or the states will set the rules. This is not the only contention relative to the rules, and would seem to be a reason not to try and convene such a convention. It can be done, but to gain harmony would be nearly impossible; the contention would be nearly violent in the current political atmosphere.

Article V of the Constitution specifically says that it will be the Congress that will call such a convention at the request of the states. At the conclusion of Article I, Section 8 the language indicates that Congress will set the rules for such a convention. The advocates of using a convention argue that the convention would set the rules.

One of the problems with the modern move for a convention is that the more-constitutionally minded think they will control such a conclave. The Left has been advocating a constitutional convention for decades, advocating conservative-appearing issues, including a balanced budget amendment. They have other amendments in mind once the convention is seated, and their influence in the process has always been there, growing behind the scenes.

Increasingly, organizations led by members of the Council on Foreign Relations are involving themselves in the process, and there is a strong hint of those groups who want a major shift in the Second Amendment.

An initial convention could be held to produce a benign constitutional revision, which would allay the fears of those worried about the runaway process. Then, after the process had been shown to "work," another convention could be called to change the Constitution substantially from its original intent.

If politicians ignore the Constitution now, what makes anyone think that they will honor a new amendment(s) that limits their ability to do as they please? The Constitution already limits them and they ignore it. The solution is re-instilling respect for the law and that has to begin at the grassroots level in order to elect people into Congress who will respect it and obey their oath of office.

Shall we revise the Ten Commandments because so many people ignore them? Or, should we work at getting people to obey them?

One of the main reasons behind a call for a conference or convention of the states is to establish a balanced budget amendment. Will it provide for tax monies in versus tax monies out? Or, will it ignore entitlements, the main cause of American indebtedness — which by law are off-budget? Many states have a balanced budget as part of their constitution, yet use imaginative accounting procedures to declare their state budgets balanced when they are in fact not balanced.[9]

There can be no talk about balancing the budget unless the Federal Reserve is taken into account. How can the budget be balanced in the true sense of the term if the Fed is allowed to continue an independent policy of running the printing presses for the various reasons they do, such as bailing out foreign banks? Members of Congress are very concerned over this secretive process. This process is disruptive of the economy and has a bearing on the ability of Congress to balance a system over which it has no real control.

It would make more sense to abolish the Fed than it would be to pass a balanced budget amendment if the Congress or any "convention" were serious about it.

Another argument against a balanced budget amendment is that spending would no longer be based upon whether it was constitutional, but whether it would affect the budget. It also would make spending subject to the whims of the people, rather than the constitution. This may seem a rather silly point until you think about it. While the Congress may not pay any attention to the Constitution now relative to how they spend the peoples' money, a balanced budget amendment would codify the process forever.

In other words, a balanced budget should only include those things authorized by the Constitution. Frankly, if they did that now, it would balance the budget.

A balanced budget that does not take into account the powers of the Executive branch and Supreme Court will also fail. No proposed balanced budget addresses these two problems. The president has used his powers to make items such as the Affordable Care Act exempt from sequestered budget cuts. The courts have also redefined the idea of what constitutes a tax, fee, etc., thus changing the entire idea of a budget.

---

9 Off budget items include Social Security, Medicare, the U.S. Postal Service, Freddy Mac, Fannie Mae, Obamacare, etc. These entities are bankrupting our country yet are not even included in some "balanced budget" amendment proposals.

A balanced budget amendment must address all of the above or it is useless. And, if it does, it will require an amendment half as long as the Constitution itself.

There has been a modern push for some years to convene a meeting that looks suspiciously like a constitutional convention. The same people have put millions of dollars behind it, over and over again, altering the proposal in their attempts to get enough people behind their initiative. They use all manner of arguments professing they have no intention of altering the basic fundamentals of our Constitution; however, no matter what device they use to convene and appoint or elect the delegates, the caliber of men who would attend would never measure up to the wisdom and understanding of the men who were sent to the original Constitutional Convention — even if their hearts and intentions were pure. Where are the Madison's, Washington's, Mason's, Hamilton's, et al., of today?

Indeed, some of the politicians flying around the country in support of a convention, calling their opponents mistaken in their beliefs, with very few exceptions are the same ones who are calling conservatives mistaken about their opposition to Common Core and foreign entanglements.

No one seems to know where the millions come from that finance the modern constitutional convention movement. Even if it comes from so-called conservative donors, one has to realize that many of these donors are heavily involved with business in China and Russia and support other initiatives which will lead to negating the Constitution in the long run. It would entail another book to document and expose this hypocrisy.

With only one or two exceptions, there does not exist today any legislature or body of voting electorate that would elect a good assembly of people to any conclave intended to solve the constitutional problems that need to be addressed. This can only happen when enough people have the education and understanding to do so. Once we reach that point, through a concerted education program among the people, the problems would disappear in the light of the knowledgeable citizenry applying pressure on their representatives and electing those who will obey their oath to the Constitution. At that point, there would be no reason for a convention.

With an informed electorate the problems would disappear. Without an informed electorate there can be no solution that will work, since they will continue to elect those who would find a way around the Constitution to not only "give the store away," but give the country away as well.

Do not think that the Conspiracy is wringing its hands over the prospect of a meeting of the states to offer amendments to the Constitution. It is a program they have long supported and would use to the best of their ability. They have been busy attempting to form coalitions with conservatives to work for such a convention, with increasing success.

Too many conservatives, especially the newly awaken and involved, do not have the historical background and experience to stand up to the socialists face to face. To honestly believe that any convention would simply be composed of conservatives is a fantasy.

Ask yourself who would represent your state in such a convention. Do you trust your legislature or the voters in your state to send an actual constitutionally minded delegate? If you do not know who would represent you, how can you possibly feel comfortable about the process? And not just your state, but delegates from every liberal state in the country.

The purpose of this tome is not to argue current issues; however, the reader should do an online search for those organizations that are backed by leftists who want a constitutional convention and call it by that name. The number and their work with seemingly conservative organizations will be somewhat surprising. [10]

While this battle may seem to be a current event, it is simply a modern extension of the arguments,

---

10   See "Working Together to Rewrite the Constitution," by Christian Gomez, *The New American* magazine, June 9, 2014.

tactics, and organizations that were in play during the ratification of the U.S. Constitution.

The battle to ratify the Constitution was based on whether it gave too much power to the federal government. One of the main arguments against ratification was the provision for a single executive, yet history had amply demonstrated that the single executive was more stable. Any government that had any style of multiple executives always ended up with one executive anyway after either a civil war, or at the minimum, an internal struggle.

The danger was in the accumulation of power in the executive regardless of form, and the framers of the Constitution felt they had solved that problem as long as the Constitution was alive and well through a separation of powers within the executive, Congress, and the Supreme Court, *as well as the electoral college*.

The original form of the electoral college had embedded within it a check and balance that was lost very early on: the two top vote receivers were to be the president and vice-president, and they did not necessarily have to come from the same faction. In other words, they would not always agree to a party line or agenda. This provided a check and balance within the executive. This was changed very soon in favor of a partisan outcome of electing party candidates for both executive offices.

While the first president and vice-president were more or less in agreement, this was not true of the second president and vice-president, John Adams and Thomas Jefferson. While Adams supported Washington and his policies, Jefferson did a great deal to undermine Washington and Adams and their policies — which we will show further on.

The vote to ratify the new Constitution was a great deal closer in several states than most realize today. In only three states was it unanimous.

From the beginning, Illuminist and foreign-driven initiatives used every issue and contention to try to wrest control of our fledgling country, split it apart, and/or take control of our western and southern frontiers. This included the debate over and implementation of the Constitution.

Similarly, disharmony over amendments considered during a modern convention could be used to divide and polarize the country.

The American War for Independence produced a country that in many respects was the opposite of what would be produced by the French Revolution. It became a struggle between two opposing forces, good and evil, manifested in their governments, and as a result a struggle over the New World geography and people that the New and the Old World governments would govern. The Illuminati, which had produced revolutionary France, now intensified their program, intent on gaining control in America.

Keep in mind as we proceed that what was happening in France with the Reign of Terror was what agents of conspiratorially controlled France likewise wanted to inject into America, with the elimination of their opposition here in the same manner. What caused them to fail included the fact that their agents were too removed from their leadership at the top of the Conspiracy in Europe; this in some instances resulted in problems with the timely direction of their minions.

Nor had the American people been degraded enough by the downturn in general morality as a result of the War for Independence to want to behead Americans that fought for independence simply because they disagreed on becoming part of revolutionary France. This statement may seem extreme; however, the agents of France and their minions constantly used *rhetoric* that indicated that they wanted the elimination of their opposition by any means possible, including assassination.

The actions of their minions, the Jacobins, likewise using harsh rhetoric and in many cases violence in the streets, were an indication of the methods the Conspiracy was using to divide the people and then "punish" their enemies.

The Jacobins were a front organization of Illuminati leadership in France and were imported to the United States. Lenin used to say that the Bolsheviks were the Jacobins of the 20th century, which is more of a description of both the French and American Jacobins than many would feel comfortable with, but accurate.

The Jacobins were named after the Jacobin Club of Paris, those who attended the meetings of the Société des Amis de la Constitution, and then those who attended the network of clubs that grew up in the provinces of France. The general revolutionary philosophy within the club was held by all, but later rivalries for power split it into factions. These factions' leaders found themselves killed by other leaders at the guillotine, until the events got out of hand and Robespierre and his immediate coterie — including Saint-Just — were themselves executed.

Antoine Saint-Just was the "president" of the Jacobins and the youngest member of the National Convention of 1792. He spearheaded the movement to execute King Louis XVI. He organized for Robespierre the arrests and prosecutions of many of the famous figures of the revolution who were rivals to their leadership, not that they were part of the old regime of royalty or clergy, but they simply had the potential to provide leadership for a counterrevolution against Robespierre.

The fall of Robespierre, besides ending the Reign of Terror, heralded the end of the Jacobin experiment of a controlled economy in France.

Again, the problems within the Jacobins were more personal rivalry than philosophical differences, although there were those who disagreed with the excess of executions. Also, just as there were those more violent in their application of their philosophy that led directly to the communist movement in Europe, there were American Jacobins that agreed on philosophy but not the tactics of how to achieve their aims. Lodges in France became Jacobin, some of which were formed of Catholic priests and leaders.

The American Democratic Clubs led by the Jacobin movement from revolutionary France provided organization to foment and lead opposition to George Washington and the Constitution, particularly after it was ratified. Many good people were caught up in the debates, most visibly those who wanted less power vested in the federal government, and they were used as dupes by the Jacobins. And, to be successful, the Conspiracy always works both sides.

While there were already Illuminati units established in America, many of these were due to a direct German influence. The French wing of Illuminism manifested itself through the Jacobin Clubs with anti-Christian organizations from France and England, and was more vocal and visible.

The first Jacobin Club was formed in Philadelphia, the capital at the time, in June 1792. The clubs were most active in 1793 and 1794, ultimately numbering about 42 groups, with nine in Pennsylvania alone. They were partisans for revolutionary France, calling themselves "Citizen" or "Citizeness" and singing the *La Marseillaise*, calling themselves Republicans, even though they called the clubs *democratic*.

The formation of these Jacobin and Democratic Clubs demonstrated the influence and groundwork laid by the Illuminati circles already established in America before the French Revolution.

The modern student does not understand the significance of these groups calling themselves "democratic" clubs. This is because today the difference between a democracy and a republic is rarely taught. Therefore, since the idea called *democracy* has become ingrained in our population, the image the student of today has of such groups and their actions is seen through a befogged looking glass.

What they see is Democracy: good. Federalism: bad.

The United States had recognized revolutionary France when no other government would in 1793. They paid us back by infiltrating their agents into our country. In addition, they and the French representatives often went around the federal government directly to the American people to try to incite the public against their government.[11]

In France, Jacques-Pierre Brissot had formed the Gallo-American Society ostensively to promote friendship with America *prior* to the French Revolution. On a trip to America he established chapters of the organization. With the onset of revolution in France, the members in America started to call themselves Jacobins.

While the Gallo-American Society was short-lived, it was aided in France by the Lodge of the Nine Sisters, and many of its members segued into the French Society of the Friends of the Blacks. Brissot was a friend of Jean-Paul Marat, and they were both close to Lafayette and engaged with him in his promotion of mesmerism, simply another way to sell the ideas of Illuminism. Brissot was also part of the Illuminist Mirabeau's writing stable that turned out all sorts of propaganda in print. In addition to propaganda, Mirabeau was involved in publishing pornography and was a notorious seducer of women.

The Gallo-American Society helped introduce all of these ideas into America in their *radical* form: revolution, mesmerism, and anti-slavery. In this case, it was not so much that the organization was important as it was the people who were involved.

Jefferson, to his credit, worked against mesmerism and sent pamphlets from France to America to refute such ideas.

The Friends of the Blacks, while supposedly an abolitionist movement against the slave trade, was in reality a conduit for radicalism by Mirabeau. Members took up a correspondence with American radicals and had an influence on the direction of the abolitionists here. The Friends were finally absorbed into the Cercle Social.

The influence of the Jacobins and Democratic Societies led directly to the founding of the Republican Party, which was later renamed the Democrat Party. They also stirred up the populace into armed rebellion in league with French revolutionary plans over real or imaginary issues. One of the more famous was the Whiskey Rebellion.

Quoting the New York Senate report of 1920, *Revolutionary Radicalism*, page 501:

As an illustration of the effect of European movements upon the United States, we may make reference to the influence which the Jacobin Clubs of the French Revolution had upon the malcontents in the United States in the later part of the eighteenth century.

The Whiskey Rebellion of Western Pennsylvania was the outgrowth of agitation carried on by so-called democratic societies acting under the guise of protectors of civil liberties, which received their inspiration from the French revolutionary societies.

Washington, in a letter to John Jay, put it this way:

That the self-created societies who have spread themselves over this country have been laboring

---

11 The same results always ensue with the recognition of communist states. One in particular, Cuba, will again infiltrate their agents into the U.S. with the use of diplomatic immunity through its consulates with the recognition of Cuba by Obama. This was one of the reasons that diplomatic relations were cut in the first place. Also, the Cuban government will be very active in propagandizing Americans against our government, police, and constitutionally minded politicians. They were a main force behind the scenes during the violence of the 1960s and 1970s, training and coordinating terrorism and violent communist movements. The Cuban Intelligence Service is the mainstay and controlling factor in Venezuela, having taken the reins of operating the police, army, and other important government offices as "advisors." The recognition by Obama of Cuba and the communist regime is payback to the revolutionaries and terrorists trained by Cuba that were the friends and mainstay of Obama's early political career. This latter information is readily available online.

incessantly to sow the seeds of distrust, jealousy, and, of course, discontent, hoping thereby to effect some revolution in the Government, is not unknown to you. That they have been the fomenters of the western disturbances admits of no doubt in the mind of any one who will examine their conduct.

The U.S. Senate, in its reply to Washington's speech at the opening of Congress, November 19, 1794, also referred to secret societies fomenting insurrection. According to Washington, the Whiskey Rebellion was the "first ripe fruit" of the democratic societies when the Jacobins used the issue of the imposition of a tax on distilling whiskey.

It was believed by Washington that Hugh Henry Brackenridge, William Findley, and especially Albert Gallatin were behind the rebellion, fomenting the general population that did not own property or even a still for making whiskey. Gallatin, as a youth, had visited Voltaire, and his grandparents, particularly his grandmother, were intimate friends of Voltaire.

The insurrectionists created their own militia of armed patrols who saw fit to punish anyone, government agent or citizen, who tried to comply with the law. The "regulars," as they were called, were very brutal and terrorized the whole area. These bands were also known as "tinkers."

Violence grew — citizen against citizen — until some of the rebellious leaders wanted to calm down the violence, while others wanted to form up the militia and take up arms against the federal government.

The final straw for the Washington administration was the takeover of Pittsburgh, and he sent in federally led militia. When the federal troops marched into Harrisburg, Pennsylvania to put down the rebellion, they found the French flag flying over the court house.

One of the least reported aspects of the Whiskey Rebellion was the effort to suppress the clergy as the French had done. The French had not only eliminated Catholic clergy, but Protestant ministers as well. The Rebellion never went to the extent of the French, but the seed had been sown.

The main propaganda argument used against the American clergy by the Illuminati was that they were using the pulpit to preach "politics," the same argument used by the "liberals" today against the Christian Right. Apparently it is all right if they use the pulpit to support socialist initiatives, but not constitutional ones.

Washington believed that the democratic societies — with the help of revolutionary France — would destroy the United States by revolution. Meanwhile, James Madison and Thomas Jefferson criticized Washington for attacking the democratic societies.

There was considerable evidence of collusion between Whiskey Rebellion leaders and other portions of the country to use the excise tax as an excuse to promote anti-Federalism, and in turn promote the party friendly to revolutionary France.

One of the situations that played into the hands of the subversives was the geographic separation of the Western territory from the East. In modern times, the distance is not that great. In the late 1700s, the distance was a problem due to the primitive travel conditions and the lack of timely communication. It would serve as a dividing point between the two areas for two decades.

Jefferson defended the revolutionaries and even went so far as to write letters of apology for Weishaupt, the Illuminati, and the likes of Sterling Price and Joseph Priestly, who were part of the Philanthropist movement, a direct result of Illuminism. At the same time, he chastised Robison, Morse, and Barruel, who wrote against the Illuminati.

In a famous letter to Bishop James Madison on January 31, 1800, Jefferson called Abbé Barruel's writing the "ravings of a Bedlamite," meaning insane, and went on to defend Weishaupt.

On the other hand, this is what Washington had to say about it in a letter to a minister who obviously was concerned about the Illuminati:

Reverend Sir:

It was not my intention to doubt that the doctrine of the Illuminati, and the principles of Jacobinism, had not spread in the United States. On the contrary, no one is more satisfied of this fact than I am.

The idea I meant to convey was that I did not believe the Lodges of Freemasons in this country had, as societies, endeavored to propagate the *Diabolical* tenets of the former, or the *Pernicious* principles of the latter, *if they are susceptible of separation.* That individuals of them may have done it, or that the founder, or instruments employed to found the *Democratic* societies in the United States may have had this object, and actually had a separation of the people from their government in view, *is too evident to be questioned.*

With respect, I remain, Sir, etc....
George Washington
— Letter to Reverend G. W. Snyder, September 25, 1798

You will notice in the language used, particularly the italicized clause in the first sentence of the second paragraph, that Washington did not believe that there was a separation between the Illuminati and the Jacobins who formed the Democratic societies.

Washington's main point was that he was not convinced that Illuminism had as yet penetrated American Masonic lodges. At that time, these lodges were not of the Grand Orient and were organized on the classic Masonic foundation. The problems caused by grafting the Grand Orient onto American Masonry were not evident enough to cause Washington concern. However, we are aware that certain Americans returning from Europe were attempting to inject Illuminism into Masonry, though this was not yet obvious to men like Washington.

Propaganda against Washington over the Whiskey Rebellion persists today. There are those who claim that Washington opposed the Whiskey Rebellion in order to gain precedence in the whiskey trade for his distillates. Washington paid the tax and the argument was just another swipe at him by his enemies involved in the Jacobin movement.

It is amazing that many conservatives today have been led to believe these sorts of distortions, and this is one of the reasons for this tome. Jacobin propaganda that evolved into communist propaganda has made great inroads into modern thought.

Under the leadership of Edmond Charles Genet ("Citizen Genet"), the French ambassador, the overall program was to turn our newly formed nation into allies with revolutionary France, and regardless to wrest the Western territories from the United States, using democratic and Jacobin associations of the Atlantic states, then drawing America into war with England. The Whiskey Rebellion was a part of this process.

Part of Genet's tactics to work his strategy was to outfit privateers, American vessels of war, "to cruise and commit hostilities on nations with whom the United States were at peace." This he engaged in before he even presented his credentials to Washington, fitting out four privateers that sailed out to assail British and Spanish shipping.

Likewise, Genet established French courts and engaged in hiring soldiers — all on American soil. He tried to raise two armies in America to invade Florida and the Mississippi Valley for revolutionary France.

He was able to procure George Rogers Clark to command the Kentucky army as major general in the army of France, and commander in chief of the expedition, in violation of U.S. law.

Genet demanded that Washington convene the Congress to debate neutrality or war. He demanded that Hamilton finance his army and cannons from Gen. Henry Knox to arm it. Knox replied that the United States would not loan him a pistol let alone a cannon.

These French armies ultimately failed because of a lack of funding. Genet, as the French minister, was using funds from our federal government due *Royal* France for weapons and loans during the War for Independence. These funds he used for the expedition and Jacobin activities. Hamilton put a stop to these funds.

It is surprising that Hamilton had not cut off these funds much earlier, since they were used by Genet to organize Jacobin clubs, democratic societies, and journals in opposition to Hamilton and Washington. The personalities of these two men meant that they gave a "lot of rope" to people to hang themselves rather than confront them immediately.

The extramarital affair of Hamilton with Maria Reynolds may have played a behind-the-scenes role in Hamilton's actions over a period of time — which we will explain later.

Such actions by Genet could well have plunged the United States into a war with either England or France — or both. George Washington was not pleased. However, Secretary of State Jefferson was pleased, defending Genet, at least privately. Genet was publically critical of Jefferson having "a language official, and a language confidential." In other words: playing both sides.

When Genet thought Washington would move to stop his actions, Genet threatened Washington with revolution if his plans were countermanded.

There was still a great amount of animosity directed at America from Britain and the idea of privateers working out of American ports for the French was too much. As it was, the British retaliated against American shipping since the American navy was nearly non-existent and could do nothing to stop the French "American" privateers from sailing in and out of our ports. With the use of the Democratic Societies working for the French, it was also difficult for port authorities to stop them.

Such activity played into the hands of the English, who wanted to seize American ships and shipping, and who took American sailors off our ships and pressed them into indentured service on British vessels. It provided them with an excuse. Another reason for this activity by Britain was an embargo on trade with Europe, which England had imposed as part of their tactics in an attempt to strangle France. Any merchantman trading with French-controlled states was seized. This ultimately played a major role in starting the War of 1812.

We became involved in a war between England and France due to the actions of the French-led Jacobin Democratic Societies. This ultimately manifested into a war between us and England.

Genet had been the French revolutionary ambassador to Russia. He was declared *persona non grata* by Catherine the Great for his revolutionary activities there, forming Jacobin Clubs in St. Petersburg. When named the ambassador to the United States, rather than going to the national capital, he landed in Charleston, S.C. where he was wildly welcomed by the people and by the governor of South Carolina, William Moultrie, a Federalist. There Genet proceeded to help foment agitation against the administration of Washington, helping spread the influence of the radical Democratic Clubs.

Diplomatic protocol demanded that any ambassador present his credentials to the head of state before engaging in any activities or pronouncements. Genet deliberately violated that courtesy by immediately attacking Washington and the constituted government the moment he landed on American soil.

Genet founded the Philadelphia Society, the "mother lodge" of the Democratic Societies fronting for the Jacobins. Washington said of these clubs in a letter to Henry Lee on August 26, 1794,

> ... the most diabolical attempt to destroy the best fabric of human government and happiness, that has ever been presented for the acceptance of mankind.

Philadelphia was the center of French émigrés and became our capital for a time. The former aides to Lafayette settled in Philadelphia, and there was considerable travel back and forth of French Americans to revolutionary France.

Demonstrations and rallies were held in every town for Genet on the way from Charleston to Philadelphia, organized by the Democratic Clubs. The continual theme was alliance with revolutionary France and against George Washington. The way was "paved" by aides riding ahead of the Genet party to spread the word that he was coming thorough their town, and it did not hurt to spread a little free rum about in the process.

Not only were these events attended by Genet, but at all fetes which were given him, French revolutionary red caps of liberty appeared and circulated. This obviously indicated organization, not spontaneity. Also, toasts were given as flattering to the French revolution as they were vituperative of the American government under George Washington.

To describe what was going on in American ports by French seamen at this time would be nearly impossible to believe in an American city, and demonstrated the lack of morality by Americans as a result of the War for Independence that we discuss in another section. The Washington administration was powerless to enforce order on this level, particularly since much of it was a local and state issue, not a federally enforceable issue.

As a result of this agitation, Genet was able to whip crowds in Philadelphia into a frenzy, encouraging them to unite with France in "the revolution of the World."

In New York, Gov. George Clinton marched with Genet through the streets of Manhattan while the crowds yelled to enthrone Genet as the head of the country.

The fever of revolution was in the air in most places except New England — as was treason.

The Philip Freneau affair was a case in point. Freneau was a clerk in the State Department, while at the same time editor of the Philadelphia, *National Gazette*, and was in league with Genet. Freneau was privy to state secrets that would have been to the benefit of Genet and enhanced his initiatives. It was obvious that Freneau was giving information to Genet, and his newspaper office had become a meeting place for French sympathizers. Freneau was a deist who attacked Washington while an employee of the Washington administration.

Washington wanted him fired but Jefferson, the secretary of state, needed to do it, as Freneau was a State Department employee. Jefferson refused.

In other words, there was a traitor in the federal government, supplying the French and Jacobins with government information, and Jefferson refused to fire the person responsible. There would be at least one more.

There was actually more to the Freneau story that put Jefferson in a difficult position. There was a group that came together to oppose Hamilton and the proposed National Bank. These men included Jefferson, Madison, Burr, and Gov. Clinton of New York.

They hatched a movement to remove Hamilton from all influence in the Washington administration, including support for a new newspaper, the *National Gazette*, set up by Jefferson to counter Hamilton's paper, the *Gazette of the United States*. Jefferson put an appointee in his State Department, Philip Freneau, on as its editor on the recommendation of Madison and Henry Lee.

The *National Gazette* became the flagship of a series of newspapers which included the New York *Argus*, the Richmond *Examiner*, and the Boston *Independent Chronicle*. All of these newspapers were started with the intent of stopping Hamilton and opposing Washington, and were the linchpins of Jacobin propaganda.

Jefferson could not fire Freneau from the State Department, since a disgruntled Freneau might have disclosed too much about Jefferson's double-dealing within the Washington administration.

Freneau was not simply an employee; he was a key link in the system of Democratic Clubs raising funds for their efforts and those in France. Firing Freneau would have possibly revealed far too much of what was behind the Jacobin movement in America.

Freneau became an agent of the French Society of Patriots in America and raised funds to send to Jacobin France. He was active in organizing and hosting some of Genet's meetings and tour when Genet first arrived in America. He was also involved in the Whiskey Rebellion and knew intimately many men prominent in early American politics. Even Madison courted his sister at one time.

Freneau wrote an attack on the Society of Cincinnatus which was translated and highly praised by the Illuminist Mirabeau in France. It may have contributed to the murder by the Jacobins of the members of the society in France, Frenchmen who had participated in the American War for Independence. There is reason to believe that the members in America would feel the same threat from American Jacobins, both in rhetoric and actions taken by them in various melees in the towns run over by the Jacobin fever.

Saying it in another way, *the French revolutionaries murdered the French officers who had helped us win American independence*. The Society of Cincinnatus was composed exclusively of such officers. They were a threat to the French Illuminists' amoral revolution.

The *Aurora* replaced the *National Gazette* as the leading Democrat-Republican paper in the country when the *Gazette* was mismanaged out of existence. Both had a top circulation of 1,700, displaying that it is not numbers but who and how they are organized that matter.

After helping found the *Gazette* and supporting other such efforts, some years later Jefferson was to say, "The man who reads nothing at all is better educated than the man who reads nothing but newspapers" a sentiment agreed upon by a vast majority of political activists.

The reader may wish to acquaint himself with the Reynolds affair of Hamilton. The short story is that Hamilton had an affair with James Reynolds' wife, Maria, and paid Reynolds to keep it quiet. Reynolds told associates of Burr, who held it over Hamilton's head for several years. This included Jefferson. What actions that Hamilton may have taken in those years that he did not wish to do as a result of this sword of Damocles held by the Jacobin leadership are not known.

What is known is the hush money that was paid. It defies logic not to think that the affair was used to influence Hamilton to do things he wished otherwise to do while it was still a secret. Once it came out, Hamilton confessed the affair and publicly apologized.

The affair finally ended Hamilton's public life and it had all of the earmarks of a setup; one clue was that Maria's divorce lawyer was Aaron Burr, not the lawyer for the injured husband. It was she who had approached Hamilton and let him know that such an affair was welcome.

There is reason to believe that some of the actions by Hamilton were forced upon him by Burr, and Burr was able to build support for the Democratic movement as a result.

Jefferson, as a member of Washington's administration, not only ignored problems among his employees — he tried to fill the administration with his partisans. A steadfast friend of Thomas Paine to the end, Jefferson tried to get him appointed postmaster general by Washington. Washington refused. At this time Paine wrote Washington an open letter from France, part of which read,

> And as to you, Sir, treacherous in private friendship, and a hypocrite in public life, the world will be puzzled to decide whether you are an apostate or imposter; whether you have abandoned good principles, or whether you ever had any.
> — "Letter to George Washington," Paris, summer of 1793

On January 25, 1797, Jefferson wrote to Italian patriot Philip Mazzei. Mazzei had been a visitor to America and despised Washington. He helped purchase arms for Virginia during the War for Independence. This may seem to be an admirable enterprise, but such men were known to make a good amount of money doing so. He became somewhat of a roving ambassador for the American cause in Europe. Later, he became active in the politics of the French Revolution under the Directorate.

The letter to Mazzei was published in the Paris *Moniteur* and was used as an excuse to deny the recognition of the American ambassador to France, and it was hoped it would influence the rise of the "triumph of the party of good republicans, the Friends of France" back in America.

It also exposed Jefferson as an enemy of Washington at a time he was still playing both sides.

When he was recalled by the French government at the request of Washington, Genet remained in the U.S., since a change in power had taken place in France and Robespierre was waiting to send him to the guillotine. It is a testimony to the Washington government that they would not give him up to the Reign of Terror that awaited him, even though it was obvious that he would continue his animosity toward Washington. Genet married the daughter of New York Governor George Clinton and became an American citizen. When she died, he married Martha Brandon Osgood, the daughter of the first Post Master General Samuel Osgood, who would go on to be the first president of City Bank of New York, later named Citibank and then Citigroup. He was also a prominent member of the American Philosophical Society.

The situation with Osgood would have driven any modern intelligence officer crazy. Washington resided in his home in New York during the brief time that New York served as the capital, from 1789-1790. It was the best house in New York at the time, and it appears that Osgood felt that the residence of the president demanded the best.

Osgood's daughter was later married to an obvious enemy of the United States, and while an enemy of Robespierre, Genet was at least a Jacobin and a minion of the Illuminati-run French Revolution. How many of Osgood's servants remained in his home, if any, and would they have overheard private conversations between Washington and others in the house? We know that Burr seemed to know state secrets before even the best of the Federalists. Was this the beginning of such intelligence? This is all speculation, but as stated, any intelligence officer would want to know the answer to such questions.

In the years we are discussing, it was rare that a daughter ever married someone the father did not approve of, and many marriages were more or less arranged by the parents in the upper middle class, at the minimum having far more to do with the decision than is done today. Osgood had to have approved his daughter's marriage to Genet — at least there is no evidence that he did not.

What we are speculating is that the process of espionage against the Washington administration, culminating in the problems with the French ambassadors, may have started earlier than people imagine — even before the French Revolution. We do know, even if Washington did not, that Illuminati organization already existed in our country long before the fall of France to their minions. It is obvious that Washington and others had no clue what was beginning to be a problem for the future fledgling state. The Conspiracy had already started to infiltrate their minions into strategic positions before the government was even founded. After all, Lafayette — a member of the Illuminati — worked closely with Washington during the war and ingratiating himself into the good graces of countless Americans.

After all that Genet did to destroy the Washington administration and the fledgling country, Hamilton still urged Washington to give asylum to Genet rather than have him return to France to a certain death by Robespierre.

Noah Webster explained in a newspaper article that the purpose of the Democratic Clubs was to gain a controlling influence over the United States by fomenting revolution, overthrowing the Washington government, and eventually uniting France and the United States in war against England. He stated:

> The most effective means of carrying their point in this country was ... gradually and secretly to acquire numbers and strength till they were able to bid defiance to the constitutional authorities.
> — *The Life and Times of Noah Webster: An American Patriot*

Webster stated that the clubs formed

> ... a league of societies, disciplined to the orders of chiefs, whose views were concealed, even from the members themselves, and which must be crushed in its infancy or it would certainly crush the government.
>
> — *Ibid.*

Further, he said it was one of "the most daring projects of throwing the world into confusion that had been exhibited since the incursions of the Goths and Vandals." Note that he said *the world into confusion.*

Once Gallatin and other key leaders saw that their Whiskey Rebellion would fail, and that an army from the federal government was marching on them, they immediately ingratiated themselves with the other side. They became the moderates.[12]

Many of the leaders in the Whiskey Rebellion went on to become part of the federal government. In 1794, Gallatin was named by the state Legislature as a U.S. Senator. He was at first rejected by the Senate because he lacked the necessary qualifications: he had not been a resident of the United States long enough. Gallatin ultimately became the secretary of the Treasury under Jefferson.

Interestingly, while Jefferson was publicly opposed to the U.S. Bank, he nonetheless named Gallatin as Treasury secretary — who was for it!

Albert Gallatin was born in Switzerland to an aristocratic family and educated in Enlightenment ideals. He came to America in 1780 and became a Republican (Democrat) and active in politics, serving many positions in his state and federal government. By 1831 he was president of John Jacob Astor's National Bank in New York City until 1839.

As noted, Jefferson went through a period of support for the Illuminati, to the point of writing letters of apology for the founder of the Illuminati, Adam Weishaupt. Jefferson fell under their influence during

---

12 Even today there are "moderate" organizations and individuals who have the same goals as the radical organizations but don the cloak of compromise, moderation, even benevolence. Examples would be the NAACP vs. the Black Panthers, the establishment Republicans vs. the establishment Democrats, and sex education in the schools vs. pornography.

the time that he spent in France. He was not involved in the debates for the Constitution at its birth in the Constitutional Convention; he was in France at the time.

Jefferson is quoted widely by the lovers of liberty. Nearly all the quotes are good; however, some are not used today *in the context of the time* they were written. Just as with many politicians, the rhetoric may not always match the action. Patriots may continue to use the quotes, but they also must understand that history is not always as it seems or what has been taught.

During the height of the agitation between the Federalists and the Jacobins, Jefferson was denounced as a red Republican, an atheist, a leveler, a radical, and a revolutionary friend of France. In other words, the religious people at the time were not as enamored with Jefferson in those years as many religious leaders are today.

In France, Jefferson was involved with a number of people who were Illuminists. For instance, during the fall and winter of 1789, one of the leading Illuminists in France at the time, Mirabeau, tried to build up a friendship with Lafayette, meeting him frequently at the home of Thomas Jefferson. Also, it is known that Jefferson attended meetings of the Lodge of the Nine Sisters and interacted with their members, whether he was a member or not.

Mirabeau and Lafayette were both members of the Illuminati, but that did not mean that they were friends.

It is known that Jefferson possessed and read Nicholas Bonneville's *De L'espirt des Religions*. This book promoted a universal brotherhood of man, but it also contained the idea of a civic religion based on the worship of reason rather than a Supreme Being.

In America, Jefferson became the titular head of the Democratic Societies, if not the actual American head, who apparently was Alexander James Dallas, the secretary of state for Pennsylvania. These societies continued to have constant contact with Genet, the French ambassador.

Dallas was born in Jamaica and educated in England, where he met Franklin. Later, his family would marry into Franklin's. He moved to Philadelphia in 1783. After Gallatin left the Treasury under Madison, Dallas took over and solidified the second U.S. Bank. He was a member of the American Philosophical Society.

George Washington's attorney general, Edmund Randolph of Virginia (who was a second cousin of Jefferson) was a friend of the Whiskey Rebellion insurrection leaders and in league with Gallatin and Genet. Randolph personally met with Fauchet in his home, who had by that time become the French ambassador, and asked him for money to win over four men who were teetering: Thomas Mifflin (governor of Pennsylvania), Dallas, Jefferson, and Randolph himself.

Upon Jefferson's resignation, Randolph became secretary of state in the Washington Cabinet and privy to private papers and any dealings having to do with foreign relations. Randolph opposed the U.S. Bank.

Captured dispatches of Fauchet exposed Randolph's collusion with Fauchet. The British had captured the letters after intercepting a French sloop on the high seas. The dispatches were thrown overboard, but a British seaman dove in and recovered them before they sank.

The British presented these captured documents to Washington showing that Randolph was furnishing Fauchet with information on the inner debates of the Cabinet, and that both were heavily involved in the Western Rebellion.

In one of the letters addressed *to the French Committee of Public Safety,* Fauchet gives them information that the secret service money, which he carried with him to America … had been well employed in cementing stronger the bonds of amity between France and America, and acknowledged himself much indebted to Mr. Randolph, the American Secretary of State, and to a Gentleman of high office in the State of Pennsylvania.

— *The European Magazine and London Review*, January 1796

In the presence of the entire Cabinet, Washington handed the French minister's letter to Randolph and asked him to explain it. Randolph was speechless and resigned forthwith. If not guilty, why resign?

Fauchet fled the country immediately once the letters were made public.

Other documents produced years later supposedly exonerated the four men, but whether these papers were factual or conveniently invented, the men were supportive of the rebellion, whether they were "on the take" or not. Both the British Foreign Service and the Jacobins were known to invent documents.

Apparently, the decision was made by the four to "prudently retire" from the affair to later hatch greater things — one step backward. The actions of both Randolph and Fauchet upon exposure indicate that they at least acted guilty, even if they were vindicated later by "new" evidence. One would think their actions would have been different had they been innocent.

It should be remembered that it was Randolph who, at the opening of what became the Constitutional Convention, offered the Virginia plan to the assembled. Rather than follow their instructions from their state legislatures to amend the Articles of Confederation, the delegates decided to write an entirely new Constitution. While the document was something all should have been able to support, the process for ratification was in violation of the law at the time, until ratification had occurred, since the articles were still in effect and the states bound to obey them. The articles called for a unanimous decision for any change but the delegates used the new Constitution rules to declare ratification by nine states — which was not yet the law of the land.[13]

Gallatin would go on to become an important influence in and out of government. John Austin Stevens penned a tribute to Gallatin which has a great deal of meaning within its lines, and will become more important as you read through this tome:

To a higher degree than any American, native or foreign born, unless Franklin, with whose broad nature he had many traits in common, Albert Gallatin deserves the proud title, aimed at by many, reached by few, of Citizen of the World.

— *Albert Gallatin, American Statesman Series*, 1888

While Jefferson and his friends purportedly supported state sovereignty, in reality they desired democracy and the rights of "Man", disguised as individual rights — a human, collective right rather than an individual God-given right. For many years, Jefferson never supported religion that came close to the Judeo-Christian God that the country's philosophy is based on. Even his attack on Mesmerism was an attack on religion, as bad as Mesmerism was. Earlier, as a college student, he was close to being an atheist.

The idea embodied in the Declaration of Independence attributed to Jefferson, that we are endowed by our Creator of certain unalienable rights, can be interpreted to mean either the individual or Man. At the time, the general interpretation was that it meant the individual — yes all men, but as individuals, not

---

13   This event has been used by those who oppose a new Constitutional Convention under Article V to show that a new convention could do the same sort of maneuver to adopt changes that an easy majority would ratify. Indeed, some proposed amendments call for a two-thirds majority rather than a three-quarters majority for the approval process of an amendment.

a collective. This individual interpretation was not universally applied by all Americans, and this opinion became obvious in the pen of Thomas Paine and others.

The quote is: "We hold these Truths to be self-evident, that all Men are created equal, that they are endowed by their Creator with certain unalienable Rights." It can be interpreted either in the singular or plural sense. Almost all interpret it in the singular and believe that is what it meant — as it should — that each man is endowed. The enemies of our system do not.

No better modern example exists than the Conspiracy's progeny, the American Civil Liberties Union, or ACLU. We express it this way because the ACLU is a direct evolution from this period and the revolutionary thinking and organizations at work at the time.

While the ACLU professes to champion the Bill of Rights, it challenges the basic principle of it, namely the Judeo-Christian basis that the Bill of Rights only protects God-given rights — it does not grant the rights. In other words, rights come from God, not government. However, the ACLU behaves otherwise.

The ACLU has long challenged the Christian religion, whether they express it precisely that way or not. They have been the visible vanguard in eliminating God from public life. Yet, the ACLU would not have been successful if they did not maintain a level of rhetoric and action that makes them appear as if they are the defenders of the people and their rights.

In addition, the writings of the ACLU, when studied in the light of individual vs. collective rights, are quite revealing. Roger Baldwin was the executive director of the ACLU for 50 years, from its onset. He stated that, "Communism, of course, is the goal." He later supposedly became disaffected with Russian communism and purged the ACLU of communists. The latter is fiction. In 1981, he was awarded the Medal of Freedom by President Jimmy Carter.[14]

Any comprehensive study of Jefferson will reveal that he was the same in his actions as Paine was, until he started to change once he became president.

To quote John Austin Stevens again,

> Jefferson returned from France deeply imbued with the spirit of the French Revolution.... Democratic societies organized on the plan of the French Jacobin clubs extended French influence, and no doubt were aided in a practical way by Genet, whose recent marriage with the daughter of George Clinton, the head of the Republican Party in New York, was an additional link in the bond of alliance.

Later Jefferson became the grand man that he had been during the period of the War for Independence, and after this retransformation he reconciled with John Adams. The gulf between the two had grown due to the adverse influences on Jefferson and the reaction against Illuminist populism by Adams.

During this time, the secret societies and French faction had brought about a crisis. Kentucky stood ready to secede from Virginia, with a convention for that purpose held in 1788. The Jacobin associations had brought their plans to such a head that treason was ready to burst upon the country, bringing with it war with Britain and a division of the country. The Whiskey Rebellion was only one aspect of the general revolt in the West.

---

14   This author was active in infiltrating Marxist organizations in the 1960s, and belonged to the ACLU as a result. I have personal knowledge that members of the Communist Party in the leadership of the ACLU was commonplace. Many studies of this problem have been published over the years since their founding. It should not be difficult for the Doubting Thomas to find several books and scores of articles online which document the communist involvement in the organization and activities of the ACLU.

This strategy changed later due to the changes in the government of France, with a new strategy for world empire, discussed in a later chapter.

The conspiracy has always looked for an existing issue or one they could invent to promote a battle for democracy, and then used a gullible majority to promote an authoritarian government.

The United States is a republic. The Constitution guarantees — indeed mandates — a republican form of government for each state. The word *democracy* is never used in the federal Constitution or in any state constitution. It is true that our nation's founders used the word democracy often — to condemn it. You can find no framer of the Constitution who advocated democracy *at the time* of the construction of the Constitution.

John Adams, in a letter to John Taylor in 1814, said:

Democracy never lasts long. It soon wastes, exhausts and murders itself. There never was a democracy that did not commit suicide.

As a side note, the word *democracy* is creeping into the language of some calls for a constitutional convention, both in the language of the state resolutions and proposed amendments. This is illustrative of the idea that we do not have the wisdom of our Founders pushing the agenda, let alone those who would be delegates to a convention.

In a republic, the government and those in it are bound down from mischief with the chains of a constitution, which is something Jefferson said well. It is a contract between the people, through their states, and the federal government. The federal government is to be allowed only to do what the contract says. It is specific, and written for every citizen to understand without a degree in law. It is extremely rare that the Constitution limits the people, business, or property rights.

Regrettably, our government regulates people, business, and property with near abandon today, in violation of the Constitution. This has come about as a result of the communist movement inside the U.S., as we shall demonstrate.

The other aspect of our system is that it is representative. We have government by representation, not direct involvement. We do it through our elected representatives at all levels — Congress, legislature, city council, etc.

The Founders felt that the direct election of the president by the people would be dangerous to liberty, and the people did not want the Congress to do so. It was not that our Founders distrusted the people per se, it was that they understood that people could be manipulated due to their ignorance of the personalities and the intentions of the personalities' organizational backers — what became the political parties.

There was and is no way the average citizen can be acquainted with a person running for a national office. The people would have to rely on the press and the candidates' organized campaigns — a very dangerous prospect in 1787, as it is today. People believe they have all the information they need because of the proliferation of news media, but this is seriously slanted. Couple this with the allure of benefits promised by candidates, and the general populace is a dangerous pool from which to directly elect the president.

Our Founders came up with a system designed to do three things, only two of which are usually discussed: 1) The state legislatures would name the electors in most cases, or there would be the election of local, politically active people, known to local citizens as trustworthy, who in turn were personally aware of the candidates for president. These electors would then vote for the president as the representatives of the people.

2) Since the apportionment was based on population plus two electors for the state, it would be harder for large states to completely dominate the federal executive, and thereby the federal government.

3) Lastly, the system *as originally organized* created a check and balance within the executive, a position much feared by those who objected to the new Constitution.

Commentaries today state that a flaw existed in the electoral college process: if a tie occurred in the vote it was necessary that it be settled by the Congress. In addition, the idea that the person with the most votes was elected president and the man who came in second was made vice-president — they did not necessarily come from the same faction or have the same goals — and that they might not even get along is likewise promoted as a flaw.

What a check and balance within the executive! But it is never presented in that light.

This was soon changed so that a *party* was elected just as much as any person, because different people ran for the two executive positions. Whichever party had the majority vote elected both positions. Therefore the party came to dominate the process, with the candidate increasingly an instrument of the party rather than an independent person. It was convenient, it stopped the squabbling within the executive branch to a large extent — and it was dangerous.

As Madison pointed out, once a particular faction gained control of the three branches of government, it was tantamount to a dictatorship since no real checks or balances would exist. It is the process of this condition — using partisan politics — that has altered our system over time.

James Madison wrote:

> The accumulation of all powers, legislative, executive, and judiciary, in the same hands, whether of one, a few, or many, and whether hereditary, self-appointed, or elective, may justly be pronounced the very definition of tyranny.
>
> — *The Federalist Papers, No. 47*

Certainly more harm has been done to our way of life, the Constitution, and system of government when the three branches of government were controlled by the same party — and it has not mattered which party it was, as we will show further along. Power corrupts.

The election of electors was such a part of the process of checks that in some states, mostly in the South, even into the mid-20th century candidates for elector were still listed on the ballot rather than the presidential candidates.

The idea of political parties was addressed by Washington in his Farewell Address. He was disturbed by the process he started to see building in the political arena and how it could affect the future of the country. John Adams was likewise disturbed:

> There is nothing which I dread so much as a division of the republic into two great parties, each arranged under its leader, and concerting measures in opposition to each other. This, in my humble apprehension, is to be dreaded as the greatest political evil under our Constitution.
>
> — Letter to Jonathon Jackson, October 2, 1789

Yet this was the direction the Democratic Societies took the young nation. They formed a party promoting democracy, necessitating a party in opposition.

In the beginning of our country, local elected representation would elect the next level up of government, except for the House of Representatives. The states' legislators elected the U.S. senators as representatives of the state governments. The legislators usually elected the governors as well.

Gradually, in the name of the people, in order to produce steps toward implementing a democracy, the governors were elected by the people.

Over time, the executives of the states, as well as of the federal government, took on more power, since they had no real ongoing check on them "by the people" between elections. By being appointed by the legislature, a governor would have a direct and constant oversight by the legislature. Also, when the legislatures were directly involved in the election of U.S. senators, this served as a direct and constant influence by the Senate against the federal government doing much harm, or a governor if the legislature elected him.

Under the original Articles of Confederation, the legislatures could recall a senator at any time if they felt he was not representing the state. The Constitution did not contain this provision, and this served as one of the arguments against its ratification.

Gradually, in the name of democracy, representative government was broken down and executives, whether state or federal, took on more power. This in turn diminished the power at the state level and eroded the sovereignty of the states.

A pure democracy involves the people at every turn. It is by mass. The people are directly involved in all decisions by mass vote. It leads to mobocracy, and who ever sways the mob rules. It will always be the superior organization and/or the media. If a secret combination controls both, the results are disastrous. This is the direction of those who desire to mislead the people, and it leads to a dictatorship of the proletariat, the first step in the Marxist program as outlined in *The Communist Manifesto*.

Even if the transition is without violence, once the majority finds out that they can tax the minority for whatever purpose, they will, and it becomes destructive of the economic system. Here too the superior organization and/or the media will use this propensity on the part of the "have-nots" to determine the course of the nation.

In a real democracy, freedom dies in favor of the majority. There are no protections for the minority. The majority can do whatever they like to the minority, whether the minority is an economic status, race, or religion.

Today, there is a move to elect the president by popular vote on the Internet. There are several variations proposed, both for primary and general elections. Regardless, it would forever eliminate the checks and balances on the executive and produce a major step away from a republic into a democracy, an unstable form of government. Of course, the Internet would be compromised at some point by unscrupulous forces if the "people" were ready to elect someone with character.

A democracy is unstable because of all of the reasons stated above: the majority will vote themselves some advantage to the detriment of the minority(s).

Marx and Engels recognized the instability of a democracy, but they also recognized the advantages of propagandizing for democracy in the name of the people. Never believe that their use of the term was phony. They really do want democracy as the first step toward a totalitarian government; because of its instability they can then manipulate it into a communist party-led government.

To call someone a Democrat around the time of our founding (and for years after) meant that person was an advocate of democracy. It was even used as a term in Europe advocating socialism, and to a lesser extent in the United States. The use of the term for the Jacobin Democratic Clubs came about at the suggestion of Citizen Genet.

In *Horace Greeley and Other Pioneers of American Socialism*, by the socialist historian Charles Sotheran, published in 1892, it says this about the use of the term:

> In those days to be called a "democrat" was considered quite as insulting and infamous as being styled now-a-days an "Anarchist," and it was not half so respectable in the public opinion as even now is thought to be that grossly misrepresented individual "a Socialist." But fashions and opinions change.

That does not mean that all Democrats held the core beliefs of the leadership. The grassroots of both parties have always been misused by their leaders, and policies instituted by the leadership were not always what the people supported or elected them to do. The leaders have gotten away with it because people tend to listen to the rhetoric rather than look at the fruit of the actions of their leaders, or the actions have been sold as a compromise between two opposing forces. Usually, the fix is at the top and the rest is show business.[15]

Since the revolutionaries could not find support among the American people to engage in a socialist revolution, the battle from the beginning of our nation was to change us into a democracy first. Why? Karl Marx and Frederick Engels, the co-authors of *The Communist Manifesto,* put it well in their small book seventy years after our founding:

> … the first step in the revolution of the working class, is to raise the proletariat to the position of ruling class, to win the battle of democracy.

The battle of democracy is to be the *first step* in the revolution.

It is interesting that the mob enlisted by the communists has never asked what the next steps are — nor did the Americans in the Democratic Societies.

Note also that they were to become the *ruling class* — so much for the common idea of a democracy for all people.

Once the republic is destroyed through democracy, the next step in the revolution is to use the majority to eliminate all opposition to communism, generally by mob action. Enemies of the Conspiracy will be isolated and executed.

Once *effective* opposition to the conspiracy is eliminated, the third step — a dictatorship — is established over everyone, including the mob: a so-called dictatorship of the proletariat.

And, it is all done by a secret organization who knows what it is doing and where it wants to take the people. Engels said so himself in the foreword of the 1872 edition of the *Manifesto*.

This has been the case throughout history, but it has been almost purged from the record so that the innocent do not realize what is going on. Our Founders knew history, however, and were fearful of such machinations.

The fourth step outlined by *The Communist Manifesto* was a *world government through a union of the communist parties*.

This latter point is important. The world rule was to be established by the party, not the so-called gov-

---

15   The best references to a republic are the DVD *Overview of America*; the booklet *Republics and Democracies*, by Robert Welch; and *Back to the Republic*, by Harry Atwood, Laird & Lee, Inc. Publishers, Chicago, 1918. The latter is particularly recommended, but the former are easier to procure at www.jbs.org.

ernments in the various countries or any union of governments. The union of the governments would be dangerous in and of itself, but the real power would be held by the Inner Party.

While Jefferson embraced the conspirators, Washington and Adams became very aware and concerned about them, specifically calling out the Illuminati, or its spawn the Democratic Clubs, as the source behind early agitation for democracy in the United States. Washington and Adams were the Conspiracy's chief targets at the beginning of our nation, not simply because they were good men, which they were, but because they realized the source of the problem, did not hesitate to identify it, and would not bend to it.[16]

According to John Adams in a letter to Jefferson on June 30, 1793, at one point a mob of 10,000 in Philadelphia was stirred up by the Jacobins and Genet, threatening to drag out Washington from his house and effect a revolution. Mobocracy at its finest!

This was at a time when the population of the city was just over 25,000 residents. Philadelphia had a history of agitation that went back to the War of Independence with what was called the Radical Patriots. This group was in charge throughout the war, even behind the scenes during British occupation, and made the economic situation in Philadelphia very difficult due to what we would call today Marxian regulations. This chapter of our history is relatively unknown among libertarians today. They even hanged a couple of people who were not that enthusiastic about the war. This type of public sentiment carried on for many years after the war.

The number of people that comprised the mob in ratio to the number of residents indicates that non-residents were employed by the organizers of the mob to increase its numbers — people from out of town. This tactic of rent-a-mob, getting people from other places to come in and either create or swell a crowd, is still used today to make local citizens believe that the majority of the local people are for or against some issue and therefore acquiesce to it.

The most adept at this today are the homosexual activists who hold gay parades and other events. Most people come from other communities, but the local citizens see the large crowd at a "local" parade and assume that most are local citizens.

Mobs are rarely a spontaneous manifestation of discontent. They are almost always fomented by organization into becoming a mob.

This is true no matter the time or place around the world, and is a hidden truism that distorts how the American people perceive events and can be manipulated into looking at affairs in the wrong light. If Americans understood that it takes organization to bring together a mob, then they would realize that organization always plays into the equation. Once they understood that, then they would realize that they are being manipulated into thinking the changes in politics are a result of happenstance rather than secret combinations.

Thousands or even hundreds of people do not decide in and of themselves to meet at a specific location at a specific time on a specific date. ESP or some other mental process does not cause this. Nor do cellphones, although they can be used to enhance the process. They are planned events and are organized to happen. *Someone has to decide where and when a crowd will meet!*

This author was involved in stopping a planned riot in his large city in the 1960s. Due to intelligence that a riot was being planned — and who was planning it — a few dedicated citizens door-belled the city and warned parents to keep their children home and be prepared for violence in their neighborhoods.

---

16 It is the same today. The most important organization that stands for the Constitution and teaches all aspects of history, including the fact of a conspiracy, which for all modern purposes started with the Illuminati, is The John Birch Society. As a result, it has sustained a half century of vilification from the media, academia, leftist, and neoconservative organizations.

It was to be in the name of racial equality. Too many Americans today do not know the origins of the violence — on both sides — of the civil rights movement and how many civil rights leaders lauded today were actually involved in militant socialist movements.

The parents stayed home with their children, and the crowds necessary for a riot never assembled. As a result, although nearly every large city in the country was set ablaze simultaneously by radical Black Panthers or other related communist organizations, the author's city experienced one of the quietest weekends in a long time. The mass media said that the *simultaneous* blazes all over the country on the same day were simply coincidence, a spontaneous national reaction to injustice.

The same holds true for the many demonstrations held across the United States and Europe supposedly in sympathy with a black man who was killed by a policeman in Ferguson, Missouri, in late 2014. Close examination showed that militant socialist organizations such as the Socialist Workers and their break-off party were active in stirring up the mobs, whether in Ferguson or London.

Nearly every city across America had participants carrying signs which told onlookers to go to revcom.us. Once they did, they found that this was the website of the Revolutionary Communist Party (RCP), for many years part of the hate-the-police genre in minority neighborhoods and colleges. At one time, the RCP was part of the Socialist Workers Party (SWP) of Trotskyites.

Back to Philadelphia, the general reason that the mob was agitated into a dangerous state after days and weeks of fevered propaganda was to effect a change in the neutrality of the Washington government, to align with revolutionary France, and if not, to change the government. Remember, this was the seat of the federal government at the time.

The general radicalization of the city was such that it was not long before the first trade union in the country rose in Philadelphia. In 1786 the printers union there went on strike. What can be called the first American labor movement made its appearance there in 1827. At first it worked for shorter hours, but it soon converted into a political movement demanding public education. Within a decade and a half, this was used to foment riots against the Catholic community.

The example of Philadelphia riots, while appalling, was only one example of the desire by the French to use their influence to seek out and destroy American opposition. In the harbor at Boston a French ship had a banner which flew from the masthead which listed eleven names of prominent Americans as "aristocrats" and enemies of France. Of course, all knew what the French did with aristocrats.

Nothing was done by local authorities to stop these practices by the French. And, the small American navy was too impotent to do anything about this, just as they were powerless to do anything about the French "American" privateers going freely in and out of American ports.

Americans today might ask why nothing effective was done. In most people's lifetime, the same problem existed with the Communist Party USA. They took their orders from the USSR, a foreign communist power. Indeed, the oath of a communist contained verbiage of loyalty to the USSR at one time. Yet, too many people felt that what they did came under the Bill of Rights — they had the freedom to do and say just about anything, even though the end in mind was violence or arson, and was deliberately calculated to result in treason and an adherence to a foreign government.

And, when the state and federal government at all levels tried to expose this fact, there arose a hue and cry that these minions of Russia were just freedom-loving patriots, trying to seek equality for all people.

Ultimately, the communists and their allies in government were able to stop investigations into internal communism or terrorism by any governmental initiative. The investigations in the 1950s and 1960s never did violate the rights of anyone, it was simply exposure. Once many of these communists were able to infiltrate sufficiently into the federal government, in the name of a War on Terror, they started to violate the Bill of Rights they claimed to defend.

In other words, the attempt was made to stop communist infiltration into American government *by simply exposing it*. Once this was prevented, the communists and their allies started to do what they accused the government of doing. The only communists who served prison time for their membership did so because they had denied their membership under oath. It was for *perjury* that they were sentenced.

The first attempt to stop this conspiracy in the United States was done by the Congress with the passage of the Alien and Sedition Acts.

Alien and Sedition Acts

Jefferson and Adams had a falling out over the direction of the federal government, and their disagreement reached its zenith over the Alien and Sedition Acts. The Acts were passed as a solution to the immigration of French agents and Illuminist minions into the United States stirring up trouble to the point of organizing mobs trying to attack Adams and Washington. These were the days when an American politician had no protection; they behaved like and were treated just a little better than the average citizen, something that has not been the case for the last 150 years, when we have treated our politicians increasingly like potentates.

In other words, they had no protection; the Secret Service did not come on the scene until Lincoln's administration.

Recall that England did the same by passage of the Unlawful Societies Act just after we had done so in America, and for the same reasons.

At the time of the passage of the Alien and Sedition Acts, America had approximately 200 newspapers. Ten percent of them supported the Democratic Societies, and nearly all of these were under the control of aliens and tended to cluster in the mid to southern portion of the country.

In addition, it was not unusual for the Philadelphia *Aurora* newspaper to print private correspondence between our government and the French revolutionary government and the *results* of this correspondence between the two governments before they were received by the President of the United States. This information was provided by French agents and was used to incite the public against our own government.

The *Aurora* was owned by the grandson of Benjamin Franklin, Benjamin Franklin Bache, who was raised and educated in France in his youth. He died before he was 30 from yellow fever.

John Adams stated years later to Jefferson after they had resumed their friendship that he felt that the only thing that saved the nation was the yellow fever epidemic that befell Philadelphia at the time. As a result, the people stayed home and shuttered their windows, and non-residents shunned the area, thereby denying the agitators the numbers needed to form up more mobs in the streets.

You can well imagine, with this sort of problem swirling around the country led by French agents, why the Congress passed the Alien and Sedition Acts to arrest seditious individuals, particularly aliens. It was the wrong solution, but it fit well into one of the tactics of the conspiracy: the action is in the reaction.

The important aspect of "the action is in the reaction" is the *reaction* to some action, such as a crisis, on the part of the people. If the action is acute enough, the people react, and are programmed into demanding a new law or regulation which was the intent of those who initiated the action to begin with.

James Madison recognized "the general tendency of insurrection to increase the momentum of power." This is due to the reaction. The majority of people who are not involved in insurrection and want peace in the streets will demand law and order, and those who want to rule are more than happy to comply. Hitler gave the Germans all the law and order they could handle in reaction to street violence the Nazis themselves initiated. What *should* be demanded is justice. In a free, moral society, justice leads to principled law and order.

While the Alien and Sedition Acts are an example of this reaction in our early years, the action and reaction of the 9/11 terrorist act would be a modern example. Osama bin Laden stated immediately after the attack,

> (T)he battle has moved to inside America.... I tell you, freedom and human rights in America are doomed. The U.S. Government will lead the American people — and the West in general — into an unbearable hell and choking life.
>
> — CNN Interview, aired January 31, 2002

Here he states that the reason for the attack was to change America from a free country to an authoritarian one. The reaction, the Department of Homeland Security and its increasing violation of the Bill of Rights, was the result.

Recall that al Zawahiri, the second in command under Osama bin Laden, is a trained asset of Russia. Bin Laden himself came out of the Muslim Brotherhood of Egypt, itself a Marxist-centered entity disguised as Muslim. There is more to terrorism than the media or our government is saying.

It is interesting to note that the hundreds of pages of the so-called Patriot Act had already been written long before the 9/11 attack, waiting for a convenient time to place it before Congress. It was passed in the heat of the moment without anyone reading it in its entirety.

One congressman on the committee through which the bill had to pass on its way to the floor of the House noticed that the writ of habeas corpus was to be suspended if passed in its original form. Happily, he was able to have this provision struck from the bill. Had it passed with the suspension, it would have codified it for a long time to come, if not forever. Habeas corpus was suspended under Lincoln, but reverted back after the war. The Patriot Act has been in force much longer, and as of this writing there is no end in sight.

At of the time of this writing, the War on Terror has lasted longer than the accumulative span of World War I and II, Korea, the Persian Gulf War, Kosovo, and the Spanish-American War combined. Yet terrorism has grown, not diminished, and the resultant effect in the Muslim countries of this "war" has been militancy and destabilization both in the Middle East and Europe where this has happened due to migration into Europe by millions of non-Europeans. This is not the road to victory.[17]

As an extension of the War on Terror, the private communications of all Americans have come under the scrutiny of the National Security Agency, or NSA. It is interesting to see the various opinions of federal judges as to whether this program is constitutional or not. Any person with the ability to think and read the Constitution and the Fourth Amendment can decide this for himself.

While the suspension of habeas corpus may have been stricken from the Patriot Act, nonetheless the federal government has been in the practice of violating this law for some time. Neoconservatives hail this practice as necessary to stop terrorism, never contemplating that they may be the target of such practices in the future once it becomes the norm.

"The action is in the reaction" tactic was used by Hitler to start World War II by faking an attack on a German radio station by German troops disguised as Poles. The German people not only fell for the ploy,

---

17 If you are reading this after 2016, you may throw in the War of 1812 as well, if the War on Terror continues. After that, it will be the perpetual war as outlined in the novel *1984*. The war just seems to move around from Afghanistan to Iraq, back to Afghanistan, then Iraq again, etc.

they literally went out into the streets shouting with joy over Hitler's "response" to the fake attack, which, by the way, was done at the end of a number of *seeming* border violations and insults from Poland. The stage had been set for the German people to say, "Enough!"

From the Versailles Treaty on, the German people felt that they had been pushed around as a country, and they were more than tired of it. Hitler manipulated the people as a result of this feeling, coupled with the desire to "restore" the boundaries of the German Empire — the Western portion of Poland had been the Prussia of the German Empire before World War I. In this case, the so-called reaction became World War II.

Another, but *simplistic* example of the action being in the reaction, is the action of a street mob, where *agents provocateurs* attack the police, inviting a reaction by the police. The police reaction is videoed or photographed and this is the image one sees in the media: a seemingly violent, unruly act by the police — not what provoked it. These images are then used as evidence to curtail police departments, and even in some cases have led to leftist control of local police through the establishment of civilian police review boards to answer the "need" for police oversight due to "police brutality." At this point, the police under leftist leadership do begin to behave badly.

Further, the psychology of the situation if compounded over a length of time creates a "them vs. us" attitude on the part of both sides: the police and the civilian population. The tactics tend to polarize the two until they no longer communicate with one another, and this results in alienation. This then sets the stage for the nationalization of the police, though not as representatives and protectors of the local people, because they have lost touch with one another.

This same tactic has been used to produce sympathy by Americans for communist revolutionaries in the streets of foreign nations, with television news only showing the reaction of the police on the demonstrators, while hiding the fact that they are led by communists.

Correspondents have rarely put the blame on red radicals. The modern ploy is to blame the massing of people in the streets on Twitter, Facebook, or the latest current social networking fad. We are to believe that all the poor masses of Third World countries can afford cellular telephones and the service necessary to use them, and are just waiting for a call to run into the streets. If they are ready to take such action, then what set the stage for them to be ready for it?

The American people would be shocked to realize that more often than not, street rallies in foreign countries just happen to have socialist and communist flags on parade. Rarely are these flags shown in the U.S. media or television images. From Russia to Turkey to Iraq to Egypt, communist flags spontaneously appear at street rallies, but Americans never see them on their news broadcasts because they are edited out. If Americans did see them, they would better understand what was going on. We will explain why further on.

These images we refer to may be seen online by surfing for news and photography in foreign news sources just after demonstrations, rallies, etc., are held. One exception occurred after the victory of the militant socialist party in Greece in January 2015. the *Wall Street Journal* published on their front page a picture of the victory rally in Athens that showed the hammer and sickle on display on their flags and banners.

The same thing existed in the conflict between the Ukraine, Russia, and Crimea in 2014. There were demonstrations, diverse in size, decorum, and support for their independence or a return to Russia, and in all three areas the hammer and sickle flag was flown. No matter which side you chose, you lost, because all of the leaders were "ex-communist" leaders. Yet, unless you went online and did a search, you would never have seen these flags, certainly not in your local paper or network news.

It has not been unusual to have banners of the hammer and sickle airbrushed out before the photograph of a major personality standing in front of the banner is printed in the American press. Today it is done by what is called "photo shopping." The images of the banners and flags at a demonstration will tell the viewer far more than the commentator or article written about the event about what it is all about and who is behind it.

This is done because, far more than any commentary or article covering a rally or protest, the banners and flags reveal the demonstrator's purpose and backers.

Returning to 9/11 again, a congressman who sat on the committee that investigated the attack told this author that he could not tell me any detail, but that I was free to surmise why the federal government asked that 26 pages of the report be taken out for security reasons. This congressman believed in liberty and that it could not thrive unless the truth was a constant. My assumption was that the 26 pages contained information detrimental to the federal intelligence agencies.

History taught in government schools today relates how the Alien and Sedition Acts were aimed at the people in such a way to imply that the Federalists were elitists and, if not against the people at least so separated from them as to have been irrelevant. This sets the stage for sympathy toward the Democrats in the minds of history students. The extent of the agitation and who and what were behind it, which led Congress to pass the Acts, are rarely taught. Congress was placed in a state of panic over the future of the country due to Jacobin-influenced lawlessness.

The Acts were also passed out of fear of the Jacobin and democratic societies' alliance with France if we went to war with France — which was a distinct possibility at the time — that these persons and groups would serve as a Fifth Column during a time of war with France, if it should come to that. It was not dissimilar to the Nazi Bund in America prior to our involvement in the Second World War, a Fifth Column within our country, except that the agitation by the Jacobins was more widespread and violent.

The level of support for a non-allied foreign power never again reached the level of the Jacobins until the war in Vietnam. The anti-war movement of the 1960-1970s was completely dominated by the communists, and turned from being a movement against war to support for the enemy. This made it difficult for those who truly questioned the war from getting any traction among the bulk of the American people, because they could not create a separation between the communist movement and themselves in the public's mind.

The prospect of invasion by France as part of the alien unrest during Adams' administration in the minds of the government was such that Washington, after serving as president, was once again called upon to be commissioned commander in chief of a non-existent army. He accepted, but never felt such an event would take place.

At that time, the Department of the Navy was created and a force authorized by law of 30 cruisers. The Constitution mandates a navy; it does not mandate a standing army. Recall this as we discuss the Jefferson administration.

This was the atmosphere in which the acts were passed — an overreaction that created an even bigger reaction as a result, which led to a change of government.

The opposition to these acts began the process of what became known as nullification. On the behest of Jefferson, Madison put forward in the Virginia Legislature that the federal union was a compact, uniting the power of the federal government. At the time, both Jefferson and Madison believed in the right of secession, but Madison was to change his mind later.

Not all Virginians or others agreed with Jefferson and Madison relative to the acts. John Quincy Adams wrote:

If Jefferson and Madison deemed the alien and sedition acts plain and palpable infractions of the Constitution, Washington and Patrick Henry held them to be good and wholesome laws.
— *History of the United States: From the Earliest Period to the Administration of President Johnson, Volume II*

Not many people were arrested under the acts; even so, Hamilton opposed their excesses, contrary to his image today.

By getting the government to overreact, the organizers gained that much more fuel to further inflame the mob by demonstrating that the new government was seeking more power and stifling dissent.

In addition, if conspirators come to power even after using the reaction against onerous government edicts, they do not always change the law; they often just use it to their own ends. The endgame is, after all, the accumulation of power in the hands of the few. Usually what happens is the mob trusts the new leaders and allows them to use the laws — fairly of course — and that usually means against the deposed leaders and their followers, and anyone else who opposes the new leaders.

Again, this is generally what happened in the 20th century with the communists once they accumulated enough power in the federal government — oppose supposed violations of the Bill of Rights, and then once they are in enough control in government actually violate the Bill of Rights. This condition can then be used to build yet another bloc they can manipulate, and do so all in the name of liberty. It is part of the tactic of creating your own opposition.

The Conspiracy's minions in government create the excuse for their minions in the streets to recruit against the government, controlling both sides. This tactic will be further explained with examples in a later chapter.

This tactic was used extensively during the Obama administration. Communists occupied positions of power and instituted draconian regulations, which implemented the above agitation and led to a number of political blocs on both sides, which were subsequently used to move government down the road to further controls.

If the reader is unfamiliar with the number of communists that came to be known as "czars" in Barack Obama's administration, simply start to explore the problem on the Internet. Several were exposed and resigned; several did not. Only the brazen were eliminated, not the subtle.

Another problem that existed from the beginning of the Carbonari, a direct descendant of the Illuminati, was the infiltration of their members into local law enforcement and government. In this manner, they would be immune from arrest and prosecution for their actions. Also, they could perform acts in their positions of authority which would create a reaction against the government by the people and serve as a recruiting base for revolution. It would be difficult to believe that this tactic is not in play today.

No law should be passed for an emergency situation that takes away the liberty of the American people, no matter what the reason. Emergency legislation tends to become permanent. Once codified into the system, it remains.

In the case of the Alien and Sedition Acts, thankfully common sense prevailed and the laws were only enacted for a two-year span. However, as a result of the acts, the backlash among the people was one of the reasons that helped propel Jefferson into the presidency and a Republican majority into both houses of Congress. In addition, mistakes made by Adams, his differences with Hamilton, and high taxation helped turn the vote to the Republicans, except in New England.

Generally, acts of violence and other crimes associated with subversion are covered under the normal criminal codes of cities and states. New laws are not needed. The only problem would be in areas where the local authorities have been subverted by conspiratorial forces and refuse to arrest and prosecute crimes carried out during activities sponsored by the Left. For instance, throwing a brick through a window is a crime whether it is politically motivated or for any other reason — or lack of reason.

While the acts were a prime example of where the solution can sometimes be worse than the problem for the liberty of the people, they did lead to many French agents packing up and leaving before the acts phased out, and succeeded in dispersing a great deal of the subversive influence of the *American* Jacobins.

Jefferson wrote:

> The threatening appearances from the alien bills have so alarmed the French who are among us, that they are going off. A ship, chartered for this purpose, will sail within a fortnight, for France, with as many as she can carry. Among them, I believe, will be Volney, who has in truth been the principle object aimed at by the law.
>
> *— The Writings of Thomas Jefferson, Volume XVI*

At the time, Count Constautine de Volney lived in America. His name is a contraction of *Voltaire* and *Ferney*. He was a friend of Franklin and Condorcet. For several years he lived in the Middle East, and probably came into contact with the more esoteric movements that emanated from that region since he was one of the first to question the historicity of Jesus, and thereby the accuracy of Gospel texts. The beginnings of the formal denial of even the existence of Jesus can be traced to the late 18th century, and specifically Volney.

In 1797, John Adams' administration accused Volney of being a French spy sent to prepare for the reoccupation of Louisiana by the French. Volney had been associated with Bonneville and the Society of the Friends of Truth in Paris. Thus, Volney had to flee the enforcement of the acts.

Jefferson's interest in Volney was more than superficial. He and Volney had entered into a secret pact for Jefferson to translate Volney's *Ruins of Empires* into English. The book's central theme is not as important as the fact that Jefferson was worried that, if it were known that he had anything to do with its publication in English, he would be accused of being an atheist since the book called into question all religion.

This latter fact, coupled with the idea promoted in the work of establishing a "General Assembly of Nations," dovetailed nicely with Illuminist aims: the elimination of all religion and the founding of a New World Order. The book concludes with a call for an absolute separation of church and state.

Jefferson had to be careful at this point since he was vice president under Adams and was readying for a bid for the presidency. He ran out of time, concentrating instead on his candidacy, and so the last four chapters were translated by Joel Barlow while living in Paris. Barlow's name then became associated with the translation, and Jefferson's name was left out of any conversation in reference to the work.

The Mississippi Valley
Prior to ascending to the presidency, again while vice president, Jefferson conspired in October 1798 at Monticello with the Nicholas brothers of Kentucky, Wilson C. and George, and with John Breckinridge to assert state sovereignty as a means to promote a secessionist movement. Jefferson drew up what became known as the States Rights Resolutions of 1798, or simply the Kentucky Resolutions, attributed at the time to George Nicholas. Jefferson's role was kept secret until 20 years later when Nicholas' son pressured his father to tell the truth.

At the time, George Nicholas was under a Spanish *pension*, a word used during the period for being on the payroll. In other words, he was working for Spain — and Spain wanted control of the entire Mississippi Valley. The separation of Kentucky from the United States would have helped them accomplish this.

Had the role of Jefferson been known at the time, the U.S. government could have charged him under the Alien and Sedition Acts with sedition if he had openly associated himself with a protest movement: to declare two laws of the current Congress unconstitutional as an incentive to separate Kentucky from the United States. Jefferson was convinced that the laws were aimed at him and his followers more than the aliens, even though he stated differently from time to time.

It is interesting that, generally speaking, Jefferson's role in this affair is well known today, and the role of Spanish-paid American radicals is not at all. Yet for the first twenty years, this was reversed.

The original resolutions were rejected by the Kentucky Legislature due to their vicious language, and they had to be amended before their passage. What is read today is the watered down version that passed, and the role of authorship is attributed to Jefferson.

There can be no doubt that Jefferson and Burr gave their cooperation to France in its schemes against the United States and George Washington. Naturally, Jefferson, Burr, and many others would be concerned over the acts, constitutional or not.

Many initiatives such as the Kentucky Resolutions over the years have seemed to be in support of state sovereignty or constitutional law, but had as their original intent the movement of people from this initial position on down the road to open rebellion. Keep in mind that one of the key people involved was in the pay of Spain. The same man's grandson would later play a key role in the Carbonari, the Civil War, and the plot to assassinate Lincoln. In modern times, these events are portrayed as libertarian rather than what the conspiratorial forces actually had in mind at the time.

The resolutions stir the hearts of liberty-minded Americans today, just as they were designed to do when they were penned. This ardor was then to be used for a purpose not well known today.

The Kentucky Resolutions, therefore, cannot be looked at in isolation. They were an integral part of the attempt to separate the U.S. from its western frontier by Spain, and many of these leaders were adherents to French designs for the area. Whether Spain or France, the idea was to weaken these United States, then rule. Today this is rarely mentioned when referring to the resolutions; this was not true of histories written for several years after the events. These historical accounts went down the memory hole.

Several initiatives for more power to the states and against the federal government were proposed by Jefferson and his friends. All were rejected by Jefferson and Co. *after they came to power*. Some of these initiatives remained active for a time since they could not be stopped completely just because the fountainhead was dried up — they had propagandized too many people over an extended period of time for the ideas to simply go away once they had served the purpose of wresting power from one to give to another, plus the expansion of the United States was complete over the disputed territory that had given rise to several treasonous initiatives financed by the belligerent powers. One example of the latter would be the Burr Conspiracy.

When one refers to the Burr Conspiracy, everyone thinks of the intrigue of Burr with others to break off the Mississippi Valley as an independent fiefdom to be ruled by Burr. However, Burr's whole life was one of intrigue and conspiracy. He did not gain the presidency of the federal government, so he searched elsewhere to satisfy his desire to rule.

The conspiracy of Burr is an example of leaders who worked together against our government in league with minions of the Conspiracy — if not actually part of the Conspiracy themselves. Since Burr tied with Jefferson in the Electoral College for president and then lost the vote in the Congress, the Democratic Societies split over the *personalities* of Jefferson and Burr, not with their general policies, and then

Burr looked for satisfaction for his ambitions elsewhere.

There is little question that Burr as a leader of the Republicans knew the political moves the Federalists were going to make during the Adams administration almost as soon as they did. As a result, the Federalists were thwarted in every move. The only way he could have known was to have had someone on the inside of the Federalist camp and close to the top. In today's vernacular: a mole.

We asked the question earlier of whether it could have been a servant in the home where Washington resided in New York or later. This may have been the situation under Adams; however, as we have already shown there were many people who did not expose their politics when they served in the Washington and Adams administrations and worked against them on the inside.

It may have even been in the Hamilton household, and why this may have been the case is due to something the author knows but cannot document.

Servant or high-level politician, it does not matter. All we know is that Burr had someone close enough to the Federalist leaders to be informed of their every move.

The 10th Amendment does protect the sovereignty of the states, but in the above instance of Kentucky, the aim was not really the protection of state sovereignty as promoted publicly. Secession was the private agenda *if power was not given to the leaders of the Democratic Societies.* Once they achieved power, they abandoned the movement.

The secession faction who bred the movement, a design for the misuse of state sovereignty, grew out of a desire on the part of Jefferson and Co. to hold power no matter how they achieved it, even if it meant disunion of the country. The end in mind was the opposite of the stated purpose.

Chief Justice John Marshall said this about the above Kentucky initiative:

> To me it seems that they are men who will hold power by any means rather than not hold it, and would prefer dissolution of the Union to the continuance of an administration not of their own party. They will risk all the ills which may result from the most dangerous experiments rather than permit that happiness to be enjoyed which is dispensed by other hands than their own.
> — *The Comprehensive History of the Southern Rebellion and the War for the Union*

Washington put it this way:

> You could just as soon scrub the blackamore white, as to change the principles of a professed Democrat; and that he will leave nothing unattempted to overturn the Government of this Country.
> — *Letter to James Henry*, September 30, 1798

Once in the presidency, Jefferson began a complete about face. In his inaugural address, he said:

> We are all Republicans — all Federalists.
> If there be any among us who wish to dissolve this Union, or to change its republican form, let them stand undisturbed as monuments of the safety with which errors of opinion may be tolerated when reason is left to control it.

This was a turning point in Jefferson's life. As he became more moderate in his actions and his appointments to federal office by and large, he lost the support of many of his former allies. He would do unconstitutional and unethical acts as president, but ultimately revert to his early principles — except for his opinion on Christianity.

The so-called *Jefferson Bible* is a chronological compilation of the Gospels, bringing them together in one cohesive narration of the life of Christ. The difference between Scripture and Jefferson's version is that in Jefferson's the end of the narration is when the rock is rolled over the entrance to the tomb — no Resurrection. If there is no Resurrection, there is no Christ, just a teacher.

There were times that Jefferson had carried the Illuminist water when it came to breaking down Christianity. He once wrote,

> Fix reason firmly on her seat, and call to her tribunal every fact, every opinion. Question with boldness even the existence of a God; because if there be one, he must more approve of the homage of reason than that of blindfolded fear.
>
> — *Letter to Peter Carr*, August 10, 1787

This and other Jeffersonian writings are quoted by modern atheists to convince people of the absurdity of faith in any god. Some of the modern writings are so anti-God that it is most disheartening to read them. It is rare that the mainstream citizen even knows of their existence, let alone having read them. It is not that the authors simply are atheists, they hate God. They take one from doubt to atheism, then on to becoming an enemy of God.

It is interesting how often the above quote is split. Some will quote the first sentence but not the second. Others will quote the second sentence but not the first — each for their own reasons and slant.

In a letter to Dr. Benjamin Rush of Philadelphia on September 23, 1800, Jefferson noted the hostility of the clergy of the country toward him and his principles. He looked upon them as a group which limited freedom of thought and expression: " … and they [the clergy] believe rightly; for I have sworn upon the altar of God eternal hostility against every form of tyranny over the mind of man." He seemed convinced that as a group, the clergy wanted a union between church and state.

Given the nature of the clergy, the differences in dogma and jealousies, the fights over one nuance or another, the idea of a national denomination was impossible as long as the country held together. Further, many colonies had official sects of Christianity as part of their government, and this was done more or less at the beginning of the establishment of the colonies. They would never have agreed to any sect other than their own at the time. There could never have been an agreement as to what it would be aside from the common belief in Christianity, with government tolerance for all religion.

The words and writings of Jefferson indicate that he did not believe in the divinity of Christ, but only as a master teacher in the esoteric sense.

The idea of separation of church and state was designed for and eventually became the separation of God and state. Read the 1st Amendment. It protects religion it does not separate it from the state. It was designed to protect religion from the state. Read it — while divorcing from your mind the pronouncements of the politicians trying to tell you what it means.

There was a more long-lasting problem that began at this time which is rarely reported in history books.

Washington's Farewell Address was noted for generations as a guideline for future American governance. The address was a document which served as an example for the government for nearly two centuries. However, while the student read it and understood it, the government rarely followed it.

One aspect was immediately ignored, and that was the division of American politics into political parties — as Washington expressed it, *factions*. He said that factions would hurt our country.

The building of factions, now known as political parties, accomplished what Madison feared. The parties became the controlling factor over the executive and the Congress, and then crept into the federal judiciary. And simultaneously, steps were taken to weaken the electoral college in favor of party politics.

Madison helped develop what he feared the most because of his distrust of Hamilton and his policies. He was reacted into the Republican movement and became a part of the accumulation of power into one party at the federal level. How much was legitimate concern and how much members of the Conspiracy whispered in his ear to influence his opinions of people is not known. But to believe that he was not targeted by the Conspiracy to affect his thinking is too improbable to believe given the evidence of the democratic movement and its personalities at the time.

At this time, forgeries attributed to Hamilton were penned which are still used today to discredit him. Likewise, his writings were misinterpreted and broadcast with definitions out of context, which distorted his intent. In a couple of instances it would have been wiser to use different words than he did. Nonetheless, the Jacobin leadership adopted the methods of the Illuminati to malign Hamilton, probably the most active political figure who was trying to thwart their designs. Many of these writings are still in use today to discredit Hamilton as being a monarchist, just as forged letters attributed to Washington were used during his administration to convince people that Washington was not neutral but pro-British.

Since libertarians and conservatives had no clue as to the machinations of the Conspiracy then, let alone today, they repeat this "history" over and over again. Keep in mind, the country and experiment in liberty were new; they were starting the transition from centuries of royalty and absolute rule into self-rule. Couple this with the agitation of the Jacobins at every turn, and it was unlikely that they would go from total government to libertarian overnight. It wasn't just the Alien and Sedition Acts that were used. Hamilton and others were trying to find a way to solve the problem of the federal debts incurred by the war and of tying a federation together that seemed at any moment would fracture due to the Jacobins, and at the same time trying to do all those things necessary to have a functioning government.

The Federalists were kept busy with the attacks on them at every turn, and the Jacobins seemed to know every move they were going to make before they made them.

While there were many things that would bother constitutionalists and moral individuals today about Hamilton, the hangover of the Illuminati against Hamilton lingers today in such a manner as to cause them to reject all of Hamilton's advice. This is a mistake. As fallible as Hamilton was, he was well aware of the danger of not working to expose and defeat the forces of the Illuminati and their allies.

The rejection of Hamilton's advice means that many will miss the wisdom of the writings contained in *The Federalist Papers* by either not reading the book or by skipping Hamilton's essays. In either case, a modern student of our system of government and the principles on which it is based would be missing a great deal relative to the thinking of the Founders of our country. This may be one of the purposes: to negate the reading and influence in *The Federalist Papers*.

Men like Washington, Adams, and Hamilton knew that if anything divided the fledgling country, one of three, or all three countries (England, France, and Spain) would come in and subjugate the country. It was a time of desperation on the part of many, and several things were done or advocated that are looked upon today as draconian, when they were simply trying to hold the country together.

To help build a political machine, John Beckley worked within a secret organization to amass votes for Jefferson. The secret campaign published disinformation and false polls. He wrote letters, pamphlets, and speeches, often under a pseudonym. He was an early proponent of attack advertising. Circulars were printed and passed between agents of this secret organization for distribution. It formed the beginning of an apparently localized political party, but one which was actually controlled from a national committee.

Beckley was the first clerk of the U.S. House of Representatives, as well as the first librarian of Congress. These are two positions to hold if you mean to control the records of Congress.

Beckley was instrumental in the destruction of the political career of Alexander Hamilton. Republicans were generally thought of as being in opposition to Hamilton, but their primary target was Washington. The same holds true today: the socialists attack a few of the early American leaders without a direct attack on Washington. This is usually extended to those who remained loyal to Washington. In this manner, it is an indirect attack on the Washington years. Regrettably, too many conservatives and constitutionalists fall for it and help promote the propaganda of the Left without realizing it.

The Left has become very adept at lowering the public perception of people while appearing to be in support of them. Two modern examples of this technique are, first, the saying about Robert Taft in his bid for the presidency in 1952: I like Taft but he can't win. This was how they destroyed his chances for the nomination. It was a well-orchestrated campaign. Robert Taft, while a Bonesman, was not the father or the grandfather when it came to supporting the agenda of the conspiracy.

The second is the television miniseries *John Adams*. The series was based on the book by David McCullough, a personable man who attended Yale and was a member of Skull and Bones. The actor who portrayed Adams was Paul Giamatti, also a member of Skull and Bones. Giamatti's father was Angelo Barlett Giamatti, who was tapped by Scroll and Key and ultimately became the president of Yale, as well as baseball commissioner.

The subtlety of the writing, the portraying of Adams, and some of the events portrayed can be disturbing to those who understand the background of Adams, Washington, Jefferson, Franklin. To demonstrate the influence of the Conspiracy, we invite the reader to visit the memorial to John Adams one of the Jacobin-Illuminati's greatest adversaries in Washington, D.C. — it doesn't exist.

Many libertarians fault Hamilton and "his" bank. First, there had to be a means to finance the United States and pay off the debt incurred both by the Congress and the individual states which the federal government had agreed to assume. Second, it was not his original idea; it was Robert Morris', the man who helped finance the War for Independence and the creation of these United States along with Gouverneur Morris (no relation), who was a prominent member of the Constitutional Convention. It is true, however, that Hamilton endorsed and promoted the bank. Regardless, it became Hamilton's duty in accordance *with an order from Congress* to prepare a plan for the payments of the debts contracted by the Continental Congress.

Robert Morris had been made the superintendent of finance from 1781 to 1784. Three days before taking the office, he proposed a national bank. Later, Washington wanted to appoint Morris as secretary of the treasury, but Morris declined and recommended Hamilton.

Keep in mind that this appointment and bank were during the Washington administration. Washington and the Cabinet were part of the process of approval and implementation. This initially included Jefferson, Randolph, and others who later formed the Republican Party.

The debt was massive for the day and the government seemed ready to collapse from the weight of the debts, and the economy was in shambles. Confidence and credit were restored with the establishment of the U.S. Bank. Did it outlive its purpose? Yes, but once it became a political tool, both political sides endorsed it or railed against it, depending on whether they were in or out of office.

Most libertarians read the anti-bank writings without realizing that many of the personages rocked back and forth in their support or, lack of it, based on whether they were in or out of power. In other words, they were political hypocrites. People today do not seem to notice this aspect of the early anti-bank movement.

Interwoven into the *private* arguments against the bank was who controlled the power of the purse — them or us — not necessarily the principle of the institution itself. Jefferson, for example, was concerned that the shareholders owned newspapers in opposition to the Republican-Democrats, and wanted government funds disbursed out to more banks to diffuse this power.

As we shall see, whatever political party was "in" supported the bank. Whoever was "out" did not — until Andrew Jackson found a way to keep the financial power while making it appear that he broke up the power by breaking the bank.

With the focus becoming partisan, soon both the president and vice president came from the same party, rather than who gathered the most votes, first and second in the electoral college regardless of party. Other changes were made to a system that was designed originally to prevent the accumulation of power by any faction in the executive branch of government, thus enabling partisan politics to rule. Today, a majority of people do not understand the college and have no idea how it was changed to benefit *party* rather than *country*, and that the original wisdom of our Founders needs to be restored. However, as much as it has been changed, it still retains a great deal of the structure to prevent the accumulation of power into the executive by any section of the country or states over other states — or, the democratization of the election process.

From almost the beginning, moves were being taken to accumulate power in the executive, as many had feared and which our Founders thought they had made provisions to prevent. But, because the people did not well understand the wisdom of the electoral system, they allowed the changes to take place.

At this time, the aim of Spain was to stop the expansion of the United States westward into and down the Mississippi River Valley. This was also the design of revolutionary France, with a few twists.

The most serious of the schemes to break off territories in the West to stop the expansion of the United States came as a result of the revolutionary French ambassadors Genet and Pierre-Auguste Adet.

In addition to the initiatives of the French ambassadors in the West, there was a scientific survey by André Michaux, a French botanist, that was little more than a cover for political intrigue.

The French ambassador charged Michaux with a mission in regard to a French occupation of Kentucky, where Spanish influence had to be neutralized first. He traveled 1,200 miles through the territory in pursuit of the mission, no light task in those days even with the best of roads and conveyance.

Jefferson asked Michaux in 1793 to undertake an exploratory mission of the western frontier similar to what he asked Meriwether Lewis to do on a grander scale ten years later. Genet, however, had Michaux evaluate a plan by George Rogers Clark to organize a militia to take over the Louisiana territory from the Spanish. Michaux was then to be the liaison between Clark and Genet. The plan did not succeed because Clark could not raise the militia, and the monies to be used for that purpose dried up. These monies came from the U.S. Treasury in payment for Royal France's help and loans during the War for Independence, and Hamilton stopped payment once the schemes were exposed.

Michaux also engaged in trying to rouse the western inhabitants around St. Louis to rise up against Spanish authorities down the Mississippi. According to established historians, when Jefferson found out about it, Michaux was expelled from the country. This was not true, and while Jefferson disagreed with Genet's plans, he nonetheless gave letters of introduction to Michaux to present to Kentucky citizens in the Mississippi Valley.

The involvement of Jefferson, Burr, and General James Wilkinson in regard to the Mississippi Valley is another example of the cross purposes of the individuals involved for their own ambitions.

The French freethinkers had more influence percentage-wise on the Western frontier than they did within the cities of the original thirteen states, with a few exceptions. They planned a break-off state in the West to be called *Franklin* as another facet of the Western initiative of the Jacobins. The plan moved forward for a time but then phased out for a variety of reasons, one of which was the growing power of Republicans in government. Once this occurred, there was no reason to split from the country since it was no longer under the Washington-Adams administrations, and the Jacobins had seemingly won the day with the Republicans in power over the executive branch and Congress.

However, while they were trying to form this new state, and since the state was to be formed out of the territory of the State of North Carolina, that state objected, even sending in a military force, which was attacked by the rebels, with disastrous results for the Franklin forces.

The Franklin forces had elected a governor and legislature, and had drawn up a constitution which barred ministers and lawyers from holding office. The Franklin forces went one step further than the Whiskey Rebellion against the clergy; they did not like lawyers as well. What gained support among the population for the enterprise was the desire to form a government to bring security to the area from the less-than-friendly Indians.

A petition was submitted to the U.S. Congress to recognize Franklin as the 14th state, but it did not receive the necessary votes because of the opposition of North Carolina to the enterprise.

Western agitation was centered within the Republican ranks, and when this party began to accumulate power within the federal government there was no longer any need for the disturbance, since it served no real benefit for those who sought power — except Burr.

The French had a great influence on the American Philosophical Society, established by Benjamin Franklin. And the takeover of the Grand Orient Masonry in Europe by the Illuminati had an effect on American Masonry when French Masons emigrated to the U.S., bringing the Grand Orient with them. Both initiatives had an effect on American intellectual life. They had only sporadic successes trying to take control of American Masonry.

The American Philosophical Society would welcome such evenings as Lafayette extolling the wonders of mesmerism. He was an avid disciple of the craft, claiming to have been initiated into its secret, although he was not at liberty to reveal it. The society was influenced by French scientific materialism in its infancy.

Many people turned to mesmerism to fill a void in their lives. However, its leaders really didn't have any power or secret to share; they primarily used the movement to break down Christian faith and morality as a means to fill their abnormal lust for sex and power.

Mesmerism is named after Franz Anton Mesmer, an Austrian Rosicrucian. He attended the University of Ingolstadt in 1759 and was influenced in his study by Adam Weishaupt's adoptive father, the Baron von Ickstatt, who was known to be very interested in the occult and secret societies.

Mesmer said that he represented the Order of the Illuminati of Bavaria and formed 20 Harmony lodges all over France modeled on Freemasonry, but they were never actually affiliated with Masonry.

Mesmerism was based on two ideas. One was animal magnetism, and the other a magnetic fluid that could be transferred to heal another by the laying on of hands with spiritual forces and a life-energy, and it could involve shakings and tremors. This is not to be confused with Pentecostalism, in which they profess the use of the Holy Spirit. With mesmerism, God was never a consideration.

The animal magnetism aspect was simply an excuse for being drawn to another person beyond one's self control; in other words, an excuse for immorality. The idea of a magnetic fluid was debunked by a French Royal Commission (including Benjamin Franklin) named by the king.

American Illuminism

Notable men such as President Dwight of Yale; Rev. David Tappan, professor of divinity at Harvard; Rev. Jedidiah Morse; and others claimed the Democratic Societies were establishing the principles of Illuminism in America, and that they were trying to take over American Masonry. In his 4th of July, 1798 discourse at Harvard, Dwight asserted that the Illuminati existed in the U.S., after it was supposedly dead according to most modern historians.

Morse started his sermons of concern about the Illuminati about the same time the volumes exposing the order by Barruel and Robison were published. We do know that he was very upset about the rise of Jacobins in American politics and the ensuing violence and breakdown of public morality. He received letters from George Washington and others stating their support for his sermons, as they had similar concerns.

Morse received a letter from Dr. John Erskine of Edinburgh in 1797, wherein he says:

A Society was created first under the name of the "Illuminati;" and, when they had been prohibited under that name, they found means, under the name of the German Union, to get control of the greater part of the literary journals, periodical publications, circulating libraries, and reading clubs, nay even of printers and booksellers through Germany, so as to prevent, as much as possible, the sale and spread of pieces of any ability, in which the doctrines of true Christianity were defended.

Dr. Morse preached and published the following in May 1799:

There are too many evidences that this order [of Illuminati] has had its branches established in some form or other, and its emissaries secretly at work in this country for several years past. From their private papers which have been discovered and are now published, it appears that, as early as 1786, they had several Societies in America. And it is well known that some men, high in office, have expressed sentiments accordant to the principles and views of this Society.

— Boston Library Archives

Earlier in the same year, John Jay wrote Dr. Morse:

Infidelity has become a political engine, alarming both by the force and the extent of its operations.... Much ill use has been and will yet be made of Secret Societies. I think with you that they should not be encouraged, and that the most virtuous and innocent among them would do well to concur in their suspension for the present.

— *The Life of John Jay, Volume II*

George Washington, undoubtedly speaking of the problem of the Illuminati and their ilk, said:

Of all the dispositions and habits which lead to political prosperity, religion and morality are indispensable support. In vain would that man claim the tribute of patriotism who should labor to subvert these great pillars.

— Farewell Address

Just as the tactic used today, extremists on both sides exaggerated the influence and/or the existence of the Illuminati. This made the task of informing the people that more difficult. Accusations and assertions were made that the enemies of the Illuminati were actually Illuminists themselves! The *Aurora* played no small part in this campaign.

The *Aurora* published articles on the Illuminati which outlined the Illuminist goals but cast suspicion on many of the enemies of Illuminism.

Benjamin Franklin, like Jefferson, became enamored of the French revolutionaries while in France. His friends included Voltaire and Mirabeau, an important agent of the Illuminati in France, and Lafayette.

On April 9, 1778, the dying Voltaire entered the Nine Sisters Lodge, under the control of the Illuminati, on the arm of Franklin, for one of the most significant Masonic initiations in history. Six months after Voltaire's death, on November 28, 1778, Voltaire was proclaimed a god by the Nine Sisters in a mixed ritual of pagan and Christian rites before 200 guests. Crowns of laurel were placed on the heads of Franklin and other eulogists.

Franklin served in this Lodge with the likes of Bonneville and other Illuminists prior to the revolution in France. Records of this organization were seized and possibly destroyed by the Gestapo in World War II. One can only guess what they contained and it is a loss to the record of American involvement, since we know that Franklin was a leader in the lodge, with Jefferson and Paine at least having floated around it.

Franklin used the Illuminist Mirabeau as his own agent to ghostwrite some of his work that he did not want attributed to himself as an emissary of America to France. This included a letter attacking George Washington.

The close relationship of Franklin and Mirabeau gives one pause to speculate as to whether the Mirabeau-Gramscian technique was not imported to America by the friends of Franklin. Franklin's actions in England and France were extremely immoral and conspiratorial, and he was celebrated as much for his impropriety among the degenerate wings of these two societies as he was for his intellect.

His sex habits in Europe and conspiratorial intrigues with the likes of his Illuminist friends were so profound that it is difficult to imagine a total abandonment of them upon his return home. Perhaps his age played a role in dampening his ardor on one hand, but did it likewise do the same for his intrigue? There are hints in both directions.

For instance, Franklin called for prayer during a particularly hard impasse in the deliberations during the Constitutional Convention. On the other hand, he was known to have suggested changes in Scripture in Europe that were blasphemous. Then too, there was the American Philosophical Society, an organization he helped found which had a decidedly Gramscian bent.[18]

The Nine Sisters Lodge had grown in its effrontery and public immorality so much that the king of France was going to order it dissolved. Franklin was then elected the Grand Master of this Illuminati-controlled lodge, preventing the king from committing an insult to America by so doing.

Franklin is portrayed as a master diplomat in regard to his bringing France into the War for Independence. One has to ask how much shorter time would it have taken if Franklin had not been involved in the immoral activities he was known for. It was not the type of image the average American would have wanted to present to the French court. Keep in mind, while there were many French royals who were decadent, the king and is wife were not part of that ilk.

The story today is that the French were enamored of Franklin. Franklin was not known for his ability to

---

18 No one seems to realize that Franklin's motion at the convention was not seconded; there was no vote taken and no prayer given according to Madison's notes. Yet ministers all over the country repeat this story as if they held a prayer meeting.

fit into "polite company," and his French was terrible. For those of you who have ever been to France, you know how the French treat those who are not proficient in their language and mores, particularly in Paris.

The image of Franklin was built up by the Illuminists in Europe, and this image was likewise built by their agents in America. Their agents within the French government — coupled with those who wanted to do just about anything to tweak the nose of England — had a great deal to do with France becoming an ally of the fledgling country-to-be.

There is no doubt that Franklin was a gifted man, but he had serious failings. It is a dirty little secret used by the forces we battle even today, that men of great leadership have drives that propel them into leadership. Usually one of them is a strong sex drive. It is a matter of whether a man, or woman, can get this energy under control and use it for good. The Conspiracy will always test major personalities as to whether they can be compromised by these desires.

This author has read dozens of books on leadership published in the United States. In only one was this aspect of a leader's personality even briefly discussed. It appears to be a taboo subject, yet it explains why so many in positions of power or authority have a failing when it comes to controlling this urge. In our history, it started with Franklin, Jefferson, and Hamilton, followed by hundreds of men and women in leadership. Only with Hamilton was it a once-in-a-lifetime occurrence.

The conspirators in the French Court were doing a great deal to help American independence behind the back of the king. They could have moved more boldly and overtly perhaps if Franklin was known to the king as a gentleman in all respects. Established "history" attributes the success of French involvement in our war to Franklin. In reality, the entire operation of gaining French aid was a secret conspiracy among Franklin, Illuminists, and other American representatives and counterparts in the Royal French government working behind the king's back.

The French diplomats, aside from the conspirators, had their reasons to support American independence. It would mean the blooding of the English and the formation of a lasting thorn in England's side. They understood that America could one day become a serious rival, but that was someday. The rivalry with England was now.

Adams, in France for a time with Franklin, was appalled at Franklin's behavior. Little was really known about America among these conspirators and Franklin did little to help them to understand. In fact, much of Franklin's work was propaganda to convince the French that America was more than the reality of our condition.

Indeed, there was a move by John Adams and Arthur Lee to have Congress recall Franklin. Lee accused Franklin of drunkenness, whoring, and accepting bribes. There were even rumors of British bribes paid to Franklin. There are articles written today that say that this was far more than rumor, but the evidence could be more convincing.

The French looked at Franklin and saw in him America. They did not see the moral underpinnings that were the hallmark of American society. In the end, the French help worked to our favor, but it led to the destruction of Royal France partly due to foreign aid to America: It added to the financial burdens of the royal court at a time they could ill afford it.

Then too, the success of the American independence movement gave impetus to the revolution being planned in France: If the Americans can do it, we can do it. It increased the morale and audacity of the allies of, and the useful idiots employed by, the Conspiracy. But it was a *social revolution* in France, not a War for Independence as in America.

After the French Revolution, France took a long time to recover from the slaughter of the truly intellectual and religious class at the guillotine. Some say they never have.

The next step in the Conspiracy's design was to have a social revolution in the United States and the formation of French-led countries carved out of the American frontier if they could not revolutionize the entire American government. They worked on both initiatives at the same time.

Part of these designs by the French-led American Jacobins was an independent West Pennsylvania and the formation of a league of states, both on our frontier as well as with established states, to unite with France in opening the Mississippi River and to form a French American republic, or a French alliance with such a republic if it maintained its independence.

Jefferson, while in France, likewise grew close to Illuminists and supported the revolution, but was appalled by the excesses of Robespierre. However, he was not initially horrorstruck by French republican extremes. It is surprising, therefore, that he lent so much support for the Jacobin movement that arose in America directed by these forces, as we will show.

Not all of the men who rallied behind the Democratic Clubs understood what they were supporting. Just as today, few people can believe that a conspiracy exists and what their goals really are. Some of the best men in America were fooled.

Some of the enemies of the Jacobins were Washington, Hamilton, John Adams, Marshall, and Jay. Jefferson, the supporter of the Democratic Clubs, withdrew from Washington's administration and became recognized as the administration's opposition. James Madison, James Monroe, George Clinton, Chancellor Livingston, and Aaron Burr were his partisans and cast their weight of influence in the French faction. Out of this group came the Republican Party, later called the Democrats. Later, Madison and Monroe had a change of heart relative to the French.

As minister to France, Monroe was friendly to the French Revolution, and Washington had to recall him when he was convinced of this. As mentioned, later in life Monroe would change his opinion.

Washington's Attorney General Randolph was found to be in direct league with Gallatin and Findley of the Whiskey Rebellion. He issued opinions which tied the hands of Washington, Hamilton, and federal excise officers.

Washington, in addition to the problems he already had within his Cabinet, was under constant pressure to appoint men who were sympathetic to the French Revolution. Much of this pressure revolved around Aaron Burr. Gouverneur Morris, whom Washington appointed to France, was not sympathetic to the revolution, and the Republicans nominated Burr to replace him.

Madison and Monroe went to Washington twice as delegates of the Republicans to get him to appoint Burr, who was sympathetic to the revolution. Washington refused and appointed Monroe — although he in turn became too close to the revolution and was replaced.

The actions and pressures of the European countries played a major part in how Washington and Adams handled foreign policy. The Conspiracy played a role in trying to shape the foreign policy of everyone. What made it so difficult were the shifting sands the Conspiracy produced during their attempts to take over country after country.

For instance, France and Spain were allies against England during our War for Independence. Spain became an enemy of both France and England after the French Revolution. Then Spain was helped by England in its battle against Napoleon. Finally, the fleet at Trafalgar beaten by Lord Nelson was a combined French-Spanish fleet. In a few short years, much could change.

It was only one of the reasons Washington, and later Jefferson, would advise against foreign entanglements — you didn't know what could change in the future and we might be bound by a treaty that we wish we had never entered into.

The same is the case with the Middle East and Europe today. The government leaders change, the types of governments change, and the ambitions and rivalries, even within the Muslim World, keep the rest of the world on edge, as do the plethora of "ex"-communists vying for power between Russia, Germany, Ukraine, etc. And, it is no different in the Far East with the government of communist China. To form alliances or entanglements within this nest of vipers could lead to suicide.

And in the mix, whether the year is 1800 or 2000, is the Conspiracy that is moving the world toward the establishment of their New World Order.

Just as the actions of the Muslims may seem confusing today, the actions of France, Spain, the Illuminists, Burr, Jefferson, Wilkinson, et al. in regard to the Mississippi may seem to have been contradictory. The bottom line is that when seeking power and the territory that manifests that power, all want it and will conspire for it, doing one thing one day and an alternative on another day — but each in his own way wanting to win.

A modern example would be Sen. John McCain, who pushed for support for the Muslim rebels in Syria against a Russian surrogate government in Damascus. Then a major element of these so-called Syrian rebels "invaded" neighboring Iraq using some of the arms we provided. They marched toward Baghdad to overthrow the government there, an ally of Iran, another Russian surrogate, and then McCain screamed on the floor of the Senate that Obama has to do something!

It was McCain's influence that helped produce the situation that he then opposed. McCain and those who surround him were instrumental in upsetting the balance of power throughout the Middle East. Too often they were in support of the most radical Muslims until it became obvious to all and the story changed. McCain has been a decades-long member of the New World Order-supporting organization, the Council on Foreign Relations, and oversaw the International Republican Institute, laden with CFR members and indirectly financed by the State Department.

We use this as an example to show that it can get confusing and that the people who want an international order include those with conservative images. In regard to John McCain, a whole book could be written to show why many say that where McCain went, jihad was sure to follow. A book could be written to show this problem of McCain's involvement and duplicity from Libya to Egypt to Syria and Iran.

The unethical and immoral will change their direction any way possible to achieve their ends. The one thing they will never change is the overall strategy, which we have shown before: the dual goal of world government and eliminating religion, or making religion over as an instrument of the state.

New Orleans, near the mouth of the Mississippi, was a French city founded in the early 1700s. France later ceded it to Spain. France reacquired New Orleans with the victory over Spain in 1800 by Napoleon; who then sold it three years later to the United States; this led to the vast expansion of the United States into the Northwest Territories explored by Meriwether Lewis and William Clark. Napoleon did this not only to raise money for war against England, but to keep America as an ally of France within Republican circles and the Jefferson administration. American money bought a vast territory, but it also helped France against England. Jefferson liked both ideas.

Incidentally, the purchase was unconstitutional since it did not have the approval of Congress for the scheme until after the fact. However, the benefits outweighed the negatives and Congress acquiesced — after more debate than most realize today — and went along with the idea.

The treaty of trade in 1785 with the Spanish government had prevented English and American trade traffic through New Orleans for a period of 25 years. John Jay negotiated the treaty to gain trade concessions for the Atlantic and sacrificed the primitive Mississippi Valley in the process, since it was not as important to the overall welfare of the country *at the time*.

Since the Mississippi was the most effective means for supplying the "West," and in turn trading with the East Coast by water rather than the hardships of transporting wagons overland, the pioneers connected to the Mississippi resented Spanish authority. Yet as we have seen and will see more, many traitors within America cooperated with and accepted pensions from the Spanish to further Spanish initiatives in the Western Territories.

Treason relative to French influence tended to be ideological, whereas with Spain it was greed with the use of "pensions" — if the Spanish money also helped the ideologues, so much the better.

Another treaty with Spain was concluded in 1795 which secured rights in New Orleans for three years, and this caused many plots in the Mississippi Valley to lose their strength.

When Louisiana became a possession of the United States in 1803, this helped quiet many of the problems in Kentucky and down the Mississippi that were stirred up by Spain and France. Yet, the arch-conspirator in the secession movement in the West, Gen. James Wilkinson, was named the governor of Louisiana by Jefferson. It was at Aaron Burr's suggestion that Wilkinson was appointed. Burr and Wilkinson had been communicating in cipher for years.

During the years of imbroglio, Burr and Hamilton were at odds. Hamilton was the most effective in the Washington administration against the Jacobins and this meant his bumping heads with Burr, even in light of Hamilton's transgressions. It would eventually be settled on the field of honor.

The famous duel between Hamilton and Burr led to Hamilton's death. Warrants for murder were taken out against Burr in the states of New York and New Jersey, but even so Burr was hailed as a hero in the South and Virginia because he killed Hamilton. Even with warrants against him for his arrest because it was an illegal duel, he presided over the U.S. Senate as vice president after the duel up to March 1805. When it comes to justice, some are more equal than others.

He was not arrested until his attempt at wresting the Mississippi for himself against the Jefferson-led United States.

When Jefferson became president he wrote Paine a letter. According to J.A. Spencer, D.D. in *The History of the United States* in 1866, in the letter Jefferson gave Paine his "assurances of his high esteem, and affectionate attachment," and offered this reviler of both George Washington and the Christian religion "a passage home in the United States sloop of war *Maryland.*"

After Genet was recalled, Jean Antoine Joseph Fauchet, who became a member of the Sophisians, was named by Robespierre as the French ambassador to the United States. He would later be involved in helping install Napoleon as the leader of France. His intent was to create a split in America by more subtle means than Genet. He claimed in his captured dispatches that the Whiskey Rebellion was premature and should have been successful if he had been able to finance the operation to raise an army to supplement the movement.[19]

At the beginning of 1797, Pierre Auguste Adet was named the French ambassador. By and large, he picked up and continued the activities of Genet. In addition, he campaigned for Thomas Jefferson as president, warning the American people that if they did not support Jefferson, there would be war with France.

When he came to America, he presented a French flag to Washington, which he wanted to be displayed in the House of Representatives. This was not done, but years later, in 1858, a symbol of revolutionary France

---

19 The Sacred Order of the Sophisians was a pseudo-Egyptian secret society of Isis cult worshipers that came out of the Egyptian campaign of Napoleon. Many of Napoleon's officer corps belonged, as well as government officials. Cagliostro, an Illuminist was involved.

was substituted, with a larger-than-life portrait of Lafayette prominently displayed in front of the just-completed House Chamber opposite George Washington, on the same level with Washington in size and position.

Adet had a nasty habit of sending official letters to Washington and sending a copy at the same time to the *Aurora* newspaper in Philadelphia, in an attempt to propagandize the American people.

The *Aurora* stole state papers and invented stories, doing all it could to destroy the party that coalesced around the administration, the Federalists. It was for all practical purposes the organ of Adet and was nothing more than a mouthpiece for the Jacobins.

The *Aurora* continued to be a propaganda piece for radicalism its entire existence. Robert Owen, the Scottish industrialist who founded communist communes both in Scotland and in America, wrote articles for the *Aurora* long before he came to the United States.

When Washington retired from office, the *Aurora* published,

The man who is the source of all the misfortunes of our country is this day reduced to a level with his fellow citizens and is no longer possessed of power, to multiply evils upon the United States. If ever there was a period for rejoicing this is the moment.

The *Aurora* found echoes in other journals: the Richmond *Examiner*, New York *Argus* and *Boston Chronicle*. The *Aurora* is still hailed by liberals today as an example of good journalism in the books and articles published about the early years of our country.

Not all anti-Federalists were lovers of revolutionary France. Patrick Henry summed it up in 1799 that France's conduct "has made it the interest of the great family of mankind to wish the downfall of her present government".... for she destroys "the great pillars of all government and social life, — I mean virtue, morality & religion. This is the armor, my friend, & this alone, that renders us invincible."

In 1798, France broke off diplomatic relations with the U.S., and Adet presented a note from the French Directory declaring that France would treat neutrals, meaning the United States, as they allowed themselves to be treated by the English. In other words, they meant to seize American shipping and impress our sailors. Before leaving, Adet directed an address to the American people intended to inflame them against their government.

At the time, a declared war with France and/or England was a real possibility. For all practical purposes, they were already at war with us. As it turned out, French Illuminist influence on Americans helped convince Congress to declare war against England by 1812. Less under French influence and for economic reasons, New England wanted war with France rather than England; many leaders in New England wanted to pull out of the United States, holding a secession convention for that purpose, although the common people were not enthusiastic about the idea. Apparently secession was considered as an option in New England in 1814, but not considered justified in the South by the New England leaders thirty-six years later.

Another ironic twist of history is that *Royal* France helped America achieve independence, while a few years later *Revolutionary* France became the enemy of our country. It is true; however, if it had not been for Illuminist influence *within* the Royal government, the king would more than likely have never supported our cause.

How much help we received as a direct result of European revolutionaries desiring a successful revolution in America is not well documented. There was far more help from France before the king agreed to it than is told in history books and on the *History Channel*. It was done within the Royal government by declaring Royal arms surplus and then smuggling them to America — past both the English *and* French authorities.

In addition, the main thrust of the Conspiracy in America in the revolutionary years came from the German influence in the Illuminati. In this regard, there is virtually no domestic evidence whatsoever for the Illuminati circles established in America as a result of the German stimulus, even though we know from German sources that such circles existed. This was established and documented by the Bavarian government in its investigations. Rapidly, the French wing of Illuminist influence became more dominant as French assistance entered the war.

The German Illuminati influence was far more sophisticated and worked with more secrecy than the French branch. Indications are, by the later build-up of Teutonic influence among the intellectual circles surrounding the likes of Everett and Emerson, Bancroft, et al., that the ties to the German roots of the conspiracy ultimately became more important.

This influence lasted up to the period just before World War II, with prominent Americans helping the build-up of Nazi Germany.

Most of the concentration on the exposure of the Illuminati in America was on the French. The German roots, while well known, seemed to elude the anti-conspirators, since the French agitation was so heavy that their focus was on that wing of Illuminism. The German wing grew and bored into American society during the period when all eyes were on the French "problem."

There was no opposition to the Illuminati in America until the Jacobin agitation brought attention to the root of the movement, to what was behind it. Even then, knowing that the root of Illuminism was in Germany, it appears that while they talked about Weishaupt, opponents concentrated on the French aspect. Yet we know that the Bavarian government had the testimony of two Illuminati members that circles existed in the U.S. long before the outbreak of Jacobin agitation led by French agents.

The German influence began the tactic of a series of steps toward implementing their goals in a covert manner. The French influence was more oriented toward public agitation, violence, and revolution. Thus the attention was given to the overt rather than the covert programs of the Illuminists, at least initially.

It is similar today when the conservatives see the street communists but cannot seem to fathom that the real problem resides higher in society and government, even including individuals and organizations within the modern Republican Party. It is likewise a problem when any patriotic American sees that the street radical is for or against something, recognizes that the radicals are behind it, and then believes that he is doing well by advocating the opposite.

Free trade is a modern example. The patriotic American thinks free trade is something to endorse, due to its title on a variety of agreements and the fact that the communists in the streets appear to be against it. This happened in regard to the Free Trade Area of the Americas pact in the early 2000s. The so-called Battle in Seattle against free trade by the street communists convinced many businessmen to support free trade without looking into what free trade was all about and recognizing the fact that the high-level communists in the governments involved were for it.

Again, the action is in the reaction.

To back up this tactic logically, if the American government is moving us toward a domestic policy of socialism, they must also be moving us toward a foreign policy of socialism. They are, after all, the same people implementing both policies. One has to also ask that, if we are engaging with trade deals with socialist and even communist nations who do not believe in free enterprise, why then do they call it free trade? A study of the agreements will show that what is really going on is forming regional unions, abrogating the independence of the United States and *economically integrating* us with socialist countries.

The revolutionary organizations had many who felt that it was hopeless for revolution in Europe and looked to success in America for the future. They did not come here as the vast majority of immigrants did, looking for opportunity and liberty. They came to assist in a world revolution, using America as the base from which to do so. Many of these people came to America to help during the latter part of the war, but there is not any good documentation as to their numbers and individuals. Great pains have been taken over the years to erase the record of conspiratorial machinations in the United States, unlike in Europe where more is known in spite of efforts to conceal it.

In other words, the Conspiracy was so embedded in relatively open fronts and widespread within such countries as Germany and France, that much of the evidence of their membership and activities could not be erased. The initial efforts of the Conspiracy in America have always been well hidden, even though we know they existed.

The primary difference between the two areas is that in Europe it is next to impossible to change the problems brought about by the Conspiracy, since the systems of government make it difficult at best and next to impossible at worst in some countries. We will not elaborate other than to say that the American system was designed to limit government and provide protection of the liberty of the people. As a result, the American people when properly informed can remedy the problems they understand. In Europe they cannot, and it is one of the reasons that both Washington and Jefferson said that we should not be embroiled in their problems.

So, in Europe, generally speaking, it is less of a problem for the Conspiracy because the people cannot really do much about it if their system does not allow the opportunity to do so, or if their system makes it more difficult. The parliamentary system, for instance, makes it more difficult for the people to change anything.

In Austria, as an example, candidates do not run for office as they do in the U.S. The party selects those seeking office. So the real power is held in the parties, and that means that one must build a movement to take over the parties. This is a long and difficult road and one in which any conspiracy excels.

Since the American people have the opportunity to make changes when properly informed and applied, it has been a major initiative to make sure that information about the Conspiracy has been suppressed. Researchers who involve themselves in this hunt will find this to be the case, but continued research and effort will bring to the surface and detail more of what is contained in this tome — and additional information, it is hoped.

Prior to Jackson defeating the British at New Orleans, he was deeply involved in the Burr conspiracy in Mississippi.

Jackson's image in history is one which has distorted context or a great deal missing from the narrative. As a result, both modern libertarians as well as Democrats look upon him as a hero. This does not compute, as they say, since the factions are opposites.

For many years the Democrats were divided into two basic camps that identified themselves as either Jeffersonian or Jacksonian Democrats. Generally speaking, Jeffersonians were states-rights oriented and the Jacksonians were nationalists.

Jackson made Burr's acquaintance while in Congress, and when Burr launched his scheme to wrest and then rule the Mississippi he contracted with Jackson for boats. We will discuss the Burr plot more in depth in Chapter Four.

Once the scheme became known, Jackson did not know whether to support or oppose Burr. In the end, he remained a friend of Burr and spoke out against Gen. Wilkinson, and attended the Burr trial and made a speech there against President Thomas Jefferson over the affair.

4

THE JEFFERSON YEARS

Once Jefferson was elected to the presidency, he increasingly lost his revolutionary fervor. After all, a revolutionary cannot be against himself as the head of state. And, many problems stirred up by his revolutionary friends became a problem for him as president. Some of Jefferson's earlier adherents split off from him as a result, such as William Duane of the *Aurora*, and Congressman Michael Leib of Philadelphia, who had been mentored by Franklin. The rivalry between Jefferson and Burr also played into Democrats being divided.

As an example of these problems stirred up by radicals, it was believed the Jacobins were behind the attempted slave revolt led by a slave named Gabriel in Virginia in 1804, where 1100 slaves were involved. While this was never proven, apparently whites were to be killed *except* those of French origin.

One of Jefferson's biggest domestic problems was Vice President Aaron Burr, who became involved in a conspiracy to divide the Western portion of the United States, along with the Mississippi Valley, into a separate country over which he would rule. In this conspiracy were included a few notable men, including the head of the United States Army, General Wilkinson, and Andrew Jackson, and the remnants of the Spanish and French influence in the area. Some plans varied in what exact territory Burr had in mind, ranging from Florida, across the Gulf Mexico's northern shore line, and into Texas and Mexico.

The conspiracy involved too many people over an extended period of time to be the work of a lone individual, namely Burr. He was in communication and contact with a large number of people about his plans for some time, including governors and U.S. senators, and even the British Plenipotentiary resident in the U.S., who communicated Burr's plan to his government.

Burr was in touch with Spanish and French authorities in an attempt to form an alliance and to have them finance his scheme to weaken American interest and growth in the Mississippi Valley. The Spanish ambassador gave him $10,000 before his government told him to have nothing to do with Burr and his plans.

It is generally thought, based on Burr's approaching the Spanish and French, plus his subsequent actions, that his scheme had more to do with treason than wresting territory from Spain. Burr had been festering due to his loss of the presidential race to Jefferson. It was a tie in the electoral college, and he lost the battle in the Congress when Hamilton moved the Federalists to vote for Jefferson as the lesser of two evils.

Burr loomed larger in the American scene than is generally realized today. He was more of the activist within the Jacobin circle than Jefferson. While Jefferson generally operated behind the scenes, Burr was always out front, and his style of leadership would probably have led to violence. Be that as it may, had Burr bided his time as vice president, he may well have become president after Jefferson rather than Madison.

Burr stayed with Andrew Jackson twice during the period of the conspiracy, once for a week.

Letters in cipher from Burr carried by Dr. Justus Erich Bollman and Samuel Swartwout to Gen. Wilkinson about his plans led to Gen. Wilkinson ultimately betraying Burr to Jefferson, and Jefferson issued a proclamation for Burr's apprehension on November 27, 1806.

Burr apparently was unaware of the fact that Gen. Wilkinson was in the pay of Spain as head of the U.S. Army, and Wilkinson betrayed Burr to protect Spanish interests. However, there was evidence that Wilkinson was more concerned about Burr thwarting his own plans for the area.

Dr. Justus Erich Bollman, who had helped Lafayette try to escape Austria, was one of Burr's trusted lieutenants. Dr. Bollman had studied medicine at Göttingen, and Bollman was influential in American Jacobin circles promoting the French style of liberty.

Henry Clay became Burr's attorney upon his initial arrest before Judge Harry Innis at Frankfort, Kentucky. At the time, Clay was assured by Burr that it was all a misunderstanding.

Innis was in league with Wilkinson in a Spanish conspiracy to wrest control of the Mississippi Valley for Spain. Innis had been a vocal proponent of Kentucky's separation from Virginia. He had received his appointment as judge from George Washington.

One of Burr's confederates, Harman Blennerhassett, also engaged Clay for his trial. After Burr was released, Blennerhassett was also released. He was described as a "liberalist of the French school," and was from England. He ultimately removed to England.

There was evidence of Spanish pensions for Innis, George Nicholas of the Jefferson States Rights Resolutions of 1798, and others. It was not absolutely proven until later that Wilkinson, while the head of the U.S. Army, was also in the pay of Spain, although it was generally "known." The pay vouchers for the money paid to Wilkinson were in the archives in Havana when U.S. troops occupied Cuba during the Spanish-American War one hundred years later.

Accusations were brought against Innis as a judge, but the Republican (Democrat) Congress refused to impeach. In the Burr case, Innis had agreed to the motions by the defense representing Burr, but none by the prosecution. Edmund Randolph, former Secretary of State under Washington, was Burr's attorney at his trial. Recall that Randolph was friendly with the Whiskey Rebellion leaders and second cousin to Jefferson. Randolph also opposed Hamilton's first bank.

Henry Clay would go on to support the U.S. Bank and the involvement of government in public works.

Henry Clay's bust would later grace the office of Horace Greeley as, in Greeley's opinion, Clay was the best politician produced in America. Abraham Lincoln would also follow the views of Clay in the Whig party. Lincoln and Greeley had much in common as fellow members of the House of Representatives. They both opposed the war with Mexico and considered themselves nationalists rather than sectionalists. Likewise, at the time, they were not abolitionists as much as they were against the extension of slavery. In addition, Lincoln *was active* in colonialization and repeatedly stated his entire life that his opinion was to send the Negroes back to Africa or to some spot in Latin America, anywhere but here.

The evidence for this is overwhelming. For years, Lincoln sat as one of the eleven managers of the Illinois Colonization Society. Their initial desire was to remove the slaves to Liberia, and that African country was established specifically to serve as the area for the colonization of Africans from America.

Keep in mind that Greeley was a member of Congress when he was a prominent leader of the socialist movement in America.

Later, along with Edmund Randolph, Luther Martin was one of the lawyers engaged by Burr for his trial on the charge of treason. Martin was a delegate from Maryland to the U.S. Constitutional Convention, but he opposed it and left without signing it. His stated reason was twofold: The Constitution did not protect state sovereignty, and it was in effect a coup d'état since the convention was called only to amend the Articles of Confederation, not to write a whole new system.

He was an ally of Thomas Jefferson but switched his alliance to the Federalists after Jefferson referred to him in derogatory terms. He spent his last days in Burr's home, paralyzed.

When the Burr conspiracy was first made public, a reign of terror by the Jefferson government prevailed against citizens who may have been involved. Searches and seizures were illegally carried out until no "invasion" by U.S. citizens of any western territories occurred. Even the judge who issued writs of habeas corpus to protect citizens' rights was arrested for doing so.

The U.S. Senate secretly suspended habeas corpus for three months to put the whole country into the hands of Jefferson; however, the House rejected the bill and made it public. Even so, Jefferson used the military to arrest material witnesses, and held them without access to an attorney until they had told all they knew or how they were involved.

These actions are completely contrary to the image of Jefferson as a libertarian.

The Burr conspiracy evolved publicly into a plan for an invasion of Mexico, which at the time included Texas and related territory. This created a number of problems for the United States with Spain. However, according to the testimony of Gen. William Eaton, whom Burr had drawn into the conspiracy, the real intent of Burr was to bring the West into revolt, establish a monarchy and use it as a base for taking over all the United States, assassinate the president, absolve the Congress, and rule.

Establishing a monarchy is what Burr accused Hamilton of trying to do. The people were not that far removed from being ruled by a monarch, and all of the countries surrounding the United States were ruled by monarchs. It was not an idea that did not have support. Even during the War for Independence, a third of the people wanted to stay under the king, a third could have cared less who ruled them, while the remaining third were for breaking away from England.

The only thing that even makes this plausible, or any part of the conspiracy, is that Burr was obsessively ambitious to be the president of the United States. Those plans were foiled. It does not explain the involvement of all the other individuals, unless the point by the master Conspiracy was to use any scheme to destroy the government of the United States and to substitute an Illuminist one.

Burr had a list of over 4,000 people, primarily in the West, whom he felt would rally to his cause. The Pittsburgh *Commonwealth*, a Democrat newspaper, reopened the discussion of the democratic societies' independence movement in the West after Burr's appearance there. *The Gazette* of Chillicothe, Ohio, the state capital at the time, published articles written by Burr to show the necessity of separation from the union and of establishing a confederation composed of the states west of the Alleghenies, the Mississippi, and the Gulf ports.

Jefferson had papers in his possession important to the case, but he did not turn them over to the court. Speculation was that this led to Burr's acquittal. The original verdict read, " ... Burr is not proved to be guilty under the indictment by any evidence submitted to us. We, therefore, find him not guilty." The court ordered a simple "Not guilty" entered into the journal. There were jurors who thought him guilty but under the law could not vote so.

The wording of what constitutes treason is very specific in the Constitution, and apparently Burr was not guilty under the specifics, even though many felt that he was guilty in spirit.

When it was all over, the trial of Burr for treason was a sham and all involved got off. Jefferson played a large role in making sure that this was the final outcome, contrary to his public pronouncements calling Burr a traitor. Speculation was that full disclosure would have revealed things that would have been embarrassing to Jefferson and the whole Jacobin movement.

John Randolph was the foreman of the jury and a partisan of the radical Democrats, but was angry at

Jefferson by the end of the trial for Jefferson's support of Gen. James Wilkinson. Randolph did not feel the general was trustworthy.

John Randolph would go on to be one of the three founder's, with Henry Clay, of the American Colonization Society in 1816 with Clay. He never reached puberty due to his lifelong bout with tuberculosis, which settled into his genital tract as a boy. He took opium to deaden the pain. He became enamored of Andrew Jackson as a result of the trial, led a successful career in politics, and was named minister to Russia by Jackson in 1830.

More than likely, and this is purely speculation, due to the number of U.S. senators, governors, and other men of influence that were involved with Burr, had the trial gone any further and the whole plot been exposed, it would have devastated the Democrat Party and returned the Federalists to power. As a result of the acquittal, many of the men who surrounded Wilkinson and Burr would go on to become federal officeholders. This is probably the reason Jefferson withheld evidence. Not only that, but questions probably would have been asked about Jefferson's previous involvement in the affair. Jefferson, like so many others, wanted to expand the United States out into territory held by other countries, not just wilderness.

The same problem of the need to withhold evidence would manifest itself later with the new Republicans in regard to the John Brown conspiracy.

An outline of the Burr plot summarized in *History of American Conspiracies, A Record of Treason, Insurrection, Rebellion, &c. in the United States of America from 1760 to 1860*, published in 1863, is:

1. Wilkinson worked for years to separate the West from the East.
2. He, along with other leading citizens, took Spanish money and plotted to betray Kentucky into Spanish hands.
3. His accomplices were retained in federal office after their guilt became known.
4. One of them, George Nicholas, acted as Jefferson's chief instrument in forcing through the Kentucky Legislature's solutions of 1798.
5. Wilkinson played a role in the Burr conspiracy.
6. Burr's only "crime" was trying to lead a design by Wilkinson-Jefferson to usurp their leadership.
7. Jefferson not only wanted to take Florida and Mexico, but Cuba as well.

Jefferson's involvement in providing cover for the guilty was also demonstrated in the cover-up of the murder (a few years later) of his personal secretary Meriwether Lewis. Lewis was put in charge of a mission into the Northwest Territory by Jefferson, and every American has heard of the famous Lewis and Clark Expedition. The expedition was somewhat secretive at the time because of not only the great danger from the British, but more so from the Spanish who sent two expeditions to attempt to intercept Lewis and Clark and eliminate the exploration party.

The Spanish authorities were informed by the traitor Gen. Wilkinson of the aims of the expedition, its primary route, and the scheduled departure. The Spanish parties reached the upper Missouri too late to stop them, both in coming and in going.

The Spanish were concerned since there was a less-than-definitive border that had been negotiated between Spain and France concerning the western boundary of the French possession where it abutted Spanish territory, most of it being unexplored. The Spanish did not want the Lewis and Clark Expedition to serve as a basis to redraw the boundaries into what they considered Spanish territory, thus the missions to intercept them.

Had the Spanish intercepted Lewis and Clark and eliminated them in the wilderness, it could have been blamed on Indians, or simply that they had disappeared never to return. It is not known how long this would have delayed the opening up of the West, but it would have delayed it for an indeterminate time.

After the trial, Burr went to England, where he was feted by the rich and powerful until he was exiled from Britain. We may never know the extent of Burr's conspiracy and those who helped him. Matthew L. Davis was put in charge by Burr of his papers, to compile a memoir, and on Burr's death, Davis stated he burned a great deal of Burr's correspondence.

Davis stated that the correspondence could be harmful to Burr and his associates, but for some reason Burr would not allow Davis to destroy the correspondence during his life. The information contained in them — and what harm would have ensued — was reduced to ashes.

The habit of destroying letters and papers before or after the demise of key personages in this narrative will show up again and again. Also, letters and papers would disappear only to reappear and then disappear again. This would be the case with the raid on Harper's Ferry by John Brown, the Lincoln assassination, the records of the Confederate Secret Service, etc. This practice by the participants has made ferreting out the truth difficult.

After the Lewis and Clark Expedition was completed, Lewis was appointed governor of the Northwest Territory, following General Wilkinson, and found information that he felt President Madison needed to know, apparently about Wilkinson. On his trip to Washington, he was ambushed and murdered. Official history says that he committed suicide — by first shooting himself in the chest, then the head. Not many people try to commit suicide in that fashion. Jefferson helped the official story by saying that his friend Lewis always had a serious drinking problem and was moody. Many contemporary histories promote the idea that Lewis suffered from depression his entire life and this which led to his suicide.

Modern television has carried stories of the death of Lewis speculating that he was killed to keep secret any information he may have found on his expedition that would have given weight to a Welsh claim on the territory, predating the claims of America, France, Spain, etc. This was supposedly due to stories of Welsh settlements in the New World prior to the Columbian period. All of this was never proven and carried about as much credence as Sasquatch sightings.

Other television histories depict Lewis as a victim of depression. These programs and writings are a more modern depiction of Lewis and are difficult to find in histories written before the 20th century.

There was never any public disclosure of what Lewis knew. It may have been that Gen. Wilkinson was in the pay of the Spanish government while the head of the American army and that he had a history of involvement in conspiracies.[20]

By the end of his administration Jefferson had changed a great deal, though he had performed many acts that were unconstitutional. In his retirement he changed even more; however, he was not looked upon with universal esteem at the time as you can well imagine, and the problems that he created or did not solve left a bad taste in many mouths.

Many of the issues at the time are not recorded in modern history books, and every one of these issues would constitute a chapter. However, in January 1809, a report of a committee of the Legislature of Massachusetts depicted Jefferson's administration as follows:

Our agriculture is discouraged; the fisheries abandoned; navigation forbidden; our commerce at

---

20 See *The Jefferson Conspiracies, A President's Role in the Assassination of Meriwether Lewis*, by David Leon Chandler, William Morrow and Company, Inc., New York, 1994.

home restrained, if-not annihilated; our commerce abroad cut off; our navy sold, dismantled, or degraded to the service of cutters or gunboats; the revenue extinguished; the cause of justice interrupted; the military power exalted above the civil, *and by setting up a standard of political faith, unknown to the Constitution*, the nation is weakened by internal animosities and divisions, at the moment when it is unnecessarily and improvidently exposed to war with Great Britain, France, and Spain. (Emphasis added.)

History of the United States, Spencer, 1866

Several old history books have similar reports of Jefferson's tenure. It is not a far-fetched view that the policies of Jefferson as president paved the way for the near defeat of the U.S. in the War of 1812 during the tenure of his successor Madison.

This is not the history taught in the schools today — any school. And, as already mentioned, it would take a chapter to explain each issue above. However, the issue with the Navy put the position of the U.S. in peril when we went to war with England. Nor, did it help with our ability to protect American shipping, which led to the war in the first place.

The Constitution does not call for a standing army, but it does mandate a navy, something Jefferson, for whatever reason, neglected.

The power of Democratic Societies, led by the Jacobins, had been waning and virtually disappeared after Robespierre was taken to the guillotine, and the political power of the revolutionary clubs of France was destroyed. In referring to this condition, John Marshall in his *Life of Washington*, 1832, said, "No more certain is it that the boldest streams must disappear, if the fountains which feed them be emptied than was the dissolution of the democratic societies of America, when the Jacobin Clubs were denounced by France."

This lack of "fountains" to feed the Democratic Societies of America also had a calming influence on the radicalism of Jefferson's followers. This in turn had a waning influence on the desire of Jefferson to support radical politics. No politician curries the favor of a waning movement.

The rise of the Jacobins led to the formation of the Democratic-Republican Party and put this party in power. The election of 1800 was a turning point in national politics, and the tie between Jefferson and Burr in the Electoral College led to changes far-reaching for the future, and the opposite image of Jefferson and Madison that libertarians have of these men.

They were the authors of the Kentucky and Virginia Resolutions for states rights. Yet, during the period of 1800 to 1817, their four presidential terms did little to advance the cause of states rights. In fact, much was done to weaken these rights.

To Jefferson's credit, he opposed the increase of the power of the federal judiciary led by Federalist Chief Justice John Marshall. However, Jefferson expanded federal powers with the acquisition of the Louisiana Territory and with his use of a national embargo designed to prevent our involvement in a European war.

Madison, in 1809, used troops to enforce a Supreme Court decision in Pennsylvania, appointed a nationalist, Joseph Story to the court, signed the bill creating the second Bank of the United States, and called for a constitutional amendment to promote internal improvements. The latter would have opened the gates to all manner of federal intrusion into the economic life of the country in the long run. Intrusion came over time in any case, but Madison's amendment would have codified the movement much earlier.

These men said one thing when not in power but did another when given the chance, changing their stances on such things as the federalists, the U.S. Bank, states' sovereignty, and property rights. They now propounded internal improvements that would necessitate the use of eminent domain, and portrayed a socialistic attitude toward commerce and the economy.

We must weigh all of the facts when judging our heroes, not just our schoolboy image, in order to understand what has happened and is happening to our country, and how we were put on the path early on toward altering the system our Founders gave to us. Too often, many of these men began the process of supporting what benefited them directly, rather than adhering to policies that benefited all in the long run.

It is human nature — and the reason the Constitution was written to curtail such ambitions with the use of government.

5

WAR AND JACKSON

A few years after the Lewis and Clark Expedition, we were engaged in the War of 1812 with England. Later, the English would do a great deal to dissuade Americans from going across the Oregon Trail by enlisting Indians to harass the initial wagon trains, just as they had done earlier along the western boundary of the colonies during and shortly after the War for Independence.

The Lewis and Clark Expedition and the opening of the Pacific Northwest by the inclusion of John Jacob Astor's fur trading enterprises into the area showed that people could make it across the country and settle onto fertile land.

There was an increasing influence and occupation by the British in the Oregon Territory and they did not want a bunch of illegal aliens from America settling there to wrest it away from them.

British-American relationships in our early years were marked by the enlistment of American Indians against either side. Some tribes or nations were allied with us, most with England. This situation presented a problem for American pioneers for decades, with hard feelings due to the ravages of Indian attacks that ran on for many years, not just feelings against the Indians, but against the British who enlisted them as well.

What is not as well known is that the British forces at the end of either war did not withdraw immediately. In a few cases, their armies were still encamped within our territory for some period of time. This caused a great deal of animosity in those regions.

There were many reasons why we would be at odds with the British: harassment of American shipping, the impressment and treatment of American sailors, curtailment of trade by British authorities in some areas of the world, exploration and expansion of Americans into British-held territory, competition for territories not held by either party, vying for influence and possession in Latin American countries, etc.

In addition to these things, Americans had memories of the incredibly harsh treatment of American soldiers and civilians during the War for Independence, particularly in the South and as prisoners of war, and the encouragement of the slaughter of civilians by the Indians for several years, etc. Most Americans today are not aware of the cruel treatment which led to disease and starvation of Americans by the British in prison ships and camps during the War for Independence.

In the Anglophile world we live in today, less and less reference to the history of U.S.-British antagonism after the War of 1812 appears in school texts. Americans today have no idea that we were, for all practical purposes, an enemy of England up to the time that we allied with them during the First World War. The 20th century has all but erased this fact.

In addition, since we became allies of the British during World War I, Hollywood has romanticized the exploits of Britain in just about every conflict they were in, whether they were defending themselves or conquering their British Empire. It is amazing how a conquering England has been made by Hollywood to look like the victim when indigenous peoples tried to maintain their independence from inclusion into the British Empire.

Our people have come under a blanket of propaganda to convince us that England is our sister, sometimes our mother, even though they may use the term cousin. This propaganda has been used to engage our country in very dangerous foreign entanglements with modern Great Britain and Europe for one hundred years.

The English people, while a pleasant race, have not always had pleasant people rule them — any more than we have.

We went to war with the English in 1812 for many of the same reasons war with the French could have been waged. The difference was that the English worked to gain a favorable position among the Federalists, but not as a revolutionary movement and not to destroy the old social order. And, they had initiatives aimed at negating the influence of America, and possibly regaining it, as a possession of England.

John Henry, an Irishman, lived in America for a number of years and served in the U.S. Army during the initial period of trouble with France. He wrote articles against the republican system of government, and this brought him to the attention of the governor general of Canada, Sir James Henry Craig. He employed Henry in 1809 to find out to what extent of dissatisfaction there was in the New England states and what the outcome might be there if a war with England were take place — would they stand with the rest of the country, or, would they go so far as to break off and secede? The possibility of using New England's dissatisfaction as a means of weakening the United States was the end in mind.

An extract of Governor Craig's letter:

> I request you to proceed with the earliest conveyance to Boston.... The known intelligence and ability of several of its leading men, must give it a considerable influence over the other states, and will probably lead them in the part they are to take.... It has been supposed that if the Federalists of the Eastern States should be successful, and obtain the decided influence which may enable them to direct public opinion, it is not improbable that, rather than submit, they will exert that influence to bring about a *separation from the general Union*.... I enclose a credential, but you must not use it unless you are satisfied it will lead to more confidential communications.
> — *A Youth's History of the Great Civil War in the United States, From 1861 to 1865*, Horton, 1866

Once the plot became known to President Madison, his message to Congress on the subject read:

> I lay before Congress copies of certain documents (that) prove that ... the British Government, through its public minister here, a secret agent of that government was employed, in certain states, more especially at the seat of government in Massachusetts, in fomenting disaffection to the constituted authorities of the country; and intrigued with the disaffected, for the purpose of bringing about resistance to the laws, and eventually, in concert with a British force, of destroying the Union, and forming the eastern part thereof into a political connection with Great Britain.
> — *From James Madison to Congress, March 9, 1812*, Archives.gov

There were a number of prominent men in New England who were strongly opposed to the Union due to the course the country had been taking toward democracy and declared so in no uncertain terms, some going well beyond what we would consider today to have been prudent. It was similar to the problems that Burr was able to capitalize on in his plot in the West, except the dissatisfaction there was in *support* of democracy rather than opposed to it.

Henry wrote back to the authorities in Canada that, although he found disunion among the leaders of the Federalists in New England, it was not found among the common people; he hinted that slavery might be used as a device to eventually disaffect the common man into disunion in time. Whether this became a goal of the British foreign service or not, there was an English bent to American abolition in the years to come.

Subsequent events caused Henry to reveal his mission to the federal government, and this was broadcast as another reason to be at war with England. There was speculation that it was a ploy to enable the administration to use the story to justify the war with England rather than France. Events that followed concerning Henry gave credence to the original story.

History as taught in American schools tells the story of our war with England, but rarely talks about the *level and breadth* of French agitation that existed at the same time.

The War of 1812 elevated Andrew Jackson into a national hero as a result of his victory over the English at New Orleans. His reputation remains thus today, but few know aspects of Jackson's life that would raise the eyebrows of modern readers.

For instance, Jackson engaged in the slave trade and one time transported slaves across Indian land, which was against the law. Silas Dinsmore, an Indian agent in Tennessee, enforced the law that Negroes could not pass through Indian lands without passports. Jackson had done so while Dinsmore was away, and it led to an argument because Dinsmore was trying to uphold the law. Through Jackson's influence, Dinsmore was replaced and reduced to a state of poverty. Jackson also had a low opinion of Indians, not just of slaves.

Jackson was known for his temper and considered even friends who offered advice contrary to his opinion as enemies. His appointment as the head of the Tennessee militia was marked as much by his getting into loggerheads with other military commanders as it was his final victory over the British at New Orleans.

Due to Jackson's political involvement with people who were friendly with revolutionary France, it would have been interesting to see if he would have been as aggressive against France if we had been at war with them instead of Britain in the War of 1812. It is highly unlikely he would have had the assistance of Jean Lafitte and the French-influenced Louisiana citizens if the enemy had been France, as he did because it was the British he was fighting.

Even so, there were traitors in New Orleans who gave information to the British, and many of the French were not too happy about being in the middle of a war. Jackson declared martial law and ordered the French inhabitants into the interior. He drafted men to fight and went house to house to find anything that could be used to defend the area and confiscated it. He arrested a judge who had issued writs of habeas corpus as a result of the arbitrary arrest and confinement of citizens without warrant. After the war Jackson was fined $1,000 for his actions, a sizable sum at the time. Later, in 1843, the Congress paid him back with interest.

The benefit of Jackson's victory was that it gave respect for America as an adversary. Other than that, the goals desired by bellicose Americans for the war were never met, such as the conquering of Canada. Plus we sided with the loser in Europe — Napoleon.

Another problem that came of the war was the terrible financial situation it produced, much of it due to Treasury Secretary Albert Gallatin. He had promised the war could be waged without raising taxes, and then went to Russia without quitting his post so that his replacement could not be named immediately to fill a very necessary office.

The truth of the matter was that America was in no shape to fight either France or England, yet we had ample cause to fight both. Washington and Adams knew this and they did all they could to prevent war while they held office. Later politicians were not as prudent and used the war fever for their own purposes.

After the Treaty of Ghent had been signed ending the war, the English kept agents in Florida, the

Northwest, and the Pacific Coast to stir up trouble for the U.S. One of the longest ongoing problems with England came as a result of these agents in the Pacific Northwest aiming at the settlers who went west by what became known as the Oregon Trail.

The treaty was negotiated by a team that included Jonathan Russell, John Quincy Adams, James A. Bayard, Henry Clay, and Albert Gallatin. Russell was Charge d'Affairs in Paris and was later replaced by Joel Barlow, the friend of Paine who was heavily involved in the French revolutionary schemes.

The war against England in 1812 was financed by loans proposed by Gallatin. These loans were disastrous failures, and made money for a small group of men while destroying others. The federal government was generally impotent and it was the states that raised the arms and men.

The party then in power, which had criticized Hamilton's bank and taxation, now supported the bank and began to discuss these measures and more. On the day the news of the Treaty of Ghent reached Washington City, February 13th, they were discussing a paper-money bank.

Alexander J. Dallas, part of the Jacobins years before, promoted the scheme for a national bank after the war. In his later years, Gallatin was hired by John Jacob Astor to head his National Bank of New York. Thus, in the beginning, the radicals were against the U.S. Bank and chastised Hamilton over it, but many were for it later when they held the reins of power or could benefit themselves financially.

As a result of emigration to the Oregon territory, we came very close to war with England again due to the dispute over the border between the United States and British Canada. The settlement of Americans in what became Oregon and Washington States made it obvious that the territory was going to be American; the question of how much of it led to the friction. One of the campaign slogans during the day was, "Fifty-four Forty or Fight." This referred to the 54°40′ latitude desired by the Manifest Destiny-Young America group as the northern border. It would have included all of the productive landscape of Western Canada. It was settled at 49° except for the southern tip of Vancouver Island.

After the Democratic Societies evolved into a political party and gained control of the federal government, two of the major issues that would have a major impact on the future of the United States were the initial changes in the electoral college and the requirements for citizenship. The former elevated the political parties into power; the latter was the first step in the process of lowering the standards among the electorate. The Federalists had a requirement of 14 years residency before citizenship could be attained. This was part of the Alien and Sedition Acts initiative to check the Jacobins. The Democrats changed this to five years, the ramifications of which we shall see later on. The next major change in the government structure occurred in the Andrew Jackson era.

Andrew Jackson built his reputation by bellicose means, making sure that all good Indians were dead Indians, or at least displaced Indians. His treatment of and lack of keeping his word to them was a scandal to some, a blessing to others. His blatant disregard for the Constitution in these affairs was breathtaking. Regardless, his reputation rose among those less concerned about constitutional government due to his victories over Indian tribes.

Jackson was a notorious adulterer and a man who had to have his own way. He invaded Florida against orders, almost putting us on the path to war with Spain. An attempt was made to censure him in the Congress as a result of both his invasion of Florida and his execution of two Englishmen. The measure failed, but the sentiment was expressed by Henry Clay, who was astounded by the violence and lawlessness of Jackson's actions:

> I hope gentlemen will deliberately survey the awful isthmus on which we stand ... they may

bear down all opposition; they may even vote the general the public thanks; they may carry him triumphantly through this House; but if they do, in my humble judgment, it will be the triumph of the principle of insubordination, a triumph of the military over the civil authority, a triumph over the powers of this House, a triumph over the Constitution of the land. And I pray most devoutly to heaven, that it may not prove, in its ultimate effects and consequences, a triumph over the liberties of the people.

— *The Life and Speeches of Henry Clay*, Volume I, 1843

The man behind Jackson for president was William B. Lewis. While William Graham Sumner, the Order, was not what we would call a constitutionalist, nonetheless in his book *Andrew Jackson* in 1892 said this about Lewis:

Lewis was the great father of wire-pullers. He first practiced in a masterly and scientific way the art of starting movements, apparently spontaneous, at a distance, and in a quarter from which they win prestige or popularity, in order that these movements may produce, at the proper time and place, the effects intended by the true agent, who, in the mean time, prepares to be acted on by the movement in the direction in which, from the beginning, he desired to go. On this system political activity is rendered theatrical. The personal initiative is concealed. There is an adjustment of *roles*, a *mise en scène*, and a constant consideration of effect. Each person acts on the other in prearranged waves. Cues are given and taken, and the effect depends on the fidelity of each to his part. The perfection of the representation is reached when the audience or spectators are disregarded until the finale, when the chief actor, having reached the *dènoument* towards which he and his comrades have so long been laboring, comes to the footlights and bows to the "will of the people." Lewis showed great acuteness in his manaeuvres.

If Sumner isn't describing a *conspiracy* then the word has no meaning. Lewis was the husband of one of Mrs. Jackson's nieces.

Sumner was an example of members of the Order who could take either side of the argument to serve the general goals of the Order.

He was an advocate of laissez-faire economics, an opponent of socialism, but was frequently described as a social-Darwinist. Man was nothing more, or had no more rights than any other animal according to him. He promoted Nature rather than God.

By his above quoted passage, it appears that the tactic of assuming the leadership of both sides was in play. Jackson was moving the country away from the Constitution and his opponents were doing the same. Such later writings by the likes of Sumner, telling the truth about Jackson and his political machine, served to criticize the Democrats so as to make the Republicans look good.

Sumner had all of the attributes of a man who helped lead the intellectual thought of conservatives, but whose theories would ultimately destroy the social order. Modern conservatives have such men in abundance. In 1876, he was named to teach a new course called *sociology* at Yale.

In other words, Sumner was able to become a leader in the conservative movement by advocating free enterprise and other economic aspects of the conservatives, but at the same time was able to inject into the movement a philosophy that had in mind the destruction of the Judeo-Christian foundation on which the Constitution was laid. The long view was the death of Christianity and Judaism.

This is a twist of a similar situation where those who advocate all the right things, including the social issues connected to Christianity, will at the same time support internationalism that will destroy the Constitution and the very social issues they profess to support in the long run.

In both scenarios, the average person only listens to the rhetoric and supports the leader, and does not extend the lines out to the inevitable end of what is being sold as conservatism.

The Constitution has always been a problem for the Conspiracy. It has proven to be a steady rock in a sea of political machinations. Once the Jacobins gained control of the federal government, they were stymied by its provisions. The same situation exists today, and many are hard at work trying to find ways to change, rewrite, or simply ignore the document. What stands in the way is the general understanding level of the Constitution among the American electorate.

By the late 1820s, the issue was between strict constitutionalists and those who wanted the federal government to promote industry, schools, transportation, and nationalism. This would place more power into the government, and the early conspirators used this platform to create propaganda to the level that the state sovereignty advocates and strict constitutionalists were called "radicals."

This is similar to constitutionalists being called extremists by the leadership of both the political parties in the 20th and 21st centuries. The constitutionalists simply wanted the government to live up to the oath taken by all public servants and politicians.

Early in our history it was to the advantage of the Conspiracy to want to divide the country. The movement then evolved into two camps: those who advocated state sovereignty and those who advocated nationalism. By the 1820s, the Conspiracy ruled both. These camps would come to manifest themselves as the Young America group and the communists, albeit they were united in a common goal of world government, just using different means.

One had to be careful not to lend weight to the subversive aspects of either movement if they genuinely believed in either position. In reality the leadership of both camps had the same goals, but the Young Americans ultimately used the states rights issue to foment division in the country as a means to react people into supporting a situation that would result in exactly the opposite — nationalism, and from there, empire.

The nationalists tended to rally to the flag of Andrew Jackson for the presidency.

DeWitt Clinton fell in line for the presidential bid by Jackson, as did Edward Livingston, who had joined Jackson as one of the men in Congress who opposed the policies of George Washington.

Clinton and Jackson later would have personal ambitions to be named to an office of general grand commander or general grand high priest of the union in their branch of Masonry. This created a split in the political movement that needed a remedy. The remedy was found in the Anti-Masonic Party we will address later.

Many rallied to the side of Jackson because they believed New England was plotting secession, as some had tried to do during the fever of the War of 1812. Some opposed him because they believed that the Jackson candidacy would unite "the purse and the sword," since what he wanted was a government-operated bank.

Apparently the men who controlled the bank felt that he was anti-bank, regardless of the impression others may have had, at least anti-bank in its original form. They even used bank funds to support Henry Clay against the Jackson candidacy.

Each party regarded the bank as an available power in politics, and each tried to get control of it. The party that failed originally (the Democrats) then denounced the bank as dangerous to the state. While some of the stock was owned by foreign interests, the bank would not publish a list of its stockholders. This created a problem for the states because they could not tax stockholders in their states, and "loans" were extended to congressmen before crucial votes on the bank.

The same is suspected today of the Federal Reserve in regard to both domestic and foreign bankers who control the Fed, since too many politicians retire as multi-millionaires having started their political career as average investors, particularly U.S. senators. There was and still is evidence of powerful senators ramming through legislation that enhances their investments, and more evidence of powerful men using their positions to aggrandize their personal fortune or that of their immediate family. This was certainly true of Stephen Douglas before the Civil War, and accusations currently exist today against Harry Reid.

The bank also gave "loans" to newspapers that opposed the bank, in order to get them to change their position.

Some of the men close to Jackson convinced him to oppose the bank. Jackson wanted the bank to be part of the Treasury, not privately owned, and it would have provided government control over all of the banks. It wasn't really a matter of being against economic control per se, but how to control and who would wield the power.

This may have been the reason some opposed Jackson — He was a man who wanted the government to have a hands-on relationship with the bank and use it for the political ends of the government, exclusive of any other controls. Couple this with his bellicose generalship, and many feared him as a result.

The accumulation of power into the executive branch under Jackson was huge for its day. Sen. Peleg Sprague, in the Senate on January 29, 1834, in reference to Jackson said:

I may be deemed an alarmist. There is cause for alarm. When one man, encroaching upon Congress, the Senate, and the judiciary, arrests and rolls back the course of legislation; interprets laws, treaties, and constitutions; assumes the sole power of appointment, — holding at the same time absolute power over the army, the navy, the post office, an affiliated press, and the whole swarm of executive officers, — and now superadded to all this, tremendous money power, the fiscal agency engrafted upon banking capital, — can liberty be safe? Safe — when a boa-constrictor is closing around her his crawling and crushing folds?
— *Speech of Mr. Sprague on the removal of the deposits: delivered in the Senate of the United States, January, 1834*

Regarding Jackson's plan to eliminate the Bank of the U.S. and replace it with a government national bank, House Ways and Means Chairman George McDuffie said:

Such control would introduce more corruption in the government than all the patronage now belonging to it. It was a desperate financial experiment, without parallel in the history of the world.

It was without parallel at the time — 1913 and the establishment of the Federal Reserve were a long way off.

The first U.S. bank was established by the Washington administration, with Hamilton at the helm of the Treasury Department. The bank was established because there was a need for funding, taxes could not be collected with proficiency at the time, and the federal government had assumed the war debts of the states. The solution was a bank.

The main issue with it among many politicians of the day was who would control it, rather than it being detrimental to the general economic well-being of the country. Once the opponents of the bank got into power, they supported it.

Modern economists and historians are not in universal agreement as to the value of the U.S. Bank to the economy and society in early America.

Jackson simply wanted to use it for his own purposes and was thwarted, and so became an opponent of the bank. *His rhetoric regarding its abolition was generally sound*, but the reality of destroying the "bankers" was fiction. He just moved the money power out of the public eye by the closure of the bank. The monies were then deposited in seven state-chartered "pet" banks that were owned by men who were friendly to the administration.

From this time on, the money power resided within the hands of a select few families. This has remained the case up to the administration of Franklin D. Roosevelt and beyond.

An example of the type of men who had a great deal of influence in the bank was Stephen Girard, a director of the second U.S. Bank, and its largest investor. He was a disbeliever in Christianity. He bequeathed his estate to build Girard College for orphans, and stipulated that no ecclesiastic missionary or minister of any sect whatever was to hold any connection with the college, or be admitted to the premises, even as a visitor.

Nicholas Biddle, the head of the bank, was important in the establishment of Girard College under the provisions of Girard's will.

The electoral college underwent another change during the Jackson era, from a congressional caucus to more like the system we see today, and the power of the executive branch also grew in both the federal and state governments during this period.

For all the pronouncements of the democratic movement in the first half of the 1800s, the one prominent feature was the growth of the executive and the diminishing of the legislative power all across the states and federal government — the opposite of what they professed to stand for.

Much of the popular support for such an accumulation of power was that the public was willing to entrust power to one man but was jealous of the authority of a legislative aristocracy or "banking aristocracy." In other words, the people were manipulated into giving power to the executive as opposed to Congress in the name of ridding the country of the U.S. Bank. This in part was how it was sold.

The historian Raymond G. Gettell wrote about the ascendency of Jacksonian politics in this manner:

The election of Jackson in 1828 marked the success of the movement of separation of church and state, a hostile attitude toward the landed interests by the removal of property and religious qualifications, direct control by the people, and a nationalistic movement away from states rights.
— *History of Political Thought*, 1924

Removal of property and religious qualifications referred to the property qualification to vote and the religious qualifications to hold state offices in some states.

By the end of the Jackson era the country was in great flux politically, with the coming and going of several new political parties. The influx of immigrants with a socialist agenda was beginning to become a problem. The American society that produced the United States was undergoing change. Politics became a petri dish of experimentation, both in and out of government.

What ultimately emerged were two primary strategies for world government within American politics.

6

THE RISE OF "TWO" CONSPIRACIES

During the period from 1820 up to the Civil War, a variety of movements arose expanding on Illuminist aims, most with overlapping leadership.

Socialism, anti-Christianity, abolitionism, etc., became noticeable all across American society. They had been relatively insignificant movements for some time after the demise of the Democratic Societies, but after 1820 exploded on the scene as a result of painstaking organizing.

There was still a residual influence due to the French Jacobins, even though their wing of the Conspiracy had waned. The ideas they propagated lingered while their sons and protégés carried on, slowly amassing influence without the visible street agitation.

From this time on until 1848, the impetus for radicalizing America came primarily from Germany through Americans educated there, and later from England due to the influence of Chartists and the leadership of the Continental communists and Carbonari sojourning in London. The Continent had become a very dangerous place for most radical leaders, so many had been moving in and out of England for decades. London became their hub until it moved to the United States after the Civil War.

These American organizations all had one thing in common besides their overlapping leadership: overthrowing the old social order. All had high sounding causes, particularly abolition. The majority of Americans did not believe in slavery, but rational solutions would not be allowed to prevail.

The idea that slaves were property became the means for the radical abolitionists to attack property rights in general. Abolition became the issue through which the socialists meant to destroy the whole idea of private property rights. This campaign, primarily in the North, drove a wedge between them and their brethren in the South. In the South, organizations were established to counter these ideas. By no means, however, was the North devoid of agitation and unrest as a result of this subversion of the principle of property rights.

And in it all was an unseen hand guiding and fueling the fire on both sides of the issue.

Immigration also played a major role in the deterioration of our Republic and Constitution. The first wave *came as agents* of the government of Revolutionary France. Later, this reversed itself as radical elements started to come to the United States *fleeing* the reprisal of European governments after attempting revolutions, rather than being representatives of a successful revolution. The conspirators and their followers were always buried within a large wave of immigrants that ebbed and flowed into America. These tended to be German, English, and to an extent Irish in the first half of the 1800s.

The modern equivalent is the migration of peoples from Latin America, particularly Mexico. Within these millions of migrants are thousands of radicals and cartel minions whose purpose is the subversion of our Republic. Outside of the communities that have a substantial Hispanic population, the average American does not see the Atzlan movement — which is based in Marxism and is agitating for the return to Mexico of all Spanish territory claimed by the U.S. since the Lewis and Clark Expedition.

Were the United States to become involved in what has been nicknamed the North American Union — the merger of the three countries of Canada, the United States, and Mexico — the United States would only be part of something called North America. The movement of Latinos across our borders would not be hindered — there would be no borders. In addition, there would be no independence, hence no Constitution.

Most Americans are aware of the immigration of Germans and Irish to our shores in the 1800s, but there was also an influx of British citizens as a result of failed Chartist schemes. While there were many Germans who returned to Germany after living here for some time, there were even more English who returned to Britain. One does not know if they were on assignment as socialist leaders or whether they simply changed their minds about living here after getting homesick. In most of these cases, they had to flee their mother country and never really had the desire to remain here after things calmed down at home regarding their arrest and imprisonment.

Many of these revolutionaries returned home in triumph due to the changed political atmosphere in their country.

The radicals that stayed had a history of internal strife within any organization they formed, but they had one goal in common: to reinvent the United States in their image, and then use the United States as a base to establish their revolution around the world.

In this they have been increasingly successful, but they have never been able to consolidate absolute control over American citizens, and in turn the world, as a result of not being able to subjugate the American people.

The primary reason has been the layers of strength embedded within American society and the resilience of our Constitution. The people, as often as they were misled, nonetheless had a base of morality and a love of the Constitution that has been difficult to subvert. The social order, even though having been under attack, until the mid-20th century was stable enough to thwart totalitarianism since it was based on Judeo-Christian values, and these values were taught in the home, church, and schools, albeit less and less so over time.

With each new massive wave of immigration, coupled with native subversion, the social structure, religious zeal, and culture in general changed and slowly over time became very different from the society that founded the country.

Another reason for not being able to consolidate control was that radicals rarely got along for any length of time, with each one of them wanting to be the leader. This substantially blunted their efforts and success over the decades because they have never gotten along well enough to put the cause first over their personal ambitions — Burr is a case in point.

Recall that even Voltaire complained about this condition among those who comprised the members of the Conspiracy in his day. Of course, he was complaining about those who would not follow his every word! It was the same with Marx, Lenin, Stalin, etc.

On top of it all, throw in the biases against race, social status, etc. among the revolutionary leaders, and this has slowed their timetable considerably over the past two hundred years. They did not all want to work with "inferiors." It continues to be a problem for them today in their attempts to tie the earth into one neat political package.

Another more strategically-based reason may be *the look of failure* by the Conspiracy in America. As we shall see, the thought would be sustained by at least one arm of the Conspiracy to use the might and wealth of America to subvert the rest of the globe. If America sustained an Illuminist-style revolution, it would by its nature destroy the might and wealth of our people. If Americans could be fooled into playing into Illuminist hands with an international policy made to look "American," using America to subvert other countries, then it would behoove the Conspiracy to leave the United States with a modicum of freedom domestically and, in the process build control over the rest of the world to the point where the American people could not stop a combined international revolutionary force if they woke up domestically to what was going on and tried to stop the New World Order.

This could be accomplished by the use of foreign entanglements, something warned against by our Founders, including Washington and ultimately Jefferson. The United States had freed itself from all permanent foreign entanglements from 1800 until the formation of the United Nations and NATO. Since the formation of NATO, it has been rare that we were not at war somewhere around the globe under United Nations mandates made to appear as American initiatives, or in defense against aggression which was aided and abetted by certain Americans up to the first shot. In other words, we have helped build our own enemies.

NATO, the North Atlantic Treaty Organization, originally formed to protect Europe from the USSR, has been used to lead armed incursions into areas outside of Europe where we were told that the need for NATO existed, such as Iraq and Afghanistan. Now, quietly behind the scenes an initiative to expand NATO all around the globe, to include Asia, has been pushed forward by such American organizations that support the New World Order including the Council on Foreign Relations. Americans should look up the NATO treaty online and then extend the lines based on the subordination to the UN that exists within the first eight sections.

A totalitarian regime by its nature sucks the life out of a country; no such regime can last long without the infusion of capital or a foreign conquest to instill "patriotism" into the population to fight the foreign regime. This is a counterweight to the population not wanting to serve the state, due to either a totally socialist or a heavily taxed environment. Then there is the fact that in a "nanny state" the people only do what they have to and no more, even if they love statism. Either condition causes the economic situation to deteriorate to an unsustainable level without a fiercely patriotic initiative, such as a war — unless, as stated, there is an influx of foreign capital. This happened over and over again to the Union of Soviet Socialist Republics, or Russia. Today, Russia is sustained by the sale of natural gas and oil to Europe and its formal partnership with the United States. The same situation continues in communist China, with direct sales of Chinese goods to the West fueling their economy. Foreign capital keeps communist governments in power, otherwise the system is unsustainable.

In Russia, the American people helped finance communism through a variety of foreign aid, material and equipment, construction of factories, etc., all generally unbeknownst to the American people.[21]

The Republican administration under Richard Nixon and Henry Kissinger opened up America to

---

21 See *Western Technology and Soviet Economic Development*, in three volumes, published in 1968-1973. Also, *National Suicide: Military Aid to the Soviet Union*, 1973, both written by Antony Sutton. The latter is more mainstream reading. The first three volumes are very lengthy and detailed, intended for the scholar and researcher. Also, during the Vietnam War, massive amounts of aid in the form of material and supplies emanating from the United States and channeled through a variety of communist satellite countries found their way into North Vietnamese hands. So much so that The John Birch Society circulated a petition to stop aid and trade with communist countries at that time that garnered several million signatures, which were delivered to Congress.

The process continues with the signing of three partnership agreements (Bush, Clinton, and Bush) that spell out economic integration with Russia. These can be accessed using the Internet. In addition, R & D in fighter aircraft development and space exploration has been a cooperative venture between Russia and the United States through labs established by major American aircraft firms, both in Russia and China. Even the space lab is a joint venture. The situation is far more serious to the defense of the United States than even seasoned political activists can imagine.

Why would such conditions exist? As we will show over and over again, we have never had a real enemy we did not create after World War I. No country could stand up to the power of the United States unless we provided the means for them to do so and at the same time weakened our defenses.

This author was personally asked by a major aircraft manufacturer to work on selling quick-change cargo aircraft to two communist countries in the middle of the Vietnam War. Apparently, war materiel was not getting to the North Vietnamese quick enough by cargo ships. The author refused, and the company apparently either never did succeed in selling the planes or altered their plans.

China, ostensibly to block Russia, and once they started to ship cheap imports into America, the coffers of communist China became glutted — to be used against the American people as well as the nations of the Far East: Japan, South Korea, the Philippines, Vietnam, etc.[22]

During the height of the so-called Sino-Russian split, a friend of the author won a Ford Motor Company tour into communist China for selling a lot of Fords. The tour bus driver took the wrong turn and ended up at the fence line of a Chinese air force base. All of the planes parked on the other side of the fence were the latest model of Russian MIGs.

Also, we express the idea herein that America was opened up to China rather than the Establishment rhetoric of opening up China to America. It is a big difference and the rhetoric belied the reality of what really happened.

If one were desirous to use the might of America to conquer the world, the condition for retaining and capitalizing on that economic might had to be retained. A system of minimal, but adequate control and subterfuge would be necessary to complete that task.

This may seem to be contradictory. Yet one idea was to build up the communist empire with American might with the American people supporting the initiative because it was made to look like an *American* expansion of influence and territory. This then would become part of the *1984* model of the construction of the three regions of the world fighting each other to fool the people into doing anything to win the war, and another war, and another.

This would be accomplished by making the initiative appear to be anti-communist, thwarting the growth of communism around the world — except that our own government, while apparently supporting anti-communism, would be helping the growth of communism out of sight of the American people. Since World War I, we have never had an enemy that Americans did not help create — and, there has never been a country that became communist that our State Department or military did not assist in the process. This would take another book to document. Many, many books were written in the 1950s and 1960s detailing this astonishing statement, but they documented only one country at a time. A book needs to be written that ties them all together to show the pattern and personalities involved.

As we go forward, these strategies will become quite apparent. Keep in mind as well that we are dealing with a force that will zig and zag depending on what will further their agenda at any given moment. Never take your eye off their goal and you will have a better chance of figuring out the end result of any global problem you see in the media, regardless of how it plays out or who is involved playing friend or foe.

All this being said, domestically the steady growth in the number of domestic and foreign radicals has continued unabated from our nation's birth. Several American political parties have come and gone as a result. Due to an anti-Christian agenda as one of the main thrusts of this radicalism, Transcendentalism, deism, and spiritualism came on the scene decades before the Civil War and had a huge influence on the Christian population. Indeed, spiritualism had grown so influential just before the Civil War that there were religious leaders at the time who claimed that the war was its result — God punishing America.

As only one example, the Unitarian Church in the beginning was not as radical as it became. It was the work of Ralph Waldo Emerson and his friends that changed the sacraments, boiled down the very essence of Christianity into something called God — but in the steam boiled off Christ — and became centers for the socialization of America.

---

22 The whole idea of Russia and China being opposed to one another has been a myth, a tactic used to convince Americas to help communist China. This has been exposed many times by defecting KGB personnel. As well, attention to the many agreements between Russia and China would have also exposed the tactic as a lie.

Emerson's poetry was well accepted by the American people in his lifetime, as well as today. Who could not be stirred by his poem etched on the Minuteman Statue at the Concord Bridge? As a result of this status and the promotion of his reputation by socialist leaders such as Horace Greeley and George Henry Evans, his organizing and other writings did great harm.

One of the leaders of the Unitarians in their sect who opposed Emerson and Adin Ballou was Paul Dean, the leader of the Restorationist faction. He was one of the most important Masons before the Civil War as Grand General High Priest of the United States in his branch of Masonry. As important as he was, he lost his fight to restore the Unitarian Church to its roots, even losing his position as a minister over his flock, further demonstrating that Masonry is not the center of the Conspiracy.

There are historians who claim that Emerson was an anti-socialist; however, in criticizing the socialists, Emerson had high praise for them at the same time — and the reality was that he worked with them his entire life in organizations and in support of a variety of initiatives:

> I honor the generous ideas of the Socialists, the magnificence of their theories, and the enthusiasm with which they have been urged.
> — *The Works of Ralph Waldo Emerson: Lectures and Biographical Sketches*

In addition, Emerson lauded the key revolutionaries of the day, placing Mazzini on the side of freedom and effusively praised Kossuth. Emerson never criticized the Chartists of Britain. Indeed, his experiences in Europe during the 1848 revolutions moved him into the role of a radical revolutionary in the antebellum period.

Many of the changes brought about by radicals in our early history seem tame today looking back through our modern eyes, which have become habituated to the changes. Modern man has grown used to many of them and look upon these changes as normal, even as American. However, these changes set us upon a course that has led us to a modern America where the people are lacking in basic constitutional studies and government ethics, and in general relegate God to the back burner in public life.

The process is delineated in Karl Marx and Frederick Engels' 1848 book, *The Communist Manifesto*, and made it clear that certain steps once taken lead to further "despotic inroads on the old social order."

Others describe the process as "patient gradualism," moving forward a salami slice at a time. This is even accomplished by trying to move a radical agenda two steps forward and then taking one step back, producing an easing of tension and a "compromise." This tactic ensures that the radical agenda keeps moving forward a step at a time. It has an advantage of making one political party look radical and the other moderate, giving a home to both sides of the political spectrum while actually moving both in the same direction.

The process worked so well that by the time of the Eisenhower Republican administration in the 1950s, the Socialist Party stopped fielding a presidential candidate. Its leader, Norman Thomas said that so much progress had been made even under the Eisenhower years that there was no longer a need to do so.

Instead, the Socialist Party began to concentrate on the *original* characteristic of their work: organizing within the political process and the political parties to do their work *covertly*. By 2010, 70 congressmen openly declared themselves Social Democrats, the new name of the Socialist Party and the official representative to the Socialist International founded by Marx. At least another 12 did not come out into the open. In other words, over 15% of the congressmen were *organized* to promote the socialist agenda. This does not count those who belonged to other organizations whose purpose was to surrender United States sovereignty to something they call a New World Order, such as the Council on Foreign Relations.[23]

In addition, the official spokesman of the Communist Party USA declared in early 2015 that the CPUSA would continue to work within the Democrat Party since their success in doing so had far outstripped their ability to work openly as the CPUSA, and that their program was going forward disguised as being Democrat.

Yet, where did you read about this socialist coterie or the communist declaration in your local paper, or hear about it on any major television network? As to the CPUSA, they openly bragged about their tactics in their official newspaper. It is not a secret, except to those who only read and view the major media — even when it is fair and balanced.

When you consider that taking over a country by a socialist entity has never required more than 3% of the population — due to the socialists' ability to organize — 15% in the Congress is a very large number.

This is a modern manifestation of a problem that has been around from the very beginning. They never campaign on the platform of open socialism; rather they fool the people with their rhetoric, telling them what they want to hear.

Much has been done over the years and been widely accepted, even glorified, as part of a process of laying Lilliputian threads over the American system of government and society. The example of the life of Robert Dale Owen, which we will discuss later, provides an illustration of the subtleties of this process prior to the Civil War even though he was very open about his affiliations. Once these threads are numerous enough, they will be drawn tight.

During the late 1840s a new party came onto the scene, the Equal Rights Party (better known as the Locofocos, the reason why is not important). They represented the radical wing of the Democrat Party and wanted an even more egalitarian movement.

They were built on an anti-bank, anti-paper money, and anti-monopoly platform. Considering the people who were involved, it would seem to be a contradiction. The core formed out of an anti-Tammany movement and the Working Men's Party. They supported Andrew Jackson.

The leaders included Alexander Ming, Jr., William Leggett, William Cullen Bryant, John Commerford, and Walt Whitman. Bryant would die many years later from complications from a fall he sustained when leaving a ceremony in Central Park in honor of the revolutionary Carbonari leader Mazzini.

Remember that the communists and socialists state that they are against "Wall Street" and the bankers, yet one of their main platforms is the centralization of banking, credit, and money into the hands of the state. They campaign against *private monopoly* but their solution is a *government monopoly*.

Another man prominent in the movement was Henry K. Smith, a participant in the Patriot War. This was a rebellion on both sides of the border with Canada in 1838-39. The short story is that it came about due to the work of the Canadian Alliance Society, which was a Canadian Owenite association (as in Robert Owen). It evolved into open rebellion.

On the American side, the Hunters' Lodge was formed, a secret anti-British, America militia in the states surrounding the Great Lakes. This organization supplied some of the army that was ultimately defeated by the British. Smith was a captain in this force of volunteers. He went on to become the mayor of Buffalo, New York.

---

23 Use the Internet to find Social Democrats in Congress. Likewise, go to the Council on Foreign Relations and compare their membership list with the membership in Congress. Also, consult the recommended reading list at the end of this book to fully acquaint yourself with the CFR. If you carry this study even further into globalist organizations, you will be shocked at just how many congressmen on both sides of the aisle are involved in subverting the independence of the United States.

Few Americans have ever heard of this war or other initiatives to promote the idea of conquering our neighbors. Surprisingly, neither have Canadians.

Perhaps no organization involved in schemes to occupy our neighbors has had a more profound effect on the nation in the long run than Young America (YA). Yet as important as it was, very few mainstream histories published even give it a mention, let alone relate its origins, influence, and the personalities who were the leaders of the movement.

Even the four or five comprehensive volumes published on YA either obfuscate or do not grasp the conspiratorial aspects of the subject, never mentioning that YA was directly linked to the "Young" movement of the Carbonari in Europe. If any mention of the Carbonari is raised, it is simply written off as "inspiring" the rise of YA.

We know that there were a number of *Americans* who fought with the Carbonari army led by Garibaldi all through the 1840s. How many there were and if they rotated through back to America and became prominent in the YA movement is relatively unknown. It was likewise the case in the so-called democratic revolutions of 1848-49 all over Europe. With the latter, however, we do have a little knowledge as it pertained to YA participation.

We have information as to the men who served as *leaders* with Garibaldi who served on both sides of the Civil War — most with the South — but who are relatively unrecognized by modern readers. As we shall see, the Northern armies contained communists in leadership, while the Southern armies had a number of those who served in the Carbonari units in Europe: two conspiracies, supposedly in opposition, but in reality two fingers on the same hand. However, the North was not devoid of Garibaldi men in uniform.

Perhaps the most famous of those serving in the Union Army were what became known as Lincoln's Foreign Legion, the 39th New York Infantry. It was called the Garibaldi Guard at the time. Formed by a motley crew of former Garibaldi men, it contained nationals from all European countries. These men were communists, revolutionary deserters from European armies, and officers of dubious character.

We also know little about the men who were not Americans who fled to the United States after Garibaldi disbanded his legion. At the time, Garibaldi was ordered to flee to America or face arrest by the Austrians. He came.

We know that thousands of members of the secret societies of Europe came to the United States after the failed revolutions. We also know enough to tie YA with the Carbonari, even without a comprehensive study based on the people we can identify.

In the mid-1800s Western world only three major countries were not nationalized. These countries were Germany, Italy, and the United States. In each case, when they became nationalized the Young movement played a major role, and in only one was that role recognized and made an historical reality: Italy.

In all three cases, independent sovereign states coalesced into a centralized union. The unification of Germany in 1870 was, in the end, peaceful. The conspiracy had been working so long and successfully within the German Confederation and the people had grown so tired of conflict, that it was simply a matter of time. The cap on nationalism came with Adolf Hitler, whose conspiracy wiped out the last vestiges of the independence of the former German Confederation "states."

In Italy it was bellicose, but not to the extent it was in the United States. In America it cost the lives of well over a half a million men-at-arms in a Civil War — plus an untold number of civilians, black and white.

The YA movement came out of what was known as the Carbonari, a direct descendant of the Illuminati. There was linkage by the communist movement to the Carbonari and they did cooperate since they came from the same source, but they became distinctly separate.

History books generally say that Mazzini was the head of the organization, and some claim that it was Albert Pike, an American, who ultimately became the behind-the-scenes leader. Garibaldi was the leader of the Carbonari's military arm but was always a problem for the organization due to his fierce ego and his inability to moderate his *public* views.

Next to Lafayette, who was the leader of the French Carbonari for a time, it is difficult to find a personage who belonged to more secret cabals than Pike. During the Civil War, he was a brigadier general in the Confederate Army. The Indian soldiers under his command committed such atrocities on Union troops (plus there were charges of malfeasance of funds) that he was forced to resign his commission early in the war. After the war he helped form the Ku Klux Klan in Arkansas, according to two sources. This is disputed by Freemasonry. However, he was a decidedly pro-slavery man and held anti-Catholic and racial prejudices.

It is known that he united with Mazzini openly in the 1870s, associated with Helena Blavatsky, and used socialism as a front for Satanism.

Interestingly, one of the subjects of antique books and archives that have disappeared from libraries and archives around the country is KKK records and documentation.

Pike's Masonic activities are the best known of his public activities. He started out as a member of the Order of Odd Fellows, and then became a Mason. He was the Grand Master of the Masonic Lodge in the nation's capital in 1852, and an obscure statue of him exists not far from the Capitol on the edge of Liberty Square. It is rather ironic that the statue is mostly hidden from the street by low-lying tree branches. One must climb up to the statue to actually see it.

In 1859 he was elevated to the Grand Commander of the Supreme Council of the 33°, Southern Jurisdiction, headquartered in Charleston, South Carolina. His "manual," if you will, for the degree, *Morals and Dogma*, proliferates in the used bookstores and libraries across the country, indicating that it is not as important as some would believe in the scheme of secret societies; otherwise, it would be rare, meant for the initiated, not the profane. It has references of Lucifer being the Prince of Light and the guiding spirit. Lucifer is only another name for Satan.

We wish to remind the reader that Pike was the leader of both the 33° and a major leader of the international Carbonari at the same time. The Carbonari was a direct descendant of the Illuminati; it is difficult to document the antecedents of the 33°.

Printing and circulating the number of copies of Pike's *Morals and Dogma* well beyond Masonic membership should tell anyone that it cannot be the real inner ritual and creed. It is too public, so there has to be more to the story.

Plus, no one asks the questions, "What about the Northern jurisdiction? Where is their manual, and who headed it up?"

There was an attempt to form a Northern jurisdiction outside of "normal" Masonary by Harry J. Seymour of New York, who in 1852 visited Europe and was advanced by the Misraim and Memphis Masons to the 96°. He tried to make himself the leader of the Scottish Rite in the North at the time. Established American Masonry (particularly Pike and the rest of the Scottish Rite) considered these organizations and degrees to be spurious, and wrote that there was no degree higher than the 33°. The only famous individual known to be part of this "spurious" rite was Louis Blanc.

These latter rites have been hotbeds of contention, with individuals passing degrees around almost like hotcakes and with various attempts to take over the rites as the supreme leader for personal gain. This has led to a history of internal friction for nearly 200 years.

The York Rite, which is the oldest and more basic rite, says that there are only three degrees of true Masonry. Most Grand Lodges did not consider the 33° to be a legitimate order for decades.

The Northern Jurisdiction of the 33° started with the initiation of Masons from the North into the Southern Jurisdiction in 1813-1815. The current body was formed in 1867 by merging with the Cerneau Supreme Council in New York, a rival group. Benjamin Butler was initiated into the Northern 33° in 1864.

The Carbonari was a violent secret society that took blood oaths. It was started in 1807 by Jean-Pierre Briot. The ritual order of the modern Mafia is based on the Carbonari and the fasces became a symbol for them as it did Mussolini and his Black Shirts. Mussolini used the fasces as the symbol of fascism; that is the etymology of the word *fascism*. There are many clues that Mussolini's movement was simply a revitalized extension of the Carbonari. The symbols and slogans were too similar — either it was an extension or it was a copy.

If it was an extension, it shows the continuation of direct, rather than indirect influence of the Illuminati. We do know that Mussolini was a socialist first and a friend of Lenin before forming the "new" style of socialism called fascism. The Conspiracy has always altered the rhetoric and appearance of their initiatives to fit the targeted audience.

The peoples of Italy and Germany were not ready to allow the imposition of communism on their countries, so they were fooled into basically the same style of governments in the name of anti-communism. There is more than enough evidence that both Mussolini and Hitler were part of the socialist/communist international movement before changing into fascists.

The fasces was several rods bound together around an axe handle as one, with the head of the axe protruding out from it; it was the emblem of Roman power. We use it in Congress as an emblem on the pillars in the House Chamber, and it was placed on the old U.S. silver dime as well. It is a symbol that denotes strength in unity. One rod is easily broken; several rods bound together cannot be broken. The symbolism was relative to the unity of the states.

By 1812, the Carbonari extended all over Italy and had assumed their structure of secret local cells ruled by one: the Alta Vendita. Long after the waning of the larger Carbonari organization, it is apparent that the Alta Vendita carried on into the 20th century, particularly as an enemy of the Catholic Church. It gained considerable influence by infiltrating the Church over time.

Many believed that the Catholic Church could not be infiltrated due to the large amount of time that would be devoted to becoming ordained a priest. In addition, given the nature of those who would be doing the infiltrating, it was assumed that it would be highly unlikely they could remain celibate as required within the clergy. These people did not understand the depravity of the conspirators and that there were forms of sexual release that could be hidden from view within the walls of those cloistered seminaries controlled by these conspirators.

Modern man has concerned himself with the sexual deviations of certain clergy instead of asking an even bigger question: What is the true nature of the network of pedophiles? Is it simply sex, or is there another, more sinister aspect to what has been exposed in the 21st century?

The same could well be asked of the same situation within the modern Republican Party. There appears to be a network of similar propensities among the RINO (Republican In Name Only) and neoconservative wings of the GOP.

All throughout history, such proclivities in those who occupy positions of responsibility and power have led to totalitarian government coupled with the elimination of innocent citizens. There is more than one reason they are called deviants.

The Internet is rife with information on the modern Alta Vendita but again, one has to be careful to sift fact from fiction and racism. We know of no definitive study of the effect of the Alta Vendita on the fascist movement in the early 20th century. There are some "studies" that negate the influence of the Carbonari, even from Catholic sources. Most of them are anti-Semitic and next to worthless, not only due to the fact that they are racist, but because what facts are known are skewed by them.

In 1818, the Illuminati Fillipo Michele Buonarroti went into the Carbonari and had considerable influence on their direction and leadership. The third degree of the Carbonari was a carbon copy of the other organizations that were direct descendants of the Illuminati.

If this is the case, there can be little doubt the Carbonari is an extension of the Illuminati, as Leon Trotsky stated — unless one claims that Buonarroti was not an Illuminist. In any case, he became part of the leadership soon on and played a heavy role in the early years of the Carbonari. Considering the aims of the Carbonari there seems little doubt that other Illuminati were involved, with Buonarroti being the most notable.

There is no question that Buonarroti incorporated Illuminati structure, rhetoric, and symbolism into his efforts before and during his sojourn with the Carbonari. There is much evidence that after Weishaupt left Bavaria he had a great deal of direct influence on new subjects, one of them being Buonarroti.

The Carbonari used the art of infiltration and recruitment of the local officials and police. In this manner it prevented the authorities from exercising their duties when it came to the lawlessness of the Carbonari. And, just as with the Illuminati, their second-tier members were encouraged to form their own organizations; many revolutionary societies came from this effort.

Adam Weishaupt died in 1830, having served as a professor at Göttingen University. It seems doubtful that he did not engage in the same activities he did as the head of the Illuminati in Bavaria; that was his nature. It is amazing how many noteworthy American conspirators studied at this university in Germany.

By 1820, the Carbonari had led their first attempt at revolution in Naples, but it was suppressed by Austria.

The oaths and articles of Young Italy were quite revealing, and since this was a front group, the oaths of the parent Carbonari must have been worse. Article 30 of Young Italy stated: "Those who refuse obedience to the orders of this secret society, or reveal its mysteries, die by the dagger without mercy." This is indicative of the remaining articles.

The endgame was a socialist government wherever they could wrest control, and the process was a continuation of the goals of the Illuminati, particularly in regard to hatred of the Christian religion. The Carbonari were particularly vicious toward Catholicism, and even attempted to isolate and then destroy the Vatican with Garibaldi's army. The plan failed ultimately, but Garibaldi never wavered in his hatred for all things Catholic.

This hatred was such that even his fellow conspirators backed away from his rhetoric and open venom. They may have agreed with him, but not in such a brazen and open manner. Considering this, why did he become so adulated by American politicians as he was? The answer we leave to you.

The goals of the Carbonari were identical to those of the Illuminati. It is regrettable that so many references to the Carbonari and/or Mazzini refer to them as nationalists. This creates a false image of what they really were. It is true that the first step they wanted in many countries was nationalism, but only as a first step toward their goal of internationalism.

This use of semantics convinced the reader that the Carbonari's goals were different than what they actually were. More importantly, using the term *nationalist* created a disconnect in the reader's mind of any thought behind their actions in league with an international master conspiracy.

They at first established "Young" groups all over Europe as nationalist organizations, but then coalesced them into Young Europe as internationalists wanting a unified Europe: from nationalism to regionalism to internationalism.

For a time, the Illuminati Lafayette was the leader of the Carbonari in France in the early years of its formation, playing a role in the Revolution of 1830. Lafayette belonged to so many secret societies it is hard to document them all. He was one of the founders of the Society of 1789, limited to 600 members including Mirabeau, DuPont de Nemours, and Marquis de Condorcet.

Thomas Jefferson, as minister to France, contributed to the overthrow of Louis XVI. He became a coadjutor of the revolutionists, opening his doors to Jacobins and agents of Condorcet and Mirabeau.

Jefferson, by his actions and especially by his advice to Lafayette (contrary to the advice of Washington), hastened the downfall of the royal French government and installation of the revolutionary cabal. The actions, for any reader to research, would include his support for Jacques Necker and comte de Mirabeau, his attack on comte de Vergennes and the Farmers-General, stifling the offer to buy flour from American merchants and Robert Morris' French business connections, etc.

Lafayette had started out as a member of the Jacobins but later left them. Many organizations and prominent members originally helped start the revolution in France and then quit to profess loyalty to king and constitution once the revolution was inevitable. This became the tactic years later in America, where conspirators would promote disunion (civil war) until it become a reality and then became strict unionists. In the South they were staunch secessionists who then became disruptive of the new Confederate government.

Members of the nobility who were non-conspirators looked upon Lafayette as a revolutionary responsible for the deaths of the king and others. The Austrians imprisoned him after he fled to their country and treated him badly, since they had the same opinion. They also had a list of members of the Illuminati that contained his name.

The man who helped Lafayette escape from Austria was Dr. Justus Erich Bollman, who later ended up in the scheme of Aaron Burr to separate the western territory from the United States. When the scheme fell apart, Lafayette sent a letter to Jefferson to intercede on behalf of Bollman on April 29, 1807; Bollman had been arrested in connection with the Burr plot.

The French Carbonari under Lafayette formed a kinship with the Grand Orient Masons of France and Italy. Initially Lafayette joined the Masonic Grand Orient in France, not the American Masonry as some histories state.

The Scottish-born American Frances "Fanny" Wright became an intimate of Lafayette after he read her book, *Views of Society and Manners in America*, in 1821. She lived in his home for three years and participated with him in his Carbonari activities. She also traveled with Lafayette for most of the time during his visit back to America.

She often wrote Lafayette in cipher during their Carbonari intrigues. She supported Jackson in the 1830s and was an advocate of many socialist initiatives, such as promoting the idea that children should be taken away from their parents at age two and raised and educated in publicly supported schools. She, Amos Bronson Alcott, and the Owenites promoted this idea until it became — and remains today — a main ingredient in the agenda of the socialist leaders in education, albeit a hidden agenda from the public.

While Lafayette was the head of the Carbonari in France, he wrote to the person whom the Carbonari had installed as leader of Greece in a revolution, that the Carbonari expected, he would hope, for the "formation of one Vast and Powerful Republic." This is reminiscent of the goal of the Illuminati and a precursor of the European Union.

During the period of the Italian campaign, Carbonari leaders laughed at the zeal of common members who sacrificed themselves for Italian liberty. This is usual for any secret society whose aim is revolution. The minions die while the leaders flourish, and the leaders hold them in more contempt than they do their enemies since they are dupes.

More recently, many black Americans left the communist movement after they discovered this attitude among the hierarchy of the Communist Party. These included Manning Johnson, who was a member of the U.S. Communist Party Central Committee.

A friend of Johnson, Leonard Patterson, trained at the main communist training school in Moscow and roomed with Gus Hall, who became the leader of the U.S. Communist Party. Later Patterson left the party and toured the United States for The John Birch Society to tell the American people, particularly his race, what was really going on inside the so-called civil rights organizations.

Both of these men, Patterson and Manning, used the term "cannon fodder" in reference to how the communists planned to use colored races for agitation and revolution in the United States and other countries around the world.

The most classic example of using people for a goal entirely different than what they believe is the Assassins of the Middle East during the Middle Ages. The minions would carry out assassination assignments that were suicidal. They were told they would go to Islamic heaven if they did the bidding of the Master of the Assassins, and died in the process.

What they would do is get young adherents intoxicated, apparently by drugs, and have them wake up in a garden valley with young women, wine, etc. The adherents would wander the valley and imbibe of the "nectar" of the garden — which they were forbidden to do in "real" life — and then be put to sleep again. Upon revival, they would be told that the Master had allowed them to see heaven and if they did as they were commanded to do and should die in the process, what they had just experienced would be their eternal reward.

The dupes would carry out the bidding of the "Old Man," or the "Lord of the Mountain" as the Master was referred to, thinking they were going to attain heaven. Some were so indoctrinated that they would commit suicide on command as an example to outsiders of the absolute obedience to the Master by his minions, and thus by demonstration would give the message to the outsider that the Master could have his minions do anything, anytime, anywhere to implement his will.

Is this preposterous, or does it have a familiar ring to the modern mind?

Its leaders would profess Islam and the young men would believe it. But the hierarchy was not Islamic. It was a ruse to enlist the zeal of young Muslims to die for the purpose of accumulating power into the Assassin leadership. The lower ranks of this secret society were Islamic. The higher one went in the order, the more it had to do with power that the leaders believed in, not Islam. By the third degree the initiate was shown the absurdities of the Koran.

At one point the organization held sway over much of the Arabic Muslim world. It was broken up, supposedly, during the Crusades. However, texts published in the 1800s claim the sect survived here and there, even as far east as India. Some believe that the Thuggees were the descendants of the Assassins, and the Thugs themselves claimed to be descended from Muslim tribes in the Middle East.

The roots of the Assassins were in the Shiah sect of Islam, which had built the power of the Imams. In the beginning the power within the sect was centered in a conspiracy not unlike the modern secret societies.

It began with young devoted Muslims, but by the eighth degree, the devotees had to believe that all religion, philosophy, and the like were fraudulent. Complete obedience to the chief of the sect was substituted. Once the power of the Shiah sect started to wane, the leader of the Assassins built his empire on that structure.

The reason most school children have never heard of this is that it is strikingly similar to the situation in the late 20th century, and knowledge of it would wake up Americans to what is truly going on in the 21st century in the Muslim nations. Terrorist organizations have nothing to do with Islam except as a ruse to fool people and keep them from looking beyond the surface to find the real source and leadership. They have everything to do with gaining power, using the Islamic faith to motivate those who would not die simply to bring megalomaniacs to power. The epicenter of Islamic terror is not in Mecca.

Any organization seeking power will usually take on the trappings of the religion or minority religion of any country or area targeted as a means of gaining adherents and minions at the entry level of the movement. At the leadership level the religion means nothing, since it is a façade.

There have been television programs in recent years to discredit the entire idea that the Assassins ever existed, that they are mythology. In this manner they prevent any curious student from looking into the "myth" and realizing as a result that the same type of organization may exist today in the Muslim world. Once this conclusion is reached, the next question would be, who is running it? And, the answer to that necessitates another book to document the hard-to-believe conclusion.

Young Italy, Young Ireland, Young Germany, Young Europe, Young America, etc. were all fronts of the Carbonari. Since the Carbonari demanded absolute obedience, many would unite under the Young movement without becoming directly involved in the even more secretive and violent aspects or the oath to the Carbonari.

The Young movements appearing to be nationalistic served two more basic purposes besides the obfuscation of conspiratorial connections: One, to start the adherent out from a position of patriotism for his country, indoctrinating him until he became an internationalist. Two, to serve as the basis for changing the system within the particular country into a national government as opposed to a royal government or confederation. The indoctrination would continue to facilitate the next major stage of the leadership's aim of world domination: a united socialist Europe.

A modern manifestation of the Young movement also occurred in a Muslim society during the early 20th century under Ataturk, the leader of the Young Turks, and led to the modern Turkish secular government. The stage was set for this event by the defeat of the Turks in Palestine. Almost everywhere else, the Turks as allies of Germany beat the British badly during World War I, although the average American has no idea that this was the case, in part due to the story of Lawrence of Arabia taking their eyes off the bulk of the Turkish campaign.

As we have mentioned, modern historians refer to Mazzini and the Carbonari movement as essentially nationalists. This is only true relative to their immediate goals in any given country. They named each Young organization after the country in order to project this façade at first. But their goals were always internationalism, a one-world government, and that included the U.S.

Famous individuals who were members of the Carbonari included Napoleon III, Lafayette, Garibaldi, Andre Ledru-Rollin, and Madame Blavatsky, the occultist. Just because people were members of the Carbonari did not mean that they always got along or agreed as to which tactics to use. In the case of Napoleon III, he used the Carbonari for his own benefit to help him come to power in France. This the Carbonari resented after he took power in France, with some Carbonari trying to assassinate him, and more than one embryonic plan was led by Americans.

Recall that Garibaldi, the Carbonari military commander in Italy, was exiled and resided for a time in the United States before reaching the zenith of his fame.

Garibaldi lived in New York on a pension given him by the Sardinian government, then worked in a friend's candle factory. While in New York, he attended meetings of the Brotherhood of the Union but kept a low profile. He then traveled for three years on a trading vessel using an American passport, having declared his desire to become an American citizen. Some, including Garibaldi himself, claim that he actually did become a citizen. This would lend credence to Lincoln's request that Garibaldi lead the Union Army or an army corps at the beginning of the Civil War.

He later traveled to London and reunited with Mazzini. Garibaldi was a follower of the teaching of the socialist Fourier and a womanizer. It was thought that he had murdered his wife, but never proven.

Garibaldi has been honored longer and perhaps more than any other revolutionary commander and historians differ widely about the incidences in his life. For one, he is said to have left the Carbonari, yet his lifetime goals matched the aims of the Conspiracy for Europe and the world. He formed the International Legion, to liberate Europe and unite it. Within its leadership was Gustave-Paul Cluseret. He made Ludwik Adam Mierostawski the head of the organization. Associates of Louis Blanc and Louis Auguste Blanqui assisted in its formation.

The line from the Illuminati was Bode to Blanc, and Buonarroti to Blanqui.

Mierostawski participated in several uprisings of Polish patriots and in 1848-1849 fought for the communists in Baden and the Electrol Palatinate. He was a member of the Carbonari and Young Poland.

Garibaldi in his declining years formed the League of Democracy and was made Grand Master of the Grand Orient of Italy.

Some anti-Catholic groups said that the work of Garibaldi fulfilled biblical prophecy against the Pope. It is amazing how many of the Christian organizations who profess biblical knowledge seem to lack understanding of the conspiratorial forces arrayed against Christianity, thereby giving these forces influence not just within history but contemporarily. By saying that some personage is the antichrist, the Conspiracy thereby creates a condition in the Christian mind that there is nothing he can do about the situation, since it is all prophesied. Thus, it helps the Conspiracy achieve their goals due a lack of sufficient opposition. The reader must realize that this is a deliberate tactic by those who intend to rule.

Since the mid-eighteenth century, Americans have been increasingly influenced by certain sects to do nothing to oppose evil, since what is "happening now," whether in 1860, 1914, 1939, 1970, or in the 21st century, has all been prophesied and the only thing that will stop it is Christs' return. The problems in those years resulted in catastrophic wars that could have been prevented had Christians worked to oppose an evil they deemed inevitable.

This author believes in Christ's return, but no amount of research has exposed when that will be. Many in the past have professed to know when that would have been, only to be finally discredited — after they had neutralized the very people needed to oppose the conspiracy.

It is amazing how often the same people will prophesy over and over again, fail in that prophecy, and still have adherents who follow them into failure after failure. Prophesying the imminent return of Christ since the advent of the exposure of the Conspiracy has been injected into Christendom for over 50 years, neutralizing from action the very people who could have stopped the Conspiracy in its tracks had they had good leadership.

It is interesting that no one has ever done research on the background of those who own Christian publishing houses. There has been some work done on the "author" of one version of the Bible, questioning his motivation and his associations. But, we leave that for the reader to ferret out for himself, since it is our wish not to point fingers at specific religious sects, but to have the reader understand the Conspiracy enough for him to make up his own mind.

Just about every dictator or major socialist leader who had a following beyond his immediate area from 1850 on has been called the antichrist.

When the Carbonari first started its conspiratorial drive, the recruiters in Italy and Switzerland traveled as agents of the Bible Society, demonstrating not only their ingenuity to look like something they were not, but the hypocrisy of their actions. Here again, it demonstrates that the Conspiracy uses the religion of the targeted state to fool the people as to their real aims.

Considering the ability of these men to pose as something they were not, one does have to at least ask the question as to how much of Christian thought about the end times is influenced by such a conspiracy.

There is a great deal of evidence that the interpretation of such meanings in Scripture has been planted by the Conspiracy itself to blunt and/or negate the efforts to fight them by their opposition: the Christian. After all, if the outcome is inevitable what can one do?

All of Scripture is an admonition to fight evil, in ourselves and in the world — and the consequences of not doing so. If the Christian, particularly, can be convinced that there is nothing he can do in his lifetime, he will do nothing or next to nothing — and his conscience will not bother him.

There is even more evidence that certain Christian leaders serve something other than Christ. Included in this number are those who are elevated by the mainstream media as representing the responsible leadership of the Christian world. Today, some are so blatant as to have started their careers as communist organizers. Then when communism "died" in the early 1990s they became Christian ministers, Rabbis, or Imams, depending on their particular race or ethnic background. Their politics did not change, only their façade.

If the main target of the Conspiracy is Christianity, it would only make sense that they would target the centers of Christianity and make them over to fit their purposes, confuse their opposition, and control the debate — and to use ministers to do so — as well as centers such as seminaries, Christian organizations, and particularly publishing houses.

The same goes for the Jewish faith.

In America, this infiltration was particularly true in our early history. Extreme examples were Emerson and the abolitionist William Garrison, but as you will see, they were far from the only examples.

Rev. Andrew T. Foss, a follower of Garrison said,

"I hate the Union" ... "I hate Jesus Christ."
—*Daily Evening Traveller*, Boston, July 29, 1857.

There were more subtle people that moved the seminaries and mainstream churches along. They had to be subtle. The extremists would draw everyone's attention to them, and this made the more subtle of the "Christian" leaders look moderate as they moved the agenda forward across a wide swath of American life.

Early on, the English government under Lord Palmerston gave moral support to the Carbonari to the extent that the Austrian conservatives had a saying:

If the devil has a son,
Surely it's Lord Palmerston

In German, of course — but it still rhymes.

The Palmerston government also helped the Comuneros movement in Spain as part of their opposition to the French. During Garibaldi's confinement, Lord Palmerston sent him an easy chair.

The concept that "the enemy of my enemy is my friend" can be flawed and lead to dire consequences in the long run. Perhaps this was the motivation of Palmerston. There are those who claim that Palmerston was part of a conspiracy that included Bismarck of Germany, the Order of the Palladium. We do not doubt the possibility, but the evidence could be more definitive.

The reader may wish to research this order and decide for himself. It is said that Albert Pike was its Grand Master after the war. Again, use common sense and logic to help separate the facts from the fantasy.

In 1867 a Conference of Peace was held in Geneva, and Garibaldi was the honorary president of the assembly. His suggestions before the assemblage were the foundations for a future League of Nations. He felt that "The papacy, being the most harmful of all secret societies, ought to be abolished." This last point, number five, in his proposed screed was directed at the papacy as the most dangerous sect in Europe. For this reason, this point and all the rest of his proposals were rejected.

Depending on the source, this peace conference was attended by anywhere from 5,000 to well over 10,000. We have also read that this conference was held in 1863 and in Genoa — an example of trying to track the history of conspiracy with quite diverse "facts" in the history books.

One of those in attendance was Fyodor Dostoevsky, one of the greatest literary giants of Russia. He wrote:

> When I arrived here the Peace Conference was just beginning, to which Garibaldi himself came.... It was really incredible how these socialist and revolutionary gentlemen ... sat and flung down lies from the platform to their audience of five thousand!...That they may attain peace on earth, they want to root out the Christian faith ... to abolish capital, declare that all property is common to all.... Only when fire and sword have exterminated everything, can, in their belief, eternal peace ensue.
> — *Letters of Fyodor Michailovitch Dostoevsky to his Family and Friends*

This was a "peace" conference. Such is the definition of *peace* in the mind of a socialist, then and today: fire and sword to eliminate their enemies. They will use the word *peace* only as a tool to fool the gullible into surrendering their ability to defend themselves.

Garibaldi ended his life fighting with France against Prussia, and cherished the idea of a league of nations and a world court of justice.

There is a great deal of conflicting information regarding his life, and strange omissions exist in some accounts so as to make him appear to be more of a hero of liberty rather than a radical, one-world proponent. It should be enough to say that there is a memorial to him that has stood for years in the USSR.

In the United States the Young America movement was in a constant state of inner turmoil. Again, the game of power is rife with individuals who know how to get power and will engage with others to achieve that goal, but each wants to be the leader and the personality clashes are constant. They cannot stand each other any more than they can tolerate those they want to rule.

In the United States, the YA *movement*, sometimes referred to as the New Democracy, included August Belmont, Stephen A. Douglas, George Bancroft, James K. Polk, Franklin Pierce, and a host of Democrat Party politicians of the day, particularly in the South. One of the literary lights was Walt Whitman.

Perhaps the most notorious at the time was George Nicholas Sanders, but try to find information on him. In any index of almost all histories written about the age it is difficult to find Young America, and even more difficult when it comes to George Sanders. Given the importance of Young America and Sanders, it is clear by this exclusion that their roles are being intentionally hidden from Americans.

When you see the involvement of Sanders in the narrative, you may want to recall the above; it will become an indication to you that the basic thesis of this tome — that a conspiracy existed and exists in America — has to be true.

The advent of the Internet makes research of the Sanders of the world easier to document, but there are still many gaps. The memory hole has been circumvented to a large extent by the Internet, and the systematic elimination of information by conspiratorial means has been frustrated. However, if you are the victim of an education that does not even hint at what you should be looking for, the Internet is next to useless. You have to be able to ask the right questions and seek out the right people.

While the Internet is a great tool, there are many archived papers and books that have never made it onto the Internet, for a variety of reasons. In some cases, this material has been used in this book and is unavailable to the reader. Some libraries have made it more difficult to access this material for the average person, requiring some sort of "academic" credential and purpose to gain access. This is true for such institutions as the Library of Congress, the Boston Library, etc.

The biggest hurdle to learning is that, if you do not know that YA and Sanders existed, why would you look them up on the Internet? It is the same for similar situations or personalities. You would not, simply because you do not know about them; therefore, you are incapable of asking about an entity that you do not even know exists. This is the purpose behind so many aspects of history and economics not taught today — if you do not know, you cannot ask about them. This applies to the positive hidden aspects as well as the negative.

By the way, the teachers have been the victims of this ignorance as well over time. If they were not taught certain critical ideas, events, and personalities, they then cannot teach them to you. This is the result of two centuries of systematic, concerted education, and publication of history under the influence and/or control of the Conspiracy.

Sanders was a Southerner whose maternal grandfather was George Nicholas of the Kentucky Resolutions, who was in the pay of the Spanish government, worked with Jefferson, and helped assist the Jacobin societies in Kentucky.

George Sanders fought with the communists at the barricades in Paris in June 1848.

Later, Sanders was named our consul in London by President Pierce. He failed to receive Senate confirmation when news filtered back to Congress of his activities, which included entertaining European firebrands at James Buchanan's residence, or his own home. The future president was our ambassador to the Court of St. James at the time.

In London, Sanders issued a public "Address to the People of France" urging the overthrow of Napoleon III, probably because he was no longer a Carbonari, and, like his more famous uncle, Napoleon III had used the Conspiracy to further his own ambition to rule. Sanders openly called for Napoleon's assassination. This outraged the U.S. Senate so that Sanders wasn't confirmed in his post; nonetheless, Stephen Douglas voted for him.

Such firebrand dinner guests of Sanders and Buchanan included Mazzini, Kossuth, Ledru-Rollin, Garibaldi, Felice Orsini, Louis Blanc, and others. Sanders called for the assassination not only of Napoleon, but of other European leaders and the overthrow of European governments, not exactly the flowery language of tact expected from one of our representatives overseas. They toasted the world republic as well. After dinner, the *La Marseillaise* was sung.

Keep this attitude toward assassination as a tool by Sanders in mind in regard to later events in his life. Orsini would later go on to try to assassinate Napoleon III and die at the guillotine as a result, having failed in his mission. Such were those entertained by the future president and our man in London, Sanders.

The invitation that went out to these firebrands to have them come to dine and then have them show up indicates the importance of Sanders in the scheme of things. Sanders had manned the barricades in 1848, as many Americans did, traveling there to participate even before the outbreaks. This indicates the planning was done well in advance, that it was not a spontaneous uprising of the people, and that it was international in scope with Americans at least involved, if not in the leadership. At the time Sanders was also trying to be an arms dealer to the revolution.

You might say the same about Buchanan, except it was Sanders' contacts with these revolutionaries that got them to attend. It was an indication that not all in the American government were really enemies of the communist revolutionaries.

Marx was not there, since he had not yet become as important as he did later. At the time he was simply a revolutionary on the way up, and had not yet achieved the heights he later would attain in the Conspiracy. Mazzini, Kossuth, and others were far more important at the time.

The revolutionaries in London were allowed to use the London American legation seal to send letters throughout Europe to other revolutionaries. Some of these letters fell into French hands and caused quite a stir, since the revolutionaries were using American Foreign Service diplomatic immunity to communicate.

While in London, Sanders served as the London correspondent for the *New York Herald* newspaper. This has always been a problem with the American media: revolutionary cadres serving as correspondents as if they are unbiased reporters. We will show even more blatant examples as we proceed.

Sanders lost the confirmation vote of the Senate in July 1854 by a vote of 29 to 10. However, he remained in London until replaced in the autumn. After he became president Buchanan wanted Sanders back in London, but Sanders said only with Senate confirmation. Since there were not enough votes to accomplish this Buchanan appointed him Navy agent at New York — which was a nice job to have if you were part of the conspiracy preparing for war.

Can you imagine the president wanting Sanders back in London? It answers a lot of questions about Buchanan's actions in his term of office that helped set the stage for the American conflict. As you will see, the aim of the Conspiracy was to promote a war between the North and South. While there is no definitive evidence of Buchanan's involvement in the Conspiracy, this at least exposes his mind-set.

Keep in mind that the events involving Sanders and Buchanan in London were less than ten years after the violent upheavals of 1848-1849, and the European governments must have been aware of Sanders' involvement. The governments of Europe were in no mood to encourage the European revolutionaries or have others encourage them. You can imagine what effect these sorts of events, coupled with the Ostend Manifesto, had on our relations with European nations.

Ralph Waldo Emerson also found it convenient to travel to Europe during the revolutions of 1848. Coincidences take a lot of planning. While there, Emerson attended lectures by Victor Cousin, who also influenced Proudhon, and met with many of the revolutionaries of the day.

While there were many Americans who found it convenient to be in Europe at this time, prominent Americans at home lauded the upheavals in Paris of that year. Minister to France Richard Rush immediately recognized the provisional government, and at home Senate Democrats like Lewis Cass, YA; William

Allen; YA, Edward Hannegan, YA; Stephen Douglas, YA; and Daniel Dickinson supported the revolution. Nearly all of Congress voted congratulations to the revolution.

John Calhoun did not.

James Gordon Bennett, YA, of the *New York Herald* wanted to send military help to the 48ers and at the same time use the opportunity, while Europe was tied up in revolution, to expand the United States into Cuba, Canada, and the West Indies.

A book could be written about the Americans in the 1800s who were appointed our ambassadors who openly advocated the overthrow of various countries, even the ones they were assigned to. In some cases, these Americans were immigrants who fled Europe to escape punishment for being communist revolutionaries, who were involved in violent revolution and were sent back as our representatives. Probably the most famous of the latter was Carl Schurz, but Elentario Felice Foresti is likewise an example.

Foresti was a Carbonari who was condemned to death in Italy, but his sentence was commuted with perpetual exile to the U.S., where he became a professor of Italian at Columbia University. In 1858, he was appointed U.S. counsel to Genoa, where he died. To believe that he did not help the revolutionaries as our ambassador is too illogical.

Two other revolutionary examples were Max von Weber, a 48cr under Franz Sigel who became a Union general and after the war worked for the IRS, then was sent to Nantes as U.S. consul; and Peter Osterhaus, a 48er Union general who was sent to France as U.S. consul in 1866. Of course, a 48er was a person who participated in the communist revolutions of 1848 in Europe.

Even so, to send a revolutionary back to Europe to represent the U.S. would not seem to be the best tactic if you are trying to establish or maintain good relations with the government he is talking to as our representative.

An incident that illustrates the problem of American ambassadors is the Ostend Manifesto, drawn up ostensibly by three American ambassadors, Pierre Soulé and John Y. Mason, both of YA, and James Buchanan, in 1854. The three met in Ostend, Belgium, with other YA adherents. The manifesto called for the purchase of Cuba by the U.S., and if Spain refused, to use force to seize Cuba; this caused a firestorm amongst European governments since it called for the takeover of Spanish territory. If the United States could invade Cuba, then whose territory in the Americas would be next?

August Belmont was apparently one of the first, if not the first to propose the Cuban scheme to Buchanan. Belmont, as agent for the European Rothschilds, felt that he could get the Rothschilds to support the American acquisition of Cuba.

The German-born Belmont came to America as an agent of the Rothschilds. He married the daughter of Commodore Matthew C. Perry, who opened up Japan to the world. He was our minister to the Netherlands during the Pierce administration, and was a member of the Tammany Society and then the Union League of New York. During a period which included much of the Civil War, he was the chairman of the Democrat Party.

The French born Soulé was involved in a revolution against King Charles X at age fifteen. He was condemned to the guillotine, escaped from prison, and fled, but was pardoned and returned to France. He was then arrested for his writings and chose exile as his punishment. He became an itinerant wandering in the Americas until he just happened to become a guest in Andrew Jackson's home, at which time he got involved in American politics.

Once he received his appointment as our ambassador to Spain, the so-called liberals there hailed his coming. He apparently got too close to the revolutionaries, and did damage to U.S.-French relations by shooting the French minister to Madrid in a quarrel over the minister's wife. He had to resign his position in June of 1855, and returned to New Orleans. Then he got involved in several Knights of the Golden Circle filibuster initiatives and became the attorney for William Walker, accused of violating the Neutrality Act of 1794.

The official story of the Ostend Manifesto is that President Pierce instructed his Secretary of State Marcy to direct ambassadors Buchanan (London), Mason (Paris), and Soulé (Madrid) to convene somewhere in Europe to confer with each other relative to gaining Cuba for the U.S. It was Daniel E. Sickles who carried the message from Pierce for Buchanan, Mason, and Soulé to put together the manifesto.

Sickles was a friend of August Belmont, and the two of them gathered in the resort town of Ostend to produce the manifesto, which was nothing more than the Manifest Destiny agenda of Young America. Sickles also worked very closely with George Sanders as Sanders' messenger between the communist exiles in England and the revolutionaries remaining on the Continent.

This was not how the Ostend Manifesto was taught to this author in school, but that it had been merely the reflection of American foreign policy at the time to free the countries of the West Indies.

Sickles was a member of Tammany and first started practicing law in the office of Benjamin Butler. He courted the land reformers during the antebellum days.

Butler had been instrumental in the establishment of the *Democratic Review*, which served the fledgling Young America movement, when he was active in Democratic circles. In the Democratic nomination convention of 1860, he supported Breckenridge, then Jefferson Davis. He would be another Democratic leader to switch and become an *uber* Republican after the war started.

Once Buchanan arrived home from London, a special train was awaiting him to carry him from Philadelphia to Lancaster, made ready by the superintendent of the state railroad, Joseph B. Baker. It bore the name "Young America," and had been draped with bunting and signs reading "Welcome Home, Pennsylvania's Favorite Son."

At the time there were several private American forces of what were known as *filibusters*, who were arming to take over sections of Mexico, as well as countries such as Nicaragua, Cuba, and others. All of this came out of the agitation of YA and their program of Manifest Destiny to build an American empire, but it would be used to help destroy the Constitution from *within* by the tactic of war and empire building, just as had been done to ancient Rome, and then to use the American empire to revolutionize the world.

Nowhere was this author taught these schemes in school.

The communist finger on the hand of the Conspiracy also was at first overtly involved in trying to make the United States into a world republic.

One of the initiatives toward this end was the German Revolutionary League, founded in Philadelphia in 1849 with the support of radical Hegelian Arnold Ruge and an apostle of tyrannicide, Karl Heinzen. The plan advocated a messianic world federalism led by the United States. Cuba and Santo Domingo were to be annexed first, then Mexico and Latin America. This was to be followed up with the inclusion of Europe, starting with England.

In the 1850s, *over 1,000 revolutionary societies* in America advocated that the United States take over North and South America, annex Europe, and absorb Asia, Africa, and Australia into a new world state, establishing the Universal Republic of United Mankind for eternal peace on earth.

A congress was called at Wheeling for September 12, 1852 for this purpose. One thousand, one hundred and twelve German American revolutionary societies answered the call, but when it came to convening the congress only 13 delegates showed up, with another three from Wheeling, including C. Göpp.

Several resolutions were passed including the idea that marriage was to be abolished, and children were to be trained, brought up, and educated by the State, and the U.S. should annex Europe. By 1853, the societies had dissolved; the communists would play a different role.

YA would be the entity to promote the American empire, and this goal would evolve over the years into the role played by the Establishment of the two major parties. By the time of Theodore Roosevelt, Wilson, FDR, and on, American empire became the overriding aspect of American foreign policy. Meanwhile, the communists would assume the role of foil against Yankee imperialism, both at home and abroad — for and against, controlled by the same hand.

At first the role played was to acquire territory, such as Puerto Rico, the Philippines, Guam, Midway, Samoa, the Virgin Islands, Hawai'i, etc. Later, rather than occupy territory, the Conspirators used entangling alliances and controlling a country's finances to essentially do the same thing — without the outward appearance of control.

One arm of the conspiracy would work to involve the American people more and more in foreign entanglements, while another arm would protest it and use these entanglements to recruit communist revolutionaries wherever American interference created problems. They would also formulate the entanglements in such a manner to use the agreements to assist the upper echelons of the communist movement in country after country while making it appear as if it was being done to stop the threat of the street-level communist.

Street-level communists have very rarely understood what was behind their movement. On the occasion when people have risen high enough in the communist organizations to glimpse behind the curtain, some have fallen away, disillusioned. Two or three have written books, some have testified before Congress, most have faded away.

This did not mean that when convenient or necessary, all fingers of the conspiratorial hand would not work openly together, for national as well as international schemes, such as in the formation of the League of Nations and then the United Nations — even cooperation in the U.S. foreign entanglements that would create the reaction the communists could then use overseas to recruit minions against America.

In certain instances the communists would object to a treaty with their controlled unions, for example free trade, objecting that it did not give adequate protection of the unions, or some such argument. This tactic was then used as an excuse to make the treaties even more onerous and internationalist in the name of protecting the American worker by including the unions into international union organizations. Meanwhile, professional organizations would sell it to the businessman as necessary for the economy.

In these types of ploys, the rank and file of the unions and professionals would rarely see the stratagem or the collusion between the two movements' leadership and the U.S. Foreign Service.

At the same time, these treaties could be used to subvert the United States Constitution. All treaties since World War II cede control to the United Nations, for instance. One only needs to read them to see this fact within the language. In some instances it is right up front, such as in the NATO Treaty. In the case of NAFTA, it takes a while to get into the agreement before one stumbles across references to UN oversight. And in some agreements it takes more of a carom from one treaty to the next before it ends up in the lap of the UN.

Legislation often overrules other legislation by amending, expanding, or abolishing existing law. The process is often so complicated that the average American cannot read a new proposed law without going into several other laws to see how it all changes — a very complicated procedure.

The larger and more comprehensive the legislation, the more apt this process is to occur. This was one of the problems with the Affordable Care Act, better known as Obamacare. The changes made to other laws were so complicated that no one could decipher what Obamacare would do. And, as Nancy Pelosi said, we need to pass it to find out what is in it.

The same conditions are at work in regard to treaties, pacts, agreements, and partnerships. With NAFTA this was especially true and even after two decades, the American people are just beginning to find out what this free trade agreement contains.

Most Americans are unaware how these foreign entanglements cede power not only to international bodies, but to the executive branch as well. This in turn erodes the balance of power between the three branches of our government.

The intertwining of a host of international trade treaties which other nations are involved in and bring to the table, entering into another agreement with the United States, is bewildering. There are literally dozens of major agreements, and deciphering them in relationship to any new agreement the U.S. enters into is next to impossible. For instance, one dangerous aspect is that should the U.S. wish to impose sanctions against another country, it would be next to impossible since one country could simply ship whatever has been sanctioned from us to the third sanctioned country because of trade agreements signed before.

The most dangerous aspect of the so-called free trade policies of our government has been that they have decimated our ability to produce war materiel without dependence on the countries which could well be our enemies in the future: Russia and China. It is a fact that is receiving increased notoriety that 80 percent of the components of American weaponry are now produced by foreign sources. This entails a book to document, as well, as it goes much further than hinted at herein.

Prior to our involvement in the United Nations, the idea that a treaty superseded the Constitution was not entertained among Americans. A campaign to make this the opinion of Americans was started with the failed attempt to engage the U.S. in the League of Nations. Some of the men surrounding Wilson formed an organization to promote U.S. membership in a new world order. This became the Council on Foreign Relations, and one of the prominent men was John Foster Dulles.

Dulles always promoted the idea of the U.S. becoming subordinated to a world government, and to that end he propagated the idea that treaties supersede the Constitution. In a speech before a regional meeting of the American Bar Association in Louisville, Kentucky he asserted:

> Treaties make international law and they also make domestic law. Under our Constitution, treaties become the supreme law of the land.... Treaties, for example, can take powers away from the Congress and give them to the federal government or to some international body, and they can cut across the rights given to the people by the constitutional Bill of Rights.

Shortly after this, in 1952 he was appointed secretary of state by Dwight David Eisenhower.

It is illogical to believe the words of Dulles since it takes both houses of Congress to pass a law, amend the Constitution, etc. It makes no sense that only one house would be capable of ratifying treaties if the treaties could overrule the Constitution and its provisions. For years before World War II, Dulles was involved in Christian Socialist circles, a movement we shall discuss later.

Incidentally, you can find several statements by Jefferson, Hamilton, Madison, and others, that treaties could not supersede the Constitution. These statements by our Founders are conveniently forgotten by those who occupy positions of power in the federal government and on our various federal courts.

By the communists lending their cooperation for a treaty they knew would create a negative reaction overseas, they would help their overall cause. Most Americans have no idea how other peoples will react to our interference. And, even if it is a minority in a country, it is a minority the communists can use to their benefit.

As stated, such tactics are usually confined to the upper echelons of the conspiracy while the street level minions are unaware of the collusion. The street level usually has no clue that their leaders are manipulating and working both ends against the middle.

This tactic is used very well in the War on Terror. In the name of a few, go in and push everyone around, stay around as foreign troops where the average citizen of that country starts to resent your presence, and soon the terrorists have a fertile hunting ground for recruits into the terrorist organizations. For the average reader that believes this is the way to handle the problem, we recommend reading the author's work on the real terror problem.

Another advantage for the conspiracy is that when conservative people see the street-level socialists for or against something, they will almost automatically take the opposite position. So the conspiracy will have a goal, have the street-level minions come out against it, and thereby automatically get the business community, religious people, etc. behind the conspiracy's agenda. There is no greater example of this than in the area of foreign entanglements, especially the modern free trade agreements.

No one seems to ask why we are in such a hurry to have trade agreements with countries that are socialist, even communist, and call it free trade. Socialists do not believe in free enterprise, so why would they believe in free trade as Americans think of free trade?

This tactic would never work if most of the time the street-level communist movement did not advocate some very onerous policies. By them so advocating, the business and professional community has an automatic bias against the communists. They assume, therefore, that everything they do must be a danger to American liberty and interests. And they usually are, but in a manner that most do not understand. They look at the overt, not the covert.

One of the main points George Washington made in his Farewell Address was that we should not get involved in foreign entanglements. They will always diminish the independence of the American people and their ability to control their own destiny. Washington may or may not have understood how American interference and/or alliance with certain governments could be used to create ill will among foreign citizens against the United States. It was certain, however, that he understood how entanglements could and would diminish the ability of the American people to make their own decisions as an independent country.

After Jefferson had served as president and had changed back to his old self, he said this in a letter to President James Monroe:

Our first and fundamental maxim should be, never to entangle ourselves in the broils of Europe; our second, never to suffer Europe to intermeddle with (Trans)-Atlantic affairs.

Foreign entanglements are sold by our government today to the American people as beneficial for us as well as for whatever foreign entity is involved; the media likewise plays a role in selling the entanglements, and Americans have a difficult time discerning the problem. Throw in the fact that *our own Foreign Service officials are part of the quandary*, and it is a real mess. The examples of the latter problem will escalate as we proceed.

We have dwelt on this problem to this extent because the modern extension of the YA increasingly uses this tactic. It serves the purpose of gaining world control, and at the same time uses this control to lay the Lilliputian strings over the American people until one day we wake up and see ourselves part of a world government with no way out — and it all looks American, until the end.

In 1854, after George Sanders' activities in Europe caught the attention of the U.S. Senate and he was denied confirmation, upon returning to our shores Sanders reaffirmed his close association with Mazzini, Orsini, Kossuth, Garibaldi, and Andre Ledru-Rollin. He was deeply impressed with Mazzini's "theory of the dagger" and that tyrannicide was justified. the *New York Herald* reported that he said he was of the Ledru-Rollin school: death to tyrants.

Again, this was before he was asked by Buchanan to return to London.

Kossuth was one of Sanders' revolutionary idols. Kossuth was so popular in America that when he was made a *state visitor* he got away with criticizing George Washington. He was a guest of the U.S. government as a revolutionary leader, not as the head of any state. This policy of the U.S. government continued on into the 20th century, with revolutionary leaders being feted in Washington before they became their countries' leaders — or, conversely, banning true anti-communists from visiting America.

Sanders, the Knights of the Golden Circle (of which Sanders was also a member), and others in the YA movement split the Democrat Party in order to ensure the election of what had become the more radical party, the Republicans, and start a war. The candidates for office in 1860 were Abraham Lincoln, Republican; the two Democrats, Stephen A. Douglas and John C. Breckinridge; and John Bell, the candidate of the Constitution Union Party, which contained remnants of the Whig and Know-Nothings who wanted nothing to do with the other two parties.

Breckinridge was an inspector of the 33° of the Southern Jurisdiction of the Scottish Rite Masonry under Albert Pike. He was also a member of the Knights of the Golden Circle. He had been vice president under Buchanan.

Of the four candidates, Bell was the most reasonable, but he was saddled with Edward Everett as his vice-presidential candidate. Considering this, if he had been elected, one could rightly speculate just how long he would have been fit for office only to be replaced by his vice president.

Of the four candidates for president in 1860, only Lincoln was not a member of the Masonic Order. If it was strictly a Masonic conspiracy, you would have thought that Lincoln would have lost.

During the Civil War, Sanders apparently was under the direct orders of Jefferson Davis and became an *ex-officio* member of the Confederate Commissioners to Canada. This man, renowned for his advocacy of assassination, met with John Wilkes Booth just prior to the assassination of Lincoln. He was originally on the list of co-conspirators to be arrested in connection with the assassination, but was soon dropped off the list.

After the war, he fled overseas; he associated with the leaders of the 1871 Paris Commune who seized hostages including the Archbishop of Paris and shot them. He faded from American public view even after his return several years later, as did YA as an organization (although their aims became entrenched in establishment political circles). Meanwhile, communism had replaced its *overt* radical influence.

A great number of members of the Carbonari and other radical socialist secret societies had moved to America, and Mazzini needed a man to pull these people together. These were an asset that could not be allowed to languish. He sent Hugh Forbes to America to draw them together into a cohesive unit. At the same time, Forbes attempted to unite American organizations into the overall coalition. It was to be called the Universal Democratic Republicans.

Hugh Forbes was an Englishman who had served with Garibaldi in Italy and had become a reliable leader in the revolution. Once he received his orders, he proceeded to England, where many revolutionaries had moved, mostly the Carbonari type of subversives. He contacted the most radical of the Chartists to raise money to go to the U.S.

En route to England, William J. Linton, Anglo-American diplomat, traveled with him to Lausanne, Switzerland. Linton was a Carbonari friend of Mazzini and had written political verses for the *Dublin Nation* which he signed as Spartacus, reminiscent of Weishaupt's underground moniker. He helped found the International League and in 1867 moved to America where he helped organize the British Colony of Republicans of Mazzini followers in Montana.

At Paris, Forbes met American abolitionist Maria Weston Chapmann. She had been on the original executive committee of the American Anti-Slavery Society. She was a Garrisonian come-outer, meaning out of the American union. She resided in Paris about the time of the commune and solicited funds for American abolition from such personalities as Alexis de Tocqueville and Victor Hugo.

Somewhere along the road, Forbes was able to have Theodore Dwight write a letter of introduction for contacts in New York. Theodore Dwight was a member of the New England Dwight family and was an advocate of Garibaldi.

The New York Tribune noted that Forbes "commenced a tour in the interior of the State of New York … under the auspices of Mazzini and other friends of Italian Liberty."

Forbes would play an important role later in the affair of John Brown.

The Brotherhood of the Union
In 1846, the Brotherhood of the Union (BU), or Continental Union, was organized by George Lippard in Philadelphia, and they embraced the revolutionary forces of Europe as their own. They toasted these leaders and one example went: "Kossuth, Louis Blanc, Ledru-Rollin, Jules Lechevalier, Mazzini — the heroes and apostles of Brotherhood in the Old World."

Lippard had cooperated with George H. Evans' National Reform Association, which adopted the term Young America and had an even more radical vision than Mazzini. They proposed a new fraternal secret society. It was out of this association that Lippard formed the Brotherhood.

The Brotherhood had too many Chartists, communists, spiritualists, land reformers, and Fourierists in the leadership and organizing the units for it to have been looked upon as anything less than an umbrella group to tie all radical elements together. Well-known radicals such as Albert Brisbane and John Commerford were prominent in the organization, and Brisbane was a speaker for the Brotherhood.

The Brotherhood publicized the writings of Wilhelm Weitling and Joseph Weydemeyer, the ideological successor to Buonarroti, and dominated the National Industrial Congress in Cleveland in 1855. In other words, the BU participated in just about anything that promoted any level of socialism and the breakdown of the old social order, from organizing socialist groups in New York to the abolitionist war in Kansas.

Lippard described his Brotherhood as a modern work of the Rosicrucians. The opening ritual of the Brotherhood was a declaration against the Declaration of Independence and the Gospel of Nazareth — again fulfilling Illuminist plans for world government and opposition to Christianity. Indeed, Lippard would claim that its roots went back to the Illuminati.

One of Lippard's publications, *Quaker City*, carried articles by Louis Blanc on the Illuminati.

The Brotherhood was to be a sort of "poor man's Masonry." According to the Rosicrucians, it contained a secret inner degree known to but a very few and patterned after the *L'Ordre du Lis* of France and the Order of the Rose in England.

The Brotherhood organization probably contained more leaders of the various movements embodied in this narrative than any other American association. The membership helped in forming just about every organization on the Left after its creation.

According to one of the leading encyclopedic references at the end of the 19th century, *Appleton's Cyclopedia of American Biography*, it was one of the strongest organizations prior to the Civil War, yet you do not hear much about it today.

As mentioned, Lippard participated in National Reform and their congress of 1848 and the 8th National Industrial Congress of 1853. He was involved with communists such as George Henry Evans, was a member of Weitling's Arbeiterbund, and professed to be one of the three leaders of the Rosicrucians. The modern Rosicrucians back his claim, yet Lippard was a very young man at the time. The congress was primarily a land reform movement, with members of the Brotherhood of the Union playing a very prominent role.

Lippard was one of the most prolific antebellum writers of historic events as fictional novels, and many of the embellishments he wrote into his books have become "fact" in the public mind over the years. One of these so-called facts was that the Liberty Bell was rung at the reading of the Declaration of Independence and it was that event that caused the crack in the bell. His writings were designed to create a different picture of major American events than the reality, usually with shadowy unknown figures who led our Founders into independence. This was intended to convey a secret-society aspect to our liberty rather than what really happened.

Lippard's works served as the basis for linking the esoteric with socialism.

He did this all, of course, to set the stage for his own secret organization and activities on two levels: One, to make people think that a since a secret society was behind our independence, there must be something out there behind the scenes that can be beneficial for the people, and two, many would want to be part of this organization — or what they thought was the organization: George Lippard's Brotherhood, and from there into the Rosicrucians.

The Brotherhood of the Union had many thousands of members during Lippard's life; the true figure is not known, but it had 146 circles in 1850. If they marched to the same drummer, they would have constituted a major force on the political scene.

While the BU was a secret organization, just like the Masons, a diligent person can find out the names of a surprising number of their members. In some New Jersey histories, for instance, they actually list the members of the sections of the BU that were established in the state at the time of Lippard's initial organizing of the order. The lists contain an amazing array of the locally prominent that carried the work of the BU forward.

Benjamin M. Braker, a personal friend of Lippard and Walt Whitman, was an example. He participated in the Free Soil Party and then helped organize the Republican Party in New Jersey. He became a justice of the peace and then a member of the New Jersey State Assembly, and was an official of the BU in New Jersey.

Garibaldi, when he lived in New York, attended their meetings but kept a low profile. The BU members helped John Brown, and more than one rode with him.

As stated, the BU was such an important organization yet few have ever heard of it. It was also known as the Continental Union. Then too, it did operate under different names at the local level at times, which probably threw people off track. The use of different local names for the circles, plus the fact that so many members were also involved in other prominent movements, made difficult the discernment of what

CHART FOUR
The most famous American Communist Communes and their supporters

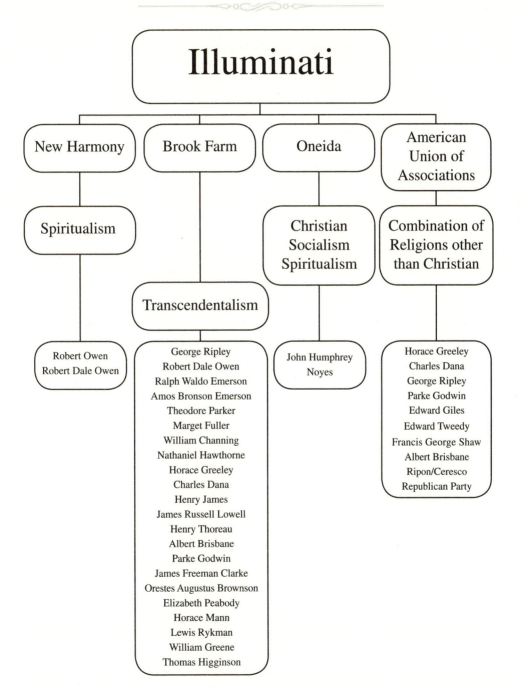

organization was really being represented at any given time. Perhaps the most important unit was the one organized in New York City.

The BU grew to 30,000 strong by 1917 — long after Lippard's death — and died out in 1994. The membership at one time was represented in the House of Representatives by Thomas Birch Florence, who was a member of the House from Pennsylvania from 1851 to 1861 and was also part of Tammany. After leaving the House, he published the *Constitutional Union* and the *Sunday Gazette* in Washington.

One of the last public events Lippard engaged in was giving a speech on the 115th birthday of Thomas Paine, attempting to redeem Paine's political legacy, which was still in disrepute at that time.

The Brotherhood and the American branch of the communist international (IWA) spawned many organizations together, and in some circles it was difficult to separate the two. Much of the movement later evolved into the Greenback movement.

The Order of Patriarchs, a radical spiritualist-led organization, evolved into the Sacred Order of Unionists, and many helped organize the Brotherhood. The original organizers of the Patriarchs were Stephen Pearl Andrews, John Murray Spear, John Orvis, John Allen, and Ellen Lazarus. The organization was particularly active in Philadelphia.

Andrews was one of the first Americans to publish *The Communist Manifesto*. He was an attorney, spiritualist, and anarchist. Due to his scientific achievements, he was elected an associate fellow to the American Academy of Arts and Sciences.

Orvis was the leader of the Sovereigns of Industry and became the president of the New England Labor Reform League, whose meetings were attended by B. Alcott, Lysander Spooner, the anarchist William Bradford Greene, and Charles T. Fowler. This evolved into the American Labor Reform League.

The latter had Greene as president and Orvis, Albert Brisbane, and Elizabeth C. Stanton as vice presidents. Their publication was *The Word*, whose contributors included John Humphrey Noyes, William Denton, Frederick William Evans, Wendell Phillips, and Henry Ward Beecher.

Leaders in the Labor Reform League included: Stephen P. Andrews, Victoria Woodhull, J. K. Ingalls, Lewis Masquerier, Harry Beeney, the Owenite socialist John Francis Bray, Josiah Warren, William Rowe, and labor leader A. W. St. John.

Evans was an American Shaker leader who had been influenced by Owenites while still a resident of Britain. William Denton was a Chartist speaker and some sort of spiritual medium, delivering his brand of hocus-pocus to anyone who would provide him a platform.

Bray was an American who went to England and became a Chartist and Owenite; returning, he went on to support the Socialist Labor Party and the Knights of Labor. Karl Marx quoted his writing at length in his attack on Proudhon, *The Poverty of Philosophy*. He has been called both the Benjamin Franklin of American labor and the Grand Old Man of American socialism.

Josiah Warren started out at New Harmony Owenite commune in 1825 to 1826.

An attempt was made to form an international alliance of the BU with Blanc, Alexander Herzen, English Chartists, Hugh Forbes, Marx, and Engels in 1857. This initiative was driven primarily by the New York circle. They held a meeting that drew 1,200 people, at which Friedrich Adolph Sorge played a role. This international association had units in Boston, Cincinnati, Chicago, St. Louis, New Orleans, and New York.

The BU declared itself a secret society, but it is surprising just how easy it is to find the names of so many of its members. You, the reader, are challenged to find out information on the BU in any standard history book. It is not there. However, once on the trail in a very few books and on the Internet, it becomes quite revealing. The BU was clearly an umbrella organization incorporating all the groups working toward the primary goals of the Illuminati.

What we see in so much of the activities of radicals is an interlocking leadership, a repetitive leadership, all working together for a common goal over the years, using different means and issues to reach those goals.

The Brotherhood was only a visible manifestation of this as well as of other organizations that attempted the same tactic. The *invisible* aspects of this activity lay within the secret organizations that gave impetus to the public action.

We have the word of Engels, who said that the secret organization behind the public Communist Party never was dissolved, although he attempted to claim at one time that it was. We also have the word of Dr. Bella Dodd that it was a few important industrialists who apparently had the power to give orders to the U.S. communist leaders just after World War II. We have the testimony of Benjamin Gitlow, the former editor of the communist organ *The Worker*, that there were shadowy forces behind the upper echelon of the U.S. Communist Party that he could never see, though he witnessed the results of their influence while on their Central Committee.

A modern umbrella group would be the Council on Foreign Relations, embracing a wide number of leaders within their membership from all walks of life. But it would be a mistake to call the CFR the conspiracy. It is too visible. Yet it has to contain a small group of individuals who actually set the agenda and lead the membership on the path toward the goal of a New World Order.

A few CFR members are also members of similar, very influential organizations. A study of some of these organizations was done some years back to determine who the overlapping people were, to see if there was a clue as to who really dominated these groups. At the time, five men were members of all, and none of them were recognizable as being important. This information was given to this author orally by Gary Allen, the primary author of the immensely popular book *None Dare Call It Conspiracy*. Fading memory has erased who these men were. Such a study today would be made easier by the Internet.

Over the last 250 years, the Conspiracy has obviously moved from Continental Europe, primarily Germany and France, into London and thence to New York.

Without key witnesses coming out and exposing what they were involved in, or actually infiltrating the inner ranks of such a secret organization, no one can document who the real Insiders were. In the 20th century we had many people who came out or defected who exposed a great deal of the communist secret apparatus, but never the people behind it. There were hints and clues, but never anything one could put into print.

Since the initial exposure of the Illuminati, much of which was based on the Bavarian government's investigations, no such government exposure has ever been instigated or published. Some individuals in the 20th century have claimed to have inside information, but these narratives are extremely bizarre, and if true, they had to have been in the "smoke filled room." It is doubtful they could have attained that level considering their personalities. Also, to gain the level necessary to have this knowledge would mean power and depravity well beyond the average criminal. Plus, if true and their revelations were true, they would not be allowed to live any more than Trotsky or other leaders close to the top if they betrayed the Insiders.

A hint of these modern revelations being suspect is that they never reveal the upper echelon of their supposed inner circle. If such an inner group were exposed, it might lead to a deranged patriot feeling that our problems could be solved by the simple assassination of these leaders, just as radicals have felt about Napoleon, Czar Alexander, etc.

Interestingly, there were no contemporary revelations of Illuminati influence or organization after the era of Rev. Jedidiah Morris that were opposed to the Illuminati, until the subject became the object of interest as a result of the republication in the 1960s of *Proofs of a Conspiracy*, and the writings of the founder of The John Birch Society about a conspiracy within America to subvert our society and system of government.

Too many modern revelations have had all of the appearance of disinformation designed to throw people off the track and to exaggerate the problem, in order to make those who believe that such a conspiracy exists look like people just a little off bubble — all of these coming after the exposés of Robert Welch.

Robert Welch, the founder of The John Birch Society, was very cautious in his writing and most of his works were based on logic, observation, and pointing out the interlocking of key personnel involved in subverting the Constitution into a web of subversion through organizations that had all of the appearance of being fronts for the New World Order, such as the Council on Foreign Relations. He established a research department to help build a picture of this web of subversion, and to help write articles through *Society* magazines documenting the facts.

For these reasons, he and his organization suffered a smear campaign aimed at silencing them by the communists, establishment media, and neoconservatives.

The elimination of those who help a dictatorship come to power is done to keep their mouths shut about secret cabals behind the scenes and those involved, as well as the fear of them usurping the new socialist leadership. This is what makes the history of Rudolf Hess, deputy Reichsführer under Hitler, rather intriguing. Once he landed in Britain, no one was ever allowed to speak to him in private for the rest of Hess' life. Hess was kept in solitary confinement for decades until he committed suicide or was "suicided."

The cabal behind Hitler was probably well known to Hess; he spent time with Hitler in Landsberg prison, helped him write *Mein Kampf*, and served as his deputy Füehrer. He had to know a lot about how Hitler was helped to power, literally up from the gutter to the head of Germany. We do know of powerful Americans and English citizens who helped the Nazis. What do we not know?

Hitler, like Obama, never really held any employment or engaged in experience that would prepare him for high office or even serve as the basis for people to support him. Both were essentially street organizers. At least Obama served in lower office, straight from the street to the Legislature and then the Senate. Who elevated these men as the executives of their respective adopted countries? People do not decide one day to run for office, alone, without help; it is a lesson in how to lose.

Conspiracies work differently than most people imagine. It only takes a few dedicated individuals who work in concert to manipulate large numbers. For instance, imagine that Messrs. A, B, and C decided to buy up a number of media outlets. They have Mr. C go out and find a Mr. D to front for them, buying the outlets and finding the editors or producers (E-Z), to manage the outlets.

Messrs. E-Z only report to Mr. D. They have no idea that A, B, and C exist. Everyone involved below the managers have no idea about D. They just do what they are told, just as any employee does. Even D may not know about A and B. D simply passes on the editorial policy that C dictates for the small cabal.

The same is true in fields such as education. If a conspiracy, using the method described above, captures the major publishing houses for school textbooks, they can control education without a single school teacher being in on the game since it would be done slowly, a step at a time. If, at the same time, they control the teachers' unions, the circle is nearly complete.

It is not just the students that fall victim to such a system — the teachers are victims as well.

What we see today is evolving into a more centralized means of control over education by the federal

Department of Education, the significance of which will be discussed a little further on.

The same would apply for Christian publishing houses. If you were part of the conspiracy, would you not want to control the publishing of your main nemesis?

You do not need to change a word; all you have to do is to set the dials of their thinking so that they do nothing to oppose you.

7
COMMUNES

Communism was well established in America by the time of the Civil War. There were a number of communist communes established around the country, but these were simply manifestations of a layer of support that went far beyond the number of people in the communes. The number of people in these communes at one time exceeded 20,000.

The equivalent numbers when measured by the population then versus the population today would be fourteen times 20,000 — 280,000. Keep in mind that any numbers around 1850 would be multiplied by approximately 14 to give you today's equivalent of the numbers influencing the population.

Many communist leaders such as Marx were not in favor of the use of communes to build the movement. For one thing, they were too insular and lacked outreach, with a few notable exceptions; the more well-known communes became well known because they did have outreach programs.

As an indication of the support for socialism and communism in America by 1848, a great Revolutionsfest took place in New York in support of the communist revolutions in Europe as they were waning. It was preceded by a hundred-gun salute, and a parade marched down Broadway for *hours*. A ceremony followed the parade where the mayor presided and a slate of socialist and communist leaders spoke to the gathered, including Albert Brisbane and Hermann Kriege, who had been denounced by Marx for deviating from the Communist Party line — a denunciation usually meant the individual did not support Marx personally. Funds for the revolution were solicited with an appeal for the German revolutionaries and Americans to unite and send cadres to Europe.

Similar, but smaller celebrations occurred all over the country, with funds raised to send to revolutionaries, primarily to Germany. It is not known if these funds ever reached their intended beneficiaries.

Keep in mind as you read further on, these events *came before* the influx of German 48ers into the United States.

Kriege came to the U.S. in 1845, founding the German Young America Community and the Social Reform Association, which affiliated with the National Reformers. The Social Reform Association grew to have one thousand members in New York. Remember, the ratio to the population in today's numbers would be in excess of 14,000, a formidable influence.

Even though Marx chastised Kriege for deviating from pure communism, he and Engels knew the communists had to work with the National Reformers:

> … just as in England the workers form a political party under the name of the Chartists, so do the workers in North America under the name of the National Reformers.
> — Marx, *Deutsche Brusseler Zeitung*, November 1847

Wilhelm Weitling, too, would join the National Reformers.

When Kriege was expelled from the communist international movement by Marx in 1846, he joined Tammany.

The National Reform Association (NRA) was a link between a number of communes and the broader land-reform movement. It was founded by George H. Evans, who had immigrated to America and become involved in a wide variety of radical movements. A list of the newspapers he edited tells the story: *Workingman's Advocate, The Radical, The Man, The Peoples' Rights*, and *Young America*.[24]

The NRA had strong links to Fourierist leaders such as Horace Greeley, and worked to have a closer relationship between land ownership and the government. Their work aided considerably the passage of the Homestead Act of 1862.

While such efforts as this wielded considerable influence, communes had the problem of isolating the communists in most cases. They hunkered down into enclaves (communes) and tried to build communism by being isolated from the general community. In order to propagate any idea, the people who promote the ideas must have an organization that has an outreach aspect as its primary tactic. Communes were not an outreach program, and this is why the more astute communist leaders did not like them.

As stated, three of the four communes that had an influence on America were the most famous — simply because they did have an influence. On the other hand, the fourth commune that had the most influence on America is relatively unknown — simply because the influence was so profound and widespread that the conspiracy does not want Americans to know about it and whence that influence came. We will begin to examine this at the end of this chapter, and in more detail later.

The three most famous communes were New Harmony, established by the Scottish industrialist Robert Owen, Oneida Colony, and Brook Farm.

Brook Farm

Brook Farm had great influence on the intellectuals of the day that are now prominent in our history books as being the norm for their time. This was not true that they were the norm, but since the conspiracy has gained control of history, it appears to be true. Certainly as the conspiracy founded and gained control of more publications, their influence began to have its effect. The famous names who were involved were Nathaniel Hawthorne, Ralph Waldo Emerson, Amos Alcott, George Ripley, Dr. J. C. Warren, Theodore Parker, Margaret Fuller, Dr. William E. Channing, William H. Channing (who published the Fourierist paper, *Present*), et al.

Emerson said of Brook Farm that "It was a perpetual picnic, a French Revolution in a small Age of Reason in a patty pan."

Not all who were connected to the communes actually lived there. These "off campus" socialist intellectuals helped raise funds for them, wrote articles for them, gave speeches promoting them, and in general did all they could to propagate a specific commune or series of communes without enduring the hardships that most communes experienced. After all, one cannot expect the higher-ups to actually do what they recommend to others!

Due to the influence of the conspiracy, these people at the time attempted to dominate the intellectual pursuits of literature, history, philosophy, etc. by eliminating from the public scene and then from American history other non-socialist intellectuals as much as possible. This was done primarily by a series of interlocking intellectual circles or clubs rather than the actual communal system.

---

24   The NRA should not be confused with a later organization of the same name which wanted to establish Christian language to the Constitution and coinage just before and after the Civil War. They wanted recognition in the Preamble of the Constitution of the rule of Jesus Christ as the supreme law of the land.

These associations followed the precepts for taking over such pursuits handed down from Voltaire, the Illuminati, and the Illuminati's protégé, the German Union. Gradually, these individuals and other socialists had become the predominant influence on letters and the arts by the late 1800s due to their organizing toward that end.

Into the 20th century, these authors and those who surrounded them were the predominant authors, poets, and philosophers studied in the public schools.

It is apparent that a small group of intellectuals in New England set about early on to dominate the American intellectual and publishing pursuits. One of the visible organizations was called the Saturday Club, and Edward Waldo Emerson, Ralph Waldo Emerson's youngest son, referred to it as "These brave illuminators." Members referred to it as a circle, or as Ralph Waldo Emerson said, a club of the club.

Its motto translated into English was: "And each inspired one here I'll count a god."

The Saturday Club was only an extension of earlier social circles, symposiums, etc., and contained a mixture of freethinkers and socialists, most of whom had studied in Germany or France, or had studied under men who had. Not all participants would have been part of the inner circle which ran it. The members included Longfellow, Hawthorne, O.W. Holmes, Charles Sumner, and Louis Agassiz.

It was reminiscent of the blueprint of the German Union for the reading societies expanding into all intellectual pursuits.

Out of the Saturday Club radiated a circle of influence that encompassed literature, newspapers, journals, foreign service, government, the Supreme Court, many sciences, medicine, education, and particularly "religion" that seemed to worship nature, not dissimilar to the environmentalist of today. Other circles were also formed by its members, such as the Adirondack Club, the Radical Club, and the Atlantic Club which led to the *Atlantic* magazine. Yet, by Emerson's comment, the Saturday Club apparently was only an extension of some other organization.

There have been adverse influences on some of the most basic references we use in our intellectual pursuits. We will cite examples later of this influence on Scripture, but it extended into encyclopedias and dictionaries as well. Subtle changes over time or complete reversals of definitions can alter the thinking of students.

As an example of contributors to reference materials, *Appleton's Cyclopaedia of American Biography* was a widely used reference for short biographies of influential Americans. It was published in 1886. It is surprising that some of the names in our history are never mentioned in its volumes, yet it purports to be a comprehensive compilation of important American personages. Sometimes pertinent facts are withheld, distorted, or presented in a different light. Once you look at the contributors or expert historians listed in this encyclopedia, it becomes apparent that many were involved in the socialist movement.

As for changing definitions, for instance, if an author or politician used a word that is read by students years later and the definition has changed, the students get a completely different picture of what the writer had in mind years before. Words like *inflation, general welfare, democracy*, and many more have changed to the point that the enemies of our system of government can move their agenda along among the now-ignorant students.

Every dictionary worth its salt has a listing of individuals who have assisted in the compilation of the dictionary. This is done to impress the user, who usually doesn't have a clue of who these people are except for their listed credentials. For instance, Thomas A. Thacher, the Order, was a professor of Latin at Yale and helped teach English to the Crown Prince of Prussia. He assisted in the compilation of a later edition of *Webster's Dictionary*, as did Chester Smith Lyman, member of the Order, and professor of mathematics at Yale. In 1846-47 he was in charge of the Royal school in Honolulu.

The Conspiracy has learned to move in small steps. In this regard the dictionaries have made subtle, almost imperceptible changes in the definitions at any one time, changing the definitions over a period of decades, not just in one edition. The definition of *inflation* is a good example. School dictionaries over a period of 60 years changed the definition in each decade, from the issuing of paper currency by the government without linkage to precious metals, to finally it being a rise in wages and prices in some dictionaries.

Looking at several school dictionaries all at once from the 1910s to today demonstrates this tactic vividly. Changing the definition made it very difficult for the American student to understand that it is government that causes inflation, and then based on that knowledge, to ask the question why.

Not all companies that published dictionaries followed suit, but even many of those who didn't changed to a double definition, using both the classical definition and the modern error, simply to keep up with the manipulated change in usage.

One thing Americans need to understand is that newspapers and journals are rarely established for purely entrepreneurial reasons. They almost always have some sort of an agenda. With most it is political, and with some it is the simple desire to sell an idea, product, and/or lifestyle. In some areas, the honest newspapers were destroyed over time with campaigns against the editors and their presses. This was done on a wholesale basis during the Civil War, wiping out much of the reasonable opposition to what was going on at the time.

The tactic used was to whip up the population into rioting against the newspaper offices, or *make an organized political effort seem to be a riot*, or simply have the army arrest the editor and destroy his machinery. The first thing to die in a war is the truth; the second is the First Amendment — which is necessary to re-establish the new "truth."

After the Civil War and into the first half of the 20th century, Mafia- and communist-controlled unions were used increasingly to bring newspapers into line by eroding their profits, setting the stage for financial failure through slowdowns of labor, diminishing the supply of newsprint, and other techniques. In some instances, newsboys were attacked in the streets for selling opposition newspapers. This set the stage for the consolidation of many newspapers into huge conglomerates — the honest newspapers would sell out due to the coercive tactics that led to their financial failure.

Sometimes the reason for the inability for a publication to survive was so subtle that the owners scarcely understood their problem. The *Saturday Evening Post* started out as a radical magazine but over time evolved into a mildly conservative entity, at which time it started to have trouble surviving. This change was evident in the cover illustrations of Norman Rockwell in family and patriotic themes. Their trouble came due to the control of advertising that went into mainstream publications. Ads started to be withheld, then dropped, and then the magazine had to shut its doors.

Prior to the Civil War there were several times when public disorder resulted in the destruction of radical abolitionist presses as well as the beating and tarring of their editors. In one case, the abolitionist editor Elijah Lovejoy was killed. This happened because of the rhetoric used by the abolitionists and their calling for the destruction of the Constitution and the attack on property rights in general, all in the name of eliminating slavery. The killing caused such a public backlash against the violence and in support of free speech that other presses of the Conspiracy's organizations generally thereafter went unmolested.

What is the sacrifice of one editor if it means that in the reaction the rest of the field is left unmolested? But this was not true regarding the Conspiracy's opposition. Freedom of speech is only valid if it attacks morality and the Constitution, not if it supports these things it seems. It is called "political correctness." It has been an increasing problem in our country, where freedom of speech means upholding anything that attacks our society, but nothing that supports it. This type of hypocrisy has manifested itself on more than one occasion in our history, and it is practiced with abandon in the mainstream media today.

One has to wonder whether the terrorist attack on the magazine *Charlie Hebdo* in Paris in January 2015 wasn't done to create a reaction against criticizing the radical media. From then on, any radical magazine could get away with saying anything, even if libelous. We do not pretend to know, and it may be too soon to ask such a question. However, the spontaneous demonstrations that took place immediately following the attack, using the same placards all over Europe at the same time, do cause one to pause and make some interesting mental observations.

The net result of the attack and subsequent demonstrations was a reaction against radical Muslims, demanding once more that we engage in war against an enemy hard to isolate and thus destroy, as well as sympathy for communist-led publications that attack Christianity more than Islam.

Since the incidences that caused the public to rise up against those who opposed the Constitution before the Civil War were exploited to cause a revulsion against such lawlessness, as in the case of Elijah Lovejoy, the general public in America never again attacked a newspaper that advocated any anti-Constitutional opinions — even up to today. Plus, the conspirators learned how to move their agenda along without being so open and brazen. Their rhetoric became more sophisticated.

The creation of martyrs, or the exploitation of martyrs, is an essential tactic of the Conspiracy. It is a prime method of creating a reaction of the public to stand still for the political beliefs of the martyr by creating revulsion to the violence, or disgust for the methods of their opposition, if one of their opposition uses tactics or rhetoric which seems extreme, or is made to seem extreme. Or, *if it is thought that an opponent created the martyr.*

The caning of Sen. Charles Sumner served as a catalyst to silence opposition to abolition and polarize Americans. Preston Brooks caned Sumner on the floor of the Senate over a speech Sumner gave against slavery in very offensive language on a personal level. It led Brooks, a relative of the man mentioned in Sumner's speech, to attack Sumner quite viciously and without warning. It took Sumner several years to recover, and he was absent from his duties off and on for a few years.

The reaction against the incident led to sympathy for the abolitionist leaders as well as Sumner. Moreover, it gave Sumner added weight to his Radical leadership in the ensuing years as a martyr for the cause.

Over the years, socialists have gained the expertise to use martyrs as a weapon to silence their opposition. The conspiratorial media focus public attention on the opposition as malevolent as a result of one lone act of violence, playing it into a national outcry. It becomes politically incorrect, therefore, to stand up for what is right. It also produces a "guilt trip" in the minds of those who oppose socialism, who then have less of a stomach for the fight.

It additionally leads directly to the label of "extremist" being attached to anyone who may hold the opinions or any part of the opinions of the perpetrator — or seeming perpetrator. The socialists have never been adverse to committing criminal acts and posing as their own opposition. After all, we are dealing with some very immoral people and they are not above using any means to win.

Brook Farm played a role in all of the above through the intellectual personnel associated with it.

A related tactic used by radicals in government to silence opposition has been the misuse of the Internal Revenue Service and other tax-collecting agencies throughout our history, as we will show. The problems of the 2010s in regard to such entities as the Tea Parties are not new. Such problems have reared their head from time to time, but usually it has been more subtle, and word of such actions did not get widely broadcast before the use of social media.

A question to ask is: Why is it okay for a tax-deductible entity to support a government or socialist program, but illegal for one to oppose such programs? Hundreds of tax-deductible organizations are involved in support of the socialist agenda and are not harassed by the IRS.

Oneida

Oneida commune is a lesson in how Christians can be manipulated from their religious beliefs into Christian Socialism and then to ultimately renouncing Christ. In the past 200 years, Christian Socialism has played a large role in moving American Christian churches more toward egalitarianism rather than the literal interpretation of the Scripture. Socialism has often been sold as pure Christianity through the misinterpretation of Scripture or the deliberate dis-interpretation.

Religious leaders who were part of the Conspiracy promoted the idea that Christianity was socialism. The modern adaptation has a more subtle argument of looking to government solutions for all social and economic ills rather than outwardly calling it socialism.

The founder of Oneida, John Humphrey Noyes, first cousin of President Rutherford Hayes, was a believer in spiritualism, or belief in communication with the spirit world, and this belief was essential to the "religious liberty" of community. He called "communication with the heavens" the "palladium of conservatism in the introduction of the *new social order*." (Emphasis added.)

Oneida practiced communal free love marriage.

When Noyes was first ordained as a minister, he climbed the pulpit and proclaimed, "I am perfect." The church expelled him at age 23.

Noyes called his movement Perfectionism. Garrison, the abolitionist leader, was an adherent of this group. By 1861, they were calling their system *communism*.

One of the most notorious members of Oneida was Charles Guiteau, who was encouraged to attend when the commune was formed. His father, Luther, was a disciple of Noyes. It was claimed that Charles was a misfit. Several years later, Charles Guiteau would assassinate President Garfield.

Over the years, Oneida played a role as a major part of the root that produced a very large and important movement called *spiritualism*, which we will return to in depth in later chapters.

New Harmony

New Harmony, established by Scottish industrialist Robert Owen, was an experiment that had a more practical side for the communists and that led to many mainstream initiatives that we look at today as essentially American: the public library, geodetic surveys, public schools, etc. Out of New Harmony and allied communes, Robert Owen and the Illuminist Johann Pestalozzi's pupil, Prof. Joseph Neef, promoted Pestalozzi's system of education which became prominent across America by 1900.

Robert Owen had become familiar with Pestalozzi sometime before the formation of New Harmony and had visited with him in Switzerland. Two of Owen's sons would marry the daughters of Joseph Neef.

The primary purpose of the first group at New Harmony was to become missionaries to form other communist communities. The Commune was dominated by the idea of enlightened atheism.

Infant schools were established at New Harmony by Robert Owen and conducted throughout the lifetime of communist experiments, and were the first of their kind in America. New Harmony became the greatest scientific center in America at the time, producing several people who were the fathers of American geology, zoology, and ichthyology, and became the headquarters of the U.S. Geological Survey (USGS).

It is necessary when changing society to infiltrate all aspects of society.

Through William Maclure, one of the founders of the Philadelphia Academy of Natural Sciences, a system of mechanic's libraries was established in more than 150 communities. These libraries were launched with the help of A. P. Hovey, who became the governor of Indiana. They served as the model for setting up libraries all across America.

Maclure had visited New Lanard in Scotland in 1824, Owen's commune there, and become an Owenite. His connection to Owen became so notorious that the relationship had to become secret in order to maintain his influence.

While New Harmony professed to be the center of sciences and education, the *New Harmony Gazette*, the official organ of the commune, stated on October 1, 1825, "that individuality detracts largely from the sum of human happiness." It also professed that "This society regards education as public property."

In other words, education is the property of the state: The state decides everything in regard to education. This fit nicely with their attitude about individuality. However, without individuality, in the long run science and education cannot advance.

The socialists then and now promoted diversity, as well as an ersatz individualism, so long as it progressed along lines that promoted international socialism. Diversity became a cover for subversion. If the individuality moved in the direction of being against the socialist agenda, then it was and is attacked.

Individualism is essential to invention. Individualists think out of the box, statists usually do not unless for a state reason, such as the invention of government initiatives or war machinery. While New Harmony led to advances in some sciences, it was advanced by individuals who were not yet debilitated by their total immersion in the communal system.

Socialists who operate within a free society will have the ability to invent. But, a socialist society will in the end stifle invention since all are trained to be alike. This is the problem with the modern educational system known as Common Core, where one size fits all. While the problem with Common Core is noticeable to the modern parent, the truth of the matter is that such a philosophy has long been the goal of the hierarchy of education in this country for a very long time.

If the internationalists in our midst are not successful in permanently establishing Common Core in the schools, they will simply change its name and come at the local schools again, claiming to fix the problems with a now deteriorating system. Each step will be a regression in the ability of outstanding students to learn any more than the lowest common denominator in the class. This then, will stifle invention.

Many modern histories of the communes use exhaustive quotes and philosophy to dazzle the reader with more information than what the reader wanted before cracking open the book. This serves to confuse the reader as to the aims and goals of the various personalities and organizations which established the communes. Herein, and throughout, we attempt to boil these down to the essence of their purpose.

Robert Owen established an organization in Europe and elsewhere called the Association of All Classes of All Nations, and they professed in their "Social Hymns" that "Community is Heaven." The goal was to replace God with government. In 1839, the organization changed its name to the Universal Community of Society of Rational Religionists. In 1845 Robert Owen called for an international socialist convention in New York, but it became an insignificant event.

The importance of the word "community" is that while to most people it has a benign meaning, it is anything but. *Community* means a common people united by the same government. Many dictionaries have this definition or something close to it. When people use the word *community* in their initiative, such as calling for a community of nations, they really mean one nation out of many, usually to be ruled by a government they put together. In the case of it involving the United States, it would mean the dissolution of the Constitution and the end of the independence of the American people.

As a modern example, Dr. Robert Pastor, the initial front man for the Council on Foreign Relations' initiative to form a North American Community in the 21st century, knew full well this definition. He protested that they were not about forming a new nation — only a community. If you read their publications there is no doubt what they are doing: trying to form a new nation to the detriment of the independence of the American people, including the death of the U.S. Constitution.

This is likewise true of those attempting to create an Atlantic Community between the U.S. and the European Union. There have been organizations trying to effect this end, such as the Atlantic Council, which was chaired by Republican Sen. Chuck Hagel, one of President Obama's secretaries of defense, and the Transatlantic Policy Network, in which Rep. John Boehner, speaker of the House, had a hand.

They also use the word "partnership" in their agreements. Partnership is, in a word, merger. These agreements are unions, just as is the North American Union.

Owen considered it an absurdity to promise never-ending love in marriage. In his Declaration of Mental Independence, Owen said that man is a slave to a trinity of evils:

> I refer to private or individual property, absurd and irrational systems of religion, and marriage founded upon individual property, combined with some of these irrational systems of religion.

A secret society was established, the New Harmony Philanthropic Lodge of Masons, among the 1,000 inhabitants. One of its ostensible purposes was to promote government schools. In reality it was patterned after a socialistic model of the Carbonari and had as its purpose *obtaining control* of the public school system.

Owenite communes existed in New Hampshire, New York (3), Kentucky, Pennsylvania, Ohio (2), Indiana (12), Illinois, and Tennessee. In the New Hampshire commune, the children belonged to the community from their second year and were all brought up together. This school was based on the idea that

> There should be free, equal, and universal schools to which at an early age children should be surrendered and in which they should be clothed, fed, sheltered and educated at the public expense.[25]

The commune was visited by personages and princes from Europe, and Albert Gallatin declared the New Harmony system of education to be the best in the world in 1826.

New Harmony represented the second initiative of the Pestalozzian system injected into America, close on the heels of Round Hill. The third was an extension of New Harmony, and it invaded New England championed by such individuals as Horace Mann, who went on to promote public education. He was not enthusiastic about doing so, but was finally convinced to become the leader in promoting government education. When Mann was appointed to the presidency of Antioch College, the most influential man on the board of trustees was Alphonso Taft, the co-founder of the Order.

---

25   This author was on the mailing list of the Socialist Party in the 1960s. As a result, a new local organization sent him a mimeographed letter outlining their aims which were essentially the same as this quote. When they went public, they hid their real intentions and for a time were successful in influencing changes in the school system in a major metropolitan area. It never came close to achieving the hidden goal of having children barracked away from their parents; it was too much of a stretch.

Horace Mann was an advocate of the religious school of Emerson. His ideas on education were steeled in Germany as the result of a trip there to visit and study German schools. The public education system that he envisioned had no place for puritanism. He was a politician and an abolitionist, having dealings with the New England Transcendentalists, which included his relatives since his sister-in-law was Elizabeth Peabody.

The person that Mann employed to run the schools was the radical Unitarian minister Samuel J. May, who became the principal of the Girls' Normal School in Lexington, Massachusetts. May was secretary of the Massachusetts Anti-Slavery Society, a Garrisonian, a founder of the American Peace Society, and a leader in the 1857 Disunion Convention.

Happy to be relieved of the responsibility for the hands-on education of their children, few parents realized that the government schools would rarely teach anything that questioned government prerogatives, and that if socialists became the teachers, it would be worse.

Robert Owen became so influential that he presented his scheme of communism in the Hall of the House of Representatives at Washington on February 25 and March 7, 1825. In attendance were almost all of the members of both houses of Congress, judges of the Supreme Court, several members of the Cabinet, and other men of distinction.

This was a few months after Lafayette spoke in 1824 before a joint session of Congress, the first foreign dignitary and Illuminist to do so.

Owen became intimately associated with President Andrew Jackson and Secretary of State Van Buren.

Owen wanted Britain, Canada, and the U.S. to federate as a forerunner of a union of nations to encompass the entire world. This became essentially the plan of Cecil Rhodes — with the caveat that it be ruled by England — who financed the Rhodes Scholarships to indoctrinate English-speaking scholars toward that end.

This information is documented in several places and is easily accessed online. It is the reason that many politically active people tend to distrust Rhodes Scholars. At best, they tend to be internationalists. At one time when this author was researching subversive organizations, it was noticed that it was not always scholarship that played a role in determining who was awarded a Rhodes Scholarship, but young men were chosen who were politically active in organizations that leaned more to the Left without being overtly radical.

Rhodes' first will proposed a secret society to bring the entire globe under British rule, using his estate to finance the endeavor.

The *Atlantic Journal* was started by Constantine Samuel Raffin, who was a frequent visitor to New Harmony.

Smithsonian Institute

Robert Dale Owen, like his father, Robert Owen, was an open advocate of communism. He likewise was a spiritualist — and was vociferous about both. He was elected to the Indiana State Legislature and helped write the state constitution as a known communist. In 1852, he became the chairman of the Indiana Legislative Assembly's Committee on Education. Later he was elected to the House of Representatives, where he sponsored the bill that led to the Smithsonian Institute. And all the voters in Indiana knew what he stood for.

In regard to setting up the Smithsonian, Owen said, "To effect permanent good we must reach the minds and hearts of the masses...." His idea of permanent good was different than most as a communist and spiritualist. As part of this effort, he and his associates urged the establishment of a teacher training school and distribution of cheap tracts and books on a variety of subjects.

The Smithsonian's facilities were not to be used, officially, for religious or political matters. As is the case with government, certain people are more equal than others, and soon the lecture hall was hosting abolitionists. Among the speakers were Greeley, Henry Ward Beecher, and Wendell Phillips.

Owen was put in charge of appointing the Smithsonian trustees as prescribed by law and the building of the institute's first edifice. Today, it is difficult to ferret out his involvement in modern references to the Smithsonian. The goal of those behind this organization was to establish a center of official government science. In this manner, as an example, they could slowly work to ostracize those who believed in anything the communists did not want people to believe in, such as Creation, and to promote the beliefs of Darwin, all using government money and sanction, and doing so exceedingly well.

On December 19, 1860, Karl Marx wrote to Engels,

> During my time of trial, these last four weeks, I have read all sorts of things. Among others Darwin's book on Natural Selection. Although it is developed in the crude English style, this is the book which contains the basis in natural history for our view.

At Marx's funeral, Engels said at the gravesite, "Just as Darwin discovered the law of evolution in organic nature, so Marx discovered the law of evolution in human history."

Today, no one who *openly* believes in the idea of intelligent design in the formation of man and animals, let alone a Creator, is allowed to work for the Smithsonian in a position of responsibility.

The movie *Expelled*, produced in 2008 by Ben Stein, is a modern documentation of this fact. The film documents the support for eugenics that is at the core of the evolution theory. Indeed, the original edition of Darwin's *On the Origin of Species* had as its subtitle: *By Means of Natural Selection, or the Preservation of Favoured Races in the Struggle for Life*. Favored races? The logical end of this kind of thinking is the concentration camp.

The communist support for the hypothesis of Darwin served as the platform to enable them to completely overthrow society. Since Western Civilization was based on Christianity, which believed in Creation, destroying the idea of Creation in the minds of the people meant the ultimate destruction of scriptural Christianity itself. After all, if the basic premise of Scripture is the creation of man supernaturally by God and this premise is destroyed, the whole idea of God is at least diminished in the minds of the student as a huge step toward the elimination of God entirely. If Creation is wrong, what else? Socialist teachers give their answer, and thereby the Conspiracy injects their brand of religion as an interim step for the people to become dependent on and look to the state as god.

The same is the case for Judaism. Jews too believe in Creation. So the entire Judeo-Christian foundation for the system of government in the United States could be destroyed in the minds of students by using Darwin to question the very idea of there being a God — we are simply creatures of accident *with no God-given rights*. This would ultimately become the basis for modern education.

Yes, they could teach the idea of God-given rights, but if at the same time you preach ideas that diminish God in the minds of the student, the ancillary aspects of our system of government will be of little worth.

If in doubt, think about it for a moment: If Scripture is wrong about Creation, what else is it wrong about? How about the Resurrection? What about the miracles in Egypt? Soon the entire idea of the basis of Christianity and Judaism is in doubt. Soon Scripture is reduced to an accumulation of fairy tales and all respect for religion is destroyed, at least Judeo-Christian religion.

For those who believe in evolution, they should try to figure the odds of such a system. There is no roll of paper in the world big enough to hold the zeros in the odds of moving from slime to human. It is not simply the odds of change and the billions of changes, but the direction of the changes. It is mathematically impossible as well as historically impossible: there is not enough time to accomplish the changes unless measured in the billions of years.[26]

The Smithsonian Committee appointed Adolf Cluss' architect firm to build the original U.S. National Museum building. Cluss was a member of the Communist League with Marx and Engels, and was a personal friend of Marx. After the Civil War he became the most influential architect in Washington. The city government at Washington proudly proclaimed these facts at the one hundredth anniversary of Cluss' death, at which time they had exhibitions of his work.

The Smithsonian trustees were to consist of the chief justice of the Supreme Court, the vice president, three each from the Senate and the House, and nine citizens. Some of the original trustees were U.S. Senator Jefferson Davis, who went on to become the president of the Confederacy and an avid supporter of the institute; Alexander Dallas Bache, grandson of Benjamin Franklin, who served as the first president of Girard College and served on the U.S. Sanitary Commission; Richard Rush, a former Anti-Mason Party member; Rufus Choate, who had studied law in William Wirt's office; and Robert Dale Owen.

The man who presided over the first meeting of the Smithsonian Regents was George M. Dallas, who had served as Albert Gallatin's private secretary for a time, was counsel to the Second Bank of the U.S., and believed in a central bank. He was made grand master of the Pennsylvania Masons in 1835 and served as Polk's vice president.

Regardless of who may serve as a regent, the Smithsonian started as the first step toward the involvement of government into the sciences and the interference of government into what would become "official," government-sanctioned science and progress. The idea has become so ingrained within the American psyche that no one questions government oversight of science by way of the Smithsonian.

They do a great job of presenting all manner of studies in print and media. Subtly embedded in all of them are the ideas of evolution, sustainable development, climate change, etc., with all of these subjects being used to enhance the belief that government is needed to control people's use of private property, ultimately leading to no private property.

There is no better modern example of the latter than the Smithsonian television series *Aerial America*. It is a beautifully presented view of the states by air. Intermingled are ten to twenty percent political correctness and the issues listed above.

Likewise, they interject what have become known as liberal political ideas and personages in their presentations. Again, this is usually done in a subtle manner so as not to rile the conservatives in Congress or in the population enough to want to them make an issue of it.

The U.S. Geological Survey headquarters remained at the New Harmony commune until after the

---

[26] Calculate how many millions-to-one it would take for the formation of life out of a soup of just the right minerals and water by itself and/or by the use of low levels of electricity. Keep in mind that the soup had to be the right concoction and have a source, some spark of life. Then calculate the next step: the ability to sustain that life. What would it take in as sustenance and how would it know to even perform this act since it had no existence or experience to tell it anything? The next step: reproduction. But let's skip ahead several millennia. What if the creature wanted eyes? How would it even know that there was light to see, or even know what *see* meant? How many eyes? Where to locate them? And, the eye is a very complicated organ — and on and on. Calculate this plus all of the advancements from an amoeba to the human structure and you are beginning to see the problem. Actually, there is no roll of paper large enough to even document the billions of steps necessary to progress from one cell to an integral structure such as a human being, let alone the odds. The study of evolution and its promotion are actually tools of those who want to establish a basis for certain human beings to be more progressed in development than other human beings, so they may denigrate the others into extinction. If you do not believe this, then study the makeup of the eugenics movement, the people who started it and who have used it since Darwin to eliminate human beings they deem inferior.

building of the Smithsonian, when it was moved there. In other words, the socialists started this enterprise and then created the Smithsonian as a means to move the Geological Survey step by step into a government enterprise.

The creation of this government entity was a huge first step toward the control of all property by government. As in all things socialist, the first step seems benign; however, the last steps become quite onerous. For instance, the USGS has led to a situation today that has placed U.S. historical and environmental sites under the control of the United Nations. This was accomplished a small step at a time and would take an overview of at least 4,000 words to describe. It is an archetype of an Agenda 21 for historical and wilderness areas.[27]

The problem with the Smithsonian is that of so many other things: It has become so institutionalized and respected, demonstrating the wonderful depth and breadth of science, that to criticize it as too much government or misplaced government is difficult. "What harm could supporting such an institution be?" would be the reply from most people. The harm is that it gives control over science to government, when it should be free from control. Control in the long run leads to monopoly and the stifling of science, particularly when exercised by socialists.

It is difficult to point these things out when one of the highlights of visiting Washington is to take in the Smithsonian Institute and its marvelous displays. Do not forget that one of the means used by statists is the use of display to dazzle the citizens. This can range from banners and flags, to monuments and monoliths, to overwhelming the doubting citizen with experts — all with the citizens' taxes.

Returning to Darwin, his work served as the basis for the elimination of God from science. Once a person is convinced of evolution, he experiences a paradigm shift and his thought processes begin to gravitate toward the ultimate goal of the Illuminati: the elimination of God in everything. In reference to individual rights alone, if we were not created by God, do our rights come from him? This idea of God-given rights is the fundamental basis of American-style liberty as proclaimed in the Declaration of Independence. Erase this basis from the American mind and you set the stage for completely altering the American system.

There have been a large number of books debunking Darwin and evolution. They are easy to access online. These volumes use science, geography, physiology, etc. to show that what people believe to be scientific facts are in reality myth, but we have been so steadily programmed to believe the myth that Creation is looked upon as the absurdity. While these books are written by well-credentialed scientists, they rarely understand the conspiracy behind the promotion of evolution.

Robert Dale Owen was the originator of the 14th Amendment, although today others are given credit. The amendment was given over to Rep. Thaddeus Stevens to push through, and it was adopted without addressing black suffrage, which was granted by the 15th Amendment. We will discuss this amendment as being illegally adopted further on. It is interesting that today some who profess a knowledge of constitutional law use this amendment for the basis of their arguments.

American Union of Associations

While history books tend to focus on the foregoing famous communist communes, there were much larger communal initiatives to establish the revolution in America which in some ways were more important due to their number and organization.

---

27 Go to the Internet and reference Agenda 21, or visit www.jbs.org/Agenda21.

The largest communist organization, which sponsored close to 50 communes around the country, was the American Union of Associations. Less is known of this initiative than the three aforementioned communal efforts primarily due to the people involved — they had a profound influence on the future of our country, and this influence had to be obfuscated for modern students of history since the knowledge would expose too much of this influence on modern politics.

Two men prominently involved with the initiative were Charles Dana and the group's president at its founding, Horace Greeley, both of the *New York Tribune*. These communes were formed to produce the vanguard of the revolution based on the teachings of Fourier and Babeuf of France. They were not so much experiments as they were training camps.

One of their communes was established at what became Ripon, Wisconsin. It was here that the Republican Party was founded, primarily by leaders of the commune. This commune was the most important commune established in America as a result of this initiative, yet few have ever heard of it.

The State of Wisconsin gave birth to at least 12 utopian experiments. Most communes that existed across the country prior to the Civil War, of all types except religious such as the Shakers, registered with the communist First International when the commune movement started to wane.

The Republican Party grew rapidly and ultimately led to the demise of the Whig Party when politicians such as Lincoln became Republicans. Lincoln had nothing to do with the formation of the Republican Party as many Republicans believe — at least not overtly.

The name *republican* at the time had the connotation of being a violent democrat, especially in Europe, not an advocate of the true republican system as established by our Constitution. It was another use of semantics to fool the people.

The original name of the Democrat Party was Republican. The use of the name again was an obvious reference to Jacobinism, as we shall see.

We will revisit the story of the Republican Party origins in more depth later.

8
1830 — 1865: An Overview

In the period of 1830 — 1850, the flow of German radicals into the United States became a major problem, particularly after 1848. The so-called democratic revolutions of 1848 and 1849 had failed. Those who were involved had to leave their countries or face the consequences of their actions.

The democratic revolutions were part of what Marx referred to when he talked about democracy. In fact, *The Communist Manifesto* was written to be used during these revolutions to enlist more people into the communist movement. It was commissioned by the League of the Just in 1847, edited, and then published just before the outbreak of the revolutions in February, 1848.

The *Manifesto's* publication was part of the planning by the League of the Just, another direct descendant of the Illuminati, which fomented the revolutionary period and further demonstrates the falsehood that the revolutions were a spontaneous uprising of the downtrodden. The revolution of 1848 was a well-planned event, and they wrote this small book to serve as a guide for the activists during the upcoming revolution.

People do not just decide to have a revolution: "Hmm. I think we should have a revolution — let's have it tomorrow — next week at the latest!" doesn't work. These things are planned.

Modern historians make it seem that the revolutions were simply the uprising of people spontaneously with no real organization behind them. People do not revolt spontaneously across an entire continent involving several countries and governments. People who do not speak to one another because of the differences in language, culture, society, government, and ability to travel, at least not at the level we are told the grassroots decided to revolt at the same time. There were no phones and social media in those days that we are told result in the same happenings today.

The League of the Just formed as a secret society in 1836 as an offshoot of an earlier organization called the League of Outlaws.

This tactic has not changed in 200 years and explains why so many social and community organizations seem to engage in political activity promoting government and/or socialism.

And, just as Mirabeau and the Illuminati suggested, this secret society changed their name three times from 1836 to 1848 in order to throw the authorities off track, as well as to mark changes in leadership: the League of Outlaws, the League of the Just, and finally, the Communist League.

The German League of Outlaws, and then the Just, at first cooperated with the Carbonari, another descendant of the Illuminati, but came out of an alliance with Mazzini to engage in pure communism, becoming even more violent in outlook during the period of 1837-1838. However, they would still cooperate from time to time as the need arose.

Friedrich Engels said that the League of Outlaws was "in reality not much more than a German branch of the French secret societies and especially of the *Société des Saisons*" (Society of the Seasons), with goals "the same as those of other Parisian secret societies of the period." These goals were Illuminist, against God and for the establishment of the New World Order. The implementation of the tactics to reach these goals by the followers of Blanqui was always violent and the organization was too small to serve as a catalyst for taking over the government, but it was instrumental in producing reactions by the government that served the Conspiracy's purpose.

The Bund der Geächteten, or League of Outlaws, was founded in Paris by German exiles. The founder, Theodor Schuster, based it on the Carbonari and Philadelphes of Buonarroti in 1834. It had around 100 members in Paris and another 50 in Frankfurt. It fragmented into the Bund der Gerechten, or the League of the Just, in 1838. One of the leading members who was an associate of Buonarroti, Johann Höckerig, moved it from Paris to London.

Initially, it took on the appearance of being Christian and converting Christianity into communism. Following the plan of Mirabeau, the nuclei of the league were camouflaged in innocent "surface" groups, such as singing, educational, and sports clubs. However, those who were in the same camp as Marx and Engels won out and the organization reverted to being Illuminist in orientation, rejecting any thought of religion. Wilhelm (William) Weitling and Goodwyn Barmby, who were the initial leaders of promoting a Christian base to communism, lost out and retired from the organization to follow different paths for the establishment of a communist base.

The progression from the Illuminati was through the Cercle Social of Bonneville. It followed Babeuf, then Buonarroti, Höckerig, and Theodor Schuster, and ultimately Marx and Engels.

The principal manifesto of the Just had been written by William Weitling before Marx and Engels wrote *The Communist Manifesto*. Fourier's utopian socialism also influenced the league. Weitling was the most influential man within the league until Marx and Engels took the leadership roles. Weitling immigrated to the United States, where he was active in promoting communism. The League moved out of Germany to France, ending up in London after being expelled from France in 1839.

In London, prior to the revolutions of 1848, it took on a more international flavor, reversing the earlier nationalism of the movement and this would serve as the basis for the two strategies of the Master Conspiracy going into the 1850s.

They formed a front called the Educational Society for German Workmen in 1840. They were able to recruit over 1,000 members by 1847, including 250 in other countries of Europe and Latin America. They converted this organization into a communist entity.

Marx and Engels were not the primary leaders at this time, although they had influence enough to rid the organization of those they disapproved of — this ultimately helped built the conditions for their ascendency. Once they had enough of a leadership role, the Communist League put their names on the *Manifesto* as the authors. For some time, the small book was printed as being written anonymously.

The league set about infiltrating or cooperating with several other organizations and fronts, with an interlocking leadership that gave coordination to the revolution.

After arriving in the U.S., Wilhelm (William) Weitling pulled the Arbeiterbund (Workers' League) together in 1850 with groups of communists that had been formed in over a dozen major cities around the country, from New York to Detroit, from Milwaukee to Louisville.

Secret members of the league helped the National Industrial Congress in New York, which led to forming a Social Reform Association within the National Reform Association in New York. They had a German-language journal that first appeared in January 1846 under Babeuf's title, *Tribune of the People* or *Volktribun*, addressed to "the poor, the supplicants, the oppressed."

As you read the evidence of radical organizations in this period, you will realize that communism did not start with Marx as many believe, although this falsehood has been taught and propagated in books and reports on communism that would fill a room from wall to wall and floor to ceiling.

The idea that communism started with Marx and Engels is to hide the truth that secret societies, the Enlightenment, and particularly the Illuminati and its offspring, were the sires of nearly all of our problems in regard to the deterioration of our Republic.

By believing the myth of Marx as sire of communism, a person cannot then understand why some seem to oppose Marx and still work to destroy the United States. Many communists opposed Marx in the formative years of the open communist movement. They may have disagreed with a nuance or the personality, but they worked to subvert their countries nonetheless.

There was no leader of a European revolutionary movement or organization whose name has come down to us over history that did not form a secret society as the main tenet of his movement: Weishaupt, Voltaire, Bonneville, Babeuf, Considerant, Lafayette, Mazzini, etc. The same was the case for many of their offspring in America.

The German Confederation contained the most widespread number of cities involved in the revolutions of 1848 to 1849. Unlike France, which was already a nationalist government, Germany was a confederation of independent principalities, requiring a revolution in all of them to be successful. Since France had a centralized government, they only needed a revolution in Paris to affect all of France.

The German revolutionaries who after their defeat fled their country to the United States started many newspapers and ingratiated themselves into the political process even before they became citizens. Carl Schurz was looked upon by Americans as the prominent leader of the so-called German vote within the Republican Party. He was placed in that position more by American politicians than the Germans. He was no more than an underling and subaltern until he left Germany and came under the direction of Mazzini as one of his emissaries to the U.S.

Schurz came to America a couple of years after fleeing Baden, Germany, where he was second in command, under the German communist, Friederich Anneke, of a brigade that tried to seize a government arsenal to gain weapons for German revolutionaries in 1848. Anneke was a close associate of Marx and Engels. Anneke's brother Emil served as the first Republican auditor general for the State of Michigan.

After coming to the United States, Schurz, Anneke, and other communists were appointed to high military positions in the Union Army. *At least 40 German radical leaders* attained the rank of general by appointment or promotion by war's end.

There were at least 78 foreign-born officers that were brevetted general in the Union Army, *in addition to the Germans*, for a minimum of 118. The Confederate Army had a total of only 10 generals who were foreign born. Several of the Union generals returned to Europe and continued their revolutionary activities, such as Gustave-Paul Cluseret, who served under Generals McClellan and Fremont then became a friend of Marx.

Union Secretary of War Edwin Stanton had been a member of Buchanan's Southern Rights Cabinet, but switched sides to become a member of Lincoln's Cabinet. He was accused by many as acting with the secessionists until he joined hands with the Radicals and won a seat in Lincoln's Cabinet; he was one of those who promoted secession until it was a fact, and then became a unionist.

Montgomery Blair and Caleb Cushing were among those who said that Stanton was a secessionist while working for Buchanan. There are very few men with the lack of character of Stanton. When it came to loyalty, Stanton demanded it but rarely gave it. Even after he joined Lincoln's Cabinet, he initially spoke of Lincoln with a sneer and found him a "low, cunning clown."

The communist leader Charles Dana was to join Stanton in the War Department as one of his undersecretaries. Most of the communist military appointments, however, were made prior to Dana joining the War Department, demonstrating the radical influence that prevailed and became overt in filling even the civilian positions in the Department with openly communist leaders.

Another undersecretary was Peter H. Watson, who went on to become one of John D. Rockefeller's attorneys and helped build the South Improvement Company. This was later broken up via an antitrust suit into several divisions of Standard Oil, all with the majority of stock held by Rockefeller!

After the war, while Watson helped Rockefeller build his empire, Dana became the leader of the anti-Rockefeller forces. The Rockefellers would go on to become a prominent part of building the New World Order. It reminds one of the conspiratorial tactic: Assume the leadership of your own opposition; where none exists, create it.

While there are many who claim that Rockefeller was Jewish, it would seem out of character therefore, if he was, that he would hire Watson who was anti-Semitic, as were Stanton and Dana.

Watson was involved with Stanton and Lincoln in the McCormick reaper patent case (Cyrus H. McCormick vs. John H. Manny) in 1855. Manny initially hired Lincoln to be part of the legal team. When Manny and Lincoln met Stanton in his office, Stanton in no uncertain terms insulted Lincoln's character and ability, apparently not even greeting him.

Stanton continued this insulting manner even when he wrote to Buchanan some years later portraying "the painful imbecility of Lincoln."

Peter H. Watson as part of the Manny team corresponded with Lincoln concerning the case. Lincoln did considerable work on it, but was prohibited by Stanton from participation in the trial.

It prompts the question as to what possessed Lincoln to name Stanton as Secretary of War — or, better put, what power may have forced him to?

While there was no love between Stanton and Lincoln, they and others all worked together to build a draconian government over time, during and after the Civil War. Again, it makes one wonder what power there was to get Lincoln to name Stanton as secretary of war, especially since Stanton had served as attorney general under Buchanan and was a lawyer, not a military sort.

Sen. Sumner, later to officially join the First International, said of Stanton during the confirmation of Stanton's appointment in the Senate that he was "one of us."

A little known incident is reported in a book on the life of Clement L. Vallandigham by his brother. He states that Col. Thomas Key called on Vallandigham; during their conversation Vallandigham brought up Stanton and said that he had a high esteem for the man. They had been "close intimate friends" for years.

Key abruptly stood, concluding the conversation, and immediately departed. Vallandigham never knew the purpose of the visit or the reason for the abrupt departure. Apparently, McClellan was looking for a recommendation for secretary of war to recommend to Lincoln. Key was so impressed by Vallandigham's praise that he immediately left to inform McClellan, and this led to the chain of events by which Stanton was asked by Lincoln to serve.

If true this is very interesting, since what we know of the relationship between Lincoln and Stanton; the fact that Stanton was a close friend of Vallandigham, whom we will address further on as a member of the Knights of the Golden Circle; Key being a member of the Order, etc., makes a rare stew.

Actually, the circle of personalities becomes a Hydra. We know the Conspiracy is a single body, but the heads that stand out appear to the observer to be separate from one another, when in fact they are not.

The initial call for troops in the North was answered by the German Turnverein, or Turner Societies.

Many, if not most, Turner groups had militia and trained them in preparation for the future Civil War, some over a ten year period. They prepared for the war just as they had prepared beforehand for the "democratic" revolution at home in Germany, where the Turner organizations flocked to the banners of the revolution.

Joseph Gerhardt, a 48er, founded the Turner Company in Washington, D.C., just before the war. It had the distinction of being the first volunteer group assembled after Lincoln's call for troops, and served as the honor guard and body guard at Lincoln's first inauguration.

The initial use of German brigades in the call-up of troops became so embarrassing that the Germans sometimes tried to find men with English names to become the commanding officers, since the appearance was that the Union Army was German. This image changed after more states raised their militias and the military draft was established.

An English-named commander was used in St. Louis. In Ohio, the first German regiment was commanded by Robert L. McCook, law partner of John Bernhard Stallo. The real military man was August Willich and the early volunteers were Turnverein.

Stallo was an Ohio Hegelian and a close friend of revolutionaries including August Willich, who had fought alongside Engels in 1848. Willich was one of the founders of the Communist League with Marx and Engels, and as a Union general marched with Sherman through Georgia.

Both foreign-born and American-born radical general officers were present in the Union Army. William Tecumseh Sherman, like so many Union generals, had no problem with communists directly under his command. In fact, according to the book *Lincoln's Marxists*, Sherman was listed in a communist publication as a member of an "approved" list of socialists/communists. Considering his actions, both during the war and later, this would fit.

Gen. William Birney had participated in the Paris uprising of 1848. He was known as a freethinker at a time when being called an atheist was not in one's interest, and in 1874 he moved to Washington and became the attorney for the District of Columbia.

During the Civil War both sides participated in unconstitutional acts, albeit the South operated under their Confederation.

The North was the worse violator, suspending habeas corpus, jailing any leader or editor critical of federal policy, declaring military law over large territories of civilian rule, issuing paper money contrary to the Constitution, and so forth. Often this military rule was commanded by the likes of Gen. Joseph Weydemeyer, a personal friend of Karl Marx.

There were violations of common decency and what we would think of as the rules of the Geneva Convention today by both sides, but it was more widespread in the North.

The acts of violence performed by Union troops under German Marxist command against civilian personnel and property became an ironic argument used 80 years later in the German Wehrmacht propaganda magazine *Signal* in World War II. They documented the behavior of these Union troops to make the case for total resistance by the Germans against the American army since the "American" soldier was so brutal — one dare not surrender. It strengthened the resolve of the German soldier to fight on when it was obvious the war had been lost, prolonging the war and leading to many of our soldiers dying as a result.

Many, if not most, of the atrocities performed on Confederate prisoners of war were done by German Marxists or under such leadership. The deprivation on both sides in POW camps was bad, and the treatment varied from camp to camp. A case can be made in many instances that the Southern-run camps were a problem due to a lack of supply (although there were brutal exceptions) whereas in certain Northern-run camps the deliberate, systematic torture and killing of Confederate soldiers occurred. This was done not by their captors, but by those into whose hands they were interred who were not combat soldiers but German Turner camp guards, forerunners of the same ilk in Germany in the 1940s.

After the Civil War, the Conspiracy did all it could to codify the consolidation of control implemented during the war rather than revert to a constitutional system. We have never recovered from it.

The Greenback Party gave political reality to the socialist-produced pressure to retain paper money rather than revert back to the *constitutionally mandated* gold and silver. The party was influenced by the position of Proudhon on credit and the monetary system. In 1880, the Socialist Labor Party supported the Greenback Party.

Civil service came about through the same leadership. Opponents of small government called the previous system the "spoils system which helped promote the building of the federal bureaucracy." The term had been used widely by Young America since the Jackson administration's misuse of the appointment system.

Jefferson started the process of eliminating people from the employ of his administration if they disagreed with him. Washington, to a fault, did not until they resigned in the face of exposure as being false to the government.

Jefferson eliminated 39 people. The five presidents before Jackson let a total of 35 people go. Jackson fired nearly 700 in his first year alone. This was done not to reduce the size of government but to make room for Jackson's adherents. These were the days when the federal government counted their employees within various departments by the score, not the thousands; however, there were several thousand in total in the combination of all federal employment which included those working in the postal service by the time of the Civil War. Today it is millions.

Once Civil Service was established, making it more difficult to release government employees, the national government became larger and larger, with professional bureaucrats always working to find ways to grow the government. When it came to running the government the bureaucrats took on more and more power in the executive branch, becoming competitive with Congress. Increasingly Congress became reliant on the bureaucrats to offer advice, write bills, formulate the budget, and provide support for any government initiative. The bureaucrats became virtually a fourth branch of government, with little in the way of checks and balances against their growth of power.

As government grew, took on more unconstitutional responsibilities, and became more complicated, Congress was more than happy to at first allow and then rely on the bureaucrats to plan and run things.

In modern times, bureaucrats violate the law and use regulations to control or harass political opposition, and in the process protect each other from congressional investigation; in other words, protecting each other's posterior. This is particularly true when the administration is corrupt. The use of the IRS, for instance, has been a recurring problem since the agency was founded. Our country's Founders recognized the possibility of such things happening when they wrote the Constitution, thereby making it against the law for the federal government to directly tax individuals. They did not want the federal government to be able to directly control the individual through taxation and enforcement. Thus, the Constitution needed to be amended to allow the income tax and the IRS to enforce it.

Carl Schurz toured the South on the recommendation of President Johnson after the war to learn what needed to be done to rebuild the South. Rebuilding the South was not on the minds of the Radicals; to them "Reconstruction" was needed to dissuade the pesky Southerners from demanding adherence to the Constitution. It was to be reconstruction, not restoration or rebuilding. It was to be the elimination of "the old social order," not simply the elimination of slavery. That had already been accomplished.

In true leftist form, Schurz returned recommending land reform similar to what the Chinese communist Mao Zedong would claim his reforms were a century later, taking land from the rich and giving it to the poor, or in the case of the South, to the ex-slaves as well. Land reform would have totally changed the old social order and laid the foundation to totally socialize the South.

One has to ask two questions: What gives the right to government to take property from one and give it to another? And, were the freed slaves capable of handling commercial property if it would have been handed to them? If the answer to the second question is no, then it would have been irresponsible to do so and may have led not only to their failure, but the failure of the entire agrarian system that was the South. If the answer is yes, then what does that say about the education of the slaves that they would have been capable of doing all that it takes to manage as well as work property? It would mean that the image propagated today of an ignorant slave population was false. We believe the answer lies somewhere in between the two.

Johnson, although an early supporter of land reform years before, rejected the recommendation, which became just one of the real reasons he was later impeached by the Radical-led Congress. It must have come as a real shock to the land-reform movement, because they at one time considered Johnson to be one of them. He was even considered as a candidate for a land-reform political ticket.

Congress, however, ordered 100,000 copies of the Schurz report to be printed and distributed. It became an important tool of the Radical Republicans.

Such a production today by a political majority in Congress to propagandize the population would be the equivalent of 1,300,000 copies.

Part of the official charges of impeachment against Johnson was that he had fired Edwin Stanton, the Secretary of War. Since Lincoln had appointed him, it was said by the Radicals that the succeeding president could not fire him, only Congress could do that.

Andrew Johnson, as a senator and as governor of Tennessee, had seen the Conspiracy at work in the South and publicly exposed it before he became vice president under Lincoln. In regard to the Southern conspirators, Johnson said on January 31, 1862:

There has been a deliberate design for years to change the nature and genius of this government.
— *The Great Conspiracy: Its Origin and History*,
John A. Logan, 1886, page 240

When he saw the problem in the South, he was elevated in the North. When he saw it in the North, he was smeared. He did not see the extent of the Conspiracy at work in the North until a few weeks into his presidency. As president, he started to see what was really happening. As vice president he had been out of the loop so to speak, with his office being more of a ceremonial position, unlike how it is treated today. He subsequently started a speaking tour as president to expose this fact and was well received by large crowds until the Conspiracy organized mobs to shout him down and force him off the circuit.

Johnson was only one of four presidents who attempted to fight the Conspiracy (Washington, Adams, and Harding being the others). Although he did a great many things that constitutionalists would disagree with, he did see an internal conspiracy at work and not being part of it tried to stop it. Some school history books have pictured Johnson as a drunk, and as far as they are concerned that is all you need to know about the man.

The mere fact that he asked Schurz to tour the South and devise recommendations illustrates his ignorance of and involvement in something the depth of which he little understood.

Johnson claimed that there was a conspiracy in the Radical Republican Congress to bring about an autocracy or dictatorship, and that they had organized riots in the South, specifically New Orleans, as part of this plan, to give an excuse for continued and increased military crackdown over the Southern civilian population, even the Border States.

There were always radical influences in New Orleans, and the history of our early country was greatly influenced out of that area, especially when it was held by Spain or France. The political climate was always volatile, and it was not devoid of communist influence. For instance, residing there was Sebastian Seiler, the publisher of the *New Orleans Journal*, a German communist newspaper that was published there in 1860 until Seiler had to flee the city in November. Seiler was an acquaintance of Marx and a member of the League of the Just. Like Marx, he had little regard for his family, abandoning them to creditors when he fled England for America.

Seiler was an associate of Wilhelm Weitling, who visited the city on one occasion. Seiler was a member of the Brussels Communist Correspondence Committee of Marx in 1846. In other words he was close to the top leadership of the communist movement, since the Correspondence Committee was not that large at the time. He served as a stenographer for the French National Assembly in 1846 and 1847, and then took part in the revolutions of 1848 as a member of the Communist League.

Seiler made the statement that he felt that the entire blame for the Civil War was due to the radical German influence in the North, although he supported abolition. He obviously looked at the situation through a glass that was limited by his experience. He was correct — as far as it went.

There were Turner units in New Orleans, and other cities throughout the South. They were more disorganized than those in the North and at first were reluctant to take part in the war, but came around and served in the Confederate Army. Just as in New Orleans, their ranks were swelled with others besides Germans to fill the quota for recognition as battalions.

One of the Turners in New Orleans, Dr. Grall, was employed at one time by Jefferson Davis as a doctor.

In some areas of the South, the Turners remained radically attached to Northern politics and were ostracized, even attacked by Southern citizens.

In 1868, Johnson chose William Maxwell Evarts as chief counsel in his impeachment trial before the Senate. Evarts was a member of the Order. Since the president was impeached, we are not sure how effectively this member of the Order defended him. Considering how the proceedings were handled, there probably was nothing that could have been done to stop the impeachment. Rep. Benjamin Butler was a raging bull, using the power of the Radicals to do just about anything short of shooting Johnson on the floor of the House. Sen. Orris Sanford Ferry, of the Order, voted Johnson guilty. In other words, Johnson was surrounded on both sides by the enemies of the Constitution, both in Congress and on his own defense team.

You get a good sense as to why Johnson was impeached when you read quotes from the "impeachment papers" of Andrew Johnson.

Evarts would later become the attorney general under Johnson, then secretary of state under Rutherford Hayes. He was a founding member of the New York City Bar Association and served as its first president, from 1870 to 1879. A founding member of Skull and Bones, Frederick Ellsworth Mather, was also involved in the formation of the Bar Association.

It is interesting that the Senate confirmed Evarts as attorney general after he served as Johnson's attorney against the radicals in the Congress. One would have thought he would never have gained confirmation considering the politics of the day, but then, one has to understand the Conspiracy.

Evarts was to say ten years after the war that such organizations as Skull and Bones led to snobbery, yet his son Maxwell was tagged for membership. Another son Allen Wardner Evarts supported the founding of Wolf's Head. And, the elder Evarts went on to play a role in many enterprises run by those who played a dominant part in building the power in government and industry.

Johnson went on a tour to inform the people how the Radicals in Congress were doing all they could to prevent the restoration of representative government in the South. Recent events in New Orleans and elsewhere were being used to inflame the Northern citizens against the restoration of state governments in the South and to continue, even increase, the army's control over the Southern states.

The first few stops where he spoke he was greeted by enthusiastic crowds. The initial flush of anger over Lincoln's assassination and holding the entire South to blame were subsiding. The majority of the people wanted to return to a true peace, welcoming back their Southern brothers into the Union. The Conspiracy had something else in mind. Agitators were organized to shout Johnson down until he was forced to quit the "swing," as the tour was known, referring to the swing around the bulk of the Northern-populated areas.

By the time he appeared in Indianapolis, the hecklers opened the meeting by tearing down the transparencies, firing shots, killing one man and wounding others, and forcing the president to quit the place without uttering a word. Similar tactics were attempted in the 2016 presidential campaign.

The impeachment papers cited a portion of the speech that Johnson gave on August 18, 1866:

We have witnessed in one department of the Government every endeavor to prevent the restoration of peace, harmony, and union. We have seen hanging upon the verge of the Government, as it were, a body called, or which assumes to be, the Congress of the United States, while in fact is only a part of the States. We have seen this Congress pretend to be for the Union, when its every step and act tended to perpetuate disunion and make a disruption of the States inevitable. * * * We have seen Congress gradually encroach, step by step, upon constitutional rights, and violate, day after day and month after month, fundamental principles of the Government. We have seen a Congress that seemed to forget that there was a limit to the sphere and scope of legislation. We have seen a Congress in a minority assume to exercise power which, allowed to be consummated, would result in despotism or monarchy itself.

Continuing in the papers:

Go on. Perhaps if you had a word or two on the subject of New Orleans you might understand more about it than you do. And if you will go back — if you will go back and ascertain the cause of the riot at New Orleans, perhaps you will not be so prompt in calling out "New Orleans." If you will take up the riot at New Orleans and trace it back to its source or its immediate cause, you will find out who was responsible for the blood that was shed there. If you will take up the riot at New Orleans and trace it back to the Radical Congress, you will find that the riot at New Orleans was substantially planned.

Further:

You will also find that that convention did assemble, in violation of law, and the intention of that convention was to supersede the reorganized authorities in the State government of Louisiana, which had been recognized by the Government of the United States; and every man engaged in that rebellion in that convention, with the intention of superseding and upturning the civil government which had been recognized by the Government of the United States, I say that he was a traitor to the Constitution of the United States; and hence you find another rebellion was commenced, *having its origin in the Radical Congress. [emphasis added.]*

These quotes were used to make it look as if Johnson were unstable and a "conspiracy theorist": "It is just silly to believe that conspirators in government and the army would contrive to start a riot in New Orleans as an excuse to bring about authoritarian rule. He must be a drunk!" — was the general theme.

The convention Johnson was referring to was an attempt to form a government to supersede the legitimate state government, similar to what had happened in Kansas before the war. Such constitutional conventions have been attempted several times in our history in an effort to either take over the government or rewrite the state or federal constitutions by radical forces.

It is just one of the reasons many are opposed to a modern constitutional convention or convention of the states, or convention of any other name. Too many times in our history, rogue conventions have been held which have led to consequences that put constituted government into chaos. It has happened in states and federally. It has not been unusual for a state to have more than one convention at the same time by opposing political forces, and this has led to decisions by the federal government recognizing one over the other, a very dangerous thing if the Congress is radical.

This technique was used to repeal prohibition. For instance, the Utah Legislature especially had no desire to stop prohibition. A convention was held to ratify the repealing amendment; it was recognized as legal by the Congress and thus they declared prohibition over due to the "necessary" states ratifying the repeal. We shall see that such things have happened more than once, making any idea of a constitutional convention or convention of the states very dangerous.

Whereas Johnson thought he could fire Stanton, whose conspiratorial history was long, he couldn't fire Thaddeus Stevens, the leader of the Radical Republicans in Congress, and this would mar his presidency.

The first bill of impeachment against Johnson submitted by James Monroe Ashley, a Radical Republican, was defeated. Ashley tried to prove that Johnson assassinated Lincoln.

One of the reasons that Johnson was not found guilty in his trial before the Senate was that some senators did not want to see Benjamin Wade made president. Wade would have succeeded Johnson under the rules of succession at the time. From 1792 to 1886, the line of succession was vice president then president *pro tempore* of the U.S. Senate, and Wade was president *pro tempore* at the time of the trial.

The pressure to find Johnson guilty was immense. The tactic of depriving members of Congress their seats was used if they were suspected of wanting to vote for Johnson, as was done with John Potter Stockton of New Jersey. This first coercive tactic prevented the necessity of using it on others who were so inclined.

There were at least six senators who wanted to vote not guilty but were pressured into voting guilty. Even the Methodist Church got involved in pressuring Waitman T. Willey of West Virginia, who was a Methodist. He had indicated that regardless of his opinion, he was going to live by the Constitution, but once his vote was not needed to "acquit," he voted guilty.

The Methodist General Conference that was held in Chicago in 1868 tried to pray for President Johnson's conviction. It was objected to but they went ahead and did so anyway.

The senators who did not vote guilty suffered socially and in business, and were driven out of politics. Had more of the senators who wanted to vote not guilty done so, the number on that side of the ledger would have been greater and perhaps those who stood alone would not have fared as badly as they did.

If a true history is ever written about Johnson, there will be much more to admire about the man than history books would indicate, even though one may disagree wholeheartedly with some of his political positions.

If Johnson would have won his battle with the Radicals, it is improbable that the Constitution would have been amended as it was over the next few years; there may have been no Reconstruction, with the South escaping 10 years of harsh treatment; and the "Solid South" would never have been formed on the political scene as a reaction against the North due to Reconstruction. The Solid South were Democrats who voted as a bloc against Republicans; they remained a part of the Congress for the next 100 years.

During this post war decade, arrests of private individuals were common and served as examples to all that resistance to U.S. Army rule was forbidden, even with the pen of editors, or court writs of judges. In areas occupied by the Army, not only in the North, but especially in the South, newspapers would not be allowed freedom of the press or judges the ability to uphold the U.S. Constitution. The only real authority was the Radicals backed up by the army.

As to amendments brought forward, recall that the originator of the 14th Amendment was Robert Dale Owen, who gave it to Thaddeus Stevens to push through Congress.

We do not mean to imply that the elimination of slavery by changing the Constitution was not necessary. It is the language and means used to change the Constitution that was a problem.

In December 1865, many Southern senators and congressmen presented their credentials to Congress to be seated under Johnson's terms of reconstruction but Thaddeus Stevens prevented these men from being seated. What helped Stevens convince others was that too many were former CSA (Confederate States of America) officials and generals.

Another problem Johnson had with the Radicals was that he was opposed to the execution of Emperor Maximilian after he was defeated in Mexico. Maximilian, an Austrian, had been forced on Mexico basically due to the machinations of Napoleon III. This is a story in itself which would require a volume to document. The basic story line is that the European powers of Spain, England, and France wanted to regain Mexico as a buffer to the United States in Latin America, and to do it while we were involved in a civil war so we could not prevent it. All backed out except Napoleon III, who installed Maximilian as emperor. He and the French forces in Mexico were ultimately defeated, leading to the execution of Maximilian.

Our ambassador was authorized to commit the use of U.S. troops for the Mexican leader Benito Juarez' assistance if need be after the war. The troops were not needed. Johnson's belief that Maximilian should not be executed, but exiled home to Austria, led to the resignation of our ambassador, Lewis Davis Campbell.

The support of Juarez, the revolutionary leader of Mexico, by Gen. Philip Sheridan included 30,000 muskets from the Baton Rouge Arsenal alone during 1866. Sheridan did feign an invasion, which had a direct influence on the actions of the Imperialists under Maximilian.

In the 1820s and 1830s, the Comuneros (Communist) movement flourished in Spain and was exported to Mexico. It had a detrimental effect on both nations. In Spain, it eventually led to the Spanish Civil War in the 1930s. Robert Owen, in the same decade that he started his famous American commune, traveled to Mexico to promote communism there as well.

In Mexico, such agitation led to almost perpetual revolution for 75 years, until the communists were permanently installed in the Mexican government in 1914 — three years prior to this being done in Russia — a fact virtually unknown to American citizens. The history of the revolutionary turmoil in Mexico is the record of communism within its borders. It is the reason that Trotsky fled to Mexico after falling out with Stalin — it was another communist-led state.

The reader may wonder why he is either unaware of these facts, or doubt that they are true. The reason he is unaware is that the Conspiracy has never wanted the American people to wake up to what has been going on slowly, a step at a time, particularly right next door. Knowing that a communist government existed in Mexico would have awakened the American people.

As an example, it is not unusual for open communists to be in the Mexican national cabinet. One of the largest and expanding sea ports on the western coast of Mexico, Lazaro Cardenas, was renamed after the president of Mexico, who served for some years, ending in 1940. He was awarded by Stalin, the Stalin Peace Prize which later was renamed the Lenin Peace Prize. They do not award such medals to non-communists. Cardenas was president during Trotsky's sojourn in Mexico.

The traditional policy of the United States was to back up anti-clerics and revolutionaries, not only in Mexico but in all of the Latin American countries. This policy has continued up to today, albeit sometimes cloaked as a corporate initiative. Buchanan, as the darling of Young America, gave valuable assistance to the first "liberal" leader in Mexico, who carried out wholesale pillage of the Catholic Church.

Buchanan even used the U.S. Navy to seize Mexican naval vessels under the command of the Miramon government off the Mexican coast, had them taken to New Orleans, and then made them a present to Juarez. A general blockage of arms and supplies to Miramon was maintained by Buchanan, allowing Juarez to be constantly refurbished.

These were acts of war without the consent of Congress, setting a precedent for administrations that followed.

The ignorance of the American people as to the history of Mexico is worse than their knowledge of Europe, yet it is right next door. Mexico and its people have been used as a punching bag for extreme socialist leaders for a long time. The last several decades have been relatively stable only because of the Conspiracy having what they want in that sad country. *Relatively* stable compared to its past history, that is.[28]

Regrettably, Mexico has taken a turn toward violence that rivals the Middle East in amount, style, and breadth of terrorism. This is easily verifiable online, but the author recommends that one does not do this. The images that one can see will scar a normal person for life — particularly what they are doing to women. And yet there is not one word in the American media.

A section of this volume could include the radical influence on Mexico from the United States. Constant revolution within Mexico has been carried out by communists and agents of secret societies for a long time. As an example of the problems in Mexico, the president of Mexico at the time of the Civil War, as mentioned, was Benito Juarez, who came to power in the "normal" manner: revolution. Juarez was such a hero of the international socialists that a socialist in Italy named Mussolini named his son *Benito* after him.

Juarez' hero was Lincoln.

Europe played games with Mexico while our country was bogged down in the Civil War, and the people of Mexico suffered under all of their leaders, native or foreign. Some leaders were so anti-clerical they slaughtered priests and nuns; this included the forces of Juarez. This continued off and on into the 1920s under the then current party leadership of Mexico. Considering the slaughter of clergy for over a two-hundred-year span, it is amazing that the Catholic religion has survived there.

It can be stated that the policies of our own government from the time of Monroe led to Mexico being

---

28   This author was engaged in a conversation with a gentleman, describing the secrecy of the powers in the United States, the organizations they belong to, and what these organizations stand for. We were interrupted by another gentleman, a Mexican small-business man, who had been listening to us and who said: "The reason your leaders hide their doings is because you can do something about it. In my country, they hide nothing because there is nothing we can do about it."

radicalized, with massive immigration into our country as a result, and led to Mexico being nominally pro-German in the First World War — certainly anti-U.S. — and subsequently serving as the ploy for the British to entangle the U.S. into World War I. Most of the oil used by the British during the war came from Mexico. This also had a great influence on the Mexican government.

These policies would seem contradictory, but then we see that as a constant today in American foreign policy. When one keeps their mind on the endgame, it makes sense; if not, it does not make any sense.

The problem with taking sides in Mexico as a lover of liberty is that no matter what side you would take, you'd lose. Both sides had a bad habit of slaughtering their opponents, even after the cessation of hostilities.

The smear attacks by the Conspiracy against Andrew Johnson have lasted for nearly 150 years — all because he dared defy the plans of the Conspiracy once he realized what was going on.

There are many historians who believe that Stanton or someone in Stanton's office played a hand in the assassination of Lincoln. One reason this is believed is that the telegraph lines out of Washington were controlled by Stanton's office. There is conflicting evidence as to whether these lines were or were not shut down at the time of the assassination, depending on the source.

A student of George Bancroft's at Round Hill likewise played a role in the mess that became the assassination investigation. Surgeon General J. K. Barnes, who for whatever reason, cut out a section of vertebrae from John Wilkes Booth's spinal column in the neck, and this may have played an adverse role in the formal identification of Booth's body.

There never was an autopsy performed, even though the record says that there was. No record of an autopsy exists in the Army and Navy Medical Museum, which would house such a document, nor was the bullet that killed Booth — more on this later.

Preservation of a corpse was not well done in those days and facial features would become somewhat distorted within a short time — enough to alter an identification if the corpse looked anything like the individual identified as Booth.

Stanton gave orders as to the disposition of the corpse, as it had begun to putrefy.

Stories about the Lincoln assassination and subsequent events continue to swirl around in publishing and television because so many things were done by disagreeable personalities at all levels who obfuscated, rather than revealed the whole story. Innocents were punished and some of the guilty went free. Booth's sister claimed that her brother remained alive for many years. Truth or fiction, who knows? What is known is that it is impossible to discern fact from fiction today in much of the assassination story. Many people have written books trying to explain this or that about the assassination, and they are contradictory, adding confusion to much of the story.

One fact that lessens the idea that Booth lived is that assassins who work for conspiracies do not have a very long life span — they know too much. Often assassins are themselves assassinated soon after the event if it involves a high-profile victim and if it can expose the conspiracy behind the "lone gunman" — unless the person is under strict discipline or held virtually incognito in isolation. The trail leading to those who gave the order is usually cut off one way or another.

In Booth's case, the evidence is overwhelming that others were involved and that it constituted a much larger conspiracy than the few that were either killed or hanged.

Another consideration is that Booth's personality would probably not have allowed him to live in obscurity — he always sought the limelight and adoration of others.

The ramifications of the war have lasted up to our own time. The semantics battle waged over the years has been won by the Conspiracy, leading to their "official" history of events. One semantics battle mentioned was the use of the term "spoils system" to help bring about a permanent bureaucracy by planting a negative image of the practice of letting the previous administration's lackeys go to make room for the new administration's lackeys. Civil-service legislation came about after the war; this was helped by this use of semantics.

One of the most successful terms used has been "states rights." The term used before the Civil War was more often state sovereignty. There is a big difference between the two. The thirteen sovereign states, or countries, started the federal government, not the other way around. The term *state* had always been used to mean a country. Americans have been conditioned to think of a state as a subordinate unit within a country, not a country itself. The word was never changed, just the definition — at least in the minds of Americans.

It is true that after the original thirteen states formed the United States, Congress accepted the petitions of the citizens in the new territories for statehood, but they were to be sovereign states after establishing a republican government as required by the federal Constitution. It is impossible to have a *republic* as it is mandated for each state in the Constitution without state sovereignty — with the exception of those responsibilities delineated in the Constitution as delegated to the federal government.

Since the average American today does not understand the term *republic*, this concept is lost. Our schools and politicians have ingrained in the people the concept of *democracy* rather than *republic*. This simple idea, misused, changes the entire thinking of our citizens from what we are supposed to be to what the Conspiracy wants as the first step toward a totalitarian government as outlined in The *Communist Manifesto*.

Since 1958, there has been a full-court press by The John Birch Society to educate more and more people about the difference between a republic and a democracy, so the situation has begun to shift in the minds of tens of millions of Americans. But, it is difficult to overcome the millions of students' educated in the public schools that are taught democracy and nothing but democracy. Many private and home-school curricula do teach the difference.

This author was taught in public school that there is no difference between a republic and a democracy, only a preference of which word you used. This is nearly a direct quote of my civics teacher in the early 1950s.

Lincoln, as a member of the Illinois Legislature, voted to establish their second state seal, which proclaimed state sovereignty, and this was a state that had joined the United States after the original thirteen. As President Lincoln some years later, he denied that states were sovereign. The Illinois seal changed again after the Civil War, but the motto of the state remains "State Sovereignty — National Union" as it was then.

States' rights imply that the states have rights *under or within* the federal government. *State sovereignty* means the federal government is held together by consent of the states. The war did not settle the issue, only forced the issue. To maintain a national government that wanted the states to lose their sovereignty, the mind of the public was trained to use the term *states' rights* along with *democracy*.

The Conspiracy has moved a free people a long way mentally from the system we started.

America started out as a Christian country, but legally tolerant of other religions. Much has been done to eliminate this fact from the history of America and the minds of American students. In addition to the pronouncements of our Founders, six states of the thirteen required the governor to be of some form of Christian. Seven states required it of their legislators. In some states there was also a religious requirement to vote. This was all gone by the late 1820s.

Over the two centuries that have passed since the founding of our nation, much has been lost from the public memory. One such loss is that the colonies were diverse in their systems of government, and the relationship between the royal governors and provincial assemblies were different save one: the assemblies enjoyed the privilege and right to enact laws pertaining to their internal needs for justice and taxation.

The significance of the mandate agreed upon by the states and in our Constitution that each state enjoy a government that is a republic is lost on modern America. Each state, by necessity, had to change its system from what it was to what it should be, a republic.

It was not simply a matter of the federal government feeling its way along from thirteen colonies independent of each other to uniting under one system, it was that each colony had been in a state of flux, in varying degrees, from what it had been to what it had become by the end of the War for Independence. Even today, the states have differences in their structure, laws, and enforcement.

While no original state has a unicameral system, Nebraska and the territories of Guam and the Virgin Islands do. (So do all the states of Mexico.) This is a real departure from what was intended and illustrates one aspect of the differences that can exist within our system at the state level.

Into this atmosphere came the agents of the Illuminati to begin to break down all the vestiges of our American system and social order. It was an experiment in liberty, and it had to be nipped in the bud if the Conspiracy was to succeed.

The movement toward democracy and the accumulation of powers started with the states. This was the easiest to do since the states had been in the previously mentioned flux and used to change. Also, the sovereign states were the foundation blocks of a federal system. Chip away the foundation and the edifice falls. From 1789 to 1850 the selection of governor by legislatures was taken away in the "name of the people", the term of office was lengthened, and veto power and a larger share of the appointing power were invested in the governor.

Likewise a change came in suffrage. In the beginning, owning property or equivalent capital was the necessary ingredient to suffrage. The idea was that property owners would not vote to take something from one to give to another, or vote for other ideas destructive of property rights. For property rights, as one of the main bulwarks of liberty, is one of the main enemies of communism. Proudhon, the anarchist, published *What Is Property?* His answer was: property is theft. *The Communist Manifesto* condemned private property.

In order to subvert private property rights, the qualifications for voting were altered to allow non-property owners, or the equivalent capital holders, to vote in the name of democracy.

Suffrage changed and, besides the qualification of citizenship, manhood became the measure of suffrage from 1810 to 1852. John Adams, Daniel Webster, James Madison, James Monroe, John Marshall, Edmund Randolph, and others opposed these measures to no avail. The last state that had the property requirement was Rhode Island, and they changed the rules in the wake of the Dorr Rebellion in 1842, which was in support of a "Peoples' constitution."

We see similar cries today from those on the Left who want a new constitutional convention. Part of their agenda is to lower even further the qualifications for voting.

A side effect of this idea of suffrage became the feminist movement. After all, if the men have the vote, why not the women? Then the cry came for a lowering of the age requirement. Today, we hear voices advocating that all in the country vote, whether citizen or not. This is a part of the agenda of the Marxist Aztlan movement.

Another aspect to this movement is allowing non-citizens to monitor polling places, serve on juries, etc. Much of this agenda has found a home in places such as California, with only partial success, so far.

The colonies/states had operated under previous royal systems. The nation and federal government were entirely new and untested.

Once the original idea of suffrage changed, radicalism in the legislatures rose and some candidates campaigned as men bearing gifts.

Likewise, there was a simultaneous agenda to change the state governments in the selection of the governors, their length of office, appointing power, etc., all done from 1789 to 1850. In general, more and more power was invested in the state executive in the name of democracy and being more receptive to the people, the exact opposite of what it became. This too played a role in altering suffrage and placing more power into the executive of the states rather than the legislatures. It was a judo movement, creating the exact opposite of what had been the governmental structures within the states, and centralized the power.

We see the same tactic being used today to take responsibility away from the legislative branch and install into the executive branch. The propaganda mill has convinced a sizable percentage of the American people that the Congress is the problem and that more power needs to be vested in the executive. The Obama administration did not invent this strategy. The idea had been implied for some time and the groundwork laid by the media and political pundits, and it broke into the open and was put into practice during the Obama's tenure.

At the onset of our country, the counties within the states had more independence, but the process of taking away this independence in favor of the states was well on its way by 1830. Today, after a long process, in practice the counties are not much more than adjuncts of the state. The power of the sheriff remains but is rarely exercised due to the sheriffs' ignorance of their powers, intimidation by state and federal governments, or the petition by sheriffs for grants from the federal government to help augment their budgets. This not only makes them servants of the state, it makes them instruments of the federal government. Grants are only granted if you are doing what the government wants.[29]

The next step was to nationalize the states, as opposed to a federation, or federal government. The future aim is to regionalize the United States into a United Nations subsidiary. Every step removes the government further away from the citizen and any ability he may have to influence his government.

The same example can be used regarding the schools, with the consolidation programs carried out since the end of World War II. These consolidations have moved the parents further and further away from the proximity of the classroom — and thereby parental involvement — unless the access is controlled by the schools.

It is not unusual for the United Nations to mandate to the United States. This is usually carried out through the bureaucracy, bypassing the Congress and out of view of the citizen. Then, the Congress mandates to the legislatures and in turn, they to the counties and cities.[30]

The following chapters will deal with all the above in greater detail. Even so, the reality of the situation is that the United States has nearly come under total conspiratorial control on more than one occasion. It has been the layers of strength and morality within the American people and the body politic that have prevented this from happening — this and the problems the conspiracy has had within its own ranks.

We came dangerously close to this total control in the 20th century as a result of two centuries of Lilliputian threads laid not only over the entire body politic, but over American society as a whole. Only one thing prevented this, but this is for a later discussion.

---

29 As part of the continuing process to eliminate true republican principles and government structure, the process of local government consolidation is being used. A multitude of excuses for this initiative are in play, but the fact is that consolidation moves local government further away from local citizens. In the process, the elective office of sheriff is under threat of being eliminated in favor of larger units of regional law enforcement run by appointed leaders not directly answerable to the voter, as is the sheriff.

In regard to the states, as much as two-thirds of some state budgets comes from the federal coffers. This creates an adverse amount of pressure on the states to not object to unconstitutional federal laws and agencies that operate within their states.

30 This author once sat on a city council where a vote was taken on six different issues during one session. Five of the votes were forced upon the council by the legislature due to mandates.

9

THE USE OF MANY FRONTS

While it seems a far-fetched view today, from the beginning many Americans believed that the country would inevitably divide in two. This belief was the result of several initiatives, from the agitation in what was known as the West during the 1780s to today. There still exist pockets of citizens today who want to move their state into secession, and it flares up from time to time and moves from state to state. It is based on the fear that the government has grown too large and intrusive. This fear has always been used by the well-intentioned as well as those who have a different agenda than the welfare of local citizens.

Indeed, there are at least two independence movements in America today that have ties to "ex-communist" organizations within Russia and the Ukraine. Such links do not bode well for truly independent, liberty-minded leadership in the long run.

In the early years this desire for local autonomy came about because Eastern politicians would not allow the Western territories enough autonomy to run all of their own local affairs. This was a problem since the transportation and communication in those days hindered the ability of the coastal areas to play an immediate role in an emergency or perceived emergency in the interior, such as an Indian war.

The people had just fought to rid themselves of a power that had an entire ocean between them. The mountains and primitive aspects of the roads provided the same gulf in the minds of the Western inhabitants: a classic "them and us" outlook, rather than thinking of themselves as one country. In other words, communication and transportation had not grown to a level of uniting people together either as neighbors or as the United States.

Some of the original states at this time were much larger in area than today and involved great distances for the times, including rivers and mountains, which separated the people out to the west. Much of the territories that constituted the states were later broken off into new states, particularly the Southern states such as Virginia, North Carolina, etc.

To the extent the same was true relative to the distances that separated the two major sections, North and South. The means of conveyance over the roads or ocean coast were still slow and also tended to separate the citizens of early America. People did not travel to the extent that we do today, and the type and speed of travel that we have at our disposal was nearly impossible to imagine in that period. The time and distance were a source of division. Nor did early Americans have the convenience of instant communication that now serves to unite us, such as radio, television, the Internet, and the ever-present cell phone.

As an example of the time it took to travel in this time period, it was a marvel for Lloyds of London to receive news from France across the English Channel in five minutes using semaphore and telescopes, versus a two-day crossing across the English Channel, from the time they boarded ship to debarkation — just over 30 miles.

The states began as separate *countries*, and were not a union before the War for Independence. It took many years for citizens to consider themselves United States citizens before state citizens. Even in the youth of this author, it was not unusual for people to reply when they were asked where they were from, "I am a citizen of," then naming the state.

There was also a notable movement for secession in the Vermont, New Hampshire, and Maine area with the Shayites and Ethan Allen. All of these desires by local citizens were used by both the Jacobin Clubs and foreign powers for their own ends.

No definitive study has been made of the monies and agents from England, Spain, and France and their influence on American politics over the years *since* the initial upheavals before the War of 1812. The history of these three countries is rife with secret intelligence services being used to subvert the political aims of their rivals, and America has always been their rival. No historian seems to have considered this possibility.

When Spain, England, and France were not quarreling with each other, they agreed to harass us — actually even when they were quarreling with each other!

Ultimately the internal influence in America of Spain waned as she lost more and more territory in the Western Hemisphere. However, Spain was under constant vigilance due to American initiatives that threatened her territories, such as Mexico, Cuba, the rest of the Caribbean, and ultimately the Philippines. She must have been active in some capacity inside the U.S. to thwart these incursions. She certainly was during the early years relative to the Mississippi River, Florida, and the Lewis and Clark Expedition.

The influence of France also waxed and waned as she lost more territory in the Americas or had a chance to regain territory.

In addition, there was heavy investment in the U.S. from English businessmen, particularly in railroads and finance. In regard to the future of these two sectors, the politics of Congress and the states had considerable weight. The policies of Congress relative to the routes railroads would take could make or break an enterprise, have bearing on the investment in land speculation, reflect on the future geography of states, and determine when these states would be admitted. These businessmen needed to maintain an influence on American politics at least as it pertained to their businesses.

We are aware of several Chartists from Britain who worked on or managed American railroads, such as James Carlton, an English Social Democrat, who managed the Chicago-Alton Railroad. Social Democrat was just another name for socialist.

We will also show that a prominent Chartist was put in charge of the security of several important railroads before the Civil War — Allen Pinkerton.

But, as we said, no definitive study has ever surfaced that documents their foreign intelligence operations within the United States and how they may have helped political movements and leaders over the 1800s particularly.

One cannot look at the War for Independence or the War of 1812 in the isolation of America. The politics of Europe played an important role. All the main sea powers, England, France, and Spain, knew that the U.S. would ultimately rival and possibly surpass their power. Each in their way tried to prevent this.

The defeat of the combined French and Spanish fleet at Trafalgar by the British on October 21, 1805, prevented an American war with Spain. From 1803 to 1811, England had captured 900 American vessels with 6,000 sailors. The French figures were similar, and on March 23, 1810, Napoleon confiscated every American ship entering any French, port in addition to the 150 vessels they already held.

The effect on the American people brought us close to civil war at the time, since New England had no use for the French, and the South disdained the English. This difference created a tremendous split in the country, which intensified up to the time of the Civil War and continued for many decades thereafter.

However, England's interest in America never waned. Considering the War for Independence, the War of 1812, threats to British interests in Canada and Central America from American politicians and socialists, and the imbroglio in the Pacific Northwest, England had to maintain an influence here just to hang on to her possessions. Her behavior in other countries suggests she was engaged in espionage here as well.

Both France and England used this split to their own advantage, for financial or political reasons. Although history books rarely mention it, many congressional initiatives relative to the railroads and new territory involved British investment.

While many Southern leaders had an affinity for the French Revolution early on, the main reason for the hatred of the English was due to the behavior of the British forces in regard to the civilian population during the War for Independence, particularly in the Southern regions. The Mel Gibson movie *The Patriot* was not far removed from fact.

There are those who believe, based on some degree of evidence that exists, that British influence (through her secret service) weighed heavily in the process of the United States entering into the First World War and becoming England's ally. If we had stayed out of it, the 20th century would have been much different — with no USSR, no Hitler, no World War II in Europe, and the avoidance of a long list of tragic events. The influences that caused this chain of events would require another book.

Even today, when you ask, most people will say that we declared war with Germany and entered World War I because the Germans sank the *Lusitania*. However, this act was done a year and a half before we declared war, and the *Lusitania* was a British vessel, not an American one. The Germans had even advertised in the newspapers warning Americans away from booking passage on the vessel, since they knew it was carrying arms and ammunition and intended to sink it if possible.[31]

The War for Independence, the War of 1812, the Pacific Northwest dispute, the growth of American influence, our interference with English initiatives in Canada and in Central America, even various attempts at invasion of Canada before and after the Civil War — all these things placed England in an opposing position. The only time Great Britain has been a friend is when it has been in her interest to be so. Regarding the First World War, as an example, the British did all they could to bring us into a war that was none of our business, using the same tactics developed during the Civil War: buying journalists, developing public relation initiatives, plying the business community, wooing the government, and helping to create secret organizations. The latter particularly became a major initiative after World War I from the Royal Institute of International Affairs, or Round Table groups.

This played out in the formation of the Council on Foreign Relations in New York, part of the Chatham House network of the aforementioned Royal Institute. To give one a sense of the real center of American influence, the CFR was headquartered in and membership was part of New York, not Washington. Only in the past few decades has the core membership expanded beyond New York to the extent of opening up an office in Washington, D.C, during Secretary of State Hillary Clinton's tenure. The ceremony marking this event resulted in her famous quote that they would not have to go to New York any longer to know what to do.

When the CFR was started as an American cousin of the Royal Institute, the main American figure

---

31 One of the most definitive works on the tragedy was *The Lusitania: Finally the Startling Truth About One of the Most Fateful of All Disasters of the Sea*, Colin Simpson, Little, Brown & Co., Boston, 1972. It is based on British documents that were released after the 50-year ban on the public release of state secrets had expired in regard to this incident.

who was instrumental in its formation was Edward Mandell House, Wilson's alter ego who wrote a book, *Philip Dru, Administrator*, that declared his desire for a government as dreamed of by Karl Marx.

We became involved in a war with Germany in 1917 when we had nothing to gain, we had no quarrel with anyone, and none of it was any of our business. In fact, the behavior of the British against *American shipping* could well have prompted our declaration of war against her. The only incident that resulted in media coverage instigated by the Germans was on the English vessel the *Lusitania*. There were several instances of British capture of American vessels that never garnered attention outside of shipping owners circles and that earned only weak-hearted protests by the Department of State to the Court of St. James.

Our postwar involvement set the stage for another war with terrible consequences for all — no matter which side won: the world would be ruled by either fascists/national socialists or international socialists.

Anyone who honestly believes that a chain of events that started with the assassination of the Austrian archduke by a Serbian belonging to a secret society in Serbia led to millions of French, Russians, Germans, English, Americans, Romanians, Turks, Japanese, etc. being killed will listen to anything in a so-called history class. Somebody wanted a war and several books have been written about the influence of secret cabals in the process.

One can only speculate as to the total influence other countries had in the conflict that became the American Civil War, especially England and France. Much has been written about the foreign policy initiatives of these two countries in relationship to America, but nothing about any covert operations that were at work inside the United States. We say "were" because it is the history of these two countries to have intelligence operations in rival countries. That is what intelligence operations are for, not simply gathering information. And, the flip side of intelligence services is undercover activities.

The epitome of such operations is the Russian KGB and FSB. Government and private reports abound of the Russian intelligence services gathering intelligence from America *and their espionage operations*. The latter have been primarily focused on setting American policy. No one has ever asked what happened to these networks inside the U.S. after the so-called collapse of Russian communism.

Not one American engaged in this Soviet espionage ever came forward after the fact, and we know there were several spy rings led by the KGB in the U.S. because defecting Russians have told us so. Plus, Russian rings have been discovered and shut down. This lack of confession by any American is indicative that the networks probably continued on. There are those who would conclude that if no one stepped forward, no networks existed. However, our government arrested individuals whom they expelled to Russia for spying in 2011. Someone must have helped them — you do not simply walk into a country and leave with secrets unless someone helped you gain access to those secrets.

Strange that the media never mentioned Americans who may have cooperated with these expelled Russian spies. We are supposed to believe that they operated in a vacuum, other than their girlfriends who were only interested in undercover operations of a different kind.

Why devote so much space to an issue that came after the time frame of this tome? Simply to show that such espionage has always existed, but few have even considered that it may have played a role in our history when we were not actually at war with one or more of these countries.

Just as with this modern example, the majority of the citizens of the United States did not ask too many questions about British espionage after the War of 1812, although some did about British "influence" on some political movements.

It is in the nature of countries to play the Great Game, as the English have referred to espionage — especially those countries that have a system of government that is not what we Americans would consider as free.

One of the hypocrisies of most of the movements of the early years, whether abolitionist, peace societies, women's rights, etc., was that they all argued against war, secession and/or revolution unless it was in support of *their* cause.

It remained the same in the 20th century when communist front groups campaigned against the war effort unless the war helped Russia. As an example, the communists helped the America First organization to keep America out of World War II while the Hitler-Stalin Pact was in force; however, when Hitler attacked Russia the communists flipped and started to promote an all-out effort to get into us into the war against Hitler, instead of just letting the adversaries exhaust each other. However, the America First organization remained true to their effort to keep us out of a European war until the attack on Pearl Harbor.

Once the Japanese attacked, our world changed. But it would have been a different world had there been no World War I and our subsequent involvement.

The point is, the subversive organizations claim one thing but do another depending on how it furthers their agenda and for no other reason — and so do countries.

Tammany

A very influential political entity in American politics started three weeks after the Constitution went into effect: Tammany of New York. And, it started as a secret society. Every original state had a Tammany Society, but New York's would be the enduring unit and most famous. The first Tammany was started before the war, in Philadelphia in 1772.

Many felt the celebrations that Tammany held around so-called St. Tammany were actually aimed at destroying "the force of the Christian religion." Certainly some of the original members in New York, such as John Pintard, were opposed to Christianity. Also, Tammany allowed the use of their hall to the Society of Moral Philanthropists at which Benjamin Offen, who wrote *Biblical Criticisms* and supported the *Free Inquirer*, was a frequent lecturer.

In May 1789, a few weeks after the Constitution went into effect, William Mooney organized the New York Tammany Society, or Columbian Order. During the War for Independence Mooney had been charged with desertion from the American army. After the war he became a "patriot."

Ostensibly the Tammany Society was founded to honor Tammany and Columbus. It was founded on the principles of republicanism and was a secret organization. One of the principal objects was to combat Alexander Hamilton, his associates, and the Federalists. Toasts were given to Thomas Paine, the *Rights of Man*, Lafayette, and the French Revolution. Tammany Hall in the beginning was the nucleus of French revolutionary thought in New York. This continued on with the inclusion of communists, land reformers, and Brotherhood of the Union adherents over the ensuing years, and Tammany had a lock on New York politics for some decades.

Aaron Burr was a close friend of Mooney, and they used Tammany to get Burr elected to the position of vice president and nearly the presidency; the election was tied and had to go to the Congress to decide, and Congress voted for Jefferson on Hamilton's advice. While there is no evidence that Burr was actually a member, his close allies Matthew L. Davis, William Van Ness, John Greenwood, and the Swartwouts were leaders in Tammany.

When Washington's Farewell Address mentioned the dangers and corrupting tendency of political combinations and associations, he was referring to the Democratic Societies and organizations such as Tammany.

Hamilton saw the problems of such associations and wanted to form an organization in opposition.

He wanted to call it the "Christian Constitutional Society." The object was to support the Christian religion and the Constitution of the United States, and the main activity was to educate through newspapers and pamphlets.

He did not receive much encouragement for this initiative, and then was killed in the famous duel. Hamilton received little support because men did not believe that people would unite in an altruistic endeavor to fight organizations led by fanatics that rewarded their followers with favors and economic advantages. No such organization was formed until nearly two hundred years later, although it would include people of all backgrounds and faiths.

Hamilton had another problem: a well-publicized liaison that brought into question his ability to be a leader of a moral institution helping to promote Christianity in the community.

Two members of Tammany leadership were with Burr at the duel where he killed Hamilton.

At first, *the public image* of Tammany was pro-American, anti-alien and supportive of American industry. After a while, they started the men's suffrage movement to remove the requirement for property ownership qualification to vote. It was to be the first step in eliminating all property distinctions.

Over time the American people have lost the knowledge of the progression of the methods and qualifications for voting. For years, secret ballots were the exception rather than the rule; men had to publicly declare their allegiances. This is where the term "stand-up man" came from. If a voter said one thing and stood for it in an election, he was a "stand up man," someone who stood by his word. Subsequently the term took on a general definition of honesty and responsibility.

Once the secret ballot came in, it was accompanied by an erosion of honesty in elections. At first the vote counts were done publicly and immediately after the polls closed in most colonies and states, but over time, sometimes due to apathy by poll watchers or sometimes by the public being barred from observing vote counts the count became a private affair. At that point, it did not matter how a person voted, only who counted the ballots.

The next major change occurred in the general timeframe of the late 1880s and 1890s when the so-called Australian ballot, where the government printed the ballots, came into general use. This gave control to government over who was even allowed on the ballot.

A modern example of this being a problem was the election of 2000, when the conservative columnist Pat Buchanan won the nomination of the Reform Party, which had been started by Ross Perot. Some state governments put Buchanan's challenger in the Reform Party on the ballot because they did not like the politics of Buchanan or his running mate, who was a black woman who had close ties to The John Birch Society. This was done even though Buchanan had won the nomination of the party in open convention and the Federal Election Commission had ruled Buchanan the candidate as a result of a court challenge by his opponent. Buchanan's opponent in the Reform Party was into transcendental meditation and esoteric yoga — and was apparently considered more "mainstream" by some state authorities.

Prior to the Australian ballot, newspapers or parties could publish ballots to get a person to use a party-line vote. The reader would simply tear out a ballot out of a newspaper or be handed a ballot (popularly known as tickets) by a campaign worker and deposit it in the ballot box. It did not matter what the ballot was or who printed it, only the vote.

After this, the voting machine was ushered in. These machines could be set to give or take away votes from the candidates. The primary way of preventing fraud was for strong-willed poll watchers to demand that the machines be opened and physically inspected before the polls opened — a rare occurrence. In a close race this could be a deciding factor. Since the voting machines were in the hands of election officials who were appointed by the incumbents in most cases, the machines could be used to give the "ins" the advantage. In this age, the local voting judges at the precinct counted the machine votes after the polls closed and posted the results at the polling place before taking them to the county or city hall.

Then computerized voting came in with the famous "chad" cases. It has been said with computerized voting, "only the programmer knew for sure who won" and there were documented cases of voter fraud by the computer programmer. The votes are counted at a central location, away from the voter.

But even that is an understatement of the problem as computerized vote counting equipment is susceptible to tampering after it leaves the manufacturer's loading dock, and while it sits in a storage room between elections. These security weaknesses are made worse when ballots are transported to a central location for counting.

Although many innovations have been made since the initial computerized voting, more are needed to fully guarantee an accurate vote. Voices are being raised asking for a national primary online, and even the final election online. We are assured that no American hacker could alter a nationally sponsored online election, but there is no mention of Chinese or Russian hackers.

By the way, Russia well surpasses the Chinese when it comes to state-sponsored hacking, as they are far more sophisticated. This is rarely mentioned in the media.

Problems with voter fraud have led many to ask that we at least go back to paper ballots, counted at the local precinct by local citizens, leaving a paper trail throughout the entire process in cases of doubt. It may take longer to know the outcome, but it would be well worth the peace of mind.

Early on, members of Tammany were involved in local corruption in addition to voter fraud. Samuel Swartwout, collector for the Port of New York, fled to Europe after he defrauded funds. William H. Rice, U.S. district attorney for the Southern District of New York, joined Swartwout after stealing from the government.

Voter corruption by Tammany became so bad that they would arm members to keep non-Tammany voters from casting ballots.

They supported Burr and Andrew Jackson for the presidency. This was how Samuel Swartwout received his appointment as the collector of customs for the Port of New York in the first place. Swartwout was involved in the Burr conspiracy, and was arrested by Gen. Wilkinson in New Orleans when the Burr scheme blew up. Wilkinson by this time had become a friend of government to promote the idea that he was never involved in the plot.

Swartwout was released after a hearing but appeared at Burr's trial as a prosecution witness, where he challenged Wilkinson to a duel but was refused. By that time he had come to know Andrew Jackson, and he was a close associate in politics afterward.

So at least one Swartwout of Tammany was mixed up with Burr in his conspiracy, and then helped lead Tammany into support for Jackson.

The first Tammany partisan who turned against them to become a political antagonist was the Illuminist DeWitt Clinton, who was a leader in Tammany but quit over a quarrel with Burr. Again, these people simply could not get along personally. They had few differences politically.

Burr and Clinton were rivals for control of New York State and City. Clinton wanted to be president (if not himself then his uncle, George Clinton), but was beaten by Jefferson — who used Tammany for that purpose — breaking Clinton's power in New York.

DeWitt Clinton was mayor of New York City and governor of New York State. He was an admirer of Thomas Paine and became a friend of Lafayette, awarding him an honorary membership in the Literary and Philosophical Society of New York.

The rivalry of Burr and Clinton was based on personal ambition, not any meaningful difference in political philosophy.

Fanny Wright's Working Men's Party organized in New York City polled 30% of the vote in 1829. She preached economic freedom and unrestricted sexual intercourse. Due to her early success at the polls, Tammany endorsed some of her ideas and carried them into law.

When the Working Men's Party split between the Wright/Owen wing and the wing of Thomas Skidmore, a disciple of Paine, many of the members went into Tammany. There are some early historians who claim the Working Men's Party actually came out of Tammany to begin with. The party platform included support for the abolition of imprisonment for debts, universal education (government schools), and limiting the hours of the work day.

By the 1840s, Tammany, had all the elements of corruption as well as the socialist agenda. They fought one another, then pulled together, then fought again, in a seemingly unending cycle. Tammany was influenced by Young America (YA) and in October 1851 they ratified the principle of "no more neutrality, active alliance with European republicanism throughout the world." George H. Evans was in Tammany at the time.

Note that they said "European republicanism throughout the world." In other words, they wanted an alliance with the forces that emanated out of Europe into all corners of the world. Not simply for revolution, but a bond with a conspiracy of Illuminati for a world alliance.

In 1857, George Sanders, an important leader of YA, Postmaster Isaac V. Fowler, District Attorney John McKeon, Congressman Daniel Sickles, and John Cochrane took control of Tammany.

Over the ensuing years, the association became more corrupt rather than revolutionary in nature, using just about any cause that could enhance their power.

The last significant thing they did that bears on the subject of this volume was facilitating the election of Fernando Wood as mayor of New York. At the beginning of the Civil War, led by Wood, Tammany wanted to declare New York a "free city," holding allegiance to neither the North nor the South. Wood, in his inaugural address, gave essentially a socialist speech, according to the socialist historian Sotheran.

Wood's neutrality was rather lopsided at the onset of the war. Wood met with one of the Confederate Commissioners in Canada, Jacob Thompson. Jefferson Davis had assigned Thompson the task of leading the initiative for a breakaway republic from the area now known as the Upper Midwest as a Northwest Republic. Wood and Thompson met in Niagara Falls, and Wood helped assemble arms for this plot.

Once this scheme broke down — or simply served as another temporary means to further the agenda of the Conspiracy to get a *prolonged* war going — Wood and Tammany became super-patriots.

Abolition

Abolition was used to promote and deepen sectionalism, leading ultimately to a split in the country. This festered more and more as states were admitted to the country and each side more or less demanded an equal number of states to keep a political balance in the Senate — slave state vs. free state. Finally, the situation became nearly intolerable with the admission of Missouri and Kansas, since they were "border" states and the battle raged over not only how they would be admitted, but who would settle in them to vote and then petition Congress for admission. This battle over the balance of states began very early in the 1800s and only ended just before the Civil War.

The basic strategy of sectionalism is encapsulated in one quote from a letter by Jefferson to Lafayette, albeit with Jefferson's slant on the subject:

On the eclipse of Federalism with us, although not its extinction, its leaders got up the Missouri question under the false front of lessening the measure of slavery, but with the real view of producing *a geographical division of parties* which might ensure them the next president. The people of the North went blindfold into the snare. [Emphasis added]

A popular opinion in the early 1800s was that the abolitionists were agents of England, and there were a few who viewed them as an extension of the Illuminati. The masthead of the *Liberator*, William Lloyd Garrison's abolitionist newspaper, reinforced this latter idea. The initial slogan on the paper was: "Our Country is the world — Our Countrymen are Mankind." On the other hand, in abolitionist literature it was common to link the Slave Power with the Northern money power because of the close ties of the slave trade with Northern financiers and shipping companies.

In the 1790s, British writers linked the anti-slavery movement in the West Indies with Thomas Paine and the French Revolution. Part of this reasoning came about due to the work of the secret society, the Friends of the Blacks, which was linked to Illuminists.

The propaganda linking the slave power with Northern money also played into the hands of the English mercantile leaders, since it would have lessened the power and influence of the American center of commerce to the advantage of the British, by citizens shipping on English ships rather than American vessels if they were opposed to slavery. It would have been a self-imposed boycott by those who were opposed to slavery of using any American company suspected of dealing in the slave trade.

The idea of Britain using the slavery issue against America was a long held idea, stemming from the time that the Declaration of Independence was crafted. The Declaration denounced King George for exciting "domestic insurrections." This was thought to include slave revolts. There was a deep feeling among many Americans that the work of the English agent George Thompson and others in the anti-slavery movement was designed to prepare the way for the dissolution of the union.

During the War of 1812, in order to gain support, an English admiral issued a proclamation,

… in order to excite the slaves to insurrection, and promised them his aid and protection as 'persons desirous to emigrate from the United States.'
— *History of the United States*, J.B. Spencer, 1866, Vol. III, Page 275

At the same time the British tried to enlist the help of the horde of smugglers and pirates on the island of Barataria under Jean Lafitte against America. They were unable to do this and Lafitte instead helped Andrew Jackson defeat the British.

The peace movement also involved a number of people who worked with the English.

Many of the early American leaders were opposed to slavery but could not see a way out of it without destroying the possibility of uniting the colonies, which at the time was more important in their minds. Alexander Hamilton was one of these men. While he is chastised as a totalitarian by certain libertarian circles today, he was an officer in the New York Abolition Society before the abolitionist movement was taken over and used as a radicalized platform for social change all across the board, working for a solution to slavery that would not upset the public weal.

Likewise, men such as Benjamin Franklin, Dr. Benjamin Rush, and John Jay were very active in anti-slavery organizations.

Yet, Hamilton's greatest nemesis, Jefferson, the libertarian, was a slave holder who would not even free them in his death.

To put the abolitionist movement into a modern perspective, while opposition to slavery was a good thing, it did not make all who advocated doing away with it men of honor. Americans can stand for civil rights without following the Black Panthers, the American Civil Liberties Union, or the communist-dominated National Lawyers Guild, all of which profess to stand for civil rights.

It was the same in the antebellum period. People were opposed to slavery, but most had no use for the abolitionist leadership. The New England Anti-Slavery Society leadership was partial to many of the then-considered un-American "isms" of the day.

In addition to the abolitionists' extreme positions and anti-Constitution nature, there were a number of incidents in the twenty years preceding the Civil War which gave credibility to the common charge that they were the tools of the British. This helped take people's eyes off the real target, the Conspiracy.

William Lloyd Garrison's publicized first visit to England in 1833 coincided with the last triumphant stage of British abolition; there he made disparaging remarks against his country in general, not just about the issue of slavery. Someone had to organize this visit in England. You did not just get off the boat and start planning your speeches. Politically motivated organizations set them up by what were called *lyceums*, which were associations for discussion and instruction by lectures and other means. These organizations gave weight to the idea of British interference in American politics.

These lyceums were copies of the Illuminist organizations on the European continent.

Garrison's trip was made to raise money for a manual training school for Negroes, to combat the more moderate approach of colonization, and to establish regular communications with British abolitionists.

No school was started, but as a result of this trip he came home the leader of the abolition movement in America; this lasted for years until many under his leadership could no longer stand his style of radicalism. Also, forming new anti-slavery groups *by friends of Garrison* that appeared to be moderate helped push the agenda forward among people who could not stand Garrison and his followers' anti-Americanism but would promote the same agenda under more "acceptable" leadership.

In other words, Garrisonians set up Garrison's opposition within abolitionism making it appear as if they were moderates but giving control to the entire anti-slavery movement by the same "ism" and leadership behind the scenes.

Another indication of British influence was the Englishman George Thompson's tour across our country after being invited here by Garrison. Thompson was a Chartist abolitionist leader, and there was the fact that the British had been using the anti-slavery issue as an excuse to stifle the trade and industry of other countries in rivalry with England, such as Brazil, which also had slavery. They were the last country in the Americas to end it — in 1888, twenty-three years after our Civil War.

Garrison's relationship with Thompson was so close that he named his son George Thompson Garrison after this Englishman.

There were many communist Chartists who came to the United States from 1839 through the early 1840s. Many of their leaders returned to Great Britain later. While they were here, they had a circle of influence, particularly in New York.

Likewise, Americans traveled widely and spoke across Great Britain and Ireland, such as Henry B. Stanton, an agent for the American Anti-Slavery Society.

The exodus from Great Britain was so high that Chartists, like their German counterparts later, formed emigration clubs to help people to move to America and stay in contact with like-minded people after they did. In this manner, American English and Scottish Chartist communities helped fashion

American politics just as the Germans would do a decade later.

While millions signed the Chartist petition in Britain, few actually engaged in revolutionary activities. Many of those that did served time in prison or fled, mostly to America. Chartists became very active in the union movement in America, especially mining unions. After a time, the immigration back to Britain by Chartists reached the tens of thousands, since most came over fleeing British justice for their revolutionary activities and enough time had passed to allow them to return without punishment for their earlier involvement.

Many of the Chartists were active in the Odd Fellows organization, and it was not unusual for this society to provide financial assistance for Chartist members to either remove to America or return to Britain.

Likewise, many Chartists became active in the National Reform Movement and the Fenians. Thomas Ainange Devyr was an example. He was a Chartist guerilla in Britain and edited the Democrat newspaper in Williamsburg, New York, until fired. He then organized the Anti-Rent Party. He edited the Fenian newspaper *The Irish People* and also wrote for *The New York Tribune*.

Rev. Joseph Barker immigrated to the U.S. in 1853. He attended socialist meetings in Wales and was expelled from the Methodist New Connection in 1841; he took out 29 churches with him, and most became Chartist. He published the *Apostle and Chronicle of the Communist Church*. By the mid-20th century, the Methodist ministry in the United States had several hundred ministers involved in communist front organizations, and many were actually Communist Party members.[32]

As much as possible, the socialist movement has always professed to look to Christ or whatever religion is prominent in the country in which they operate to fool the gullible. Chartists claimed to look to Christ, Thomas Paine, and Robert Owen. As we know, this was impossible as the three are incompatible.

The same is the case in the Muslim world to such a degree that it is astonishing how little is reported in the media about it. As one example, when the American troops took Baghdad, Iraq, in the Second Gulf War, the people demonstrated in glee at the fall of Saddam Hussein. The video images on CNN television showed some black but mostly red flags being carried in the crowds in several cities *simultaneously* across Iraq. Once the video cameras got closer, it became obvious the red flags also had the hammer and sickle on them. Yet there was no mention of this by the CNN crews. The obvious questions that should have been going through the viewer's mind were, where did these flags come from all of a sudden, who organized the crowds to show up at the same time at the same place simultaneously in the larger cities across Iraq, etc.

Before Saddam Hussein came to power, Iraq had the largest membership in the Communist Party in the Islamic world outside of the USSR. They posed as Muslims, and they were no more Muslim than communists are Christian in Christian countries. This problem has entered into the instability of Iraq ever since we occupied and then left the country. The bad guys are always made to appear to be jihadists or Sunnis or Shiite extremists by the media and State Department — even the neoconservatives.

It is also true that the militant Muslim Brotherhood is more than what meets the eye. When the elections occurred in Egypt to elect a new government dominated by the Brotherhood, the first country the newly elected president Mohamed Morsi visited was communist China, in 2012. Yet, this change in Egypt with the Brotherhood in control occurred with the vital help of three organizations funded by the U.S.

---

32   The first communist affair this author infiltrated was a private birthday party for an octogenarian who was a party member as well as a Methodist minister. His bishop and archbishop were party members as well. Several other party members were there, including the lawyer-son of the "man of honor." He was a former state representative who was a suspect in the "suicide" of a Legislative colleague, a communist, who supposedly committed suicide the weekend before he was to testify about communist infiltration into his state Legislature. The dead legislator was going to testify openly and remorsefully as to his involvement. The legislator supposedly committed suicide in his bedroom while the communist who came to convince him not to testify was in the living room. Such was the story.

government and led by Council on Foreign Relations members.

Once Morsi and the Muslim Brotherhood were deposed by the military, leaders of these three organizations went to Egypt to demand that "democracy" be restored — in other words, restore the Morsi government based on the Muslim Brotherhood. The most notable were Republican Senator John McCain, a longtime member of the CFR, and Republican Senator Lindsey Graham, two prominent neoconservatives.

Even in the 21st century, some socialist and communist organizations put up images of Christianity on their websites to fool those who come online to check them out. Anyone who has much to do with them knows that it is a façade and it has always been (unless they are part of the overt anti-God movement and are very open about what they believe in — rather, do not believe in). The façade allows them to appear to be the moderates in comparison to the more volatile communists. In the end, the goal is the same.

Back to England, it was not simply that the English were interfering inside our country. In the late 1700s and early 1800s it was a common sentiment amongst American seamen that France and England used the slave issue to harass American shipping. They established way stations on the West Coast of Africa, ostensibly to stop slavery, but in reality to secure all trade from the continent. In the name of interdicting and inspecting shipping, supposedly to stop the slave trade, Britain was able to control the shipping along key shipping lanes.

We almost went to war with England and British Canada over the Northwest Territories and free trade during the period of 1844-45. Considering all of these problems with England, and more, the Garrisonians having as much to do with the English in the 1840s as they did appeared to be treasonous to Americans.

One of the situations in what became part of the South that added weight to the idea of English influence in the anti-slavery movement was when the Texas lawyer Stephen P. Andrews traveled to England in 1843 to try to raise money to buy slaves in Texas to set them free. The English government felt that this would lead to war with the United States, and his mission failed.

This was one of the events that helped move Texas into annexation as a state. Andrews would later become a disciple of Josiah Warren, the anarchist leader. He also became a contributor of letters on love, marriage, and divorce to the *New York Tribune* and joined the NY Liberal Club. He also wrote for the *New Nation*. He would later advocate a universal language and a religion of "Universology." He was a spiritualist leader and was apparently the first to use the term *Scientology*.

In 1847, the press for the black abolitionist Frederick Douglass' *North Star* paper came from England. He was also given cash for his efforts. Douglass had been in Ireland and England on a speaker's tour for abolition in the U.S. Interestingly, the major Chartist newspaper in Britain was called the *Northern Star*.

Later, Douglass was to merge his paper with Gerrit Smith's *Liberty Party Paper* to form the *Frederick Douglass Paper*.

"English gold" gave argument by all parties against abolition. It was "common knowledge" that Lewis Tappan, a heavy financier of abolition, was a conduit for Englishmen to involve themselves with American abolition.

The end of the line of the Underground Railroad was Canada. There was considerable intercourse between Canadians and Americans in the process. Americans lived in Canada to educate the freed slaves living there, and just in the general scheme of things Canadians had to have had an influence in the American movement. Canada at that time was an English possession, not the Canada that we think of today as a more independent part of the British Commonwealth.

You can see how Americans could believe that the abolition movement was the work of the English, considering all of these facts. However, this just hid the real impetus behind the abolition movement.

We must not forget that the epicenter of the Conspiracy had increasingly moved out of the Continent into England after 1800. Gradually, the leadership and top minions of all the Conspiracy's second generation organizations were ensconced in London: Mazzini, Marx, etc. From there, the epicenter moved to New York in the last half of the 18th century.

In other words, we have to temper our research with the idea that, although many of the problems America was beset with did come from England, they were not necessarily "English," but part of the Conspiracy making it look English. If you have the wrong target, you cannot hit the bull's eye.[33]

The largest organization against slavery was the American Anti-Slavery Society. They were, for all practical purposes, the abolition movement. They had agents all across America, and their 250,000 members were influential in the founding of several small colleges and institutions. They were formed into 2,000 local chapters and had 20 journals. An equivalent membership today would be the National Rifle Association, except the NRA is not organized as well locally as was the Anti-Slavery Society.

This was a tremendous amount of influence, and when you become more acquainted with the people in the leadership you see that the issue was not simply confined to anti-slavery. It is astonishing that they captured so many members, considering what they stood for besides anti-slavery. It demonstrates that over our entire history Americans have been buffaloed into movements that have consequences the members do not foresee. Too many people do not have the ability to connect the dots or extend the lines politically. This is due to the manner in which they have been educated, being taught what to think rather than how to think logically, and the innate tendency on the part of good people to be too trusting of political leaders.

Its founders were such men as Arthur Tappan, William Lloyd Garrison and Elizur Wright, one of the original national secretaries. To illustrate how the thinking of individuals was changed by working with such organizations and leaders over time, Wright started out as a Congregationalist. Over time he became an atheist and a contributor to *Freethinker's* magazine, and by 1876, he helped form the National Liberal League of atheists.

By 1840, Garrison was in control and moved the headquarters to Boston from New York. The New York group then organized the American and Foreign Anti-Slavery Society.

The organization started to wane once the followers became involved in politics through the Liberty Party, the Free Soil Party, and ultimately the Republican Party. Their concentration became politics rather than educating and organizing among the rank and file. The leaders engaged in self-aggrandizement by running for office rather than organizing. Then too, the American citizens were getting tired of the un-American rhetoric of the movement. Nonetheless, the educational efforts of the society permeated American society as a whole to a large extent in the North — and created a reaction against them in the South.

Like all American activist organizations that have an initial flush of success and widespread support, the Anti-Slavery organizations atrophied down to a hard core, which gradually withered away into other movements. This phenomenon has occurred many times, including in the 20th century with a variety of Left and Right organizations. The ones that have lasted the longest have been the inner core of the Conspiracy and the only Americanist, constitutionalist organization, The John Birch Society, due to the manner in which it is organized.

---

33 Typical of the attitude of many in the North who recognized European conspiracy in America was the claim by Robert A. Parrish, Jr. against the government of Napoleon III. He saw the problems with the John Brown conspiracy, Young America, the Knights of the Golden Circle, the Fenian Brotherhood, etc. He believed that the impetus for these entities and the Civil War came from France, the Jews, and the Catholics. He had a good understanding of part of the problem but not whence it came. He wrote about it in his published *Details of An Unpaid Claim on France for 24,000,000 Francs, Guaranteed by the Parole of Napoleon III* in 1869. He never mentioned the Illuminati. With the wrong target, it doesn't matter how well you can "shoot."

Even though many of the leaders of the Anti-Slavery Society quit organizing, enough work had been done to ingratiate their ideas into the Northern American psyche. By no means was the North devoid of pro-slavery thinking before this time. The massive effort to promote abolition ultimately found fertile soil in the North even though most rejected the extremism of the abolitionist leaders.

Samuel Gridley Howe was a social reformer who was prominent in many issues, including anti-slavery organizations. Howe had traveled in Germany in the company of Albert Brisbane, the communist, and he had a knack for showing up at revolutionary insurrections in Europe. His idea of aid to anti-slavery men in Kansas was guns. He was involved in trying to save John Brown after the Harper's Ferry insurrection. Later Howe was a leader in the Emancipation League, attempting to get Lincoln to issue an emancipation proclamation.

Out of the league, Secretary of War Edwin Stanton appointed a three-man board to investigate the emancipation of Negroes and recommend measures to place them in a position of self-support. The three were Howe, Robert Dale Owen, and Col. James McKaye of New York.

While in Europe, Howe was the head of an American Committee in Paris, which was helped and funded by the Illuminist Lafayette and played a role in the Polish revolution in the early 1830s. The committee met in James Fenimore Cooper's house. During the revolution in Paris in 1830, Howe was part of the group that helped lead Lafayette to safety at his residence at the Hotel de Ville during a chaotic period.

Howe was close to Henry Longfellow, a founder of the *Atlantic Monthly*, and Charles Sumner. Sumner was a Radical Republican Senator. In 1845 Sumner sneered at an exaggerated love of country and called the military academy at West Point a seminary of idleness and vice. During 1848 he wanted to meet Mazzini, but did not. He also was an intimate of Horace Mann, the man some trace back erroneously as the founder of public education in America, although he played a major role in implementing the system. Sumner advocated the commonwealth of nations and a world court, the goals of the Illuminati.

McKaye, the third man appointed by Stanton, was associated with the New England Anti-Slavery movement and by 1864 was arguing in favor of the confiscation of land in the South and its redistribution as absolutely essential for poor whites and Negroes. He got his start by being a junior partner in a law firm with Millard Fillmore.

It was apparently Sumner's idea for the American Freedmen's Inquiry Commission, and the three appointed by Stanton were friends of his and Gov. John A. Andrew.

Before and during the Civil War, Sumner was the chairman of the Senate Foreign Relations Committee and joined the First International.

Sumner knew more about the John Brown plot that led to Harper's Ferry than was legal and helped protect the conspirators. For years he was an advocate of peace, but would not allow any compromise or concession to avert war with the South. The first paper he ever subscribed to was Garrison's *Liberator*. He was chairman in 1849 of the Peace Committee of the U.S., and was yet another who did not mind a war to stop secession.

The *Atlantic Monthly* was founded in 1857 by Longfellow, Emerson, Oliver Wendell Holmes, and James Russell Lowell. The character of what the magazine would become was discussed and molded in Emerson's study. It was the culmination of the idea of uniting the literary force of the North with the Free Soil movement.

Free Soil had a double meaning: against the expansion of slavery and for free land for the people. It had abolitionists within its ranks, but the broader political appeal was against the *expansion* of the vice of slavery, more than its elimination.

Oliver Wendell Holmes grew up around radicals and many were his classmates at Harvard as well. He was a Unitarian of the Emerson school. His son was appointed to the Supreme Court by President Taft.

Lowell was a Fourierist, Transcendentalist, and abolitionist. He wrote for the *Dial*, *Harbinger*, and *Democratic Review*.

Abolitionist leaders quoted Scripture, but most practiced some form of heresy. They lauded the United States while plotting its demise through disunion and promoted a world government in some form, all in the name of wiping out slavery.

Spiritualism

The anti-Christian movement moved down two roads: the immediate total rejection of religion (the radical), and the more subtle method of moving people a step at a time toward total rejection (the moderate.) Both were scheduled to arrive at the same destination, just by different routes.

Many believe that the conspiracy at work to bring totalitarianism to America is basically a Satanic conspiracy. When looking at the evidence of who and what has been involved, it is difficult to dismiss. Others believe that the elimination of religion is simply to replace God with the state and those who run the state, similar to past regimes that tried to convince the people that the head of state was a god, thereby demanding obedience to the head of state as the state religion.

In either case, the result is the same on earth.

This belief destroys the very foundation of Americanism, with the belief that our rights come from God, as declared in the Declaration of Independence. Also, this is the basis for obedience to a high moral standard rather than a human, statist standard.

Modern adaptations of this idea are exhibited in the government of Hitler, Stalin, Mao, and others, to the extent that portraits of these men were placed in the schoolrooms and daily devotions to them sung in the classrooms. We marvel at the ignorance of ancients in Egypt and Rome that would even consider their pharaoh or emperor to have been a god, yet modern man has done much the same thing after the Illuminist organizations have taken over a country.

If people do their research, they will discover that the modern Common Core curriculum likewise moves the student away from parental and religious guidance into a condition of dependence on the state for leadership and assistance.

The use of what was known as Transcendentalism and spiritualism in the 1800s was designed to break down the existing social and religious structure. The reason this is necessary from the perspective of revolution is best outlined by quoting Napoleon I:

> There are certain moral combinations always necessary to produce revolution; and if they do not exist it is impossible to revolutionize a government or interrupt its peaceful administration.
> — *Martyrdom in Missouri*

He made it seem moral. If he had said, "There are certain *amoral* combinations ... ," he would have been accurate. *It is the breakdown of morality and the social order that must be changed for a revolution in the modern sense to be successful.*

And, what Napoleon meant by revolution's "peaceful administration" was for it to be peaceful for the revolutionary leaders to administer their changes and oppression. Peace in the mind of any socialist has always meant the lack of opposition by their opponents.

As we will make the point over and over again, it is society and its morals and mores that are under attack by the Conspiracy. Marx always referred to changing the social order, not revolutionizing the government. Any society will always determine the system of government over it. A moral society will be free. An immoral or amoral society will be ruled by a totalitarian government. It is that simple, and yet this reality eludes too many good people who believe sincerely that they need not pay any attention to social issues.

Napoleon was a creation of the Illuminati conspiracy, and he had their support until he abandoned them once he thought he could rule on his own. As all who think so, he found out differently. Such men are disgraced, imprisoned, and/or killed no matter how well they served their masters before.

Remember, Napoleon was a nobody, just like Hitler, Stalin, Mao, and Obama. They were "made" by others who elevated them and put them in power as the front man for the conspiratorial forces. It also demonstrates that the Conspiracy can lose control for a time over their minions.

Let us clear up one thing: The American War for Independence was not a revolution in the modern sense. It was done for the *preservation* of our social order and institutions. Initially, the movement was in defense of colonial government as *contracted* with the Crown. It was done to preserve the colonies, not to form a new government, until it became obvious that the Crown had no intention of allowing the colonies to keep their liberty. They realized that they had to unite in order to be strong enough to stand up to the world's super power at the time.

The use of the term *revolution* in connection with the War for Independence has served the semantic battle the Conspiracy uses to affect the mind-set of the people and to prepare them to listen to those who advocate a *social* revolution. After all, "We formed our government with a revolution — it's an American tradition, right?", is the idea put into the students' mind. They have not been taught the difference between what our Founders did and what the communists do.

Revolution at the time of the War for Independence meant the separation from the government or the replacement of the government, not what the meaning has become: social change as well as regime change.

One of the first recorded instruments designed to change the mind-set of Americans from understanding a war of the colonial states for independence to thinking in terms of it having been a national revolution in the modern sense, was a book authored by an Italian nationalist who had become a French revolutionary activist, Carlo Botta, in 1809: *History of the Independence of the United States of America*. The title indicated it was about the War for Independence, but it inculcated a romantic nationalism into the students when it was used at Harvard in 1839.

The work was immensely popular in its day, with many editions published in France and Italy, and by 1848 there were ten American editions promoted by those who wanted to imbue a different slant to our history. Due to the success of his *History* in America by 1816 Botta was inducted into the Philadelphia Philosophical Society, yet today he is relatively unknown.

Another use of semantics to indoctrinate was the use of the terms denoting our country. Presidents before Lincoln generally avoided the term "nation." After the Civil War, the wholesale adoption of the term and the tendency to refer to these United States as plural was changed to the singular, *the* United States, not *these* United States.

Of all things American, the one thing that separated us the most from Europe was the level of involvement of the average individual in religious belief and hands-on involvement in their local church. This had to change and/or the *church* had to be changed if the Conspiracy was to be successful.

Anti-Christian organization and propagation was rarely done by those other than socialists. It was to be part of the destruction of the old social order leading to a socialist revolution. Rev. W. M. Leftwich, in his book *Martyrdom in Missouri* in 1870, said this of spiritualists:

> They commissioned mediums to write, women and men indiscriminately to preach, to heal the sick, to see through the material and reveal the spiritual, to break up the marriage relation, to destroy parental affection, to form new standards of private and social virtue, to disturb and destroy old foundations and safeguards of society, and reconstruct the social system upon the modern ideas of socialism and the most offensive forms of free-loveism.

He had this to say about the influx of German rationalists and socialists into America:

> It could not be expected that German rationalists, who could barely speak English well enough to carry on the most ordinary traffic, would understand, or care to understand, those institutions of the State which characterized the State as a Christian commonwealth.

After the Civil War began, it was not unusual for Union troops in the contested Border States to arrest ministers who were neutral and to heap abuse on them, some to the point of death. This problem was more widespread than most can imagine today, and was primarily done by troops under the command of rationalists and socialists. It was one of the means used to try to "cleanse" religious leaders who believed in serving all people instead of taking sides — which was being forced on everyone to do.

Some of the positions taken by ministers in opposition to the changes in religious practices seem a bit strident by today's standards. We have moved a far distance from what our forefathers practiced. Some changes have been for the better, and some have not.

The anti-God movement came about very early in our history. To give you a perspective of the opinions that prevailed, let us quote from one volume published less than a hundred years after our founding: *Religion in America*, by Robert Baird, 1856. Speaking of the French revolutionaries' influence, Baird said:

> At the head of these, in the United States, stood Mr. Jefferson, who was President from 1801 to 1809, and who in conversation, and by his writings did more than any other man that ever lived among us to propagate irreligion in the most influential part of the community. In the same cause, and about the same period, labored Mr. Thomas Paine, and at a later date, Mr. Thomas Cooper, who endeavored to train to infidelity by sophistical reasoning, and still more, by contemptible sarcasm and sneers, the youth whom it was his duty to teach better things.

In his day Thomas Cooper was influential, and yet his name has been lost to modern students of history. Born in England, he left his home because of his support for the French Revolution and immigrated to America. His sympathies were with the Girondists. In the United States he became an anti-Federalist and was arrested and confined under the Alien and Sedition Acts. He was highly esteemed by Jefferson, and Jefferson was able to secure him a professorship at the University of Virginia. Cooper resigned that position after a fierce attack by the Virginia clergy. He was an agnostic and freethinker.

He went on to a number of academic positions, always butting heads against local and state clergy. He served as the president of what became the University of South Carolina from 1821 to 1833, but was once again obliged to resign his position.

He may well have been the first man to suggest the secession of South Carolina over the nullification fight against the federal government by the state. He held some good views on government, but on balance was a firebrand in addition to his religious beliefs. The idea of nullification was to invoke the 10th Amendment, but people like Cooper wanted to secede and tried to use the movement toward that end.

His close friend was Joseph Priestly, the scientific wizard and Unitarian minister. Priestly rejected the divinity of Christ and was a supporter of the French Revolution.

Since war has a negative effect on morality, this was the result of the War for Independence. In one of Rev. Jedidiah Morse's speeches, he referred to the war and how it caused deterioration in public and private morality, from which the nation had not yet recovered at the time of his speech. The same sentiment was expressed by many men of religious belief. It took several years following the war for Christianity to overcome the war's demoralizing effects.

The efforts of Morse were very important to the exposure of the work of the Illuminati in the United States. As a result, history brands him as a fanatic, an alarmist who tried to excite American citizens against a false conspiracy. Such charges seem similar to today's against sound exposure by responsible people and organizations of what is happening to our nation with the politically correct slogan: There is no conspiracy.

Rev. Morse was by no means the only man who recognized this breakdown in the general morality. In the small book *The French and American Revolutions Compared*, by Friedrich Gentz, 1800, appears this passage as translated by John Quincy Adams:

Even the morals and the character of the people, had been essentially, and not in every aspect advantageously affected by the revolution. Although we can draw no conclusion from this circumstance with regard to futurity, yet history must remark with attention, and preserve with care, the confession, which comes from the pen of a calm and impartial witness, the best of all writers upon the American revolution hitherto (Ramsey): "That by this revolution, the *political*, *military*, and *literary* talents of the people of the United States, were improved, but their *moral* qualities were deteriorated."

Robert Baird in his 1856 book, *Religion in America*, exposes a great deal of the hardship Christianity suffered as a result of the war, most of which is unknown to today's American:

Unfavorable to the promotion of religion as were the whole twenty-five years from 1775 to 1800, the first spent in hostilities with England were pre-eminently so. The effects of war on the churches of all communions were extensively and variously disastrous. To say nothing of the distraction of the mind from the subject of salvation, its more palpable influences were seen and felt everywhere. Young men were called away from the seclusion and protection of the parental roof, and from the vicinity of the oracle of God, to the demoralizing atmosphere of a camp; congregations were sometimes entirely broken up; churches were burned, or converted into barracks or hospitals, by one or other of the belligerent armies, often by both successively; in more than one instance pastors were murdered; the usual ministerial intercourse was interrupted; efforts for the dissemination of the Gospel were, in a great measure, suspended; colleges and other seminaries of learning were closed for want of students and professors; and the public morals in various respects, and in almost all possible ways, deteriorated. Christianity is a religion of peace, and the tempest of war never fails to blast and scatter the leaves of the Tree which was planted for the healing of the nations.

Notice that Baird refers to the 25 years from 1775 to 1800. This was the time of the war, including the Jacobin imbroglios mingled with the efforts of Americans who, for whatever reason, were enemies of the church in general. This is quite the opposite of what is taught by many today concerning these times.

Transcendentalism on the surface was a rational, or reason-oriented philosophy seeking truth, but in reality a transition from Christ to anti-christ. The early influence came from Voltaire, Rousseau, and Diderot. It was then influenced by Victor Cousin, Fourier, and German Illuminism. Some of the American leaders early on were George Ripley, an editor at the *New York Tribune*; William E. Channing; John S. Dwight; Margaret Fuller; Ralph Waldo Emerson; Henry Wadsworth Longfellow; Theodore Parker; Henry Thoreau; Bret Harte; Walt Whitman; John G. Whittier; and William Henry Channing.

George Ripley became the president of the National Convention of Associationists, often referred to as the American Union of Associations. Dwight was a Fourierist and for years ran the only American musical journal, *Dwight's Journal of Music*. Channing advocated guerilla war against slavery, and he also advocated the redistribution of property and a new economic system, becoming a leader in the Christian socialist movement. He was chosen the chaplain of the U.S. Senate for the last two years of the Civil War.

Early adherents of Transcendentalism included Ralph Waldo Emerson and George Bancroft. They were very close to Theodore Parker. He had a disbelief in the miracles of the New Testament and said that Jesus was not the Son of God but a great teacher. This belief has been propagated by many secret societies and occult organizations, but not all. Parker began to deny the traditional teachings of Christianity as a student of German liberal theologians such as Friedrich Schleiermacher, who had tremendous influence on Illuminists, a free-lover who held the same basic belief about marriage as Robert Owen, that it was an unnatural bond; and David Friederich Strauss, who played a large role in questioning the divinity of Christ.

Parker went further. He compared Scripture with the works of Newton, Descartes, the *Veda*, and the *Koran*. He denied sin and the atonement. He summarized God as goodness, and "each man as his own Christ." His sermons echoed the socialists of Europe of the 1840s. He also said that slaves have the right to kill for freedom, and he welded the revolutionary doctrines of Europe to abolition.

It is interesting that the Christian Socialists have used the doctrine of the second coming for their own purposes since the 1780s and a great deal of their teachings has permeated mainstream Christianity without the Christian community realizing it, thereby neutralizing opposition to socialism. By the 1880s, the Christian Socialists prophesied that the Kingdom of Heaven was about to descend, and Christ would reappear with the dissolution of capitalism, the "logical" culmination of the social gospel.

By January 1846, Parker's supporters formed a congregation in Boston and installed him as its minister. Among his flock were Louisa May Alcott, William Lloyd Garrison, Julia Ward Howe, Elizabeth Cady Stanton, Samuel Gridley Howe, and William C. Nell. Depending on the source, it is claimed his congregation grew to somewhere from two to over three thousand people — quite a large congregation of "Christians" who had a pastor who did not believe in Christ — about three percent of the people living there at the time.

Indeed, it appears that many ministers of the Unitarian variety simply used the freedom of their office and responsibility to be free enough to work for socialism and ultimately atheism by one path or another.

In 1889, a volume titled, *A Biographical Dictionary of Freethinkers of all ages and Nations* was published by J. M. Wheeler. It was a substantial list of atheists, anti-Christians, and those who debunked any kind of religion. Elizabeth Cady Stanton was among those listed. This volume is essential for the research of the anti-Christian movement around the world in the 1700s to 1800s. It does omit many important Illuminati and other conspirators for whatever reason.

Many trace Lincoln's phraseology in the Gettysburg Address to Parker, who used it in 1850: "A democracy, — of all the people, by all the people, for all the people." It is known that Lincoln's protégé William H. Herndon was in constant communication with Parker.

The best literary achievements of the Transcendentalists were exhibited in the *Dial*, the journal of the movement in New England. Contributors included Emerson, Margaret Fuller, Bronson Alcott, Henry Thoreau, and Channing.

Margaret Fuller lived for a time in the home of Horace Greeley while she was a literary critic at the *Tribune*. She went to Europe in 1847 and was there in 1848, at which time she became involved in the Italian revolution and became a friend of Mazzini.

Those who used to gather in Emerson's study came to represent the flower of American intellectual achievement for the age, according to the history books. These included Margaret Fuller, Nathaniel Hawthorne, Amos Bronson Alcott, Fuller's brother-in-law William Ellery Channing, Henry James, Bret Harte, John Greenleaf Whittier, Walt Whitman, Henry Wadsworth Longfellow, and Henry Thoreau.

Channing was especially taken with the French freethinkers such as Rousseau and the Englishman William Godwin. Hawthorne was a Transcendentalist Fourierist who broke off with the organization but remained friends with Emerson. He was involved with YA and served as consul in Liverpool in the Pierce administration.

Whitman became known as the man who influenced Ella Reeve Bloor in her youth on a visit to her home. When she grew up, she became "Mother Bloor" within the leadership of the U.S. Communist Party in the 20th century.

Channing was a founder of the Massachusetts Peace Society, which was organized in his home, was sympathetic to communal experiments, and was a contributor to Brook Farm's *Harbinger*.

Henry James, while professing the deity of God, was a student of Swedenborgianism and socialism, writing for the *New York Tribune* from time to time.

Bret Harte went on to become more noted in the West, and established *The Californian* newspaper with co-editor James F. Bowman. They both went on to be some of the founders of the Bohemian Club in 1872, with Bowman as its secretary in 1876.[34]

Brook Farm commune was a Transcendentalist enclave which followed the teaching of Fourier socialism. Its publication was *The Harbinger*. Contributors included the Channings, Horace Greeley, Charles Dana, Henry James, Rev. Thomas Wentworth Higginson, John G. Whittier, Nathaniel Hawthorne, Theodore Parker, James Russell Lowell, William Wetmore Story, Henry David Thoreau, Albert Brisbane, Parke Godwin, Amos Bronson Alcott, James Freeman Clarke, Robert Dale Owen, Frederic Henry Hedge, George William Curtis, and Orestes Augustus Brownson.

Charles Dana was a vice president of the National Convention of Associations. He was a member of the Proudhonian Club, nicknamed the 48ers of America, composed mainly of Americans who had participated in the revolution of 1848-1849 in Europe. In 1848, he spent eight months in Europe covering the revolutions for the *New York Tribune*, and he shared Marx's views. Dana wrote that the purpose

---

34   Information on the Bohemian Club abounds on the Internet. It should be of interest to the modern reader relative to men in high places and their propensity for the bizarre. Use caution in believing all of what you will see; the truth is bad enough.

of the uprisings was "not simply to change the form of government, but to change the form of society." He did more than report.

Dana is but one example of reporters who participated in revolutionary activities and then posed as impartial observers as "reporters." This has long been a tactic of the Left, and continues to this day. Ten years after the above, such activities reached a zenith with the "reporters" who accompanied John Brown and participated in the murder and mayhem while sending dispatches to several newspapers in the Midwest and East.

At first, Brook Farm had a Swedenborgian bent, which they promoted it as a new religion, and then they evolved into spiritualism. "Swedenborgism went deeper into the hearts of the people than Socialism that introduced it, because it was a *religion*," according to the socialist chronicler John Humphrey Noyes.

Andrew Jackson Davis, an American Swedenborgian, claimed he met Emanuel Swedenborg's ghost in a graveyard near Poughkeepsie in 1844, and again in 1846. Swedenborg himself claimed he had talked to angels and demons while visiting heaven and hell.

Swedenborg's work was called an "illumination" by many people involved in it. It was known in the U.S. as the Illuminati of Stockholm.

Noyes claimed that "Unitarianism produced Transcendentalism; Transcendentalism produced Brook Farm; Brook Farm married and propagated Fourierism; Fourierism had Swedenborgism for its religion; and Swedenborgism led to modern Spiritualism."

Swedenborgism had been introduced into America in 1748. By 1817, seventeen "New Church" societies united to form the General Convention of the Church of the New Jerusalem. It participated in Fourierism, Christian Socialism, and the Single Tax Movement, in which the government would own the land and rent it to the people.

Amos Bronson Alcott was considered to be a "god-made priest" by those around him. He formed Temple School in Boston with Elizabeth Peabody in the Masonic hall. When it failed he was invited by Emerson to move to Concord.

Alcott was influenced by the Illuminist Pestalozzi in his educational experiments, even calling one of his attempts the Cheshire Pestalozzi School.

Alcott made two attempts at communal living, and both failed. His Fruitlands was founded as a "consociate family," a "New Eden" near Harvard. Its ideas were communal ownership of property, no clothing produced by slave labor or animal skins, cold water bathing, and vegetarianism. Fruitlands became a way station on the Underground Railroad, transporting runaway slaves.

When Fruitlands fell apart the Alcotts moved back to Concord. By 1860, Alcott was named the superintendent of the Concord public schools.

Some of the ideas of Alcott are commonplace in American schools today. In addition to his abstract philosophy (no absolutes), he felt grammar to be a "waste study" (its only for I and we), frowned on textbooks (then the parents would know what is being taught), preferred individualized reading (it is not a well-rounded education to only read what you think you might enjoy), encouraged undirected scribbling on paper (modern art), pushed art education (for the lower grades it does not prepare the student for life, and some art should not be viewed by impressionable children), and conducted field trips and nature studies during school hours (just as environmentalists do today).

Years later, when asked to explain himself to an audience in St. Louis, he replied that "only a Christ can interpret a Christ."

Only fiction needs to be credible!

Elizabeth Peabody was important in the movement. She taught school at Brook Farm commune and her sisters married Nathaniel Hawthorne and Horace Mann. She became a fast friend of Carl Schurz.

She was a Transcendentalist and was a secretary to William Ellery Channing for a time. As a disciple of the German Friedrich Fröbel, she founded and was president of the American Fröbel Union and started a kindergarten based on his system in 1860.

Friedrich Fröbel was a student of the Illuminati member Pestalozzi and had studied under him in Switzerland. Fröbel developed the concept of the kindergarten and coined the word now used in German and English. While his overall concept found appeal among socialists and freethinkers, the Prussian government banned it in 1851 as "atheistic and demagogic" for its alleged "destructive tendencies in the areas of religion and politics." Other German states followed suit.

One of his students, the wife of Carl Schurz, founded the first American kindergarten in Watertown, Wisconsin. She apparently inspired Peabody's interest as a result. The German immigrant Adolph Douai founded a kindergarten later in Boston in 1859, but it was short-lived.

Kindergarten was part of the breakdown of the social order and the indoctrination of children at an ever younger age *away from their parents*. As the socialists in communes took two-year-olds and raised them communally, kindergarten was the "moderate" thing to do toward this end, a salami-slice toward their ultimate goal.

Teaching children as young as possible is no vice, and in fact is preferable unless it is to give them the mind-set of socialism and statism which will enslave them in the long run. The idea of teaching children by the government schools at an ever younger age crops up from time to time in an attempt to reach the socialist goal just outlined. This was a trial balloon of the Obama agenda in 2013; it did not meet with opposition and was funded in 2014.[35]

Douai was a socialist 48er who left Germany after his release from prison and became an abolitionist editor in Texas. He removed to Boston, teaching there, and then moved to the New York-Newark area, where he again was engaged in teaching in a variety of schools. None of these employments lasted very long.

He was an early and prominent member of the Socialist Labor Party of America, which was established as the Working Men's Party of the United States as part of the First International. He was going to translate Marx's *Das Kapital* into English but did not complete the work.

Transcendentalists ranged from moderates to radicals, from preaching to forming communes to revolution. Robert Dale Owen, Fanny Wright, and Orestes Brownson, close to the extreme end of Transcendentalism, organized the Working Man's Party, a communist organization in New York. (This was not the party of Weydemeyer.)

The Transcendental Club of Boston was nicknamed the Hedge Club after Frederic Henry Hedge. A short biography: Hedge had been sent to Germany under the care of George Bancroft at the age of 13. He spent four years in Germany, starting his education at Göttingen. Upon his return, he went to the school of divinity at Harvard. The only time the club met was when Hedge made it to Boston from Maine. This club became a powerhouse within the Unitarian Church.

Just as there was moderate versus extreme in socialism, Transcendentalism became two movements, with a large part becoming spiritualist. By and large these two movements were linked through interlocking leadership.

---

35 *Fact Sheet President Obama's Plan for Early Education for all Americans*, issued by the White House, February 13, 2013, advocated birth to four-year-old education and care by state agencies and/or federal grants. Several videos of Obama's Education Secretary Arne Duncan advocating the boarding and raising of small children on through their entire education by the government exist online.

The leaders of the socialist/communist movement who actually practiced communal living were also spiritualists, such as Robert Owen and his son.

As part of the spiritualist movement, séances became a parlor game to some and a serious spiritual experience to others among the middle and upper classes that tended toward rationalism and socialism. It wasn't an innocent amusement as it may seem today, since it was done at a time of strict religious beliefs which did not believe in ghosts or spirits in any fashion except that they came from Hell.

Cornelius Vanderbilt attended them and through his interest in spiritualism met and became a close patron of the communist sisters Victoria Woodhull and Tennessee Claflin, who were supposedly spiritualist mediums and magnetic healers. Vanderbilt at one time wished to marry Claflin.

During an interview for a newspaper, Vanderbilt was asked how he had made millions on the stock market. "Do as I do, consult the spirits!" was his response. Then he added that his stock was "bound to go up ... Mrs. Woodhull said so in a trance."

William Cullen Bryant and Wendell Phillips also attended séances.

Phillips, a radical abolitionist, true to the conspiracy model, advocated disunion at first. After it became a reality, he became a unionist. Early in the Civil War he gave a speech that was printed in the *London Times*. He called for the dissolution of the union due to the poor leadership of McClellan and Lincoln and putting another nation in its place, the cornerstone of which would be written: "Political equality for all the citizens of the world."

Bryant was interested in socialist movements. He was the editor of the *New York Evening Post* and one of the original founders of the Union League of New York. Later he was to be a founder of the Liberal Republican Party and "president" of Manifest Destiny. His last public appearance was at an unveiling of a bust of Mazzini in Central Park in May 1878.

History says that after the death of Mary Lincoln's son, séances were held in the White House at her desire. This is not entirely accurate. Lincoln himself attended séances on trips to New York without her long before he was elected. Indeed, even the story of his dream which foretold of his own demise is a bit strange.

J. B. Conklin was a medium. Upon Lincoln's election, he recognized Lincoln as a frequent guest at séances in New York prior to his election. Conklin stated in the *Cleveland Plainview* that Lincoln was a spiritualist. Lincoln was shown the article and instead of contradicting it, said, "The only falsehood in the statement is that the half of it has not been told. This article does not begin to tell the wonderful things I have witnessed."

On four successive Sundays prior to the issue of the Emancipation Proclamation, Conklin was a guest at the White House and tried to take credit for the proclamation. Accurate or not, and there were many other influences, a number of spiritualists urged Lincoln to issue the Emancipation Proclamation. Just about every other person of influence on the Left tried to take some credit for it after it was *fait accompli*.

Mary Lincoln attended many séances with three different mediums after moving to Washington, and Lincoln accompanied her on occasion in and out of the White House.

Indeed, both the Lincolns and Stanton behaved rather strangely when it came to those they loved who died, Stanton particularly.

Stanton lived in a boarding house in Columbus, Ohio, managed a bookstore and was infatuated with the daughter of the boarding house's owner. One day she fell ill and died rapidly of cholera. As was the practice at the time, victims of cholera were interred as rapidly as possible to help prevent the spread of the disease. So Stanton left for work in the morning and by the time he came home, she had exhibited the symptoms of the disease, died, and been buried. It was not unusual for people to exhibit the symptoms of cholera and die within eight hours. He could not believe that she was dead and disinterred her to make sure.

Years later, in 1841, after his daughter had died and been buried for a year, he had the body exhumed and laid out in a special metal container for another year in his living room. His wife died in 1844, and for a short time he kept dressing and undressing her in her wedding gown, also in the living room. At night, he arranged his wife's nightcap and gown beside him in bed. He finally was persuaded by friends to bury both together.

Madness apparently ran in the Stanton family — his brother, Darwin, would commit suicide by cutting his own throat.

Lincoln likewise disinterred his son, Willie, to look upon him after his death. He had been embalmed, a new process at the time.

The God-is-dead movement is not a modern phenomenon. At the onset of our country, organizations were formed to promote the idea. Elihu Palmer was a Unitarian minister and a friend of Thomas Paine. In 1794 he organized the Theistical Society in New York among a group of enthusiasts of the French Revolution. After Jefferson was elected, he started a journal called the *Triumph of Reason*.

The Theistical Society was nicknamed the Columbian Illuminati by John Wood, who wrote "A Full Exhibition of the Clintonian Faction, etc." in 1802. He pointed out that the society had to be connected to the Bavarian Illuminati since the character of the members, the oaths, and their constitutions were too similar not to be.

Wood professed to know 95 members' names, but only revealed a handful: DeWitt and George Clinton and a few unrecognizable to citizens today, such as Alexander Ming, John Fellows, and Thomas Hertell. There were ties to Paine and Jefferson, even claims of membership.

Hertell was a New York City judge and member of the New York State Assembly, and was known as a Jacksonian as well as a freethinker writing works against Christian theology and exerted his influence in favor of State secularization. Ming was Thomas Skidmore's closest ally in the Working Men's Party in 1830 and published many of Skidmore's works.

Wood pointed out that DeWitt Clinton had family ties through marriage to the Girondist Edmund Genet; he was the first leader of the General Chapter of the Royal Arch Masons, and a friend of Thomas Smith Webb, a prominent influence on American Masonry.

The society rejected Christianity and every Christian. They renounced all forms of government except pure democracy, and the society spread from New York to Philadelphia. They had three degrees, the first being ignorant of the other members who were of a higher degree. The third degree was the only one allowed to communicate with Palmer himself.

There were many spiritualist journals in the early 1800s. One was led by Andrew Jackson Davis, a Swedenborgian spiritualist. His journal's motto was, "The establishment of a universal system of truth, the *reform and reorganization* of society." (Emphasis added.) William M. Channing succeeded its publication with *The Present Age*, mainly a socialist organ.

There were at least 50 spiritualist publications in operation at one time. *The Banner of Light* alone had a circulation of 25,000. Edited by William Colby of the *Boston Post*, it was sympathetic to the communist First International, as were the spiritualist publications *The American Spiritualist* and *Hull's Crucible*. The "free thought" publication in Boston, the *Investigator*, was likewise sympathetic to the International.

The telltale title of the spiritualist publication *Lucifer*, in Kansas, edited by Moses Harmon, was influenced by a disciple of Proudhon, Benjamin Tucker. Edwin C. Walker also edited *Lucifer* and the publication *Fair Play*. Helena Blavatsky was also to name a publication *Lucifer*, in London during the last years of her life.

The Fox sisters were the rage for a time among spiritualists. They got their start by professing that they heard tapping's from the dead in their home. When they replied in the same manner, the tapping's would repeat. Their fame spread and they too became involved in the parlor game of séances.

At one of the Fox sisters' séances, their supporters Horace Greeley, Rev. Dr. Rufus Wilmot Griswold, George Bancroft, James Fenimore Cooper, Bigelow of the *Evening Post*, Rev. Dr. Francis Hawkes, Dr. J. W. Francis, Dr. Marck, the poets Nathaniel Parker Willis and Bryant, and Gen. Lyman were in attendance.

At a later affair, Gov. Tallmadge of Wisconsin was supposed to have levitated.

Nathaniel P. Tallmadge, U.S. Senator in 1833-34 and governor of Wisconsin 1844-46, was a spiritualist. In April 1854, a memorial was presented to Congress by James Shields asking for an inquiry into the truth of spiritualism, containing 13,000 signatures. Gov. Tallmadge's signature was the first.

Tallmadge claimed to be able to communicate with the deceased former Vice President John Calhoun.

Spiritualism even extended to the New York Supreme Court in the person of Justice John W. Edmonds. He served in the New York Legislature, including serving as president of the Senate. He was forced to resign his position on the court due to his spiritualist beliefs. He became a medium, and he professed to communicate with the dead Swedenborg and Francis Bacon.

Not to be outdone by the dead Swedenborg, Robert Owen communicated with Emma Hardinge Britten and gave her *The Principles of Spiritualism* after he was dead! At least, that was her story.

Henry Steel Olcott was an associate editor on the *New York Tribune* who was a special commissioner during the Civil War with the rank of colonel. He met Madame Blavatsky and they together went on to found the Theosophical Society, a spiritualist cum Buddhist organization, in 1875. They too believed in universal brotherhood. He was commissioned by the president to report on trade relations between the U.S. and India in 1878, and Olcott and Blavatsky moved the headquarters of the society to India in 1879.

Blavatsky relied heavily on the works of the Rosicrucian Paschal Beverly Randolph, among others, to formulate her theology and writings.

James Martin Peebles, another noted spiritualist, was on intimate terms with Emerson, Thomas Carlyle, Victor Hugo, Walt Whitman, John Bright, Theodore Parker, H. W. Beecher, and Gerald Massey. He was the owner and editor of at least three spiritualist newspapers.

Henry Ward Beecher had as one of his parishioners in New York a member of the Order, Henry W. Sage. Beecher had tremendous influence over this man and ordered him to put up the money for one young man's education in Europe. Sage also established the "Lyman Beecher lectureship" at Yale where his son, Harry, delivered the first three annual courses. Rev. Lyman Beecher, Henry's father, had been put on trial for heresy but was acquitted.

Paschal Beverly Randolph, spiritualist, was purportedly the founder of Rosicrucian sects in America. He edited two publications, and was a trance medium. His branch of Rosicrucians was absorbed in the 20th century by a more modern order, which was allowed to advertise in the *National Review* magazine of the neo-conservatives in the 1960s looking for adherents among their readers.

Over the years, Americans influenced the rise of spiritualism in the British Empire, especially England late in the 1800s. Spiritualism began in the U.S. and spread to Britain among the Owenites.

One of England's most prominent spiritualists was Dr. Alfred Russel Wallace. He was the co-originator with Darwin on the natural selection theory of evolution. Wallace was also involved in socialist theory and activism. His youthful education that started him on this path included reading the works of Robert Owen and Thomas Paine.

In other words, there was a socialist influence on the development of the theory of Darwin, and it was tied to spiritualism.

Another example of American spiritualist influence was on the Imperial Council to the Czar, who became a spiritualist by reading Andrew Jackson Davis' *Nature's Divine Revelations* in 1855.

Perhaps the greatest influence on an existing church was that of Emerson and his coterie on the Unitarians. Emerson studied at the feet of German-educated theologians and became the leader of the "German School" of American Unitarianism. He became a Unitarian minister but left over the administering of communion and public prayer — he was against both. By 1848 he had left the ministry entirely. He became America's "death-of-God" theologian.

By 1885, all of Unitarianism was of the persuasion of Emerson and Theodore Parker and was heavily influenced by the entire spectrum of the Left and anti-God movements.

The purpose for infiltrating the churches was not to destroy Christianity alone. The intent was to use the organizational remnants for the purpose of "Illuminizing" the population that had a conscience; further, there were many socialist leaders, such as Horace Greeley, who felt that Americans would not support socialism unless it was tied to religion.

People will always have a conscience, and means must be taken to either numb it, creating an amoral people, or to create a salve for people to do things they would not normally do or support. There is no better salve than a false religion.[36]

The Christian church may preach repentance and forgiveness, but they also preach sin and its consequences. If the "New Church" can change sin from a scriptural and Mosaic basis to being just a human trait to be accepted, then this serves the state and those who run the state.

As an example, the Christian says that sex outside of marriage is a sin. On the other hand, not only did the fascist socialist states of Italy and Germany tell the wives of the nation to breed more sons, rewarding such breeding, but the Nazis encouraged the breeding of young girls and SS men to produce Aryan children out of wedlock.

These children were then taken from the mothers and raised as children of the state. No one talks about what happened to these children once World War II was over. They were not old enough to take care of themselves, the oldest not yet teenagers.

All sorts of television documentaries on such networks as the *History* and *Military Channels* show the bred babies and their state-employed nurses in the late 1930s and early 1940s. In their early, formative years they were immersed in national socialist education. However, these TV documentaries never mention what happened to the children — all imbued with National Socialism from their birth. Some were adopted out to good Nazi families.

While socialists in American government do not go that far, the Department of Education helps finance the breakdown of morality and sexuality in the schools by national standards now being implemented through Common Core.

American schools have begun the process through national standards for sex education to teach that

---

36 In the late 1960's, this author attended an outdoor rock festival amassing evidence of the involvement of communists and Satanists (you read it right) working together to subvert the youth. At this well-attended affair, a "church" tent had been erected providing 24-hour marriages for girls who had the need to salve their consciences about having sexual relations with someone out of wedlock. The existing photos taken at the time provide a shocking look at what goes on when parents do not have a clue of the influences such events have on their children.

sexuality in nearly all of its forms is natural and normal, even to the extent, before they reach puberty, of teaching the "natural" method of self-gratification once they do. It will not take the researcher very long to satisfy himself that this is true, and worse. The problem exists in varying levels across the country.[37]

The ultimate state-sponsored sin is the murder of innocents simply because they are not the same race or religion of those that rule the state. Again, we can look to the Nazis as the epitome of such a policy. Hitler looked to those who employed such a policy before him; Nazis thanked Americans for their model of eugenics and honored the Illuminati Christoph Meiners as a founder of racial theory.

Meiners wrote against Jews, blacks, women, and slaves in *Göttingisches Historisches Magazin,* which he co-founded with fellow Illuminist Ludwig Timotheus Spittler. Both were professors at Göttingen University.

There are many other examples that could be cited as to how the state actually promotes sin as a state-sponsored activity. Having a church in league with the government is a distinct advantage to those who want power over the people.

This is why the Founders of our country did not want state-approved *churches*; this has become known as the separation of church and state. It was never intended to be for the limitation of Christianity or its practice either in public or private. There are too many pronouncements of our Founders for the need of Christianity to be the conscience of the nation for the separation of church and state to really mean the suppression of Christianity from public life.

Let us not forget that the term "separation of church and state" was coined by Jefferson, and this idea has been drummed into the heads of Americans over and over again by the enemies of religion until even the religious believe it.

In the beginning of our country many states had laws on the books that forbade the practice of opposing Christianity. These laws disappeared soon after our founding.

Nonetheless, if the Illuminists could take over church after church and change them into arms of the conspiracy as well as the state, they would achieve their goals in any case. Or, if they could convince those that *they did not take over* to refrain from getting involved in "politics," their opposition would be minimal and perhaps ineffective. Today, the attitude that conservative ministers should not preach politics prevails. This is largely due to the idea of the separation of church and state having been ingrained into the thinking of conservative ministers.

On the other hand, liberal ministers have no problem preaching the socialist agenda. They pay scant attention to the idea of staying out of politics. It is interesting that the use of 501.c.3 tax-deductible money may be used to support a government program, but the use of tax-deductible money to oppose a government program is unlawful.[38]

And, as stated before, just infiltrating Christian and Jewish publishing houses would serve the agenda of the Conspiracy simply by creating the idea that what was happening was none of the church's business, that ministers and rabbis had to focus on the things of God rather than politics, and lastly that it was all inevitable and prophesied — there was nothing you could do about it anyway. A school of thought also arose and persists that a Christian getting involved in politics will somehow slow down the return of Christ and

---

37   See *National Sexuality Educational Standards, Core Content and Skills, K-12,* January 2012. As you read it, note that it declares that it is a part of the Common Core standards. Read it carefully to see that it recommends classroom time to practice sexuality skills. Note also the school and professional organizations who wrote it. Nowhere in its pages does it point out the dangers of disease or psychological trauma by engaging in sex at a young age.
38   In 2014, the IRS agreed to monitor the sermons of ministers in order to challenge their tax-deductible status. This came about as part of a settlement of a suit against the IRS by the atheist organization Freedom From Religion Foundation of Wisconsin and was made part of the court record. The suit was apparently instigated to curtail conservative and pro-life ministers preaching against state-sponsored sin.

thereby be guilty of delaying God's plan. The earthly result: evil wins.

The Illuminists and their descendants always had as a main tactic of capturing not only the public schools, colleges, and publishing houses, but the seminaries and Christian publishing houses as well. Relative to the latter, they need not destroy faith as much as they need to neutralize Christians from effective opposition either by advocating not getting involved in politics, for whatever reason, or by advocating false solutions based on the lack of historical perspective by the Christian community who have been educated in the public schools.

A bad education has just as much effect on the Christian as it does everyone else. They may have a better moral perspective, but they can still lack the necessary information to make critical decisions for their country.

By the mid-20th century, the infiltration of communist organizations and ideology into the mainstream denominations was wide-spread. Literally thousands of ministers belonged to communist fronts, and hundreds were actual communist party members. The Church League of America documented and published the communist involvement of thousands of these so-called "servants of Christ" in the 1960s. They were never sued for liable after publishing several volumes of documentation naming names. Copies of these volumes are rare today, and no organization exists today which researches the problem.

Once the Illuminists take over, they feel that they can eliminate the faithful by extermination just as they have done in France, Mexico, the Middle East, etc., should they no longer need their cooperation.

We have refrained from documenting the infiltration of most major sects in order not to appear biased against them in a religious sense. Once the reader understands the goals and techniques of the Conspiracy, he will arrive by himself at the conclusion of whether a sect has been neutralized or not. Again, they need not destroy faith, they only need to neutralize the religious from opposing the Conspiracy through ignorance or a lack of resolve.

In September 1836, the Transcendental Club first met at the parsonage of George Ripley, Purchase Street Church, in Boston. In attendance were Bronson Alcott, Orestes Brownson, James Freeman Clarke, Ralph Waldo Emerson, Convers Francis, and Frederic Henry Hedge; all but Alcott were Unitarian ministers.

Many organizations were formed by anti-Christians that ultimately became "mainstream" in the general population. Thomas Wildey was a member of the United Ancient Order of Druids formed in London in 1781. It came to America in 1834. Its ritual was based on ancient Druid priesthood rituals and sacrifice. Wildey would go on to found the Independent Order of Odd Fellows. Early on, the Odd Fellows had many associations with British Chartist leaders; however, they seem to be more mainstream today.

The Druids were also formed in America by John Skey Eustace of the *Cercle Social*, changing a Masonic lodge into the Druids when he immigrated here. Eustace had close ties to Paine and he served in the revolutionary French army as a major general before he returned to the U.S. in 1800.

It may seem silly to the casual reader that people would actually engage in pagan Druid rituals, yet even today the practice persists in Great Britain and rituals take place at places such as Stonehenge and other prehistoric monoliths that dot the British landscape. One wonders about Americans who have built replicas of such pagan sites in the United States. Are they fascinated with them, or does their fascination carry them further into paganism?

Spiritualism has been the fundamental mystery of most secret societies, and drug traffic was its chief commercial secret for many years as part of the whole genre of seeking a higher state of mind through the use of drugs. Spiritualism was also an element of the drug scene in the heyday of the hippie movement of the 1960s. One could not tell where one began and the other ended, they were so interwoven.

It is quite possible that the so-called sightings and other "religious" experiences of some of the spiritualist leaders in the 1800s were actually drug induced. This is certainly true of some American Indian rituals.

Spiritualism remains a part of American society, although more subtly than in the 1800's.[39]

We see many manifestations of the idea of Lucifer being the prince of light and the source of enlightenment running through the teachings of spiritualists, *occult* Masons such as Albert Pike, and modern New Age ideas. Lucifer is simply a more-accepted way of saying Satan.

The idea that Satan is god is not new and permeates much of the radical philosophy, but it is generally hidden from the public. Goodwyn Barmby, one of the English ministers who was influenced by Robert Owen and who is considered one of the fathers of modern communism, said,

"In the holy Communist Church, the devil will be converted into God ... "
— "Karl Marx: Communist as Religious Eschatologist"
Murray N. Rothbard, *Requiem for Marx*

Barmby collaborated with Weitling, the leader of the League of Just Men, but their views on Christianity were not accepted within the majority of the group and Weitling lost his leadership. Weitling left for America, and Barmby became a Unitarian minister in France and friend of Mazzini.

We see here that the idea of including Christianity in the communist movement by Weitling was nothing more than a façade. Even so, Marx and his followers did not even want that much "religion" in the mix to sell communism.

The Satanic aspects of the movement are revealed in the youthful poetry of Karl Marx, who was raised a devout Christian Jew but had his faith destroyed at college. In a poem dedicated to his father called "The Fiddler," Marx penned,

With Satan I have struck my deal,
He chalks the signs, beats time for me
I play the death march fast and free

— *Requiem for Marx*

Such are the clues we see when studying the Conspiracy and its minions. And, we have just scratched the surface of Americans who edited spiritualist papers and were involved with influential groups and individuals.

It was too much too fast for the average American. For them not to reject it wholesale, the people had to be influenced a step at a time rather than at the fast pace that was going on. Many institutions that the citizens relied on for guidance and the education of their children could and would be subverted from the inside, out of the view of the citizens. This happened primarily at colleges, where the students were away

---

39 When involved in the early 1960s infiltrating Marxist organizations, this author stumbled upon modern spiritualism, one branch better known as the New Age movement. In the metropolitan area where he lived, he found three bookstores, unknown to the general public, that sold their publications and held seminars. The general belief was in what was called "white witchcraft," or looking to Lucifer as the light. This was the name of Satan before he fell; hard to believe but true. Today, 40 years later, the New Age movement is frontline and is less obviously related to white witchcraft, but it serves as a first step into Luciferian dogma.

As a result of knowing the captain in charge of a local police drug squad, the author was taken to a site outside of the urban area into a Satanist enclave the police had discovered during a drug investigation. The man who owned the property was questioned by the author with the chief, and what came out of this is too bizarre for the reader to believe without having actually been there. It did not involve the stories of human sacrifice that float around; rather, it involved drug trafficking and the means to change teenagers into amoral citizens.

from home, turning the students from Christian-based education to Hegelian-based Illuminist thought. The son the parents got back after college was not the boy they had sent there.

Spiritualists came to teach at prestigious colleges such as Smith, Harvard, Duke, Brown, Columbia, and many, many more. The students after graduating then permeated into the professions, including the law, politics, and teaching. Over time, these thoughts and beliefs became more the norm among a large segment of the educated class of people, who over time were hired into nearly all of the colleges as instructors.

The spiritualists would not have been as successful as they were if the Transcendentalists had not helped prepare the way. And they would not have been successful if the Palmers, Jeffersons, and Paines of America had not preceded them.

The changes made in higher education were led by Transcendentalists early on by the breakdown in liberal arts education, by moving the student away from the study of Greek and Latin, the two languages of our Western heritage. Not studying these two languages makes it difficult to study the philosophy of the Greeks and Scripture *in the original*. In both instances, the student is held hostage to the translator rather than the author.

Latin lingered for many decades, but Greek as a mandatory subject was eliminated in the latter half of the 19th century. Latin became an elective, and finally disappeared in school after school in the 20th century.

Transcendentalism professed a sort of Christianity while it set about breaking down Christianity. The Transcendentalists worked their influence on the *intelligentsia*. Once you have them, you have the foundations of the educational system. Rationalism became the "religion" of the establishment intellectuals.

Orestes Brownson was a leader in the Transcendentalist movement. Once he broke with them and converted to Catholicism, he stated that what the Transcendentalist movement was really all about was Fourierism and Owenite communism, and that the leadership constituted a secret movement within Transcendentalism to promote those ends. Part of this network was the Society for the Mutual Instruction. It was a secret society of Owenites to promote centralized public education, socialism, and anti-Christianity.

As a Unitarian minister before his conversion, Brownson also had formed the Society for Christian Union and Progress to advocate free inquiry, and a Church of the Future.

By now the idea of how wide and deep the influence of spiritualism was must be apparent to you. The number of people involved in spiritualism and the level of acceptance of it in the period of 1850 to 1880 would astonish the average person today. We will touch on it again in the post-bellum period.

Peace

William E. Channing was looked upon as the "bishop" of Transcendentalism by Transcendentalists such as Ralph Waldo Emerson. It was in Channing's home that the Massachusetts Peace Society was organized. This led to the American Peace Society organized by William Ladd of Maine.

Founded in New York City, the American Peace Society promoted a world "Congress and High Court of Nations" to avert war. It was formed from 50 local groups from New York, Massachusetts, New Hampshire, Maine, and Pennsylvania that coalesced into the society. It was originally headquartered in Hartford, but soon moved to Boston. It had the same international goals as the Illuminati and what became the United Nations.

Its organ was *World Affairs*, and remains so today. All of this is reminiscent of the modern Council on Foreign Relations and its organ, *Foreign Affairs*.

Through the efforts of Ladd, a prize of $1,000 was offered for the best essay on the subject of "'A

Congress of Nations,' for the termination of national disputes." This was a considerable amount of money at the time. The prize was divided among five authors, one of whom was John Quincy Adams.

As usual, the leadership of the Peace Society split and formed other organizations more radical, which made the original look less radical and more moderate. In 1838, William Lloyd Garrison, abolitionist; John Humphrey Noyes, socialist; Adin Ballou; and Bronson Alcott, father of Louise May Alcott, formed a new organization, the New England Non-Resistance Society. Then in 1866, the Universal Peace Union was formed out of it as well.

The American Peace Society had a strong Christian message for peace — that it was the Christians' duty to support some form of peace activism. The arguments were quite sound and based on orthodox Christianity even though many liberal pastors were in the leadership. One has to remember however, that the country was still based in Christianity, as Alexis de Tocqueville pointed out in his *Democracy in America* — the arguments had to be aimed at the Christian population.

It was astonishing that people did not notice that many of the peace leaders were also the leaders in spiritualism. Just as the Carbonari propagated their organization posing as a Bible Society in Europe, the conspiracy in America used Christian arguments to build a movement wherein the rank and file had no clue where they were being led.

The society did an excellent job of documenting the atrocities of war over the two centuries before and during its early existence, information which is generally lost to Americans today. This documentation would make any decent person repulsed by war and its aftermath.

The arguments for the desire for peace were sound, but the solution was something that no student of the horrors of big government could abide: world government and the power that would be accumulated in it, becoming, at the minimum, a corrupt institution with no recourse left for decent people to stand up to it. It would substitute war between states or people into perpetual war by an all-powerful government on the peoples of the earth in order to keep them subjugated. In other words, Orwell's *1984*.

It is a primary example of the ability to state a problem, get general agreement that the problem exists and at the level it exists, then sell a false solution due to the inability of people to extend the lines and realize how they are being used to establish the goals of the Conspiracy.

The American Peace Society is also an example of the leaders stating that they want peace, but when it came to the Civil War, they endorsed the conflict on the side of the "Federals." It was, after all, a just war, since the North was fighting against the slave power. There were leaders who did not hold this position, but they had little standing in the face of the war fever.

It is amazing how often peace leaders of the socialist persuasion over the last two hundred years have endorsed war if it furthers the socialist agenda. There have been others who were not that hypocritical.

Adin Ballou, a spiritualist and Unitarian minister in Milford, Massachusetts, formed the Hopedale Community, a "Christian republic" commune, in 1841. He was a Christian anarchist who believed that it was a Christian's duty to disobey all temporal authority if by doing so he is following God's will. He was also a leader in the New England Anti-Slavery Society. He authored *Practical Christian Socialism*. He was an early ally of Garrison until Garrison advocated violence to end slavery. He serves as an example of how anarchists always seem to end up socialists or communists. In reality, anarchism is just another tool of the same conspiracy behind socialism.

In 1846 another organization, international in scope, was formed by Elihu Burritt of Natick, Massachusetts, to promote pacifism called the League of Universal Brotherhood. In 1842 he had started the *Christian Citizen*, a weekly journal devoted to anti-slavery, peace, temperance, and self-culture.

After forming the brotherhood, he traveled to Europe for three years where he cooperated with English peace advocates. He was prominent in organizing the 1st Peace Conference and took part in two subsequent congresses in 1849 and 1850. There were five substantial congresses held all over Western Europe in that time frame.

The 1st Peace Conference was sponsored primarily by the English Peace Society in 1843. It was attended by 150 delegates, 18 of whom were Americans.

By 1852, Burritt was the editor of the *Citizen of the World*, in Philadelphia. His peace advocacy had evolved openly into the Illuminist idea of one world. In 1865, he was appointed as U.S. consul in Birmingham, England.

The peace movement of the 19th century was strikingly similar to the communist front groups that promoted peace in the 20th century. The interlocking of so-called peace groups was in reality only a manifestation of international socialism/communism in the English-speaking countries, something that continues to exist into the 21st century.

We will illustrate this with many examples as we proceed through this narrative.

Recall that the peace conference held in Geneva in 1867, chaired by Garibaldi, became nothing more than a mass meeting to promote socialism and anti-Catholicism. While the conference rejected Garibaldi's extreme position against the pope, nonetheless the overwhelming sentiment was anti-Catholic, only disagreeing on the extent of the punishment that should be levied against the church and property of the church.

Peace to a militant socialist means the peace of the grave of his opposition. In other words, in the socialist lexicon, peace means no opposition to socialism. There are many such words which carry a much different meaning than the normal definition among socialists, and they can communicate among themselves and have a much different message they hear or read than the non-socialist.

At the same time, Harvard and Yale were being subverted by the same groups, turning them from strong Christian-based institutions to Transcendentalism and internationalism in the name of peace and security.

Anti-Masonry

The Anti-Masonic movement had more to it than the simple reaction against Masonry. There was a natural aversion by some citizens toward those in Masonry who seemed to have a fraternal lock on politics and business in many areas. Even into the 20th century, the voting blocs in some rural areas had leadership that broke down into more of a Mason vs. Catholic vote rather than Republican or Democrat.

Then there was always the suspicion of any organization that kept secrets from the public, whether it was the Masons or the Knights of Columbus.

The apparent murder of the Mason William Morgan in New York served as the catalyst for the sudden upheaval of anti-Masonic feeling. Morgan threatened to expose the real secrets of Masonry and was killed by Masons to prevent the disclosure — at least that is the story. The evidence weighs on both sides and the truth will probably never be known for sure. The main problems are that the witnesses on both sides were less than reliable. It is so mixed up that other than to say that the incident was used for a number of reasons by those who wanted power would be speculation.

There is just too much uncertainty in the evidence to warrant discussing it, and in the general scheme of things, it is not important to the discussion. All we need to know is that the incident was used to agitate the populace into a widespread anti-Masonic reaction, and that the national movement grew too rapidly with coordinated press impetus to be spontaneous.

The anti-Masonic movement (along with the anti-Jackson sentiment) led ultimately to the organization of the Whig Party and elevated to prominence such men as Thurlow Weed, Millard Fillmore, William Henry Seward, Benjamin Wade, William Wirt, and others.

First, the anti-Masonic movement was used to enlist the average citizen into a political movement apart from the mainstream organizations in an attempt to move them one more step away from constitutional government than what had already been done through the then-existing major parties.

Second, the Masons had a great deal of influence and a large membership, so large that coupled with the manner in which Masonry was organized it would have been very difficult to take them over with a small coterie of infiltrators. Whereas the Grand Orient of Europe had a more centralized aspect to it through their conventions, their membership was never large, and they were more inclined toward subversion. Something was needed to try and make American Masonry over to make it more susceptible to infiltration and control by the Conspiracy.

In 1816, there were approximately 850 lodges in America. By 1826, there were over 1,290 lodges with as many as 60,000 members. This would be the ratio of influence at the equivalent of 1.4 million today, about a third of the National Rifle Association membership.

The public outcry that was produced and the smear tactics against American Masonry caused nearly 90% of its members to quit in some states, particularly New York. There were 600 lodges in New York when the furor started, and by the end of 1834 only 50 remained active. The members could not stand the heat in the kitchen, as Harry Truman was apt to say.

This Masonic membership was primarily the non-conspiratorial type not occult Masonry. The latter did keep their membership, since they were more secretive, and probably even helped to shrink the influence of primitive Masons.

The smear tactic has always been used by the Conspiracy to prevent growth in their enemies' organizations, as well as the loss of their members because most people cannot stand up to controversy.

To give you an idea of how large American Masonry was at the time and how difficult it would have been to subvert, one state alone, New York, had nearly as many lodges as all of Europe had in the Grand Orient.

A smaller organization could be easier to infiltrate and take over.

Third, the anti-masonic movement was a means for relatively unknown individuals to take leadership positions in forming the Anti-Masonic Party, and through it rise to public notoriety.

One such individual was Thaddeus Stevens. He and William H. Seward became fast friends in the movement, so much so that they roomed together at the anti-Masonic convention that nominated for president William Wirt, one of the prosecutors in the Aaron Burr trial. Wirt was a member of the Jacobin Democratic Societies and used to sing *La Marseillaise*, not a Masons-are-to-blame-for-everything type that the anti-Masons would seem to want.

Later, President Andrew Johnson would refer to the leaders of the Radical Congress, Stevens, Charles Sumner, and Wendell Phillips as those men who were trying to destroy the fundamental principles of government. This should be no surprise when you take into account that the First International sent Cesare Orsini to America briefly during 1866, where he had interviews with Sumner, Phillips, and Horace Greeley. All three joined the International. Keep in mind, this was done while Sumner was chairman of the Senate Foreign Relations Committee.

Cesare Orsini was the younger brother of the assassin Felice Orsini, who had been guillotined for his attempt on the life of Napoleon III in January of 1858. The bomb attempt took several lives and wounded nearly 150 bystanders, but did no harm to Napoleon.

Seward would later lie about not knowing about the Harper's Ferry raid beforehand. He was one of the men who were put forward as a presidential candidate over Lincoln by the Radicals. He was a fast friend of Thurlow Weed. Much to his credit, he would oppose the impeachment of Johnson.

Stevens had been rejected twice for membership in the Masonic order as a young man. There were other problems between him and Masons regarding his reputation early on. All these things may have played a role in his enthusiasm for the anti-Masonic movement.

This enthusiasm soon was redirected after his conversion to abolitionism as a political career by the Unitarian minister Jonathon Blanchard.

Thurlow Weed was the editor of the *Anti-Masonic Review*. He was one of the campaign managers of William Harrison, along with Nicholas Biddle, the head of the U.S. Bank. With William H. Seward, he helped form the People's Party convention to nominate DeWitt Clinton for governor of New York.

Since the whole idea of the anti-Masonic movement was to be against secret societies, it is rather interesting that some of the leading lights of the anti-Masonic movement would endorse Masons and individuals well known for their involvement in Illuminist circles, such as Clinton and Wirt. The anti-Masonic movement did more to damage Masonry than it did to hurt the Conspiracy, and one has to ask the question why. One of the answers, again, has to be to trim the size of the Masonic orders in order to attempt to control them or curtail their influence. Members of Masonry were very influential in building the United States to begin with.

One has to always recall that the aim of the Conspiracy is to assume the leadership of their opposition. Plus, not every fight is really a fight. It's Punch and Judy.

The Anti-Masonic Party drew votes away from Clay leading to the re-election of Andrew Jackson in 1832. Jackson was a Mason and so the splitting of the vote resulted in the exact opposite of one of the public goals of the Anti-Masonic Party: the elimination of Masons in the political realm. Considering the background of many of its leaders, this may have been one of the multiple gains for the democratizing of America in forming the party in the first place.

Jackson at one point was attempting to become the leader of all Masonry in the United States, to not only become the leader, but to unite all of Masonry in the process.

The Anti-Masonic Party which was composed largely of the old Clinton party in New York indicates that not everyone's motivation was really anti-Masonic. Some of the early leaders of the party were Masons themselves. The Anti-Masonic Party dissolved in 1833, with most of its leaders going into the anti-slavery movement.

Interestingly, the rival to Jackson becoming the head of American Masonry was DeWitt Clinton, another clue as to the possible motivation of the Anti-Masonic Party. In any case, it did not happen.

Spencer, in his *History of the United States*, summed it up this way:

In the autumn of 1826, the abduction of Morgan ... (caused a stir) for some three or four years, the masonic fraternity was freely denounced, and numerous politicians made use of this topic, as a means of advancing ends in which they had an interest.

Anarchism

Anarchism was also a movement within all of the movements. It had many of the attributes of the libertarian philosophy, without the foundations and principles seen in mainstream libertarianism today. A love-hate relationship with the communists has always existed, and on most occasions through the last two centuries the anarchists have cooperated with the communist movement.

Today, some anarchists have a foot in both communist and libertarian causes. This situation in the past has always helped lead to the failure of the libertarians, since the anarchist involvement is obvious enough to conservatives and constitutionalists to make them shy away from their involvement with them; therefore, since the anarchists are visibly involved with the libertarians, they reject them as well. There is a difference, but generally if conservative people see some aspect of a movement they do not like, they usually reject the whole.

While this played a major role in the rejection of libertarianism, another aspect also played an equal, if not greater a role in its rejection by conservative Americans. That is the general dismissal by libertarians of moral issues. We have discussed that morality plays a dominant role in the makeup of any society. Many Founders of our country can be quoted saying that morality or religion was the foundation of our free society and government, and that without it our system would not only be inadequate but collapse.

It is interesting that modern libertarians often quote Jefferson but rarely quote Washington and Adams. You may visit events sponsored by political conservatives and libertarians and find very little literature and material about Washington and Adams or their quotes, but the booths and tables assembled to reach out to the participants will be laden with items promoting Jefferson.

This does not mean that the quotes and materials are not wise, but often the material is taken out of context, or certain facts are missing from the narrative that would shed a different light on the original motivation of depicted events and speeches. Most of these outlets of information do not believe in conspiracy per se, and tend to ignore anything that would expose a cabal unless the exposure is aimed against Alexander Hamilton or other enemies of the Jacobins. One has to ask why.

Such is the modern movement, and they will disagree with this evaluation vehemently. And, they also believe that moral issues are a distraction from the real fight, usually meaning economics. Yet economics without morality is a disaster and is destructive of freedom.

There is a widespread rejection of any idea of a conspiracy within the libertarian movement, which causes them to be blindsided from time to time. A modern manifestation of this problem is that certain wings of libertarians were temporarily more inclined toward Russia and Putin than the United States government. This has also shown up in Christian circles based on the false idea that Putin is more moral than the U.S. government due to his anti-homosexual stance.

One wonders if they would have thought the same about Hitler putting effeminate homosexuals in concentration camps.

There are other solutions that are supported due to a fundamental lack of education.

Americans need to also remember that in modern times the action of politicians has not met the rhetoric. This has always been the case. Today there are many socialist and communists who have been quoted extensively in the media and within academia without the corresponding information about the motivation behind such people. What we see in history is that the rhetoric has survived but the actions have been sanitized, just as today.

William Bradford Greene, an anarchist, was a graduate of West Point and served in the Seminole campaign and later in the Civil War as a Union colonel. He lived in France, met Proudhon, and studied there from 1853 until the start of the war. At some point he became a member of the French Section of the First International. After the war, he became active in labor unions. Before going to Europe, he was a member of the Massachusetts Constitutional Convention.

He had this to say about socialism in 1849:

> In socialism, there is but one master, which is the state, but the State is not a living person, capable of suffering and happiness. Socialism benefits none but demagogues, and is emphatically the organization of universal misery. Socialism gives us but one class, a class of slaves.
> — *The Expositors of Individualist Anarchism in America*

Yet, later he joined the French Section of the communist First International. It is rare that anarchists remain anarchists, and they usually end up joining some form of socialist organization, yesterday, today, and probably tomorrow.

Anarchists serve the purpose of either creating a vacuum or a reaction on the part of the people and/or government. They advocate no government at all and will even engage in acts of violence ostensibly to bring down the state. All they ever really do is set the stage for either a reaction on the part of government or a condition where an organization can take over in a period of chaos. In either case, power is centralized and accumulated. They are useful idiots, as Lenin would say. Their actions produce the exact opposite of their professed desires by the reaction created.

This is why it can sometimes be difficult to recognize the true anarchists from the ones who are only advocating the philosophy to produce the necessary conditions for power to come out of chaos. Almost always, the anarchist leaders serve the same master as the communist, and are but a little finger on the master hand.

And, they will be in the streets shoulder to shoulder with communists. It has been indeed rare that anarchists are not represented at demonstrations organized by the communists. This was the condition during the period covered by this tome, and it remains the case today.

By now, you are beginning to see the interlocking aspect of organizations and key leaders that formed the Conspiracy's cadre.

10

NEO-RADICALS

One tactical aspect of subverting freedom that the enemies of freedom use is not putting all their eggs in one basket. They diversify. As mentioned earlier, the Conspiracy needs to work all sides in order to control the agenda.

One side will be radical, the other side less radical and/or compromising. The second side will take many of the positions of the freedom movement to gain the confidence of those who defend liberty in order to sell them out in the future and/or simply move the agenda along a small step at a time when necessary using the tactic of compromise. The latter is not always easy to expose since it is difficult to tell if an individual is purposeful in his betrayal or simply misguided.

In America the more visible aspects of the conspiracy that were not endeavors promoting intellectual change and were more of the lower tier began to coalesce around two historic organizations in the 1840s and 1850s: communism and the Carbonari.

The Carbonari's Young America (YA) reached its ascendency in the late 1850s and played a key role in laying the groundwork for a future civil war. After the Civil War they faded *as a visible organization,* even though their ideas have never faded from the American scene, as witnessed by the Spanish-American War and the modern neoconservative movement. YA aims since the Civil War have been generally carried out by the establishment of the major political parties.

In other words, the goals of YA became the established American foreign policy without being a *visible movement* from the Civil War until 1921, with the formation of the Council on Foreign Relations (CFR), when their tactics again became obvious, even as a more visible *organization* than before the Civil War. By the mid-20th century there were several elite organizations promoting the YA goals, all with interlocking directorates and membership.

Just as the average American patriot did not see through the rhetoric of the YA leadership before the Civil War, they do not see through the rhetoric of the neo-con leadership currently. It is a failure to extend the lines to the logical conclusion of a neo-con foreign policy which has led to, among other negative things, a backlash against Americans and Christians in countries that once tolerated Christians, particularly Muslim countries that had Christian communities extending back two thousand years.

The communists and the Carbonari were at odds from time to time, yet they cooperated when it came to the goals they held in common on orders from the Insiders. Likewise, there have been communists among the Council on Foreign Relations, the Carnegie Foundation, and other elite organizations who have helped move the agenda along contemporarily.

Remember that the only real difference between Marxism and the Carbonari was the tactics and personalities at the top. The end in mind was the same, and it remains the same today. It matters little if you call the totalitarian government communist, socialist, fascist, corporate, or otherwise. The effect on the people is the same because the control over the people ultimately has to be the same if it is a totalitarian state.

In order to control the people, they must use the same methodology, structure, etc. that produce this control. This includes control over property rights, freedom of movement, communication, religion, anything and everything that individuals would use to oppose the state. Keep in mind that *control* is the operative word. It does not matter if a person believes that they own property, for instance, if the state controls everything about its use and taxes the "owner" for the privilege of ownership.

There is little difference between the state owning property and renting it to the people, and people owning property and paying taxes. In either case, if you do not pay the rent or the taxes, you are off the property. In some cases not only may property be controlled through a web of regulations and zoning, but the property may be confiscated if it does not conform to the "purpose" of government.

An example of men who had public differences, particularly regarding slavery, but had the same goals in the end, was George Sanders and Horace Greeley. From time to time they cooperated on political initiatives, and both worked with Young America. However, ostensibly one worked for the South, and the other worked for the North. One was a socialist cum communist leader, the other a Carbonari.

By the end of the Civil War, the main radical influence in America became what we call Marxism today. We will discuss the forces of Marxism later. YA as an organization faded from the public view to a large extent because so many of its leaders were Southern, and Southern influence waned. It is ironic that as the influence of the South came back in the 20th century, many of the goals of YA became embodied in the neoconservative movement, which was started primarily by Irving Kristol, a former Trotskyite communist, and interwoven with the CFR, of which Kristol was a member.

Neoconservatism is not new, only renamed and packaged for the modern conservative. Its initial sales job was to sell the conservative constitutionalist movement on the idea that they needed to change their public image in order to succeed in the 1960s. In changing that image, they adopted the image of compromise as the first step toward implementing the same internationalism as the communists, only with a cosmetic applied.

In addition, the reason for YA waning was that the foundation of the impetus for YA, the Carbonari, was waning in Europe, with its leadership less revolutionary and becoming more occult about the time of the Civil War and especially after, although it retained enough influence in Italy to achieve its goals. Likewise, it started a long trek toward infiltrating the Catholic hierarchy rather than attacking it head on, and this was achieved to a startling extent by the mid-20th century through the Alta Vendita.

Many of the policies of YA later became embodied in the aims of Cecil Rhodes and the group of Lord Alfred Milner of England, with an Anglo-Saxon bent, with the Rhodes faction in America basically being Anglophile. In other words, Rhodes wanted Britain to be the controlling factor in world government rather than the U.S.

The YA adherents, along with the major revolutionaries of the day, were active in England, where the headquarters for the Conspiracy appeared to be centered before the Civil War, ultimately moving to New York after the war. Most of the major international revolutionary leaders lived in England prior to the American Civil War.

An article written anonymously by a YA adherent in England in July of 1854 — possibly Sanders — referred to America playing a role for the ascendency of " ... Anglo-Saxonism throughout the world...."

The CFR was established as the American equivalent of the English Royal Institute of International Affairs. It was the continuation of English influence on U.S. politics, but in the long run the roles became reversed, with the American wing calling the shots.

Whether the reader believes all of this or not, the one commonality is that regardless of the leadership of these wings, or the ostensible goals, they all seem to end up at the same place at the same time. The United Nations is a good example. The communists, socialists, peace organizations, American and Russian foreign service, etc., while appearing to be in opposition, formed an organization together supposedly to prevent a war amongst themselves!

This is illogical, but modern America hasn't been thinking logically enough to see through the plot. Those who mean to rule and be the ruling leadership do not form organizations to curtail their activities. They form organizations to curtail their adversaries.

Since its foundation, the UN has *presided* over more wars than at any time in modern history. And even when there was no fighting, they still called it a war: the Cold War, using this condition to establish more controls over the American people — which would require another book to tell the story.

Remarkably, the Carbonari was anti-royal, yet their "revolution" led to the ascendency of Victor Emmanuel to the throne of a united Italy. Those "behind the throne" know what they are doing, even if the rabble does not. A study of the French Revolution will also reveal that a certain portion of the conspirators simply wanted to bring down the king only to establish another on the throne: the Duc d'Orleans. This ambition by the Duc and his followers ultimately served the goals of the Illuminati.

Throughout Europe Carbonari front groups sprang up in league with other secret societies and cults in countries other than Italy. The line from the Illuminati to these groups was in most cases organizational, with a few others philosophical, and they formed Young Europe, an umbrella group for the wide, diverse lower ranks of conspiracy-controlled connections.

In the United States, Young America was formed. Since the power behind the YA was secretive and great pains have been taken to conceal the American wings of the Conspiracy, it has been difficult to ferret out the actual beginnings of YA and the initiation of the leaders of YA that are known.

We have never had an *effective* American government investigation — by any other entity, for that matter, except for private author's — into any arm of the Conspiracy, with the exception of the Knights of the Golden Circle (KGC). Any such investigation almost always produced a report which limited the time frame of the beginning of the organization to an ambivalent time of Marx or some other personality, and with no connection to the Illuminati. And then, only as the organization pertained to communism. This limited the scope of any investigation to a point of near irrelevance relative to the overall problem.

With the government investigation of the KGC, no connection was made to a conspiracy outside of the ranks of the American pro-slavers. While it exposed a great deal about the KGC, it was more propaganda against the South and the Confederacy rather than an exposé of the forces dividing the country on both sides of the ledger.

We have seen in the 20th century the same deficiency in certain conservative leaders, who will confess that there are conspiracies, but that they are limited to a few communist spies. Any mentions of conspiracies that are wider in scope or include entities that are not openly communist are looked at with skepticism, if not derision. This attitude was particularly true of the former CIA operative William F. Buckley and those who surrounded him in his magazine, *National Review,* and in the Republican Party.

We do know that George Sanders was a founder of YA, that his family had befriended Aaron Burr, and that his grandfather was a traitor in the pay of Spain who worked with Jefferson to attempt to separate Kentucky from the United States. Sanders would form a bond with Mazzini and other radical European revolutionaries who were Carbonari leaders. Sanders admitted that he was a friend of Louis Blanqui, a Carbonari leader, and had joined the "Club Blanqui" at Paris.

In other words, Sanders was associated with Blanqui, who worked with Buonarroti, who was under the direct influence of Weishaupt.

Blanqui served as a leader of the Carbonari and founded the Democratic Association for the Unification of All Countries in 1847. Karl Marx was its vice president. While it did not have a significant influence immediately, it nonetheless displayed by its goals a very modern idea.

The idea was to establish a series of smaller confederacies to expand over time into regional governments, starting with Europe. These regional governments would then merge into a one-world government. This is what happened — and is continuing to happen — with the European Union. It is also the program of the North American Union and the sinew of the modern free trade partnerships.

We know that the *Young America* newspaper was founded by George H. Evans in 1845. Evans started his publishing career by issuing a monthly, called *Radical*. Thomas Skidmore and William Leggett worked with Evans at that time. *Young America* started out as *People's Rights* in March 1844, and in 1845 was changed to *YA*. Evans was associated with it until 1849 and died in 1855. He was assisted by John Windt, Lewis Masquerier, and Alvan E. Bovay, who went on to found the Republican Party.

Masquerier was active for many years in land reform movements. When he joined Evans at the magazine, he "entertained the communistic views of (Robert) Owen," in his own words.

Behind the scenes, *Young America* was assisted by Judge William S. Waite of Illinois, Sen. Isaac P. Walker of Wisconsin, Lewis Ryckman, and Gerrit Smith of New York, all advocates of land reform.

Edwin de Leon was an editor of John O'Sullivan's *Democratic Review*, a party organ for the Democrat Party that became the intellectual center of the YA movement. De Leon was a member of the Carbonari under the Blanqui/Mazzini leadership. The *Democratic Review*, started in 1837, promoted the writings of Ralph Waldo Emerson, Henry D. Thoreau, Walt Whitman, and Nathaniel Hawthorne. Benjamin Butler was instrumental in the establishment of the paper, and George Bancroft and a select group of Transcendentalists praised O'Sullivan and assisted him behind the scenes.[40]

While holding many paradoxical positions, O'Sullivan supported the idea of a "Congress of Nations" in the name of peace, desired American intervention into any country where liberty was in danger, and advocated the forceful acquisition of additional territory for the United States.

You can see that his positions contradicted one another, yet they form the position of modern neoconservatives. Senator John McCain, for instance, has advocated armed intervention just about everywhere in the name of liberty and has endorsed the idea of a League (or Concert) of Democracies. This league or concert would be more than a military alliance and would be the basis for political alliance. McCain has been a longstanding member of the Council on Foreign Relations, and headed up the International Republican Institute (IRI) funded indirectly by the U.S. State Department. He is a leading neo-con.

O'Sullivan's desire was for a Congress of Nations in the name of peace, but he was quite ready to send American armed forces into other countries and territories. The modern neo-con supports the principle of the United Nations while advocating the same regarding the use of American armed forces, always under the leadership of the UN. *All wars where America troops have been committed since 1945 have been waged under UN resolutions and jurisdiction,* rubberstamped and made to look like American initiatives by the president and congressional leaders.

Since modern American conservatives have become increasingly skeptical, even fearful of the United Nations, neoconservatives such as John McCain have therefore advocated this new League of Democra-

---

40 Edwin De Leon is sometimes referred to as Edward DeLeone by some writers. Alvan Earle Bovay's name has alternately appeared as Alan or Allen, Earl or Earle in myriad history books.

cies to produce the same result as the UN but under a different name. Most have seen through this charade.

George Law and August Belmont, the Rothschild agent, acquired a financial interest in the *Democratic Review,* and in 1851 handed George Sanders, one of the founders of YA, a share in it as co-owner. At this time it surged into a firebrand style of rhetoric.

In the newspaper, Sanders called for the invasion of Europe and the destruction of its crowned heads, targeting Napoleon III especially. He glorified Mazzini and gave support to the terrorist group the Knights of the Silver Star. He also approved of his partner's ship, George Law's *The Crescent City,* sailing to Havana loaded with cannon and muskets to launch a YA campaign to take Cuba. The prominent Southern lawyer Judah Benjamin also approved.

About the same time that Sanders took over the operation of the *Democratic Review,* he started a group called Young Cuba as an extension of the Carbonari YA.

William Corry, a longtime associate of Sanders, in a biography of Sanders, said Sanders was directly involved in an assassination attempt on Napoleon III.

Contributors to the *Democratic Review* under Sanders included Samuel Tilden, William Cullen Bryant, and YA members Nathaniel Hawthorne and Edgar Allen Poe, who apparently did not support communism.

As the Civil War came, *the New York Tribune* and Horace Greeley took on the mantle of YA as the movement's representative. In this example we see the re-bonding of the people who supported both Marx and Mazzini.

O'Sullivan was elected to the New York Assembly in 1841, and among other things he proposed a Congress of Nations as an arbiter to war. He worked for many years to make Cuba a possession of the United States, or that failing, an independent state. He was put on trial for raising funds for Narciso Lopez, which was a violation of the Neutrality Law. He became a Confederate during the war.

Again, we see the hypocrisy of the people who led the radical movements. They profess to not want war, advocating a Congress of Nations in this case, but have no problem in supporting the building of empire by force or creating problems that will lead to war. Once the problems are created, then they can advocate a "compromise" through their established organizations for peace. The compromise will always be a step toward their goal of world dominance.

Americans have had a problem, then and now, understanding that people involved in the Conspiracy will do and say anything that will further their agenda. This is a problem for honest people who, without enough experience to rely on to gain a history of those they work with in the political or social arena, are misled by the rhetoric of those who pretend to be their allies and friends.

This is a particular problem among conservative Republican activists who either do not have the background to recognize the end result of particular actions, or lack the experience to know who may be trusted to mean what they say.

Since they do not usually have access to information that shows the "behind the scenes" activities or endorsement of initiatives in opposition to constitutional principles, they will almost always listen to the rhetoric and ignore the actions of politicians professing to be their leaders in whatever branch of the conservative movement.

It takes time and experience, or access to alternative publications, to gain an insight into who are honest and forthright in their political lives.

Edwin de Leon became the U.S. consul general to Egypt, and it was there that he heard that the war had broken out. He was a major diplomat for the Confederacy until he was forced to resign.

As an extension of the Illuminati, Carbonari aims were the overthrow of established order (*regard-*

less of what it was) religion, and the middle class, followed by the establishment of nationalism as a step toward regionalism, and then on to a world government. YA adopted and adapted the Carbonari program to suit an American audience.

One of the early leaders of YA, George Henry Evans, was the founder of the National Reform Association (NRA) in 1844 and the National Reform Congress in 1845. Evans, like Marx, talked about a world revolution:

> The Chartists of Great Britain, the Repealers of Ireland, the Republican Associationists of France, and the Communists of Germany — Noble Pioneers of the good time coming! When National Reform for a Free Soil shall be triumphant throughout the world ...
> — *Young America: Land, Labor, and the Republican Community*

Allies of the National Reform Movement were the American Union of Associations of Greeley, Brook Farm leaders, the New England Workingmen's Association, the secret society called the Mechanics Mutual Protection Association, the Brotherhood of the Union, the Arbeiterbund, the Spartan Band under the Irishman Mike Walsh, and, of course, the communists. (The American Union of Associations was sometimes referred to as the National Convention of Associations.)

Walsh and some of his Spartan Band were involved in the Dorr Rebellion in Rhode Island in 1841, which aided in the battle to eliminate the last vestiges of the property requirement to vote. He published the *Subterranean* in 1843, merged it into G. H. Evans' *Workingman's Advocate* for a short time in 1844, and then pulled out. In 1847 it went under due to a libel suit. He was a New York State Assemblyman from 1846 to 1852, then went to Congress as the Tammany candidate in 1852. He was defeated in the next election by Tammany for his lack of support for abolition.

One of the leaders in the National Reform Association was London emigrant Gilbert Vale, who published the paper *Citizen of the World* and wrote a biography of Thomas Paine. There were many Chartist leaders from Great Britain who involved themselves in the NRA after immigrating to America.

The president of the NRA convention was Lewis Ryckman from Brook Farm. The secretary of the NRA in 1848 was Alvan Bovay, who went on to form the Republican Party six years later.

The New England Workingmen's Association had such luminaries in its ranks as Horace Greeley, Robert Owen, and Albert Brisbane. They re-named their organization the New England Labor Reform League, but this is not to be confused with the organization of the same name that was formed in 1869. The latter had some overlapping goals, but were more anarchist than socialist under the leadership of William Greene and Ezra Heywood.

William Greene was a Unitarian minister who came through Brook Farm on his road to anarchism. He was influenced by the writings of Proudhon and became his personal friend. He, as most radicals do, involved himself in promoting a change in the economic system and worked for a mutual banking system. He was educated at Harvard Divinity School.

Ezra Heywood was the editor of their periodical, *The Word*, which also held the writings of the Anti-Tax League, Union Reform League, and Free Love League. He labored against the use of gold as money, and his organization had an influence on Susan B. Anthony's National Woman Suffrage Association.

The spiritualists launched the Order of Eternal Progress and helped both the American section of the IWA and Heywood's Labor Reform League.

CHART FIVE
The influence of the Illuminati on the Carbonari and Young America

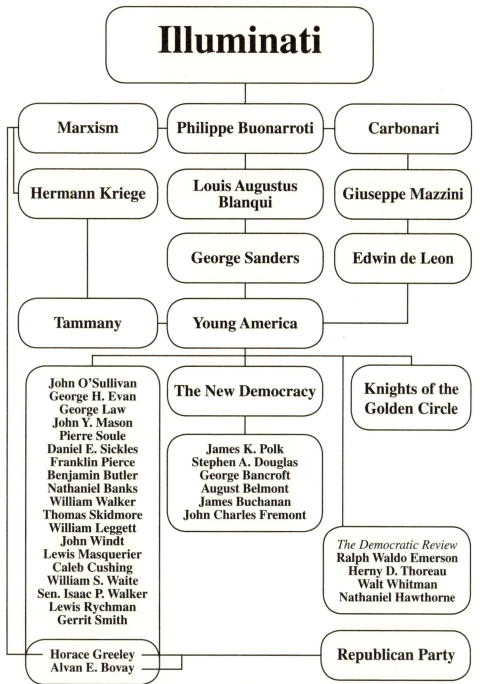

In case the point has not yet been made, this is what Friedrich Engels had to say in his *Principles of Communism*:

> In America, where the democratic constitution has been established, the communists must make common cause with the party that is utilizing this constitution in the interest of the proletariat and against the bourgeoisie, that is with the agrarian National Reformers.

The Young Men's Committee of Tammany Hall also played a role in YA. This came about through the foundation laid by William Leggett, a friend and partner of William Cullen Bryant. They were also instrumental in the memorializing of Andrew Jackson with a statue in New York.

The widespread YA movement was a direct result of the young men within the Democrat Party and the many adherents of Andrew Jackson. In addition, there were connections with the communist finger on the hand of the Master Conspiracy.

In other words, there was an inner core of men and women who were *conspirators* of the Carbonari, and they were successful in producing a much wider YA *movement* of non-initiates.

Lafayette may have helped plant the seeds of the Carbonari fifteen years earlier on his visit to America, at which time he was the Carbonari leader in France. Lafayette was a prisoner of the crown; nonetheless, the Congress through Monroe invited him to America as part of the 50th anniversary of the founding of the United States.

Lafayette wanted to visit the United States, but could not until his debts were paid. Of the three men who paid his debts, two were Americans: James Brown, Minister to France, and Jean Francois Girod, citizen of New Orleans. A hostage to the French to ensure Lafayette's return had to be arranged for and held until Lafayette's return. James Brown served as that hostage.

The Congress also voted a sum of $20,000 and land as a gift for Lafayette, a handsome amount at the time.

Some of the key people he stayed or met with were: Gov. William Eustis, Sen. James Lloyd, Jr., and Judge Levi Lincoln, Jr., Worcester, all of Massachusetts; Robert L. Livingston, Gov. Joseph C. Yates, DeWitt Clinton, all of New York; Gov. Isaac H. Williamson and Joseph Bonaparte in New Jersey; Nicholas Biddle and Judge Richard Peters in Pennsylvania; and Gov. Samuel Sprigg of Maryland. Lafayette gave the bride away at Charles I. DuPont's wedding.

Judge Levi Lincoln, the son of Jefferson's attorney general, was the host of a dinner party with the guest of honor an Abraham Lincoln from Illinois, who was on tour as a speaker for the Whig Party in 1848. At this dinner Abraham Lincoln met luminaries such as George S. Hillard; George Ashmun, who would later chair the Republican Party convention that would nominate Lincoln; Henry Gardner; Emory Washburn; and Alexander H. Bullock; the latter three future governors of Massachusetts.

John Quincy Adams hardly left Lafayette's side while he was running for president. After the election, Adams had Lafayette stay in the White House for some time until arrangements could be made for his trip home.

Andrew Jackson became close friends of Lafayette and spent a good deal of time with him, as did Frances "Fanny" Wright. Lafayette stayed with Jackson at the Hermitage in Nashville, Jackson's home. Later, Fanny Wright formed a group of trustees to manage her estate which included Lafayette, Robert Owen, Robert Dale Owen, and other likeminded people.

Once home, Lafayette continued his revolutionary activities, and the goal was to establish the Duc d'Orleans on the French throne. This was the original aim of some of the Jacobins used by the Illuminati, and subsequently the French Carbonari.

The term *Manifest Destiny* was coined by Massachusetts Congressman Robert C. Winthrop and picked up as a slogan by John O'Sullivan, also editor at the time of the strongly anti-British and intensely patriotic *New York Morning News*. YA always had the appearance of being pro-American and fiercely patriotic.

YA quickly adopted the motto, and American expansion with the foreign interference strategy of YA became known as Manifest Destiny, as if there was some sort of divine providence for the United States to rule the Western Hemisphere and to overthrow the old governments of Europe. This appealed to the patriotic nature of Americans in the 19th century just as it appeals to the neo-conservatives in the 20th and 21st centuries, who advocate getting involved in foreign entanglements and supporting the overthrow of a variety of governments by force in the name of democracy.

Albert Gallatin was opposed to Manifest Destiny, probably because it was so American oriented. He was, after all, a citizen of the world. Then again, there has always been a debate among conspirator leadership as to the best method for achieving world government.

Filibusters

Americans forget that the reason there were so many wars in Europe was due to fierce nationalism, blind patriotism, and aggressive national personalities rather than adherence to liberty for all under a system that limits government. Ambitious men used these traits to first subjugate their own people and then attempt to do likewise to their neighbors. It is a wonderful thing to be patriotic, but not blindly.

It was one thing for Americans to want to expand the nation out into the frontier, but Manifest Destiny became much more, including the filibuster movement. *Filibuster* today refers to the tactic in the Senate of holding the floor against a majority. In the 1800s, a filibusterer was a mercenary, yet another example of how a word can evolve into a different definition.

Filibuster armies were formed to invade Cuba, Mexico, Nicaragua, and other Central American states, similar to what had been attempted against our infant country by the radical French ambassadors in the late 1700s, and then later by Aaron Burr.

The three most prominent filibusters were Narciso Lopez, John A. Quitman, and William Walker, who led the most famous enterprise. He had invaded Baja and Sonora, and there had instituted a short-lived so-called republic. He led an expedition called the "La Falange Americana" (The American Phalanx), reminiscent of Fourier, which for a time actually held Nicaragua until Cornelius Vanderbilt, who wanted the country for his own shipping interests, and the British worked together to finally capture Walker and have him executed.

Walker had allied himself with the rivals of Vanderbilt on the advice of his longtime friend Edmund Randolph, with whom he had practiced law. Randolph was the grandson of George Washington's attorney general who resigned when it was discovered he was in collusion with the Revolutionary French ambassador.

Nicaragua was considered by many as a linchpin in the quest for a world empire. The original idea was to build what became the Panama Canal through Nicaragua rather than Panama. As far as American interests were concerned, Nicaragua was a battleground between the financiers Vanderbilt and Charles Morgan and his partner Cornelius K. Garrison, and then the Young America leader George Law, all very much involved in shipping. Each wanted the country for his personal benefit.

A canal through Nicaragua would have been a boon to American interests, and whoever would have controlled such an enterprise and seen the project through to establish a canal from ocean to ocean would more than likely have become the richest man in the world. If in addition he got to decide who could use it, he could have immense control and power over trade in the hemisphere and beyond.

Here we have an example of where men of industry and commerce may have the same basic political goals but are at odds for control for their own ambitious ends. They may be personal enemies, but the end will be the same no matter who wins. And, it is a very graphic illustration that whether it comes from the Left or corporate, it is the same and interlocking. Power is the motivator, not philosophy.

Note that while the leader Walker was part of the socialist revolution, he was backed by corporate heads. The same is in play today with such examples as George Soros. Meanwhile, another man of industry, Vanderbilt, was the enemy of these men but by no means adverse to communism, having supported the activities of the Woodhull and Claflin sisters.

Conservative Americans simply have to divorce themselves from the thought that capitalism is an enemy of communism — moral capitalism is, immoral capitalism is not. And, while we are thinking about it, there is no economic system that exists that is not capitalistic; it is a matter of who controls it, individuals or the state or those behind the state.

Capital is defined as the means of production or the tools for such means, and it includes the tools and land for agriculture. Communists do not destroy capital — they assume control over it; ergo they are capitalists. They beguile the masses into thinking that they are not, and this is one of the most egregious teachings in the government schools because it hides what is really going on.

In the early 21st century, the allure of a Nicaraguan canal persists, with interest by the Chinese communists in building a canal through Nicaragua after the communist Sandinistas regained the government there by convincing enough people that the radical Daniel Ortega had had a change of heart and was no longer the communist he had been in the 1980s, and they voted him into power. Ortega lied. The more things change, the more they stay the same.

In 2013, the government of Nicaragua voted to allow the Chinese to construct a 40-to 50-billion-dollar canal through their country. A groundbreaking ceremony was held in December of 2014.

Walker was interested in mesmerism and medicine, and studied in European universities, including Göttingen. While there, he participated in the peripheries of the revolutions. He fell under the influence of the more radical revolutionaries of the day.

When he became the editor of the *New Orleans Crescent*, he promoted the European revolutions of 1848 and stood further left than most radicals of the day, to the point of wearing a Kossuth hat. Even Lincoln wore one for a time.

Under his editorship, the *Crescent* declared its willingness "to lay ourselves open to the accusation of radicalism, jacobinism, agrarianism and … other names." It held abolitionist feelings, although very subdued. It was considered a Yankee newspaper.

Prior to Walker's expedition to Nicaragua, he led an expedition into the Mexican state of Sonora. Edmund Randolph and Parker Crittenden were supporters of the cause. This expedition was one of the pressures on the Mexican government that led them to cede territory in the Gadsden Treaty. There were other expeditions, including one by French immigrants to California, who had fled there due to the revolutions in France.

Walker intended to establish an independent state and then merge it into the United States, just as had been done with Texas. This tactic was to be used in other countries as well, but never accomplished.

The base of operations was in California, where Walker edited more than one newspaper. Col. John C. Fremont was a supporter of Walker's leftist enterprise until Walker became a supporter of slavery. At the time of Walker's incursion into Nicaragua, the firebrands of the South supported him, but the moderates did not.

Walker again serves as an example of the Left not being against slavery, even though modern leftists claim they have always been against the oppression of the people. How can they be against slavery when they want to subjugate everyone? How can they believe the different races of people of the world are equal when they believe in Darwinism? All their public pronouncements and positions are phony and are used as a means to organize people into initiatives they little understand.

California from the beginning was a hotbed of leaders who had radical ideas, so nothing has changed over the years. The governor from 1852-1856 was John Bigler, a member of the Knights of the Golden Circle expansionist organization.

Walker called his expedition *La Falange Americana*, the American Phalanx. This appears to be a reference to the phalanx movement of the socialist Fourier. Walker's adherents wore red ribbons to signify their democratic allegiance, and Walker's flag had a large, red, five pointed star in the center, reminiscent of modern communist revolutionaries, with light blue striping across the top and bottom.

In addition, while there is no overt evidence that the Walker expeditions were part of a Master Conspiracy, hints of their ideas are rampant in the whole enterprise, as well as in Walker's history in Europe. There is the example of the American Phalanx and a later group who went in support of Walker, which organized themselves into the Young America Pioneer Club, ostensibly to provide a club for them and to establish reading rooms, so say some authors on the matter. Then there was the editorial position he always took in his newspapers in support of the Conspiracy's agenda.

There were men associated with Walker who were members of the Knights of the Golden Circle, from officers in his army, such as Robert Charles Tyler, to top lieutenants, such as Sam A. Lockridge, Chatham Roberdeau Wheat, Hugh McLeod, and Charles Frederick Henningsen.

Walker declared Nicaragua a slave state. This was apparently on the advice of Soulé, who said to Walker that by so doing he would gain a great deal of support from below the Mason-Dixon Line. The *Richmond Enquirer* welcomed the news and looked forward to the day that Nicaragua would be "added to the South, in or out of the Union." Walker made it appear that he supported slavery all along, in spite of his earlier writings against it.

In the midst of the controversy the leaders of Tammany co-hosted a rally for Walker and helped raise money for his exhibition. So on one hand Tammany supported abolition, but at the same time they supported Walker, even though he wanted Nicaragua to be a slave state.

To make a long story short, Walker lost Nicaragua and was wined and dined on his return to the United States. He met with President Buchanan privately. He had support in the Senate in the persons of Senators John Weller of California and Lewis Cass of Michigan. Once the support for Walker waned, due in no small part to the pressure from England, Cass, as secretary of state, turned on Walker.

Returning to Nicaragua, Walker was arrested by an American naval officer and placed on trial in New Orleans for violating the Neutrality Act. His attorney was Soulé. He walked away from that and returned again to Nicaragua.

The financier George Law, YA, sent Charles Frederick Henningsen to help Walker. Henningsen was a close friend and key officer with Kossuth in 1848 during the Hungarian revolution. Henningsen was the head of the New York Central American League. He was urged by Secretary of War J. B. Floyd to start a revolution in Mexico. Later he became a brigadier in the Confederate Army.

With Henningsen went thousands of muskets and howitzers and much ammunition, donated by Law.

Law saw an opportunity to try to cover the initiative for a canal for his shipping interests, because he thought that Vanderbilt, Charles Morgan, and Cornelius K. Garrison were exhausting themselves in their business rivalry. Plus, Law was an important leader in Young America. He was mistaken in his assessment of Vanderbilt's resources. He underestimated them by far.

Even so, Vanderbilt carried a grudge. Morgan and Garrison were involved in a stock manipulation which had injured Vanderbilt. His answer: "I won't sue you, for the law is too slow. I will ruin you."

Pierre Soulé had Lawrence Oliphant join an expedition to reinforce Walker, but he was arrested by the English. Oliphant had participated in the Carbonari revolution in Italy before touring the South, making many friends. After his arrest, he rose in the British Foreign Service, became a member of Parliament, and then resigned to join the Brotherhood of Life in New York. The Brotherhood was a commune in Wassaic, N.Y., founded by the Swedenborgian Universalist Thomas Lake Harris, who taught that God was bisexual. Harris was a spiritualist leader and had formed three communes from 1851 to 1875 that advocated no marriage. Oliphant then returned to England, were he promoted the settlement of Palestine by Hebrew colonies.

Recall that Soulé was involved in more than one initiative in league with YA and Carbonari leaders to wrest other Latin American territory to add to the United States.

The British finally stopped Walker (thereby stopping American expansion), capturing him and turning him over to a Honduran firing squad.

Walker represented YA, but was personally very ambitious. It is difficult to say what Vanderbilt represented except himself; however, he had formed an "understanding" with the British, a de facto alliance. Vanderbilt was not anti-socialist since he was the patron of Victoria Woodhull, who was a member of the Communist League and who published the first English edition of *The Communist Manifesto* in the U.S. in the *Woodhull and Claflin Weekly* in 1872. From this edition was translated a French edition published in the New York, *Le Socialiste*.

With the backing of Vanderbilt, Woodhull and her sister Tennessee Claflin started the first female stock brokerage on Wall Street, and with the money they made started the aforementioned newspaper. It carried ads from all of the reputable brokerage houses in New York. They lost everything when they published the infidelity of H.W. Beecher in their pages and were arrested for publishing lurid material. The disclosure of the affair led to Theodore Tilton, the husband of the woman who had the affair, suing Beecher.

As a result of this affair, Tilton strayed from his faith and in 1871 started the *Golden Age,* which became a vehicle to promote Greeley for president. The *Golden Age* likewise endorsed the First International.

The fact that Woodhull and Claflin started a stock brokerage and a newspaper in support of the stock market is another example that belies the propaganda of the Left that they oppose Wall Street. On the street they do; at the upper levels they are part of it, desiring to manipulate the economy.

The Walker enterprise in Nicaragua is an example of how those who either dabbled in the Conspiracy or were part of it had personal ambitions and differences of opinion. The enterprise was further complicated by the interests of other countries, and thus it failed.

Walker's expanding ambitions were to apparently create a nation out of five Central American countries, invade Cuba and then to build a canal.

While Walker's enterprise was the better-known initiative, John A. Quitman was probably the most famous individual who was involved in filibuster enterprises. His efforts never went as far as Walker's, although if they had they would have been more successful. Quitman was a major general in the U.S. Army, having fought in the Mexican War. He was a member of Congress, and was governor of Mississippi at the time he helped Lopez raise the wherewithal for his Cuban expedition.

The federal administration first wanted this expedition to go forward, but then changed its position and the whole affair fell apart. Quitman was tried for violating the neutrality of the United States, but two hung juries ended his problem.

During the 1840s, Quitman was a member of the Supreme Council of the 33°, Southern Jurisdiction. Likewise, he was a member of the Order of the Lone Star.

In 1856, Viscount Palmerston ordered troops to Canada, about 20,000, because the entire Caribbean-Central American ambitions of Young America ingrained in our government and the filibusters were leading to war talk. Palmerston may have been sympathetic to the Conspiracy, but would have been more so if it were under his leadership, not the Americans.

There was a story of a Paladin society of which Palmerston and Otto von Bismarck were supposedly members. The evidence tends to be a bit sketchy. As we know, Palmerston was helpful to other conspiracy-centered causes and individuals. Bismarck was ultimately the leader under which the German Confederation became a national government.

John Thomas Pickett was an American army officer who while studying in Hungary joined with Kossuth, the Hungarian 48er, then became engaged in several filibuster initiatives in the Americas, and was a friend of Walker. Pickett became an intimate with John C. Breckenridge, John Forsyth, Judah P. Benjamin, and John Slidell, all prominent men who became leaders of the Confederacy. He was appointed Confederate consul at Vera Cruz, where he hated the Mexican revolutionary leader Juarez.

He was to obtain a favorable treaty with Mexico and perform other tasks that would help the Confederacy gain war materiel through Mexico across the Rio Grande. None of these things were accomplished because Jefferson Davis did the same as U.S. presidents had done before him: sent the worse ambassadors possible when it came to men who wanted to overthrow the existing governments. No one believed Pickett was a friend of the Mexican government and they knew he wanted Mexico to become part of the United States before the war.

Pickett's communications with Richmond were intercepted by Mexican authorities and handed over to the U.S. ambassador after being read by Juarez. But soon Juarez was in flight due to European interference, especially by Napoleon III, with the Austrian prince Maximilian installed by the French as emperor of Mexico.

Pickett went into the Confederate Army, and at the end of the war five trunk loads of Confederate records came into his hands. He sold them to the U.S. government for $75,000. How many he destroyed before handing them over, if any, is unknown, nor is it known how many were destroyed by Washington once they had them in their hands. We will point out later that a European revolutionary, Francis Lieber, was put in charge of the Confederate records. *To the victor go the myths and monuments.*

It is interesting that the government paid Pickett handsomely for the records, rather than simply seizing them as war records of the enemy.

Lincoln, in contrast to Davis, sent an ambassador south who practically sided with Mexico during the Mexican-American War and displayed his sentiment by saying that Mexicans should welcome American soldiers "to hospitable graves." The appointment of this type of man automatically made the Union ambassador welcome over the Confederate representative.

It didn't hurt U.S.-Mexican relations either that Lincoln had been an opponent of the Mexican War when he was a congressman.

We are aware of the tremendous influence Lincoln's secretaries had for a period of time, but few have asked if Jefferson Davis' private secretary had much influence. Indeed, few people even know his name.

Burton Norvell Harrison, who was Davis' secretary from February 1862 until the end of the war, was a member of the Order: Skull and Bones.

Two of the four filibuster expeditions led by Lopez into Cuba ultimately failed, and in one case the American participants were executed. This led to riots in New Orleans, with the burning of the Spanish flag and the sacking of shops owned by Spanish-speaking citizens.

The other two of the Lopez filibuster initiatives were stopped by the U.S. government before they were able to reach Cuba. One group that did make it to Cuba came from a Kentucky initiative. This expedition's battle flag became the Cuban national emblem on May 20, 1902.

One of the Kentucky men who led this group was the aforementioned Lt. Col. John Thomas Pickett. After the expedition, he was appointed U.S. consul to Veracruz, Mexico, and later commissioner to Mexico for the Confederacy. He married the daughter of the Grand Master of the District of Columbia Masonic lodge, Kate Keyworth.

After the war, he worked with the former head of Mexico, Santa Anna of Alamo fame, on behalf of the U.S. government in a failed attempt to place him at the head of the Mexican government. Santa Anna had been living on Staten Island, New York, before returning to Mexico. One would have thought that, given the reputation of Santa Anna in regard to the Alamo, he would have been unwelcome in the U.S.

During the time of one of Lopez' expeditions against Cuba, our ambassador there was Allen Ferdinand Owen, an attorney who had served as a U.S. congressman and was a member of the Order.

Young Americans in Government

To review, the major goal of YA was the expansion of the United States into all of the Americas, then into Europe, the Pacific, etc. The U.S. government was to be the base from which to segue into a world government, and YA was simply an arm of the Master Conspiracy having its roots in Illuminism. There were several initiatives to implement this policy in and out of our government.

There were major figures in the American government and politics who were YA adherents, particularly in the Pierce and Buchanan administrations. Many radical socialists of the day had their feet in both YA and communism, as was the case in Young Europe for a time.

The most famous public pronouncement by YA members desiring to expand the United States into foreign countries in the Americas was the Ostend Manifesto. What made this so outrageous to the governments of Europe was that it was signed by three American ambassadors to Europe, James Buchanan, Pierre Soulé, and John Mason.

There were a variety of schemes with a goal of annexing Mexico to the United States that did not go very far. The dream did not die out until long after the Civil War. George Bancroft worked for expansion into Mexico while a minister in Europe. Buchanan, (when Secretary of State), Secretary of the Treasury Walker, Vice President George M. Dallas, and Senators Edward A. Hannegan and Daniel S. Dickinson all wanted to annex Mexico.

Rep. Nathaniel Banks, as chairman of the Committee on Foreign Affairs, promoted the idea of the islands in the Gulf of Mexico becoming a part of the U.S. in 1869.

All of these people were part of YA or sympathetic to it before the Civil War, including Banks.

If politicians were not looking with covetous eyes south, they were doing so north. The acquisition of Canada came under the spell of Whig Senators William H. Seward, John P. Hale, John Chandler, and John Bell.

The last series of threats to Canada came in 1866, 1870, and 1871, coming from the radical Irish

Fenians, which had been founded in America. The initial attack in 1866 of 1,500 men was foiled by troops interdicted on Grant's orders. It all had its roots in Young Ireland and the revolutions of 1848, with participants immigrating to the U.S. and forming the Fenians. Most of the men in the Fenian invasion force had served in the Civil War under radical Irish officers.

The Irish Republican Brotherhood, or Fenians, was organized in Tammany Hall in New York City on St. Patrick's Day in 1858 and was based on the Carbonari Young Ireland group. (*Fenians* refers to the legendary Irish warriors of antiquity.) Its branches were called circles and the oath of membership called for obeying the orders of Fenian commanders.

The first modern submarine built in the U.S. was commissioned the *Fenian Ram* and was used for secret missions to Ireland.

The Fenians had many communists within their ranks, such as John Devoy and J. P. McDonnell, who represented the Irish at the First International in New York after it was moved there by Marx. During Orsini's visit to America in 1866, the Irish Fenian leader James Stephens joined the International.

Marx told Siegfried Meyer and August Vogt to form an alliance with the Irish to grow communism in America. Meyer helped organize the German workers' movement in New York as a member of the IWA. Marx would subsequently fall out with Vogt, accusing him of being an agent of the Bonapartists.

The organizations of militant Irish can be traced from the Illuminati in an unbroken line to today.

The United Irishmen, founded in 1791, had established links with revolutionary France. In 1795 they reorganized and created an organization closely resembling the Illuminati. From there, the Irish radical organizations can all be traced.

Of all the generals who led Irish troops in the Civil War, Thomas Francis Meagher was probably the most famous. A member of the Young Ireland movement in 1846 and a revolutionary leader, in 1848 he was entrusted with the responsibility to carry a message from the Irish Confederation to the provisional revolutionary government in Paris. He was arrested twice in 1848 for treason by the British government and condemned to death, but the sentence was commuted to banishment for life to Australia, whence he came to the U.S.

Meagher studied the law and at first was a Southern sympathizer, until the war started. He was a friend of Daniel Sickles and part of Tammany. At the conclusion of the war, he was appointed secretary of the Montana Territory and served briefly as its governor. While engaged in protecting settlers from hostile Indians, he fell from the deck of a steamer into the Missouri River and drowned.

There were American politicians, such as Calhoun, who did not want to expand into Latin areas for fear that the move would erode American-style liberty, since the populations did not have the educational or spiritual base that American citizens possessed.

The last president to have no interest in the expansion of empire was Zachary Taylor. He respected congressional rights, resisted filibusters to overthrow Spain in Cuba, was a pre-war unionist, and felt that the California and Oregon territory might be better as an independent country since they were too far away to administer well (at least at that time, without the advances of transportation and communication that were invented a short time later).

The election of Franklin Pierce was an endorsement of expansionism. "Pierce and Cuba" was just one of the election slogans. The *New York Herald* of June 10, 1852 reported that Pierce was a "discreet representative of Young America."

Pierce was under the influence of YA through two men, George Sanders and Jefferson Davis, who were very influential in the Democrat Party, to the extent that he appointed many YA adherents to important posts both overseas and domestically, such as Caleb Cushing as attorney general.

Cushing was a contributor to the *Democratic Review,* which had become George Sanders' YA newspaper. Cushing went on to chair *both* Democratic conventions of 1860, the Douglas party and the Breckinridge party. He was sent by Buchanan to South Carolina with a letter to Gov. Francis Pickens urging the people of the state to await the action of the Congress before seceding.

The fact that Cushing chaired both Democratic conventions illustrates the fact that conspirators split the party to ensure the election of the Republican Party candidate, regardless of who that candidate would have been. The reaction of such an election led to the average Southerner believing that secession was the only solution to saving Southern culture and the principles of the Constitution. Slavery was an issue, but not the overwhelming reason for secession. More on this tactic later.

A delegate to both of these Democrat conventions was Richard Jacobs Haldeman. He studied in Heidelberg and Berlin after attending Yale, where he had become a member of the Order. He was a U.S. congressman from Pennsylvania, and was our attaché at the legation in Paris in 1853 and then at St. Petersburg and Vienna.

The YA individuals whom Pierce appointed as representatives to Europe were: Daniel E. Sickles from New York as our London consular attaché and 1st secretary, who would later murder the son of the composer of *The Star Spangled Banner* and get off scot-free; August Belmont as minister to the Netherlands, where he was able to help his bosses, the Rothschilds, at the same time; Pierre Soulé to Spain; John L. O'Sullivan, minister to Portugal, where he harbored the assassin Victor Frond, whom Sanders had hired to attempt to kill Napoleon III; John Y. Mason to Paris; George Sanders as consul to London, where he created a groundswell of anti-American feeling among the leaders of the European nations along with James Buchanan as minister to the Court of St. James; Nathaniel Hawthorne as consul to Liverpool; Edwin de Leon as consul to Egypt; and while, not a Carbonari, the communist leader Robert Dale Owen as U.S. minister to the Kingdom of Naples.

We have not gone out of our way to spend time looking at the specific problem of ambassadors. These men appointed by Pierce have been the obvious ones as this work was researched on the whole. Later presidents continued the problem. A full-scale investigation would probably reveal far more men who did not have the historical reputation to stand out as revolutionaries. If these men stood out, how many did not but were part of the conspiratorial forces as representatives of the U.S.?

The appointment of Pierre Soulé was especially vexing to the government of Spain. Soulé was a close friend of George Sanders and an adherent of YA. His role in the affairs surrounding the filibusters in Spanish Cuba and Nicaragua was well known. It was only one of the diplomatic slaps in the face to Spain and other European governments by the American government over several administrations starting with Pierce, intensifying under Lincoln, and continuing on through today, when most Americans have no idea of the background of the men and women we are sending to represent the American people. Ask yourself: pick a country, any country, and try to think of who our representative is. It is a sad state of affairs when only some politically active people can name our ambassador to the United Nations but not any other post.

As a result, presidents have gotten away with sending some of the worst people to represent the American people. We strongly suspect that the Congress has not taken the time to note whom they have confirmed, unless they have stood out by their reputation.

The suspicion of Spain regarding Soulé became justified when he became one of the American ambassadors to sign and issue the Ostend Manifesto. Keep in mind that Soulé had a history of trying to take Spanish territory away from Spain and helped revolutionaries all over America and south of the border, and this was the insult to Spain by appointing him. Ambassadors are supposed to be able to represent our country, engage in negotiation, and in general use tactful language and actions to do so. It was a slap in the face and could only have resulted in bad feelings and ultimately war if such appointments continued.

You can well imagine the shock to European leaders when Pierce appointed Robert Dale Owen, American communist and atheist leader as the U.S. ambassador to Naples in 1854. This was an independent country at the time, not yet united under Italy. The appointment was to become typical.

When Sanders landed in London as our consul in November 1853, he immediately became involved in the Central Democratic Committee, a 600-member-strong organization whose main purpose was a death-to-tyrants society — this generally meant all European leaders, whether royal or not. Victor Hugo, Mazzini, and Kossuth were members as well. It was modeled after the Maximilien Robespierre style of revolution.

In a speech in New York on September 22, 1855 George Sanders was to advocate the use of the guillotine, so loved by Robespierre, to kill Napoleon III. The meeting was in celebration of the birthday of the French revolutionary republic. He said that he would be willing to operate it powered "by steam, by God."

While many in YA held the beliefs of Sanders, they doubted Sanders' ability to move the agenda forward due to his vituperative language and disdain for what he termed the "old fogies." Nonetheless, Sanders' influence was considerable. He was not only active in Democrat circles; he had influence in the Know-Nothings as well through his contacts.

In other words, certain leaders of YA felt that moving the agenda forward without making waves or harsh rhetoric would accomplish more. This usually is done by forming very radical organizations and putting forward radical leaders to take the heat off the real culprits, who operate behind the curtain, handling the dials of Oz — and who are equally as yellow as the Wizard when exposed.

Sanders, along with other YAs, pushed the candidacy of Stephen Douglas for the presidency in 1852. In his paper he wrote an article titled, "Eighteen-Fifty-Two and the Presidency." In it he heralded 1852 as the year of the liberation of the oppressed masses of Europe and the U.S. It called for the statesmen of the previous generation to "get out of the way."

Douglas was disappointed in such language and said, "While I am a radical and progressive Democrat, I fear the *Review* goes too far in that direction — especially in regard to European affairs." He tried to tone down Sanders, but to no avail.

After the 1852 campaign YA cooled on Douglas, but rallied back by 1860.

While the Buchanan administration was opposed to William Walker, this does not mean that they were opposed to Manifest Destiny. According to Walker, Buchanan's Secretary of War John B. Floyd urged Charles Frederick Henningsen to aid a revolution in Mexico and incite a war with Spain so as to provide a pretext to annex Cuba. When Henningsen went to Mexico, the Southern people believed Walker's story.

The Central American League became the Southern Emigration Society to help raise men and money for Walker. The play between Vanderbilt and Walker included others that did not want to see Vanderbilt succeed and thus helped Walker to a limited extent.

There were those who felt that Buchanan had become an English agent during his sojourn in England as our ambassador. There was an attempt on his life by poisoning at the National Hotel at this time, but no one was implicated — at least no one on the record. In any regard, Buchanan finally stood up to the British after they started to board American ships in the Caribbean just as they had been doing in the early 1800's, which led to the War of 1812.

It wasn't until the battleship *Maine* exploded in Havana Harbor that the excuse for war finally led to the Spanish-American War and the acquisition of several territories, the most prominent being the Philippines and Puerto Rico. Cuba was left more or less to its own devices, and it ultimately became the center for Latin American terrorism and communism as a surrogate for Russian-led communism.

Cuba also served for two decades as center for African terrorism, until the communists could build up a reliable African state to serve as a base. Russia made it a habit to create surrogate states to implement their terrorist and espionage activities. In this manner, with one or two countries in the linkage, the Russians could claim deniability for acts of violence or espionage. The practice continues today.

Cuba also played a role in the street terrorism that befell America in the 1960s and 70s through the training of Americans in Cuba, such as the Venceremos Brigade, and Cuban intelligence officers handling radical leaders within the civil rights and peace movements. This was one of the reasons for isolating Cuba. With the opening up of Cuba by Obama, many fear that the same tactics will again be used in the heat of recent anti-police feelings among both Left and Right.

The Venceremos Brigade was founded by the Students for a Democratic Society and the communist government of Cuba, and prominent in their ranks were the terrorists Bernardine Dohrn and her husband, Bill Ayers. The friendship of Obama with these two individuals his entire adult life probably played a role in his decision to recognize communist Cuba in late 2014 which led to hundreds of thousands of un-vetted Cubans coming into the United States through Mexico in 2015 and 2016.

Americans in the Eisenhower administration and the media, particularly the *New York Times*, played a large role in turning that unhappy island over to Castro. Once that betrayal became fact many of those involved professed ignorance, but it was finally exposed that they had ample warning of Castro being a communist agent, both publically and privately.

Robert Welch, later the founder of The John Birch Society, used his magazine and considerable influence in conservative circles to warn early on that Castro was a lifelong communist months before he came to power in Cuba. Ezra Taft Benson, later the head of the Mormon Church and secretary of agriculture at the time, did the same within the government — to no avail. When one studies the life of Eisenhower's secretary of state, John Foster Dulles, it is surprising that all of Latin America did not go communist. Dulles was a founding member of the Council on Foreign Relations and active in Christian socialist circles.

Manifest Destiny was not an idea confined to the Western Hemisphere. It included the scheme to overthrow European powers by helping arm European revolutionaries. Sanders was involved in this activity before he became our consul in London.

Manifest Destiny was also sold to Christians using a Christian-style argument. The Calvinistic worldview was replaced with a grander vision:

> The Manifest destiny of a Christian America: Men of all walks of life believed that the sovereign Holy Spirit was endowing the nation with resources sufficient to convert and civilize the globe, to purge human society of all its evils, and to usher in Christ's reign on earth. Religious doctrines which Paine, in his Book, *The Age of Reason*, had discarded as the tattered vestment of an outworn aristocracy, became the wedding garb of a democratized church, bent on preparing men and institutions for a kind of proletarian marriage in support of the Lamb.
>
> Timothy L. Smith, *Revivalism and Social Reform in Mid-Nineteenth Century America*

YA was not confined to native Americans. Immigrants likewise were involved in the YA fervor. In November 1845, members of the secret society the League of the Just, the forerunner of the Communist Party, helped the National Industrial Congress in New York. Called the "German Commune of Young America," they led the German community in New York to form a special Social Reform Association within the National Reform Association in America.

Their German-language journal *Tribune of the People*, in January 1846, addressed itself to "the poor, the supplicants, the oppressed." This attracted attention in German immigrant communities from Boston to Milwaukee to St. Louis.

Communists Who Influenced America Politics:

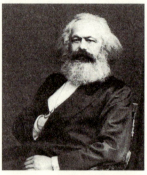

Karl Marx. Became the front man for communism and socialism. Moved the International Workingmen's Association (First International) to New York in 1972.

Wendell Phillips. Lawyer. Abolition and political leader. Member of the Communist International.

Senator Charles Sumner. Republican. Chairman of the U.S. Senate Committee on Foreign Relations, 1861-1871. Member of the Communist International.

Horace Greeley. Publisher of The *New York Tribune*. Member of the Communist International. Employer of Karl Marx. Posted bail for Jefferson Davis along with Cornelius Vanderbilt and Gerrit Smith. With Alvan Bovey provided the impetus for the formation of the modern Republican Party.

Robert Dale Owen. Son of Robert Owen. American communist and spiritualist leader. As a U.S. Representative from Indiana he sponsored the bill establishing the Smithsonian Institute.

Victoria Woodhull. Leader of Section 12 of the Communist International, New York City, 1972.

Friedrich Sorge. Leader under Marx of the Communist International world headquarters in New York City.

11
REPUBLICAN PARTY ORIGINS

We have been taught in public education that certain individuals and movements were essentially the paragon of Americanism. We have already demonstrated the fallacy of this idea in regard to several people and ideas held in our youthful ignorance. The same is true of the political parties. While not everyone who believes in the agenda of the Illuminists due to their education is actually part of a conspiracy, nonetheless the origins of the political parties are part of this problem.

The Conspiracy cannot allow a truly constitutional outlook to prevail within any political movement. To ignore this on their part would destroy them. This is true even if the people never understood that they were the target of a coordinated effort to socialize the country.

By *constitutional*, we mean after the style of the U.S. Constitution in its original intent. Even so, there is a basis in law for any constitution and if this law prevents the Conspiracy from implementing their agenda, that law, or constitution, must make way if they are to be successful. This is one of the reasons constitutions do not last long in other countries. The more free and educated the people, the more limitations on the government by a constitution, the less likely the instrument will be changed. This is why our Constitution has lasted so long.

The constitutional outlook, *if widely taught*, would ultimately prevail since it is based on truth resulting in liberty. The enemies of our Constitution cannot allow this and work to the best of their abilities to prevent this education. It behooves any constitutionally-oriented organization, therefore, to have as its prime objective educating as many people as possible about the foundation and purpose of the Constitution.

As you will see, the constitutional base within the Republican Party came long after its founding. The modern reputation of the Republican Party is that of conservatism which is today an ill-defined term since it means many things to different people. Generally, it has come to mean anything that is not Democrat.

The very beginnings of the Republican Party before it started to attract conservatives are much different than Americans even imagine.

In the late 1840s and early 1850s, an organization called alternately the American Union of Associations or National Convention of Associations founded nearly 50 communist communes around the United States. The initial leaders of the associations were Horace Greeley, George Ripley, Parke Godwin, Edward Giles, and Edward Tweedy. Later, many of Greeley's employees were involved, including Charles Dana. In fact, almost every member of the *Tribune's* editorial staff during the first decade of its existence came from Brook Farm commune, and they were out and out socialists at best.

One of these communes was established in Wisconsin about 50 miles northwest of Milwaukee. They called it Ceresco after Ceres, the ancient Roman goddess of agriculture. After this commune gained its notoriety as we shall describe below, several other socialist initiatives adopted some modern derivative of the name of the goddess Ceres.

The guiding light of the Wisconsin commune was Warren Chase. Chase was an advocate of Fourier socialism, spiritualism, land reform, and free love. It is strange that a man who believed in free love renounced alcohol, tobacco, coffee, tea, pork, *and* sexual relations with his wife. His life as a reformer was frustrated by his unsupportive wife. Better put, his life as a reformer was thwarted by his frustrated wife.

As happened with all communes, Ceresco failed as a communist enterprise, but the inhabitants remained and were very politically involved. Three members of the commune went on to be elected to the Wisconsin State Legislature. A group of people established a small town adjacent to the communal area and after the commune was dissolved they named the town Ripon; it is known as the town where the Republican Party was founded in 1854.[41]

Since more and more people are taking notice of the early Marxist history in America, there has been a movement to claim that the origins of the Republican Party lay elsewhere, rather than in Ripon and with the men who actually started the Party.

The communal site for Ceresco was originally proposed by Warren Chase in letters to Horace Greeley. Later, as a state senator, Chase was involved in the two Wisconsin State Constitutional Conventions that wrote the original state constitution. He also ran for governor of Wisconsin.

The Wisconsin State Constitution impressed the British Chartists so much that it was printed in their newspaper *Northern Star* which served as an incentive for communist Chartists to move to America.

The leadership of the commune was very instrumental in the founding of the Republican Party, particularly Alvan Earle Bovay, a late arrival. Bovay served on the staff of the newspaper *Young America* before he served on the staff of the *Tribune*. He also served as the secretary of the National Reform Association. The socialist historian Charles Sotheran claims that Young America was a joint effort of George H. Evans and Greeley; the evidence supports this claim. But there was more to it than this simple, albeit relatively unknown aspect of the party's founding.

Before proceeding further, due to what has already been laid out and what will come out further into this chapter, the reader should take the time to go to the Internet and look up the term *Radical Republican*. What you will find is that this was the wing of the Republican Party that controlled the Congress during the Civil War. In reality, it *was* the Republican Party leadership. It provides only a hint but it gives the reader an idea that maybe something else was going on in the early years of the Republican Party that may be important for him to understand and learn more about, especially since they were called *Radical* Republicans.

One of Lincoln's secretaries, John Hay, referred to the radical leaders in the Republican Congress as the Jacobin Club, as represented by congressman Lyman Trumbull, John Chandler, and Benjamin Wade. Wade was a religious "skeptic"; he was an abolitionist but disliked Negroes. He supported all of the socialist agenda at the time, including women's suffrage, trade unions, and "free land," and was critical of capitalism.

Since most people are unfamiliar with the value and results of organization, no one seems to ask the question why and how the Republican Party was so successful in forming and proliferating throughout the northern portion of the United States so quickly, as if it was something that happened spontaneously. They accept the history books at face value.

At the time, the two major parties were the Democrat and the Whig. It is true that there were serious contentions within both parties over the issues of slavery and economics to the point of possibly splitting them internally, providing the opportunity for a new party, but that is only part of the story. This divisiveness was fueled by the Conspiracy working both sides.

---

41 The citizens pronounce *Ripon* much differently than others around the country. Its pronunciation is Rip'n.

In addition, several third parties had come and gone, most of them started by the radicals. The main contender in the early 1850s was the Know-Nothings, or American Party.

The American Party founded in New York in 1844 came out of the American Brotherhood, and then changed its name to the Order of United Americans. It was anti-Catholic, anti-foreign born, and anti-communist, or at least its members thought so. Yet it had a great deal of influence on its policies by those who helped YA and communist movements. It was a secret society fronting as a political party.

Like all secret societies, it had elaborate rituals. After the Order came the Grand Council of the United States of America, a secret organization formed after the 1852 election of Pierce. From this came the nickname the Know-Nothings. When members were queried about the group, its purposes, aims, etc., the members always replied that they knew nothing, hence the nickname.

By 1854, the body directing the Know-Nothings was called the Grand Council of the Supreme Star Spangled Banner. Their power grew until they attained elective power through the American Party, electing through their support several governors and U.S. senators, and a hundred U.S. Representatives, not all actually running on the Know-Nothing ticket.

It was able to amass a large following, organizationally, by a common interest in destroying the Whig Party, and was a step toward negating property rights. While publicly for abolition, privately they were against equal rights for Negroes.

Anti-Catholicism was high within certain American quarters, and this was fueled by age-old animosities from Europe, by the backlash against the high immigration from Catholic countries, and by the Conspiracy as well, since the church was still their only well-organized nemesis. The Know-Nothings capitalized on these feelings.

The year that the Know-Nothings were established, 1844, was the year of the worst anti-Catholic riots in our history, and they occurred in Philadelphia. They started with the local bishop asking the school authorities to allow the Catholic children to use the *Douay Bible* in the classroom rather than a Protestant one. The situation escalated and rumors flew until enough people were convinced that the Catholics were actually trying to ban the *Bible* from the schools. It wasn't true, but the situation had escalated to a point where the truth did not matter. It led to churches being burned, and Catholics became the targets of harm.

The solution to this disorder and the net result was that the city of Philadelphia consolidated additional surrounding towns into their incorporated area, as part of establishing and being able to support a large police force, and in general a larger government. Usually the results are what someone had in mind to begin with.

Finally, the Catholics established their own schools, which further separated the population into political blocs since the Catholics from this time on in the area became isolated from the general population; however, they were able to maintain the integrity of their religion, free from the march away from all religious teaching that was just beginning and increasingly becoming the direction of the public schools.

Thus we see the depth of anti-Catholic feeling that could be stirred up and the results. Since the Catholic Church at the time was the only organizational opposition to the Conspiracy, any anti-Catholic feelings, if allowed to run unchecked, would only serve the purposes of the Conspiracy, one way or the other.

On the other hand, Catholics as a result of the above could be led by their reaction into doing things that served the Conspiracy as well.

YA had a great deal of influence within the ranks of the Know-Nothings through Nathaniel Banks, George Law, George Sanders, and Albert Pike. Law was looked upon as the chief financier of YA and was a prominent Mason. As we stated, the Know-Nothings had a public image on one hand, and a private goal on the other.

Before the 1852 elections, both the *New York Tribune* and *New York Herald*, owned by YA adherents and socialists, supported Know-Nothing candidates. James Gordon Bennett, the owner of the *Herald,* was a man who hated Jews.

In 1856, the Northern Know-Nothings nominated Nathaniel Banks, YA, for president, *to withdraw in favor of Fremont if the Republicans nominated him,* as part of a scheme to throw the party into the new Republican camp. Banks had been named speaker of the House in a bitter fight that went on for three months in the Congress. He had stated that he had no fetish for the Union and was willing to "let it slide" under certain conditions. Garrison called the election of Banks as speaker "the first gun at Lexington of the new revolution," since the socialists had a great deal of faith in Banks as supportive of their agenda.

This scheme to withdraw the Know-Nothings into the Republican Party was started at a meeting held at the Silver Springs, Maryland, estate of Francis Preston Blair on Christmas Day in 1855 between Gamaliel Bailey, Charles Sumner, Salmon Chase, Banks, and Preston King, radical New York Democrats, to plan an organization of anti-Northeast Democrats. Blair had been a confidant of Andrew Jackson.

A ruse was needed to move as many people as possible into the new Republican Party since many of the radical Democrats did not want to use the name Republican or unite under the Republican Party. This was a means to get them into the Republican Party, at least in the North. This included the anti-slavery partisans of the American Party that met in New York prior to the Republican convention.

Banks withdrew immediately upon his nomination as the American Party candidate, and subsequently the delegates nominated Fremont, who also became the nominee of the Republican Party.

Meanwhile, the Southern wing nominated Millard Fillmore, who had already served as president and was a Unitarian and former Anti-Mason Party adherent. He was a little more moderate in his politics than the others in these movements, yet had served as a mentor to several men who went on the serve the Conspiracy.

Banks, in company with Francis P. Blair, promoted Fremont for president on the Republican ticket.

Early in 1856, Thomas Spooner, a Know-Nothing leader, wrote, "The American party is no longer a unit. The National Council is gone to pieces, Raise the Republican Banner, the North Americans are with you."

The American Union of Associations was formed by men who today have a prominent reputation in history but who were far from being what could be considered Americanists, such as Horace Greeley and his editorial staff.

Charles Dana, one of Greeley's editors, knew Karl Marx from when he met him during the so-called democratic revolutions in Europe in 1848-1849. He met Marx in Köln while Marx was the editor of the radical *Neue Rheinische Zeitung*. Dana wrote that he saw the uprisings in Germany and Europe as "not simply to change the form of government, but to challenge the form of society."

Greeley traveled to Europe after the revolutions. In London, in 1851, he helped celebrate the 80th birthday of Robert Owen, who was an intimate friend.

Dana and Greeley hired Karl Marx in 1851 to be a European correspondent for the *Tribune;* he worked for a period of eleven years and wrote over 500 articles for the paper. He was not the only foreign or domestic communist who wrote for the paper. After the Civil War started, the newspapers had to let go many of their foreign correspondents to make payroll for war correspondents to cover the Civil War for their readers. In the case of the *Tribune*, Marx was reluctantly the last foreign correspondent to be let go, in 1862.

One of the errands that Dana performed while in Europe in 1848 was to deliver gold from Greeley to the communist leader Heinrich Börnstein as payment for his articles in the *Tribune*. Börnstein would later immigrate to the American Midwest and form the Society of Free Men as a framework for education and anti-Christian agitation.

The very name *Tribune* came about as a result of communist influence. Nicholas Bonneville, an Illuminist communist, said that the revolution must be led by a "tribune of the people." His disciple, Gracchus Babeuf called his journal, *The Tribune of the People*. One of Babeuf's philosophical followers, Greeley, established his *Tribune* later. The position of *tribune* in Rome, thus the name, meant the advocate of the people.

It was likewise the idea of Babeuf to establish phalanxes, or communes, which would become part of a future revolution. Greeley and company were simply following in his footsteps. The fact that Greeley was a socialist long before he established the *Tribune* has never been denied by friend or foe.

Babeuf represented the more violent wing of the French Revolution. He was even denied membership in the Jacobins because, as they expressed it, he was a "throat-cutter." It is interesting that he should serve as the example for the likes of Greeley.

As outlined in an earlier chapter, the phalanx movement was an outgrowth of the teachings of the socialist Charles Fourier, whose chief disciple in the United States was Albert Brisbane, who had gone to Paris in 1842 and studied under Fourier. Brisbane was made an editor of the *New York Tribune* by Greeley.

It was Brisbane who introduced Greeley to Fourierism. Brisbane wrote a magazine called *Future*, which Greeley published. In any case, regardless of the form, Greeley was a socialist years before he started the *Tribune*.

Albert Brisbane recruited eleven others to spread Fourierism in the America: Greeley, Osborne Macdaniel, Parke Godwin, George Ripley, William Henry Channing, John Sullivan Dwight, Charles Dana, Marx Edgeworth Lazarus, Lewis Ryckman, John Orvis, and John Allen. These men shaped the American movement.

The North American Phalanx was founded in 1843 by Albert Brisbane, Horace Greeley, William Ellery Channing, and George Ripley. It was only one of the many communes that would be established by these men, as well as others who worked with them, into the 1850s.

Brisbane was in Europe during the revolutions of 1848 and played a leadership role in the revolution in Germany. He was, for instance, the keynote speaker at a rally controlled by Marx and Engels of 10,000 people which was assembled to form a Red Republic at Warrington on September 17, 1848, while an editor of the *Tribune*. In other words, two editors of the *Tribune* were in Europe to cover the revolutions and played a role in them. One, Dana, went on to lead an organization of Americans who had participated in the 1848-1849 revolutions.

Again we have an example of newspapermen reporting on events in which they were playing a role while hiding the fact that they were not only involved, but involved at a leadership level.

There were editors who joined the *Tribune* later who also held radical views. Sydney Howard Gay was on the staff as an editor in 1857, and was the managing editor during the war after Dana was appointed undersecretary of war by Lincoln. He had been an attorney, but had abandoned the law since he did not want to swear to uphold the Constitution of the U.S. as an abolitionist. He would go on to be the managing editor of the *Chicago Tribune*, then on the editorial staff of the *New York Evening Post* in the 1870s. William Cullen Bryant later asked that he write an illustrated history of the United States with him.

The *Chicago Tribune* went through a period in the mid-20th century when it was known as a conservative publication. However, during the period of the mid to late 1800s, it was anything but, and by the last years of the 20th century had reverted to its earlier heritage.

Horace White was an abolitionist reporter with the *New York Tribune* at the beginning of the Civil War. On December 30, 1860, he said, "We live in revolutionary times and I say God bless the revolutionary." By 1864, he was one of the owners. He went on to become involved with Henry Villard in business, and when Villard took over the *New York Evening Post* and *The Nation* in 1881, White managed the enterprise with Edwin L. Godwin and Carl Schurz.

In 1852, Greeley met with Alvan Bovay in New York City and the two of them discussed the formation of a new party. It would be called the Republican Party, at Greeley's suggestion. Even more than the word *democrat*, the word *republican* had become synonymous with a volatile person who advocated democracy. The name also hearkened back to when the original Democrats called themselves Republicans while under the direct influence of the Jacobins.

These terms, *so defined*, are alien to our ears and sensibilities today since we have grown so used to them, and the parties have become mainstream. In their embryonic state this was not so.

The idea of these socialists came at a propitious moment in time. The political atmosphere was alive and in flux. While the radicals controlled large swaths of the parties, the infighting among them prevented the full implementation of their agenda. And, a new party was needed to manipulate the voter and serve as a catalyst to split the United States apart politically and then physically.

Organization meetings by Bovay were held in Ripon in February and March, and on March 20, 1854 the party was established locally. He was the leader in the famous "founding" meeting in the little white church-house in Ripon, and became one of the initial five-member committee of the new party. Another communist, Jacob Woodruff, was also on the committee.

Once the party was formed, Bovay notified Greeley, who started to promote the new party in his paper — so the story goes.

All of this information is readily available today in Ripon, as well as in several skewed accounts in history books and on the Internet, but the significance of Bovay, Woodruff, and Greeley, what they believed in and their purpose of the new party, is sanitized. For years, this author had a difficult time finding out who had started the party in any major library. It took a trip many years ago to Ripon to find out. This was, of course, before the helpful Internet.

Interestingly, Carrie Chapman Catt, the founder of the League of Women Voters, was born in this small town just a few years before the founding of the Republican Party.

The person who started something will usually tell the story more than anything else, for if you know the personages and their philosophy, you know the real goals they want to achieve with anything they organize, regardless of their publically stated goals. This is the reason today that socialists of all stripes hate to be exposed and why The John Birch Society was hit so hard in the media in the early 1960s — they exposed the communists and socialists. In politics, if the people know the actors, they understand the play.

For instance, the founder of the Republican Party, Bovay, was an editor with the magazine *Young America*, was secretary of the National Reform Association, and was involved with the American Union of Associations with Horace Greeley. Only a person with a very shallow amount of logical thinking would believe that the purpose that Bovay had in mind for forming the Republican Party with Greeley was to form a conservative political movement.

People such as Bovay show the linkage between these various organizations, and he is by no means the only example. Through this linkage, they can present a broad front for initiating their goals and they can make any movement seem irresistible.

It also serves as an example of interlocking directors between seemingly diverse groups, and how a few can influence the many.

At this point in time, although primarily a daily, *the* Tribune *was the largest-circulation newspaper in the country* with its weekly edition. It had grown to this level with the help of the communist-socialist network patronizing and promoting it through their activities in a wide number of organizations.

Immediately, the communist and other subversive organizations rallied behind the new party and threw their weight into spreading the news, and started organizing local units of the Republican Party, at first as Republican Clubs. Many of these groups also organized paramilitary organizations known as the Wide Awake Republicans which had some of the traits of the Turner groups of Germans but did not engage in the level of military training of the latter.

And now you understand why in the mid-20th century many of the so-called liberal Republicans who organized to fight the constitutionalists within the party called themselves the Ripon Society. At the time they said they intended to take the party back to its true roots. Most Republicans had no clue as to what they meant and brushed it off as simply rhetoric. The roots were socialist.

Six years after founding the Republican Party, Bovay was involved in a small but violent armed insurrection against the United States government. It involved a situation in Milwaukee where the editor of the *Free Democrat*, Sherman W. Booth, called upon the citizens of Milwaukee to storm the jail as if it were the Bastille to free a prisoner who was a fugitive slave. When this happened, the federal authorities held Booth responsible for inciting violence.

The federal authorities were involved because it was a violation of federal law, the Fugitive Slave Act.

Booth was involved in several scrapes with federal authorities as a result of his agitation. He was accused of raping the babysitter who was hired to watch his children. He got off, but his wife did not believe his story and divorced him. About this time Booth went to Ripon, where he was to address a gathering of Republicans. There a deputy U.S. marshal tried to effect his arrest for unpaid fines at the public meeting and the deputy was stabbed several times. Afterwards, Bovay offered a resolution, "Resolved, that Mr. Booth shall not be arrested in Ripon."

Subsequently, on the spot, they organized a League of Freedom and enrolled 120 people, with Bovay as president. Another communist, W. Starr, was named head of the Vigilance Committee, formed out of the league to keep Booth from being arrested. This they did along with the local chapter of the Wide Awake Republicans.

The Booth story is used by many today as an example of the feeling of the people against the fugitive slave law that existed at the time and the need for people to get involved against unjust laws today. While slavery was wrong and the Fugitive Slave Act was something that would be difficult for anyone to sympathize with today, it was the law at the time. The feeling against the law was used by the Conspiracy to get Northern citizens to speak and act against the law in such a manner to react the Southern citizens into secession more than it was to get the law repealed.

If the law had been repealed, it would not have served as the catalyst for agitation that it was. It was the same tactic all over again that the Jacobins used against the Alien and Sedition Acts during the Adams administration.

Do not misunderstand: the law (as well as slavery) was bad, but many of the leaders opposing the law were more interested in how they could use the reaction to the law than they were in an effective solution. The communists have always used a just cause to arouse the people and recruit into their party. It is rare that the leaders have any real desire to remedy the problem, unless it is to provide a platform for more government regulation.

That being said, the law was effectively nullified since the Northern citizens and state governments refused to obey it.

Never told is communist involvement in the Booth incident or other events the communists used for their advantage to react people into supporting separation and then a war. We will cite additional examples further on.

The Booth incident is likewise an example of people being stampeded into supporting those who have a very dubious moral background, overlooking this simply because the person involved is a partisan or leader of the "cause." The most famous example in the 18th century was Henry Ward Beecher — in the 20th century it was Bill Clinton.

This problem of human nature is not confined to liberals or atheists, and many famous conservatives and ministers who got involved in moral problems still maintained a large following.

Bovay went on to be elected to the Wisconsin State Assembly and served as a major in the Union Army.

The first presidential candidate put forward in 1856 by the Republicans was John Charles Fremont, who was instrumental in bringing California into the United States through the use of force. He was an advocate of Young America, who supported the Walker filibuster campaign prior to Walker coming out for slavery. Fremont was a belligerent man who rarely respected higher command as a military officer, either before or during the Civil War.

During the conquest of California, Fremont, with his right-hand man Kit Carson, killed three unarmed Hispanic residents, sons of prominent families, simply because he did not want to be bothered by taking any prisoners. He became the first U.S. senator from California, and after the Civil War became governor of the territory of Arizona.

During the Civil War Lincoln had to rescind some of Fremont's orders because of the problems they created, and as a major general Fremont had generals and colonels under his command who were Marxist Germans and Hungarians, such as Franz Sigel, Louis Blenker, and Carl Schurz. Blenker was appointed American consul to Nantes, France, after the war. All activities of Fremont from 1856 on attracted radical socialists to his cause like flies to honey.

By 1856, many anti-slavery politicians jumped on the bandwagon of the new Republican Party. The convention of 1856 had delegates as diverse as James G. Blaine; Thaddeus Stevens; Alphonso Taft, the co-founder of the Skull and Bones Order; John Edward Seeley, also of the Order; Joshua R. Giddings; Rufus King; Z. Chandler; Francis W. Bird; and Owen Lovejoy.

At this convention, Lincoln came in second for the nomination of vice president.

The radical Germans flocked to the Fremont ticket, with notable German revolutionaries speaking on his behalf.

The people had the choice between three men for president in 1856: one who was right at home with radicals, Fremont; a man who had co-hosted a dinner in London for the Conspiracy's radical leaders, Buchanan; or Millard Fillmore on the Southern wing of the American Party, or Know-Nothings, who had mentored radicals. The election choices have not changed much over the years.

If Fremont would have been elected, there were Southern states that were ready to pull out of the Union at that time, such as North and South Carolina and Louisiana, according to a letter to Jefferson Davis, secretary of war at the time, from James M. Mason of Virginia. The South was afraid of the Republican Party and it would not have mattered who was nominated and elected, as we shall see.

Before Greeley was in the publishing business on his own, he was given his start by Thurlow Weed in his propaganda-oriented publications supporting William H. Seward for president. Then Harrison and Weed put Greeley in as the editor of The *Log Cabin* in support of Harrison. The *Log Cabin's* circulation grew to 80,000. With this success, Greeley wrote for the *New Yorker*.[42]

Yet, Thurlow Weed later would deny his protégé Greeley the U.S. Senate seat from New York in 1861 by amassing enough legislative votes against him.

The second Republican candidate for president was Lincoln. The convention that nominated him was broader in political scope and experience by this time since most of the Whig Party in the North, which had ceased to exist, went into the Republican Party but still had delegates that included Carl Schurz, Horace Greeley, Joshua R. Giddings, William M. Evarts of the Order, and other radicals, including 42 German-born delegates.

The front-runner was William H. Seward, but the radical preference was Salmon Chase, who was nominated by Evarts and seconded by Austin Blair, John W. North, and Carl Schurz. But neither Seward nor Chase could get a majority. Finally, on the third ballot, Lincoln came in with only 1½ votes needed for the nomination, and four changed their vote and put him over the top. The modern perception is that Lincoln was the Republican nominee without much opposition and was overwhelmingly supported by the Party.

Lincoln had been nominated by Norman B. Judd and seconded by Caleb B. Smith, Columbus Delano, and William M. Stone.

Judd became a friend and business partner of sorts with Smith, a Masonic leader in Indiana, and Delano; they all later served at one time or another as the secretary of interior. The latter had to resign in disgrace over the corruption in his department, especially in the Bureau of Indian Affairs during the Grant administration.

What is not so well known is that bogus gallery tickets were printed that filled the Wigwam convention center with Lincoln supporters. This jammed the galleries with Illinois supporters of Lincoln. How much they swayed the delegates cannot be determined.

Lincoln did not run for re-election during the war on the Republican ticket per se. The wartime ticket he ran on was the National Union Party. By 1864 Lincoln did not believe that he could get re-elected on the Radical Republican ticket, and so a National Union Party was conceived with its primary purpose being the re-election of Lincoln. If you ask most Americans today, they know nothing of this development and believe that Lincoln always ran on the Republican ticket for president.

The Radical Republicans formed the Radical Democracy Party and ran Fremont. The Democrats ran Gen. McClellan.

Fremont made a deal with Lincoln shortly before the election and withdrew.

The whole exercise was another ruse to gain votes for the Radical agenda while making it appear to be something else. There was little question at the time that the national re-election of the Radical Republicans was in serious doubt across the North. Therefore, they repeated the strategy of 1856 used by Nathaniel Banks, again with Fremont, plus an added twist.

Since the Radicals probably could not get elected, they made it appear as if the Republicans had split and nominated Lincoln on one ticket and Fremont on a more radical one, and then had Fremont "reluctantly" withdraw in favor of the more "moderate" Lincoln.

It worked. It worked so well that historians cannot believe the idea was a ruse. The majority then (and

---

42   Whether there is any connection to the name of this paper or not, it is interesting that the modern homosexual organization of Republicans is called the Log Cabin Republicans. There are clues all along the way when one looks at what the organizers of groups call themselves; in this case, it was after a publication edited by a prominent socialist leader. In both the incidences of "liberal" Republican organization, the names can be traced back to the efforts of Horace Greeley: Ripon Society and Log Cabin Republicans. Of course the latter claim it is in reference to Lincoln.

now) did not seem to notice that the War Cabinet and the entire structure of the administration never had an exodus of Radicals — quite the opposite. There was never any indication that the Radicals in government were not going to be kept there by Lincoln. It again was show business.

There are those who make a case that in fact Lincoln was not re-elected in 1864 due to vote fraud involving absentee ballots from the army. (A similar situation existed in the 2012 elections, when military ballots were not counted due to their late arrival from overseas. It was obvious that the delay came as a result of those who did not want them counted due to the low percentage of our armed forces who supported Obama — by the end of 2014 only 15% supported Obama in our services, according to reputable polls taken at the time.)

In 1864, ballots of those voting in the Union Army from southern Ohio were declared as overwhelmingly in favor of Lincoln. However, these ballots were later discovered in the files of the Ohio Historical Society individually sealed and never having been counted.

Once Lincoln was re-elected, Fremont sent a letter to Lincoln congratulating him, part of which read:

> From the very beginning of the titanic American strife, the workers of Europe instinctively felt that the star-spangled banner carried the destiny of their class.... The workers of Europe feel that, as the American war of Independence initiated a new era of ascendency for the middle class, so the American war against slavery will do it for the working class.

The Radical Democracy Party leadership that nominated Fremont was Wendell Phillips, Charles Sumner, Gen. Gustave-Paul Cluseret, and, of course, Fremont himself.

Cluseret had won his reputation and the Legion of Honor for his repression of revolutionaries in 1848, but after this his life was one of revolution and he served with Garibaldi's Red Shirts. During the Civil War he served under Fremont and as aide-de-camp to McClellan. He was a friend and advisor to Gen. Sheridan.

After the war he worked with the Irish Fenian underground in the U.S., and tried to lead an Irish uprising in England.

He edited the *New Nation* in New York City in 1866, and again advocated the election of Fremont. The *New Nation* published Albert Brisbane, Thomas Jefferson Durant, a Southern socialist; and Stephen P. Andrews. In it, Cluseret promoted the idea of "a diminution of the powers of the Executive, and that Cabinet ministers be made in a greater degree responsible to Congress."

He was the minister of war in the Paris Commune in 1871, where he was referred to as the "red general," but had a falling out with its other leaders. He joined the IWA and was a friend of Karl Marx in the 1870s. Lenin's seizure of power in St. Petersburg in 1917 was based on the rough blueprint of Cluseret.

Cluseret was the man behind much of the bloody warfare that took place during the Civil War. His idea was a new kind of total warfare where "no quarter is to be expected since none is to be given." He advocated an "Ultimate Reconstruction": "We desire the creation of a nation in place of a confederation," with "national education and national institutions."

After Fremont withdrew from the race based on a deal with Lincoln, Lincoln won re-election. It is interesting that August Belmont, the Rothschild agent, backed McClellan. For those who believe in a Jewish conspiracy, the North was anti-Semitic, particularly people such as Grant, Stanton, and Wade. The South gained loans from a Jewish banking house, and many of their politicians were Jewish. There were no Jews *in the Northern government*, aside from a clerk of lower rank.

If it was a Jewish conspiracy, McClellan would have won, and the South as well.

There are those who believe that all modern conflicts have been manipulated by the Jews or by the Rothschilds, yet their agent in America, Belmont, spent a fair amount of time writing to his personal contacts in the South urging them to hold their states in the union. "Secession means war, to be followed by a total disintegration of the whole fabric, after endless sacrifices of blood and treasure." This belies the theory that the Rothschilds *always promote war* in order to gain political and/or monetary profit. They may do so, but not always, obviously.

Keep in mind, Belmont was part of YA, which wanted an American empire, not a depleted country, although that was not the strategic plan of those in control. First they had to change the system of government by the use of a prolonged war. *This does not mean that they all agreed as to the tactics to achieve the end they had in mind.*

The immigrants before the formation of the new Republican Party had generally gravitated toward the Democrats, mainly because of the name; however, radical leaders were able to bring most of the recent immigrants into the new party. It would swing back again in the ensuing years.

The Germans formed the Turnverein, or Turner Societies. On the surface, these were intellectual and athletic social clubs steeped in rationalism. Many formed armed militia organizations and trained in all manner of military formations, bayonet practice, weapons training, etc. They were preparing for war, but not as a local militia.

Several Turnvereins came together in October 1850 and formed the Associated Gymnastic Unions of North America, but this title was changed the following year to the Socialist Gymnastic Union. Turner organizations were formed all over the United States, from New York City to Sacramento. It was rare that they were not led by socialists of some type, from what may be called ultra-liberal to communist.

The Turners moved en masse into the Republican Party.

The Turner militias formed the backbone of the Union Army during the initial call for troops by Lincoln at the onset of the Civil War. At least 250,000 immigrant Germans served in the Union Army. In the spring of 1861, enrollment in the Union Army was 80% German, 12% American born, and 8% other.

Mrs. Jefferson Davis stated repeatedly after the war, that without the Germans, the North could never have overcome the armies of the Confederacy. At the same time, she said that had this not happened, North America would have been a theater of continuous war instead of a home of peace.

Aggravated by the Conspiracy, the political situation became untenable in the 1850s and the Democrat and Whig parties split along sectional differences, North and South.

The Know-Nothing party in the North went into the Republican Party for the most part. The Whig Party faded away, and this is when Lincoln became a part of the Republican Party. He had run on the Whig Party ticket in November 1854, seven months after the founding of the Republican Party, and was elected to the Legislature but rejected the seat when he found that a sitting member of the Legislature could not be elected to the U.S. Senate. Before the 17th Amendment the state legislatures elected the senators, and based on Illinois law they could not elect one of their own.

Lincoln's friends Ichabod Codding and William Herndon, his protégé, were in the Republican Party at its inception in 1854, but Lincoln remained aloof. It wasn't until May of 1856 that he quit being a Whig and became a Republican.

At the beginning of the war the Northern Democrats split between War Democrats and those who had little sympathy for the war.

Lincoln is generally thought of as the founder of the Republican Party. The modern Republicans hold Lincoln Day dinners to celebrate the party's origins, of which they have no clue. In 1854, he had protested against his name being used to organize the Republican Party in Illinois. It was six years after the party was formed that Lincoln became its standard bearer.

Think about this for a moment: We are told that this backwoods, rail-splitting country lawyer was nominated by the Republican Party without his campaigning for it or appearing at the convention. At least that is the schoolboy history.

Since when has anyone ever been nominated without a powerful organization behind him?

At the convention of 1860, Carl Schurz, along with Prescott King, escorted the permanent chairman, George Ashmun, to the front of the Wigwam convention center in Chicago, where the convention met. Schurz served on the platform committee and became a member of the Republican National Committee. Other radicals represented their states.

Meanwhile, over on the Democrat side, Young America and the Knights of the Golden Circle were busy splitting the party, ensuring the election of the Republicans, all in the name of nominating a true pro-slavery man. The 1860 candidates became Stephen A. Douglas, the Northern Democrat; John C. Breckinridge, the Southern Democrat; John Bell, of the Constitutional Union party; and of course, Abraham Lincoln.

The mainstream opinion is that the splitting of the Democrats would have made no difference in the election because the Republicans had such a grip on the majority of the electoral votes due to the states that they would carry. This simply was not true, although the election results would imply it.

The Democrat Party was split prior to the Republican convention and there was no certainty that Lincoln would be the candidate, especially since there were more prominent men vying for the nod, most of them radical. It was best to be safe and make sure the Republican Party candidate would win *regardless* of who was nominated. In fact, the first Alabama resolution regarding secession (in April 1860, two months before Lincoln was nominated and when he was not the front-runner) referred to the Republican Party, not any specific candidate.

One of the means by which the Republican Party was assured of victory was by the flooding into the Northwest (today's Midwest) of German immigrants under the influence of the 48ers. All manner of enticements were given to them by the railroads to move into this area the decade before 1860. The main railroad involved in this process was the Illinois Central Railroad, the same railroad the attorney Lincoln represented. McClellan, Banks, and many others who were main characters in the Civil War were also connected to this railroad.

A considerable amount of British capital was invested in American enterprises, particularly in railroads such as the Illinois Central. Here we have a clue that the Brits may have had an influence in American politics. Again, no attempt has ever been made to ferret out the influence of England on American politics since the War of 1812. This investment was also placed in New York and Philadelphia banks, such as the Manhattan Company and Girard's.

There was a consensus at the time that German immigrants under the leadership of the 48ers put Lincoln over the top in six key Midwest states. This fact has been expunged from the history books.

Douglas was very popular in the Midwest, and he had just defeated Lincoln for the U.S. Senate based on that popularity. To further ensure that the vote would turn out as the radicals wanted, in the states of Indiana, Michigan, Ohio, Minnesota, and Wisconsin, non-citizens were allowed to vote. This was done on the basis of a mix of one or more of the following: a declaration of intent to become a citizen, residency from 4 to 30 months, and/or payment of property tax.

German immigrant population in these areas ranged from 5% to 15%. It is estimated that between

450,000 and 600,000 German immigrants in this area voted based on the foregoing formulae. In 1860, fully 50% of the German-language newspapers were run by 48ers promoting the Republican Party. This gave an inordinate amount of influence to the socialist leadership compared to their actual number. Capture of the information services (media) has always been one of their goals — it remains so today.

Without the German vote in 1860, Douglas would have been elected president. Without the *illegal* German vote, Douglas would have been president.

One of the radical Germans who served as an elector for Lincoln in 1860 in New York was Friedrich Kapp, an attorney there from 1850-1870. He had been active in the Republican Party early on. He returned to Germany and was elected to the German Diet in 1871. He said that America "will occupy a decidedly higher place as soon as it gets rid of Christianity."

By this you can see that illegal-immigrant voting is not new and has been used by the Conspiracy off and on to further their agenda at the polls. It usually happens during periods of a high influx of immigrants, when it is relatively easy to bring the immigrants together and organize them. If immigration is low, it is difficult to use them in elections to turn the tide in the manner desired by the Conspiracy, and the effort is not usually worth the return.

The mass influx of immigrants has always been a problem at the ballot box, with people either voting illegally or not yet assimilated completely. This has also served as the basis of radical agitation and violence. Early in our history, the Federalists understood this and made the time necessary for citizenship to be in residence for over a decade. The Republican-Democrats understood this as well, but wanted to take advantage of it.

When the Federalists were the majority in the Congress, the obligation for citizenship was enacted as 14 years of residency, with the thinking that it would serve as the necessary time for an immigrant to assimilate to our system of government *as well as our society*. A second reason was to deprive the radicals from Europe of the ability to swing elections by using recent arrivals to our shores.

When the Republicans (Democrats) became the congressional majority, one of the first things that they did was to change the law, making it a five-year requirement.

Today there is less emphasis on assimilation, and immigrant communities are encouraged. In addition, blocs are formed by the encouragement of ethnicity or color. It is the old divide-and-conquer technique.

Young American August Belmont was in support of Douglas. He was the head of the National Committee of the Democrat Party during the war, and a national leader for a decade after, an incredible position for a Rothschild agent. Another leader of Young America and a financial agent of Belmont was George N. Sanders, who also pushed Douglas.

Sanders tried to get a prominent Southern-rights man as the Vice-presidential candidate on the Douglas ticket, to no avail. Sanders had manned the barricades in Europe during the revolutions of 1848 and was intimate with many of the revolutionary leaders. His family had a long history of Jacobin and conspiratorial involvement, dating back to the 1790s.

Colonel John Singleton Mosby, of Mosby's Raiders, stated in *Leslie's Weekly*, April 6, 1911, that the only reason Breckinridge was made a candidate was to split the Democrat Party in order to elect Lincoln. Mosby had been a leader in the Southern army. After the war he became a Republican and was appointed consul to Hong Kong by Rutherford Hayes, finally settling down in San Francisco.

It is interesting that this Confederate-turned-Republican was active in the Confederate Secret Service. There is ample evidence that he was involved in the plot against Lincoln. For someone who was so dedicated to the Confederacy, he changed sides quickly and thoroughly. Taking an oath to the government of the U.S. was one thing, becoming a Republican was something entirely different — or was it?

The only thing wrong with Mosby's statement is that Lincoln was not the candidate when the Democrats split. It would have been more accurate to say that the Democrats were split to ensure the election of the Republican Party.

It was the opinion of Douglas that the North would not vote sufficiently for Breckinridge if he should withdraw, but the South would vote for him if Breckinridge should withdraw. Neither did.

August Belmont was very active with Southern radical politicians before the war. At one time Slidell tried to get him to become our ambassador to Spain, but Belmont turned down the spot and Judah Benjamin took it instead. Belmont was the husband of Slidell's niece.

Slidell's oldest daughter married Baron Emile Erlanger, the head of a European banking house, said to have been one of the most influential men with Napoleon III.

Slidell in his political heyday in New Orleans was accused by opposition newspapers of political ruffianism in every way as "Gallatin street assassinations and thuggery." His reputation across the South was one of buying up votes, either in his state or throughout the Democrat Party at conventions.

Slidell's family contacts were influential. While he was looked upon as Jewish, he married an Irish woman who was descended from a Jacobite member of the Mackenzie clan. He immigrated to America. His sister married Commodore Perry, the man who opened up Japan. His wife's sister was married to Gen. Pierre Beauregard, the Southern general who ordered the firing on Ft. Sumter.

As you can see, it is not just interlocking directorates that are a problem in politics, but family ties as well.

The South had its own problems with radicals, who pointed to the volatile radicals and immigrants of the North as examples of why secession was necessary, not so much to save slavery, but more to save constitutional liberty — even though many in the Southern political leadership had no intention of actually supporting the Constitution. This rings strange today in light of the way history has been taught for so many years, both in the North and South.

The problem was that the people in both sections were standing in quicksand and instead of their leadership helping to pull them out, they did the opposite.

There was a movement within the Republican Party to form militias to participate in the coming war. They were known as the Wide Awake Republicans. While they were not overt in their military training, they were organized more as shock troops for the party — their acronym said it all: WAR.

Elmer Ellsworth worked in the Lincoln law office in Springfield, Illinois studying law. He had formed a company of Zouaves and toured 20 Northern cities to promote the Wide Awake forces being formed before Lincoln declared as a Republican. Zouaves were military units who wore the colorful French-style of North African uniforms.

While Lincoln was still campaigning as a Whig and not a Republican, the two men in his office working for him were building the Republican Party: Herndon and Ellsworth.

The WAR also had a secret society attached to it, which Allan Pinkerton put in motion, that actually ran the organization. It used the Eye of Horus — which was also the symbol of Pinkerton's detective agency, the All Seeing Eye. The motto of his agency was, "We Never Sleep." The eye was used on the certificates issued by WAR clubs to certify membership and on their banners used in parades.

In addition, both on Wide Awake and Republican banners and posters, the French revolutionary flag appeared far too often on one side, with the U.S. flag on the other and the Eye of Horus in between.

While it may seem wild speculation, the banners used were designed to be remarkably similar to the winged disc of Horus, with the flags semi-furled and positioned as the wings of Horus. There have been some who claim that it was graphic code for the secret society of the Columbian Illuminati, but there is no proof.

The Columbian Illuminati was the nickname of the Theistical Society started by Elihu Palmer in New York in 1801. He had studied divinity but became a deist in 1791. The Theistical Society developed ties to the Jacobin democratic societies. Their organs were *The Beacon, The Temple of Reason, and The Philanthropist,* and their deistic gospel was carried on by British residents in the U.S. including George Houston, Robert Owen, and Francis Wright. These three laid a great deal of the groundwork for the labor movement in New York and other cities in the 1820s. The New York *Beacon*, by 1840, coupled the cause of labor with the rejection of all religious theories.

Palmer had become blind in 1793 as the result of an attack of the yellow fever. He wrote Principles of Nature in 1802, an anti-Christian work reprinted by Carlile in 1819.

The joke made during those days was that the Wide Awakes' eye was actually the Eye of Horace, meaning Horace Greeley. While that was the joke, the guiding light behind the scenes was Pinkerton who used the eye as his logo for his detective agency,

The difference in the Wide Awakes and previous campaign organizations was the use of a military motif for the group. This had never been done before in the history of American campaigning; militant, yes, but not military by wearing uniforms or in their intent. One needs to remember the acronym of the Wide Awake Republicans: WAR.

Stretching just from central Illinois to southern Wisconsin the organization contained approximately 250 companies! Mass meetings were held in the major northern cities, at one time drawing 70,000 WAR members. To accomplish this takes organization and media hype. Consider also that the population of our country was decidedly less in those days — 70,000 was a huge number in that area. Today, even to draw those numbers to anything other than a football game would be significant.

The *New York Herald* estimated that nationally there were 400,000 WAR members in 1860. Based on the ratio of the population then vs. today, that would be four million in the North alone. Here again, we have to ask the reader if they have ever heard of this organization, and if not, why not? This kind of influence would seem to garner at least a paragraph in school history books.

Recruiting into the WAR units had a decidedly paramilitary bent, with talk of moving into the South and destroying all but Republicans. The Wide Awakes had become the street soldiers of revolution. One is reminded of similar conditions in 20th century Europe using party auxiliaries.

With the outbreak of hostilities, it is safe to say that without the WAR members in the St. Louis area, Missouri would have linked up with the Confederacy. They gave great help to Francis Preston Blair, Jr. in his fight to save Missouri for the Union.

As we said, the WAR movement was so large that it is remarkable that the average history student of today has never heard of them. It is not as if they were unknown or insignificant to the story of the Republican Party. If they were to be included in history textbooks, the manner in which they were organized and used would raise serious questions in the mind of the student, leading to more questions that would need to be answered. Thus, they are rarely, if ever, mentioned in school texts.

From Congressman Owen Lovejoy, Sen. William Seward, and others came the call to either invade and slay Southern leaders or impose the will of the Republicans on the South.

If the Southerners looking at this development had not been afraid for the future before, they were then. And they reacted accordingly, with their own militancy. Soon, Minutemen militias were forming in the South as a counter to the WAR groups. These militias *are* recorded in school history books, since they fit the politically correct image the establishment historians want of a belligerent South to help explain the origins of the Civil War.

The recruiting and growth of the WAR companies did not abate after the 1860 election. They continued to grow. It was obvious that regardless of what the Southern states did, the intent among those who had come to power was to use the force of arms against the South and to use it to overthrow the old social order, particularly in the South but in the North as well.

Remember that units of the Northern areas of the Democrat Party were not averse to injecting French revolutionary ideas into their programs. Radical Germans were active in the Democrat Party as well. As a reminder, in Iowa, the Democratic Platform of 1854 declared as its mission "to sustain and advance among us constitutional 'Liberty, equality and fraternity,' " the French revolutionary slogan.

It was not unusual for radicals to move back and forth among the parties of the day as they promoted their agenda. Salmon Chase, who ended his career as the chief justice of the Supreme Court, started out as a radical. He was a leader of the Liberty Party as well as the Anti-Slavery Society. He went from senator to governor of the State of Ohio. He belonged to several parties, and was the main candidate of the radicals for the nomination for the Republican Party in 1864 until he declared for Lincoln. In 1868 the Democrats considered him for their candidate.

As governor of Ohio, he gave a letter of endorsement for John Brown and was supportive of Brown's work in Kansas. He was a friend of Adam Gurowski. Along with Ashley and Wade of Ohio, Chase set out to see to it that the Southern states did not return to the Union with full voting powers that would doom Radical Republicanism.

Chase was appointed the secretary of the treasury in the Lincoln administration, and as such he agitated for an "improved" banking system. He oversaw the issuing of bonds, the Greenback, the National Banking Act and other aspects of changes in the economy during the war.

Carl Schurz conferred with Chase, Sumner, and Stanton before Schurz toured the South after the war. Chase himself toured the South electioneering among Negroes for radical votes.

After he was appointed to the court he slowly began to moderate and ruled against the Greenback and the income tax; one stayed in force and the other disappeared — for a time.

Chase was only one example of the many radicals who served in the leadership of many political movements and parties, demonstrating the interlocking of leadership among the various minions of the Conspiracy.

Allan Pinkerton, the man who formed the secret society within the WAR movement, was born in Scotland. Even though his policeman father was injured in a Chartist riot, Pinkerton became an ardent Chartist by age 19, plotting and rioting. He founded the Glasgow Democratic Club, and had to leave England due to involvement in the communist Chartist movement when the British authorities started to arrest Chartist activists. In America he became an associate of the terrorist John Brown.

After immigrating he settled in Chicago, where he came in contact with Elijah Lovejoy, Philo Carpenter, Doctor Dyer, and L. C. Freer, aggressive leaders of the abolition movement. Pinkerton became a leader in the Underground Railroad. Lovejoy was later to serve as a martyr for the abolitionist cause in Alton, Illinois.

After Brown's capture at Harper's Ferry, Pinkerton, Timothy Webster, and other Pinkerton detectives moved into Charleston to try to free Brown, but had to abandon the effort.

While modern historians may write of the Wide Awakes as a type of police for Republican rallies, their intent went much further as they served as a sort of recruiting medium for the upcoming conflict. They met secretly but marched openly. Upon Lincoln's call for troops in the opening days of the war, the

Wide Awakes enlisted en masse but needed to be organized into military units, unlike the Turners, who already were so organized.

The radicals of Young America and the Knights of the Golden Circle controlled enough of the political process in the South to be able to use the Southern reaction to the radicalism of the Northern firebrands to inflame the South into going it alone. This was a very bad mistake for the Southern people. Had the South remained in Congress, they had the political clout to prevent much of what came to pass, but that was not the plan of the radicals on both sides. They wanted war.

Modern Republicanism

The Democrat Party started out as the radical party, originally using the title *Republican*. By the time of the formation of the second Republican Party, the Democrat Party had gone into an era of relative moderation *in comparison* to the new Republicans.

Red republicans from Europe turned to the "Republican" Party (Democrats) during the time of Jefferson. Under the leadership of DeWitt Clinton and others, European immigrants continued to be welcomed into the Democrat Party.

This tradition went on for some years. Andrew Jackson's populist appeals on behalf of "the masses versus the classes" kept the European radical immigrants within their ranks.

The slogan among radical Democrats and radical Germans within the party in the early 1850s hearkened back to the French Revolution. Again, there is the example of the Iowa Democrat Party Platform of 1854 "to sustain and advance among us constitutional 'Liberty, equality and fraternity,' " the slogan of the French revolutionaries. Also YA leaders held dominant roles in Democratic leadership.

Through it all, was the essence of *German radical demands* of popular sovereignty versus God's sovereignty. Some of the planks the Germans supported were free government schools, homesteading, anti-slavery, and term limits.

Let us explain the difference between homesteading, which seems to be a good thing, and what had been done up to that time: simply going out into the wilderness and staking out a claim before anyone else got there. While there were inequities in the latter, as there always are when people enjoy freedom, the systematic homesteading of the frontier placed the acquisition of all land into the hands and control of the federal government. Property became a matter of state control, rather than an essential ingredient of liberty, and then a matter of federal control with the help of the Homestead Act.

Also, the use of term limits as a solution to bad government needs to be discussed. The United States already has term limits — they are called elections. In a free country, the people are allowed to vote for whomever they please. Term limits curtail that right. If a politician is bad, term limits will only get rid of one bad politician with the substitution of another if the electorate does not change. The ignorant majority will simply elect the same type of politician.

The use of term limits within state politics has produced some benefits, but they are only temporary. In this author's home state, term limits actually worked against constitutional forces because in many areas the people had been educated to vote for conservatively-minded candidates. Once conservatives were elected, the activists went back to sleep relative to educating the voter since they felt their job had been done. The conservatives coasted along until term limits kicked in and the constitutionalists were out of office, and the people reverted to voting in socialists.

The presidency has term limits. Have we had better presidents since this amendment to the Constitution, or worse?

The key to good government is not to change the system, it is to systematically educate the voter with an organization designed to do so — continually. This takes work, and most political activists will not take the time and effort to engage in it.

The only reason that the more conservative activists gravitated toward the Republican Party after the Wilson campaign is because the Democrat Party started to revert back to the more radical of the two in the 20th century. This was due in part to progressive or socialist movement within the Republican Party breaking off for a time to follow Teddy Roosevelt, forming the Progressive Party. But at the top, the Republican Party has never been in alignment with the image it has projected to its own grassroots activists or public, and has always done all it can to ensure that constitutionalists' influence is negated or isolated within the party. This is done almost always out of the view of the majority of the average party activists or voters, behind the scenes.

The establishment of the Republican Party has never, ever allowed constitutionalists into positions of power or influence. They never allow a strict constitutionalist to assume the leadership of a congressional committee. Any story to the contrary is simply myth in order to either cover up the reality or hold on to their constituents, with two exceptions.

The modern school texts often call the Progressive Party by its nickname, the "Bull Moose Party," to help cloak the real purpose of the party: socialism. The Roosevelt idea of "Walk softly but carry a big stick" is thought only to pertain to Roosevelt's foreign policy. It applied to his domestic policy as well.

Teddy Roosevelt's policies fit into the mold of Young America. A person reading the speeches he delivered after he served as president can only come to the conclusion that he was a socialist at best. Roosevelt's environmental policies, for instance, rushed the federal government into locking down huge sections of the country from private ownership, and the process has gone on almost unabated ever since.

It was a direct attack on state sovereignty and private property, all done in the name of the people and environment.

It does not matter how high an ideal is, once the government gets involved, the government agency always will grow higher, wider, and deeper, becoming just another bureaucracy exerting control over the people.

In the case of land, the government does not really control the land; *it controls the people* in relationship to the land. Government does not alter the land or divert any dangers to the environment. One example is that they will not allow anyone to clear the forests of fallen trees and branches which build up into wide swaths of tinder, ready to be lit by a stroke of lightning and spread uncontrollably.

There are other examples of government creating environmental problems with the diversion of water, such as in Florida.

Private ownership only wishes to improve the land or utilize its resources for profit. This will always result in benefits for the people in the long run, even if the local land is altered. What comes out of it benefits the economy, thereby all people eventually.

All of the Roosevelts promoted socialism except one or two family members, who became ostracized from the family. Yet Teddy has an image of conservatism among Americans primarily due to his war record during the Spanish-American War and the famous charge on San Juan Hill. This has been cultivated and fits the pattern of modern neoconservatives promoting candidates and policies based on foreign belligerent initiatives.

To reinforce the idea that Teddy Roosevelt was a socialist, one only needs to read his speech he delivered at the dedication of the John Brown Memorial Park and Museum in Osawatomie, Kansas, on the fiftieth anniversary of Brown's execution. In essence, he sent a message to the progressive forces in the Republican Party that led to the campaign of 1912.

By the way, there never was any proof that the Spanish blew up the battleship *Maine* in Havana Harbor in Cuba, which served as the basis for us to declare war against Spain. If you think about it logically, would the Spanish do something so obvious in their own backyard that they knew would lead to war and the loss of not only Cuba, but Puerto Rico, the Philippines, and so many of their possessions in the Americas and Pacific Ocean?

Well, the citizens of the U.S. were reacted into thinking so by the mass media. The powers-that-be convinced enough of the American people that the Spanish were that stupid. They just could not believe that an American sailor was dumb enough the sneak a cigarette in the magazine, forgot to open a valve on the main engines, or whatever else could have caused the sinking.

Back to the declaring of national parks and forests; one of the little known aspects of federal land is its use by Mexican drug cartels to infiltrate drugs into our country. The U.S. Border Patrol is denied access to the federal lands without forewarning the appropriate authorities. The corruption within these authorities alerts the cartels and they are rarely interdicted as a result.

While the setting aside of national parks and forests was supposedly for their preservation, this was actually the means for the federal government to gain back land that had become state and private property as territories were admitted as states. In the State of Arizona alone, about half of the border with Mexico is federal land. The people who smuggle drugs and personnel into the U.S. do so with abandon in these areas. A quick, guided tour by someone who has had border responsibility in the area will immediately convince anyone of these details. A U.S. congressman personally filled in this author on the details of such a tour, complete with photographs.

While Manifest Destiny had taken on a Southern flavor due to the fact that many involved wanted to expand south and annex new slave states in Latin America, the program did not cease with the demise of the Confederacy. In 1892, the Republican Party platform stated, "We reaffirm our approval of the Monroe Doctrine and believe in the achievement of the *manifest destiny* of the Republic in its *broadest sense*." (Emphasis added.)

In other words, we will oppose any European involvement and acquisitions in the Western Hemisphere — because we want it.

While they lost the election that year, in 1896 the Republicans returned to power and Manifest Destiny was cited to promote overseas expansion. President William McKinley, Republican, advocated the annexation of Hawai'i in 1898. He said, "We need Hawai'i as much as and a good deal more than we did California. It is manifest destiny."

Based on what you have read about the filibuster campaigns and other aspects of Manifest Destiny, you must realize that Cuba was always in their sights. The reaction to the sinking of the battleship *Maine* provided the catalyst for the ultimate campaign to engage in Manifest Destiny and the acquisition of territory. This continued on until after World War I, when we acquired other territories in the Pacific Ocean, either outright or as protectorates. This policy underwent a change to exercising control over, rather than ownership of countries and territory.

Most rank-and-file conservatives think of *conservatism* to mean something akin to a constitutional outlook on politics. However, the conservative *movement* shifted from a near-constitutional model in the early 20th century to neoconservatism by the end of that century, due to a well-orchestrated program by those posing as constitutionalists with their rhetoric but not in their actions.

This began to happen by the end of the Barry Goldwater candidacy due to the efforts of men within the party who did not want Goldwater elected, including the Rockefellers and George Romney, who was comfortable working with and befriending people like Saul Alinsky, the model-maker for ACORN and similar community activist groups promoting a socialist agenda. This latter fact is easily verifiable online.

Neoconservatism was the name that Irving Kristol and other "former" Trotskyite communists adopted after they realized that they could further their agenda better by grafting themselves onto the Republican Party, rather than working within the Democrat Party, appearing to be something they were not: conservative. The neoconservative agenda, as we have seen, is in reality nothing new, only the name is new. It is a repackaged YA program.

This was accomplished as a backlash against the Goldwater forces within the Republican Party who had taken control of the movement largely under the philosophical influence of members of The John Birch Society. Although the JBS did not engage in politics as an organization, its members had a great deal of influence in and on the party by 1964. The battle for the nomination of Goldwater was bitter and probably would have never happened except for the favorable, albeit cautious mention of Goldwater as a good, possible candidate for president by Robert Welch in the widely distributed JBS founding document known as *The Blue Book,* which prompted members of the Society to work for his nomination.

While Goldwater became the candidate in 1964, the establishment retained control over the party leadership itself and helped scuttle the campaign through inept campaigning. This included certain members of the Left who infiltrated the party, positioning themselves to even write speeches for Goldwater using the technique of addressing two audiences at the same time. The conservative was enthusiastic at the end of the speeches, the fence sitter appalled. The conservatives were none the wiser.

One of the more famous phrases from Goldwater's acceptance speech for the nomination sent thrills through his supporters and shudders through those who had doubts about his leadership: "Extremism in the defense of liberty is no vice." His supporters heard "defense of liberty is no vice." Others heard, "Extremism." They had been programmed by the media to believe he was an extremist, and as far as they were concerned, he had just admitted it. The Democrat opposition built their campaign on calling Goldwater an "extremist."

One of Goldwater's speechwriters was a member of the Students for a Democratic Society at the time. Goldwater had no idea. The SDS was led by communists and very militant socialists. The communists even ran a "photo-shopped" picture in the *Peoples' World* communist organ of Goldwater giving the communist salute at the Republican convention. The altered photo was a message to the Red readership that Goldwater had been *surrounded and neutralized*, not that Goldwater was a mole.

Even at the grassroots level, once the Draft Goldwater movement started to gather momentum it was infiltrated by opportunistic individuals who rose to local leadership and who exposed themselves in the aftermath as very liberal Republicans. They practiced the tactic of getting in front of a wave to ride it to influence.

At the end of the campaign, you could not find a liberal Republican who did not profess to have been a Goldwater supporter — once the threat of constitutional leadership had been beaten down. They wanted to fool the newcomers to the GOP into believing that they were conservatives. The tactic was repeated in the Reagan campaign when the wave of grassroots conservatism overwhelmed the establishment.

Few looked into the background of a very young man elevated to the heights of philosophical leadership of the conservative movement well beyond his years of experience and age by the establishment and the *government's television network* with a weekly program of conservatism: William F. Buckley. No one seemed to notice that no other "conservative" need apply for a spot on PBS, the Public Broadcasting System. Buckley was a CIA agent involved in covert activities in Mexico before anyone had ever heard of him. His book *God and Man at Yale* gave him a conservative image, when all the while he was a member of the Order, having been tapped into Skull and Bones as an Eli.

Buckley gained the reputation of having "kicked" The John Birch Society out of the conservative movement. He also was behind the scenes doing all that he could to convince prominent people to leave their membership in the Society, both through individual contact and orchestrated events.

His magazine became the home for a variety of ex-communist and neoconservative writers.[43]

The neoconservative movement reminds one of a passage in Shakespeare's *Macbeth*:

In often times, to win us to our harm, the instruments of darkness, tell us truths, win us with trifles, to betray us in consequence.

— Shakespeare, *Macbeth*, Act I, Scene 3

The Republican Party has not always been the paragon of virtue and conservatism that many rank-and-file Republicans believe.

A century later, the campaign of 2012 exposed to the party activists some of the problems within the upper echelons of the Republican Party and the control they have to ensure that true constitutionalists cannot get the nomination for president. A book could be written about this fiasco that is relatively unknown to the average Republican voter, but well known to those involved in the attempt to nominate individuals the party hierarchy did not want to get the nomination.

The campaign of 2016 only demonstrated this even more.

The trouble with too many Republican politicians is that they cannot get their heads around the idea of conspiracy and that people on the Left will infiltrate their organization to scuttle any chance a viable candidate may have to rise to an effective level of influence. It is not only the Republican establishment, but members of constitutional candidates' entourages that can contain people whose aim is to destroy any hope of success by their candidates. This author has seen this process acted out at least four times, but was never able to convince the candidates until after it was too late.

This process of infiltration into the organizations of constitutionally oriented candidates who have the potential of winning continues unabated, as it does into conservative organizations.

---

43 The best study of the life and influence of Buckley is the book by John F. McManus, *William F. Buckley, Jr.: Pied Piper for the Establishment*. It is a well-documented book showing that his reputation was the opposite of his actions and possible motivation. It was written and published several years before Buckley's passing, and was never refuted by Buckley.

12

SLAVERY

The average Southerner did not own slaves, and knew that slavery was wrong and could not last. When the original abolition movement was started, a great deal of it was centered in the South. Once the abolitionists started to get traction, the more radical moved the center of agitation to the North, where they became outside agitators to Southerners rather than neighbors who wanted to end a tragic condition in our country.

By doing this, they set the stage for agitating the people toward sectionalism more than what was already the case.

Many of our country's Founders, such as Alexander Hamilton and John Jay, wanted to end slavery as judiciously as possible. Jay was president of the Society for Promoting the Manumission of Slaves, and his son was an abolitionist. Manumission societies existed throughout Southern states, often under the leadership of Quakers and Presbyterians, two of the most prominent religious sects during the War for Independence.

Benjamin Franklin was president of the Pennsylvania Abolition Society in 1790.

Northern states such as New York and Pennsylvania passed laws that overcame the condition of slavery through a gradual process. In the light of today's thinking, these laws did not acknowledge the rights of humanity as we would deem proper. But, in the framework of the first decade of the 19th century, they ultimately freed all slaves over time in their states without the violent upheavals that came fifty years later.

In 1832, the Virginia Legislature brought up the issue of slavery, and emancipation was openly and strongly urged by many. Such discussions would later become impassioned rejection of any talk of eliminating slavery, due to the agitation of radicals in the North, who included socialism, land reform, and attacks against all property in the course of advocating the elimination of slavery.

Prior to Garrison, abolition organizations, by and large, tended to be colonizers — in other words, those who wanted to remove the slaves back to Africa or to countries south of the United States in a colonization program. Southern abolitionists complained about Northern abolitionists being detrimental to their efforts to gain headway toward any program designed to put an end to slavery.

Colonization was not confined to just foreign enterprises, and involved the idea of moving slaves into territory, at the time, on our frontier. The most notable was the idea of doing this in Louisiana when that area was essentially a wilderness. Today that would not seem as bold as it was in the late 1700s. This scheme actually helped boost the formation of the American Colonization Society.

The American Colonization Society was organized in all states except South Carolina. It had many prominent men in its ranks, such as Henry Clay and John Randolph of Roanoke. As a result of their work, Congress passed the Anti-slave Trade Act in 1819. The founding of the nation of Liberia in Africa was also influenced by their work. Their capital of Monroeville was named after President Monroe, an ardent supporter of colonization.

Fourteen state legislatures, the great majority at the time, instructed their congressmen to work for colonization, and the U.S. government actually appointed three agents to colonize Africa with Negroes under the auspices of the American Colonization Society. Two of the three died on the trip to Africa and Samuel Bacon, the third agent, died soon after due to the hardships of the venture.

Colonization was still alive in the 1850s and 1860s, particularly in New York among the liberal establishment. Lincoln was a longtime, active supporter of colonization with a scheme he considered carrying out during the Civil War. Conditions were such that the plans could not be put in motion.

Colonization's last gasp as far as men in government were concerned came in 1870, when Grant had negotiated a treaty to purchase the Dominican Republic as a U.S. possession and it could have served as a place for the freed slaves to migrate. It was the most serious attempt by the government to institute colonization, although it was promoted for other reasons as well, one of which was the lure of mineral wealth that the Dominican Republic might contain. It was stopped in the Senate Foreign Relations Committee by Sen. Sumner, a member of the International. Moving freedmen out of the country could not be used as a source of agitation later by the communists.

In other words, by eliminating all or a large portion of the Negro population from the United States, the communists would not be able to incite racial hatred between the races, nor would they have been able to propose the formation of a communist "Negro Republic" in the so-called Black Belt of the South. This became one of Stalin's plans in the late 1920s as a means to divide and conquer America. The USSR actually sent agents to the U.S. to work this agenda.

Whether they actually intended to put this government together or not, it was used as one of the sources of agitation from the 1930s up to the 1960s. Many books were written, pamphlets printed, and organizations formed promoting such a scheme, but generally the communities outside of the black areas did not see the campaign in action since it was actually designed to attract Negroes to the communist cause.

There has been much written to discredit looking into this Soviet initiative, since to follow it and the trail it paved would lead directly to many people who are still active in communist activity whom they wish to protect today, including members of Congress.

You can trace the economic destruction of Detroit by following this record.

At the same time, the communists and their allies worked within the KKK and like-minded organizations to create hatred in the Southern white population.[44]

The commission that Grant appointed to determine the feasibility of the American annexation of the Dominican Republic consisted of Andrew Dickson White of the Order, and the Radicals Benjamin Wade and Samuel Howe.

Amazingly, one of the envoys sent there by the government to actually start the negotiations for annexation included Burton Norvell Harrison of the Order, Jefferson Davis' private secretary during the war.

In other words, the Conspiracy got in front of both sides of the issue in order to control its direction.

Before the war, the work of the Conspiracy in radicalizing abolition was destructive of the work that had already been done, and what could have been done, to bring a peaceful end to the sin of slavery. The communists always adopted policies which would serve to widen the gap between the races and did nothing to alleviate the problem. They wanted no part of colonization since it would have alleviated the problem and thus stood in the way of their initiatives.

In any case, it would not have been fair to the Negroes who had been forcibly seized, then exported here from their own countries, to uproot them forcibly again to places unknown, even if they volun-

---

44 The best documentary on this entire scheme is the movie, now a video, *Anarchy U.S.A.* on YouTube. There is far more evidence, but this is a good start.

teered. By the beginning of the Civil War most slaves had been born here, and removing them to poorer countries would have probably made their condition worse. And, as far as voluntary removal is concerned, government has a bad habit of making "voluntary" look a great deal like "coercion". It would not only have been unfair to them; it would have been unfair to the people already inhabiting the territory into which they would have been injected. It would have had a great destabilizing influence on that country, socially and economically.

Having said this, there were black American organizations well into the 20th century that were formed to promote colonization. Most came to look suspiciously like schemes for raising money for their leaders rather than actually working for colonization, since their leaders lived like potentates and one claimed to be a prophet.

The English abolished slavery peacefully in 1833 and provided £20 million plus an apprenticeship for ex-slaves — a great deal cheaper than waging a war. And, they did not have to kill two-thirds of a million men-at-arms and untold numbers of civilians to accomplish the end of slavery, as the Conspiracy did in America — with no plans to help the freedmen at first. What plans there were to help were too little too late, and generally were used to promote a radical agenda, and to organize the freedmen into radical voting blocs as much as they were to help them.[45]

The attacks against the South and slavery caused a Southern reaction that ranged from apologizing for slavery to defending it. The more strident Southerners began to claim that men were not equal. Even the very idea of freedom came under attack, that liberty is not born with man, but is a privilege for which individuals and races must demonstrate their fitness — a Darwinian approach to liberty. This helped fuel the feelings of the Northern people who were on the fence against Southerners and slavery.

It became a Ping-Pong game of agitation, back and forth.

The idea that any man was not endowed with rights from God was a radical departure from the thinking and philosophy of our Founders. It demonstrates that the goals of the Illuminati were being pursued in the South as well as the North to completely change the religious foundations of American society and government.

In reality, most Northern abolitionists felt the same as the Southerners about the Negro being equal. When it came to advocating the freedom of the slaves, these same Northern people did not treat Negroes as equals, shunning them from society and preventing their employment except for the most menial of jobs. There were exceptions, but generally this was the rule. It too was a Darwinian approach.

The Negro vote was never an issue prior to the war. Most abolitionists did not believe in it above the Mason-Dixon line. It first came up as a tool of Radical Republicanism to control the South during Reconstruction. Ohio, a free state, for instance, did not give the vote to Negroes until 1870. William Jay, a typical abolitionist leader and New York lawyer, did not believe in Negro suffrage.

Louis Agassiz was also characteristic of the Northern attitude. He wanted freedom for slaves, but felt they were inferior and should not have full citizenship rights, although "with proper restraints, they could provide for themselves."

While he was friends with the members of and met with the Saturday Club, he did not believe in Darwin; he felt that the races were created by God separately and believed they were equal before God.

While the abolitionists promoted anti-slavery, they did not believe in intermarriage or even integration. And, most felt blacks inferior to Caucasians. As has been the case down through the centuries,

---

45   The apprenticeship system was abolished by Parliament in 1838 due to widespread protests as to the cost of the program.

reformers have a public image and a private one, usually racist in nature. Even Lincoln expressed these ideas prior to becoming president.

It may come as a shock to many that free Negroes were banned from entering certain Northern states, such as Ohio. Many would not allow them to testify in legal cases involving whites. These and other restrictions eased just before the Civil War but still were a problem in the minds of many people, and the reality was that the restrictions were practiced even though they had been made illegal. The feelings were so ingrained that abolitionist candidates rarely advocated such changes for fear of losing votes.

Many leftist organizations promoted the freedom of the slaves as a lofty ideal as long as one didn't have to associate with them. It is more or less the same today within socialist and quasi-socialist circles. They will pander to people of color, but really want nothing to do with them. The most notorious of these types were active in the American eugenics programs in the 20th century. They supported socialism, but they also wanted to eliminate the poor among us — as well as colored races — through mass abortion and sterilization.[46]

With this attitude, one can well imagine that many people in the North had no desire to fight a war over slavery.

In the 20th century, the reformers who wanted to do away with segregation had a strange attitude about education. They felt the Negro children could not learn without being integrated with whites. This was patently false, but it was one of the clarion calls of the civil rights movement. It revealed that the reformers did not really believe that the Negroes could do it on their own.

To make absolutely sure the reader understands: forced segregation is wrong. So is forced integration. These are things for the individual to decide, not government. The problem is mandatory, universal government education controlling the people and their children, telling them what they may or may not do, what they will or will not study, not just who sits in the classroom together.

Racial discrimination is repugnant, but the process of government making men equal in all things — except for justice — or the converse of promoting one race over another within the power of law, always leads to more government and the diminishing of liberty for all, regardless of race. Government must make sure that all men are equal in the sight of the law, forcing equality in any other circumstances accumulates power into government until government decides everything.

Black Americans should be able to decide to have a blacks only organization; whites as well. We may not like it. We may even be offended by it, but it is their right to do so or freedom has no meaning. Coercion is not freedom. This author has been asked to leave public establishments more than once by black American proprietors. Is it offensive? Yes, until you remember that it is their right to do so.

By the 21st century, because of the Somali and Hmong immigrants being allowed to have segregated public schools in Minnesota at their own request, some of the black Americans there also wanted their own segregated schools, a complete reversal of their position in the 1960s.

While Lincoln has the reputation of wanting freedom and equality for the Negro, he did not always express this as his position. During the famous Lincoln-Douglas debates when both were running for U.S. senator, at one such debate in southern Illinois, in Charleston, Lincoln said this about Negro-white relations:

> I am not, nor ever have been, in favor of bringing about in any way the social and political equality of the white and black races.... I am not nor ever have been in favor of making voters or jurors of negroes, nor of qualifying them to hold office, nor to intermarry with white people; and I say

---

[46] We suggest to the reader the acquisition of the DVD *MAAFA 21*. It is lengthy, but it proves the point made above with exhausting detail.

in addition to this that there is a physical difference between the white and black races which I believe will forever forbid the two races living together on terms of social and political equality. And inasmuch as they cannot so live, while they do remain together there must be the position of superior and inferior, and I as much as any other man am in favor of having the superior position assigned to the white race.

— *Collected Works of Abraham Lincoln, Volume 3*

Douglas won points in the senatorial selection by pointing out that Lincoln said such things in southern Illinois, and would say that all men are equal in northern Illinois. The two sections of the state were split between Northern and Southern sentiments. Note that Lincoln said that he was not in favor of Negro suffrage.

These words are a very different image of Lincoln than is taught to our children.

Much is made of these debates today and the words of Lincoln. The education system makes it appear that Lincoln won the debates. It must come as a surprise to some students that Lincoln did not win the debates and lost the race for the U.S. Senate in the Legislature.

They talk about the debates so that *certain passages* of Lincoln can be taught, but the result of the debates seems to elude them.

As an example — the above being just one — Lincoln opposed YA since his opponent, Douglas, was the darling of YA. Lincoln said that rather than the expansion of territory being the best means of creating heaven on earth (the policy of YA) it was instead the encouragement of "useful discoveries and invention."

Lincoln also pointed out that the expansion of territory would lead to immense power and would ultimately lead to the dream of unfettered world rule. Since this is the goal of the modern neoconservative Republicans, you can well imagine that this portion of the debates is not widely taught or known today.

Considering the policies of Lincoln that he would enforce later as president, some of his words would seem a little hypocritical.

The extreme position in the pro-slavery camp, but by no means without support, is demonstrated by the radical George Fitz-Hugh in his book, *Sociology for the South, or the Failure of Free Society*, 1854. He first advocated a system of anarchy, but then in this book he replaced that idea with the declaration that as civilization advances, liberty recedes, since "what is needed is good government and plenty of it — not liberty."

In common with socialism, he attacked the principle of free contract: A Southern plantation was an ideal type of a socialist society. Further, the feelings and interests of the masters prevent undue pressure on the laborers; they are protected from the evils of competition and are assured employment and support.

His only objection to socialism was "that it will not honestly admit that it owes its recent revival to the failure of universal liberty and is seeking to bring about slavery again in some form."

No effective combination of labor can be made, said Fitz-Hugh, until men are willing to surrender their liberty and subject themselves to a despotic head or ruler — "this is slavery, and toward this socialism is moving."

Gov. James Henry Hammond of South Carolina, in a letter to Calhoun in 1850, expressed the belief that "free government and all that sort of thing has been a fatal delusion and humbug from the time of Moses." He also alluded contemptuously to the "much-lauded but nowhere accredited dogma of Mr. Jefferson that all men are created equal." Hammond was a vociferous pro-slavery man.

As editor of *The Southern Times*, he wrote as early as 1844 that separation was inevitable. Even before, he was a nullifier in 1830 when some behind this movement were more interested in secession than using the Tenth Amendment for what it was intended: for the states to limit the federal government from doing anything unconstitutional, particularly against the states themselves.

Yet Hammond was friends with Samuel Hoar and Francis Lieber, men supposedly on the other side. Hammond was a spiritualist and thought the Scriptures a fraud, which fit very well with his sexual liaisons. He exhibited all the attributes of someone who had the same agenda as Northern conspirators, only with a Southern flair. It reminds one of assuming the leadership of both sides in order to control the debate and the ultimate outcome.

The radical pro-slavery advocates fell into the Darwinian theory of the survival of the fittest and believed that the Negro had not evolved to the level of the white man. Such were the theories later of Adolf Hitler. Communists, Nazis, and atheists — all have promoted Darwin. It is one of the building blocks of formulating a person's education for disrespect of others based on race that leads otherwise rational people into supporting totalitarianism. It is part of the process of changing society in order to change how men are ruled.

Since all Marxists profess a belief in Darwin, it is strange that people do not see through the rhetoric advocating justice for all races embodied in communist organizations' propaganda. ***How can Marxists advocate equality when they believe in a Darwinian system that says that all are not equal?*** It becomes obvious that Marxist leaders are lying about what they stand for in order to enlist the gullible, bleeding-heart activist.

The situation was volatile enough during the election of 1856, and the words of the extreme Southern leaders were used to convince Northerners over the next four years to want to split the country. Preston Brooks of South Carolina, for instance, said that if Fremont were elected, the South should "march to Washington, seize the archives and the Treasury of the Government, and leave the consequences to God."

The action of the people is in the reaction. Create a situation in the North to react the Southerner, at the same time do the same in the South to react the Northerner — the more vituperative the better.

By the election of 1860, the lines had been drawn and violence was in the air. It had grown so bad that James G. Blaine quoted himself in his book *Political Discussions*, from a speech he had given on July 4, 1860:

> We can felicitate ourselves that the strife between Mr. Douglas and Mr. Breckinridge will in all probability give the election to the Republicans … and that Abraham Lincoln, if he lives, will be the next President.

"If he lives" — a very cogent remark.

This is how far the American political scene had deteriorated due to the agitation of those who wanted to divide and conquer. The lines of division were drawn very deep between the leadership in the North and that in the South — with the average American caught in between, seemingly powerless.

William Lloyd Garrison played a dominant role in creating this condition. He was always in a leadership role in abolition. He started out as a temperance movement activist, and then was converted to abolitionism by Benjamin Lundy. He became a member of the Perfectionist communist church in the 1830s. He founded the paper *The Liberator* in January 1831, whose masthead supported a world system. He called for the disunion of the North and South as early as 1843. He publicly burned the Constitution in the streets of Boston in 1854. His associates actually said that the slaves had the right to cut the throats of their masters. His actions caused such a reaction that several states had rewards for his arrest, while the Georgia Senate tried him in absentia.

He was representative of the leadership of the abolition movement, and most abolition organizations held many, if not most of his views.

As a result of all of this rhetoric and the reaction to it, the United States became the only country to end slavery through civil war.

More Antebellum Agitation

Slavery needed to be abolished. The majority of citizens were opposed to it; however, they had a number of stumbling blocks on the road to abolition to overcome. For one, slavery was an unbroken reality in the history of man. Right or wrong, it was an institution, albeit one that Europe had not seen for many years as a widespread *race of people*. It was true that, in the modern sense, all Europeans were slaves in varying degrees to their own governments.

It was not simply that there was a certain amount of oppression in Europe, but there was indentured slavery as well. Many forget that America was settled in no small part by European indentured slaves: men and women served in that condition imposed upon them by the courts for a legal period of time due to tax or private debt until their indentured service paid for their debts. There were severe penalties for running from this servitude, just as there were for running from chattel slavery.

Indenture was also used as part of the criminal code.

Many of these indentured slaves where sent or carried to America to serve out their time. Many were offered at public auctions similar to those for Negroes who were chattel slaves. *Unconquered*, a movie made by Gary Cooper in 1947 which had the French and Indian War as a backdrop, included a main character played by Paulette Goddard who was an indentured servant. She could not be free until someone paid for her indenture and set her free or she worked out her indenture period.

Likewise, one of the movies nominated for the Academy Award as the best picture of the year in 1935, *Captain Blood*, starring Errol Flynn, was based on this servitude. This sort of history once was well known enough to be included in Hollywood drama. Today, it is not politically correct to even point it out since it would show that it was not just black Africans who were slaves.

Another feature of indenture included orphans, the children of people who could not afford to raise them, and those who needed to pay for their own passage to America. The latter would be done by parents or the persons themselves to pay for their food and passage. In our very early settlement, approximately two-thirds of American immigrants came as indentured servants, who endured this condition for several years after arriving on our shores to repay this debt. The practice of such indenturing tapered off rapidly but did last into the early 20th century.

It was started again in the late 20th century and early 21st century by underground organizations, such as the drug cartels and Russian mafia, paying people's way to the United States and then expecting a return in cash and/or services rendered within a certain time period. People from poor countries were poor themselves; they could not afford to simply buy a ticket and did not have the ability to find work right away, so this is how they could afford to come to America. They continue to contribute to the crime rate in a major way.

For those who are informed about how much it can cost to come into the U.S. by the use of "coyotes" across our southern border, one has to ask that, if the illegal immigrant can afford such a high price, why do they need to come here looking for work in the first place? The answer is that often they will pay later on the installment program through cash and services.

There have been instances where people have been held captive after crossing our border and could only gain their release by having a ransom paid, and of women who were promised one thing and found another, becoming slaves in organized prostitution rings. One only needs to search the Internet for such news stories.

Keep in mind that people came to America looking for a better life and to escape poverty. If they had a better life at home and had not suffered from poverty, or at least from being poor, they would have stayed home. The means to get here was some form of indenture to pay their passage, often including the money for their entire family.

Considering that early on the majority of white citizens (or their parents) came to America in some condition of servitude, one can understand why, when looking at it through this lens, most were not overwhelmingly concerned about chattel slavery; they and/or their antecedents had been able to work their way out of such a condition. Others, who may have been mistreated, felt otherwise.

In some cases entire communities were indentured, to the extent that they were sponsored by commercial entities who had contracts that needed repayment within a certain amount of time with interest. These entities paid for passage, supplies, and accouterments for the colonizers to sail to and settle areas determined on agreement by both parties.

If one takes into account the means by which people were afforded the opportunity to learn a trade in Europe and America in the years before the War for Independence, what we would consider today as slavery would even encompass this process. And, this was the case in any civilization on earth at the time in some variant.

Trade guilds in Europe had a period of servitude that was linked to the government and those who were called master craftsmen. In the German Confederation for instance, a person needed to obtain a passbook from the government and have a master craftsman sign on to accept him as an apprentice. It had to be co-signed by the local police office or office of the burgermeister.

Once the apprentice served a specified time under the master, usually two to four years, he then had to seek out another master in a different city, often a different state, and repeat the process. This became known as his *journey,* and this is how the term *journeyman* came into our language. It usually took four such entries in the apprentice's book before he became a master craftsman able to stake out his own business. And, he had better be on good terms and stay on good terms with his masters and governments involved or he would be out of luck. People who oppose government policies need not apply.

The system in which Benjamin Franklin learned a craft was a hybrid of the above. He was for all practical purposes an indentured servant to his brother in his shop in Boston. Franklin finally fled, ending up in Philadelphia. Pennsylvania perhaps had the most indentured servants of any colony, and Franklin was among the loudest in opposition to the system.

Life in general was not easy in Europe, where opportunities were slim. That, along with religious freedom, was one of the reasons the average person did what he could to come to America, where the boundaries either did not exist or were breaking down, particularly along the frontier as it moved irrepressibly westward — even if it meant being indentured for a time.

Even if European farmers held property, many of the children had to leave after growing up. The land would only support so many people and inheritance laws made it difficult for the female and younger male siblings. This was likewise the case for craftsmen with large families, as the trade guilds who would only allow so many apprentices into the system, since they did not want competition to drive down the price of their work or flood the market with too many craftsmen who could not find work.

Indenture was for some an investment in the future: an education, even if under the most strident of conditions. The education varied, from farming to mechanical to intellectual pursuits.

Yet we see that unions in this country have come full circle in their desire to be joined at the hip with government through such agencies as the Labor Department and the National Labor Relations Board. The average union member does not see how he can once again be controlled by government through such agencies. As long as these agencies appear to be pro-union, their power will be upheld by union leaders and politicians. At some point, once government achieves enough power, it will be used against all labor — union or not. This is the historical reality.

This was one of the methods that the Nazis used in Germany to come to power: organizing within the unions and gaining more and more adherents. The Nazis were just as active in the unions as any other entity, such as the communists, if not more so. It was called, after all, the German *Workers* National Socialist Party (Nationalsozialistische Deutsche Arbeiterpartei — or NSDAP). It is rarely spoken of, for if it were well known and understood by modern Americans, it would mitigate against the rise of union power linked to government here.

Likewise, the full name of the Nazis is rarely, if ever used because it in itself delineates the type of government that it was: socialist, albeit an altered form to be able to rise to power to suit the country and times. The mass media with a socialist bent does not want the people to really understand what Nazism was — it is too close to what is going on today.

The process of accumulating power seems to help the worker — until it is too late and he becomes a slave to the government. Most union leaders are socialists, but not all. Socialist union leaders work to bring about an all-powerful government which in the long run will be detrimental to the worker, *and they know it*.

The fact that teachers by and large are unionized weighs in heavily toward the teaching of unionism in public schools and the steady erosion of true history relative to unions, both good and bad.

The reader is encouraged to find a retail newspaper outlet in a major city that carries a wide variety of national and international papers, including socialist publications. Particularly in *special editions* celebrating some anniversary or personage in socialist and communist organs, the open support of unions for these publications by placing ads in the papers helping the party meet the expense of publication is evident. Here is another case of the misuse of union dues. You will be startled by the number of unions and who they are.

The attitude toward slavery in general was tough to overcome, but great intellectual strides had been made from the mid-1700s onward. In the United States it should have been simply a matter of working through the transition; after all, England had done it. However this was not going to be allowed by those who wanted to destroy the American system. Keep in mind that while this transition was going on in the United States, slavery was a more universal practice than most realize today. Just about every Western Hemisphere country (but Canada) used slaves in 1860.

The abolition movement was used by its leaders to divide the country more than to abolish slavery, since they were also involved in socialism, anti-property rights, and anti-Christian ideas. The abolitionist movement was international in scope, and some were even involved in terrorism.

The battle for abolition was actually led by those who wanted to break down the old social order, particularly to eliminate the individual prerogative for one to decide what he wanted in life, and instead tie it to the state. This was done by including in the battle a number of issues that had little to do with slavery.

Good people would fight abolition, not because of the issue of slavery but because they could not abide the attacks by abolitionists on property in general, did not want socialism, and found attacks on the Constitution and Christianity abhorrent. This then was made to look as if they were for slavery when they were not. This is what caused the martyrdom of Lovejoy, which was then used to silence opposition to the militant abolitionists in the North.

And, the inclusion of these issues in the fight against abolition guaranteed that abolition would fail to be implemented in a timely fashion and/or as a peaceful movement. Northern states had been abolishing slavery, but the more the abolitionists gained a toe hold and influence in the North rather than the South, the less likely it became that slavery would be abolished throughout the land, because of the reaction against the movement and what it stood for.

It developed sectionalism beyond what it was, and it became a "us vs. them" situation all over again.

The pushing of abolition rather than the use of colonization or some other less radical solution (at the time) was used to split churches in two, North and South, particularly the Presbyterians, Methodists, and Baptists.

In 1834, Rev. La Roy Sutherland published an *Appeal on the Subject of Slavery*. In 1836, he started *Zion's Watchman*, an anti-slavery journal, in New York. In 1842, he and Orange Scott of the Massachusetts Abolition Society helped organize the battle that split the Methodist Church into Northern and Southern branches. Sutherland finally went into spiritualism and died an atheist. It is not impossible to believe that the end result of splitting up the church was the aim all along.

There was more behind the issue than met the eye at first. One of the first things that anti-God people do is create splits within churches, using any issue at hand. Dividing the children of God is necessary to defeat them. A house divided against itself cannot stand.

Similar situations happened in other large mainstream churches prior to the war. The mainstream Christian churches suffered as a result of the infighting and lost much of their evangelicalism due to the concentration on the issue of slavery by some within their ranks. It set the stage for war in that the Christian spirit of brotherhood was broken. There are those who claim these churches never regained the evangelical fervor and became more concerned about the social gospel, this condition lasting well beyond the Civil War into modern times.

This process began with a problem that needed addressing, but was turned into a means to break down the social order by the misuse of the issue. The socialist agenda was piggybacked on the issue of slavery. If one therefore opposed the socialist agenda, he was made to look pro-slavery rather than against the socialist agenda. This point may seem redundant, but it must be driven home since the same tactics remain at play in modern issues.

The same occurred during the civil rights movement of the 1960s and 1970s. Many people opposed the socialist agenda hidden within the civil rights movement and the communists involved, and were made out to be racists as a result. Subsequently, many of the communist leaders went on to be honored with streets, buildings, and schools named after them, and pointing out their communist background prompted charges of racism by the media.

The charge of racism has long been used to counter accurate criticism of certain movements, starting with abolition and continuing through a variety of issues into modern times. If someone who is of any color is criticized due to his socialist stance, the counter-charge is that the attack is due to open or latent racism, not the actual issue at hand. It is amazing how many good people will recoil from such criticism and cease their active opposition to socialism as a result. They can't stand the heat in the kitchen.

The enemies of our country and way of life will never allow a comfort zone for their enemies. Anyone who opposes them must realize that and accept it. By so doing, they will be less prone to suffer the dire consequences to them and their children by not getting involved and losing to the Conspiracy.

A little discomfort now is better than standing in line for your gruel at a "processing center" — provided they let you get that far.

Let us make the point here that once communists come to power and consolidate that power, they started a systematic elimination of those who stand in their way, do not conform, or simply are useless eaters. Useless eaters include, for instance, salesmen (there is no surplus to sell, only rationing of the economy), lawyers (the system becomes one of arrest and disappearance, not a day in court), teachers who are honest (they cannot allow students to hear the truth), and a whole army of people who used to work in stores selling the abundance of goods and services that no longer exist under a communist system.

Too many people find out too late that it is not simply those who opposed communism who are eliminated. In Cambodia's Killing Fields 40 years ago, they eliminated entire cities, emptying them by marching them out to the country and slaughtering them by the millions. Elsewhere in Cambodia, one criterion they used was any young child who wore glasses — he obviously could read.

Even sound, solid conservatives in the 21st century have fallen for the idea that some communist leaders of the 20th century were in fact great humanitarians, due to the propaganda lying about their true involvement and motivation.

The most blatant modern example of this twisting of the truth was Nelson Mandela of South Africa. There is no question that Mandela was imprisoned as a communist terrorist, and he posed on many occasions giving the communist salute under the hammer and sickle at South African Communist Party conventions after he came to power in South Africa. Yet the average American believes something else, and being critical of Mandela makes one look like a racist, not someone concerned about communism. Mandela's image was a very well-crafted marketing campaign by the communist influence within the international media.

Once Mandela died, the Central Committee of the South African Communist Party admitted that Mandela remained a communist and on their Central Committee all the while he was the ruler of South Africa and subsequently. It was no longer necessary to continue the façade, but the propaganda was so widely believed and ingrained into the American psyche that even American conservatives ignored the revelation. Then again, it was extremely rare that the Central Committee's revelation was carried in any mainstream media.

The myth of Mandela continued after his death with the re-publication of a book about Mandela, *Long Walk to Freedom*, which was purged of his communist and terrorist record. The author, Richard Stengel, was a *Time* magazine journalist who became an undersecretary for public diplomacy in the Obama administration.

And, there were other communists of the same ilk in the United States.

Bayard Rustin was a member of the Communist Party, first joining the Young Communist League. He remained in the communist movement for a few years as an adult, then moved over into the Socialist Party, ultimately becoming its chairman. His actions seemed to support all of his communist training, even so. He was an open homosexual and served 60 days in jail for participating in a sex act in a car on the streets of Anaheim, California. Modern articles about him make it look as if he was discriminated against due to his color and his sexual preference.

Rustin was the chief organizer of the 1963 civil rights march on Washington, and he worked very closely with Martin Luther King. In 2013, President Obama awarded him the Freedom Medal posthumously.

In addition to the communist influence in the abolition movement, there were many actions, events, and leaders that also demonstrated the influence of the British in the issue of American slavery. Keep in mind that British slavery had already been abolished, and their anti-slavery organizations were aimed at the American institution more than those of other Western Hemisphere countries.

Wendell Phillips, a noted abolitionist, traveled to England for the World Anti-Slavery Convention in London in June of 1840, held in the Freemason's Hall. He was given letters of introduction to several members of the English nobility, with whom he met. He formed a friendship with George Thompson, a Chartist abolitionist and member of Parliament. He formed a great friendship with Daniel O'Connell, the Irish liberator. O'Connell was associated with the United Irishmen, but was more of a moderate. By 1847, Young Ireland had broken with O'Connell.

One reads about letters of introduction used in such cases, but the historians rarely, if ever, divulge who wrote them. In other words, who was working with men like Phillips who had enough influence and contacts in England, in this case, to be able to open doors for him?

The convention, dominated by the British and Foreign Anti-Slavery Society (B & FASS), was *aimed at American slavery*. Since the leaders of the radical abolitionists went to this convention, it was just another indication to the man on the street that the abolition movement was probably an English-dominated initiative. The B & FASS was founded by Joseph Sturge, a Chartist who helped found the Peace Society in England. He visited the U.S. with Whittier to look at American slavery, and this was yet again another indication to many people of English interference in American politics.

As we reiterate this point, keep in mind the mind-set of the average American due to the general politics surrounding British-American relations and the many times that we almost got into a war with England over the four decades prior to the Civil War. The interference smacked of treason to many. It lessened the probability of many Americans listening to the abolitionists, even if they agreed with them. As a result, it widened the gap between both sides of the issue rather than serving as a platform for moderation. Astute abolitionists would have understood that, yet they did nothing about it. Their motives were different than most realized.

Earlier, President Andrew Jackson, a former slave-trader, denounced men such as George Thompson in the course of his Seventh Annual Message to Congress, December 7, 1835:

> It is fortunate for the country that the good sense, the generous feeling, and the deep-rooted attachment of the people of the non-slaveholding States to the Union and to their fellow-citizens of the same blood in the South have given so strong and impressive a tone to the sentiments entertained against the proceedings of the misguided persons who have engaged in these unconstitutional and wicked attempts, and especially against the emissaries from foreign parts who have dared to interfere in this matter....

As we have stated before, not all those who were changing America agreed. In this case, the Southerner Jackson was a slave trader, and while he had many of the same designs on the American system, he objected to abolition and held obvious prejudices. The Conspiracy works both sides in order to confuse the people and emerges victorious no matter who wins. And, very few abolitionist leaders really felt that the Negro was his equal.

Two other delegates to London were William Lloyd Garrison and William Adams, professor of Oriental languages at Harvard. Garrison refused to take the floor in protest, however, since women — specifically the American delegates Mrs. H. G. Chapman and Lucretia Mott — were denied seats. You see, Negroes were to be free, but women were not equal. In reality the Negroes would not be equal either; abolition was not a legitimate cause for many of the leaders of the anti-slavery movement.

The American women's suffrage movement can be understood to have started at this anti-slavery convention in London, as a backlash to this policy.

It is said that this experience of Mott caused her to become even more involved in activism as a result.

She went on to help found the Universal Peace Union in 1866. The Peace Union grew out of the reaction against the compromising tactics of the American Peace Society during the Civil War. It ultimately grew to tens of thousands of members, but started with Joshua P. Blanshard, Adin Ballou, Henry C. Wright, Alfred H. Love, and Mott. Love's mentor was William Lloyd Garrison. Blanshard had helped found the Massachusetts Peace Society with William Allen, the president of Bowdoin College; the governor, William Phillips; Abiel Holmes, the father of Oliver Wendell Holmes; and William Ellery Channing.

What needs to be understood is that the peace movement in its early years was always aimed at the American people more than the government. By that we mean that as a government of the people, the people would ultimately come under the edicts of an international "peace" body through its control over their own government. It would be true that the government would change as a result, but the net effect would be more controls on the people by means of coming under international controls that would abrogate certain aspects of the Constitution, if not all of it.

After all, the primary purpose of the Constitution is to protect and preserve the independence of the American people. This primary aspect is lost on most Americans since the Constitution is no longer taught well in the public schools. We cannot even have a constitution as we know it if we are not independent enough to make our own decisions, particularly as to when we go to war.

In any case, such an initiative would diminish the independence of a free state relative to its international involvement and any mandated changes in the legislative structure.

It means little if an international body places its jurisdiction over a totalitarian state as far as its people are concerned — they do not run the government in any event.

However, if a free society forms or runs the government, the controls from an international body are placed on the free people. They cannot be truly independent and free if they have to adhere to an international criminal court or international parliament. In the name of peace, they may not be allowed to defend themselves or their country due to the restrictions placed on them by the international body. The right to life includes the right of self-defense.

A modern example would be the initiative of the United Nations to ban all firearms from being held by private citizens, only allowing governments and their armies and police to be armed. This initiative is promoted under the banner of peace and fighting crime, terrorism, and drug trafficking. But, the average citizen is not engaged in any of these illegal enterprises and must have the means to defend himself, his family, his property — and, his country.

A man who is deprived of his individual ability to defend hearth and home is not truly free.

The right to life is a God-given right. The right to defend one's life is likewise given by God. No one should be deprived at any time or level of the ability to defend himself, or those he is responsible for, by a government of any size, shape, or form.

Today, the United Nations wants an international "peace keeping" force while at the same time disarming all citizens of gun ownership except in the strictest of cases. Gun "ownership" in these cases seems to be limited to citizens belonging to the right political party and high enough in the party structure, similar to what existed (and exists) in Nazi and communist governments. Totalitarian states always disarm the general population and arm their trusted cadres. UN occupation armies have always followed this example.

It is not unusual for UN armies, or armies working under resolutions for war, such as the U.S. armed forces, to go door to door to disarm the people. It is always done with the excuse that terrorism can only be stopped by such a procedure. What it really does is deprive the citizens of their right to defend themselves from terrorists; thereby they are intimidated by the terrorists and do their bidding.

The idea that only party or government officials will have guns when the people do not *can* happen here. The beginning of the type of thinking that leads to this end exists around the country. For instance, the *Idaho Statesman* for March 18, 2015 said this about a bill before the Idaho Legislature regarding concealed weapons permits:

> State law today exempts "officials of a county, city, state of Idaho," and U.S. officials and all publicly elected officials from the requirement to have a permit to carry a concealed weapon.

In other words, anyone who works for the government is fine, but the law-abiding citizens need government permission. The end result down this path is the disarmament of the citizen and his ability to defend himself from all dangers.

Individual terrorists, just as criminals, will find a way to arm themselves. The decent, law-abiding individual cannot, and will become only a pawn in the game of who will rule. However, as we have said, organized terrorism has an arms supplier. They do not decide one day to be a terrorist and say to themselves, "Let's see, where do I get an automatic weapon and some C-4?"

After all, if they have never handled a gun or explosives before, do-it-yourself cannot be the best method of learning. In a controlled environment, someone supplies and trains them in how to use them.

On a larger scale, forcing a free society into an international peace organization, such as the UN, means that the free citizens lose their independence to defend themselves at *their* will and become beholden to whoever controls the peace organization. It is a step toward total internationalism, a government so removed from the people that it can never serve the people.

The history of those who have formed peace organizations is that of promoting whatever fit their purposes: peace or war. The consistency in these two opposites is that whatever it takes to establish the New World Order (NWO) is what will be done. It is very rare that someone who is not an advocate of a world government forms a peace or anti-war organization.

The United Nations today has waged more wars than any country known to man since its founding, yet it is supposedly a peace organization. Regrettably, the American people are generally ignorant of this fact because not all combat that UN troops have been and are engaged in gets reported in the media. It is rare that this is not the case somewhere in Africa at any given time. This is coupled with decades-long "peace keeping" initiatives in divided countries, and buffer zones that could now be called permanent in areas such as Gaza and other disputed territories.

Part of the unreported aspect of these deployments under the UN is the effect of UN troops on the population; this calls into question what is better, the UN troops or the problem that existed that warranted their presence in the first place. UN troops are notorious for crimes against citizens in countries around the world.

The leadership of the American Peace Society had no problem endorsing the Civil War, since it fit the parameters of establishing a world order in the long run. Francis Wayland, former president of the Peace Society, always condemned the recourse of war in the settling of disputes, *except for the Civil War*, and wrote to a friend in 1861 favoring it.

As a more modern example, it was discovered by the Reese Committee in Congress that during World War I the Carnegie Endowment for International Peace sent a message to President Wilson cautioning him against an early conclusion to the war. This was done since a more prolonged conflict was necessary for the goals they had of establishing an international peace organization, among other things.

The hope was that a *prolonged* revulsion against the carnage would lead to this end. This turned out to be the League of Nations, the precursor to the UN.

The people had to be prepared to accept another layer of government because of their abhorrence to war and the type of conflict war had become, killing millions. As it turned out, the American people were still not ready and the Senate refused to ratify membership in the League of Nations.

The minutes of the Carnegie Endowment showed that from their beginning in 1908, they concluded that there was no better means of altering the life of a nation than by the use of war as a catalyst. They also wanted to know how to involve the United States in a war. They concluded that as part of this process they must take over and manage the State Department, and that could only be accomplished by taking over the diplomatic service.

After World War I, they realized that they needed to change the manner in which history was taught in the schools — not just taking over the publishing arms, but the entire scope of teaching history across the country. They contacted the Rockefeller Foundation and agreed to split the responsibility for so doing between the domestic and international history, with the Carnegie group assuming the task for international history.

It is enough to remember that Alger Hiss, the Soviet communist agent who helped found the UN, was the head of the Carnegie Endowment after World War II.

Another so-called peace organization was international in scope, and its American wing was headed by Skull and Bones men and others who would later found the American Civil Liberties Union: the League to Enforce Peace. The American leader was the former President William Howard Taft, the son of the founder of the Order and a member himself. The American section carried on its American Provisional Committee a half-American youth, an author by the name of Winston Churchill. Its mission would be to enforce peace by waging war on those who wage war. In the end, it only served as a booster for the idea of a League of Nations.

These are easily documentable facts, and we bring them to you to show that the agenda of the Conspiracy did not change over the decades.

The issue of women's rights in the abolition movement eventually split the Anti-Slavery Society. Garrison retained the majority but lost the organization's organ, *The Liberator*, in the process. Both he and Phillips were anti-constitutionalists.

The anti-slavery movement often took an anti-God bent. In the book *Reflections of Wendell Phillips* by Franklin B. Sanborn, Emerson is quoted as saying:

> If the Creator of the negro has given him up to stand as a victim of the white man beside him, to stoop under his pack and to bleed under his whip — if that be the doctrine, then I say, "If He had given up his cause, then He has also given up mine, who feel his wrong and ours, who in our hearts must curse the Creator who had undone him."

Sanborn was born into a radical family and named Franklin Benjamin Sanborn as an inversion to Benjamin Franklin. He was close to John Brown and raised money for Brown because he knew Brown was ready for revolution and disunion.

He advocated a peaceful solution to the situation in Kansas during the problems there before the war. After a peaceful resolution was reached, however, his opinion was that "the officers must be immediately seized and hung — nothing milder will serve the purpose." In other words, feign conciliation and moderation, and use the opportunity to kill the leaders of the other side.

The communists of the 20th century must have read his words since they used this tactic several times.

He, along with Higginson, would flee the country into Canada to avoid prosecution in the Harper's Ferry affair. He urged violence and murder all along in private. Later in life he was active in women's rights, prohibition, and unionism. He edited the *Springfield Republican* during the war.

In November 1840, after the World Anti-Slavery Convention, a conclave was held for Universal Reform called the Chardon Street Convention. The list of names of those in attendance is quite revealing as to their depth of influence: Samuel Osgood, William Lloyd Garrison, George Ripley, Christopher Pearce Cranch, A. B. Alcott, Joshua V. Hines, Cyrus M. Burleigh, Edmund Quincy, Theodore Parker, Robert F. Wallcut, Henry C. Wright, James Russell Lowell, Ralph Waldo Emerson, John Pierpont, Abbey Kelley Foster, Thomas Davis, Oliver Johnson, Francis Jackson, Luther Lee, William Channing, and so many more. To describe the influence of these gentlemen as ministers, publicists, and activists would take several pages.

Part of the reform was the opposition to Sabbath laws, another step away from Christian and Jewish observances. However, what became known as Blue Laws (the banning of Sunday activity in certain instances, such as liquor sales) remained across America well into the 20th century in spite of the movement to do away with them. These observances seem silly to most today, but it was indicative of a morally centered society to reflect on the Creator rather than self on the Sabbath.

While the "call" for the convention was published in several newspapers and not signed by Garrison, it was still believed that he was the man behind the entire affair. It was referred to as an infidel convention, as participants gathered from different states to call into question the validity of the Sabbath, the church, and the ministry. Many felt it meant the decline of the influence of Garrison, since he identified himself with Perfectionists and Transcendentalists — all in harmonious effort against the Bible as the standard faith.

Little did the people in opposition to what was going on fathom America's ignorance as to what was really happening, for Garrison remained a viable influence for decades because of the organization he and his followers had built up. Organization will trump disorganization.

Abbey Kelley Foster, who attended the conclave for Universal Reform, was a major fundraiser for the abolitionist movement. She was very radical and believed that the whole nature of society had to be changed in order to eliminate slavery. In other words, the reverse was the real end: use the issue of slavery to overturn all of society — just as the Illuminati and the communists advocated.

The public pronouncements of both Garrison and Phillips against the churches and the Constitution created subversion. Phillips became a disunionist who would not even vote. He would not practice law because it required that he swear an oath to the Constitution. To him, it became a "covenant with death and an agreement with hell." At least he was honest. Today many take the oath and then ignore the Constitution.

In 1839, the British and American Anti-Slavery Society was organized by the Englishman Joseph Sturge of the Society of Friends. Sturge was a Chartist and also a founder of the Peace Society in England. The American unit (AASS) had been established in 1833 and financed primarily by the Tappan brothers, wealthy industrialists. Some of the money that flowed through the Tappans was from England.

It is very telling that the British organizations and agents for the anti-slavery movement were not engaged in trying to convince Americans to emulate the British method of eliminating slavery, to follow their example to a peaceful solution.

Free speech and the press were victims of the abolitionist movement. There was little in the South on this subject. These could be very dangerous in the North, but not because of the issue per se. There were several occasions when crowds destroyed anti-slavery presses and beat up editors (before the Lovejoy martyrdom) because of their anti-American attitudes and their attack on property rights and the Constitution.

Martyrs are an important part of the communist agenda. Just as with communists killing their own in New York to gain sympathy for their Party, martyrs have played a role in the movement in America well into the 20th century. In nearly all incidences of assassination of prominent men, the people who carried out the deeds had ties to communism in some manner, even when the violence was perpetrated against their own minions.[47]

The use of martyrs could also be employed in reverse: kill the enemies of the communists in such a manner as to react people into doing things against the communists that involve the people or government in illegal or unconstitutional acts. An outraged people will do just about anything — or ask the government to do just about anything — to bring justice or vengeance on the perpetrators. By this tactic, the government will be "persuaded" to do something unconstitutional and set a precedent that will come back to haunt a free society later.

This would seem to be counterproductive to the communist. However, we have to remember that the leaders look upon their minions as expendable for the greater goal of accumulating power into the state and changing society in general. In other words, the ends justify the means.

The same tactic is in use today by so-called terrorist groups against innocent people to react the American people into further foreign entanglements in the name of justice, or into domestic controls in the name of security. These terrorist groups serve a master as yet invisible to the American people; there is a coordinated purpose to their actions.

At home, the tactic is used when people such as the police are gunned down. The backlash against such a crime will almost always create a condition where the conservative population will demand more law and order. This is usually furnished by building up the law enforcement entities into larger units and requiring more strident enforcement. It invariably creates a "them vs. us" mentality, further exacerbating the problem of local police service.

The mere fact that police units are beefed up will cause the inevitable corruption of the basic law by the size of the force. It goes to the adage of Lord Acton: Power corrupts, and absolute power corrupts absolutely. The larger the government unit, regardless of what it is, the greater corruption, and it will do all that it can to grow even more and gain more responsibility and authority.

All of this plays into the hands of the communist movement whose desire is to change society and grow draconian government, which they plan to ultimately control.

An armed citizenry does not require large law-enforcement organizations.

There was an abolitionist "come-outer" movement led by Phillips, who would become AASS president, and Quincy which ultimately prevailed within the Anti-Slavery Societies. One by one, AASS chapters swung into line. Come-outers believed that "as the Constitution is pro-slavery, therefore its destruction and the Union along with it is desired": In other words, to "come out" of the union.

They did not advocate amending the Constitution as much as they wanted to do away with the law altogether. If they had a grievance against slavery, one would think that they would have wanted to just amend that out of the Constitution. Instead, an amendment banning slavery was done after the Civil War *after they had done all they could at the time to use the issue to change the old social order.*

The journals of the Anti-Slavery Societies in Boston and New York displayed headlines with the motto: "No Union with Slave-holders."

---

47   See Chapter 14.

Stephen S. Foster, a Garrisonian, wrote a pamphlet titled, "Revolution the Only Remedy for Slavery." In the North disunion became more and more a program connected to abolitionists.

Once the radicals held sway in the administration and Congress, abolitionists then swung over to become ardent unionists, supporting what they now controlled, particularly after the war started.

At one time, the AASS had 70 agents on their payroll traveling the country establishing their organization. This number dwindled as the Tappans lost a great deal of their wealth in 1836. As with most organizations, membership dues and even many small donations never keep a grassroots group going; it is the major donors that keep any sizable group afloat. It was the same with the AASS.

The ostensive purpose of most of the agents was to evangelize for Christ, but the real purpose was to propagate the AASS. In other words, they used the cloth to pose as missionaries but in reality were propagating the Anti-Slavery Society under the radicals' leadership, just as the Carbonari agents who posed as Bible Society missionaries were actually promoting the Conspiracy's agenda.

One of the initial aims of the AASS was the neutralization of the American Colonization Society, which also stood for the end of slavery but wanted to establish new settlements, usually outside of the United States and run by the ex-slaves. The ineffectiveness of the Colonization Society was sped up on the inside of the organization by individuals who were Colonization members but at the same time were members of the AASS. They were not interested in allowing any plan to exist that could prevent their goal of destroying the American system and possibly derail their agenda, even if it was a plan designed to solve their supposed concerns.

The AASS leadership was primarily a combination of ministers, writers, and Garrisonians. *Amongst the leadership*, the plan was never to solve the problem but to use the problem to promote solutions that led to establishing the Conspiracy's agenda.

The people within the AASS chapters who did not agree with Garrison's leadership generally went into the Liberty Party. A founder of and candidate for the Liberty Party for president in 1840 was James Gillespie Birney, who was married to the sister of the wife of Gerrit Smith, one of the Secret Six who aided John Brown in his raid on Harper's Ferry.

In the long run, the Liberty Party drew people out of the anti-slavery movement into political action. This resulted in the focus of the movement becoming divided, with some wanting to educate and activate, and others wanting to simply work with political means to achieve their objectives. This lack of focus hurt the movement if the real desire was to solve the problem.

Many in the anti-slavery movement sank into disbelief after starting from a position of orthodox Christianity. While Phillips did not quit his faith, he disregarded the Constitution and left the clergy for a time, and his path was a bit crooked. He apparently eschewed secret societies as well.

While he professed to remain in his faith, he tried Mesmerism on his wife as a medical cure. Mesmerism was a part of spiritualism at the time.

There was a great deal of agitation over such things as the admission of Texas to the Union as a slave state, the return of runaway slaves, etc. On one occasion a runaway slave was returned from Massachusetts. Faneuil Hall in Boston was filled by abolitionists in protest. John Q. Adams presided, Dr. Samuel G. Howe presented the facts, and John A. Andrew, later governor, presented the resolutions. Charles Sumner spoke, as did Phillips. The slave had been returned as a result of the law, and Daniel Webster was horrified at the disobedience to the law and objected strongly to Phillips on disunion:

"You prate of disunion, do you not know that disunion is Revolution?" Phillips: "Yes, we know it, and we are for revolution — a revolution in the character of the American Constitution."

— *Wendell Phillips: The Agitator*

Amazing how the Constitution can suddenly be invoked by anti-constitutionalists when required to excuse revolution.

Lending weight to the argument that the British had undue influence on the anti-slavery movement as a means of weakening America to their advantage, Lewis Tappan in the spring of 1843 attended the second World Anti-Slavery Convention in London. At the time, *he attempted to influence British statesmen to help keep the slave country Texas out of the union as a state*. Tappan met with the prime minister and foreign secretary and urged them to give a loan to Texas to enable the Texas Republic to put its finances on an independent footing and not have to enter the union to secure its future.

This was approximately a year before we almost went to war with England over the Pacific Northwest, and the agitation toward such an end was already in play. Tappan's initiative to use the English in an America squabble looked like treason to many.

The Tappan brothers had a history of supporting William L. Garrison, but finally split with him over his attacks on Christianity in general. Lewis Tappan was opposed to Presbyterianism, but promoted Congregationalism.

The definition of Christianity for many is what "I believe, not what you believe." It is no wonder that Christians cannot agree long enough to save their own hides from the anti-God movement. In this case, Tappan's attitude worked against the anti-God movement.

The worst thing a soldier can do is to ask the man in the foxhole next to him what church he belongs to and decide whether or not he will stay in the foxhole with him to fight the enemy. Those sorts of arguments can come into play after the enemy is defeated. One need not give up or compromise his faith, only work with others for the good of all, just as the Founders of our nation had done.

This should be the same attitude of those in the "trenches" today who are fighting to preserve our American system.

The history books make it appear that the South was the only one that wanted disunion. This, as you can see, is not true. In January 1857, a Disunion Convention was held in Worcester, Massachusetts. Attendants included T. W. Higginson, Wendell Phillips, William Lloyd Garrison, E. M. Hosmer, Stephen Foster, Samuel J. May, Jr., and John Brown, with Francis W. Bird as the president of the convention.

The aim was to discuss the steps necessary to dissolve the union. What it really did was to furnish yet more proof to Southern sensibilities that abolitionists were out to destroy America — at the minimum it supplied evidence that certain elements in the North would just as soon have the South out of the United States.

James Redpath covered it for the *New York Tribune*. Greeley felt that the South had the right to secede. He later recanted, but only after he had helped encourage disunion.

Theodore Parker seemed to stand in the middle between union and disunion. However, he said, "I used to think this terrible question of Freedom and Slavery would be settled without bloodshed; I believe it now no longer."

Later in the year, the AASS convention was held in New York. At this meeting, Rev. Andrew T. Foss of New Hampshire said,

> There never was an hour when this blasphemous and infamous government should be made, and now the hour was to be prayed for when that disgrace to humanity should be dashed to pieces forever.

This quote comes from the *Democratic Speaker's Handbook,* published for use in the first election after the Civil War to promote votes for Democrats by quoting extreme remarks by Republicans. While one may disagree with certain Democrat political positions, the book was a good synopsis of the violation of the Constitution by the federal government under the Radicals after the war, the spirit of the Declaration of Independence, the surrender terms of Robert E. Lee and other Confederate generals, and the war by the Radicals on Jews and Catholics — as well as the pre-war statements by Radicals in the North who wanted disunion and/or war before secession. Although this is the only quote from the book used herein, it nonetheless is indicative of some of the other quotes used from a variety of different sources.

Francis Bird, the president of the Disunion Convention, was the leader of a discussion group called the Bird Club. By 1860, it had 30 to 40 members. Usually Bird presided; otherwise, it was George L. Stearns. Members included William S. Robinson; Elizur Wright, who employed Charles Dana before Greeley; Henry L. Pierce; Dr. S. G. Howe, Frank B. Sanborn, and Stearns, three of the Secret Six; Senators Henry Wilson, who later served as vice president, and Sumner, who had foreknowledge of Harper's Ferry and would later join the First International; and Gov. John Andrews, who helped meet the defense of John Brown.

This represented a considerable amount of influence among men of letters and politics, led by a disunionist and attended by friends of John Brown and socialism. *Between this discussion group and the interlocking reading societies and forums*, it had all the appearance of the style of networking outlined by Mirabeau and Weishaupt.

Even Edwin Stanton, later to manipulate himself into the War Department under Lincoln, was for disunion while serving as the attorney general under Buchanan. Once the deed had been done, he became a Union man.

Garrison's paper, *Liberator*, had on its masthead in 1842, "A repeal of the Union between Northern Liberty and Southern slavery is essential to the abolition of the one and the preservation of the other."

The masthead that was originally on the paper was far more revealing when discussing the *origins* of his movement:

Our Country is the World — Our Countrymen are Mankind

Again, the obvious goal of one world and a universal parliament: the goal of the Illuminati. The slogan soon disappeared, since it told too much of the story as to Garrison and Company's motivation.

One of the tools used to create widespread agitation was Hinton Helper's book, *Impending Crises*, commonly referred to as *Helper's Book*. It openly advocated class war between rich and poor Southerners. It was endorsed by the leader of the Republican Party and 68 Republican members of Congress.

The book stated such things as: "Against slaveholders as a body we wage an exterminating war." "Do not reserve the strength of your arms until you are powerless to strike." "We contend that slaveholders are more criminal than common murderers." "The Negroes, nine cases out of ten, would be delighted at the opportunity to cut their masters' throats."

Helper's Book did less to enlist the North into anti-slavery (even though Wide Awakes distributed 100,000 copies, mostly to their own members) as it did to help react Southerners into secession. *The action is in the reaction*. With *Helper's Book* Southern leaders were able to demonstrate to the people of the South that the Northern leaders were so bad that the South must go it alone.

Lincoln appointed Helper as consul in Buenos Aires, and he served there from 1861 to 1866. *After the war*, Helper became a white supremacist. He wanted to build a railway from the Bering Sea to the Strait of Magellan to help populate white instead of black and brown races in the Western Hemisphere. This was essentially the platform of YA. He eventually committed suicide. It is amazing how key agitators changed their positions as the need to move the Conspiracy's agenda forward would segue onto different paths.

Seward gave *Helper's Book* his special endorsement, calling it a work of great merit. Giddings, of Ohio, said, "I look forward to the day when I shall see a servile insurrection in the South. When the black men, supplied with bayonets, shall wage a war of extermination against the whites ... " Giddings as a member of the Congress entered a petition to dissolve the union, yet he declined to attend the January 1857 Disunion Convention and disapproved of it. Giddings was a Perfectionist and spiritualist.

If the intent was to create the conditions for a war, and looking at the evidence who can doubt it, the abolitionists could not have done more by writing verses against the flag of the United States. These were circulated about the time of the founding of the Republican Party in 1854, first appearing in the *New York Tribune*:

> All hail the flaunting lie
> > The stars grow pale and dim,
> The stripes are bloody scars —
> > A lie the vaunting hymn.
>
> Tear down the flaunting lie,
> > Half-mast the starry flag,
> Insult no sunny sky
> > With hate's polluted rag.
>
> — *The Old Guard*, and *The American Quarterly Church Review*

You can well imagine the concern on the part of Southerners. Things such as these verses, the speeches of leading Republicans and abolitionists, radically-run Northern newspapers that circulated in the millions, and *Helper's Book* were used by Southern conspirators to move disunion forward in the South. The action is in the reaction.

During the election of 1860, the speakers enlisted for the Republican Party and Lincoln's candidacy helped split the sentiment between the South and the North by their rhetoric and actions. Carl Schurz, as a member of the Republican National Committee, had as his responsibility enlisting foreign-born speakers aimed at gathering votes among their former countrymen. He had no difficulty in finding radical 48ers as speakers who advocated a socialist revolution aimed at the Southern population by first electing Lincoln.

The lesson for Southerners of John Brown's campaign and the support he sustained among the leaders of the Republican Party was that he had no problem with slaughtering people, whether they were slave owners or not. You can well imagine the horror that was felt in the South about those who supported Brown and who served as speakers for the Party that came to power advocating the destruction of the South.

Notable socialists such as Parke Godwin were also speakers for the Republican Party during the election of 1860. In and around New York City, the communist and secret-society leadership was very active in the Republican campaign, organizing and speaking.

It was not simply that the federal government was going to be occupied by a radical element. The South also looked at the Northern states that were filling their state executives with radicals, such as Massachusetts and Ohio. John Andrews became the governor of Massachusetts. Following the attack and arrest of Brown at Harper's Ferry, Andrews raised funds for his defense.

Salmon Chase became governor of Ohio. He had the reputation as being the candidate of choice for the presidency by radical elements in the North.

Both of these men identified with the radical element until the end of the war. And, several other states such as Wisconsin, Indiana, etc. had similar men in power, either in the governor's mansion or within the legislatures. Communists within the legislatures or representing congressional districts were not rare.

With Northern state governments becoming more radical, the South saw that as just another indication that the only solution appeared to be secession.

Some historians make the point that the refugees from the revolutions of 1848-1849 who came to the United States brought with them a world view unknown in America. As we have seen, this is not true; this view was already here, implanted by Illuminism from Revolutionary France and German higher education in American students. Americans were very much involved in promoting communism and a world parliament long before the communist refugees landed on our shores.

It is true that from time to time variants of the means to reach the goal of a New World Order under socialism were inoculated into America from European radical leaders, each one believing he had the best philosophy and organizing powers to reach the goal. But the basis for this thought had been here from the beginning.

Let us not forget that the first English colony in Massachusetts tried socialism at the onset and almost perished as a result. The same was true in Virginia.

The truly *political* refugees from the 1848 revolutions were probably fewer than 25,000, but their influence was disproportionate to their number due to their organizing capabilities, coupled with the press they either controlled or affected while adding their influence to the Conspiracy's minions who were already here. Here we are talking about revolutionaries who carried some responsibility for and led revolutionary activities in their homeland.

In the January 1882 "Preface" to that year's Russian edition of *The Communist Manifesto,* Marx and Engels mention the radical immigration to the U.S. as: " … when the United States absorbed the surplus proletarian forces of Europe through immigration." They were basically saying that all but the main cadres had left Europe for America.

Since Marx had moved the headquarters of the IWA to the United States, a great number of the cadre had to be here as well. Also, in the 1882 Russian edition "Preface," Marx and Engels said they felt that a Russian Revolution would become the signal for a proletarian revolution in the West, which is basically what happened 35 years later.

This does not mean that the remainder of the German immigrants were not sympathetic to the revolutionaries, including the indoctrination that all immigrants had received in the German schools. This influence extended over the approximately 500,000 that came in just after the 1848-49 revolutions fleeing the unrest. It also had a great effect on the immigrants called the Grays, who had come over after the European upheavals of the 1830, although many of the Grays were already socialists, particularly in the press and publishing.

This influence was a result not only of the energy and organization of the radical leaders themselves, their way was "greased" for them. Many of these 48ers were used to promote the socialist agenda of the existing Americanized movement, particularly those *who could project* a moderate image. This in turn enhanced their reputation among the German immigrants, since they saw these leaders being accepted by their new countrymen.

Think about it. Mostly itinerant communist leaders who had to flee with literally nothing came to the United States and immediately founded publications, traveled around giving speeches, and had meetings with Americans as well as other refugee radicals, and no one asks where the money or the organizing for this activity came from.

We tend to forget that the vast majority of immigrants from Europe could barely scrape together the means to come to the U.S. Most people who came did so because they did not have the opportunity to get ahead, let alone become rich in their homeland. Property was settled in every sense of the word in Europe, and starting a business or acquiring property was a long and controlled process. Whatever the people had was liquidated to purchase their passage for them and their family, and there was not much left over to get a start in their new home. And we have already mentioned indenture, although this practice was waning at this time.

Revolutionaries had to leave — quickly. They did not have the time to dispose of their property at a reasonable price.

The money and organizing for these revolutionaries had to come from Americans. And, Americans served as the basis for building the reputation of key communist leaders among their fellow Americans. There were service and fraternal organizations which helped German, British, and Irish revolutionaries on both sides of the Atlantic.

The obvious means to accomplish this are readily apparent after one understands the network of American intellectuals, publishers, industrialists, and activists that were already at work in our country, in a position to help one of their own ilk no matter what country they came from. This hidden network becomes increasingly obvious in the number of Americans who went to Europe to help the revolutions there.

The influence of Americans who promoted Illuminism is also apparent in those who went to Europe to study. This usually meant Germany when it came to studying the liberal arts. American universities were originally Christian in orientation, actually started as Christian institutions, but they gradually changed over time. The returning students, steeped in Hegelian thought, became part of the intellectual fiber of America and transferred this thought into every nook and cranny of American society, with many becoming teachers at universities. This was the gradual approach which became known as the Gramscian strategy in the 20th century.

It is not now nor ever has been a new strategy.

George Ticknor, Joseph Green Cogswell, Edward Everett, and George Bancroft all went to advanced studies in Germany at Göttingen University. Remember that Weishaupt was a professor at Göttingen, and at least three other professors were members of the Illuminati. Everett was the first American to receive a Ph.D. from Göttingen. Emerson studied under Everett at Harvard right after Everett had returned from Germany, and Everett helped shape Emerson's worldview as the leader of the German School of American Unitarianism. Ticknor would go on to help found the Boston Public Library.

A question that needs to be asked in regard to the Conspiracy and its minions has to be: Who supports these activists until they either get traction or complete their mission?

Another aspect of this support for radicals is the instances of assassination by people who apparently have no means.

All through the 20th century, for instance, there are examples of assassins who seem to have foreknowledge of the travels of their intended victims and the ability to track them for months and engage in a great deal of travel, and all of it without any visible means of support for either themselves or their activities. The official pronouncement was always the "lone gunman" scenario, usually with a diary of the gunman which was found that supported this idea. If not a diary, then a paper or document was found after the deed. This was the pattern in the 19th century as well, as we shall see.

Somebody or some organization supports this activity. Before the Robert Kennedy assassination, no one except The John Birch Society tried to honestly *investigate these aspects* of the crimes, whether they were assassinations or terrorism. Later much work was done after the trail had gone cold, with a great deal of wild speculation based on the bias of those writing about or investigating the subject.

An interesting sidelight of the official investigation into the John F. Kennedy assassination is that the official American Communist Party newspaper, *The Worker*, editorialized that an investigative committee needed to be formed and headed by Earl Warren. This is what happened.

There are many reliable witnesses, including the doctors who worked at Parkland Hospital the day of the Kennedy assassination, that stated publicly that the Warren Commission ignored facts, including the direction of the bullet that caused the wound that killed him.[48]

Recall that George Sanders, the Carbonari American, was involved in hiring a man to try to assassinate Napoleon III. Somebody nearly always finances these activities.

The reader will have noticed that communists coming to our shores also found work in various government entities. Where an American would find it difficult to be vetted and then employed by the state or federal governments, radicals did not seem to have a problem filling tactical positions such as clerks to legislatures or the Library of Congress.

This pattern of radical employment extended into the 20th and 21st centuries. During the Vietnam War when the communists were starting to organize the anti-war movement in the 1960s, demonstrations would be held in Seattle, Washington against the war in front of the Federal Courthouse. The demonstrators' leaders did not have to travel far to demonstrate. They simply came out of the Federal Building where they were employed.

This fact and more were documented and made public by this author at the time to show that the elements in our society against our government were actually employed by or financed through grants by our government. In other words, people inside the government were involved in destroying our form of government, and those responsible either looked the other way or helped the street communists by hiring them in the first place.

One key communist leader was the editor of the federal employees' union newspaper.

Since the tactic is so important to understand, both in the past and present, we will give you another illustration of the collusion between the government and communist activity.

Another aspect of the above-mentioned research was the use of cadres to move an agenda forward while the American people were ignorant of what was going on. In this author's metropolitan area, the federal authorities hired three women who were communists to head up an organization to demand more aid to dependent children, which meant the people or parents responsible for their upbringing would get the money, not the "children."

The government then gave these three women the list of those receiving this aid, so that they could organize them into a class action suit against the federal government for more money. They used legal services lawyers paid by the federal government. Then they fought for the increases in federal court against federal lawyers employed in the government agency responsible for giving out the aid. The federal government was the common link between all parties. It should come as no surprise that they got the money.

---

48   Search online for Dr. David Stewart as one witness in the emergency room at Parkland Hospital.

Again, it was Punch and Judy. At no stage was the federal government not involved in and paying for the charade. It was even played out in the news media without the average man on the street even realizing that the fight was fixed.

There is a link between the government and communists in the community action organizations. This has been a problem for over 150 years.

The Knights of the Golden Circle

The South was heavily influenced by organizations that fueled the fires of war. *Activist* leadership in the Young America organization was more predominately Southern. Two of the leading proponents of YA who had great influence in the South were Robert Toombs, first secretary of state of the Confederacy, and Alexander H. Stephens, the vice president of the Confederacy. Another group which played a major part in undergirding the YA filibuster movement and the opposition to abolitionism was the Knights of the Golden Circle (KGC).

Stephens helped lead the Secession when it became inevitable, but along with Toombs, Robert Barnwell Rhett, Joseph Emerson Brown, and Zebulon Vance, became a leader of disorganization against the Confederacy *while being a leader* of the Confederacy. Toombs was YA, KGC, and a 33° Mason under Pike.

The League of United Southerners was suggested by Edmund Ruffin to W. L. Yancey to counter the radical organizations of the North. Robert Barnwell Rhett and these gentlemen were firebrands of secession, but their organization was more rhetoric than action, and what there was of it was effectively absorbed into the KGC.

To *counter* the radical organizations of the North, any such opposing organization would have to be active in the North *where the radicalization was taking place*. It becomes obvious that any group in opposition attempting to counter the problem (whatever and wherever the problem may be) would have to be where the problem resided and be aimed at an outreach program on those citizens. Obviously, the Southern firebrands could not or did not even try to do this. Therefore, the effort would seem to have been either made in terrible ignorance of how to get the job done, or done deliberately to further inflame Southerners.

This so-called blunder in tactics is precisely what the abolitionists did to radicalize the North while "ticking off" the South. Rather than work in the South to eliminate slavery, they moved into the North to become outsiders telling others what to do, Garrison being the obvious example.

Membership of the KGC grew rapidly and included some very notable people, such as Sam Houston, John C. Breckinridge, and Jefferson Davis. The most striking membership was in the Texas Rangers. This famous law enforcement group was heavily infiltrated by the KGC, according to research housed in the Texas Room at the public library in Houston.

Organized in 1854 in Lexington, Kentucky, by "General" George Bickley, a member of Lippard's Brotherhood of the Union, the KGC had three degrees of membership, similar to other secret societies including classic Masonry, and did not welcome volunteers. Most of their numbers came from recruiting. You could resign from the first two degrees, but not the third. They had secret signs, passwords, and grips.

The direct "parental" authority of the KGC has been debated; all we need to know is that there had to have been a conspiratorial authority above Bickley due to his background and later his removal from its leadership.

Chroniclers of the KGC are all over the map as to the date the KGC was founded, its numerical strength, whether a viable organization ever did exist, who actually belonged, and *who or what founded it.* Generally, the latter idea comes from those who weave doubt within any narrative concerning the importance of any secret organization. It is quite surprising that several books exist that document conspiracies in general that go into great detail about the organization(s) and membership, but promote the idea that the organization did not really amount to much. This is especially true of the Illuminati, but includes the KGC as well.

That being said, there was a KGC scare in the North to try and serve as a basis for the Northerners to blame someone for the war besides the real culprits. As a result, the KGC served that purpose, and many Southerners were listed in significant books and studies as KGC members. Since it was a secret organization, who really would know?

The KGC oath stated,

> … I will never reveal, or make known … any thing which my eyes may behold, or any word which my ears may hear, within this sacred Temple … "

The units of the KGC were known as *castles*. The oath goes on to state that the Knight will never reveal any member, symbol, signs, passwords, or even the name of the order. The penalty would be death. The oath was similar to the Carbonari. For this reason, and due to the fact that many YA were members of the KGC as well, some historians believe the YA was the parent organization, and that it was therefore a Southern, direct extension of the Carbonari. While it makes sense, there is no definitive documentation for this, although there is a goodly amount of circumstantial evidence.

The History of the Great Rebellion, 1863, has this to say about the KGC and secession:

> For this purpose a secret order, the "Knights of the Golden Circle," having for its primary object the extension and defense of slavery, was organized, and several degrees, as in the Masonic order, were open to the aspirant for high rank in it. To the initiated of the highest rank the whole plot was revealed, and the others, … were led on to further its designs. Among the officers and members of the higher degrees of the order were, it is said, cabinet and other officers of the government, and prominent citizens of all the Southern and some of the Northern states.

Even as late as 1886, Jefferson Davis wrote to Basil Duke not to reveal the names of Northern leaders of the KGC conspiracy. Duke was editor of the *Southern Bivouac*. Why Duke would be privy to that information is not well known.

The "public" goal of the lower degree of the KGC was to build a slave empire, a Golden Circle, with Havana in the center of this circle that extended from Pennsylvania to Panama, encompassing everything in between, including the Caribbean. The real goals of the organization were passed orally within the two upper degrees.

Many of the filibuster groups in the mid to late 1850s were under their auspices, at least at their inception. These "armies" were intended to carry out the designs of the Knights. The KGC provided a more "Southern" wing to the YA initiatives.

The activities and goals of the KGC were identical to YA's and members of both were active together, although the KGC was the pro-slavery wing of YA before the war. KGC's goals relative to expansion were slightly modest as to territory compared to YA, and were disguised as building a circle of empire surrounding the Caribbean based on slavery.

The KGC contained members of all persuasions. Dr. George Cupples, KGC, was a medical surgeon in the British army and immigrated to Texas, where he was a member of the Castro Colony. He served as a surgeon in the Mexican War and the Civil War. He organized and was the first president of the Texas Medical Association.[49]

The KGC had allies when it came to their plans for Latin America, even among those of the radical Republicans. Jacob Dolson Cox, U.S. senator then governor of Ohio, before the war praised the KGC plan for Mexico. In a speech Cox mentioned astrological projections being correct and the KGC having the magic of Prince Arthur's horn, "which could not only call his thousand liegemen at the blast, but before whose blast the enemy fell down."

Just as the Northern anti-slavery organizations stood for disunion, the KGC did likewise. A pamphlet circulated by them in mid-1860, said that the KGC "constitute a powerful military organization as a nucleus around which to hang such political considerations as which will, if well managed, lead to the disenthrallment of the cotton states from the oppressive majority of manufacturing and commercial interests of the North."

John Pendleton Kennedy, secretary of the Navy in the Fillmore administration, blamed secession on the KGC and their conspiracy. He would come to advocate a central republic of Border States as a buffer between the North and South to avert war.

Meanwhile, the work of the KGC gave the excuse to Northern agitators to be able to point their fingers at Southerners as the problem; however, both sides were guilty and both had their conspiratorial organizations. Modern history will allow some aspects of the KGC to be mentioned, but the Northern conspiracy is rarely mentioned since it had the prevailing influence for a century after the war. Mentioning the KGC superficially makes it appear that the blame for the war was on the South.

There are those who believe Northern leaders exaggerated the size and scope of the KGC, as well as its danger to the North after the war began, to discourage Northern citizens from blaming Radicals for bringing about the war in the first place, and to give weight to the need for imposing military government in the North due to KGC threats. There were KGC initiatives in the North which were troublesome, but generally speaking, these initiatives were by and large thwarted; nonetheless, the scare and its result (more government control over the citizen in violation of the Bill of Rights) were precursors to the Patriot Act which came 150 years later, at which time the actual threat to our country was much less.

The KGC in their First Degree claimed to be supportive of the Constitution and absolute protection of property and personal rights, and claimed that republics lasted only as long as the slave institutions. They supported conquest as their foreign policy. This position was contradictory. A true republic cannot last under slavery or conquest. Sooner or later these policies destroy limited government and it becomes imperialistic.

But then, those behind these two movements, YA and KGC, knew that. Many of our Founders understood this as well, but could not find a way to eliminate slavery without destroying the basis for holding our country together at the time. To have founded two nations at the time, one slave, the other free, would have meant that either one would have been too weak to stand against Britain, France, or Spain, countries that did all that they could to break up the fledgling United States.

Keep in mind that the founding of the United States and the ratification of the Constitution were still within the lifetime of many of the elderly.

---

49 Texas was not devoid of communist experiments. Victor Considerant, the chief disciple of Fourier and his successor, co-founded La Réunion phalanx near Dallas in 1855-57 at the invitation of Albert Brisbane. He returned to Paris in 1869, where he participated in the Paris Commune uprising in 1871. He was a member of the First International. There is scant research on the inhabitants of the many communist experiments once they dissolved. In the case of Ripon, Wisconsin, they remained and played a major role in local politics and it is assumed that this was the situation in most cases elsewhere around the country, including Texas.

The process of the elimination of slavery was hampered for many reasons, not the least of which was its need by the Conspiracy to serve as a basis for dividing us and using that division to bring about the slavery of all in the long run.

The KGC had three degrees: The Knights of the Iron Hand, a military degree; the Knights of the True Faith, a financial degree; and the Knights of the Columbian Star, a political degree. The first degree was a probation period before one could attain the higher degrees. Members could not even tell their wives of their membership.

They drew their ranks initially from the Southern Rights Clubs and the Order of the Lone Star. The Order of the Lone Star (OLS) was started by Dr. John V. Wren in 1850 in New Orleans, among followers of the Cuban revolutionary Lopez and Americans who wanted to bring Cuba into the United States. The ritual was formulated by John Henderson, and its membership included revolutionaries such as the 48er Louis Schlessinger. The Order never engaged physically in a filibuster enterprise, but did channel funds and arms into those who did. It ultimately merged into the KGC.

The oath of the order demanded allegiance to an unknown grand sachem, "without any reference to and in spite of any oath they may have taken to support the Constitution of the United States." They professed to want to make Cuba a possession of America without violating any laws, yet their very oath violated the law.

Some claim that Pierre Soulé was the head of the organization, and another U.S. senator, John Henderson, was involved in its leadership. There was a John Henderson involved, but the actions of Sen. Henderson later in Missouri and during the Civil War would make him a Northern sympathizer rather than someone connected with the OLS. He also co-authored the 13th Amendment to eliminate slavery. It is possible that he, like so many others, worked for one thing before the war and then became an ardent follower of the Union after the war started.

Pierre Beauregard and other U.S. Army officers took the oath. Later Beauregard was to join the KGC.

It was said the order had about 28,000 members. It may be that the number is exaggerated since most secret societies tend to portray their numbers to be larger than they are. Numbers are not as important as the members, their influence, and how well they are organized.

Southern Rights Clubs had similar foreign goals as the Order of the Lone Star. Oaths were somewhat similar as well.

Texas had the greatest percentage of KGC membership. Its population voted 76% for secession. The high percentage of KGC membership there was due to threats of invasion at the time from Mexico by revolutionaries to acquire Texan territory in the name of protecting Chicanos. Texans rallied to the KGC flag to put down this movement, either by invading Mexico or repelling an "invasion." Robert E. Lee, as the commander of the U.S. Army unit in the area before the war, did all he could to dissuade the KGC-led brigade from invading Mexico and asked them to disperse.

Texas was the last bastion of the Confederacy after the surrender of Lee. The war was not considered over in Texas for many months after Appomattox. There was never a formal surrender of the Confederacy as a unified government due to the diversity of the states involved, as well as the armies not being under a centralized command.

Surrender came week after week and month after month until the resistance in Texas ceased and President Johnson declared the war to be over in the middle of 1866.

The KGC believed slavery was a divine institution, and were against Mormons, Spiritualists, utopians of any sort, abolitionists, and Turners. At times, they promoted seemingly conflicting policies. For instance, they supported the socialist Juarez of Mexico even while forming at least two brigades to invade Mexico to make it an American territory. The plan called for a goal quite different than it seemed.

According to *Abraham Lincoln and the Fifth Column,*

> The plan was to assist the Constitutional Party under President Benito Juárez to overthrow the Clergy party under Miramón, by furnishing them men and officers, arms, munitions, and by shaping public opinion in the United States.

To this end, negotiations were carried out with representatives of the KGC and Juarez. However, the actual purpose was,

> ... the entire and speedy conquest of Mexico and the establishment of a separate and independent nation upon such a basis as to render it subservient to the march of American civilization.

Support of Juarez fulfilled the anti-Christian aspects of the Conspiracy against the Catholic Church. Juarez and other revolutionaries in Mexico were very much opposed to Christianity, and their primary target was the Catholic Church simply because it was the dominant religion in Mexico. The atrocities against congregations and clergy were astonishing. Considering all, it is amazing that the church survived. Many would say that it didn't considering the liberation theology that pervades the church in all of Latin America.

It is not a far-fetched notion that revolutionaries in Latin America allowed kindred spirits within the Catholic Church to live while killing off the true believers. In this manner, the revolutionaries would have friends in the pulpit no matter what the results of a current revolution might be.

If the KGC goal could have been achieved in Mexico and that country brought into the U.S., it would have meant the acquisition of 25 new states, 50 senators, and over 60 representatives, all supporting the slavery issue and subverting the American system in general, not only by the aforementioned, but by the fact that these new citizens would have no idea of the principles of liberty and constitutional principles upon which our country was founded.

In addition, the volatile nature of its inhabitants would forever be a problem for the rest of the United States if they had been made part of our country. It remains true today in regard to any thought of a North American Union, a "community" of the United States, Canada, and Mexico that has been proposed by the Council on Foreign Relations and similar groups.

Whether one likes to hear it or not, the crimes committed by individuals who have come into the U.S. illegally are indicative of the corruption of the entire system called Mexico.

After the election of Lincoln, the KGC organized mass meetings, torchlight parades, etc. to promote secession.

In the South, the identity of the KGC was absorbed into the Confederate Army at the beginning of the conflict. Bickley's efforts then turned north, where the group became a Copperhead and guerilla organization. While it wreaked havoc from time to time behind Union lines and caused a number of schemes to be born within Northern state governments, it was not as influential on Northern political affairs as it had been in the South.

More is known today about the KGC in the North than in the South because the work of the KGC was more important in the South and therefore kept secret, and because the establishment historians did not want anything to upset the image of the Southern citizen being a rebel by relating how a small group of people can make things happen. The rest of the people wonder what happened.

Besides, conspiracies do not make things happen — everything is an accident. Nothing is allowed that may alter that opinion among the targeted people; otherwise, they may do something to stop it.

Generally speaking, if an organization has three percent of the population, particularly among the opinion molders, and the organization has a focused leadership, that organization will achieve its goals, no matter what those goals are or how violent they may become. In some instances the percentages have been less. The key is if there is any organizational leadership opposing what is happening. If good people do nothing, it makes the conspirators' job very easy.

Over time, this idea that all Southerners were rebels became "fact" in the public mind — and the mind of the history teacher. True conspiracies hide as much as they can about themselves.

The KGC was more important before the war, and that is the time period where less is known of it due to its secrecy and the fact that its activities led to the reaction into the war the Master Conspiracy wanted. Then, after the beginning of the war, reaction to the danger of the KGC and its affiliates was used to spread alarm of armed insurrection behind Union lines. This was used to help stimulate dividing the Union into military districts, which helped clamp down on Northern citizens.

After the war started, the schemes of the KGC, either in league with the Southern Confederacy or acting alone, never amounted to anything substantial. There were countless plots and sub-plots which used up a great amount of money that went into the plotters' pockets, but there was nothing to show for it other than busying giddy minds on pie-in-the-sky activity. Ineptitude was the hallmark of these secret societies during the war, or at least the appearance of ineptitude. Their usefulness was in bringing about the war, and prolonging it but not winning it, which would have led to a sectionalized continent.

Indeed, some of the leaders of the KGC conspiracies in the wartime North later joined the Radicals in their political agenda after the war. Not exactly the actions of men who had principles. This was also the case many times in the South.

The result was a country that changed into a national government rather than a federal one, while loosening the restraints of the Constitution which limited government. Empire and all that word means were the ultimate goal.

With at least two-fifths of the Union Army composed of foreign-born people, particularly from Germany and Ireland, the use of troops to perform unconstitutional acts on our citizens was not a problem for the North. These troops did not understand constitutional law and the Bill of Rights. Having scores of foreign-born generals in the Union Army did not help this situation. If you include majors and colonels, it was in the hundreds.

There is a modern twist to this idea of foreign troops in our armed forces who do not understand our rights and Constitution. Can you imagine the problems we would have if a North American Union would become reality, with the integration of Mexican troops into an NAU consolidated armed force? Yet the Obama administration signed an agreement with Mexico and Canada on March 28, 2012 to allow their troops into the U.S. in case of a national emergency, either natural or civil. Of course, the national emergency would be called by the president, not the Congress or the people.

All of the ills outlined above and further on in our narrative would become enormous problems for American citizens interacting with these foreign troops, both during the Civil War, in its aftermath, and in any similar situation in the future.

Two-fifths became the percentage of foreign-born troops in the Union Army after the call-up of the

CHART SIX

The following aided and abetted terrorism in the person of **John Brown**, before and after the fact. This list is limited to generally recognizable individuals and newspapers due to space considerations

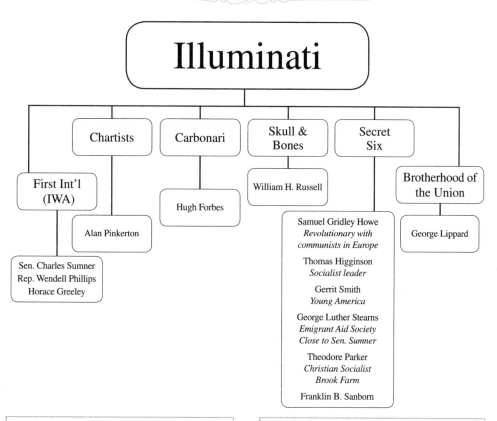

Individuals and Organizations

Kansas Aid Society
Sen. Henry Wilson
Sen. William H. Seward
Sen. John Parker Hale
Attorney General Ebenezer Hoar
Frederick Douglass
Joshua Giddings
Ralph Waldo Emerson
Henry Thoreau

Newspapers

New York Tribune
New York Evening Post
The New York Times
New York Independent
Boston Traveler
Washington National Era
Chicago Tribune
Cleveland Leader
The St. Louis Democrat
Topeka Tribune
Lawrence Kansas Republican

George Nicholas Sanders. Grandson of Spanish agent George Nicholas. A Carbonari leader of Young America. Associate of Blanqui. On the original list of Lincoln assassination conspirators.

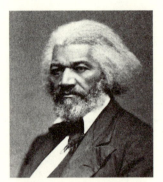

Frederick Douglass. Abolition Leader. Vice-Presidential candidate on the Equal Rights Party with Victoria Woodhull, communist leader. U.S. Marshall of Washington, D.C.

William Huntington Russell, primary co-founder of Skull and Bones and Connecticut politician and educator. One of the trustees of the terrorist John Brown's estate.

John Brown. Communist terrorist aided and abetted by prominent newspaper owners, members of Congress, industrialists, and religious leaders.

Charles Dana. Editor of The New York Tribune. American communist leader and friend of Marx. Assistant Secretary of War during the Civil War.

Carl Schurz. German revolutionary under communist leadership. Lincoln confidante. Secretary of the Interior under President Hays.

state militias had fleshed out the army and the draft was instituted. Prior to that, during the initial months of the war, the majority of troops in the Union Army were foreign born. This was during the initial consolidation of control over the Northern citizens in the first months of the war. These foreign-born troops had little appreciation for the Bill of Rights and constitutional law.

Bickley became a problem for the KGC organization and was ousted from effective control by the New Orleans castle, and became a problem elsewhere as well. Later he was arrested by Northern authorities and confined for the duration of the war. The fact that he had been ousted indicates that he never really controlled the group to begin with, and it could not have been as monolithic or as secret within the hierarchy under Bickley as it appeared. Such organizations operate monolithically and in secrecy as to who is really the "anointed one." Had he really been at the helm, he would never have been so public or vulnerable. Too much was known about the man at the time he was supposedly the leader of a secret society.

The identity of the real leader is usually held more in confidence than any other secret they may have. Sitting on the seat of power is a dangerous proposition — somebody may want the seat — so the fewer who know where that seat is, the less the danger to the man or small group who holds it.

Also, an aura of wisdom in the leadership must be maintained within the general membership. Within conspiracies, the more the leader is known, the more likely some followers will not respect the leader(s) and will plot to take over the leadership or quit.

Bickley's life was generally known, and it was not one of competence or morality. There are holes in his life that remain unknown, but enough is known that it makes it impossible to believe anyone would follow his leadership without something more behind his organization.

To logically back up what we have just said, why would the membership be held in secret if the secret society leadership was not? The real leadership had to extend into more powerful areas. Too many powerful men belonged that would never have followed Bickley's leadership.

The number and names of organizations that the KGC spawned after the war started have gone down in history within the genre of the conspiratorial history buffs: Sons of Liberty, Corps de Belgique, Circle of Honor, Order of American Knights, Mutual Protection Society, Knights of the Mighty Host, etc., all in the North or Border States.

The leading personality of the Copperhead movement, as all of these organizations were generically known during the war, was the Democrat U.S. Representative Clement L. Vallandigham, the leader of the Sons of Liberty and KGC in Ohio. Of all those who were arrested and confined for being against the war, his story is the most famous. He was denied habeas corpus, tried by a military court in Ohio, and sentenced to military prison for the duration of the war, but his sentence was commuted by Lincoln to exile to the Confederacy.

He returned before the end of the war and was generally ignored by authorities. He did not achieve political success again until after the war, when he joined forces with those he supposedly opposed during the war.

The Copperhead movement occupies a great deal of space in history books due to its visibility, but it was not as important as the pre-war activities and intrigue of the KGC and allied groups that kept their membership and actions more secret.

Too many honest historians only concentrate on the obvious. They rarely have the mind-set to look beyond what they readily see, particularly if they have been programmed to ignore any thought of conspiracy. Collusion sometimes, but not tied to an organized conspiracy that is much larger than they can even imagine. Other than a superficial identification of an obvious number of people who agreed on some issue, they never ask just what the fountainhead of any movement was. What *physically influenced* them to come together and organize is rarely studied.

Without understanding that conspiracy in politics is the norm, one cannot study history well and therefore put himself in the position of being able to ask the right questions. These conspiracies may range from a very small number of people to large units. Some will be relatively benign, simply to affect a vote in a convention or propel one of their number to a party position. Others, as we are documenting, will be dangerous.

Recall that Jefferson Davis, many years after the war, did not want the leaders of the KGC revealed, even in the North. A logical reason for this is probably that they still held positions of influence, and revealing their involvement in the KGC would have diminished that influence. They still had work to do.

One of the best examples of a large conspiracy that existed right before everyone's eyes was the activities and personnel surrounding John Brown.

Kansas and John Brown

The battleground for the opposing sides of slavery before the war became "Bleeding Kansas." It was a state that would go either for slavery or for emancipation depending on the influx of pioneers from both persuasions, both wanting to do all they could to ensure that Kansas would vote their way once admitted as a state. In addition, it was used as a means to agitate both sides in the North and South into irreconcilable differences.

While the image of Southern rights organizations tends to be more of a constitutionalist one today, this was not always the case. Virginians in Kansas made up a band called the Red Shirts, and marched under a red banner with "Southern Rights" emblazoned upon it.

Red shirts with red banners were always an indication of militant socialism, then as well as today. The Carbonari army under Garibaldi at that very time wore red shirts and was renowned for it. There was a considerable amount of sympathy in the South for Garibaldi and his legion.

We have also noted that there were several sizable secret societies that were less than constitutionally oriented and quite bellicose.

It is a generalization, but a true one, that had both sides not been financed from the outside, there would never have been a conflict in Kansas. It is particularly true that the free-state forces' leadership of a variety of "armies" would never have been involved if they had not been paid well, whether it was Gen. Jim Lane's or John Brown's bands.

The main lesson taught in schools today about Kansas and pre-war agitation is that John Brown was a fighter for the freedom of slaves and that he may have been a little eccentric, but after all, it was for a good cause — he was a martyr for what was right.

We will concentrate more on the Northern aspects of Kansas rather than the Southern. Again, this is not because the South did not have its revolutionary and/or conspiratorial aspects, but since the Northern wing of the Conspiracy had more long-range influence on America as a result of the war, and subsequently over the future of Kansas as well as the country, it is best to concentrate on this facet in Kansas. The purpose overall is to exhibit the revolutionary intent, the militant spirit, and the conspiratorial tactics that almost destroyed American liberty completely.

As an example that is indicative of the personalities as well as of the problems in Kansas, a short story of Charles Robinson is in order. In California he took part in riots in 1850 as a supporter of squatter sovereignty, was wounded, and while under indictment for conspiracy and murder, ran away and was elected to the state legislature. The charges were subsequently discharged by the court without trial.

Robinson was the Kansas agent for the New England Emigrant Aid Society, which was an organization founded to flood anti-slavery citizens into the territory and was closely allied with the usual suspects from New England who gave help to John Brown. Robinson gave a glowing letter of introduction to John Brown for his assistance in "defending" Kansas. He knew that Brown was a murderer, and had attended a meeting at which an armed invasion by John Brown was discussed.

Robinson was elected in an illegal convention as governor in opposition to the territorial governor that had been installed by the president of the United States. As a result, he, along with several others, was arrested and imprisoned.

There is a lot more, but the bottom line is that he became the first governor of Kansas after its entry into the union. He was impeached but not found guilty in a rivalry with Gen. Lane. He later became the president of the Kansas Historical Society, in charge of setting down the historical record of the state. *To the victor go the myths and monuments.*

To this day, the nickname used to identify Kansans is Jayhawks, the nickname of the anti-slavery soldiers and the men who fought for the Union from Kansas.

Kansas formed the battleground for militants of all stripes. The Emigrant Aid Societies of the North supplied arms, which they called Beecher's Bibles, after Henry Ward Beecher, the liberal preacher who had a great deal of influence among the radicals in New York. He was not a man of character and would be sued for adultery in 1874 by the accused woman's husband, but the jury could not decide *after 6 months* of trial and deliberation. Beecher's senior counsel at his trial was William Maxwell Evarts, the Order.

As a result of the notoriety, Beecher was dropped over time from every newspaper he wrote for. He later redeemed himself but never was looked upon as a paragon of virtue again as he became more and more involved with socialist leaders. Beecher became a champion of Charles Darwin's theory of evolution, which also caused his reputation among conservative ministers to wane.

Later, Judge Joseph Neilson, who presided at Beecher's adultery trial, attended Beecher's 70th birthday celebration, obviously a non-partial judge.

Beecher's father was Rev. Lyman Beecher, who had been tried for heresy but acquitted. One of his sisters was Harriet Beecher Stowe, who wrote *Uncle Tom's Cabin.*

The entire adult life of John Brown was involvement in conspiracy, including the conspiracy that had worked for years to destroy the social order of the country and replace it with Illuminist ideas. *He named as one of the trustees of his will William Russell, the founder of the Order.*

Since the growth of the Internet, the widespread reputation of Skull and Bones, the Order, has proliferated, with more and more people paying attention to such things, and some modern histories of Brown have dropped any reference to Brown's connections with William Russell. Apparently to refer to Russell in connection with Brown would raise some eyebrows.

As more modern books are published, older histories are sold off or discarded by public libraries. As this happens, more and more understanding of the forces behind certain events and personalities is lost. John Brown's history is a case in point.

Brown was the first political terrorist of his kind. Before, terrorism was a part of government, either against their own people as a means of ruling them, or against another citizenry whom they wished to influence into some form of reaction, or tribe against tribe.

Dictionaries until a few years ago stated that terrorism was a state-sponsored activity to help the state rule its people or a conquered people. Only recently has terrorism taken on a more independent look, and as a result a different definition. Even in modern times terrorism is almost always state-sponsored, but this fact is kept from the people in order to provide the conditions for subjugating the population in the name of some kind of a war on terror and to divide the world into Muslim and non-Muslim.

The exceptions are lone wolves who commit acts of terror as a result of any influence they may have come under, as a byproduct of building the terror network by those who want to recruit their minions from among the gullible. They are not directly recruited, and serve to give credence to the idea that terrorism isn't a well-coordinated activity from a centralized source.

There will always be unbalanced individual "wannabes" among any society.

If the people realized that a government or coalition of governments was behind terrorism, the excuse to wage war all over the world and to impose draconian new controls on our people would not "fly" with the American people. They would know that the enemy was another government or alliance and force the issue, as had been done in the past, by punishing the government involved.

We cannot find any evidence that terrorism today is not state sponsored, yet the public, conservative organizations, and "fair and balanced" media do not seem to notice. The terrorist organizations today are financed, trained, and armed by governments. We will leave it to the reader to ferret out just who these governments are, since to start down this road would entail another book. One clue: Look to where the terrorists get their weaponry.

Once the fountainhead of terrorism is destroyed or neutralized, terrorism cannot flourish.[50]

In the case of Brown, he was backed by those who wanted a change in government for their own purposes. He was their instrument to wage terrorist activity to react the people into accepting war and the changes wrought by that war. And, his arms were supplied by these men.

Brown had conspirators in government at the state and federal level who helped him, even though his enterprise was not sanctioned by the government. This is always a problem in modern terrorism as well, no matter in what country it may be. In fact, terrorism usually has a hard time operating within countries where the government is not infiltrated to a certain extent.

Indeed, if the federal government had done the job it was supposed to do, the army would have arrested Brown and others in the Kansas Territory who were causing the mayhem on both sides.

Brown was never totally honest in his business dealings or his abolition activities. His career as a businessman was a disaster. He was constantly roaming about among well-heeled abolitionists looking for funding for his businesses and then his activities in Kansas. The *public* amounts of the monies he received never amounted to much, but there was a considerable passage of money to him that was "off the books."

Part of John Brown's original, grandiose plan was to re-import escaped slaves residing in Canada to form the basis of an army. It never came to fruition due to a lack of substantial funds, the fact that there were not that many ex-slaves that wanted to re-enter the U.S. and risk death or a return to slavery, and the fact that Hugh Forbes sabotaged the plot and led to its suspension. Brown then segued into a different plan to attack Harper's Ferry.

The revelations by Forbes to key conspirators probably had a great deal of influence on the actions of Buchanan as president and how he handled the Kansas situation. Too many people were involved and the word more than likely got to Buchanan.

There was a considerable number of people from Canada mixed up in Brown's schemes. This too lent weight to the idea that the agitation was driven by the English, in this case from British Canada.

Brown hired Hugh Forbes, an Englishman who had fought under Garibaldi, to train his soldiers in

---

50 You may wish to consult the author's booklet and DVD on the subject of terrorism, both titled *Exposing Terrorism: Inside the Terror Triangle*, at ShopJBS.org.

1857. In most volumes about Brown, little is mentioned about Forbes except the foregoing. When looking into his background, it becomes very interesting that he linked up with Brown and subsequent events.

The story of Forbes is that he was an emissary and operative of Mazzini in the United States. He was asked to come to America in that capacity and work with the émigrés who had removed to the New World. Literally thousands of members of the European Carbonari front groups had moved to America after 1848. They needed to be pulled together into a cohesive organization to work for the goals of the Carbonari. Forbes was one of the main men tasked to do the job by Mazzini, if not the leader of the effort, to at least to pull together the lower political levels of Carbonari influence.

Forbes was pressed upon Brown by his backers in the East, specifically Joshua Leavitt of the *New York Independent*, and Brown consulted with Gerrit Smith and Thaddeus Hyatt, who was a business partner with Joshua Ingalls, about the idea. Leavitt was a Congregationalist minister who was the first secretary of the American Temperance Society and a co-founder of the New York City Anti-Slavery Society. He had turned to journalism once he became involved in abolition.

Considering that all involved knew that Forbes was working for Mazzini, it is obvious that important Americans welcomed the involvement of a key Carbonari in their operations. It was not simply a plot by Brown; it involved many prominent people who had no problem involving the Carbonari — if they too were not already part of the Carbonari conspiracy, or higher up the ladder themselves.

Here we can see that conspiratorial forces worked both sides of the conflict: within the Brown initiative and the KGC. Supposedly, the two were in opposition, but in reality they were guided by one force linking back to the Carbonari network.

Forbes became disillusioned with Brown quickly because his "army" was more bravado than substance. Forbes going to key Radicals in Washington to reveal Brown's plans may have been a move designed to force Brown to alter his original plan, which he subsequently did.

Many radicals rode with Brown. The Wattles brothers of Cincinnati, Augustus and John Otis, were members of the Truth Brotherhood and the community at Utopia; John was a spiritualist. William Addison Phillips apparently was a member of the Brotherhood of the Union. Brown also had veteran 48ers Charles Kaiser, August Bondi, and Charles W. Lenhardt who rode with him in Kansas, and the Chartist Richard J. Hinton.

Many short histories of Brown leave out any reference to the majority of the aforementioned men.

Brown was admired by Emerson, Thoreau, Theodore Parker, Gerrit Smith, Dr. Samuel Howe, and Frederick Douglass. Frederick Douglass was close enough to Brown that Brown confided in him the location of what became the raid on Harper's Ferry. After the raid, Douglass also fled temporarily to Canada for fear that he would be prosecuted for abetting. The official story is that he was worried about guilt by association. Actually, evidence captured at the time in the possession of John Brown implicated Gerrit Smith, Joshua Giddings, and Douglass.

Mothers used to say to their children that, "You are known by the company you keep." This can be said about the whole gambit of abolitionists. This adage was used by mothers to convince their children to associate only with decent people of character. It didn't work with the abolitionists; they apparently heard "only associate with characters."

Again, the conspiracy was too wide to have been something that Brown alone would have had control over. The membership in a wide variety of conspiratorial organizations just among the men who rode with Brown indicates a broad-based influence within the Left. And, as we shall demonstrate, a number of editors of substantial newspapers had also to have been involved along with their reporters.

Photographs taken of Brown showed a gradual deterioration in his face from what appears to be him going mad. He later grew a beard, which hid much of this crazed look. Drawings of Brown in textbooks show a benevolent old man kissing a Negro child as he is being led away to his execution, far different than his actual appearance.

When Brown was caught in Harper's Ferry, the comments about him became blasphemous in their adoration. Emerson said of Brown's "martyrdom, if it shall be perfected, will make the gallows as glorious as the cross."

Leonard Bacon, a schoolmate of Brown's in Ohio; Cheever, and others equated Brown with the Apostles, even Christ.

The better-known part of those involved in this conspiracy is known as the Secret Six. These men were George Luther Stearns, Gerrit Smith, Thomas Wentworth Higginson, Samuel Gridley Howe, Theodore Parker, and Franklin B. Sanborn.

These men had extensive backgrounds in subversion. Dr. Samuel Gridley Howe was a Unitarian who had served in both the Greek and July 1830 Revolutions in Paris. He was the chairman of an American Polish Committee in Paris, which assisted the Poles in their revolt against Russia. He was imprisoned in Berlin for his activities in this regard. The communist Albert Brisbane saved him at that time.

Howe helped make the song "John Brown's Body" popular. His wife, Julia Ward Howe, wrote new words to the tune, and the song has endured as "The Battle Hymn of the Republic". The words were understood to have a double meaning among abolitionists, with more meaning in regard to Brown than Christ.

Howe's idea of aid to Kansas meant guns. His and his wife's home in Boston was known as "Green Peace," and it welcomed John Brown in 1857.

Even into the early 1930s, the song "John Brown's Body" was used as a communist rally song. In 1933 the infamous Hollywood production *Gabriel Over the White House* had unemployed veterans marching to and singing the song, with the implication that their leadership was at least a socialist leadership. This movie was scripted as a rough outline reminiscent of E. M. House's book, *Philip Dru, Administrator.*

Rev. Thomas Wentworth Higginson was a socialist. He went on to help found the Intercollegiate Society of Socialists in 1905. He was a leader in the Emigrant Aid Society and the Kansas Aid Society, and as such raised money, arms, and men for Kansas. While on tour for the above organizations in Kansas, he served as a correspondent for the *New York Tribune,* the *Chicago Tribune,* and the *St. Louis Democrat,* as an unbiased observer, of course.

He was the originator of the Disunion Convention in 1857 and called for armed resistance to the U.S. government. He advocated revolution and treason. He also organized the American Woman Suffrage Association.

Higginson became a colonel during the war, commanding the first federally authorized black regiment, the 1st South Carolina Volunteers. You will not find out that he was a socialist by searching Wikipedia.

The Kansas Aid Committee, or Kansas Aid Society, was an even more radical branch of the Emigrant Aid Society and helped finance John Brown. Their number included four of the Secret Six — Higginson, Sanborn, Stearns; and Theodore Parker; and the Radicals Martin Conway, S. W. Eldridge, William Hutchinson, William A. Phillips, J. Todd, E. B. Whitman, Sen. Henry Wilson, and S. H. Wood.

Sen. Douglas denounced the Emigrant Aid Society as "a movement for the purpose of producing a collision, with the hope that civil war may be the result."

In 1856, several ex-members revealed plans of a secret military organization, the so-called Sharp's-rifle Christians, who had not only shed innocent blood for political effect, but conspired to drive North and South into civil war.

The name was a play on words. Christian Sharps invented the rifle and they used the name, reversing it to give the impression of a religiously based group.

The primary individual who formed the New England Emigrant Aid Company was Eli Thayer; the company was a merger of the organizations of the same name from Massachusetts and New York. The initiating members ranged from Thayer to Amos A. Lawrence; Edward Everett Hale, a Unitarian minister of the liberal school and nephew of Edward Everett; Horace Greeley; George L. Stearns; Dr. Samuel G. Howe; and several prominent and wealthy men.

They hired Dr. Charles Robinson to serve the company in Kansas with a few others. There was no question that one of their key goals was to arm a military force. On April 2, 1855, Robinson wrote Thayer requesting arms. One sentence stands out in the letter:

Cannot your *secret society* send us 200 Sharps' rifles ...?

(Emphasis added)

Not satisfied with simply writing letters, Robinson dispatched his clerk, George W. Deitzler, to Thayer to emphasize the need for arms. Deitzler would later serve in the Union Army as a brigadier general.

Money was raised for the arms from the usual suspects in New England and New York, including men who, while they were not directly involved in the company, were men of substance and influence committing what at the time was treason against the legitimate government appointed by the president, whether they agreed with that government or not. Frederick Law Olmsted was one of these men.

The free-state forces had tried to establish an illegal government, and connected to it was a free-state militia. In addition, they had two secret paramilitary societies: the Kansas Legion and the Kansas Regulars. There were several organizations which supplied them with arms, clothing, food, and money. These organizations did not necessarily trust one another, and there was a great deal of jealousy among their leaders.

Eli Thayer served in the U.S. House of Representatives after this activity, from 1857-1861. Before he was elected, he had also formed an anti-slavery community in what is now West Virginia, named Ceredo after Ceres, the Roman goddess of the harvest. This was reminiscent of the communist commune that had been formed a few years earlier in Wisconsin, Ceresco (also named after Ceres) which was the group that formed the Republican Party.

The Sharps rifles sent to the free-state forces gave the advantage to them, since the Southern-oriented armies were armed with older muskets and rifles. Sharpe's were the latest rifle manufactured at the time. Even so, the civil war in Kansas swung back and forth.

Government investigations were held to determine the origin of the weapons sent into Kansas, but the people involved lied until after the start of the Civil War about their involvement and were immune from any repercussions; then they bragged about it.

Many supported Brown to engage in guerilla war and terrorism for three reasons: to further the agenda of disunion, to actually make Kansas a free state, and to completely overthrow the country and replace it with a new form of government (Brown's motivation). Keep in mind that the times were different. The U.S. Army was small, designed to be beefed up by the state militias once any war was declared. So the dream of revolution, while unrealistic, was not as far-fetched as would be today against a large, well-organized, and well-armed military establishment.

His son, John Brown, Jr. is said to have become a socialist later in life; in any case he revealed that his father was a convert to communism in the 1840s. He stated that the elder Brown's "favorite theme was that of the *Community plan of cooperative industry* in which all should labor for the common good; 'having all things in common'...." Perhaps that is the reason more than any other that the Secret Six helped Brown extensively in addition to the better-organized and much-larger army of free-staters led by Gen. Lane.

The Rosicrucians claim that their leader at the time, Lippard, was instrumental in converting Brown to abolition; if so, he must have also had an influence on Brown toward communism, since Lippard was heavily involved in that movement as well.

For decades after his death, Brown was honored by such organizations as the Fenians, the First International, and assorted socialist organizations and leaders. *La Marseillaise* or *John Brown's Body* was sung at socialist/communist events. Later, in the mid-20th century, *We Shall Overcome* was added to the hymnbook of the conspiracy and increasingly became the song of choice at communist-led gatherings.

We Shall Overcome is purported to have been composed in its final form by Pete Seeger, a man who graced the pages of the communist newspapers *The Worker* and *People's World* in almost every issue during the 1960s and 70s. Yet, the tune is the same as the communist Latin American song, *Venceremos*, utilized from Cuba to Chile, and the title is translated much the same.

Another of the Secret Six, Theodore Parker, had an admirer in William Herndon, who believed Parker would help influence his increasingly important law partner, Abraham Lincoln. Herndon was the protégé of Lincoln and had extensive correspondence with Parker. In fact, Herndon was a friend with Parker, Garrison, Phillips, Sumner, and many other firebrands.

Herndon was an activist while a protégé and then a partner of Lincoln. His father had disinherited him due to political differences, and he lived with Lincoln and Joshua Speed. He organized the Springfield Library Association and brought in speakers such as Emerson, Greeley, and Henry Ward Beecher. He was a reader of Darwin and an anti-Christian, and claimed that Lincoln was as well. While he supported the Republican Party early on, he quit it to support Horace Greeley in 1872.

After the Harper's Ferry raid, the Secret Six had to hire lawyers to defend themselves. Parker's lawyer in his earlier trial for his speech against the Fugitive Slave Act, John Parker Hale, had a daughter who was engaged to John Wilkes Booth at the time of the Lincoln assassination. It's a small world, as they say.

Gerrit Smith was a very rich man as a result of the estate of his father, who was in partnership with John Jacob Astor. Smith and his father did not have a relationship at all. His two brothers suffered from mental problems that led to their deaths. Gerrit did for a time as well after it was discovered that he had helped John Brown's raid on Harper's Ferry. It was a convenient illness that helped prevent his being prosecuted.

Smith did help a number of causes and individuals, but his charitable causes included an agenda that aimed at changing the old social order rather than simply helping people out. He stood for an international court and disarmament of nations — but not in Kansas. During the war he would help organize Loyal Leagues after being active as a disunionist. In 1867, along with Cornelius Vanderbilt and Horace Greeley, he would sign Jefferson Davis' bail bond.

After a time, Smith hired Lysander Spooner as an attorney to sue those who accused him of being involved in the Brown plot. The public sentiment had reached a level where the truth was no longer relevant, but it did not help him in his suit against the *Chicago Tribune*. John Brown, Jr. had signed an affidavit that Smith had full knowledge of the operation.

Spooner denied Christianity and said that a belief in miracles was the product of a diseased imagination. He had written "A Deistic Reply to the Alleged Supernatural Evidences of Christianity" in 1836. He would become known as a leading anarchist leader. Although an abolitionist, Spooner believed that the Civil War was an entire fraud, and that the issue of slavery was used as an excuse for waging the war for the Northern industrialists.

Gerrit Smith's would ultimately give up all dogmas and wrote *The Religion of Reason*.

George Stearns was a lead pipe manufacturer. He was active with Parker in the Emigrant Aid Society. He was known to advocate, "A revolution was what the country needed." He fled to Canada with Howe after Harper's Ferry.

The Secret Six financed and were in on the plans for Brown's activities in Kansas and Harper's Ferry. They used their contacts to help build support of terrorism by providing excuses for the actions of Brown and covering up the severity of his atrocities as the mere actions of a Christian defending himself and the enslaved Negro.

Their involvement was such that they were abettors in the legal sense in Brown's terrorist activities.

This is also true of Emerson and Wendell Phillips, as accessories after the fact if not before.

The friendships and ties to certain intelligentsia and government by the Secret Six meant that more people knew what was going on than wanted to admit it. For instance, George Stearns was very close to Emerson and Sumner; he was not only part of the Bird Club, he presided over their meetings on occasion.

Brown's band of terrorists included men such as John H. Kagi, who was a newspaper reporter. He and other newsmen participated in the terrorism while they were sending dispatches to their newspapers building the reputation of Brown. Kagi was a correspondent for the *New York Tribune*, *New York Evening Post*, Washington *National Era*, Topeka *Tribune*, Lawrence Kansas *Republican*, *Chicago Tribune*, and the Cleveland *Leader*.

Richard J. Hinton, a friend of Adam Gurowski, was a correspondent for the *Chicago Tribune* and the *Boston Traveler*, and his reports were carried in Ohio and Missouri newspapers. He was an immigrant from England and learned his profession in New York. He helped organize the Republican Party in New York before going out to Kansas, where he became a field scout for John Brown.

Hinton would go on to help organize the Washington section of the First International. He served in the Civil War as officer of the First Kansas Colored Regiment, and later edited Eugene V. Debs' Socialist Party magazine.

During the war he also did a stint in secret service work in the South. At the end of the Civil War he was acting inspector general of the Freedmen's Bureau. He became the U.S. commissioner of immigration in Europe in 1867 and then inspector of U.S. consulates in Europe — another communist in foreign service.

Finally, Hinton was the special agent in charge of the Department of Agriculture from 1890-1892. The socialist aspects of the department extend this far back. It is essential for the Conspiracy to have control over the people's food supply if they mean to control the people — in the name of the people.[51]

William Hutchinson, correspondent for the *New York Times*, was an agent of the Kansas Aid Society and supplier to Brown. Henry J. Raymond, the founding editor of the *Times*, was a protégé of Greeley.

James Redpath was an example that was duplicated many times over in the 20th century with his brand of journalism. He got his start with Greeley's the *New York Tribune,* and it was he who started the newspaper build-up of John Brown as a folk hero.

---

51   The reader may wish to explore the Internet to find out just how much of the food chain the communist Chinese are purchasing — food, processing, agricultural land — and supplying for not only their own people, but Americans, and how the U.S. Department of Agriculture is helping in this process. Another, older source showing how the agriculture of America has become increasingly centralized and the end goal in mind is the book *Ill Fares the Land*. This out-of-print volume demonstrates that there has been concern since the 1960s about the centralization of the food chain into the hands of those advocating the New World Order.

While in Kansas, Redpath became of friend of Jim Lane, the abolitionist soldier, and rode with a 200-man "army" of abolitionists who were part of the Bleeding Kansas war.

He attended the Disunion Convention in January 1857 and covered it for the *Tribune*. He became a war correspondent for the *Tribune,* and marched to the sea with Sherman and later with other generals. When he came into South Carolina, he was made the superintendent of education for Charleston, organizing the school system, particularly for the freedmen.

After the war, he teamed up with Hinton for a time to work on a book that they hoped would entice pioneers out into the Colorado area to search after gold.

Have you ever asked yourself why it is that television and news reporters seem to be able to meet guerilla leaders and terrorists, even videoing some of their training, movements, and actions, when the government cannot seem to find them? The above is a clue why — too often they are participants posing as unbiased news reporters.

And, sometimes the communists who have infiltrated the government do not want them found. This was the case with the Batista government of Cuba. They could not seem to find Fidel Castro in the mountains because the Batista government was too laden with communists in the first place.

Major Pedro Diaz Lanz, the head of the revolutionary air force under Castro, told this author that he accepted the surrender of the Cuban Air Force from a general who was a member of the communist party. He said that it was the circumstances of this occasion that prompted him to realize that what he had been involved in was more communist than what he had opposed under Fulgencio Batista and that he had been duped — even while working alongside of Castro!

This was also the problem with the Nationalist Chinese government in the 1940s. It was hard to tell where the Nationalists started and the communists left off, the government was so infiltrated. After the fall of China to Mao's forces, the communists declared themselves and it was seen that much of the corruption blamed on the Nationalist government was actually due to these infiltrators.

Newspapermen have a vested interest in keeping trouble going, or even starting it. The right story can make your career. This author was at an event and witnessed a reporter and his photographer trying to get a man to slug another so they could get a picture, screaming at him, "Hit'm! Hit'm!" Character is so important, especially in a member of the media.

In the case of the young radical correspondents in Kansas, it meant a rapid rise in career, and the longer the conflict kept up, the more famous they could become. Their bias was to the North, and some were revolutionaries. Hand in hand they helped fan the heat of passion into flames of war. Many went so far as to personally take part in violent acts: property damage, kidnapping, looting, and murder. They then had the gall to report "on the scene" as if they were just impartial onlookers.

In the case of Kagi, he died in the Harper's Ferry raid after becoming an integral part of Brown's entourage. The other reporters with Brown went on to "distinguished" careers you may readily access on the Internet.

Notice as well that the so-called reporters in Kansas were pooled by a number of newspapers since it spread their costs among more than one paper. The editors may have had the appearance of having an independent editorial policy, but where the rubber hits the road, they worked together.

This example of reporters and editors working together is a twist on the tactic of interlocking directorates or leaders among conspiratorial organizations — at minimum showing collusion if not a conspiracy.

The gathering of news and the technology to broadcast it led to the formation of news bureaus that serviced hundreds and thousands of newspapers, then radio and television. This process led to a centralization of the news — local papers no longer had to send reporters out to gather the news. They could simply take it off the telegraph and then teletype. It led to wholesale control of what news was disseminated and the slant of the news by those who owned these services.

By the 1970s, ninety percent of the news read, seen, or heard was controlled by members of the Council on Foreign Relations.

Josiah Warren, the socialist, said in the mid-1800s that the press now ruled. No better case can be demonstrated than the deliberate propaganda build-up of John Brown as an *instrument* for increasing governing power. Supply the readers with "facts" to move them to think exactly as you desire. Then they will vote or react as you wish, all the while believing that they are free — and informed. And, in this example, it was coordinated among several personages behind the scenes, from the reporters and newspaper editors, to the financiers of the operation, the philosophical leaders, etc., etc. — the perfect example of a conspiracy exposed but not stopped, with the mid-level minions of it all protected from punishment by those higher up in authority.

In all of this activity, the "revolution" of John Brown did not add up to any significance other than to serve as propaganda. There were far more people involved in setting Brown up than there were members of Brown's "army" at any point. The people were reacted by the violent acts of Brown committed by a few people surrounding Brown. What made it a "big deal" was the newspaper reporting and the conspirators behind Brown, making it seem that there was more substance to Brown's enterprise than there really was.

Brown would no more have been a celebrity based on his gang or his murders without press build-up serving as the means to create a rift in the North and South. In reality, his activities did not amount to much more than the many robbery gangs that operated after the Civil War.

It was the conspiracy behind Brown that made him larger than life.

No one outside of Brown and his small party at Harper's Ferry ever received the punishment that should have followed, not those reporters who built his reputation while serving with him, those who financed him, those who destroyed evidence, or those in government who knew of the plot and did not come forward to stop it.

It was probably the largest cover-up in U.S. history up to that time based on the number of people involved and their positions in society. The Burr conspiracy was bad enough but it did not have the breadth in numbers and multiple levels of society and government actively involved.

It is a prime example of a large conspiracy that was not fully exposed at the time, and one *which was protected*. It is an example that belies the idea that a large conspiracy would in and of itself be exposed to the public. How does one expose a conspiracy if the media is part of it? It can be done, but more on this further on. Similar conspiracies have existed where the public was ignorant of them, and this is the case into modern times.

There are those who believe that a Master Conspiracy cannot exist simply because it demands the involvement of a large number of people. Conspiracies such as Burr's and Brown's belie that thinking. All it takes to hide a large conspiracy is making sure that the information highway used by the majority of people never talks about the real story.

The tactic of revolutionary newspapermen sending back reports from Europe that supported revolution had been done just ten years before, with the revolutions of 1848; we saw this with Dana, but he was not the only one. J. Gabriel Woerner came to the U.S. with his father in 1833. He was a correspondent for the *German Tribune* and the *New York Herald*. He went to Germany in 1848 because he had a desire to participate in the revolution, and he served at the same time as a reporter.

Once the revolution was suppressed, he returned to St. Louis and became the editor of the *German Tribune*. He later became an attorney, the city attorney, and served on the city council, in the state senate, and finally as judge probate for St. Louis in 1870.

Between the *New York Tribune* and the *New York Herald*, the citizens of New York got a much distorted view of what was happening in Europe, and this helped build sympathy and support for the communists. It would be some decades later that these two papers would unite into the *Herald Tribune*. This publication would then supply the news for the majority of Americans visiting or working in Europe with its international edition.

Education of the electorate has always been the aim of the Conspiracy in a country where the people have the vote. Perhaps a better phrase would be the *indoctrination* of the people.

Just as James Redpath influenced people through his newspaper reporting before the war, after the war he formed the Boston Lyceum Bureau to continue influencing how people thought. The Lyceum was a speakers' bureau that supplied performers as well as speakers all over the country. They ranged from Mark Twain to Julia Ward Howe, and included Charles Sumner, Ralph Waldo Emerson, Wendell Phillips, Henry Ward Beecher, Susan B. Anthony, and Frederick Douglass. It was one of the most successful enterprises of its type.

When Brown was finally stopped at Harper's Ferry, tried, and hanged, he refused to have a minister with him before he was hanged, yet he had used Scripture as a means to justify his activities and had started out in life considering becoming a minister. Along the line, he abandoned his faith.

He also had men with him who were vocal about their disbelief, such as Kagi, who was an agnostic and who became an important lieutenant of Brown. Aaron Dwight Stevens, who rode with Brown, was a spiritualist, as was Stewart Taylor. Two or three men may not seem like many, except that Brown never had that many people at any one time under his orders.

Brown's wife, Mary, stayed with Lucretia Mott while her husband awaited execution.

Brown's defense for his trial consisted of Samuel Chilton, of Washington, and Hiram Griswold, of Cleveland. The men were recruited to the task, and money raised for the defense, by Montgomery Blair, who became postmaster-general under Lincoln. The monies primarily came from Stearns, Amos A. Lawrence, John Murray Forbes, and other like-minded businessmen.

Blair, of all of Lincoln's Cabinet, was adamant that Ft. Sumter be resupplied, when the others said it would be confrontational and could lead to war. Stanton at that time was not a member of the Cabinet.

Prior to the aforementioned lawyers, Brown had dismissed his defense counsel except for George Henry Hoyt, but Hoyt was not up to the task as a young attorney. Hoyt had been influenced in his youth by Wendell Phillips and was more in tune with Brown than the two men dismissed. Hoyt only served briefly between the original dismissal of counsel and the inclusion of Chilton and Griswold. Hoyt was recruited originally as a volunteer on the defense to pass messages to and from Brown. He was involved in a plan for a prison break for Brown, but it was found to be unfeasible.

During the war Hoyt served in the Union Army; he then assumed command of irregulars known as the Missouri Red Leg Scouts due to the red leggings they wore.

There were at least six plans for breaking Brown out, led by individuals such as Hoyt, Samuel Howe, Alan Pinkerton, Richard Hinton, and Charles Lenhardt. Most did not go any further than to realize that it was an impossible task. The ability to free Brown with a small group was impossible due to the means by which Brown was kept under guard. Plans to use a large number of men to effect his escape never came to fruition. One plan was to use veterans of the Kansas conflict, and another German 48ers. These two plans were abandoned due to the expense and complexity.

Richard Hinton attempted to raise volunteers to free Brown that included August Wattles and members of the New York Communist Club.

Charles Lenhardt left the Cincinnati Law School and used Masonic and secret signs he had learned in his sojourn in Kansas to get past and then join the guards around Brown, to await an escape attempt that never came.

Apparently there was little or no coordination between the leaders of these attempts, and their plans may have been unknown to each other. Regardless, all plans were abandoned.

Besides, the conspirators probably thought it was better to have Brown as a martyr. He had served their purpose, he was an expensive tool, and he was too hard to control. And, he was only larger than life in the newspapers, not on the ground. His death would fill the pages of the newspapers to propagandize the North and send shivers through the South.

Martyrs have always been used to further the agenda of the Conspiracy, and they are used when the death of the men serves a more useful purpose than leaving them alive. In their death, the act can be used to react a sufficient number of people into positions they would never have held without the trauma of death, especially if it is violent and particularly if it looks as if the death was committed by the opposition to silence the rebels.

When agents of conspiracy have served their purpose, they can become catalysts for polarization, change, and even violence by their death.

A modern example of the subject at hand is Martin "Luther" King. We include the name Luther in quotes because that was not his given name. It was added later to invoke the image of a religious icon among the Protestant population. The real story is too fluid to absolutely state that he ever legally went by the name he is remembered by; it does show up on some documents in his adult life, but none in his childhood. There was no birth certificate.

King at his time of death had alienated much of his earlier following by his false pacifism, philandering, and bias for things socialist. Before he was martyred, he had gone from being an honored civil rights leader to a man leading a garbage strike in Memphis. This fact has been lost from the public consciousness since his martyrdom.

The black community at the time was rejecting his leadership, but as a result of his murder, immediately black Americans were politically polarized. Before his death, they were fragmented as a community, afterward they were as one voice, and the socialists who surrounded King channeled that voice.

In fact, just about every negative aspect of his personality and involvement has been expunged from the public mind. And, the official government reports of the FBI and Justice Department investigation of MLK were sealed for fifty years after his death. *To the victor go the myths and monuments.*

As to the black community being fragmented prior to his death, with many if not most black Americans not following his leadership, this author was involved in the black community enough to know this as a fact — at least in the author's large community. It was also true among many, many black conservative ministers who preached against the so-called pacifism of King, which was designed to provoke a reaction to then be used as bad examples of white hatred.

Laws and holidays have been passed in his name. In some homes he is honored almost as a saint. Never mind that he belonged to more communist-organized committees than most leaders of the American Communist Party, that he was a student and a teacher at a communist-run civil rights leadership school, the Highlander Folk School, or that the head of the FBI called him the most notorious liar in the country.

In his death, Martin "Luther" King is serving the cause well. One can always put words into the mouth of a dead man and not fear him contradicting them. Recall that this was and has been a method used by the Conspiracy since Voltaire advocated it.

The records of the Justice Department and the FBI were sealed from the public regarding King for 50 years after his death. This is not true of any other personage in America — suppression of records, true, but not an official government policy. Most Americans do not recall that Robert Kennedy, JFK's brother, as attorney general ordered the investigation of King in the first place, not some conservative Republican.

Finally, this author was told by more than one ex-communist, one who was an FBI agent working inside the party, that they were told in the party to look to King's leadership in the civil rights movement. One even stated that MLK was not only in attendance at a training event for communists only, but that he was one of the teachers.

Congress held an investigation of John Brown, Harper's Ferry, and those who had aided and abetted him. No papers of Brown could be found by the congressional investigators, but Wendell Phillips had a quantity of letters between Brown and his supporters. Witnesses refused to appear and evidence was suppressed.

The papers in Phillips' hands were transferred to Gov. John A. Andrew for safe keeping and were returned later to the senders. It was said that had the letters been discovered, John Brown would not have hanged alone. Considering some of those who would have been indicted, it is quite possible that much of the fervor for secession may have been averted since the letters would have exposed a conspiracy toward the agitation for such an event from the North and produced a calming effect, at least to some degree.

The Letters would also have exposed members of the Conspiracy in government and led to their resignations or even prosecution. As you can see by those involved, it would have set the Conspiracy back several decades. Some of these men were very instrumental in altering our government during the war, and were also instrumental in hiding evidence in the Lincoln assassination.

Many knew of Brown's intentions prior to the events in Kansas and Harper's Ferry. Hugh Forbes went to the Capitol and revealed the plot to Republican Senators Charles Sumner, William H. Seward, and Henry Wilson. He also filled in Horace Greeley. Some historians claim that Sen. John Parker Hale was filled in by Forbes rather than Sumner.

Wilson was later to be elected vice president under Grant. His reputation was as a philanderer, and in two cases with considerable notoriety.

The Secret Six had raised money and arms for Brown. There was a considerable correspondence between these individuals and others which raised a great deal of speculation as to just how far and wide the conspiracy went when it came to all of Brown's activities.

There were a large number of letters between Theodore Parker and William Herndon, Lincoln's law partner and protégé. Whether Lincoln knew of the plot is unknown, but a revealing book on Lincoln himself was *Herndon's Lincoln*. Historians have been discounting its value as a true picture of Lincoln as related by Herndon because it would be so devastating to Lincoln's reputation if widely read and believed.

The majority of the citizens in the North did not like the abolitionists, even if they agreed with them about slavery. Even after the war started, many were angry and did not like the abolitionist leadership running the country.

This attitude was even embodied within certain elements of the Union Army, especially within the command of Gen. McClellan.

A sizeable segment of the population also resented the war, especially after the initial blush of the war fever wore off. As the casualties mounted and along with them the hardships at home, the people rapidly grew tired of war. Men stopped volunteering in the numbers required, so a draft had to be instituted. And public opinion was suppressed.

After the war started, Wendell Phillips, Stephen Douglas, Benjamin Butler, and William Lloyd Garrison became super patriots. The hypocrisy was astonishing. On January 20, 1861, Phillips preached in Theodore Parker's church in support of the subject, "Disunion!" Just three months later Phillips gave a sermon supporting the war effort to preserve the union, on April 21, 1861.

Butler did likewise. He was a Democrat in 1860 and supported Jefferson Davis for president, then Breckinridge. By 1861, he was an abolitionist. He was offered the vice presidency by Lincoln in 1864, but he declined. He was instrumental in hiding evidence from the congressional House Committee on the Judiciary investigation into the Lincoln assassination. The evidence was found among his effects by his heirs many years later. No one seems to know what happened to it after this.

During the war he was a general and in command of New Orleans after its capture. It was there that he earned his nickname, the "Beast." He had given orders that any Southern woman that did not treat a Union soldier with deference was to be treated as a common street walker. Karl Marx had been quite taken by Butler during the Civil War, hoping that it would be he who marched into Richmond first.

The first unit into New Orleans under Butler when it was captured was commanded by Col. Henry Champion Deming, a member of the Order, and his unit was given the post of honor. Deming was installed as mayor in 1862-1863 under martial law, until he resigned. He was a U.S. congressman from Connecticut before the war. He later became a U.S. collector of internal revenue.

Butler became a Radical Republican Congressman and one of the managers of Johnson's impeachment. The historian David Saville Muzzey refers to Butler, Stephens, *et al.* at the trial of Johnson: "Like the Jacobins of the French Revolution, they urged the tribunal to punish the self-convicted traitor rather than to try the privileged defendant."

Butler became active in the National Labor Union, which had links to the First International, but he was never trusted by the Socialist Labor wing of the movement. In 1884, Butler became the candidate of the Greenback Party for president.

Again, this is the man to whom Lincoln first offered the vice presidency during the war. One shudders to think what the country would have looked like had he accepted. It also demonstrates the fact that the ploy by Lincoln to run on a National Union ticket to demonstrate his moderate politics was bogus. Lincoln never rejected radicalism unless it was politically expedient to do so.

Phillips gave speeches on the need to conquer, occupy, and re-educate the South for a generation — what essentially became Reconstruction.

In England during the Civil War, the American Anti-Slavery Society, through their British agents, was instrumental in moving English public opinion against the South. The Chartist George Thompson was their paid agent. An influential Emancipation Society was organized in London in the interest of the Union, with Thompson as the spirit behind it and his son-in-law as its executive. Members included John Stuart Mill and Herbert Spencer.

Thompson tried to get Phillips and Gerrit Smith to come to England to help create and direct public opinion. Phillips could not go; Henry Ward Beecher took his place and much was done through working class meetings.

One of the agents of the American abolitionists who worked to move England toward being sympathetic to the Union was the secularist Moncure D. Conway, one of Thomas Paine's biographers. He was a Unitarian minister who finally abandoned the "conservative" church and moved from Emerson's Transcendentalism to humanistic freethought. He was an editor of the *Dial* and ultimately remained in Britain. He was a speaker at the tribute for Robert Owen in London in 1871.

The Emancipation Proclamation and the victories of Grant and George Meade put the *coup de grace* to any idea of British intervention on the side of the South in order to split the U.S. in two.

During the war, George Thompson was received in a public reception in the House of Representatives with Lincoln and his Cabinet present.

At the end of the war, Thompson rushed back across the Atlantic to be in on the death of slavery and the war. A Boston celebration was held and the speakers were the Englishman Thompson, Garrison, and Phillips.

When once again the American flag was hoisted at Ft. Sumter after the war, a special ceremony was held. George Thompson and Garrison were there by special invitation of the National Government.

Again, it is not difficult to see how some U.S. citizens saw the hand of the English in the agitation that led to the conflict, due to their continued involvement in American domestic affairs.

After the war, the leadership of the AASS passed on to Phillips. The organization supported the 15th Amendment, and Phillips became increasingly involved in labor reform. He also wrote a letter to the New York Italians congratulating Garibaldi and Mazzini on the liberation of Italy. Mazzini had established Young Italy lodges wherever Italians were to be found. A Young Italy organization existed in New York and received their orders from Mazzini in London.

The term *Mafia* was coined by Mazzini, who used such people as enforcers, and the name evolved into use by Americans to refer to La Cosa Nostra. More research is necessary to determine the exact evolution or merger of the criminal and conspiratorial elements. It is difficult to ascertain how much they are influenced by the Conspiracy today, since the inclusion of La Cosa Nostra into politics is not unknown.

The Massachusetts Labor Party made Phillips their candidate for governor in 1870. The Prohibition Convention, of which Alvan Bovay had become a part, did the same. Thus we see the Prohibitionists as part of the overall conspiratorial orb at the time.

Phillips wanted the overthrow of the whole profit-making system and the elimination of the poverty of the masses. He grew close to Benjamin Butler, as he was part of the labor movement as well. During the campaign, Phillips openly declared himself to be a socialist.

As late as 1871, Phillips was stating that the way to handle the South was to march 30 million men, women, and children to the Gulf and hang a few generals.

When Wendell Phillips died, his pallbearers included Wendell Phillips Garrison, Theodore D. Weld, and Dr. Oliver Wendell Holmes.

13

WAR

The truth is not always palatable, and should not always be told.
General William Tecumseh Sherman, *Memoirs*.

I don't believe the truth will ever be known, and I have a great contempt for History.
Gen. George Gordon Meade,
victor of Gettysburg, Bradford, *Union Portraits*

The secret history of those days … concealing many startling revelations, has yet been sparingly written; it is doubtful if the veil will ever be more than slightly lifted.
Sen. Zachariah Chandler, (R, Michigan), *Life*

Many of the revelations … of the first few weeks (of Lincoln's incumbency) would doubtless be startling, even today, but the time has not come for their exposure.
J. G. Holland, the editor of the *Springfield Republican*,
Massachusetts, November 1865

None of these men ever revealed what they were referring to.

By the time of the political conventions in 1860, the body politic of the United States was running a fever, a war fever. There seemed to be nothing stopping it. Why? What good would war do for the country? What purpose would a war serve?

Rage, coupled with fear, had swept over the South over the idea of John Brown trying to organize a slave revolt starting in Harper's Ferry, filling the average Southern citizen with animosity toward Northern abolitionists and the politicians who supported them. To believe that Northerners in positions of influence were serious about starting a slave revolt that could engulf them all and their children became personal.

Those who wanted war knew what they were doing.

Why War?
There are a number of things that can be used to change the society or the form of government of a country, and these include some crisis, either economic, natural disaster, or bellicose, such as terrorism and war.

War is, of them all, the best means for effecting change in any people and their system of government. If a combination of crises brought about by the war can be used, more changes can be made. People will stand for just about anything and sacrifice much in the name of the war effort and the need to win the war. Not just enduring increased taxation or inconvenience — they will go to the extent that their individual liberty is curtailed.

The same has been true in the past for terrorism, but to a lesser degree — unless the terrorism was frequent and widespread within a country.

However, modern terrorism does not need to be local to have its effect on people. Once a terrorist attack is performed locally, due to the images on television, subsequent terrorism regardless of where the attack takes place — even on the other side of the world — keeps the urgency before the people so they stand still for almost anything for the sake of security, believing it's for their own good.

In other words, modern communications have brought terrorism into the living room on a daily basis, through television, the newspapers, and the Internet. This then creates the urgency to eliminate the terrorists in the minds of the people. It does not have to always be right down the block. It can be anywhere and serve the purpose of keeping fear in the frontal lobe.

And, a government that wants more power will constantly remind the people of the terror threat to enhance the fear and thereby the acquiescence to change on the part of the population. Government will always have a solution, and it will always lead to more controls over the people rather than the terrorists. It is the same idea where gun control is promoted — the innocent are the victims because they cannot be on equal terms with the criminals or the government, since they obey the law and as a result are unarmed.

Natural disasters tend to make the changes local, usually extending little beyond the effects of the disaster, unless the population can be convinced that the disaster has a major effect on the whole economy. Economic problems can be used, but only to the extent of the ignorance of the people as to economic realities and how much control the government or those behind the government have over the market place to begin with. Usually, economic controls come in steps that have been orchestrated by a few manipulators through a banking *system*.

Keep in mind that free enterprise is not a system. It is a lack of a system if it is truly free. Yet the use of the term "free enterprise system" implies that it is a system. It is, again, the use of semantics to fix the mind-set of the people. If free enterprise is a system in the minds of the people, then it is simply a matter of controlling the system if there are, or are what appear to be inequities. Thus, the free aspect of economics disappears eventually into the hands of the few through government regulation.

If a combination of any or all of the above can be orchestrated by government or those who want government to become totalitarian, all the better. The 20th century was a hundred years of examples of the combination of economic disasters, war, and terrorism designed to move whole continents into ever larger and more intrusive government.

The more obvious change as a result of war occurs on the vanquished — the less obvious on the victor.

The American Civil War came about for the same purpose of altering American society and constitutionally protected liberty, and was orchestrated by conspiratorial organizations with behind-the-scenes coordination even while appearing to be enemies of one another.

An example would be the abolitionist movement under William Lloyd Garrison and the Knights of the Golden Circle under Bickley. Both were members of the secret Brotherhood of the Union led by George Lippard. While it was obvious that Garrison ran with socialists and his newspaper, *The Liberator*, originally had a motto promoting the new world order idea, this was not as obvious with Bickley.

For Bickley to have formed chapters of the Brotherhood under Lippard, must have meant that his motivation was more than what he revealed to the KGC members. Some history books state that he tried and failed to do so in Cincinnati, but the fact is that he successfully did so in at least three places.

Did this organizing prove that Bickley could coordinate something new to those in conspiratorial leadership, and then they promoted him as leader of the KGC?

In the previous chapter we pointed out the connection between those who supported Brown, and the Carbonari, who also supported the KGC.

You cannot have a good fight unless you control both sides — one may not want to fight, and the outcome may not be what is intended unless you have working control.

And it doesn't necessarily mean that the underlings know that they are controlled by the same person, Star Chamber, or whatever entity. Two seemingly opposing organizations' members may truly believe that they are enemies, not understanding that they take orders from the same source.

A modern example would be the fact that the Communist Party USA had effective leadership over many civil rights organizations in the 1960s, and this was likewise true of various KKK and white supremacist organizations, particularly in Mississippi. While the communists were trained to start or take over civil rights organizations, at the same time they had a school for teaching communists to run KKK organizations.

Many of these training schools took their impetus from the KGB of the USSR. Over the years such schools in Russia, their satellites, and targeted countries would teach a wide variety of methods to subvert societies in Europe, Asia, and particularly America.

Perhaps the best kept "secret" of the Cold War was the agents of change that were trained by Russia and its satellite countries that they sent into Muslim countries to radicalize them and form terrorist cells. According to defecting KGB officers, the numbers were in the thousands.

You cannot have a good conflict, especially a prolonged one, unless you control both sides. The communists did work *both sides* to whip up racial hatred in order to provoke violence, which would lead to more legislation placing the federal government into areas never before regulated, such as education, hiring practices, local social mores, etc. Neither the minions in the Civil Rights movement nor the KKK members knew that their leadership sprang from the same fountainhead, only that they hated each other.

Meanwhile, the victims, the American people of all races, could only stand by and watch, not knowing what was going on or what to do about it if they did.

One of the modern situations where such tactics came into play was the Oklahoma City bombing. There were others involved that did not come to trial including individuals with ties to both Right and Left terrorism.[52]

These same tactics have continued under Putin, where Russia has sent in *agents provocateurs* to stir up situations they then could take advantage of, such as in Chechnya and the Ukraine in ± 2000.

Terrorism is usually eliminated by responsible government very quickly. If not, the government wants it to continue. While it may seem ridiculous to the reader that terrorists and government officials would work together, Rev. Al Sharpton, Attorney General Eric Holder, and the White House working together is just the tip of the iceberg. Instead of calming things down after the riots of late 2014, they made public pronouncements which initially fanned the flames, after they had visited together.

---

52 The best exposition of this event and those involved is archived in *The New American* magazine, which did an extensive study of the problem, including that fact that the government did not seem to want to pursue individuals who were foreign born or involved in extremist organizations of any stripe. As far as our government was concerned, Terry Nichols and Timothy McVeigh acted alone.

Since Lippard was very active in socialist organizations and wrote along the lines of convincing people of socialist goals, and with the inclusion of so many communist leaders in its membership, it is doubtful that the other leaders of Brotherhood of the Union would not have promoted the same. Therefore, since it is obvious that Garrison was active with socialists, and since his newspaper in the beginning carried the motto promoting the aim of a new world order, his membership in the BU is significant. Bickley, supposedly the enemy of the abolitionists, must have also had these goals as well, no matter how he disguised the goals of the Knights of the Golden Circle. Yet on the surface, to the average American, they appeared to be enemies.

Given this condition, Bickley's public persona was very different than that of the bulk of the Brotherhood's leaders, and his forming an organization that supposedly worked against aims of the BU *after forming circles of the BU* demonstrates that the people can be organized over and over again into groups that have public goals quit different from the real and hidden objectives.

People will follow leaders that come out of nowhere to guide them — as long as they say the right things. This then fools the followers into believing the rhetoric rather than the results of the action engaged in as a solution.

The reader must understand by now that the entire radical leadership, regardless of outward appearances, had been working together for some time. Often, the leadership is so interwoven it becomes confusing as to what is what. The main thing to remember during a study of the process is the final aim in mind. The rest is a bewildering mass of initiatives and leadership, deliberately designed to confuse.

To bring the strategy forward in time, in the magazine of the Council on Foreign Relations, *Foreign Affairs*, former State Department official Richard N. Gardner said this in 1974:

> In short, the "house of world order" will have to be built from the bottom up rather than from the top down. It will look like a "booming buzzing confusion" … an end run around national sovereignty, eroding it piece by piece, will accomplish more than the old-fashioned frontal assault.

It is all designed to confuse and confound their opposition.

The Left does not make mistakes when it comes to understanding the motivation of political leaders. Those on the so-called Right are fooled constantly. However, there can be no doubt to the then-current politicos that the Brotherhood contained a variety of leftist leaders and affiliates. Bickley, at the minimum, had to understand what he was involved in since he started units of the BU before the KGC.

After the war, prominent members of the KGC participated in radical causes, land reform, and socialist movements, within both the Republican and Democrat parties, indicating their motivation was different from that presented by their public images at the time or by historians today.

In 1844, George Evans organized the Reform movement to promote a modified version of Thomas Skidmore's proposed "equal division of all property, including land and capital." Skidmore's *The Rights of Man to Property* was not a mandate for individual property rights, but for Man's property rights, just as Thomas Paine advocated. Its inevitable end was the control of property by the state in the name of giving property to all.

The communist National Reform Movement promoted the "Vote Yourself a Farm" movement. The Republicans used this as one of their planks in the 1860 election, and it became the Homestead Act. This placed the federal government in charge of any new lands, rather than the enterprising individual pioneer who would suffer the hardship of going into the wilderness to tame it, as had been done originally by the states or counties.

This was a multiple gain, for it was also used during the Civil War to entice Europeans to the United States as cannon fodder for the Union Army. The promise of free land was a major enticement. Regrettably, some soldiers only received that land six feet under it.

One can measure the growth and control of government by the percentage of the land that remained in the federal government's hands when a new state was admitted to the Union. The original thirteen states had virtually no federal land in them outside of military installations and other small facilities as delineated in the Constitution. As each state was admitted going west across the continent, increasingly federal land became a larger percentage of the new state, until Alaska was admitted and the federal government retained 61.8 %.

Interestingly, the worst case happened during the Civil War under the Radical government: Nevada. It was not only the state constitution that was forced on the state as an arm of the federal government, at the same time the federal government kept 81.1 % of the land. We will visit this again in a later chapter.

The exception to the above scenario has been the growth of national parks, forests, and wilderness areas that are now being set aside as federal land. However, this mostly came about after the vast majority of the states were admitted and serves as a means to go back and get territory they did not keep when the states were admitted.

The tactic keeps the individual out or away from the land as it regards ownership. As this system grows, the individual is confined more and more into areas the government can control better. If eventually the people are confined to cities, then the government can have nearly complete control over the activities and businesses of the people through zoning, taxing, environmental regulations, etc. The smaller the confines of private ownership, the easier it is to control by government.

This is the ultimate goal of what is known as *Agenda 21*, which is under the leadership of the United Nations — the world government — but made to appear local.[53]

Secession

The agitation leading toward a civil war had been going on for decades. Secession was not a new idea in American politics, as has been pointed out. To recap: It was used as a tactic in the West during the fledgling thirteen original states by the Jacobins. It continued under the initiatives of the Nicholas brothers with Jefferson and then Aaron Burr. At one point, Jefferson called for Kentucky and Virginia to secede if the Alien and Sedition Acts continued. It was seriously considered in New England during the War of 1812, amongst leaders in South Carolina during the nullification battle, and a secession meeting was held called the Hartford Convention in the North before the South seceded. Then there was a broad-based, lengthy propaganda program by radical abolitionist "come-outers" promoting disunion.

Samuel Fessenden, an anti-Illuminist during the Rev. Morse campaign, introduced a bill in the Massachusetts Legislature to arm the militia and declare independence during the governorship of Caleb Strong. Such was the feeling of the Federalists at the time against the French influence within the U.S. stirred up by the Republican-Democrats.

In January 1850, a Nashville Convention of secessionists was held. Jefferson Davis was its chief promoter. Others included Albert Gallatin Brown of Mississippi, William Lowndes Yancey of Alabama, and Robert Barnwell Rhett of South Carolina. It did not have a common purpose, since Davis wanted a Southern Republic and Rhett wanted state sovereignty. The scheme to annex the countries south of the U.S. into a vast slave empire was also the motivation of many in attendance, if not most.

---

53   The easiest resource to access for information of this modern threat to private property is at www.JBS.org/Issues.

The general Southern sentiment was not for secession in 1850. It would take another decade of agitation in the North and South to prepare the way within the Southern electorate for their desire to separate themselves from the United States.

Disunion was a common thread that was woven into socialist solutions for decades as a means to deal with pre-conceived "problems" with America. But it was only a tactic, a step toward the end goal.

Abolitionist leaders who favored disunion as the "corner-stone of all true anti-slavery" were William L. Garrison and Wendell Phillips.

Garrison was not only hostile to the Constitution, he was also hostile to Christianity; he became a spiritualist and was convinced that a violent revolution was necessary. As a Perfectionist, he believed in communism.

Twelve years before the war, Phillips, at the American Anti-Slavery Convention in New York City in May of 1848, offered this resolution:

> That this Society deems it a duty to reiterate its convictions that only the exodus of the slave out of his present house of bondage is *over the ruins of the present American church, and the present American Union.* (Emphasis in the original.)

It passed. Note that it was not simply the disunion of the United States; it was the destruction of Christianity since there was no established church. To call, therefore, for the destruction of the American church meant all churches. *Yet there were many members of the Christian clergy that were leaders of the AASS.* When everything is taken into account, the motivation of these leaders was much different than simple abolition of slavery, and was why many who opposed slavery could not work with anti-slavery leaders.

It is obvious to anyone really studying the movement that there were many members of the clergy who were actually working for the elimination of Christianity from inside the church.

Garrison offered this resolution at the meeting of the Massachusetts Anti-Slavery Society in May of 1857:

> "Resolved: That the one great issue before the country is, The Dissolution of the Union...annulling this 'covenant with death.'"

One of the mainstays for the Union after secession became *fait accompli* was U.S. Senator Wilson, who was an incorporator of the Massachusetts Anti-Slavery Society, the disunionists. The strategy was: agitate for disunion into a war, and then become a unionist.

Lincoln himself at one time supported the right of a portion of the people to secede from their government, but was of a different opinion regarding the South. In his speech on the Mexican War in January 1848 he said:

> Any people anywhere, being inclined and having the power, have the right to rise up and shake off the existing government.

This was in reference to Texas seceding from Mexico.

The Disunion Convention of 1857 was held, and an *acceleration* of sentiment toward secession occurred from this time on until it became the solution of choice by both extremes and those they influenced.

The extreme hypocrisy was in December of 1859. The *abolitionists* in New York City adopted:

Resolved: The we invite a free correspondence with the Disunionists of the South ... to secure the dissolution of the present imperfect and inglorious union between the free and slave states.

Both sides had a desire for war, and both sides were victims of those who had a longstanding relationship with radical organizations and personalities. And, there may have been more of a connection between the two radical disunion movements than most realize based on more than this one clue above.

There were many leaders in the Southern secession movement who had close friends in the socialist circles in the North, as we have established, but not to the level we would desire since we are tending to concentrate a little more on the conspiracy in the North. The little that we have looked at that could be called Southern was organizations that before the war had a great influence on the federal government, the foreign service, and international relationships.

Reaching out to one's archenemy to dissolve the union would not seem to be what abolitionists would do. By so doing, if successful, *they would have dissolved the union but slavery would have kept going!* If the abolition of slavery was the goal, then why reach out in this manner when the end result would not have been the elimination of slavery, but the dissolution of the United States? The goal had to be secession to get a war going.

There were concerned citizens and political movements that wanted to find a means to stop the juggernaut. In 1861, the New York Democratic Party called for a convention to be held on January 31 in Albany. In its call, the Democratic State Central Committee stated:

In this emergency conservative men of all classes call upon our time-honored party, which at this moment represents the views and feelings of a majority of the people of New York, to co-operate with patriotic citizens elsewhere, and especially with the efforts of the "Border States," in putting down the agitations and *conspiracies* of the Secessionists of the South and the ultra Republicans of the North. (Emphasis added)

The party was for just about any solution for a peaceful resolution even if it meant disunion without war. Note as well that they referred to the *conspiracies* at work, *on both sides*.

A Washington Peace Conference was held to which most states sent a total of 100 delegates to try and resolve differences in order to preserve the union. Delegates ranged from those who earnestly desired to prevent a split in the country, to those who, on both sides, wanted it. One of the delegates was Judge John W. Houston of the Order. The exercise was doomed to failure since not all delegates had a desire to see it succeed.

This convention proposed amendments to the Constitution as a means to reach amity. This example is used by some today to illustrate how a Constitutional Convention would be plausible today and not become a runaway convention. They forget that it failed. Not the least of the reasons was that it contained delegates from two extremes that could not agree, with legislatures and a Congress that could not agree was well.

The same conditions would prevail today.

It is interesting that the proponents of a modern convention are adamantly opposed to the process of nullification. Yet, nullification, done correctly, would leave the Constitution intact. Any convention would change the Constitution in all cases, either through amendment or wholesale revision. Which process supports the Constitution?

In the narrative below, we *again concentrate on the Northern aspects of the situation* over the Southern because in the long run it became the Northern influence on the nation that counted, and because of the disinformation and lack of logic that prevails in schools today about the events controlled by the North.

Most people today do not realize that there would not have been a civil war, even with all the agitation for one, had not Lincoln wanted the war and performed several unconstitutional acts to force it on the citizens of America — at least not when the war did occur. It might have come later under a different administration with additional agitation. This is not what is taught in American schools today. However, in the South, this idea still lingers among the people.

Do not reject the idea that Lincoln wanted a war. It will become more convincing as we proceed.

First of all, the South did not secede en masse. They went out in groups and singularly. Every act committed by Lincoln after the initial secession of Alabama, Florida, Georgia, Louisiana, Mississippi, South Carolina, and Texas seemed designed to create a larger secession. No other idea makes sense unless it was that Lincoln was either insane or stupid, which he was not. Thirteen states ultimately seceded; however, circumstances in Missouri and Kentucky led by pro-Unionist militia and the U.S. Army prevented them from ever joining the Confederacy. It would have been fourteen had not Lincoln arrested the bulk of the Maryland legislature before they could vote.

With the evidence that the movements controlled by the Conspiracy wanted disunion as a means to create a prolonged civil war, Lincoln's actions fit the plan. At first, the communists declared disunion and worked for it, and once it became a reality they segued into super patriots demanding that the union be preserved — not only preserved, but that no state would ever be allowed to say again that they wished to be separate or in any way preserve the vestiges of state sovereignty and the balance between the federal republic and the state republics.

In the South the Conspiracy created disunion, and then a sizable portion of the leadership did all they could to make sure that the South could not win the ensuing war.

The secession of the first states occurred prior to Lincoln's inauguration. After his inauguration the Confederate States sent a peace delegation to Washington to meet with Lincoln on March 1861. He refused to see them.

According to the Constitution, only Congress has the power to call up the state militias, yet Lincoln did so without the consent of Congress in April 1861. This he did with the excuse that it was to put down an insurrection due to the firing on Ft. Sumter, when the state had not been in the union for several months. The unconstitutional calling up of the militia caused Virginia to pull out.

The firing of cannon against Ft. Sumter is the reason historians say that the war started and the reason Lincoln gave to declare an insurrection. The man who was in charge of the Confederate forces at Charleston was Gen. Pierre Beauregard, recently the commandant of West Point. He was a member of the KGC and tried to form a castle of the KGC during his brief stint as commandant at West Point.

Ft. Sumter ignited the North against the South. It was the turning point for most of the people who wanted a peaceful solution. Only one Southerner of note argued against the firing on Ft. Sumter: Robert Toombs, the Confederate secretary of state.

" … it is suicide, murder, and you will lose us every friend at the North. You will wantonly strike a hornet's nest … now quiet, will swarm out and sting us to death. It is unnecessary; it puts us in the wrong; it is fatal."

Prior to Ft. Sumter, Lincoln met with Governor Andrew Gregg Curtin of Pennsylvania and told him to prepare for war, *before Lincoln sent an expedition to Sumter*. It was this expedition that eventually led to the fateful events. Recall that of all the members of the Cabinet, only Blair, who was involved in raising money for the defense of the John Brown conspiracy, wanted to force the issue with Ft. Sumter.

In 1884, James G. Blaine wrote:

The overwhelming public desire for all was peace, and the overwhelming public opinion was against the extremists who would, by any possibility, precipitate war.

Secretary of State Seward, five days before Lincoln called out the militia, wrote the English Ambassador: "Only an imperial and despotic government could subjugate thoroughly disaffected and insurrectionary members of the state." Yet, Lincoln did exactly that.

In order for Lincoln to be justified in invading the South — for that is what happened — a situation had to occur for it to be accepted by the people. *The firing on Sumter was not the first time such an event had happened*, but it was used to ignite the war. Several posts and forts had been seized by Southern forces without incident.

The supply ship *The Star of the West*, flying the American flag, had already been fired upon when it attempted to supply Ft. Sumter. Since the flag had already been taken down from many forts and depots around the South without the public outcry that the firing on Ft. Sumter produced, the incident had all the earmarks of a staged event to inflame the North and South.

The fort was virtually the last military installation left in the South that was held by Union forces. Efforts had been made to effect its being handed over to the State of South Carolina, but all such overtures were rebuffed.

When planning an invasion, it is always better to make it look as if you are attacked. Lincoln invaded the South. On only one occasion did the South invade the North, and that was much later at Gettysburg — *all other major battles were in defense of Southern territory by the invading Union Army.*

There were some incursions into Northern territory by raiding parties, but none that were intended to be *invasions* in the meaning of the word.

If Lincoln had been serious about re-supplying Ft. Sumter, he would have given the expedition more support. The U.S. naval vessels, instead of helping the supply ship reach Ft. Sumter, stood idly by. It turned into a military disaster as to its stated intent. Yet every Union man who had participated in this military failure with any onsite responsibility was promoted immediately and continually during the war.

There was no immediate threat from the South to move north into Northern territory. Ft. Sumter was a long way away from Washington. In order to go into the North, any Confederate army would have had to traverse territory considered to be Southern but which had not seceded — in fact did not want to secede — at least not then: Virginia and Kentucky.

Kentucky was certainly in no mood to permit troops to traverse her territory to attack Washington at that time and did all it could to stay out of the conflict.

Much has been written about the Ft. Sumter affair and the blame is spread around all sides and all people connected with it. Lay that aside and look at the results logically. What happened was what someone wanted to happen.

Lincoln created an action to stimulate a reaction. Once that took place, the excuse to act unconstitutionally was in place.

Earlier, the attack on Harper's Ferry, a staged act, sparked the South. Ft. Sumter inflamed the North. Again, the action is in the reaction.

Based on the illegal call-up of the militia by Lincoln, Virginia seceded; it was trying everything it could not to, but enough was enough. Virginia looked upon the call-up of the militia on April 15, 1861 as an act of war against the Southern states *that were in no way threatening the North, had no plans to invade Northern States, and just wanted to be left alone.*

The nearest seceding state to Washington at the time of the call-up was South Carolina!

Virginia went out two days later, and North Carolina a little over a month later. Virginia left because of the illegal call-up of the militia to war on fellow Americans, and North Carolina left because of the illegal naval blockade against North Carolina imposed by Lincoln before North Carolina seceded. The blockade gave the secessionists the leverage needed to convince the average North Carolinian to support secession.

All movements for secession in the North, and there were several, died after Ft. Sumter and they became unionist.

At the outbreak of war, on April 20, 1861, the Left in New York City organized a rally in support of the Lincoln administration, and 100,000 people gathered in Union Square and listened to speeches by such people as John Commerford, Friedrich Kapp, Theodore Tilton, and John Cochrane of Tammany.

What makes the actions of the federal government onerous was that the Southern Peace Conference commissioners sent to Washington, D.C., to meet with the newly elected president were afforded every courtesy and assurances while the administration was preparing to provoke an incident at Ft. Sumter and was preparing for war against a force that did not exist — at least not one that was set to invade the North.

Later in April, Lincoln called for a naval blockade to be placed around the South. In this case, no matter how you look at the act, it was illegal. If the states were still in the union, it was illegal under international law. If the states were no longer part of the union then only Congress had the power to authorize it, for under international law it was an act of war — and only Congress has the power to declare war.

At the end of April, he extended this blockade to North Carolina which was still in the union. Again, this is what put North Carolina over the top to secede the following month.

The idea propagated in the North was that the South was going to invade the North and take the national capital, when in fact it was the other way around. The army assembling in Virginia was assembling to protect itself from the call-up of federal troops to invade the South. Recall that Virginia did not secede until the Union call-up was made.

During the early months of the war, when the army was assembled, the communications between Lincoln and McClellan were of taking Richmond, not defending the capital.

The litany of such acts and the reversal of promises made to state governments, such as honoring Kentucky's neutrality while remaining in the Union, went on for some months with a growing heavy hand of actions that were totally in violation of the Bill of Rights and the Constitution, but backed up by not only the army, heavily laden with Socialist German units, but the paramilitary units of the Republican Party WAR detachments.

To be fair, the Southern units were being egged on by the Knights of the Golden Circle in their ranks, or were made up of KGC members entirely. In both incidences, however, whether North or South, the military units were heavily influenced by conspiratorial organizations.

There were initiatives by the Border States to maintain peaceful relations, such as between Ohio and Kentucky. No one outside of the extremists wanted a war. These initiatives were dashed on the altar of war and looked upon as treason in Washington.

A "Convention of the Border Slave States" composed of states which had not passed ordinances of secession met in May 1861. From the *Journal and Proceedings of the Convention of the Border States* comes this statement of the conditions in the country at the time:

> It is a proud and grand thing for Kentucky to stand up and say, as she can, truthfully, in the face of the world "we had no hand in this thing;" our skirts are clear. And, in looking at the *terrorism* that citizens, their homesteads subjected to lawless visitation, their property confiscated, and their persons liable to incarceration and search — how grandly does she not loom up, as she proclaims to the oppressed and miserable, we offer you a refuge! Here constitutional law and respect for individual rights still exist! Here is an asylum where loyalty to the name, nation, and Flag of the Union predominate; and here is the only place, in this lately great Republic, where true freedom remains — that freedom for which our fathers fought — the citizen being free to speak, write, or publish any thing he may wish, responsible only to the laws, and not controlled by the violence of the mob.

The terrorism referred to above came as a result of Union troops enforcing the will of the federal government against any free speech in opposition to war.

It appeared that everything Lincoln and the Radicals did was designed to agitate rather than calm Southern fears. One further example is that Gen. Lane, the leader of the largest Kansas free-stater army during the conflict in the 1850s, was put in charge of the guards at the White House. There was enough blame for violence and murder in Kansas to go around on both sides, and in the heat of the day, each side pointed their finger at the other.

In this case, the action of placing Lane in this position was, as far as the South was concerned, just another indication that the worst elements of the abolitionists were in control. It was not a condition for mediation or moderation and those in charge had to have understood this and wanted it that way, performing acts, making appointments, and in general doing everything to provoke rather than heal the situation — which helped the KGC agitation in the South.

If peace or conciliation had been desired, such blatant events placing the most extreme elements in charge in the North would have never been allowed by the incoming president. There were many officers in the U.S. Army who could have served in that position who would not have stirred up the emotions that the command by Lane did. After all, the Southern papers had been carrying reports out of Kansas just as the Northern papers had done, only with a slant against the anti-slavery "armies." They knew well who Lane was, and he was just a hair above the character of John Brown.

The opposite of conciliation became the norm. There was an atmosphere of suspicion and the shutting down of any dissent or moves toward moderation.

Newspaper offices were occupied by Northern troops to prevent their publication, and the use of the postal service was denied to hundreds of Northern publications. Members of Congress were arrested, and a substantial number of the State of Maryland's Legislature was arrested and confined to prevent their voting for secession. If they had, Washington would have been surrounded by the Confederacy, with Virginia on one side and Maryland on the other.

In July, Congress convened and did just about everything Lincoln wanted and/or confirmed what he had done, including the suspension of habeas corpus. Of course, most of the Southern states had by this time withdrawn from the Congress.

As late as November 1861, the Border State of Kentucky seceded, fed up with the blatant violations of the law by the federal government.

One has to ask what Lincoln's motivation was with the actions that were unethical and immoral which exacerbated the war fever. While he stopped some generals from going too far, it was more of a political decision rather than a moral one in too many cases. Was he part of the plan, was he inept in how he handled things, or was he, like modern presidents, simply a tool of the people who put him in office who are generally unknown to the public?

In 1848, Lincoln wrote to his protégé, William H. Herndon:

Kings have always been involving … their people in wars.... This, our (constitutional) convention understood to be the most oppressive of all kingly oppressions; and they resolved to so frame the Constitution that no one man should hold the power of bringing this oppression upon us.

Yet Lincoln did not ask the Cabinet for their opinions in the final moments of the crisis. They docilely stood by while Lincoln singularly called for troops and suspended habeas corpus and all of the other congressional prerogatives that he took upon the executive branch.

Lincoln's Attorney General Edward Bates said: "Public opinion is never spontaneous … It is always a manufactured article … Bold and active rulers make it on their side."

The litany of unconstitutional acts performed by Lincoln at the beginning of his presidency makes a solid case for the fact that he had no regard for the Constitution.

The ends never justify the means. You cannot perform an immoral act to justify upholding morality. Nor can you perform a series of unconstitutional acts and proclaim that you are doing it to save the Constitution. By performing unconstitutional acts, you are in reality destroying the Constitution, particularly when it sets a precedent that can be used later if unchallenged.

One can use the argument that invasion justifies many extremes by government to repel the invader. But, the South was not an invader, yet the federal government made it seem so as an excuse to start a war. Plus, many acts by the Lincoln government were designed to provoke a violent response to further the idea of martial law, at the least, and war at the worst.

Secession is not necessarily rebellion. It is the desire to go it alone and be left alone. It can possibly include rebellion, the idea of not only leaving but taking over the remainder, and this was the image portrayed by Lincoln. There were statements by some in the South which were used to help portray this attitude, but they were the small minority.

The smallest act of secession of a societal or governmental unit, the family, is a divorce. This is rarely amicable in the full meaning of the word, but it is not necessary that one party kill the other, no matter how much they would like to. And, the one getting the divorce doesn't necessarily want the house. If they do, that's rebellion. If they also want alimony, that is total defeat by the rebel!

In the case of nations, it's called reparations.

There were many steps taken by Lincoln which did not take into account the advice of his Cabinet. The ignoring of the Confederate peace delegation by Lincoln was an obvious sign by Lincoln that he did not want a peaceful solution. Rather, those behind Lincoln who elevated him to the presidency did not want a peaceful solution. He could have at least met with them without recognizing their ability to represent the Confederacy as legitimate.

What are the negative aspects of one meeting compared to the deaths of well over a half a million men at arms?

The Southern citizen was concerned about the belligerent attitude of the men who had been elected into the federal government; the WAR units, coupled with the Turner groups' militia, and both of their leaders using the Helper book to call for the annihilation of the Southern slave holders in such a way that imperiled all Southerners; and, the statements by Radicals in Northern state governments, as well as the federal government, indicating that the South was going to come under attack. They reacted to defend themselves, and in the process served as a basis for the federal government to say that the newly formed Southern government arming itself was an act of aggression.

It was tantamount to a bully yelling that his victim is committing an act of aggression by the victim putting up his hands to defend himself. This twist is widely used today in a variety of Leftist movements against their victims. They also use it against the police. In either case, the aggressor is made to look like the victim in order to further the leftist agenda or react the situation into more draconian government.

Civil rights leaders used this tactic all the time during the 1960s and 1970s. They would perform some act of belligerence, and then call any reaction or act of defense of either a person, property, or civil law as a provocation, documenting this as proof of the belligerence of the police, local authorities, or property owners.

The unconstitutional acts by Lincoln only exacerbated the reaction by the South, leading up to a critical mass that burst on the American scene.

Keep in mind that there was already evidence that the entire affair at Ft. Sumter was staged. Those in command of the situation had shown that they were part of the organizations that were descendants of the Conspiracy.

Also, the first battles were in Virginia, where the Union Army had assembled. If the Virginians moved against the Union forces, it was to expel them from their own soil. To have allowed them to stay would have negated the sovereignty of the state.

Keep in mind the constitutional aspects of the situation and the manner in which the United States was to operate militarily. The militias were to form the vast bulk of the army, at least initially. Since the constituted authority in Virginia was the Virginian government and they had control of their militia, other state militias entering their soil without permission was an act of war, even if they called themselves the United States Army. The initial troops of the army were other militias for some months.

A short list of unconstitutional acts by Lincoln is:

- On April 13, 1861, Lincoln declared the seceding states in a condition of rebellion and called for 75,000 troops to deal with them. The Constitution says that only Congress may do this.
- On April 15, he called for Congress to return to session, *but not until well into July*, not the action of a president concerned about an emergency. Congress should have met immediately.
- On April 19, he declared a naval blockade of the South. Illegal under international law.
- On April 21, he instructed the U.S. Navy to buy five warships, an appropriations act needing congressional approval.
- On April 27, he suspended habeas corpus.
- On May 3, he called up thousands more troops for a three-year hitch — another act that could only be authorized only by Congress.
- He ordered the Department of the Treasury to pay two million dollars — a huge amount at the time, and the purchase power of billions today — to a New York company to outfit the army, which was another appropriations act that could only be authorized by Congress.

- Kentucky did not want to become involved on either side. They called a convention of the Border States in May. Lincoln promised to honor their neutrality, but then violated that promise, causing Kentucky to secede.
- He suspended the use of the mail and publishing in certain quarters and large areas of the North.

By the time Congress did meet, the war had begun, the situation was up in the air, and the president had handed the Congress a *fait accompli*, and just as today, the Congress rubberstamped the actions of the president. It had little choice, and the Radicals had the war they wanted.

Reiterating, as a Congressman, Lincoln said in January 1848 in reference to Texas seceding from Mexico:

> Any people anywhere, being inclined and having the power, have the right to rise up and shake off the existing government, and form a new one that suits them better. This is a most valuable, a most sacred right — a right which we hope and believe is to liberate the world. Nor is this right confined to cases in which the whole people of an existing government may choose to exercise it. Any portion of such people, that can, may revolutionize and make their own so much of the territory as they inhabit.

As president, he violated this right on the part of the people and states which seceded.

Keep in mind that the original thirteen states — colonies — seceded from the Crown in the first place. They may have made a formal declaration together, but each in its own right had to formally secede by its legislature/assembly/House of Burgess. And the colonies were only a portion of the English possessions in America; the provinces in Canada and elsewhere did not "secede."

The answer to the colonies that did secede from the Crown was war. It was the same response from Lincoln.

The image of Lincoln is that he was a moral man, a Christian, the best president we have ever had. He occasionally attended the Methodist or Presbyterian church in Washington, but was not known to attend any in Springfield, Illinois. Of the twenty-four ministers in Springfield, Illinois (Lincoln's home), all but three opposed his election.

We know that he cooperated with men who were anything but Christian. He attended séances, not just with his wife, but alone, before he was elected. He was very compassionate on one level, but ruthless on another. His protégé, William H. Herndon, was anything but a Christian. He worked with socialist leaders, and Lincoln worked alone with him for years and made him his partner.

When you read what Herndon had to say apologetically about Lincoln's faith, it does read as if he was at least an agnostic. Lincoln was looked at as a deist by his early political opponents. There are stories that Lincoln actually wrote a book against the Bible as a young attorney but that he destroyed it on the advice of a political friend. Some historians claim that the book was a defense of Thomas Paine's deism and that Samuel Hill, a friend of Lincoln, burned the manuscript to save Lincoln's political career.

Let us look at a letter that Herndon wrote concerning this subject:

> I told you in my letter that Mr. Lincoln once wrote a work on Infidelity so-called. This was and is true. Mr. Lincoln was told when a boy some *asserted* facts — facts that somewhat disgraced some of his dear relatives. This story clung to him during all his life, a fire shirt, scorching him;

he suffered that one suffering till 1835, when his love's death duplicated his suffering. The facts, as I can get them, are that he wrote the book on Infidelity before 1835. But from what I know of Mr. Lincoln, and his double cross, I aver that that book was a burst of despair. The book was a lofty criticism, a high spiritual rationalistic criticism, like, as I understand the various evidences … Mr. Lincoln could not believe, as a rational man, a logically-minded one too, a very logically-minded one, that the Bible was the *peculiar*, only, and *special* revelation of God, as the theologic Christian world understands it; i.e., as they preach it. He did not believe that a few chosen men were *particularly*, *specially*, excluding all other men, *inspired*, as the theologic Christian world understands it; i.e., as they preach it. It was *impossible* his mind was so organized for him to see or believe in such doctrines. Mr. Lincoln did not believe in the Miraculous Conception of Jesus.... (Emphasis in original.)

— Letter of W. H. Herndon to Mr. Cronyer, December 3, 1866

There are too many variables in Lincoln's personality to say for certain that he was or wasn't a Christian. It depends on whom you go to for your evidence. However, there are too many hurdles to jump if one is to say that he was. And, it depends on your definition of Christian. Plus, his actions and his administration relative to the Constitution, the Bill of Rights, etc. make it questionable.

This is by no means to excuse what the Buchanan administration did in the last year of his tenure to facilitate the arming and position of the Southern states.

What were Lincoln's politics? Lincoln summed up his political principles when he first ran for the Illinois State Legislature in 1832, principles he never deviated from:

I presume you all know who I am. I am humble Abraham Lincoln. My policies are short and sweet, like the old woman's dance. I am in favor of a National Bank, in favor of the Internal improvements system, and in favor of a high protective tariff.

In other words, he was for a central bank. He was for at least the portion of the socialist platform as outlined by Horace Greeley outlining government involvement of "improvements". It is no wonder that modern politicians love the image of Lincoln as being our greatest president.

The unconstitutional acts approved by Lincoln did not stop after 1861. As an example, in 1863, Gen. Thomas Ewing drew up Union Order 11, perhaps the most onerous edict of the war. It drove the rural residents of four border counties in western Missouri from their homes in an attempt to stamp out guerilla activities. There was a total suspension of the legal and constitutional rights of the state's citizens. Those who could prove their loyalty were permitted to remain but had to move to communities near military outposts. Those who could not had to remove from the counties altogether.

Lincoln approved of the order, but Ewing's superior officer forced him to drop the provision allowing loyal citizens to remain, and removed all from the area. It did not eliminate the problem, and only aggravated it by providing an example and reason for citizens to help the guerillas.

At one point, the United States almost went to war with England over the violation of international law in the seizure of two Confederate Commissioners, Mason and Slidell; this was known as the Trent Affair. The event was named after the English vessel from which the men were seized by U.S. authorities in December 1861. Some historians claim that this was a deliberately staged act on the part of the Confederacy to show the lack of regard to all law, domestic or foreign, by Lincoln. In other words, Jefferson

Davis orchestrated the event for just this incident to happen by having nearly zero security for the commissioners' travel and accommodations.

This excuse is all it is: an excuse to make the U.S. government look as if they had no choice, when they did. Interdicting another nation's vessel and boarding and seizing passengers is a serious violation of international law, and those who performed the deed understood this. It was not the only case where this happened, just the most recorded.

We as Americans have a hard time putting ourselves in another man's shoes and looking at things from his perspective. In this case, you have to look at the Trent Affair from the perspective, say, of a Dutchman.

You are told that you may no longer trade with a large portion of America. You know that the embargo and blockade is illegal. Now you see that the United States feels that it can board any vessel and do as it pleases on the high seas by seizing cargo or individuals just as any pirate would.

Put into the mix the fact that American diplomats were appointed to Europe before the war that had been engaged with communists and Carbonari revolutionaries in Europe, openly stating they supported the overthrow of European governments. At one point, along with the British consul in Rome, the American consul issued passports to some of Mazzini's Carbonari to escape from Rome when the French entered the city.

Plus, it was an open secret that the American government wanted to take the Spanish possessions in the Caribbean, looking the other way in most cases at invasions by private parties to effect this end.

Throw in the fact that the American government was preparing to launch an invasion into its own states in the South, and to you Dutch it would seem as though the American government had gone rogue.

Such an action as the Trent Affair seriously placed the U.S. government into very deep and murky diplomatic water. As a Dutchman, you would be concerned, especially if you were a shipping company owner. You would be concerned no matter what nationality you were. The American government was saying that they could board any vessel for any reason *if they suspected* the vessel was either harboring Confederate officials or cargo or doing it in international waters.

While England had done this, and more, to American vessels over the years, almost leading to war several times as it finally did in 1812, when the American Navy did so, the English were upset. One could hardly feel sorry for England, but then two wrongs did not make a right. It wasn't right when England did it, and it wasn't right when the U.S. did it.

Due to international considerations and the possibility of war with the U.S. over the matter, England starting moving troops into Canada in anticipation of a conflict over the Trent Affair. Going to war with England was not part of the plan, so the two Confederate diplomats were released.

The English proclamation of neutrality in the conflict between the Union and the Confederacy did not sit well with either side. For the South, it meant that they were not technically recognized as an independent state. For the North, it meant that England considered the South a belligerent state, an equal in many ways to the North. The latter further fueled the idea in the North that the start of the war was influenced by England.

Typical of the opinions of the North was a speech on July 4, 1861 by the grandson of John Jay, himself named John Jay, titled, "The Great Conspiracy," later published as *The Great Conspiracy and England's Neutrality* in the same year. He professed to outline a conspiracy in the South to split the country and then chastised England for naming the North and South as co-belligerents rather than naming the South as insurrectionist.

The argument would have held more validity if Jay himself was not part of the Free Democratic League, allied with men like John P. Hale and Hiram Barney. Jay served as president of the New York

Young Men's Anti-Slavery Society, as did Barney at one time, and Barney was a law partner of Benjamin Butler's son and the son-in-law of Tappan. The grandson of one of our Founders, John Jay, would go on to lead the American Historical Association in 1889. Another example that the son was not the father, and that *to the victor go the myths and monuments* by the control of history.

The proclamation of neutrality forbade British citizens from involvement on either side. Thus, there were fewer men from England involved in the American armies than from many other countries, particularly in the North. However, there is more than a little evidence that English Secret Servicemen trained Confederate Secret Service personnel in England, some even working with them in America.

Lincoln began a war against not only the Confederate Army but Southern citizens as well by asking McClellan if he could get close enough to Richmond to shell the city and its civilian population. McClellan stated that he felt the war should be against opposing armies, not against civilians.

McClellan instead issued orders to honor private property, that it could not be plundered:

> ... that this is not a contest against populations; and that it should be conducted by us upon the highest principles known to Christian civilization.
>
> *McClellan's War*

Three weeks later he was replaced; however, this was done for several reasons, not the least of which was that he had several men on his staff who wanted war against Washington as much as with the South.

Since a prolonged war was the plan of the Conspiracy, the actions of McClellan through his aide Col. Thomas M. Key are important to know. Key was a member of Skull and Bones at Yale and became a partner in the law firm of its co-founder, Alphonso Taft. In other words, very close to the top of the Order.

Long story short, Key and McClellan formed a lasting friendship before the war and Key was instrumental in getting McClellan named the head of the Ohio militia, which led to his being named the commander of what became the Army of the Potomac.

Many of the personalities who would work together during the war came together before the war by their association with the Illinois Central Railroad: Lincoln, McClellan, Pinkerton, etc. McClellan had little respect for Lincoln, calling him a "gorilla" and a "well-meaning baboon." These were similar to Stanton's invectives regarding Lincoln prior to the war. Here again, English money was invested in this railroad.

There were secret negotiations between McClellan and Southern forces, which indicate a desire not to destroy the Southern army but to arrive at a peaceful settlement. There were also men on his staff who wanted to turn the army around and capture Washington to overthrow the Radicals in charge, particularly Stanton.

Key apparently was instrumental in stopping these officers from carrying their plans forward. Key never revealed who these rebellious officers were. More importantly, Key was the man to whom Pinkerton reported in his intelligence gathering. This intelligence was shoddy and it agreed with the intelligence Key presented aside from Pinkerton — all of it giving bloated figures for Southern strength. The two became very close and in his will, Key left his watch to Pinkerton.

Key was a major part of all this activity as McClellan's alter ego, and much can be made of his role and his conversations with various people. There are no papers of his or official records regarding these issues that are definitive. All that we have are the conversations of others after the war as to his involvement. He was a very private man. No photographs exist that *definitely* can be identified as him. His personal papers were destroyed almost to a letter.

A bizarre incident occurred involving Key's brother, Major John Key. Due to a remark that John made, *he was hauled up to a court-martial in Lincoln's office* and was summarily discharged from the army. John Key had said that the reason McClellan had not pursued his advantage to destroy the Confederate Army after winning an early victory was, "That's not the game. The object is that neither army shall get much advantage of the other; that both shall be kept in the field till they are exhausted, when we will make a compromise and save slavery."

This is a rather odd comment, if true, from a member of a family who opposed slavery all along. Regardless of the reason, the strategy fits the same strategy of the Conspiracy relative to a prolonged conflict.

The bottom line is this: Thomas Key played a role in prolonging the war and then in preventing a coup d'état against the Radical government, regardless of the reasons put forth for his actions and his public positions on the issues of the day.

This was also true of McClellan, who scorned the secessionists as well as the abolitionists equally. He wrote that, "I am fighting to preserve the integrity of the Union and the power of the Gov't," and "on no other issue." It was his purpose at this time to wage war to nudge the South back into the union, not to punish the South, seize its property, or subjugate its people.

This attitude was used to help "start" a combat that would in fact prolong the conflict, regardless of his intentions.

There were too many people whose actions served this goal, knowingly or unknowingly.

Further complicating the reasons for the actions of McClellan was the history related by Carl Sandburg that Stanton showed Lincoln a letter that purported to show that McClellan was initiated into the Knights of the Golden Circle by Jefferson Davis in 1860. One can speculate, but the presidential campaign rhetoric of McClellan in 1864 as a Democrat was essentially an acceptance of the split of the country in twain. Was this his aim, or was he simply trying to lose the campaign? It is murky, since there is evidence that supports two or three motives relative to McClellan's actions from the beginning of the war to the end of the 1864 election.

The trouble with the Carl Sandburg history is that Sandburg was a socialist at best, so his history would be slanted in that direction. He joined the Social Democratic Party, the name of the Socialist Party of America in Wisconsin, and served as the secretary to the socialist mayor of Milwaukee from 1910 to 1912.

There were several initiatives by Lincoln and the Northern armies which were against the laws of war. For instance, there was an attempt to move a cavalry unit into Richmond that was authorized to assassinate Jefferson Davis and his Cabinet. The mission fell apart during its execution, but the net effect was to heighten Southern resolve against the North once the word got out as to the intent of the mission.

Lincoln turned down prisoner exchanges that were offered late in the war that would have saved the lives of many prisoners that could not or would not be fed by Confederate prison camps. The mistreatment of prisoners by the South was then used as a means to whip up Northern civilian sentiment against Southern soldiers and members of government through newspaper reports and tracts issued by such organizations as the Union League.

While the Conspiracy initially wanted disunion leading to a prolonged war, the European crowns believed such a war would weaken the United States. Most crowned heads at the time saw in Lincoln the personification of the republican ideas that had kindled the anti-monarchist revolutions in Europe. They feared him and hoped that the Civil War would destroy or weaken the United States and our government's ability to assist revolutionaries in Europe.

Napoleon III, in the first year of the war, was instrumental in forming a European coalition in favor of the South. This may have been to prolong the war, for in the end he did not do much to help the South.

It could well be that he remembered that some of the Southern leaders were involved just as much as the Northern leaders in trying to subvert the European monarchies, including advocating his assassination.

The Russian initiative of sending two fleets to the U.S. would have cooled any British ardor to join with Napoleon to break the U.S. blockade even if they had the idea of doing so. Without Britain, anything Napoleon wanted to do would fail, just as in Mexico.

Spain probably did more to help the Confederates than any other government, by allowing Confederate raiders into their Cuban ports and thereby protecting them. This was strange on the surface of it, considering what so many Southern leaders had done over the preceding two decades to wrest Spanish possessions away from Spain. Their motivation may have been to help weaken the two belligerent powers, since ultimately wiping the seas of American shipping would serve that purpose no matter who won.

They may have figured that weakening the U.S. would also weaken the desire of Americans to try and wrest territory from Spain.

It was George Sanders, after all, prominent behind the scenes in Canada with the Confederate Commissioners, who had taken an active role in trying to assassinate Napoleon when in Europe. He had also formed Young Cuba to provide the means to take Cuba from Spain. And, by no means was Sanders the only YA leader in the Confederacy who had cooperated in these schemes.

The leaders of the Holy Alliance (Austria, Belgium, etc.) looked to the U.S. as an inciter and supporter of republican revolutions, since Lincoln had supported Kossuth as early as 1848 and had spoken in favor of European revolutionaries in Congress.

While it may seem as if this European attitude is misguided, one cannot dismiss the activities of our citizens in revolutions in Poland, Germany, France, and Greece, or those of our own ambassadors to Europe. Indeed, if for no other reason, the Ostend Manifesto would have been enough to at least make the European governments wary.

Remember that we are basically talking about a little more than a decade from when all of Europe was under continual threat from the revolutionaries of 1848-1849. For European leaders, revolution was current events, not history.

Likewise, President Fillmore had sent a naval vessel to bring the Hungarian revolutionary Kossuth to the U.S. Since it was the Austro-Hungarian Empire at the time, you can imagine the attitude of Austria. It almost led to a break in diplomatic relations. Kossuth lived in America from 1851-1852.

Add to this the support of Kossuth by Lincoln in 1848, the offer of a command in the Union army to Garibaldi and other revolutionaries early in the war, and the correspondence between the American government and the First International, and it is no wonder that Europe was concerned about at least the possibility of American interference in their affairs, especially if the United States remained powerful. So it was in the general interest of European powers to see the United States weakened politically as well as from the standpoint of economic rivalry.

While the correspondence between Lincoln and the First International on his re-election and his responses by means of an American consulate does not show that Lincoln was a communist, it does show a mutual respect between Marx and Lincoln — more so on the part of Marx for Lincoln, his administration, and the war.

European leaders had much to be concerned about no matter who won the Civil War when it came to support for European revolutionaries and the diplomatic initiatives of the U.S. The control of the American diplomatic corps was well on its way to being controlled by the Conspiracy. Add to this a fear by Europe of the Garibaldi incident.

The story of the offer of a command, or the entire command, of the Union army to Garibaldi and how it never came to fruition is varied. All we know for sure is that an offer to Garibaldi to be commissioned at least a major general was made and it did not happen. One history has it that Garibaldi turned down the offer because he was not satisfied with the rank of major general and would not serve unless he was made commander in chief, a title held by the president.

The shocking thing about it is that Garibaldi was at the head of the Carbonari military. Everyone knew this and what the Carbonari stood for, yet Lincoln made the offer. It was made at the time that Lincoln was looking for a man to conduct the war in the manner he wanted. He did not find that man until Grant.

Apparently four offers to Garibaldi were made, one officially through Theodore Canisius, whom Lincoln had named as our U.S. consul to Vienna in August 1861. There are many accounts and histories relating to this incident, and they are all over the map as to whether any official offer was made. There are even accounts of an offer of ten million dollars for Garbaldi's services. Anyone doing research on this particular subject will become increasingly frustrated with the contradictions.

Be that as it may, Canisius was a 48er who immigrated right away in 1848 due to his activities. In the U.S. he bought the smaller *Staats-Anzeiger* newspaper in Springfield, Illinois. Lincoln bought the paper from Canisius and had him continue to run it as a means to influence the Germans toward the Republican Party.

In other words, Lincoln bought a newspaper run by a German 1848 revolutionary and had him remain in the editor's chair to influence the German immigrants. Lincoln then named him our consul in Vienna, and he contacted Garibaldi.

Garibaldi's reply to Canisius' request was carried in the *New York Times*, October 9, 1862:

SIR: I am a prisoner and dangerously wounded, consequently it is not possible for me to dispose of myself. Still, the moment that I have obtained my liberty, and that my wounds are healed, I shall seize the first favorable opportunity of satisfying my pleasure to serve the great American Republic, of which I am a citizen, and which is now fighting for universal liberty.

Canisius made the request public, and this was an embarrassment to the American government due to the volatile situation in France, and especially England, at the time as a result of support for Garibaldi. This support had led to demonstrations that included gun fire and stabbings between Irish who supported the pope and Garibaldi adherents. The governments of France and England were not pleased, and if the U.S. government was known to have been in communication with Garibaldi, it may have led to support for the Confederacy. The net result of all the agitation and how it was handled, however, led to a diminishing of support for the Southern government in the long run.

We will continue to mention throughout this volume several appointments by Lincoln of ambassadors that gave pause to Europe's governments. In some cases, the ambassadors were so obviously revolutionaries or opposed to the governments they were assigned to liaise with that they were refused recognition by these governments. In most cases, rather than be recalled, they were simply reassigned to other countries.

One, Anson Burlingame, a "violent radical" according to the Austrian ambassador to the U.S., was named by Lincoln to the court of Austria. He was supportive of European revolutionaries, particularly Kossuth in his revolution against Austria, and had offered legislation in recognition of an anti-Austrian Italian region. Lincoln was informed that Burlingame would not be accepted as our ambassador in Vienna and diverted him to China.

Another example, but by no means the last, was the appointment of Carl Schurz by Lincoln to Spain.

The one good thing that came out of the war for the heads of Europe was that so many revolutionaries came to the United States to fight in the war and stayed on here that it slowed down the revolution in Europe for many years.

As mentioned, Britain declared itself neutral and this was considered by the North as an unfriendly act. For England it was payback time to have the Confederacy attack Northern merchant vessels. The American ships during the War of 1812 had inflicted heavy damage on the British merchant marine, destroying a large portion of it. By the time the Civil War was over, the Confederate vessels had destroyed the American merchant marine, and it would not regain the competitive edge until the Great War, when German U-boats sank so many of the English merchant fleet.

The Confederacy acquired about 30 vessels, among them the *Alabama*, from England. The majority of the sailors of the *Alabama* were British subjects, and it alone destroyed 66 U.S. merchant ships while never entering a Confederate port. Altogether, with the *Florida, Shenandoah,* and other vessels, the Confederate Navy destroyed 257 Union vessels.

Action at sea against American vessels by Confederate ships continued for some months after the surrender of Rebel forces, since they were out of touch and lacked communication with the Confederacy, and all others, for that matter. Once they heard the news, they surrendered and decommissioned their ships, but not always to American forces.

European fears about the growing power and influence on their foreign affairs by the United States were confirmed; after the Franco-Prussian War of 1870-71, there would never be another European conflict to be settled without U.S. intervention.

What kept the crowns of Europe from playing an active role in the Civil War on the side of the South was the attitude of their own populations. The revolutionary fervor was still alive, and many of the "men on the street" were opposed to slavery.

Cotton played a role in the conduct of the war. The idea was propagated in the South that if they withheld cotton from the market, which was a vital commodity needed by England to sustain the Industrial Revolution, they would force recognition by Great Britain for the Confederacy. An embargo was established, enforced mainly by the Southern citizens themselves. The embargo had the reverse effect desired.

First, as far as the English government was concerned there were more important considerations than the availability of cotton. Second, the real negative was the effect on British workers. The workers were already inclined toward the Northern government due to the influence of the Chartists. The withholding of cotton initially put a large number of British workers out of work, and they held the South responsible. It turned into resentment rather than pressure on the government to recognize the Confederacy. The English have never been ones to knuckle under to outside pressure.

All the above could also be said for France and the French artisans. The French communists were inclined toward the North, and all French classes detested slavery. The average Frenchman was not partial to French recognition of the Confederacy.

Nonetheless, there were powerful rumblings within the population toward both sides of the conflict that led to more than one confrontation at rallies and meetings in England and France. The two governments did not need this kind of problem to fester into unrest against them.

Revolutionaries organized street demonstrations for the Union in England, France, and Austria. The crowns were afraid that just as American revolutionaries had participated and cooperated with their revolutionaries just a decade earlier, the same could happen again, only this time with the direct support of the American government since so many Radicals now occupied seats in Congress and in the administration.

At the beginning of the war, reports in the *London Times* foretold the demise of the North. Writing from America, W. H. Russell wrote that "The great republic is gone, and no serious attempt will be made by the North to save it." After the battle of Bull Run or Manassas (depending on how you look at it), which the South won, Russell said in his dispatch, "General bankruptcy is inevitable, and agrarian and socialist riots may be expected very soon." This was a complete distortion, but it shows the weight of the socialist influence on the minds of such people at the time.

Had the South shipped the cotton on hand at the very beginning of the war, the monies would have gone a long way toward outfitting the Confederate Army.

By the spring of 1862, the South changed its mind and wanted to move cotton to Europe, but the Northern blockade had been put in place. It was too late. And, cotton had not been planted at the levels that it had been before the embargo. There was no sense in planting something that would never reach a market.

The figures for the growth and export of cotton for the war years is sketchy, but it is well documented that the first years after the war the growth and exportation was approximately half of the amount exported just before the war.

Prime Minister Lord Russell had declared the Union blockade to be effective; therefore, the British government and shipping honored the blockade. This did not mean that some English shippers would not try and run the cordon, but generally they would not. A few braved the risk, and those that were successful became very rich. By so declaring the blockade as legitimate, which, under international law there was no legal basis for it, it created a precedent that the British government would use later against its enemies.

At first the blockade of the South was more of a sieve than a real blockade. Some of the ships initially used in the blockade could no more stop a row boat than they could a merchant vessel. The English declaration made the blockade a reality, at least over shipping they controlled or influenced, which at the time was substantial.

The blockade even extended over neutral ports close to America such as Matamoros, Mexico, Nassau, and the Bahamas. The principle of the "ultimate destination" also was imposed. In other words, if the cargo was intended for the Confederacy, no matter on what ship or between what ports, even neutral ports, it could be seized. This policy was used later by the English as well.

Britain did so against Germany in the First World War. At that time, before we entered the war against Germany, American vessels were seized that were bound for Holland, Denmark, and Sweden. When the American ambassador objected, Sir Edward Grey, British foreign secretary, smiled and reminded him of the federal practice during the Civil War.

British shipyards were used initially to build Confederate warships, and when this allowance was withdrawn it had all the earmarks of an English policy to provide the Confederacy enough ships to blast American shipping from the high seas, but not enough to allow them to win in a fight against the U.S. Navy.

The blockade did serve as an economic opportunity for certain blockade runners. One who became wealthy doing so was the father of "Col." Edward Mandell House, one of the most influential conspirators of the 20th century in support of a world government and court.

Because of the policies of the Confederate government, by January 1862, after ten months of existence, the South had a fractured financial structure — struggling under a mass of paper currency, crippled in its credit abroad, its people hungry for food, and the whole extent of its territory beginning to be wracked by poverty, the latter two primarily due to paper money and speculators.

Yet it is called incompetence or a series of blunders by historians.

The Erlanger loan was a scheme that did not help the image of the Southern government. Baron Emile Erlanger's son had married John Slidell's daughter and negotiated a loan based on cotton. The story was one of everyone losing on the deal except Erlanger, who was the only one to make a profit out of the venture.

The net result was that investors who would normally be inclined to help the South would stay away from any future schemes. Besides, with the obvious destruction of the credit of the Confederacy, it created the image of incompetence.

Blunders? A case can be made that the Confederate leaders were incompetent; however, all indications are that there was as much behind their actions as there is behind our leaders' financial motivation today. A number of deliberate acts by the same politicians toward a given end are not stupidity or ignorance. It may have the façade of ignorance to cloak the real motive: profit for the few.

The story of Confederate incompetence (or otherwise) in finance and foreign affairs is much too lengthy to include herein and does not lend itself to the narrative. Nor do the motivations and moves of foreign powers in regard to our conflict, except in a few instances, such as Mexico.

England, France, and Spain seized the opportunity of the Civil War to intervene in Mexico while America was concentrating on the conflict. Finally, a letter penned by Seward, on orders from Lincoln, was sent to European powers *openly warning them of intervention in Mexico and that there would be United States help to European revolutionaries* if they did not leave Mexico alone. England pulled out of Mexico by April 1862, and Spain shortly thereafter. France stayed.

Napoleon installed Maximilian as Emperor in Mexico not only to gain Mexico but just as much to ally Austria to France, since Maximilian was in line for the crown of Austria and his brother wanted him out of the way so he could reign without worrying about any rivalry.

The longer the war went on, the more England swung back to acknowledging the Northern government as the coming victor.

Several schemes were hatched by the South relative to enlisting support for the Confederacy, including the ceding of territory to French Mexico for the support of France. There were French officials and royalty who did all they could to promote war with the United States, to no avail.

On the other hand, Maximilian was thrown to the wolves by his own family as a means of ensuring that he would never return and contest any succession to the throne of Austria. In London, this reality was recognized to the point of him being called the "Archdupe" Maximilian.

The Austrian ambassador to Washington let Lincoln know that they were neutral and not to pay any attention to public or face-saving gestures, including manpower to Mexico, and that Franz Joseph would not do anything to help Maximilian.

Apparently the royal line was more important than any desire by Austria to weaken the United States by the occupation of Mexico.

Before the war there were some in the South who supported a return to monarchy as a means to stop Radicalism from the North. It was another false solution that helped fuel resentment in the North. Robert Toombs had visited Europe in 1855, returned to the U.S. supporting the British constitutional monarchy, and advocated such a system in a stormy meeting of the Georgia State Legislature just before the war in November 1860.

There were several initiatives along these lines discussed by Jefferson Davis, Toombs, and Judah Benjamin.

By the end of the war, many Southern politicians had become friends of royalty. Louisiana politician Slidell's daughter had married royalty. After the war, Judah Benjamin, who served in almost every Cabinet post in the Confederacy, went to England and was the darling of royalty until the novelty wore off.

There was a fleeting thought in the South of helping European powers invade America from Mexico to restore the monarchy across the entire country. It did not get very far.

After the war, many Confederate Army officers and units crossed south across the border, never to return. Some went to South America. While this may seem to be an extreme reaction, the atmosphere just after the war among Northern circles was to seek revenge by hanging Confederate officers, and many of these officers had grave concerns as to whether they would become victims to postwar retribution. More than one influential Northern politician stated publicly that Southern officers should be hanged.

More often than not, in other countries after a civil conflict, the losers found themselves standing by a shallow grave to be shot. This was normal just across the southern border. It would not be too much of a stretch for Southern leaders and military to believe that it could have happened to them given the nature of the men in charge of the Union and some elements of the army. Over the years, this was the result in country after country where people resisted communist radicals and where these radicals had come into permanent or temporary power.

There was a program to form a colony in Mexico based on a plan submitted to Maximilian by Confederate Commodore Matthew Fontaine Maury in the Cordoba region, which included Confederate generals John Magruder, Joseph Shelby, Sterling Price, Henry W. Allen, (governor of Louisiana), and David S. Terry (Supreme Court judge of California).

In October 1865, Maximilian cancelled the colonization project due to it provoking the anger of Washington.

Napoleon withdrew all support for Maximilian after Seward wrote an energetic note in December 1865 demanding immediate withdrawal from Mexico and President Johnson sent 50,000 troops to the Texas-Mexican border under the command of Gen. Sheridan.

The propensity of Catholic countries to engage in acts that appeared to support the South during the war helped fuel the idea that the pope was behind the assassination of Lincoln later on. This was anti-Catholic propaganda, a means to throw people off from speculating further as to who or what was behind the assassination, and at the same instant it worked against a primary adversary of the conspiracy at the time, the Catholic Church.

If it had been a papal plot, John Surratt would have been given a better reward than serving as a Vatican Zouave foot soldier. More on this later.

Economics

From our beginning, the growth of the federal government in violation of the Constitution was a concern to many, but this unease always lacked any effective organization. What organization existed usually had false leadership and used the fear as a judo move to flip the concerned citizens into further exacerbating the problem.

The Conspiracy has always been afraid of the American people waking up to what has been going on, not simply recognizing the trends, but understanding the design and organization behind the direction, that it is not all an accident of history. They have used several ruses to keep them ignorant, even supporting false solutions designed to placate them and move the Conspiracy's agenda forward at the same time.

Some progress was seemingly made from time to time to look as if an initiative was organized toward preventing the growth of the power of the central government, or those who controlled the government. A good example would be the concern over the United States Bank.

The history of the first U.S. Bank has been changed over the years to the point where good conservatives, constitutionalists, and libertarians now believe that Hamilton was the "bad guy" and Jefferson was the man who stood for liberty in all things, including banking.

Nothing could be further from the truth.

This is, again, the subject for another book, but we shall deal with it in as short a time as possible.

First of all, the major banking "problem" for Americans was the Bank of England (BOE). This continued to be a competing factor over our economy and America, in order to survive, had to create a system that not only separated itself from the BOE but addressed the problems of the people, commerce, and the Congress.

This the first U.S. Bank did. It also tended to center on the ability of local banks to facilitate commerce. This created a "them and us" between those who wanted to advance commerce, and those who had their local economy based on slavery and the provisions in the Constitution that gave a disproportionate tabulation for the electoral count to slave states while not actually treating them as citizens.

This was one of the reasons for the split between Jefferson and Hamilton; the reader knows that Hamilton was opposed to slavery and Jefferson supported it. However, Jefferson initially did not oppose the bank — in fact he was a stockholder and depositor.

The reader also knows that Jefferson supported the Jacobin movement while Hamilton opposed it.

What Jefferson opposed was the creation of solvent local banks as part of Hamilton's plan and these banks helping build local commerce and infrastructure away from the slave system.

Students of history today do not realize the chaos that existed at the end of the War for Independence. British troops did not leave all quarters of our territory until five years later. Much had been ravaged by the conflict and many were in prison due to bankruptcy for having helped fund the war. There existed only three banks for the thirteen states and the people were using fifty currencies and foreign coinage. Some order had to come out of all of this for the economy to stabilize and grow.

As a result of the bank, backed by gold, the economy started to flourish. Debts owed for the fortunes patriots had lent the government during the war were paid with interest.

Hamilton, in spite of his singular lapse of morality, was a brilliant lawyer and recognized as one of the two stellar constitutional lawyers, along with John Adams. His knowledge of commerce, banking, the causes of past economic balloons, bubbles, and bursts, coupled with his knowledge that America had to have a system completely divorced from the money interests of the BOE and Europe weighed heavily on his scheme for the bank.

As a result, he forged the system based on three components: A central bank, the Bank of the United States, and local banks designated national banks and banks of commerce. Each was to function in a role propelling America into a stable system of free enterprise.

The Bank of the U.S. could not give voting rights to any non-citizen or to any citizen who had an interest in foreign banks. This was only one of the provisions which were designed to keep the bank American. You can well imagine that the BOE and others would immediately cast aspersions on the bank and Hamilton. They wanted in, and were deprived of that ability by Hamilton.

Keep in mind the heavy investment by British interests in American companies. They still had their "finger in the pie" so to speak and wanted the best piece: banking.

Long story short, the bank's original charter expired in 1811. Had it been as powerful as claimed by modern histories, it would have found a means to continue its existence unhindered. It was not renewed primarily due to the Southern states. If it had had the power of the modern Federal Reserve, we are sure that the situation would have been different.

The result was a collapse of the economy. This created a real burden as well during the War of 1812. Madison soon learned of the need for a bank after having opposed it when he wasn't president. He enacted the policy of re-chartering the bank over the objections of Jefferson and Andrew Jackson.

Immediately, the partisans of Jefferson, Jackson, and the international bankers started a war of propaganda against the bank.

We will leave the narrative at this point in regard to the early history and invite the reader to ferret out more information from non-establishment sources on what constituted the three banks that Hamilton established.

Another thing to remember in your study is that the personalities involved would change their public persona from time to time as the political winds shifted. This makes any study of who was for or against the bank more difficult. And, as we have pointed out, those on the outside were against the bank. Those in the inside were for it. This support shifted with who and what party was elected.

Major concern over the bank led to its final abolishment under President Jackson. However, financial transactions still needed to be made by someone on behalf of the country, and now they were less visible to the average American. The end result was the transfer of the money power from one group to another — in this case the friends of Jackson — where it remained up until the time of Franklin Delano Roosevelt's administration.

When Jackson withheld federal funds from the Bank of the United States prior to and after the 1832 election and beginning the next September, he deposited them in state banks throughout the nation, known as "pet banks" due to the special relationship they had to the administration.

For this action, the U.S. Senate censured Jackson on March 28, 1834:

Senate resolves that removing the deposits the President has assumed authority not conferred by the Constitution and the laws but in derogation of both.
Harper's Encyclopedia of United States History

After heated debate, the Senate resolution vote was expunged from the record on January 16, 1837, nearly three years later. Jackson had a record of being punished by the Congress only to have it revoked years later, in this case and in his handling of the Battle of New Orleans on the civilians, the invasion of Florida, the killing of British citizens there, etc.

The use of the banking system to establish favoritism was not unique to Jackson. In 1803, the Roger Williams Bank was incorporated in Providence, Rhode Island, through the influence of Thomas Jefferson, who wanted to place government deposits in a Republican-controlled bank. The bulk of the U.S. deposits in Rhode Island remained there until 1817.

Here we see that while some opposed the U.S. Bank, they did not oppose using the money power of the state for their own political purposes. It is rarely opposition to the money power per se; it is who controls it.

Jefferson and Jackson, renowned for their opposition to the money power, in reality only wanted to use it for their own purposes. They gave false solutions to hide what was really going on behind the scenes and to build support for their policies breaking up the money power, all in the name of the people.

In a letter to the arch-conspirator Edward Mandell House, the prime organizer of the Council on Foreign Relations in the early 20th century, FDR wrote this:

> The real truth of the matter is, as you and I know, that a financial element in the larger centers has owned the Government ever since the days of Andrew Jackson — and I am not wholly excepting the Administration of W.W. The country is going through a repetition of Jackson's fight with the Bank of the United States — only on a far bigger and broader basis.
>
> President Franklin Delano Roosevelt,
> November 21, 1933, *F.D.R.: His Personal Letters*

In other words, the money power was taken from one group and handed to another, quite different from the rhetoric used by Jackson to close the Bank of the United States. And it was quite different than what the American people were led to believe was going on. Even today, conservative Americans laud Jackson for closing the "central bank." All he did was give it to the central bankers — in a manner they could control out of sight of the American citizen.

Edward Mandell House knew what FDR was talking about because of his close ties to Morgan banking interests.

The above quote shows the process of wealth transfer was happening again during the Great Depression and many books have been written outlining the fact that the Depression was contrived primarily for that purpose — as well as other benefits to the conspirators.

Note that the history books tell us that during the Depression men and businesses failed, property was lost, etc. They never tell us who picked up those businesses and property or who may have benefited due to less competition. Generally speaking, property (and all of what that word means) did not disappear, it simply transferred in ownership.

The same process happened again in 2008-2012, and this time it had the full participation of the government using taxpayer money with a so-called stimulus program. The process was actually the big fish eating the little fish with government help and money, and the result was fewer but larger fish, particularly among the bankers.

The difference between what happened in the 1930s and what happened in the 21st century was that in the 30's, America still had an industrial base to rebuild on; by the 21st century, America's industrial base had been moved out of the country, primarily to China.[54]

The Guaranty Trust Company was founded with the original capital from the Whitney, Rockefeller, Harriman, and Vanderbilt families in New York in 1864. All of these patriarchs' families were represented in the Order. The trust grew, absorbing others, until it was effectively controlled by the J. P. Morgan interests by 1912.

The Whitney family particularly was involved in the Order. John Lyman Whitney became a mainstay in the Boston Public Library, one of the premier libraries in the country. Collins Whitney did not amount to a great deal for a few years after graduation from Yale, but was the inspector of the New York Public Schools in 1872. He went on to become quite rich and the power behind President Grover Cleveland.

Another member of the Order who was an inspector and trustee of the New York Public Schools was Frederick Ellsworth Mather, a Democrat who was a member of the New York Assembly from 1854-57.

So we see the hand of the minions of the Conspiracy from the onset of the New York Public Schools

---

[54] While this author has some doubts as to the solutions offered, nonetheless the DVD *Death by China: One Lost Job at a Time* is a superlative review of the problems with trade with China and how it has resulted in a loss of jobs, industry, national security, etc.: www.DeathByChina.com.

into the period of the 1870s, from DeWitt Clinton to members of the Order.

Since it is difficult to say with absolute certainty that Morgan and a few others evolved into the Federal Reserve Bank due to the secrecy surrounding its control and stock holdings, nonetheless it is safe to say that Morgan interests had much to do with the *establishment* of the Fed based on what evidence is available.

Morgan was not alone in this scheme, and the best study available is the popular tome *The Creature From Jekyll Island*, by G. Edward Griffin.

It is ironic that modern conservatives look to Jackson as a liberator due to his battle against the Bank of the United States, but ignore the fact that he threatened South Carolina with invasion if they did not back away from nullification of a tariff. The issue was not the problem; it was that the Jackson administration negated the 10th Amendment through the threat of force.

On the other hand, nullification was used to support secession as well. There were many who looked upon nullification as treason. At the time it served the purpose of the Jackson government to promote nationalism and a central government. Robert John Walker helped push through a resolution in the Mississippi Legislature that basically said that nullification was treason. Walker was YA and a close friend of George Sanders. Both sides in this battle were manipulated for the Conspiracy's purposes.

When nullification was used to weaken the United States under Washington, they supported it. When it was used to curtail the growth of government under another of their minions, they opposed it.

Walker would be appointed governor of Kansas during the terrible time there. He was a U.S. senator for Mississippi and secretary of the treasury under Polk.

To reinforce the idea that people could hold positions on both sides depending on their reasons and motivations at the time, Jackson helped Burr, who was involved in splitting up the United States, and yet later, as president, was against nullification, claiming that it was being used to split up the United States!

Let us make the point that the states were in existence before the United States, and it was the states that formed the federal government, not the other way around. It is ludicrous to believe that the states do not have the ability under the Constitution to nullify unconstitutional federal law, policy, edicts, etc. To give power to the federal government by the states and say that they do not retain the ability to rein in that power is illogical.

Today, those who oppose the idea of nullification are those who, one way or another, support or apologize for big government. This not only includes socialists and modern Democrats, but neoconservatives as well.

There is no question that many have used the issue as a smokescreen for secession, but that does not preclude the legitimacy of the process. One only needs to read the 10th Amendment and see what it says and implies, rather than the rhetoric of case-law oriented lawyers.

The Constitution was written for all of the people to understand who have a rudimentary knowledge of English, not to be interpreted by those who have an interest in a role they may profit by, either as lawyers or politicians. What most people do not understand, including the lawyers themselves, is that the Constitution in its original intent is no longer taught in the public preparatory schools or colleges, or the postgraduate studies at almost every university.

What is taught increasingly is a distorted version of the law, even to the extent of misquoting the Constitution and Bill of Rights. For those who doubt this statement, we invite you to examine the school texts given your children regarding the Constitution. You will be shocked at what you will learn — assuming you yourself have studied the Constitution.

The election of Jackson in 1828 marked the success of the movement for separation of church and state, removing religious qualifications for holding office, adding more direct control by the people through democracy rather than through their representatives, and moving toward a nationalistic movement away from state sovereignty — less radical than France, but building on the French model.

George Bancroft, a supporter of Jackson, put it this way: "The day for the multitudes has now arrived."

Bancroft, who had appointed Orestes Brownson as collector of the Port of Boston in 1836, received a letter written September 25, 1836 from Brownson that was revealing in its outline of Brownson and Bancroft's strategy at the time:

> You are but following out the direction which modern civilization is to bring. All things tend to democracy. Those who support it are sure of the future ... I am trying to democratize religion and philosophy.

As late as 1830, the tricolor flag of the French revolution was still used by reformers. Its wide-scale use died out for a time but was revived again in the late 1850s among the Wide Awake Republicans.

In the early years of the 20th century, Democrats were known as either Jeffersonian or Jacksonian Democrats. The former meant a person more prone to advocate a balance between the states and the federal government; the latter was a person more in tune with nationalism, which negates state sovereignty, and an advocate of government solutions to economic and development problems.

Davy Crockett was defeated as a member of Congress by a member of the "Andy Jackson camp," as he expressed it to the patriots at the Alamo. The Jackson camp believed in government intervention in the economy and industry. Crockett did not.

As the socialist Horace Greeley expressed it in 1850:

> We believe that Government, like every other intelligent agency, is bound to do good to the extent of its ability — that it ought actively to promote and increase the general well being — that it should encourage and foster Industry, Science, Invention, Intellectual, Social and Physical Progress.... Such is our idea of the sphere of Government.
>
> *Horace Greeley and Other Pioneers of American Socialism*

For government to be involved in the above by those who profess not to be socialists, but agree with those who are, means that government will decide what all of these improvements will be, not the individual citizen. It means that government will decide what are the correct industry and science, what invention will go forward and be utilized, and the correct social and physical progress.

In the beginning, it can sound as if it is good for government to be involved. But in order to accomplish the above, the government must build a bureaucracy to do it. They must take taxes from everyone to implement the ideas, and build the bureaucracy. And, invention is actually stifled under government since invention requires the freedom to think outside of the box. It is freedom *from* bureaucracy that leads to invention. That is why America has been more inventive that any other country: because it has been more free.

Indeed, many of the "American" inventions came about by men who immigrated here to be able to think and invent and keep the fruits of their labor and intellect. They could not do so in the countries from which they came. They came to a *free* country and all that this word meant.

A good example of the stifling of invention would be the inventive powers of the German scientists during World War II. We have all seen the vaunted power of the various rockets and jet aircraft in movies and on television. What most do not know is that some of these inventions would have come on line much sooner by years than they did if it weren't for government interference. The war in Europe would have probably been extended by at least a year into 1946 if the scientists had been given the go-ahead to develop them sooner, or in the manner that was most conducive to their use in combat. In this case, it was an advantage for freedom that it happened the way it did. It may be the only time in history where systemic government interference and arbitrary rules helped freedom in the long run.

At the minimum such designs outlined by Greeley are fascist socialism, a welding of government and business, sometimes called *corporatism* today.

The process also involves government planning. Such an initiative may seem to be to the advantage of the citizens, but in the long run, planning leads to full-scale socialism. This is inevitable and inescapable. The onset of planning by government is so benign that the average citizen cannot imagine where the process will lead and its ultimate end.

Planning by government means the death of property rights in all forms: personal, intellectual, and landed. This is because government planning will assume control over all or part of these prerogatives in order to move their plans forward, whether it is zoning, building government projects, eminent domain, etc. The elimination of property rights means the death of all individual rights and liberty, for without the ability to control your property you lose the ability to control your future, and your means to survive as an individual, becoming dependent on the state as a result.

The point is that when the American people, or any people, are ignorant of the facts and basic lessons of economics and history, they can be manipulated. This manipulation always leads to more government to be used by the manipulators.

Almost always, grassroots organizations are formed and used by manipulators to carry these functions forward or to support false solutions to seeming or real problems. The minions rarely have a clue as to how they are misused. It was a problem in the early years of our country and exists up to today.

Once in a while, a few wake up to the fact that not all is as it appears.

Two examples from the mid-20th century we have mentioned before would be Benjamin Gitlow and Dr. Bella Dodd, both who served on the Central Committee of the Communist Party of the United States of America (CPUSA).[55]

No national organization ever existed capable of countering socialist influence until 1958. Collectivists have always organized; after all, they are collectivists. Individualists who wanted less government have not, they are individualists.

In the early 21st century, a phenomenon referred to as the Tea Parties emerged in opposition to what was seen as the inordinate growth of government. Some of these independent and not-so-independent groups were used as well by forces they did not understand, due to their lack of experience in both politics and with politicians and leaders who professed to be constitutionalists but were not. The truly independent organizations tended to be sound; those who attached themselves to Republican Party leaders were not and supported solutions the Republican establishment wanted, or ersatz conservative candidates, all the while believing they were opposing the establishment.

In the early 1800s, the necessary eruption to provide the catalyst needed to make major changes in

---

55   How Gitlow woke up to the fact that they were being used by forces he could not see is related in his book *The Whole of Their Lives*. How Dr. Dodd woke up is contained in a book by W. Cleon Skousen, *The Naked Capitalist*.

American society and the government of the United States meant that a major conflict of a *prolonged* nature had to be implemented.

Economic crisis was out of the question as a means to accomplish this since the proliferation of property in the hands of the average citizen was widespread and growing, the average American was not overwhelmed by debt, and the country was not so much in the economic grasp of a few bankers to a degree that an economic collapse would work to convince Americans to give up any of their liberty, particularly when the monetary system in use by the citizens was still based on physically held precious metal coins rather than paper controlled by central bankers or government.

A war was necessary to gain control of the entire economic sphere, and to create the conditions whereby the people would stand still for not only the loss of conveniences to achieve victory but the loss of liberty as well. The latter would mainly be the case in the North since it was a forgone conclusion by all who had any military grasp of the situation that the South's position in any conflict was untenable for many reasons; therefore, the full curtailment of Southern liberty by internal forces was unnecessary. These controls would ultimately come from the North imposed on a defeated South.

The war, by necessity, had to be on American soil, since foreign wars would not produce the psychological conditions for the people to stand still for the types of changes in American society that were needed to establish control over the people — or at least make them docile to government intrusion.

In modern times, foreign wars can supply a certain amount of the means necessary for the above due to the use of television and the Internet that brings the war into everyone's living room every day. In addition, the means to carry a war to our soil today exists in a manner not available in the 19th century.

This does not mean that years ago there were not those who saw what was going on, extended the lines, and tried to warn their fellow citizens; however, they did not have sufficient organization behind them enabling them reach enough of the people with the truth. Since they acted as loners, they were silenced one at a time.

The history books tell us that the war was over slavery; some include economic problems, but they never document the antebellum organizations and their agenda relative to the agitation against Christianity and support for socialism as part of the process.

In 1860, Reuben Davis of Mississippi wrote:

> There is not a pursuit in which man is engaged (agriculture excepted) which is not demanding legislative aid to enable it to enlarge its profits and all at the expense of the primary pursuit of man — agriculture.... Those interests having a common purpose of plunder, have united and combined to use the government as the instrument of their operation and have thus virtually converted it into a consolidated empire. Now this combined host of interests stands arrayed against the agricultural States; and this is the reason of the conflict which like an earthquake is shaking our political fabric to its foundation.
>
> — "On Southern Agriculture"

There are two things wrong with this statement. One, he did not realize that legislative aid would ultimately affect independent agriculture through adverse treaties, subsidies, and land control. Second, he did not actually see the root of the problem. All he saw was the North flourishing to the disadvantage of the Southern farmer.

In the 1870s, Davis became a member of the Greenback Party.

The same exists today: people look at the breakdown of the social order, the amassing of fortunes through government regulation, and think it is corporate rather than Illuminist. Ultimately, the goal is that gradually the individual entrepreneurs will be shoved out of business, and when there are only large corporations left they will be taken over by the state, the entity that gained power by helping the corporations. Power is not actually invested in the corporations. It is invested in government. This includes corporations that are based on agriculture.

This is essentially what happened in Nazi Germany by the end of World War II. When Hitler first became chancellor of Germany, he met with key industrialists to assure them that they could trust him to not socialize Germany's industrial base since, after all, he was a national socialist.

For those first few months he went so far as to wear formal or business attire rather than the uniform that the public was used to. It was an act put on to appear to be moderating since he knew that in the beginning of his tenure the powerful industrialists might have been able to depose him; with his reassurances, they went along with him.

He lied. And by the time the Nazis got through regulating them step by step, the government had complete control. Control is more important than ownership. It does not matter who holds title to property if the government can tell you what you may or may not do with it.

The fewer the corporations, no matter how large, the less power is diffused among the middle class; not only that, but the middle class atrophies. In order for major corporations to gain a monopoly through government regulation, more power is given to government, not the corporations. The corporations gain their power through government regulation. Sweetheart regulations that certain companies can abide by will be implemented, curtailing and then stifling the competition of those companies who cannot exist with the regulations.

In the beginning of such a process, the corporations in bed with the powers-that-be appear to have the upper hand. After the regulations hit a certain level, the regulations become, *for all practical purposes*, ownership by the government.

In the end, government will have more power than the corporations and will simply "nationalize" the few businesses that are left. The owners or managers of these few corporations will not care *if as a result they are, or are made to believe they are, part of the power behind the scenes*. Does it matter if you are employed by a large corporation or the government if your lifestyle is good and you have more privileges than the average citizen in addition?

Some of these corporate leaders will be part of the conspiracy. They will not care if their own businesses are taken over by government if they are the true government, the Inner Party.

Let us be reminded once again that what people call the middle class today is not the middle class. Just because Americans have a higher standard of living does not make them a member of the middle class. The class is actually made up of the entrepreneurial section of society, those who invent, start, and own businesses.

The reason that the conspiracy behind communism hates them is because they are the innovators, inventors, and producers that pull civilization up into a better condition for all. They are referred to by the communists using the French word: *bourgeoisie*. The Conspiracy cannot stand for this class to exist since they can and will by their very nature stand in the way of government controls and provide a standard of living that will satisfy the average man so he cannot be manipulated into a revolution by his poverty or dissatisfaction.

Communists only want two classes — themselves and the ignorant masses — a much more manageable condition. There has been a great deal of propaganda disseminated in the 20th century to convince people that they are part of the middle class when they are not. By not understanding the term, they have been manipulated into more government controls over the economy in their name.

By the 21st century, *the socialists began a campaign* to convince everyone that they wanted to help the middle class, *the very class their historic writings have said they must eliminate.* The campaign was not only false but based on a false definition of what comprises the middle class.

Again, if we use the semantics given us by the opposition, we will have already diminished our ability to fight with words the people understand. The first step in any argument is to define the terms being used so that it is a level playing field.

Secession Within Secession
The South had a problem that made waging a war difficult, and that was a lack of cohesiveness. Americans at that time tended to be difficult to control for any length of time as they considered themselves very independent, both as individuals and states. This was more so in the Southern areas.

Except for regional independence exhibited from time to time in the North, such as the Hartford Convention during the period of the second war with England and Shay's Rebellion, the more independent attitudes were imbued in the South. This was to be a major problem for the Confederacy when a difference of opinion arose as to the conduct of the war, regardless of the reason, and in the supply of men and provisions for the Confederate army.

There were many times that the North was victorious because of this problem, particularly during Sherman's March to the Sea.

Another dilemma that existed was that both sides had sympathizers on the other side. This was dealt with more vigorously by the Northern government than the Southern. Although Southern citizens and guerilla organizations handled much of this in the South and Border States, it remained a persistent problem.

The few nuisances that existed, led by the Copperhead movement in the North, were more than offset by the controls of the military governors. The South suffered more due to the Union and internal disunion influences with their borders, and did not have military governors as did the North to ensure obedience to the government.

While there is no evidence that the following fits the scenario of a sympathizer on the other side, it is interesting to speculate. Gen. James Longstreet, Lee's close friend and second in command at Gettysburg, became a Republican after the war. He then cooperated with the Radicals during Reconstruction. Some blame him for the loss at Gettysburg, and he has been called a Southern "Judas." One would at least think that he would not have later involved himself with the worst enemy of the South, let alone the country: the Northern Radicals.

Con. Clement Vallandigham, the Copperhead and Knights of the Golden Circle leader in Ohio, was another man who was in the limelight as an opponent of Radical Republicans but who after the war was quite in agreement with them in national politics. He was involved in the "New Departure" policy of the Democratic Party that led to an alliance with the Liberal Republican Party just after his death in 1871, and which nominated Horace Greeley for the presidency in 1872.

We cannot forget that Vallandigham was a close intimate friend of Stanton for years before the war.

The New Departure policy was in support of the three major constitutional amendments after the war. While the Liberal Republican Party had as one of its platforms the return to local government in the South, it was dominated by pre-war radicals and wanted to institute changes in the government that would permanently place bureaucrats in power, such as the civil service initiative.

While arrests continued in the South after the war, their Southern allies in the North, the Copperheads, were becoming increasingly involved in supporting the Greenback currency, civil service reform, and government intervention into the economy and commerce, using the excuse that it was in the interest of the general welfare.

This reminds us that the KGC was started by a man who was part of the Brotherhood of Lippard, whose ultimate goals matched the socialist agenda using a different path to get there. One would think, based on the *public* persona of the KGC, that Copperhead leaders would have opposed the Radical agenda.

The governor of Georgia during the Confederacy was Joseph Emerson Brown. He was a strong states rights advocate during the war, and held that attitude against the Confederate government as well. At first, he played a large role in swinging Georgia into the Confederacy and was a delegate to the Southern Constitutional Convention.

After the war got started, he then became a disorganization leader along with Zebulon Vance, Alexander Stephens, Robert Toombs, and Robert Rhett. Many feel that had he been turned loose with the men and equipment under his state authority to fight Gen. Sherman, Sherman would never have been able to march to the sea through Georgia. In fact, in September 1864, Brown "furloughed" his "Ten Thousand" state militia. He ordered them to drop their arms, disband, and return home.

Sherman was so astonished that he wrote to Brown for a meeting, but Brown refused. Sherman felt at the time that he might be able to bring Georgia back into the Union; that was before he launched his campaign through the state which led to the burning of Atlanta and the destruction that made Sherman famous, or infamous as the case may be.

These Southern leaders after helping bring about secession became the commanders of disorganization. This disorganization existed in contrast to a more unified Northern command.

Both the North and the South instituted the draft to fill the ranks of their armies. The South passed the Conscription Act in April 1862. The North did the same on March 3, 1863, *a year after the South*. On the same day, the Congress authorized Lincoln to suspend habeas corpus whenever he saw fit.

Brown began a systematic war against the use of draftees from his state, and went even further to prevent men from volunteering. Laws were passed to exempt certain professions, and soon these professions started to proliferate all across the state as a way out of the draft for the average young man.

Gov. Vance adopted these same tactics in North Carolina, which had the highest desertion rate of any state. The governors of Alabama, Mississippi, and Texas soon followed suit. One can argue the problem of the draft, and there are certainly sound arguments against it, but the leaders of the South were so independent and libertarian that they could not provide a common front against the socialist onslaught of the North. It became a matter of herding cats.

In the case of Brown, it went much further than that and appeared to fit the strategy of the Conspiracy to agitate for war, get it going, then serve the end of supporting more government, which in the long run meant the Northern government.

After the war Brown became a Republican and joined the carpetbaggers, becoming one of the richest men in Georgia.

He was not alone. William Woods Holden, the "father of secession" in North Carolina, became the Republican governor of the state after the war.

The Southern states worked against the Confederacy in many ways to prevent the use of the men from their states in the Confederate Army. Although the whole story would take too much space to document, it was extensive.

How much of this disorganization was influenced by the conspiratorial forces is unknown. Certainly it played into the scheme to prolong the war, and contributed to this as well as the breakdown of Southern society. This was a problem in the North as well, but the central government of the North was able to handle it and the people were more attuned to allowing the army to run roughshod over local government, the press, and just about anyone who stood in their way, and the people simply had no organization or power to stop it if they wanted to.

From 1861-1865 several secret societies grew up in the South to fight the Confederacy. Their names ranged from Peace and Constitutional Societies to Heroes of America or Red Strings. They had the usual bewildering array of passwords, signs, grips, and such.

Their objective was to obtain enlistments for the Union, prevent recruiting for the Confederacy, oppose Confederate taxation, fight Confederate conscription, stimulate desertion, and agitate for a return to the Union. Their methods were terroristic and membership was substantial. About 103,000 men deserted from the Confederate forces, according to estimates, some of them due to the work of these groups.

The one exception to the problem of agitators causing ineffectual problems in the North was the draft riots in New York City. In this case, Negroes were lynched, massive fires were set, and Union troops were called in to quell the insurrection. Until the 1960s, it remained the most violent civil insurrection in our history.

There was never again a city that sustained the corresponding level of violence that New York did in 1863, although there were many incidences in the latter half of the 1800s, such as Haymarket, and into the very early years of the 20th century. The combined organizations of Leftists in the 1960s and 1970s coordinated and carried out many acts of arson, bombing, and rioting at the same time in multiple cities across the country. The combination of these latter acts was worse than the New York riots in comparison to the times.

Even though cities were set ablaze *simultaneously*, federal officials claimed the riots of the decades of 1960-70 did not constitute any conspiracy. There were individual cases of mayhem, such as the Watts Riot in Los Angeles, but too often the riots occurred at the same time from coast to coast.

Whether the riots appeared singularly or several at a time in the 1960s and '70s, it was obvious to any experienced observer that they were centrally coordinated or influenced by communist cadres, most with connections through Cuba to Moscow. Toward the end of this period, the Chinese started to become a factor among the most violent.

There were many leaders on both sides of the Civil War that played major roles in the communist and Carbonari movements. The North had its revolutionaries but so did the South, although not close to the percentages in the North. At the unveiling of the Stars and Bars flag of the Confederacy in Montgomery, the revolutionary French song *La Marseillaise* was sung, with George Sanders in attendance. Some of the more proper Southern ladies and gentlemen were not pleased.

There were many important reasons that the South's position was untenable in the war against the North. They had no industrial base to make the various accouterments needed to wage war, not even paper to any extent, and no major shipyards. Other than small vessels, what effective warships the Confederacy acquired were built in Europe. The railroad system in the South could barely be called a system, as it used a variety of different rail gauges and was only one-third of the size and scope of the system in the North. This meant that often a boxcar could not be loaded in one area and the goods transported across the South without unloading from one car to another to accommodate the changes in the rail gauges. This was a problem in the North as well, but not to the extent as in the South, plus there was one major difference: the

South could not replenish worn out or destroyed rolling stock and engines since the factories that manufactured them were in the North. Major foodstuffs that required labor were not grown in sufficient quantity. With men at the front, food production suffered, and there was the blockade. And finally, the manpower to field an effective army over an extended amount of time was lacking, particularly in light of the desertion rate, coupled with obstruction tactics to prevent enlistments or the drafting of men. The white population in the South was much smaller than in the North and constant, large-scale immigration into the Northern ports only added to this disparity. And, the above does not even bring into account the financial problems, the lack of central command, and the many problems brought about by those in the South who wanted the North to win.

The North had fewer of these problems. Besides being the most populous section, with a four-to-one ratio to the white population in the South, the bulk of immigration into the United States entered into and stayed in the North and would continue to do so. And, this immigration was substantial. Men fit for battle could readily come from this resource more so than in the South, and they did. After all, immigrants coming to America could not run the Southern blockade, so they sailed into Northern ports.

The passage of the Homestead Act served to lure men to this country in the quest for free land, and they found themselves in the Union army. Part of the goal for passing the act was this benefit for the North. Recruiting among the multitude of immigrants into the Union Army began in Europe and extended to the docks in U.S. ports.

Another problem the South had was that they never successfully took land away from the Union. Therefore, they rarely had an opportunity to capture supplies. On the other hand, when well-equipped Union forces took land in the South, it was not unusual for them to conscript "freed' slaves into the Union Army, thereby swelling their forces.

With these problems, the South could not conduct an offensive war. One cannot wage a defensive war and expect to win, only delay the outcome. As Napoleon said, "The best defense is a good offense." Robert E. Lee tried an offensive thrust once up through Pennsylvania and found the going too rough. The North had the manpower for a completely offensive strategy — the South did not.

It was the immigration into the North of radical elements, particularly from Germany, that assisted in bringing about the war in the first place. The communist-led revolutions of 1848-1849 (which failed in their overt intent) necessitated the leaders and their armies fleeing Germany, Ireland, and to a lesser extent other pockets of revolution, in Europe. These men became the vanguard of immigrant agitation and armed units preparing for war.

The use of intelligence services was a factor in the war, as well. Both sides had effective programs. A possible clue as to a problem on the staff of Robert E. Lee is a passage in *The Civil War in the United States*, a compilation of correspondence and writings by Karl Marx, indicating that there was a major on Lee's staff in 1863 who was in direct communication with Engels. Who else might he have been in touch with?

The Turners
The most famous of the immigrant organizations preparing for a civil war were the Turnverein, or Turner Societies, that were particularly strong in the Midwest states. Their motto was, "A healthy mind in a healthy body." A healthy mind was in reality to be one based on rationalism, or socialism. A Turner was a gymnast, and this served as the public persona of the organization to the outside world at first glance.

The Turners were founded in 1811 by Professor Frederick Ludwig Jahn of Berlin University. He then took them into the Tugendbund, a military revolutionary band. This was followed by absorption into the

Burschenschaften student group, which also contained the Totenbund, or death society. The Totenbund was actually started by the Carbonari and its aim was to kill all who should oppose its aims.

While the Turners were ostensibly gymnasts, there can be no question even in the minds of those who doubt conspiracy that the Turners organized by Jahn were to consider themselves liberators against Napoleon after Napoleon had "gone rogue" from the Conspiracy. They were to be the revolutionary vanguard.

Almost all short references to the Turners skirt the fact that they were anything other than patriotic gymnasts.

Prior to the Turners, the Tugendbund, or Band of Virtue, was founded in 1810 as a successor to the Illuminati. They infiltrated the Black Knights of Jahn, the Concordists of Dr. M. Chevalier von Lang, and other secret societies of the day in Germany. They rose against the rule of Napoleon, who by that time had abandoned the conspiracy, and were suppressed. The claim is that they revived as the Burschenschaften, dove down again under cover and came back in the period of 1830-33.

The League of Youth under Karl Follen, associated with the Burschenschaften, also advocated assassination. Follen worked with the Carbonari Gioacchino Prati and the Illuminist Buonarroti on forming the league, which was to be a youth arm of the League of Men, to spread to all aspects of society. These organizations were the direct descendants of the Illuminati organizations in Germany and had links with the Carbonari.

The more radical wing of the Burschenschaften, "the Unconditionals," in their paper in Weimar, Germany, the *Patriot*, set forth their aims in the slogan: "Ein Reich...ein Gott, ein Volk, Ein Wille." (One Empire, one God, one Race, One Will.)

In Hitler's day it became Ein Volk, Ein Reich, Ein Fuehrer (One Race, One Empire, One Leader.) The most famous propaganda film building up the Nazi movement within a unified Germany was titled *Triumph of the Will*.

The only difference between the early conspiracy slogan and Nazism was that Hitler was substituted for God. They relegated God to the slogan on the belt buckle of the Wehrmacht (*Gott mit Uns*), but the oral oath of allegiance by the Wehrmacht was to Adolf Hitler. It was the end result of 150 years of radical activism in Germany.

Imagine if American soldiers — instead of taking an oath to obey the Constitution — took one to obey Obama or Bush. Rather than obey the German constitution or government, the German soldiers agreed to obey one man.

The idea of a Thousand Year Reich was not original with Hitler. In the 1820s M.L.B. Müller promoted this concept, which was expanded on by A. Dietsch, the author in 1842 of *Das tausendjährige Reich*, a twist of the concept of an earthly kingdom ruled by Christ. Both men turned from the promotion of such a millennial Reich to immigrating to the United States to realize their dream.

Likewise, Carl Schurz was for a Pan German nation before he decided to immigrate to America. As promoted by Hitler later, it was to include all Germans: Germany, Austria, the colonies of Germans to the east, etc. Most Americans are unaware that a vast number of German colonies existed in all of Central Europe and Russia, established in the late 1700s and early 1800s. These colonies generally retained their German heritage and language into the mid-20th century.

The idea of racial purity and superiority — promoting superior bodies and minds — came about as a result of such activity and philosophy over time, and was ingrained in German organizations such as the Turners. The idea of superiority over others has the psychological effect of enlisting the "superiors" into subjugating other races and countries; it is the logical progression of Darwinism and the survival of the fittest.

Hatred of other races has had a long history within the so-called progressives, another word for socialists. While their leaders profess to work for the downtrodden and minorities, they have no respect for them, and even detest them. A study of the eugenics program in the United States and Germany would confirm this.

The socialist elite in both countries have long advocated everything from abortion for the colored races and discouraging mixed offspring, to the elimination of races. The Nazis were more open about it. American liberals tend to advocate such things in the name of eliminating poverty and crime. In the final analysis they both end up at the same juncture.

From the beginning of the modern conspiracy to today, the leaders have hated other races, from Marx's and Voltaire's anti-Semitism to Frederick Engels' hatred of the Slavs, calling for their extermination. Hitler was simply implementing their ideas. Hitler got the blame for the crime, not the authors the conspirators want the impressionable to read, such as Voltaire, Marx, and Engels.

Marx was Jewish by race, raised a Christian until he entered the university, and then he rejected his own race and Christ while under the influence of his professors. He was an anti-Semitic of the most virulent kind, writing a book against the Jews titled *A World Without Jews*.

Marx had a great deal of problems with a few members of the Jewish race in the early communist organization. He almost always worked to negate their leadership. It was done partly as a desire to rule the communist movement by gaining the leadership then holding it without interference, but his anti-Semitism had to have played a role.

Both he and Engels probably derived many of their racial beliefs from Hegel, who had complete contempt for the Negro, for instance. Marx, a decade before the American Civil War, was all for the enslavement of the Negro in America until it wasn't politically expedient.

From the beginnings of socialism/communism, running through the National Socialism of Germany and the communism of the USSR, a variety of races have suffered, particularly the Jews. It is a two-fold tragedy: One, a few of the Jewish race helped build the very structure that would kill them in the end, and two, because of the spotlight placed on these particular Jews, far too many people think the conspiracy is Jewish.

It manifests as anti-Zionism. It is true that a wing of Zionism is controlled by the Conspiracy after they did all they could to eliminate the true Zionists. One of the best books on this subject is *To Eliminate the Opiate* by Rabbi Marvin S. Antelman. The work is in two volumes, with the first volume a better-documented work.

One of the aims of false Zionism is to create the appearance of being the heart of the Conspiracy in order to throw people off target as to the real motivation behind the Conspiracy. We use again the argument that if the Conspiracy is of one race or religious sect, the second or third tier of the orders would not continue to help them since they would realize that they would never be allowed to attain to the top tier, let alone the leadership. They would be forever stuck working for people they could never replace since they are not of that race or sect.

This condition may work in a normal employment atmosphere, but here we are talking about the abnormally ambitious, people who want to attain the most power possible.

From the onset, the roots of Nazism and communism are traceable to earlier Illuminism and the Age of Reason including their racial biases.

The originator of the Turners, Jahn, said in 1810, "Poles, French, priests, aristocrats and Jews are Germany's misfortune." At first Jews were not members of the Turnverein, but later they were allowed into membership.

The first American Turner group was established in 1848 in Cincinnati by Friederich Karl Franz

CHART SEVEN

Turner Organization

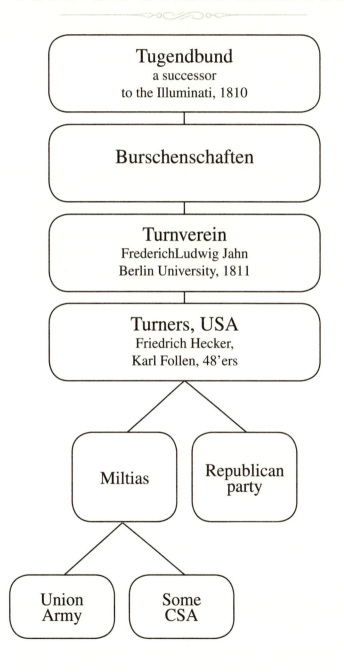

Hecker, a German revolutionary. He was a member of the extreme Left in the Baden Diet in 1846-47. He fled to the United States upon hearing that he would be executed by the government after he led the first armed insurrection in Baden, Germany, which failed.

After coming to the United States, he immersed himself in politics and later the Republican Party, helping to get it established. During the War, he became a colonel in the Union Army in Gen. Fremont's division.

Karl Follen was an extremist leader within the Burschenschaften and the Unconditionals. He also formed an alliance with Prati, an Illuminist disciple and close collaborator of Buonarroti. Buonarroti was an admirer of Robespierre. Mazzini was also close to Buonarroti.

Due to his agitation, speeches, and leadership, Follen was accused of inciting violent acts by his followers. He had to leave his country when one of his followers engaged in an assassination, and came to the United States, where he wanted to form a German state as a base for mounting revolution in Germany and the rest of Europe. He came with letters of recommendation from Lafayette, and in fact rode over on the same vessel furnished by the American government that brought Lafayette to the United States for his triumphant visit.

The Prussian historian Heinrich von Treitschke described Follen as a "petty Robespierre ... endowed with great terroristic powers."

Follen ultimately became a Unitarian minister and the first professor of German literature at Harvard University, apparently with Lafayette's help. He also became a prominent member of Garrison's Anti-Slavery Society. He was active in the establishment of Turner organizations.

Keep in mind, Follen worked with Illuminati and as a violent secret-society leader, and he ingratiated himself immediately into American politics and culture once he immigrated here.

Also, when you read in these pages of their efforts and areas of influence in the United States, remember that the Turner groups were an extension of the Illuminist efforts of German revolutionaries.

While some individuals like Follen had in mind continuing the German revolution at first, the vast majority retained their revolutionary attitude and turned their attention against the American system. If their true desire was freedom, why then did they not become partisans of the American Constitution rather than working to destroy the American social order? This is a further demonstration that liberty has never been the goal of the revolution.

The constitution of the Milwaukee Turnverein declared in favor of the "Red Flag of Socialism." In 1850, the New York Socialistischer Turnverein was formed. It changed its name to simply the New York Turnverein, but their constitution said, "We stand on a revolutionary and socialist foundation."

Some of the more interesting aspects of the platform of the New York Turner organization were: the direct election of U.S. Senators, which ultimately came about in the early 20th century; a graduated tax on ability to pay; and ultimately the abolishment of the Senate and presidency substituting in their place an executive committee of the House of Representatives — the latter essentially the government of revolutionary France. The remaining planks were the normal calls of the socialist movement of the day.

As stated, the New York unit started out as the Socialististischer Turnverein, later simply calling themselves the New York Turnverein. The first leader of the socialist organization in 1850, Sigsmund Kaufmann, later ran as the Republican Party candidate for lieutenant governor.

He was of the more radical wing of the Turners, and by 1863 the New York organization had 500 members. Lincoln offered him the post of ambassador to Italy, but he declined.

At the Turners' national convention in Philadelphia in 1854, 62 Turnverein groups were represented. At the national convention the following year in Buffalo, three major principles were adopted:

1. No voting for Know-Nothings.
2. Abolition.
3. Opposition to prohibition laws of any kind.

This caused a split, with a small minority of Southern units withdrawing from association. We will not be documenting their efforts in the South to promote a brand of socialism there. Some of these Turners supported the Union during the war, with some German communities coming under attack by Confederate citizens. One example was Fredericksburg, Texas, settled by 48ers. Others became Confederates.

Turners led by militant 48ers instilled four ideas into the German community:

1. The Union must be preserved.
2. Abolition.
3. People must live according to the laws of reason. (As opposed to Christianity.)
4. Republicanism must be entrenched in the continent. (Meaning the Jacobin definition of republicanism.)

The German revolutionary leaders such as Carl Schurz felt that secession was treason if it was the South doing the seceding. They had no problem with a revolution in Germany to overthrow their existing government, but were opposed to the right of the Southern governments, not to overthrow the existing government, but to simply go their own way.

Many of the Turner groups formed military units wherein they practiced marksmanship, drilling, and bayonet practice. By November 8, 1860, the National Turner Society ordered all groups to form military units and engage in military training as part of their gymnasium program.

These units formed the bulk of the initial brigades which became the Union Army.

After the Civil War, they changed their national name again, this time to the North American Gymnastic Union. Some locals still used *Socialistic* as part of their name and remained sympathetic to the socialist movement. Other groups remained sympathetic without the use of the term in their name.

An important source of agitation after the war was the Arbiter-Vereine, established by the communist Wilhelm Weitling. These were artisan oriented and close to being unions. The most prominent in the national organization was the Chicago unit, which included Joseph Weydemeyer in its ranks.

The Chicago organization celebrated the first anniversary of the brutal Paris Commune of 1871, and this was troubling to the local authorities.

An interesting sidebar to the Paris Commune is that George Wilkes, a famous newsman, got his start by working for a time on the *Subterranean*. He was active in politics and the Brotherhood of the Union, and helped introduce pari-mutuel betting to America. He was a friend of Mike Walsh in his youth, and as an observer at the Paris Commune hinted that it was part of the Illuminati conspiracy and that the IWA secretly pulled the strings.

The only American who actually fought in the Commune was William Dugas Trammell. There were a large number of foreigners in the Commune leadership, including men who fought in the Civil War, but with the exception of Trammell, no American citizens. Trammell was from Georgia and was a judge there, and at his death was vice president of the IWA.

Into the mid-20th century, Turner organizations became more like their public persona, a gymnastic organization holding meets and athletic events.

Radical Foreign Leaders
Many German revolutionaries went into the publishing business, and several newspapers that served the German immigrants. The majority of the well-known publishers were communist in orientation. Out of this industry came Joseph Pulitzer, after whom the annual prize for American journalism was named. Pulitzer was Carl Schurz's assistant in the *Westliche Post* newspaper in St. Louis, and if Charles Sotheran, the historian of the Socialist Labor movement is correct, Pulitzer was a member of the International.

The leader of the so-called German vote within the Republican Party was Carl Schurz. His rise to fame among Americans was due to prominent public figures helping him gain a swift reputation upon his immigration to America, apparently as an emissary of Mazzini. Among these was Louis P. Harvey, a manufacturer who became a member of the Wisconsin State Legislature and later governor. Harvey saw to it that articles appeared in newspapers relating heroic stories of Schurz. Another man, Horace Rublee, owner of the *Madison State Journal* saw to their distribution.

In Germany, Schurz, along with August Willich, had effected the escape from prison of their mutual friend Gottfried Kinkel, a member of the Communist League with Marx and Engel, who had been a teacher of Schurz at the University of Bonn. Along with Willich, Kinkel later would fall out with Marx, but not before he came to the U.S. to raise money for the revolution. He was not too successful in doing so, but did have an interview with President Millard Fillmore.

Wisconsin was a very important base for German revolutionaries, who were appointed or elected to important positions. Edward S. Salomon, one of the three revolutionary Salomon brothers, was made a regent of the University of Wisconsin as was Schurz. Salomon was elected Lieutenant Governor of Wisconsin in 1861 and served as governor after the death of his predecessor. He removed to New York City in 1869 and eventually moved back to Prussia, where he died in 1909.

Other states had similar infiltration and appointments.

In Germany, Schurz had been a student leader in democratic societies. He became so radical that many of his fraternity brothers refused to follow him after a time. Further research is needed to find out if these were the descendants of the student organizations founded by Illuminists, although obviously he was influenced by his communist teacher, Kinkel.

Schurz became an adherent of the idea of all German peoples forming one nation, a condition that became a reality for the most part under Bismarck. The larger German state almost became a temporary fact under Adolf Hitler, excluding the German colonies to the east of Moscow where the German armies could not penetrate during World War II.

These German colonies in Russia were established for the most part under Catherine the Great, who was German herself. There were many of these towns and villages that welcomed the invading German army because they were under the rule of the brutal communists. On a scale of cruelty, the Nazis were less so than the Bolsheviks in the daily lives of these villagers.

Movie clips from World War II exist showing young Russian and Ukrainian fräuleins from these colonies giving the Hitler salute while marching in review past the local German occupation authorities.

Stalin decided that the German colonies that were overrun by the Wehrmacht were a security risk to the communists, so after the war he ordered that they kill all of the males above a certain age and march the small boys, women, and girls off to Siberia. The villages were then occupied by ethnic Russians who moved in to farm the former German areas. Graveyards robbed of valuables, and churches were destroyed unless they could serve as warehouses for grain and other farm goods.

This author has seen a homemade video by a German-Russian American who went into these areas in the early 1990s to search out his origins and family tree. This search was in vain since the villages had been occupied by Russians for too long, with the subsequent destruction of church records and graveyards. The narrative regarding what was in the video does not lend itself to this book, except to simply state that what was there was abject poverty and desolation beyond what the average American can imagine among the villagers and rural people inhabiting the communal farms, all quite different than the communist propaganda depicting life in the Russian farmland at the time.

Schurz joined the communist Anneke in an attack in 1848 on the arsenal at Siegburg, which became a fiasco. He then became a lieutenant under Anneke in the larger revolutionary army, under the command of several important communists.

After fleeing Germany for his participation in the 1848 revolution, he was kicked out of France as a dangerous revolutionary in 1851. It was during this period that he became close to the Carbonari leader Mazzini. He was in the company of Mazzini, Marx, Louis Blanc (the socialist president of the 1848 Paris commission), and Louis Kossuth. At one point in his sojourn in London, Schurz was under the orders of Mazzini and appears to have been sent to America serving in that capacity; however, he would not be the only revolutionary who came to the U.S. who served directly under Mazzini.

When he came to the United States Schurz had letters of introduction to various politicians, and the one who impressed him the most was Jefferson Davis. Davis was the secretary of war under President Pierce, and he was instrumental in promoting many of the revolutionaries that received appointments to our consulates and embassies abroad in Europe. It is unknown who wrote these letters of introduction from Europe for Schurz and how they came to open doors to very influential people in the United States. The idea that they were written as part of the Carbonari underground would seem to fit the circumstances. YA was part of this apparatus.

Schurz visited with several U.S. senators and President Pierce. They apparently convinced him to move to the Midwest once he settled in America.

As a result of Schurz' travels in the United States he decided that the European revolution would have to take a back seat to eliminating slaveholders' influence in America. Something made Schurz decide that the political situation in America had to change before they could change Europe.

When he first came to the United States he also contacted German revolutionaries. It appears that he considered the slavery issue to be the best catalyst for fomenting a war in America. He then returned to London to meet with revolutionary leaders.

Upon his return to the U.S., Schurz was established as a political leader by men such as Gerrit Smith of the Secret Six, Longfellow, and John A. Andrew, who was to become governor of Massachusetts in 1860. He met many of the intellectuals of New England while on a speaking tour there — again one of the tours that seemed to blossom from nowhere. In our school history books, it is never mentioned by whom, how, and why the tours were organized — or why the particular speakers were asked to participate. It takes a lot of manpower and upfront money to put on a successful speaking tour.

To generate a speaking tour, you need a coordinating organization that has local contacts to schedule a tour. These contacts need a local organization in each area where a speech is held to set up a venue and produce local advertising and publicity to generate an audience, unless it is strictly of a popular entertainment value.

Such organization may be invisible to the average man on the street, but it does and will always exist. Speakers do not just show up or decide which cities they will appear in; someone sets it up using organization. One has to ask what that organization was — and in the case of modern times, what it is. This is a very important question that must be answered in order to understand the actual intent of the organizers.

Such arrangements might be organized by an existing lyceum, but what would prompt them to put Schurz on tour, even if they built up publicity for his appearances?

Who would want to hear a man from Germany without any real reputation except that he participated as a low-level officer in the revolution of 1848? True, he had rescued a high-level communist leader from prison; however, these tours spring from politically motivated organizations. Nonetheless, there were other men with basically the same credentials or more who participated in the revolutions of 1848 and 1849; why not ask them to speak? It was all part of the buildup of a man who would come to serve the Conspiracy in several capacities.

From 1858-1859, Schurz was placed on the board of trustees of the University of Wisconsin and made a colonel in the militia — all this in fewer than ten years in our country.

Schurz was appointed by Lincoln as our ambassador to Spain, which was not looked upon with favor by Madrid. They did not want a European Republican and abolitionist sent to Madrid to become the center of democratic conspiracies. It was bad enough when native-born Americans appointed to that position were doing the same thing. In Schurz' case, he had too many connections with the European revolutionaries for the Spanish to be comfortable with him. They could be sure, based on his history and contacts, that he would use Madrid as a base for revolutionary tactics. They had witnessed this sort of thing before with those involved in the Ostend affair.

Keep in mind that Spain had several possessions that had the institution of slavery, and having an abolitionist stirring things up was not something Spain would have welcomed.

Schurz got the appointment after being offered Lisbon. He rejected Lisbon because it was a lower station and he wanted at least $12,000 per year, a goodly sum in those days. The modern equivalent would be no less than $250,000. The idea of Schurz was to upgrade the mission to Lisbon with the increase of pay, but Congress was not in session to do that. *A number of unknown New York bankers* offered to make up the difference in salary until Congress could make the change. Secretary of State Seward refused to go along, however, and the Spanish legation was offered.

Historians do not mention who these bankers were or why they would make such an offer to assist Schurz.

It is interesting how many socialists like the good life and believe that lower stations in society and organization are beneath them. Everything is done in the name of the equality of the people, but some people seem to be more equal than others.

Upon his return Schurz advised Lincoln that the European powers would have trouble supporting the South if emancipation became the policy of the North. In this way, the general populations of Europe would resist having their governments helping the Confederacy once they witnessed the Union abolishing slavery. The grassroots of Europe were, by and large, opposed to slavery.

Before the second Lincoln inaugural, Lincoln read his speech to Schurz in advance, declaring it was "a mark of confidence I have given no other man."

Schurz' influence on Lincoln at one time allowed him to sit in on some of Lincoln's Cabinet meetings.

Schurz raised the ire of other Germans due to his rapid rise in prominence, as one could well imagine among those who wanted to be "the leader," particularly those under whom Schurz had served in the communist revolution in Germany. In Germany, Schurz was an underling. In America he was made a top leader.

It is unknown who gave him the letters of introduction and why his way was "greased" above all other Germans. Obviously it was his connection to Mazzini, if not Mazzini himself. The American connections to and respect for Mazzini were wide and deep. The evidence suggests Schurz was an emissary of Mazzini with a mission slightly different than another of Mazzini's minions, Hugh Forbes. Schurz moved in higher circles, with a political slant to his activities and free from the burden of running an organization, as Forbes had been tasked to do.

It is unknown just how many minions of Mazzini and Marx were sent to America on specific missions to help build their influence, but there were many. It would be nice to know just who the letters of introduction for Schurz were addressed to and who wrote them. Just one that Schurz used, the letter to Jefferson Davis, should raise eyebrows.

Forbes appears to have been assigned the task of pulling together the Carbonari that had immigrated to America, into an American version of the Carbonari organization apart from YA. While the mission of Schurz appears to have been to work at a higher level in the political arena, this did not mean that Forbes did not have high-level contacts in the American government as well; he did, but was never politically active with them. He maintained open communications with them but never participated in their political activities, as did Schurz.

After Spain, Schurz was given a commission as a general in the Union Army under Fremont, where Fremont's military aides were old Garibaldi officers from the Carbonari army. Schurz was a lieutenant in Germany then appointed a colonel in the Wisconsin militia by a governor who was initially involved in promoting the reputation of Schurz, then made a general by the Stanton War Office, and finally promoted to major general.

Keep in mind as you read about this man's life that in most cases he did not rise by himself, he was given a free ride by very well-placed dignitaries.

It was not unusual during the war for men to be brevetted a general if they had political connections and any previous military experience. This was done probably to confer authority on the politically correct, to avoid any widespread mutinies by units of the Union Army that may not like their orders that were in violation of common decency or the Constitution.

This continues today, as it is increasingly common to see members of the Council on Foreign Relations holding important commands and implementing CFR policy through the use of our armed forces overseas. This is why, although one would have thought that our modern generals would fight tooth and nail to stop women serving in combat roles and opening up enlistment to homosexuals, there is not a peep!

After the war, Schurz became even more prominent and instrumental in codifying many of the onerous edicts that were put in place during the Civil War. He lost his Watertown, Wisconsin farm by mortgage foreclosure in 1867, but money was raised by Emil Preetorius for Schurz to "buy" an interest in the German-language newspaper edited by Preetorius, the *Westliche Post* in St. Louis. Preetorius' law partner, James Taussig, raised the $10,000 in 24 hours. In 1869, two years after losing his farm in Wisconsin, Schurz was the U.S. senator from Missouri, elected by the state legislature — indeed, the first German immigrant to serve in the Senate. It's nice to have friends.

Carl Danziger had started the *Westliche Post* after working for the communist Heinrich Börnstein. The *Post* had more than one 48er on its staff over the years, including Theodore Olshauser, who was a member of a radical student organization at his university in Germany, and who returned to Germany in 1865.

The secretary of the *Post's* corporation, Felix Coste, went on to serve as the president of the St. Louis Board of Education.

Years after the war, Schurz was a co-founder of the *Saturday Evening Post* magazine, which became very popular in the early to mid-20th century and is better known today for its covers that were painted by the renowned artist Norman Rockwell. As stated before, the magazine gradually adopted a more conservative flair as compared to other mainstream publications such as *Life*.

Schurz and Otto von Bismarck, the unifier of Germany, later would become friends. Such friendships helped solidify Schurz' influence among the German immigrants.

This sort of influence that inflamed and manipulated the American people into a protracted war you could multiply all across the country in regard to a variety of domestic and foreign radicals. It might be worth re-reading the above paragraphs, keeping in mind that Schurz had no base in America and was nothing more than a talented revolutionary with letters of introduction. This fact reinforces the idea that the Conspiracy exists and is international in scope, and promotes its minions to positions of influence. Even his introduction into the newspaper business was bought and paid for by others.

And, Schurz was just one of many.

One of the problems of constitutionalists — or advantages, depending on how you look at it — is that constitutionalists hire people based on their capability more than their politics. The socialists do otherwise, hiring like-minded people. This helps drive the agenda and prevents their opponents from gaining traction in business, government, and media.

The influence of Carl Schurz has lasted into the 21st century, through organizations such as the Carl Schurz Memorial Foundation, founded in 1930. The first leader of this foundation was the former executive secretary of the American Friends Service Committee; supposedly a Quaker organization but one which has had close ties to the communist movement in America.

The foundation promoted the idea of American students studying in Germany in the 1930s and beyond.

The initial group of directors of the Schurz Foundation included Paul M. Warburg, who was also its first treasurer. He has been called the father of the Federal Reserve. The foundation signed a lease with the Department of the Interior to house themselves at the old Custom House in Philadelphia, home of the Second Bank of the U.S. Warburg served on the initial board of directors of the Council on Foreign Relations until his death.

Both Schurz and Warburg are buried at the Sleepy Hollow Cemetery.

You can't make this stuff up!

Another foreign revolutionary needs to be noticed since he had so much influence on many key individuals before and during the Civil War: Adam Gurowski. He was so radical that apparently he was the only man that Lincoln feared might take his life.

Gurowski studied under Hegel at the University of Berlin and was influenced by the French Revolution. He was active in Polish revolutionary activities against Russia, and as a result his property was confiscated and at one time he was condemned to death.

He became a friend of Lafayette in the 1830s in France, and may have been not only an advisor to Mazzini, but perhaps his leader at one time. While in France, he also conspired with Louis Napoleon when he was an active Carbonari. Gurowski was a Fourierist, promoting this form of socialism.

He ultimately became a Russophile, promoting Russia as the head of a Pan Slavic empire. As such he was given a reprieve by Russia, although his property was not restored.

When he came to the United States, he began to keep the company of a host of radical and intellectual notables, who all knew his background. These included George Bancroft, William C. Bryant, Edward Everett, Longfellow, Charles Sumner, Theodore Parker, the Howes, Walt Whitman, Albert Brisbane, Prescott King, Nathaniel Banks, Z. Chandler, Salmon Chase, and Lincoln's secretary, John Hay. He grew close to Edwin Stanton.

For several years he worked in the editorial offices of the *New York Tribune,* from 1851 to 1857, and rewrote the pieces sent in by Marx and Engels. He was not close to Greeley, but was close to Dana, Ripley, William Fry, and James Pike. It was in this time period that he served on the editorial staff of *The New American Cyclopedia.*

Before the war, the Peace Convention broke down as a result of Gurowski's help, along with other Republicans and secessionists. They did not want peace.

During the early years of the war, he was hired as a translator for the State Department, where he apparently spied on Seward for the Radicals, who became his only friends when the likes of Sumner severed relations with him.

Gurowski wrote his diaries, and these were published with the help of Gov. Edward Andrew and George Luther Stearns, one of the Secret Six who helped John Brown. His earlier book, *Slavery in History*, was published in 1860 by A. B. Burdick, who also published *Helper's Book.* It was Edward Everett who got Gurowski his first job in America delivering lectures and attempted to get him on the staff of the Smithsonian.

Gurowski died some months after the war of typhoid fever; had he lived longer, he would have had even more influence on the American scene. But, for foreign personalities to have influence on the United States it wasn't necessary for them to immigrate here. Many of their disciples carried their influence here for them.

Close friends of Karl Marx and founders of the communist First International were active in politics and publishing, and they did all they could to foment the war. Many were appointed to important positions in the Union Army and over civilian territory once the war started.

A prime example was Joseph Weydemeyer. He was a friend of Karl Marx, and it was in his home that Marx stayed for a time in 1849 after the failure of the revolution. Weydemeyer was a founder of the First International. He was forced to flee his country and came to the United States, where he started a German-language newspaper called *Die Revolution* in 1852. He changed the name to *Reform* rather than retain the "in your face" title, to make the paper more acceptable.

Weydemeyer also formed the first Marxist organization in the U.S., the Prolaterierbund, in 1852 with four of his friends — again, a five-man initiating team. This organization later became the American Workers League, and at the first meeting 800 people joined. While it organized German branches in New Jersey, Ohio, and Pennsylvania, it had an English local in the nation's capital. After it was founded, a secret military organization was founded within it. The surface Prolaterierbund itself was short-lived.

Having been an officer in the Prussian army, Weydemeyer he was able to get an appointment as a colonel, then general, in the Union Army. He was named by the Lincoln War Department as the commander in charge of the defense of the St. Louis area toward the end of the war.

At the beginning of the conflict, Gen. Winfield Scott, the hero of the Mexican War, was in command of the army. He advised Lincoln to continue the blockade against Southern ports and to launch a thrust down the Mississippi to cut the Confederacy in two and disrupt their supply lines. He warned Lincoln not to otherwise invade the South, as that would lead to a prolonged conflict. Lincoln did not follow his advice not to invade, and a prolonged war was started.

The little known story of how Scott became the commander of the U.S. Army was that Gen. Jacob Brown, who held the position, died in 1828. There was another general who claimed seniority for the position along with Scott. Congress could not decide between the two, so they gave it to a third gentleman. Gen. Scott resented the whole affair, and due to his actions was suspended. During this suspension he traveled to France, where he visited with Lafayette, who successfully advised him to resume his position in the army. In 1841, Scott became the commander of the army.

To further demonstrate the influence of conspiratorial circles, let us remind the reader that early in the war Lincoln offered a Union Army to Garibaldi. Garibaldi wondered if he should go, and asked the opinion of Victor Emmanuel, who answered that he should go if he wished. When the U.S. ambassador came for his decision, Garibaldi begged off since he felt that Italy needed him more. At least, that is one of the many stories circulated of this event.

Pinkerton

One of the key figures in the manipulation of the Washington government early in the Lincoln administration was Alan Pinkerton. In 1842, Pinkerton left Scotland, where he was involved in the Chartist agitation in Britain and had to flee to avoid jail just as so many other radicals from Europe.

Pinkerton was not simply involved with the Chartists; he was a leader as a young man, having formed the Glasgow Democratic Club.

He settled in Chicago into a cooper business, and was not immediately involved in the detective business that made him famous. He initially immersed himself in the secret side of the radical program in Illinois, becoming one of John Brown's contacts and a participant in what was known as the Underground Railroad, moving escaped slaves north into Canada.

Pinkerton then became one of the earliest detectives on the Chicago police force. He grew even more active in law enforcement, joining the sheriff's department.

For a variety of reasons, the railroads were having problems that required a security system. Various railroad companies, such as Galena and Chicago Union, Rock Island, and Illinois Central, decided to come together to promote Chicago's first detective agency, with Pinkerton in partnership with E. G. Rucker. The partnership dissolved after a year, but Pinkerton was left in a position to run the railroads' security with his own agency. At the time, Lincoln was an attorney for the Illinois Central Railroad. Due to McClellan's involvement in the Illinois Central, he became a friend and patron of Pinkerton. Nathaniel Banks was a vice president of the Illinois Central in the late 1850s.

Pinkerton adopted the so-called Eye of Horus, or all-seeing eye, as the logo for his detective agency. His motto was, "We never sleep," as the eye was always open. The logo led to the moniker "private-eye," meaning a detective, a nickname used so often in early 20th century detective stories, magazines, and movies.

Pinkerton's agency supplied all types of security for the railroads against theft, free-riders, robberies, etc. It also was used to keep an eye on railroad employees, particularly conductors, since they had the role of authority over the movement of who and what traveled on the trains. As a member of the Underground Railroad, it was a convenient position for Pinkerton to have.

John Brown often spent nights in Pinkerton's home, and Pinkerton helped him to move to Kansas to "invade." After Harper's Ferry, Pinkerton disguised himself as a Southern planter and learned the layout of the prison holding Brown, but concluded that he could not successfully extricate Brown from the prison.

Pinkerton was a young man who was involved in radical activities and disobeyed the law in Scotland; disobeyed the law in Chicago (no matter how onerous that law was); aided and abetted a terrorist, John Brown; and formed a detective agency. He became the main intelligence officer of the Union at the beginning of the Civil War, and helped lay the groundwork for the U.S. Secret Service.

As one wag of the day quipped, "While Pinkerton's right hand caught lawbreakers, his left hand broke the law."

Pinkerton played a major part in the psychological basis for the events that triggered the war. The agitation over the election of Lincoln was high. Lincoln was elected by the smallest percentage of the popular vote of any president; he represented the minority. Due to the structure of the electoral college and the splitting of the Democrat vote he was elected, but the majority of citizens were not happy about that, or the about platform of the Republican Party and its Radicals.

In other words, Lincoln represented the minority of Americans, and the majority was not happy about it and felt that he was elected due to a perceived weakness in the electoral system. This opinion was widely held in the North, just as it was in the South. We have already mentioned that there was illegal voting for the Republicans by immigrants in the election throughout the Midwest.

The political tension was high and the editorial attacks against the newly elected president-to-be were vituperative. Similar attacks today would more than likely draw the attention of Homeland Security.

Pinkerton told Lincoln that there was an assassination plot against him scheduled to take place on his journey to Washington for the inauguration. This led to Lincoln disguising himself and switching trains; some circulated that he was disguised as a woman, as a means to discredit Lincoln, and it became a story of derision and ridicule among Democrats and Southerners. The story never has been told the same way by those who were directly involved.

Many of those around Lincoln at the time said that there was no evidence of such a plot except in the mind of Pinkerton. Ward Hill Lamon, Lincoln's bodyguard, discredited Pinkerton's claims of a Baltimore assassination plot. There was one story of a bomb that had been placed on Lincoln's train in a carpetbag. If this had been the case, why would Lincoln abandon his family to this threat for his own safety?

True or not, and the debate goes on even today, the whole situation bred a considerable amount of paranoia in the presidential party and set the mood for the first weeks of the administration.

This state of agitation played on the minds of Lincoln and those who believed the story of a plot against his life, whether it was true or not.

Considering this, it is interesting that while Lincoln's first inaugural was heavily guarded, his second inaugural was not, when the plot to kill him was definitely real. The first inaugural was guarded by the local Turner units, with overall command in Washington under Jim Lane of Kansas. On the other hand, a photograph of the second inaugural shows John Wilkes Booth and some of his fellow conspirators standing within a few feet of an unprotected Lincoln in the middle of a war.

Booth secured a pass to the Capitol stands for the second inauguration from Sen. John P. Hale, through John Parker Hale Wentworth, Lucy Hale's first cousin. It is unknown how the other conspirators with Booth gained their positions so close to Lincoln. Hale, of course, was involved in Radical activities, which again demonstrates interesting coincidences involving overlapping personalities in both camps, before, during, and after the war.

Incidentally, Lincoln's carriage to the first inaugural procession included Edward Dickinson Baker, a man rarely mentioned in histories about Lincoln to the extent one would think necessary. Lincoln had named his son, Edward Baker Lincoln, after him.

Baker's family had immigrated to the U.S. and ended up at the New Harmony commune in Indiana in 1825. The next year they left and settled in Illinois. Young Baker studied and became an attorney, engaging in politics. He met Lincoln, and over the years they became fast friends. How much the influence of his family and New Harmony played on his thinking is unknown. Certainly the fact that the family gravitated into this commune as their first home must indicate that they were inclined toward communism. He became a U.S. senator, and ultimately died in combat as a brigadier in the first year of the war. Lincoln wept.

Pinkerton went on to be the head of Gen. McClellan's Department of Ohio's secret service under the alias of Major E. J. Allen. His secret service moved to Washington to oversee military intelligence and counterespionage, at which time Pinkerton was also asked to provide intelligence to McClellan as to the strength and disposition of the Southern forces south of Washington. The plan was for McClellan to lead the Army of the Potomac in an aggressive move against the Virginia army and crush it in a decisive battle to end the war almost as soon as it started.

Due to the intelligence that Pinkerton gathered, coupled with that of McClellan's own aides, this never happened. The reports given to McClellan by Pinkerton exaggerated the number of the Southern forces to be three times the number of Northern troops. This led to McClellan constantly calling for more men and training them to be able to mount an attack. General military wisdom at the time was that an aggressor had to have twice the number of troops to defeat an entrenched defender, assuming equity of armament.

The South did not have the forces to stop McClellan at the onset of war, and McClellan's delay allowed them the time to amass an army that defeated McClellan in the first battle. Without the work of Pinkerton and the man he directly reported to, Col. Thomas Key, the war would have been over before it began, and the prolonged conflict needed to change the old social order would never have happened.

In addition, when McClellan told Stanton of his concerns based on Pinkerton's intelligence, Stanton issued the opposite information to the press, making it look as if McClellan could easily have defeated the Southern forces. When he did not, McClellan was made to look inadequate and the press called him a disappointment.

Pinkerton reported to Col. Key as the head of McClellan's intelligence arm. Key and Pinkerton were friends and remained so all of Key's life. In his estate, Key left his watch to Pinkerton, the only person not a member of his family to receive any of his property. Key had been a law partner of Alphonso Taft, the co-founder of the Order and a Bonesman himself. Think of it, a Chartist and a Bonesman were in charge of U.S. intelligence at the beginning of the war.

A similar situation existed during World War II with the OSS when communists were recruited to serve as our agents. There are several books which detail this problem. One wonders about U.S. intelligence vis-à-vis the president today, when terrorist organizations spring up out of thin air in the Mideast without anyone seeming to notice — with a lot of finger pointing as to who is the responsible party.[56]

Interestingly, today the so-called drug cartels of Latin America, especially in Mexico, use the tactic of beheadings to intimidate people. There is virtually no mention of this in the national media, yet the practice is widespread and frequent. It is a matter of how the powers-that-be want to react the American people, or not, and keep the problems of a destabilized neighbor from the public view. The average American understanding what has been happening in Mexico would affect public opinion about the migration from that country into the United States.

The intelligence gathered by Key personally only reinforced the inflated numbers of the Confederate Army submitted to him by Pinkerton, which served as one reason McClellan held back initially from at-

---

56 One does not want to belabor the point and we have already recommended the author's work called *Exposing Terrorism: Inside the Terror Triangle*; however, it is a fact that U.S. and Russian intelligence agencies work together against terrorism. Who benefits? A good video, originally a movie made in the mid-1960s, can be seen on YouTube: Anarchy, USA. It documents the use of terror in three countries as a prelude to the establishment of communist governments. One of the countries, Algeria, had a communist revolution with the façade of it being "Muslim." It widely used the terror tactic of beheadings, which were laid out on the street for all to see. This was before social media, which can show the deed as well as the result instantaneously. It was also before the media could get away with showing such gory details due to the propriety of the social mores at the time. The point is, they are the same tactics, and have the same antecedents, whether in the 1950s or the 21st century. Communist terror always uses the façade of the religion in any country in which they operate. It tends to throw people off track as to the real culprits. We also heartily recommend www.thenewamerican.com for articles documenting the origins of terrorist organizations.

tacking the Confederate forces. Apparently McClellan believed that the intelligence he received was bona fide the rest of his life, even in the face of contrary evidence.

It was during a visit to the Key home in Cincinnati that a young Harriet Beecher, who married Calvin Ellis Stowe, witnessed a slave auction that was to influence her for the rest of her life. Here we see a tie between the Keys and the abolitionist leaders.

The Constitution Trashed

For some years the radicals had been gaining strength in the federal government, and it accelerated due to the election of Polk, Pierce, and Buchanan. While many of these radicals were Southern, their policies were such that they created a gulf between the federal government and the conservative people who recognized the problems these men were making for peaceful solutions to any number of problems, domestically as well as internationally — just as they do today.

The culmination of the radicalization came with the election of many revolutionaries in the 1860 election, and the future looked grim.

Had the Southern states not seceded, they would have had enough influence in the Congress to stop what the election of Northern radicals would have tried to change. The secession not only changed this condition, it opened up the United States government to the worst elements of the radical persuasion — **exactly the opposite effect** *the Southern politicians claimed to desire.*

T. Harry Williams, president of the Southern Historical Association, wrote:

> The Southern action created a revolutionary situation. It brought to power in the national government the radicals, doctrinaires who if the South had not left would not have had power, political types who in American politics usually hover on the edge of power rather than being at its center.
> — *Lincoln and the Radicals*

This is true, as far as it goes. In fact, while the radicals were already gaining power in the Polk, Pierce, and Buchanan administrations, the election of the Republicans brought a new breed of radical into office that had the same agenda, and it put this agenda on the fast track.

Pierce was prone to appointing YA radicals to office, and later would have Nathaniel Hawthorne, a well-known YA adherent and socialist, write his biography. Buchanan, as much as he was loved by YA, did not appoint known YA individuals to his Cabinet except for Breckinridge. In addition to Breckinridge, he named Stanton as attorney general, who was far worse in the general scheme of things.

Interestingly, a 20th century president also had a militant socialist write his memoirs: Dwight David Eisenhower's *Crusade in Europe*. The author was Joseph Fels Barnes, who was identified as a communist agent by several ex-communists under oath. It is another example of certain histories lying, saying that Eisenhower did not have a ghostwriter, when in fact he did.

It is interesting how many websites that talk about the book *Crusade in Europe*, pointedly make the comment out of the blue that "Ike" did not have a ghostwriter, a patent falsehood. If people would be aware of his ghostwriter and his background, it would raise serious questions about Eisenhower and his brother Milton, questions that have been suppressed systematically for many years. One question alone should suffice to start: Why did he appoint John Foster Dulles as his secretary of state? Any honest constitutionalist would cringe upon close study of Dulles, who was one of the founders of the Council on Foreign Relations and who publicly stated that treaties could supersede the Bill of Rights, an absolute falsehood.

The policies of Pierce and Buchanan probably produced more abolitionists than all the efforts of the abolition leaders themselves. It was the tactic again of the action being in the reaction. Whether they intentionally meant to do this or not, it was the result. They were too involved with radical YA and pro-slavery people who were an obvious embarrassment to the country.

The programmed reaction into secession by the people of the South and their governments due to the radicalism in the North, and with such machinations of the KGC and similar groups in their own states, played into the hands of the Master Conspiracy. Cooler heads would have settled the problems and preserved the Republic as it was founded sans slavery.

War fever brought about the wholesale violation of the rights of American citizens. In the Union-held territories this extended to those in state and local government. Even Chief Justice Roger Taney was concerned that he would be arrested for defying Lincoln's suspension of habeas corpus. It had been done at least twice before, during the Burr conspiracy when the Jefferson government arrested a federal judge for saying that the suspension of habeas corpus was illegal, and again under the command of Andrew Jackson.

And, that is exactly what happened. Lincoln did issue a warrant of arrest for Taney. There is scant evidence in history books for this action, but contemporary witnesses corroborate it. The federal marshal of Washington, Ward Hill Lamon, a longtime colleague of Lincoln, refused to serve it.

Obviously Lincoln did not respect the separation of powers between the three branches of the Federal government. He not only wanted to arrest the Supreme Court chief justice for upholding the Constitution, but ignored the Congress, issuing edicts that were unconstitutional before he called Congress into session to rubberstamp his actions.

Taney, then 85 years old, wrote in his decision to prevent the suspension of habeas corpus in *Ex parte Merryman*:

> If the President of the United States may suspend the writ, then the Constitution of the United States has conferred upon him more regal and absolute power over the liberty of the citizen than the people of England have thought it safe to entrust to the crown — a power which the Queen of England cannot exercise to this day, and which could not have been lawfully exercised by the sovereign even in the reign of Charles the First.

Great pains were taken by Lincoln to forestall the withdrawal of *certain* states whose governments' desired to separate from the North. The worse case was Maryland. Secessionist members of the Maryland legislature were arrested September 13-16, 1861. When the legislature met, no secessionist members were present. This prevented a bill for secession being proposed. The action also included the arrest of local officials in Maryland, including the mayor of Baltimore.

The arrested legislators were held incognito in prison until after the November election. Their guards were German-speaking Turner troops from Wisconsin. It is unknown just how many of these troops were actually citizens of the United States or how long they had been in country. Nonetheless, the troops, not being versed in the Constitution, ensured their obedience to orders in violation of constitutionally protected rights. Not only that, but communication to the outside was made more difficult due to the language barrier as well as the political differences between the legislators and the troops.

Union troops in the thousands garrisoned outside of the capital from other states voted in the November 1861 election in Maryland. Meanwhile, Maryland residents were intimidated and had to vote by passing through gauntlets of Federal troops and their bayonets.

There were many instances of the arrest of newspaper editors who published papers that were openly sympathetic to the South, as well as of those simply asking the question as to what gave the government the right to arrest any dissent.

The arrests did not stop there. Just as was later done in the 20th century communist countries, generals who failed in battle were arrested as traitors. In the battle of Ball's Bluff, Gen. Charles Stone failed in an attack across the Potomac. He was labeled a traitor by the radicals, arrested, jailed for six months without charges, and subsequently released. He served honorably for two years more, but always with a cloud over his head and under surveillance.

The Congress established the Joint Committee on the Conduct of the War. All of the generals who commanded the Army of the Potomac, except Grant, were investigated by the committee. The committee was led by Sen. Benjamin Wade until 1862, and was composed mostly of the members of the Radical wing of the Republican Party. This body put fear into the hearts of the Union officers that if they did not succeed, for any reason, they could be imprisoned.

The committee was considered by Gideon Welles "a child of Stanton's," and Stanton attended many of its sessions, cooperating fully with its work.

This committee and its power to discipline officers who did not succeed created a more aggressive officer corps in the North. This was necessary, from the Radicals' standpoint, since it was the North that was the aggressor against the South.

The North needed a dose of adrenalin in the Union Army at the beginning of the war, before the experience of war set in to create the necessary animosity against "the enemy." The fear of the Joint Committee on the Conduct of the War provided that among the non-revolutionary officers. They needed the fear factor to instill the proper motivation to attack their American brothers.

You might put yourself in the mind-set of Northerners at the time. True, there were radicals who wanted the war, but the average citizen did not really look upon the Southern American as the enemy any more than a modern American would want to invade Montana, Wyoming, Idaho, or the Dakotas and gun down their citizens should they secede.

With Northern invasion against the South, the Southerners had three advantages: they knew the land on which the battles would take place; it took twice as many Union troops as an aggressor to attack a defensive position; and the Southerners were determined to repel invaders from their lands. These three reasons helped prolong the war in spite of the disadvantages the South had, as outlined earlier.

The Communist Manifesto, in the ten steps for communizing a country, has as the fourth step, "Confiscation of the property of all emigrants and rebels." This not only punishes the individual, it isolates all opposition to communism from being able to use their resources, for whatever purpose, personal or political.

Montgomery Blair, the man who pushed forward the Ft. Sumter initiative, proposed to Lincoln the confiscation of the estates of traitors, using the money to compensate loyal slaveholders for their manumitted slaves, in late 1861. Whether this proposal ultimately led to the law which was passed by the radical Congress, fulfilling the letter of the *Manifesto*, but without compensating the loyal slave owners, is not known.

The most famous seizure was the estate of Robert E. Lee. Today the property is called Arlington Cemetery. Pierre Soule's property was also seized under this law. They were not the only ones.

A modern philosophical equivalent is the RICO (Racketeer Influenced and Corrupt Organizations) law. Originally passed to confiscate the property of organized crime bosses, it rapidly became a law the federal government used to confiscate the property of just about anyone remotely connected to a crime, and has included owners who rented property unknowingly to a criminal. This has evolved into seizure of bank accounts by the IRS if deposits appear suspicious. The business owners are never given back all the money confiscated once they are found innocent — they have to prove their innocence, a complete reversal of the Constitution, where all are innocent until proven guilty. From time to time these cases are shown on FOX News.

Without the writ of habeas corpus, the government could hold individuals for trial without first granting them their right to hear specific charges against them in court, a detriment to organizing a defense. In areas under martial law, military commissions — not civil courts — tried civilians for alleged crimes.

The reader will be able to see this being done in regard to the modern War on Terror. Similar situations existed using the power of the presidency during the Civil War that are used today. At least today, newspapers are not overtly seized by the army and shut down. The process is more subtle today, with precious few national media outlets being much more than mouthpieces for socialism.

It is regrettable that so many conservative Americans cannot see that standing still for unconstitutional means to detain terrorists can become a practice that someday may be used against them. At what point does looking the other way become the norm?

Union authorities arrested tens of thousands of civilians during the Civil War: suspected spies, enemy agents, Southern sympathizers, draft evaders, newspaper editors, public officials, and others critical of the Republican administration. Some place the figure at 38,000, a few even higher. Part of the process of arresting people was the wiretapping of telegraph lines without a warrant.

In July 1861, Lincoln ordered all Democrat newspapers in the State of New York to be denied the use of the mails to circulate their papers, over 300 of them. While Democrat newspapers were being denied the mails and their editors were being locked up, or worse, for supposedly being against the Union, Lincoln was a subscriber to the *Boston Liberator,* whose motto was still *"The Constitution is a league with death and a covenant with hell."*

It only takes a few score men of the press and in local government to be arrested to send a message to others, and most acquiesce. Too few stand up, and most think that the end justifies the means — after all, we're at war! The first victim in war is the truth.

The number arrested far exceeded a few score, however. The clamor over arrests became so loud that for a time even the lists of those arrested were kept secret.

Horatio Seymour campaigned for governor of New York as a Democrat and promised to restore freedom of the press, regardless of the hazard to him. He was elected in 1862 and served in 1863. This helped force Lincoln to recant as to the papers in New York, and by January 1, 1863 the newspapers were allowed the use of the mail again. Seymour would be the Democratic candidate for president in 1868, losing to Ulysses Grant.

Although it was no longer the official policy of the federal government, suppression of newspapers continued, implemented by local military commanders such as Gen. Burnside, and was conveniently ignored by the administration.

On occasion some of the actions of Northern newspapers who opposed Lincoln were extreme. As a result, as late as May 18, 1864, Lincoln issued the following order to Maj. Gen. John Dix:

> You will take possession by military force of the printing establishments of the New York World and Journal of Commerce ... and prevent any further publication thereof.... You are therefore commanded forthwith to arrest and imprison ... the editors, proprietors and publishers of the aforementioned newspapers.

Lincoln's actions were also extreme.

All the while, Lincoln was saying things such as: "We, the people are the rightful masters of the Congress and the courts, not to overthrow the Constitution, but to overthrow the men that pervert the Constitution." Many use this quote in regard to the problems of today, apparently not understanding what was really happening during this period. Presidents have a bad habit of saying one thing and doing another.

Also in modern times during periods of war, the federal administrations were involved in curtailing the press. Even without a war in the sense we are describing, the Obama administration in 2014 floated a proposal for the Federal Communications Commission to monitor the newsrooms of media outlets, to ask, for instance, what political philosophy the media outlet had relative to how they covered the news. It caused enough of a flap that the administration backed down.

Again, in October 2014, the Federal Communications Commission was considering fining any broadcaster who used the term *Redskin* to describe the Washington Redskins football team, as reported by FOX News. This was to be an attempt to force political correctness on the broadcast industry. If they could get away with that, then what would be the next step, and the next?

Any conceived or perceived crisis is used to attempt to increase the power of government, in Rome, in France, in Germany, in the United States.

A new tactic for propaganda purposes came on the scene which today would be known as photo-shopping. There were a number of photos later placed in books that were actually composites of more than one photo. One of the most famous of Lincoln's portraits was actually a photo of Calhoun with Lincoln's head on the body. Another of Grant on a horse before his army was actually a composite of three photos; again the only real portion of the event was Grant's head. These depictions are two of the most famous "photos," but the viewer has no idea that they are phony. They were constructed to give the appearance of stature to Lincoln and Grant and were widely used in school texts.

By 1864, the Union was nearly a complete dictatorship. Transportation and communications were for all practical purposes nationalized; the writ of habeas corpus was suspended; military tribunals replaced civilian courts in a large portion of the North and Border States; a secret police system existed in the military and the Department of the Treasury; wiretapping was performed on the telegraph lines; domestic passports were issued in order for citizens to travel in many parts of the country; and many military units were under the command of European and domestic communists — indeed, the entire Department of War was under the leadership of renowned communists like Dana.

Few have heard that the State of New Jersey passed a resolution in the legislature condemning the conduct of the war by the federal government and the creation of new states such as West Virginia. Further, the resolution contained this language:

… while abating naught in her devotion to the Union of the States and the dignity and power of the Federal Government, at no time since the commencement of the present war has this state been other than willing to terminate peacefully and honorably to all a war unnecessary in its origin, fraught with horror and suffering in its prosecution, and necessarily dangerous to the liberties of all in its continuance….

— "New Jersey Peace Resolutions," March 18, 1863

The resolution detailed a long list of violations of the Constitution by the federal government in its conduct of the war. It is well worth reading for anyone who wishes to study just what was happening to American liberty as a result of the war, and is widely accessible online from reliable sources. Yet, school history books give no mention of this resolution and the obvious sentiment among the people of sections of the North that belie the general story line promoted.

Not only was the State of West Virginia wrought out of Virginia with the help of the federal government, the State of Nevada was also brought into the Union during the war. The language required by the federal government to be in the Nevada State Constitution to receive statehood read:

> Sec. 2. Purpose of government; paramount allegiance to United States.
> ... the paramount allegiance of every citizen is due to the Federal Government ... and no power exists in the people of this or any other State of the Federal Union to dissolve their connection therewith or perform any act tending to impair, subvert, or resist the Supreme Authority of the government of the United States ... the Federal Government may employ armed force in compelling obedience to its Authority.

This is still a part of the constitution of the State of Nevada, and the United States government still lays claim to over 80% of the land in that state.

Contemplate the above in light of the so-called Obamacare legislation and presidential edicts emanating out of the White House that are more and more the norm and in violation of law and the Constitution. It could place the State of Nevada in a position where the 10th Amendment of the U.S. Constitution is null and void.

Such required acts of obedience may have been arguable in light of the conflict under any other system of government, but not with the underlying principles of the Constitution of the United States. This was the sort of attack on state sovereignty that led New Jersey to issue its resolution.

Obviously, concern over citizens' rights was not confined to the South. Subsequently, due to the dumbing down of American education in general, and particularly the real history of our country, over the next century, the American people have not had the same outlook as the citizens prior to the Civil War. However, there are recent signs that substantial numbers of people are once again posing the right questions regarding the rights of citizens and the protection of those rights under the Constitution, which indicates that more people at the grassroots are reading and understanding the Constitution once they have become adults and separated themselves from structured education.

These Americans need to learn who their friends are and whom they can trust — or not trust.

The first Internal Revenue Act of 1862 was framed on the theory that the taxpayers were the natural enemy of the government. Detectives were hired and shared in the penalties collected from delinquent taxpayers. This law phased out after the war, and a later attempt to impose an income tax on Americans was declared unconstitutional.

Tax enforcement by the federal government evolved into the National Detective Police, and finally, with the forces of Pinkerton, the Secret Service was formed under Lafayette Baker with over 2,000 men. It was free from judicial authority, and Baker could and did arrest people without warrant and confine them to cells in the basement of the Treasury building.

These general conditions exist today. Few people know that the IRS still operates outside of the normal civil or criminal court systems, and many of the procedures they engage in would not stand up in regular courts. They are the regulator, the enforcer, and the adjudicator, all in one department of government. There is no separation of powers, except in name only. And, those found guilty serve in federal prisons.

As a result of the above, the federal government can and has imprisoned people they could not have normally imprisoned through the criminal or civil courts. This has served the people well with such individuals as Al Capone, but has also been misused to eliminate, or at least start the process of eliminating, opposition to the policies of the government. And, it all begins with the ability to prevent tax exemption to certain organizations that the government would rather see out of business.

The ethics of the IRS have never been the best, but the misuse of power in the Obama administration rivaled that of the Lincoln administration with the subsequent cover-up of that misuse of power, in violation of federal law in many instances. By no means were these two administrations the only ones who used the IRS for political reasons.

Lafayette Baker was no paragon of virtue. As power is a corrupting influence, so it was the case with Baker. He spied on the Confederate forces in Virginia for Gen. Scott, who was impressed and elevated him to the rank of captain, and was made the head of the Union Intelligence Service in place of Pinkerton. He owed this appointment to Stanton, but spied on Stanton as well. When Stanton learned his telegraph lines were being tapped by Baker, he shipped him off to New York. There, Baker sold seized cotton through Chaffey Company and kept the cash. Chaffey Co. in New York was a front for smuggling into the Confederacy. John Wilkes Booth also worked with Chaffey Company.

At first the State Department under William Seward enforced the president's unconstitutional orders, even though Supreme Court Chief Justice Taney ruled that only Congress could suspend the writ of habeas corpus, which they did later. Seward organized a sort of secret police of agents and informers, with hundreds arrested and held without trial.

Neutrality within the U.S. was looked upon by Northern authorities as treason, and dealt with in the same manner. Many believed that states were sovereign and were only exercising their right to leave the union, and while they may have disagreed with secession, they did feel that armed force was uncalled for, especially when other means may have been used to woo the states back. None of these were tried and indeed were rebuffed, such as the peace delegation from the South at the time of Lincoln's first becoming president. Too often, those with influence who believed in neutrality were arrested.

In February 1862, Lincoln granted amnesty to those arrested under Secretary of State Seward's authority. He then turned control over to Stanton, secretary of war.

By this time the harm had been done and the radicals in charge had made their point.

Once Stanton found out that Baker was tapping his telegraph lines, he had Undersecretary Dana appoint Washington as the base of operations of the National Detective Police. Basically, this meant his office. There is apparently no honor among thieves, and they cannot trust one another. Interestingly, it was an open communist leader, Dana, who gave this order and apparently had some control over the police.

Jefferson Davis suspended the writ of habeas corpus as well, but the Southern Confederate Congress refused to put its stamp of approval on it as the Northern Congress ultimately did. Davis came back a couple of years later and suspended it once again.

We have stated that this work is intended to show the Conspiracy in the North, since it has had the major influence on our country as a result of the North winning the war. However, the effects of the socialist agenda of the Conspiracy were not unknown in the South. Louise B. Hill wrote the book *State Socialism in the Confederate States of America*, in 1936, documenting certain aspects of how the socialist movement was manifested, but never got close to the conspiratorial side of the problem.

Lincoln set many precedents against civilian authority and citizens that were used later by Wilson and Roosevelt when war came in the 20th century.

As students, we studied the Emancipation Proclamation and were told that it freed the slaves. Not one slave was freed by the proclamation, and if anyone reads it instead of just accepting what the books say, this is obvious. For it states that the slaves are free in only Confederate-held territory, not in Union-held land. Since the federal government had no control over Confederate land, they had no way of freeing the slaves. It was show business:

BY THE PRESIDENT OF THE UNITED STATES OF AMERICA.

A PROCLAMATION.

… That on the 1st day of January, A. D. 1863, all persons held as slaves within any State or designated part of a State the people whereof shall then be in rebellion against the United States shall be then, thenceforth, and forever free …

If the Union Army held territory, obviously the rebellion in that territory no longer existed. And only rarely were slaves freed before the Proclamation early in the war in Union-held territory, after Fremont had done so and had been overruled by Lincoln.

The Proclamation's primary purpose was to give the radicals in Europe a means to convince the European people to support the North. In this manner, the European heads of state, who distrusted the American government and/or wanted a weaker U.S., would not intervene or help in any way the Confederate government if their people would not stand for it.

The communist and Carbonari networks were strong enough to cause problems in many countries, particularly England and France, who would have been the most inclined to have been involved. They would have made it difficult for the governments to help the Confederacy.

While Lincoln was adept at splitting France and England away from helping the South, he did nothing to spread goodwill among the Southerners or to widen the rift between secessionists and the Southern Unionists, the latter being substantial in number. They were all to be treated as rebels.

It was this attitude, coupled with an unprecedented and arbitrary use of government power, that caused many to be opposed to the Proclamation. Today, Americans would be surprised that there would have been anyone opposed to it outside of the South. Since slaves were still considered property, the Proclamation addressed more than freeing the slaves; it took on the idea of government control over property. What *property*, was the next question.

We may find this position repulsive in today's light. Yet we are talking about the attitude of the average person in those days, when slavery had been the human condition all around the world since written history began. It did not mean that all Americans wanted to own slaves or treat them unkindly, but slaves were considered property at the time regardless of how one thought of the practice.

In addition, there was the fear that slaves would rise up and kill not only their masters but the white population as a whole. It is a testament to the character of the Negroes that they did not. It would take many decades for deliberate agitation among the Negro population — along with continued injustice for a sizable number — to push them into civil unrest or lawlessness.

This did not mean that organizations of militant Negroes who hated the white man did not exist; they did, but they were the minority and tended to be as pro-communist as anti-white. This statement would require another book, but several were written in the early and mid-20th century which document this fact.

No one wants to be a slave, nor should we advocate someone else being a slave. However, we have to look through the lens of the time, not how we view things today, in order to understand the reactions of people in the mid-19th century.

In light of the situation today and the happy fact that chattel slavery no longer exists in the United States, the Proclamation seems to have been the right thing to do, except that it did nothing to actually free the slaves and was only a political ploy.

The English solution to slavery upheld the idea of private property even while creating the condition for slavery to cease to exist in their empire. They took the view that the idea of slaves as property was abhorrent. They paid for their release and then said, basically, let's go forward from here and never look back.

Lincoln took a while to issue the Emancipation Proclamation because he knew the reaction that it might cause in the North, not just in Europe or the South.[57]

Even Lincoln's home state, Illinois, condemned the Proclamation. The State Legislature passed a resolution on January 7, 1863 that laid the foundation for it being illegal under both military and civilian law, and ended:

> The proclamation invites servile insurrection as an element in this emancipation crusade — a means of warfare, the inhumanity and diabolism of which are without example in civilized warfare, and which we denounce and which the civilized world will denounce as an uneffaceable disgrace to the American people.
>
> — "Resolution of the Illinois Legislature in Opposition to the Emancipation Proclamation," January 7, 1863

In other words, the Illinois Legislature feared the uprising of the slaves, and would hold the federal government responsible for such a war tactic, if that condition were to occur.

The bitterness of the conflict and the war against the whole Southern population *initially* united the white population of every seceding state against the federal government. Even so, there was never a total allegiance among Southerners for the Confederacy. The Proclamation, due to the fears outlined above, only solidified the resolve of most Southerners to stay the course. The Proclamation, therefore, helped prolong the war.

Again, it is a testimony of the Christian attitude of the Negroes at the time not to rise up and kill their masters. Then again, the myth of all masters being drunken sots who beat the male slaves and rape the females had only a small basis in reality. It may make great novels and Hollywood productions, but such a system would not have ever worked as a viable *economic* system.

This is not a justification for the system of slavery, for how could such a system be justified? It is only stating the obvious. There are those who have studied slavery who state that no matter what, the system would have collapsed of its own accord after a while since it would have become economically untenable.

After the Proclamation, as Northern forces moved into and through the South, Negroes were freed and driven off plantations by Union authorities — without any means of support. Thousands of Negroes

---

57   Contrary to what people believe, slavery still exists in some parts of the world in various forms, from chattel slavery to sex slavery. The latter exists in the United States, particularly within Latino and Somali-led crime syndicates, and includes child prostitution, with the children held as slaves. If this seems impossible, go online and research child prostitution rings. In 2013, the arrests of individuals in the United States who traded on the very young for sex online, including infants, reached an all-time high.

perished as a result. Some sources claim substantial numbers, and that white civilians and Negroes killed in the war *from all causes* were one million. We are unaware of any statistics of how many Negroes in the Confederate Army or militia perished in battle as part of this number. Nor are we aware of the number of freed slaves who were forced into the Union Army upon being given their "freedom" and perished as a result.

The problem lies in the fact that the numbers are un-documentable, since no records — or scant records — were kept during the chaotic period in the latter part of the war and subsequent occupation.

Again, it is a testament to the character of the Negroes that they did not commit wholesale crime in order to survive. Many perished rather than commit sin. These facts are almost unknown today. The Emancipation Proclamation may have seemed the catalyst that freed the slaves, when in reality it was Union troops that freed them — and the consequences were very difficult for the slaves at first. It could have been handled much better for the Negroes, even though several organizations did what they could to help the plight of the ex-slaves.

And, *the slaves were not completely freed in some areas of the North until the Constitution was amended after the war* — while the Proclamation had been in force.

One act of kindness on the part of Lincoln would have had more effect in re-establishing the union than all the victories of Lincoln's generals. And, by this time, it was obvious to all that slavery was not going to go away until it was abolished. Peaceful reconciliation based on union and emancipation would have been endorsed by most citizens.

But that was not the agenda. It was to destroy the old social order by prolonging the war, and Lincoln rejected all offers of an olive branch.

As mentioned, it is relatively unknown that Union troops, as they "freed" the slaves, would also conscript the able-bodied men into the Union Army. They went from being told by their overseers how to labor to being told by Union troops how to labor and get killed.

England openly turned against the South after the Proclamation. There was evidence that England's sentiments were for a nationalistic government rather than for sovereign states forming a union. *The Economist*, London, printed this opinion:

> The war will draw together the Northern states as they have never been drawn together yet … and finally will impress them with the absolute necessity of a closer union, a stronger central power …
> in one word, with the duty of turning the federal government into a really supreme power.

There was one aspect of the Proclamation that all seem to miss that had more influence on bad government than anything up to that time. The Proclamation was in essence an executive order, used increasingly since then by presidents to go around the Congress and establish "law" as they envision it. It was Lincoln's version of the "pen and telephone" of Obama.

One should always take into account how even doing the right thing can subvert good government. It is a matter of how things are done and their effect on future government control. The Proclamation "freed" the slaves, supposedly, but served as the basis for all to be subjugated by government in the future. This is not taught in the schools or mentioned in libertarian literature or constitutional studies, as it is not politically correct and sounds anti-black.

A great deal of real history and biography is never spoken of for this reason. We have mentioned several examples. Truth is essential to understanding.

Secret societies to thwart the Confederacy were formed throughout the South, particularly in northern Alabama, in the Army of the Tennessee, in North Carolina, and even in Virginia. This helped ensure the defeat of the South and the imposition of federal rule over them by weakening, as much as possible, the Southern strength and resolve.

In the Northern-held territories, Union generals stopped the "disloyal" from voting in elections, particularly in General Ambrose Burnside's area. Burnside also stopped the circulation in the mail of the *New York World,* and the publication of the *Chicago Times*.

Jefferson Davis' decision not to sell cotton at the beginning of the war cost the South the ability to arm 500,000 men. By the time the decision was made to sell it, the blockade became a problem and the American cotton industry sales to England had been supplanted by Egypt. After the war, American cotton was again exported to England. Regardless of the reason Davis made the decision not to sell the cotton, it was one more thing that made the South's position untenable and led to the Southern defeat.

Many in the South still refer to the Civil War as the War of Northern Aggression. With the exception of Gen. Robert E. Lee's thrust into Pennsylvania, the North was always the aggressor into the Southern states. One might argue the validity of secession, but it is difficult to claim that the South was the aggressor.

The troops originally called up by Lincoln to "defend" the Capital were actually used to invade the South.

More Than Two Republics
There were other initiatives to prolong the war and to create widespread chaos. It was the intent by some to divide the country even more. These schemes were hatched by men involved in the Knights of the Golden Circle and other, more Southern-oriented plans. One scheme was the Northwest Republic, aided by Confederate Commissioner Jacob Thompson and Mayor of New York Fernando Wood. Another was the Pacific Republic.

Joseph Lane, U.S. senator, former governor of Oregon, and running mate of Breckinridge; U.S. senators from California William Gwin and Milton Slocum Latham were all charged with trying to form the Pacific Republic. Latham said, "We in California would have reasons to induce us to become members neither of the southern confederacy, nor of the northern confederacy, and would be able to sustain for ourselves the relations of a free and independent republic." Latham was a 33° Mason of the Southern Jurisdiction.

Yet, it became obvious that Gwin was pro-slavery and tried to colonize Mexico with Americans from the South, and had contacts with Soulé in this regard. Gwin was a member of the Knights of the Golden Circle.

Latham would go on to become the president of the New York Mining and Stock Exchange in 1880 for a short time before his death.

Engaged in the scheme for a Northwest Republic was Thomas H. Hines, who resigned from the staff of the Masonic University at La Grange Kentucky at the outbreak of the war. John B. Castleman worked with Hines in this plot.

In the long run, there were five initiatives to divide the country: the Southern, the North, the Pacific, the Northwest, and the Central States. The latter overlapped the North and Northwest to some extent in the southern regions of those states affected, and were meant to be a buffer between the warring factions in an attempt to avert the war. Many in this region felt that they would become the battleground between the two regions over which the armies would wage war, and they wanted no part of it. The scheme for any kind of Border State secession failed even though the majority in those areas was, at the time, in opposition to the Lincoln government.

None of these non-Southern secessions went very far, and they may have been initiated simply to ensure the war became a prolonged one by diffusing the necessary focus on the main goal of settling the war as quickly as possible. However, it would have fit the foreign policy goals of such nations as Britain to weaken the United States by splitting us up into two, three, or four separate countries, which Britain would have probably been able to set against one another through intrigue over the ensuing years.

The Conspiracy may have debated within their ranks over growing the United States or splitting it. Although some may have wanted to split it due to America's system and layers of strength that made it difficult to totally subvert, this never reached practical application. The Constitution stood in the way many times.

And, if any wing of the Conspiracy ever had any thought of dividing the United States, the ever growing centralization of the federal government as the result of the Civil War would have ended the debate. Keep in mind that the major step between world government and what we had, was to form the earth into three major governments: the U.S., Russia, and probably China.

There have been conflicts within the Conspiracy as to just how to proceed into a one world government, but these have usually revolved around personal ambition rather than overall strategy. A study needs to be done relative to this problem as it involved Germany and Japan during the 1930-1940s. There is more than enough evidence to support the fact that they both wanted to establish the New World Order but were thwarted in their leadership in favor of the classic American, Russian, Chinese conspiratorial alignment. Both of these Axis powers used the term the New World Order in reference to their goals.

Recall that Mrs. Jefferson Davis said that even though the South had lost, if the country would have remained divided, there would probably have been continual war on the continent. Did she understand things as the wife of the president of the Confederacy that others did not?

Chief personalities of Young America, such as George Law, helped agitate California to promote an independent republic by providing firearms to the San Francisco Committee of Vigilance.

There was support for independence along the Pacific Coast. California was an independent republic for a short period, albeit with a sentiment toward the U.S. since it was Americans who had established the country against Mexican authority, just as had been done in Texas. The state flag is still the one which was flown for the California Republic. This was before the Panama Canal, and there were few means to travel to the Far West convenient for civilians. It was arduous. Communication was a problem. For many, these reasons alone constituted a case for going it alone. And, many moved there to escape the sectionalism and the looming conflict, in addition to pursuing the opportunities in mining and other business enterprises.

The West Coast residents in the 20th century did not consider themselves to be particularly Northern or Southern, even though in the 19th century the majority of troops did go into the Northern army since they considered themselves citizens of the United States. This may seem contradictory; however, Westerners could feel loyal to the country without feeling a definite Northern or Southern sentiment since they were so far removed from the sections in contention.

The end that the Conspiracy had in mind was the nationalization of the United States, and then an empire. Everything that was done by them must be viewed through this lens. Any initiative to split the U.S. was only a means to prolong the war until the necessary changes in the federal government could be made to facilitate this end.

At this point we need to reiterate that this tome is not meant to be a history of the United States.

Rather it is an attempt to augment what you already know with information that falls within the title theme of this book, so that you may begin to see history from a different angle and better understand the forces and influences on American society and political life of a handful of men and women who want to change America into a socialist entity.

14

Assassination

There is a modern perception that in the North the people loved Abraham Lincoln and that he was the greatest president that we ever had. The idea that everyone loved him in the Union was far from the truth. You can well imagine this to have been the case based on what you have already read.

The words of two prominent men in the Democratic Party illustrate the disparaging remarks about Lincoln in the political arena in 1864 and also demonstrate why Lincoln felt he could not be re-elected on the Republican Party ticket as a result of the negative feeling about the party that was widespread among the population.

August Belmont, at the National Democratic Convention in August 1864, said:

Four years of misrule by a sectional, fanatical and corrupt party have brought our country to the very verge of ruin. The past and present are sufficient warnings of the disastrous consequences if Mr. Lincoln's re-election should be made possible by want of patriotism and unity. The inevitable results of such a calamity must be the utter disintegration of our whole political position, among bloodshed and anarchy.

Political History of the United States of America During the Great Rebellion

Some delegates at the Convention talked openly of overthrowing the government. Keep in mind, this was in the North.

At the same convention, delegate Benjamin Allen, a Copperhead from Ohio or New York (depending on the source you read), said,

The people will soon rise, and if they cannot put Lincoln out of power by the ballot, they will by the bullet.

The Assassination and the History of the Conspiracy

The assassination of Lincoln has been a subject of sustained interest for nearly 150 years, probably due to the fact that so much mystery still surrounds the event.

Another reason it has been kept alive is the assassination of John F. Kennedy, since there were so many parallels between the two. There are those who believe that the reason there are so many parallels and coincidences is that the same sinister force that killed Lincoln was also behind the slaying of Kennedy.

There are too many unanswered questions regarding both events. One must always remember, however, who is in charge after all is said and done — *cui bono*: who benefits? In both instances a Johnson assumed the presidency, but both became powerless within a short time as a result of the real power brokers.

Both were "liberals," but found themselves on the outside of the room when it came to wielding the power of the presidency. Andrew Johnson discovered this immediately. With Lyndon Johnson it took a few years. They both had been promoted by and used by communists, and in the end found that they had no power at all.

Whether Lincoln or Kennedy were actually part of the Conspiracy we have been discussing has been and continues to be a matter of speculation. Evidence exists that gives weight to both sides of the argument in both cases. But, just how high up the ladder they were is debatable as well, if you do believe they were part of the Conspiracy.

There is an idea held by some that Kennedy was assassinated because he was going to stand up to the Conspiracy over some issue or another. The patriarch of the family, Joseph, and his political clout were a creation of the Conspiracy, after he gained a large fortune as a bootlegger during Prohibition.

What few know is that JFK was a confidential member of the Council on Foreign Relations. He was never listed in their public membership roster, but he admitted so in a letter to one of his constituents while a member of the U.S. Senate. This author has seen the original on U.S. Senate stationery over his signature. The CFR apparently had other members of a confidential nature, to hide the real motivation of key people whose influence would be harmed if the public knew they were members. Kennedy was more conservative than Lyndon Johnson, but still a very liberal man. The one thing that Kennedy was not involved in was the incredible corruption that surrounded Johnson.

The Kennedys were also friends of Joseph McCarthy, who was anathema to the socialists.

The CFR changed its bylaws slightly in the 1970s. The original bylaws did indicate that confidential membership would exist. Although the language used today would also indicate this in the mind of someone who does not trust them, for the innocent reader it is far too innocuous to notice.

The assumption that a conspiracy will not eliminate one of their own is erroneous. Conspirators will eliminate one of their own for a variety of reasons. The amoral principle is that the ends justify the means. If the death of a conspirator high on their ladder of authority will further the overall goals of the conspiracy as a whole without exposing the conspiracy in the process, it will be done. (Also, do not forget rivalries.)

The obvious tactic where this is in play is when conspiracies take over a country completely, they assassinate or kill off the members of the conspiracy that helped bring them to power, as did Robespierre, Hitler, Stalin, and Saddam.

Like the two Johnsons, Lincoln and Kennedy were products of the Conspiracy, but obviously not Insiders in the Conspiracy. This volume is not long enough to document the last statement except on two accounts: 1. The Kennedy family fortune and influence were the product of others. Joseph Kennedy assumed what power and influence he had as a result of working for men who were far more powerful than he. The only member of the Kennedy family that may have been an Insider would have been Teddy Kennedy, since one of the criteria for that elevated position is the performance of murder. We leave it to you to think that one through. 2. Other than the word of the Rosicrucians, there is scant evidence that Lincoln was in the hierarchy of the Conspiracy. The Rosicrucians claim he was one of the top three in their secret society and "anointed" to become president in 1848. Fact or fiction — who knows?

One of the modern examples of conspirators eliminating one of their own for the benefit of the conspiracy is described in the book by Benjamin Gitlow, *The Whole of Their Lives*.

Gitlow told the story of the rivalry of Stalin and Leon Trotsky vying for the leadership of the world communist movement. It was partially played out in the streets of New York for the control of the American communist organization, an important, if not the most important wing of the world-wide movement.

Trotsky had to flee Russia to escape the growing power of Stalin. Stalin was killing off his rivals using the excuse of a war on terrorism, which did not exist except as an excuse to be used by Stalin to kill any rival by calling him a terrorist. A few acts of terror were performed by the Soviet secret police and blamed on terrorists in order to set the stage for the removal of Stalin's rivals as being the terrorists.

The same condition exists today, according to KGB defectors. The KGB/FSB performed acts of terrorism and blamed it on Chechen terrorists to give the excuse for Russia to clamp down on Chechnya and Russian dissidents and journalists in the 21st century. Revelations by Russian journalists and defectors exposed this continuing activity, and led to these reporters being assassinated in Russia and England, Alexander Litvinenko probably being the most famous.

These tactics continued in the Ukraine, and will continue to be used going forward in the struggle to unite all of Europe eventually under Moscow's leadership.

When Trotsky left Russia the communist movement split, with those siding with Trotsky calling themselves Socialist Workers. One of the essential differences between the strategies of the two was that Trotsky wanted a worldwide revolution, whereas Stalin wanted to reach the same goal by first regionalizing the world as was proposed early in the approach of the Conspiracy. It became a war for the leadership of the organization of communists' worldwide. It played out in a small way on the streets of New York in fist fights for the best location for delivering speeches to woo a variety of sympathizers that would gather to hear communist leaders of all stripes.

At one particular location, the Stalinists started a fight with the Socialist Workers, took possession of the "soap-box," and started to address the crowd. On signal, Stalinists who were waiting on the roof at the top of the building above the site hurled down bricks onto *their own men* who had just won the battle. It killed more than one of them. The crowd just assumed that the Trotskyites had done it out of revenge, just as the Stalinist leadership planned.

The net result was that the street mobs rejected the Trotskyites and sentiment swung over to the Stalinists. No one thought that the Stalinists had actually done it to their own to win the favor of the crowd. The action is in the reaction. If necessary, they will kill their own. For them, the ends justify the means.

From that time on, the Communist Party USA regained the reputation as the premier socialist organization.

Even the assassination of Trotsky himself fits the scenario of the hierarchy eliminating one of their own as long as the overall conspiracy or their plans are not exposed in the process.

If unknown to the reader, Trotsky was higher in the "pecking order" of the communist movement than Stalin and was placed in control of the Red Army under Lenin. However, Stalin was a better conspirator and eventually supplanted Trotsky as the premier leader in Russia. Once enough of Trotsky's supporters among the communist leaders had been eliminated by Stalin, Trotsky knew he had to get out of town, so to speak.

Once Trotsky was assassinated in Mexico, the Moscow leadership began a systematic, large-scale infiltration of his organization.

We have dwelt on some of the aspects of assassination to set up in your mind the problems associated with such an act, the reasons for the act, and the ramifications of such an act. Usually these are not given a thought, and people tend to only dwell on the act in and of itself, without thinking through what may have been behind it besides the obvious killer or killers.

Let us state for the record that we have no idea with any degree of certainty who exactly was behind the assassination of either president. We are only certain of the results of such an act and therefore the likely movement that was behind the killings, even though we may not be able to identify the specific group by naming the individuals involved.

We believe that the books that dwell on the assassinations contain deliberate disinformation to further cloud the issue to the point that to specifically state what the real story is would be speculation. The gravity of the acts was such that it necessitated making the evidence murky and in doubt, so that the Conspiracy would not be exposed — thus the many books that point fingers in all directions.

The results, however, expose the *movement* behind the assassinations for those who are versed in understanding the goals, tactics, and history of the Conspiracy. We will focus on these facts.

Assassinations of prominent men that are performed by a conspiracy usually have a pattern. Unless the killing is meant to "send a message" to a number of people, the deed is made to look as if it is done by a lone, demented assassin.

The magnitude of risk connected to assassinating a high-profile individual — let alone a president of the United States — must be offset by important *multiple* gains in the results of the deed in order for the perpetrators to risk it — especially due to the possible exposure of those behind the act. Public pressure for a full investigation makes the process more difficult to hide.

Of course, the exposure would only go up the ladder of responsibility so far if there were to be a problem. The death of an individual at any rung on the ladder of responsibility would take care of that, creating a dead end to any investigation. The assassin will be killed; sometimes the killer of the assassin will likewise suffer a premature death in order to create a cul-de-sac in the investigation. The same will happen to key witnesses.

Some of the multiple gains due to the assassination of Lincoln for the Conspiracy would have been:

1. The reaction of the Northern people against the South. The country wanted to get back to normalcy. Speeches were being given by Lincoln referring to our Southern brothers. The situation could not be allowed to get back to normal if the reason for the war was to destroy the old social order.
2. In addition to the social order, many changes had been made in the federal government, which, if things went back to normal, would be changed back to a nearly constitutional level once the war was over. The assassination would create the necessary public mood to not only keep these programs but to pass even more legislation to "honor the wishes of the dead president." This was particularly true of the Kennedy assassination.
3. The reaction to the assassination would also set the stage for the elimination of the opposition to the Conspiracy, mostly by the heated political atmosphere generated. Any effective opposition would be vilified for speaking out against any radical idea of "our dear departed president", particularly since no organization existed to give coordination to the opposition. Persons known to have been in opposition to both Lincoln's and Kennedy's policies were physically attacked immediately following the assassinations, and effective opposition was rendered ineffective for a time until the immediate shock of the killing wore off. This critical time allowed the Conspiracy to consolidate changes.
4. And, if all had gone according to plan, the Conspiracy would have been in total control with the president pro tempore of the Senate, Benjamin Wade, leading the country. The situation would not have been that dissimilar to Robespierre being in charge of France.

But it did not go according to plan. Only Lincoln was assassinated. Johnson and Seward lived; one assassin would not carry out his assignment, and the other the attempt was muffed. Elaborate schemes rarely go according to plan; there are too many things that can go wrong.

Let us look at the results of the numbered gains listed above. The events following the assassination seem unreal today when chronicled.

One, Jubilation swept across the country when Lee surrendered and the spirit of reconciliation was high. Even though several Confederate armies remaining in the field had not yet surrendered, the back of Confederate resistance had been broken. Lincoln indicated that the majority of those involved in the "rebellion" would be welcomed back as brothers.

Following the assassination, this changed dramatically. Immediately after the assassination the radical Union General Benjamin Butler came out of his Washington hotel and gave a speech wherein he advocated the hanging of all Southern officers educated at West Point and Annapolis, stripping Southern politicians of all levels of their civil rights and throwing them into prison, tolerating others, and giving full rights only to freed Negroes. The crowd agreed.

The assassination occurred just before Easter, and this meant that the attendance in churches across the country would be high. The sermons that were delivered by pastors such as James Freeman Clarke, Henry Ward Beecher, *et al.* were blasphemous, or nearly so. Scores of sermons by influential pastors were recorded that referred to the need for vengeance on the South for the deed. Some went so far as to refer to Lincoln as the modern Moses or Christ, depending on the orthodoxy.

Clarke was a Transcendentalist and close to the socialist movement, but became a "conservative" Unitarian, a trustee of the Boston Library, and an overseer at Harvard.

Henry Whitney Bellows, a Unitarian of the Emerson school, called for vengeance against the South, and said that Lincoln was taken by God, his work over, like Christ. William Adams, a leader in most major interdenominational organizations who would play a pivotal role in the formation of the YMCA and president of Union Theological Seminary, said that the time for conciliation was done, it was time for vengeance.[58]

There were memorial services all across the country, including Washington, D.C., where George Bancroft delivered the main address. He also spoke in Chicago with Schuyler Colfax, where the invocation was delivered by a member of the Order.

At first, the desire was to bury Lincoln in Washington. Many states did all they could to have him interred in their soil. Finally, the State of Illinois was chosen since they had the best claim — and for another reason. To bury him in Washington meant that probably hundreds of thousands would see the body and ceremony. To do so in Illinois meant that literally millions could witness the body and partake in a prolonged ceremony by transporting his body on display through the more populous areas of the North by train to his burial plot. The path of the Lincoln train did not take the direct route to Illinois.

By doing it this way, millions could be propagandized into hatred toward the South. Stanton had ordered that the wounds on Lincoln be visible so as to inflame the onlooker toward those who were responsible. It was implied that the South as a whole was to blame.

Two, one can say that for the most part, the Radical Republican agenda during the conflict had institutionalized or begun the process toward implementing just about every aspect of The Communist Manifesto's ten planks for communizing a country. These steps could not be allowed to revert to pre-war constitutional levels.

---

58 Union Theological Seminary became a hotbed for religious liberalism and communism within Christianity. One of the links from German liberalism later in American history was Charles Augustus Briggs. After him, many personages connected to the seminary were open communist collaborators, such as Harry F. Ward.

They included:

- The establishment of an agriculture initiative that ultimately led to the Department of Agriculture. The control over the monetary system led to control over gold and silver, which led to control over the mining of these metals and ultimately to the establishment of the Bureau of Mines. Everything human beings consume or use is either grown or mined. It began the process of control over the entire economy of human existence by the state.
- An income tax, Step 2 of the *Manifesto*. It phased out, however, and a later initiative was declared unconstitutional. The Constitution was amended 50 years later to allow Marx's graduated income tax.
- An inheritance tax, which was the first in U.S. history. It was a step in the direction of total confiscation as called for in Step 3 of the *Manifesto*.
- The passage of the National Banking Act as a major step toward centralization of banking into the hands of the state and driving non-government script from circulation.[59]
- Issuance of the Greenback. It has been hailed as the means by which Lincoln saved our country from foreign interests by not taking loans from the European banking houses. It actually robbed the people of 50% of the value of all property in the United States by means of inflation through the printing of paper money. It likewise placed the monetary system into the hands of the radicals and their friends, and coupled with the half-step of the National Banking Act, finally culminated in the Federal Reserve 50 years later: Step 5 of the *Manifesto*.
- The Pacific Railway Act, which started the federal government on the road to centralizing the means of communication and transportation in the hands of the state, as called for by Step 6 of the *Manifesto*. It included a telegraph line over the same territory covered by the act for the railroad.
- The Homestead Act, which satisfied the "vote yourself a farm" movement of the socialists prior to the war, and likewise satisfied Step 7 of the *Manifesto* for the improvement and cultivation of wasteland. It placed the process of settling the West by individuals under the purview of the federal government.
- The Land Grant College Act, which gave land scrip to states for educational institutions. Much of the scrip went to colleges controlled by members of the Order. It helped solidify conspiratorial control over education and intellectual pursuits.

Various other programs placing more control over the people would be passed by claiming that the dead president wanted them and that we must honor the martyr's wishes.

One of the most onerous problems that came about due to the conflict was the issuance of internal passports, similar to the travel papers issued by communist and Nazi governments. These were handled by the State Department under Seward. This practice ceased soon after the war.

Three, there were many acts of violence against people in the North who did not display the "proper" remorse. This included two ex-presidents, editors of newspapers, etc. Anyone who represented that they were not completely behind the war became pariahs for some time. This tactic even worked against An-

---

[59] Prior to the Greenback, it was not unusual for paper script to be issued by banks and other entities as a means to facilitate cash transactions. This script was always backed by gold or silver deposited in the bank of issue. After the Greenback became the standard government "money," laws were passed which outlawed any competing currency by private institutions. Good money drives out the bad in the marketplace. Stable private script could not be allowed since it would not have allowed the federal government the ability to invisibly tax the people through inflation, nor would it have allowed the government to control the economy by controlling all money. The paper dollar was at first redeemable in gold, but gold was rarely asked for, thus allowing inflation to occur.

drew Johnson, who tried to bring some sense out of the chaos. This allowed the Reconstruction program to go forward. All U.S. senators who voted against a guilty verdict against Johnson were never again active in national politics.

Four, even though the conspirators did not eliminate the vice president and secretary of state who had been targeted, Stanton behaved as if Johnson were dead and acted against the constitutional order of succession. The vice president was to succeed the president, followed by the president pro tempore of the U.S. Senate.

Immediately after the assassination, the federal government became even more of a military dictatorship for some weeks and months.

Stanton took control, and just about every aspect of the period was run through his office. The trial of those they caught was heard by a military court rather than a civilian court, completely against the Constitution. This and more caused President Johnson to attempt to fire Stanton.

Stanton repudiated the peace terms that Gen. Sherman made at Confederate Gen. Joseph E. Johnston's surrender and ordered all of Sherman's commanders to disobey Sherman and attack all portions of Johnston's surrendered army, essentially to slaughter what were then technically POWs. This was not done again by an American commander until the conclusion of World War II.[60]

The designs of Stanton and the Radicals imposed, a dictatorship. This was the reason he assumed power on the death of Lincoln, instead of allowing the Constitutional progression of the vice president. Johnson was sworn in as president, but was powerless on many levels due to Stanton and the Radical Congress.

In the aftermath of the assassination Stanton bamboozled the Cabinet, and soon Secretary Gideon Wells wrote in his diary:

> We were all imposed on by Stanton who had a purpose. He and the Radicals were opposed to the mild policy of President Lincoln, on which Sherman had acted, and which Stanton opposed and was determined to defeat.

There can be little question, when all aspects of the "peace" are lined up, that it was an attempt to create a Radical dictatorship, culminating at that time but beginning in the Jacobin agitation from 1787. Pres. Johnson was in the way of that initiative. Had Lincoln lived, and if his words were true the last days of his life, he would have been the Radical target rather than Johnson.

Considering everything, the assassination of Lincoln made it easy for the Radicals in the War Department and Congress to impose their total will. *Cui bono*? It was not the South or the Copperheads, as the Radicals attempted to blame. It was the Radicals themselves who benefited.

---

60 See the book *And Other Losses*, published in Canada and verified in small biographies of people personally involved. The information contained therein is common knowledge among older Germans, but not younger Germans. Approximately one million German POWs were starved to death under American authority after the cessation of hostilities. We understand that this fact is difficult to believe; nonetheless, it happened. This author has read accounts of this by a German immigrant who came to the U.S. and became a citizen and businessman in North Dakota. It coincided with Operation Keelhaul, which forcibly moved Eastern and Central European refugees back under the control of Stalin after the war ended in Europe. These refugees had fled from the forces of the USSR into Central and Western Europe. The operation included civilians and soldiers from such countries as Poland who had fought on the side of the Allies during the Italian Campaign. Most, if not all, were slaughtered. All of this may seem preposterous. Look at the cover-up called Benghazi — the attack against our embassy in Libya by terrorists and the subsequent questions surrounding whether or not it could have been saved with a timely response. Without the Internet, social networking, and the cell phone, this would never have been an issue. Think of a situation where the issue of Benghazi had not come up, then years later it came out in small obscure publications. Would the general public, upon hearing of the incident, believe the revelation or continue in the belief the government may or may not have fostered? Most believe the official "history." The same question could be asked of several crises over the past few decades.

The actions of Stanton and the Radicals had a purpose other than simple retribution when they wanted Gen. Johnston's forces annihilated. They wanted to eliminate Southerners who had fought for what they believed in so that Reconstruction would have no opposition among the people, and so that the program of changing society could go forward without any possible opposition, at least any effective opposition. It was their opportunity to stifle dissent for generations to come, if not forever.

Keep in mind as well that, historically, rebellion elsewhere has usually ended with the losing side being eliminated, particularly in modern society since the communists have been in the equation. Only in the United States was this tactic the exception due to the general morality level of the population — they would never have stood for it. Yet this was precisely what Stanton wanted done to the Southern armies after Lee surrendered. And, he was not alone in Radical circles.

The Radical Republican leaders in Congress held a caucus just a few hours after Lincoln's death and proposed a reorganization of the Cabinet to rid it of moderates. They apparently did not think to ask Johnson, the new president, his opinion.

Even though one of the charges against Johnson in his impeachment by these same Radicals was that he sought to replace Stanton, and their argument was that he could not replace the appointment of a previous president without congressional approval, they had no problem trying to do the same when it fit their own plans without the approval of the president, who would have to be the nominator.

The Supreme Court stood in the way, as well. However, it was finally neutralized in 1867, when Congress passed a law forbidding the court to take jurisdiction in any Reconstruction case. After this, Congress was the Supreme Court when it came to Reconstruction, and the court could not even put a Reconstruction case on its calendar.

While Johnson's impeachment trial was proceeding, Chief Justice Chase wrote that the Senate's real purpose was to place "Congress above the Constitution."

One of the least-known aspects of the Constitution is that Congress can limit the appellate jurisdiction of the Supreme Court. This process has not been used for some time. This is one of the things that the modern Congress could do to the court should they have a problem with certain issues being made legal or illegal. It exposes the lie that Congress is powerless to stop judicial fiat and stops false interpretation of the Constitution. You would not need a federal law or an amendment, just limit the court and allow the states to decide their own laws on that issue.

The courts are not to *interpret the Constitution*. Their job is to *interpret any law* that comes before them as to it its constitutionality.

This last point seems to elude the so-called conservatives who are demanding a conference or convention under Article V of the Constitution. All they need to do is to build public pressure for the Congress to limit appellate jurisdiction over such items as the Affordable Care Act, abortion, etc. and then the states could enact their own laws as they deem fit. There is no need to change the U.S. Constitution.

Crazy People
When a study is done of the personalities surrounding the events of the assassination, it is much like studying the inhabitants of an insane asylum.

Anna Surratt, daughter of Mrs. Mary E. Surratt, tried to see President Johnson the morning of her mother's hanging. She was prevented from doing so by Sen. Preston King of New York and Sen. James H. Lane of Kansas. Six months later, King tied a bag of shot around his neck and jumped off of a Hoboken ferry. Eight months later, Lane shot himself. At least those were the stories. Henry Rathbone, in the box with Lincoln, years later killed his wife and ended up being committed to an asylum. There were several strange deaths of people involved in the Kennedy assassination as well — quite a number, in fact. These are accessible online.

The man who supposedly shot Booth, Thomas P. "Boston" Corbett, was an itinerant preacher who had seen two "women of the street" from his soapbox and was smitten with lust. He went home and gelded himself with a knife (or scissors, depending on which story you believe). He was treated at Massachusetts General Hospital for self-castration.

In the Union Army Corbett was known to berate his superior officers for using swearwords, even high-ranking commanders. He was known by his fellow soldiers as the "Glory-to-God man." Many years after the war he obtained a post through the Grand Army of the Republic as a doorkeeper at the Kansas Legislature. On February 15, 1887 he calmly locked the doors, pulled out two pistols, informed the assembled legislators that God demanded their lives and started to shoot at the legislators. He missed, was subdued, and was confined to an insane asylum. He escaped and was later found in Oklahoma.

John Wilkes Booth's family felt no animosity toward Corbett for shooting Booth to death; in fact they were grateful for his deed as a deliverer of Booth. Not exactly the feelings one would expect of family that thought Booth was dead. Nor, was Corbett punished for disobeying an order to capture Booth alive. Instead, he was given a portion of the reward money for Booth's capture.

On June 16, 1866, B. G. Harris of Maryland, in a speech on the floor of the House of Representatives, claimed that Booth's body was not intact, that his skull, heart, and spine were in three different locations and not with the remainder of his body. It is known that Booth's body was photographed. The plate and print were confiscated as soon as they were made and delivered to either Stanton or Baker — it is uncertain which. What is certain is that they were never seen again.

Mary Lincoln was so distraught she could not attend her husband's funeral. Ultimately, she was confined to an asylum. For all practical purposes she was confined and put on trial, and her civil rights were violated. In the words of the authors of *The Trial of Mary Todd Lincoln*, relative to looking into the evidence and the proceedings of the trial, "digging uncovered a strong odor of kangaroo court."

This could have been prevented by her son, Robert; instead he participated in putting her out of the way. This was done either due to her condition or because she would not keep her mouth shut; history says it was the former. It was not unusual in those days to confine relatives as punishment or to enforce the confiner's will upon them.

The net result was that she was out of the way, for whatever the reason. And, just as the history books say that President Johnson was a drunk, they also tell a story that Mary Lincoln was unreasonable, had an overbearing manner, and was crazy — don't listen to those two and just move on. Herndon says, and it appears to be the opinion of a few others as well, that Mary Lincoln never did anything crass without a purpose in mind.

Vanderbilt's committal of his wife and son for the purpose of imposing his will on them was perhaps the most famous case of such a procedure in the 1800s. We say the most famous, because what happened to Mary Lincoln is all but forgotten.

The public watched Jacqueline Kennedy for decades in the news after the assassination of her husband; Mary Lincoln became "Mary who?"

It would be an historical advantage to know what Mary Lincoln knew. The record is sparse, nearly non-existent in this regard, but there is some evidence that she blamed Johnson. In any case, she was silenced. She finished her days in Springfield, Illinois in relative obscurity.

Robert Lincoln was known to destroy evidence, and at one point was found burning some of his father's papers. The man who caught him at it said that he was destroying history. Robert's reply was that there was a traitor in his father's Cabinet and that there was no reason to bring it out. After describing the friendship of Horace G. Young with Robert T. Lincoln, and a visit Young had with Lincoln, Emanuel Hertz wrote,

> On arriving at the house he found Mr. Lincoln in a room surrounded by a number of large boxes and with many papers scattered about the floor, and with the ashes of many burnt papers visible in the fireplace. Mr. Young asked Mr. Lincoln what he was doing, and Mr. Lincoln replied that he was destroying some of the private papers and letters of his father, Abraham Lincoln. Mr. Young at once remonstrated with Mr. Lincoln and said that no one had any right to destroy such papers, Mr. Lincoln least of all. Mr. Lincoln replied that he did not intend to continue his destruction — since the papers he was destroying contained the documentary evidence of the treason of a member of Lincoln's Cabinet, and that he thought it was best for all that such evidence be destroyed.
> — *The Hidden Lincoln*

Leaving and returning, with the help of another friend, Mr. Young was able to persuade Robert Lincoln to stop. Who knows what was destroyed in the interim.

Lincoln's secretaries wrote about their experiences with Robert Lincoln. Robert's friendship with them gave him the opportunity to ask that certain aspects of his father's life go unreported; his request was honored. Since those facts were unreported, no one knows what they were; we only know that Robert's wishes were honored.

Robert went on to hold several important positions in private and public life, all the while asking many to withhold facts concerning his father.

There were also others who wished to keep details from the public. Albert J. Beveridge said:

> Sweet wrote a letter to Herndon which renders valueless parts of his published reminiscences. He admonished Herndon that the truth must not be told, because at that time, the public would disbelieve and resent it.
> — *Abraham Lincoln*

It is problematic that Beveridge did not want the truth told, because he was a "progressive" and an expansionist who knew all the right people when it came to producing historical records. He *served as the secretary of the American Historical Association* and was part of the elite class that promoted socialism. Such men report problems relative to historical fact, but do not seem to work at finding out what the omitted truths were.

Thus we see a list of people who did not want some aspect or another of Lincoln and his actions to ever become a part of written history. We can only speculate what these things would have been. *To the victor go the myths and monuments.*

Many historians believe that Stanton, or someone in his office, was involved in the assassination plot. This suspicion is in part due to the War Department control over the telegraph network in and out of Washington. The night of the assassination these lines went dead for a critical amount of time, which assisted in the initial escape of John Wilkes Booth. Some historians deny the lines were down at the time. The more that is written about this case, the more confusing it gets.

Also, the lines carried a report that the secretary of state had been killed. Was this a mistake, or a report put out based on the original plan and telegraphed before it was known that the secretary had escaped death?

Indeed, the reports of Lincoln's death and that of the two men whose assassinations were muffed seemed to fly a lot faster than the telegraph lines around the country. Many wrote of these facts and asked how this could be, and wondered whether the plot was not more known than history says it was.

Booth knew the password in order to pass through at least one Union checkpoint. Where did he get that information? Since the use of such devices had to be known by many people, it is difficult to say where the information came from; however, it is interesting that the pursuing officers following Booth did not know the password.

Years later, the sentry at the Anacostia Bridge over which Booth fled gave a sworn statement that actually *two* horsemen passed on the evening of the assassination, both knowing the password. Booth went by first and then another rider ten minutes later, apparently David Herold.

Apparently all bridges out of Washington were closed, password or not, except the one bridge by which Booth's escape was made.

There were conflicting testimonies and facts that came out years later by participants in the events that contradicted the official story and their original stories. To relate them would take up volumes and would make things even more confusing — which may be the intent. All we know for sure is that Booth killed Lincoln; what happened before and after that is not etched in stone.

Too many witnesses changed their story, either immediately or years later. Some cited pressure to conform to the official story by Baker and his men, and that it wasn't worth the trouble to say something that would not have been welcome at the time.

Booth Is an Interesting Study

A distant relative of John Wilkes Booth, John Wilkes, was an English revolutionary and a friend of Thomas Paine. He became Lord Mayor of London. (Wilkes and Benjamin Franklin were members of the Hell Fire movement together.) John Wilkes Booth is known today by his full name, but when he was alive he preferred to be called by his relative's name, Wilkes. Billing often had him as J. Wilkes Booth, or J.W. Booth. Booth's father, Junius Brutus Booth, was a Mason and an occultist. Booth himself was a Knight Templar.

Booth was also a pre-war member of the Knights of the Golden Circle, belonging to the Baltimore KGC Castle, and was a member of the militia at John Brown's execution. He enlisted in the militia just before they marched off to protect John Brown's execution from attack by those who would have wanted to free Brown, and it was his only appearance as a soldier. He was presented Brown's lance by the major in command, a strange gift to a new recruit.

During the Civil War he was a member of the Confederate Secret Service, and in his trunk in his hotel in Washington he had the Confederate uniform of a colonel along with a standard Confederate code system. Booth visited George Sanders in Canada just before the assassination. In other words, he had a great deal of contact with conspirators from before the war to the time of the shooting.

In 1865, three months before the assassination, he traveled to England and Paris. His activities just prior to the assassination indicate a large number of people were contacted and involved in the plot as financiers and advisors. These people remain unknown.

George Sanders, with Clement Clay and James Holcombe sought to arrange a peace conference in early 1864 at Clifton House in Niagara Falls. Col. Ambrose Stevens was sent there to return intelligence to Washington on the affair. In his report he states that it was crawling with Confederate agents and that one of the Confederate peace commissioners was urging a plan to assassinate Lincoln just before the November elections. He had to be referring to George Sanders, who was quite vocal about his desire to see Lincoln assassinated, just as he could not keep his mouth shut about the desire to do the same to Napoleon III. On Lincoln's orders, the matter was hushed up.

There was even talk of a conspiracy to assassinate Lincoln by friends of Gen. McClellan. Allan Pinkerton met with one of McClellan's aides, Edward H. Wright, to tell him he knew of a plot and implied it should be called off — or else. This may have been a continuation by members of McClellan's staff who wanted to perform a coup d'état early in the war.

There is a great deal of evidence that the Confederate Secret Service was involved in the plot against Lincoln, at least in the original plan, which was to kidnap Lincoln and hold him for some kind of ransom to either free Confederate prisoners or to end the war under favorable terms.

Rumors persisted of Confederate Secret Service agents being trained by British agents while they were in England. Certainly there were a number of British citizens involved throughout the war with Confederate Secret Service personnel.

Probably the most notorious incident of the English helping the Confederacy was by the British Consul in Charleston, Robert Bunch. He issued passports to Confederate agents who wished to travel as "Englishmen." George Sanders used this device during the entire conflict. Bunch also served as a Confederate spy until caught and sent packing to England where he was dismissed from the British Foreign Service.

Apparently the original idea of the Confederacy was to kidnap the president and hold him for ransoming tens of thousands of Confederate prisoners. Booth initially attempted such a plot, but circumstances made the attempt impossible. Abduction would have helped the Confederacy and their cause. Assassination helped the Conspiracy.

Booth recruited Michael O'Laughlen, who was a member of the KGC Castle in Baltimore, in the original kidnapping plot. There was not enough evidence to convict him of the assassination, but he was involved at least up to when the plot was changed to killing Lincoln rather than kidnapping him and served a life sentence, dying in prison of yellow fever.

The movements by Lincoln and those surrounding him were well known to Booth, demonstrating that Booth had to have had a number of people working to feed the information to him through some organization that extended inside the Union government.

For instance, Booth knowing the countersign at the Anacostia Bridge, over which he made his escape. Another indication that Booth had inside information relative to the movement and schedule of Lincoln was that Booth seemed to know which people were invited to attend events with Lincoln.

Booth was in Montreal, Canada, in October 1864 for ten days. While there, he deposited into a bank, a large sum of money which he used later in carrying out the assassination. It is not known where he received the funds, but he did not have them when he traveled into Canada. Speculation is that he received them from one of the Commissioners or their agent, Sanders.

Booth's fellow conspirator, John Surratt, played a major role, having been a courier for Judah Benjamin and the Confederate Secret Service. A short time before the assassination, in late January 1865, he traveled to Richmond to meet with Benjamin. Considering what happened to Surratt later, it is obvious that he was more than a major player, yet his importance is overlooked in most history books. And the events following the war and his arrest and trial indicate that he was immune from justice, or at least from the gallows.

In addition, one has to take into consideration the claim made by Surratt that he was inducted into the KGC by Booth before the war.

Booth traveled numerous times to New York City, which appears to have been the nerve center for the plot against Lincoln, whether a kidnapping or, as it turned out, an assassination. Surratt also had people in New York with whom he was in touch.

In George Atzerodt's confession, he mentions that Booth told him that if he did not get Lincoln, "the New York crowd" would. Booth also stated more than once that there were between 50 and 100 people involved in the plot.

This is not as implausible as it may sound. Recall that the John Brown conspiracy involved scores of people who were never brought to justice.

Booth, as is the case with most assassins, also kept a diary (if indeed it was his and not something put together by the Conspiracy or ordered by them for Booth to write to throw people off target). Lafayette Baker had Booth's diary in his possession for some time. He had been recalled to Washington after the assassination and was in charge of the search for Booth. Due to his work, he was elevated to brigadier general and given a reward of $100,000, which would have made him in modern times a multimillionaire comparatively.

Once Baker revealed that he had the diary Stanton demanded it, but 18 pages had been removed and it is unknown as to what was contained on them or who removed them — or even if it really was Booth's diary. No one who had possession of the diary was ever called to account for the missing pages. If Booth had written the diary, he would have destroyed it completely rather than leave it to be found, unless it was meant to be a document to throw people off target. Many at the time felt the missing pages implicated Stanton.

There are seven distinct assassination theories, one of them implicating Stanton, and one is just as good as another. The important thing to remember is that the deed went a long way toward the establishment of draconian government in its wake. The number of theories and the books written to support each theory have only obfuscated the real story — if it is even among the seven.

Baker died of arsenic poisoning a few years later. This was confirmed in modern times by an Indiana University professor using an atomic absorption spectrophotometer on the exhumed corpse. It was determined that his brother-in-law, who worked for the War Department, was most likely the means for the absorption. Of all the men connected to the assassination and its aftermath, Baker probably knew the most — other than Stanton.

Had all of the assassinations been carried out, America would be a very different place today. Not only would those who assumed power — either legally or de facto — have been different, but the feelings against the Southern people would have been even more broad, deep, and vituperative. Wiping out the top three in the federal government would have been used to justify anything the Radicals desired — not only over the South, but over the North as well. Radicals in power never allow a crisis to go unused in building power.

There has always been a mystery surrounding Booth's death and whether he actually did die in the barn. There are purportedly three different versions of his last words. Again, history can be confusing, especially if some want it to be confusing.

The famous Dr. Samuel Mudd who treated Booth during his escape, said that Booth's tibia was broken. On the corpse it was the fibula. Booth's sister, Asia Booth Clarke, said that her brother lived out his life in Oklahoma in secret. It is hard to believe that whoever was behind the assassination would have allowed Booth to live — he knew too much. Yet they allowed Surratt to get off.

Would Booth's ego have allowed him to remain incognito for decades? It seems highly doubtful. He may have escaped, but for those behind the deed to have allowed him to live, that is another story.

Surratt's ego would not allow him to remain silent, whether he told the truth or not. He changed his story too often to rely on his tale. He even traveled on a lecture circuit talking about the crime, making himself look as if he too was a victim of Booth and circumstances. The conspirators may have allowed him to live simply because he changed his story so often that no one would believe him if he had told the truth, and his stories made finding out the whole truth that much more difficult.

While the Northern authorities were looking for Booth, the Southern Secret Service was doing likewise. There is abundant evidence that John Singleton Mosby and his command were involved in the plot and the search for Booth. This is interesting in light of Mosby's life after the war. Lewis Powell, another of the conspirators, was sent to Booth from Mosby in January 1865. (See the book *Come Retribution*.)

Much of what could have been made public of the plot died with the assassination conspirators, save one, Surratt, or remained a closed secret with those who knew parts or all of the story. Assistant Secretary of War Thomas T. Eckert visited Powell in prison to question him and said afterward, "All I can say about this is, that you have not got the one-half of them."

On April 30, 1866, the House Committee on the Judiciary investigated the assassination, with emphasis on the part of Jefferson Davis. Lengthy testimony was taken. A sealed package containing the testimony was given to the House clerk and it disappeared. In 1930, the heirs of Benjamin Butler found the package among his effects. It is not known how much of it was intact or what happened to it.

By all indications, the intent of the Southern government was a kidnapping. Someone changed the orders along the line. Judah Benjamin took over the plan under Jefferson Davis, and Benjamin destroyed much of the Confederate Secret Service's papers at the end of the war.

Judah Benjamin, the so-called "Brains of the Confederacy," held many different Cabinet positions in the Confederate government. While he was of Jewish extraction, he converted to Roman Catholicism, married a non-Jewish woman, and was buried in consecrated ground.

He kept his distance from all and had a reputation of being secretive and shy. He had a habit of destroying papers to a mania. In his old age he even sought out his correspondence in all possible quarters and destroyed it. When he died, he only left half a dozen papers behind.

He was the head of the Confederate Secret Service and he obviously felt that many of the dealings he orchestrated needed to be kept from not only from contemporary eyes but from posterity as well, particularly the assassination and/or attempts that occurred at the end of the war.

Lincoln was often apprised of plots against his life, and he either dismissed them or ordered others to ignore them.

The story goes that Lincoln had a dream of his own demise. This may have been true or simply his way of preparing others for his death after finding out that there existed a plot against him. It is improbable that the plot was only from the Southern government, it had to contain Northern elements, and it is possible for him to have realized that the odds against him were too great.

This story takes on an occult nature if the Rosicrucians are correct about his involvement in that bizarre organization. Knowing one's days are numbered is not altogether rare among those who play this dangerous game.

The last major speech by Martin "Luther" King, Jr., for instance, had language in it that any student of conspiracy would recognize as indicating that he knew of his coming death (or his speechwriter did).

There are times that conspirators are called upon to sacrifice themselves for the cause. It may be to take the fall for a crime to protect a member higher in the plot, such as a Mafia Don, or to actually be killed: Nothing personal, just business, as they say.

Now this may seem implausible, yet when you are dealing with the types of people we are documenting, involved in rigid secret organizations, the occult, even some Satanic, and certainly criminal, anything relative to their deaths is plausible. While it is an illustration outside the American culture, the example of the honor code of the Samurai of Japan of suicide on order or to save face would be apropos. This attitude was imbued into the psyche of the average Japanese soldier during World War II. It was a different culture, but suicide for honor's sake is not unknown in the Western world.

Nor is it unknown to order others to commit suicide to save relatives and friends from harm. There were many examples in ancient Rome of this scenario. In the modern world, the case of the World War II German Field Marshal Erwin Rommel, who took his own life to save his family, is one example.

The author knows of one individual who took the fall for a Mafia member and served two years in prison as a result. He did this to gain favor and a position within the organization when he got out. He changed his mind during his incarceration, however, and went into the military instead to further get away from his adverse environment in the "hood."

There have been times that plots have been uncovered with certain people in authority looking as if they are innocent of any direct involvement, but sometimes responsible parties have allowed plots to go forward for their own ends. By this means they have maintained their "innocence" of the deed but have received the benefit of it by knowing what was going to happen.

The modern example would be the 9/11 terrorist attack on the World Trade Center in New York. It is obvious due to the evidence that came out that certain parties in government knew about the plot but did not stop it, and ordered members of the plot turned loose after they had been arrested. These released men went on to help carry out the terrorist attack. FBI agents involved were not allowed to testify as to what they knew in this regard. The actions of vice president Cheney also raised questions. Several wives of the victims were active in documenting these facts but were ignored not only by the media, but by many so-called Truthers as well.

All else in regard to 9/11 is conjecture, conjecture that is being helped along by too many Russians, with foreign and domestic communists. They have drawn many patriots into an argument that is a dead end. Who would investigate? The government they supposedly say caused it? If not, then who, how will the money be raised, who will control the money, etc.? Once a report is issued, will the media even look at it — and on and on.

An extensive investigation by *The New American* magazine, for instance, was done on the Oklahoma City bombing that was supposedly carried out by Timothy McVeigh. They showed that he did not act alone with Terry Nichols and that several others were involved, naming them and even saying where they could be found in some instances. The story was much broader than Oklahoma City, yet the magazine could never get traction in the mainstream media since to expose what really happened would not fit the "official" story of so-called right-wing nuts carrying out the attack. This story was needed to take the heat off the Clinton administration, which was under criticism for their attacks on innocent "right-wing nuts" as well as the slaughters at Ruby Ridge, Idaho, and the religious enclave at Waco, Texas.

The point is, just because the facts are "known" does not mean that the average American will ever see them. There are several instances where facts were brought out by one publication but never reported on by the major media and therefore not noticed by the average American.

Interestingly, those who clamor the loudest about 9/11 being a government plot were nowhere to be found when the evidence regarding Oklahoma was exposed and published. Many yelled about Ruby Ridge and Waco, but were almost totally silent about Oklahoma regarding the evidence coming from *The New American* — until about 20 years later, when it was presented as new evidence and little could be done about it.

The result of the Oklahoma attack was to take attention away from the onerous actions of the Clinton administration and turn it toward so-called right-wing extremists as the real problem. To sum it up, the real evidence showed connections to countries under the sway of Russia and their terrorist network.

The end result of the 9/11 attack was the Department of Homeland Security and the Patriot Act, written a long time before the attack. One does not need to know who specifically was behind the assault, only the results. *Cui bono?*

The same can be said of the attack on Pearl Harbor. Substantial evidence from several different sources has been brought forward that Roosevelt knew of the pending attack at least two weeks in advance, but did nothing to alert our forces in Hawai'i since he wanted to go to war without making it look as if he dragged us into it. Even the *Chicago Tribune* carried an article stating this during the 1944 elections, but said that it was a good thing for Roosevelt to have done since we needed to get the United States involved in the war. There were several non-Democrat publications during and just after the war that called the official story of a "surprise" attack into question. And many books have been published documenting in detail that it was only a surprise to those on the ground in Pearl Harbor.

Yet, establishment historians do all they can to hide these facts along with the mass media.

Had these facts become known even within a matter of weeks after our declaration of war, would it have changed anything? Probably not. The only real change would have been to expose a portion of the Conspiracy in control of the government, but they would have been replaced with lesser lights due to the general ignorance of the American people of the Conspiracy and how it works — and the control they already exerted over the political process and within both major political parties.

Sometimes even exposing the facts is an exercise in frustration, as oftentimes the situation cannot be changed when people consider it to be water under the bridge, no matter how immoral or illegal it is.[61]

Surratt

Again, John Surratt was a courier for Judah Benjamin. He carried dispatches to Confederate Gen. Edwin E. Lee in Montreal, Canada, and as such was a very important and trusted member of the Confederate Secret Service.

Surratt's escape after the assassination was helped by at least four people inside the U.S., according to him, although he never revealed their names.

Surratt had malaria and contracted pneumonia after the assassination and was bedridden for a time in Canada, allowing plenty of time for investigators to track him down and bring him back from there before he boarded a boat for Europe. The Canadian government would never have stopped this from happening under the circumstances.

---

61 A good place to start a search about Pearl Harbor is the article by John T. Flynn, "The Final Secret of Pearl Harbor," which is a summary written in October 1944, before the two books below. The two books, and by no means the only ones, written in exhaustive detail and documentation are: *The Final Secret of Pearl Harbor*, by Rear Adm. Robert Alfred Theobald, and *Infamy: Pearl Harbor and Its Aftermath*, by John Toland.

He was assisted by friends and Confederate agents in Montreal, and left for Europe. Some claim they were Catholic clergy. Either he was given enough money for a year and to carry him to Italy, or he may have used funds he was responsible for. Surratt often carried considerable amounts of cash for the Confederate Secret Service.

Considering the atmosphere after the assassination, one would think that no one would want to have any part in helping Surratt. The fact that he did receive help indicates a much greater motivation on the part of those helping than simple humanitarianism. And, there were more people involved than the history books document.

As a result of these connections he finally ended up as a Papal Zouave in Rome under the name of John Watson.

He was spotted there by an acquaintance, who informed the Vatican authorities and Rufus King, the U.S. Minister in Rome, of his true identity. Surratt was arrested and placed in prison, from which we escaped.

Rome was surrounded at the time by Carbonari-led troops who were trying to bring down the Papal government. Surratt was able to go through these elements and live with Garibaldians for a short while, and then was given safe passage to Egypt.

As the Vatican was surrounded by the anti-Catholic Garibaldi army at the time and was at war with the Catholics, it is strange that a Vatican military employee would be able to not only escape through their lines but be put up by them with safe passage.

One has to ask the question whether Surrat knew some secret sign or password of the Carbonari. Such signs or passwords are common to secret societies. Since Surratt had been initiated into the KGC by Booth, he must have known this ritual. There is a great deal of resemblance of the KGC order to the Carbonari. There is evidence that the KGC was interwoven with YA members who were Carbonari. It is known that Surratt had what was known as a Garibaldi jacket made for him in Washington that he wore; however, he apparently wore his Zouave uniform when he made his escape — which makes his escape through Garibaldi's lines even more remarkable.

Years later, Surratt in his biography would claim that Booth had initiated him into the Knights of the Golden Circle in July of 1860. Thus the relationship with Booth extended back over several years and would explain why he was so trusted by Benjamin to carry secret documents and messages. And his induction into the KGC would show his involvement in at least one secret society. The problem lies in the veracity of Surratt, as to when you could believe him and when not.

After his escape from Italy, upon arrival in Egypt, he was interdicted, arrested, and sent to America to be placed on trial.

His trial was in a civilian court, since by 1867 the Supreme Court had ruled that military courts for civil crimes in the North were unconstitutional. Several prosecution witnesses testified that he was in Washington the day of the assassination; defense witnesses said he was not. The result of the trial was a hung jury. Since many of the charges against him were beyond the statute of limitations, he was released, which, considering the crime he was involved in, was incredible.

One of the problems of Surratt's story was that he told so many lies it was impossible to know the truth about the man. He claimed he was not in Washington during the assassination, and that he was involved in the kidnapping plot but not the assassination. His mother was executed on slimmer evidence, yet he got off even though his involvement was continuous from the middle of 1864. It is difficult to believe he did not know what was in store and was not involved.

Considering his involvement, his manner of escape, lifestyle during the time he was a fugitive, and the fact that he was supplied with money for a year plus travel to Italy, one has to question his connections and how he was able to be placed in a position that was so public if he wanted to remain in hiding. Even in Italy Surratt confided that he was receiving money from London. This may have been from Americans who had moved there after the war, but exactly who they were and their nationality remains unknown. Considering who Surratt was, how would the contacts have been made, and how did either party know to make them? His story of his membership in the KGC gains credibility under the circumstances.

If his story is correct about receiving money from London, as a fugitive on the run, hiding and then settling down in Rome, how would he have been contacted by the person or persons sending him the money? Was it indeed money from Americans, or from those closer to the international radical leadership living in London? It raises a lot of questions that no historian seems to have wanted to pursue.

Far too many suspects and witnesses were allowed to flee without being stopped.

There are implications that McClellan, Belmont, Fernando Wood, and others were aware of Booth's plot to kill Lincoln. The plot had so many intelligence leaks that Pinkerton and Lamon were also aware of it and were concerned, carrying such news to Washington.

Lincoln never seemed to want to prevent attempts on his life by arresting the conspirators. There were other attempts against him before the tragic event, yet Lincoln suppressed any public notice, even allowing the plotters to remain free.

The story of the indicted co-conspirators that were originally on the list of people to be arrested and brought to trial is very interesting, particularly considering the vindictiveness that existed in the North among the Republican Radicals in power, coupled with the interlocking aspects of the American wing of the Conspiracy.

George Sanders' name was on the original list of co-conspirators, but he was dropped from the list. Jefferson Davis was also dropped, but he remained in custody to be placed on trial as responsible for the entire war and secession. His bail was raised and paid for by none other than Horace Greeley, Cornelius Vanderbilt, and Gerrit Smith. This allowed Davis to leave prison, where he had been held for two years without trial, a violation of the Bill of Rights.

Holding people thus in the War on Terror was not new. This type of arrest and confinement of American citizens continued during a variety of crises, such as the two World Wars. Probably the most intriguing was an American serviceman who knew that Washington had received word of the sneak attack before December 7, 1941. He spent his time incarcerated for the duration just to get him out of the way.

Based on what you have already read, the trio that put up Davis' bail money would seem strange unless they had a loyalty to something that was hidden from the public. Horace Greeley, a man who spent his whole life promoting socialism and communist leaders; Vanderbilt, who was the mentor of the Claflin sisters, leaders of the American Section of the First International; and, Smith, who was a member of the Secret Six, among other things. Seemingly unconnected, and yet …

The Constitution was violated in regard to Jefferson Davis since the Sixth Amendment states that a citizen has the right to a speedy trial. This is to guarantee that both parties, the prosecution and defense, have the benefit of short-term memory and witnesses staying alive to testify, and more importantly, so the government cannot simply hold people and then after a time let them go when *they no longer present a threat* to the men in government.

Over the years, this right has been diminished to the point where there are seldom quick trials, whether for a terrorist or a common murderer. This author was a minor witness in a murder case, being the first to call 911 at the time of the incident, and the process dragged out for nearly three years before it came to trial.

The confinement of Davis was an incidence that showed the lie of the federal government claiming that the South was a part of the U.S. even after secession and that they were *states in rebellion*. This would have meant that all Southerners therefore remained citizens of the U.S. under the law and should have been treated accordingly — two wrongs do not make a right. The actions of the federal government — not only in this case but in the matter of how certain amendments to the Constitution were ratified after the cessation of hostilities — belied this public position.

Punishment of rebels is what governments do, but the rights of a citizen cannot be violated. It is not the system upon which this nation was founded, and in a way demonstrates why so many felt justified in rebelling against what they saw as the inevitable path the federal government would take.

Jefferson Davis was finally released and the charges dropped. Speculation based on what reasons are known is that the trial would have revealed too many things about what had been going on in the North before and during the war, information that Davis and his defense team knew that would have been very embarrassing to key politicians, such as Seward and Sumner. What this information was is unknown.

In addition, a Supreme Court justice met with Davis' attorney and was convinced that secession would have been found legal, as there was nothing against it in the Constitution. Therefore, there would have been a not guilty verdict unless run by a "kangaroo court." After all, the precedence had been made with the secession of the original thirteen colonies from the British government. It was a principle on which our country was founded.

Also, if our contention is correct and the Conspiracy wanted a war, then conspirators in control in the North would not want certain information to come forward in a trial of Davis. Not all men look forward to the gallows, and it seems obvious by the evidence that Davis would have revealed information about key Northerners that they would not have wanted revealed (leading to perhaps their execution as well). Such a trial would have been the trial of the century, and of necessity would have been open to the public. Speculation, yes, but likely based on the evidence we have.

There seems little doubt that Sanders was involved in Lincoln's assassination and he was known to publicly advocate Lincoln's demise. There was ample evidence that Sanders knew of Booth's intentions; he certainly was in contact with Booth just prior to the assassination, and probably gave him funds to carry out the deed. Too many people who were around Sanders at the time have stated that they heard him state that Lincoln was as good as dead.

He had a reputation for not keeping his thoughts to himself, and elevated his importance by bragging about what he knew. There was enough evidence of his involvement that he felt his safety was in question, and he went abroad, staying in England, as many of the leaders of the Confederacy did for a number of years. In his case, he had a number of friends among the leading communist and Carbonari revolutionaries in London.

The problem of Sanders not keeping his cards close to his chest (which caused resentment among his colleagues) may have been one of the reasons his old cronies did not attend his funeral.

No one seems to ask how such individuals as Sanders, Benjamin, *et al.* fled the country with no visible means of support. How were they able to live in a foreign land; who gave them support; and where did their money necessary to survive come from?

Those who were not immediately exposed among the small, insignificant group surrounding Booth were allowed to walk free. One has to ask why, and what these people knew that the authorities did not want exposed to the public by open trial. Killing too many witnesses leads to people asking too many questions, and we know that Davis and Benjamin had no desire to tell what they knew unless it became necessary.

This was the case with the John Brown plot and raid — only the few who were at Harper's Ferry received punishment; the conspirators that reached even into government were never pursued.

And it remains so with the Kennedy assassination. The official story is that Lee Harvey Oswald was a lone gunman. This story continues to be questioned due to the circumstances surrounding the grassy knoll and Jack Ruby, Oswald's killer. No one has ever adequately explained Oswald's travels, his earlier attempted assassination of Gen. Edwin Walker, or his marriage to a niece of a Russian MVD colonel. At the time Marina met Oswald she lived with her uncle in Minsk and was a member of the Komsomol, the communist youth organization.

Very few facts about Ruby have been made known to the general public, the facts that are known to the few who have studied the situation raise considerable questions about Ruby's possible involvement in the assassination of Kennedy, not just Oswald. Did Ruby kill Oswald to make sure no one found out the entire truth? To continue would necessitate another book.[62]

After all is said and done, *cui bono*? The answer, whether you are talking about the Lincoln or the Kennedy assassination, is those who wanted more government.

---

62 This author was acquainted with a doctor who was in the emergency room when Kennedy was brought in to Parkland Memorial Hospital. He stated that based on what he saw, Kennedy's wound that caused his death was from the front, not the rear of his head, regardless of what the Warren Commission said. He also treated Gov. Connally and stated that in no way was there a "magic" bullet that struck Kennedy first, then Connally.

15

Reconstruction

As the federal troops marched into the South, a number of changes were made, including the widespread establishment of public education at the state level, coordinated at first from the national government. These schools were segregated between the Negroes and white children. In other words, it was the Northern activists who, while professing Negro rights, initially segregated the schools. This followed the pattern of public education in much of the North at the time.

Immediately after the war, the use of private education was at a lower percentage than before the war, due to the growth of the government system, which was largely controlled by the state rather than the local citizens.

After the war, the Reconstruction Act was passed in 1866, which divided the South into five military districts ruled by military governors under the command of the head of the U.S. Army, Ulysses S. Grant. It declared that a state of war still existed. If this is the case, the president remains the commander in chief. Whether the war was in effect or not, the authority of the president of the United States was usurped. Grant would issue all orders, for by this time the Radical Congress was also at war with the president of the United States. And, of course, Grant's boss was Stanton.

Johnson had vetoed the act, but the veto was overridden by Congress.

The law declared that a state of war still existed against the entire South nearly a year after Lee's surrender at Appomattox and the pockets of organized resistance had gradually shrunk back into Texas. However, due to the excesses performed by federal troops against property and civilians, retaliation by Southerners did not cease entirely.

The military governors were not inclined to be kind to the vanquished. The son-in-law of Benjamin Butler, Adelbert Ames, was appointed provisional governor of Mississippi in mid-1868. The manner in which suffrage was instituted enabled him to be elected by the legislature as U.S. senator, then in 1873 to the office of the governor. His administration resulted in rioting by December and the murders of Republicans, white and black.

Ames appealed for federal troops, and a year later the Democrats returned to power. Ames left under threat of impeachment and returned north to Minnesota.

Prior to the 1866 laws, the South had been divided into several military districts. One in southwest Georgia was commanded by Major General John Thomas Croxton, a member of the Order. He later was made our minister to Bolivia by Grant. The district of the Carolinas was commanded by Daniel E. Sickles, who was replaced due to the harsh treatment he dealt out to the citizens.

The five military districts that were finally established were ruled by generals who represented a cross section of Union general officers. It was not an easy time for the Southern citizen; the officers functioning under the commanders could at times be very draconian regardless of their commanders' sentiments, and treated the civilian population as if they were conquered aliens.

The civilian governments in the reconstructed states were led by men in the governors' chairs that were barely more than crooks. In one case, Franklin J. Moses, governor of South Carolina, ended his career by being arrested by New York police for playing a bunco game in 1881.

The worst corruption was probably in Louisiana, continuing the political shenanigans of the New Orleans politicians reinforced by Northern bayonets. This corruption continued into the 20th century, played out on the front pages of newspapers, and became the basis for several Hollywood dramas.

The conditions in the South became so bad that James Russell Lowell, one of the original abolitionists, wrote,

The whole condition of things in the South is shameful, and I am ready for a movement now to emancipate the whites.

Letters of James Russell Lowell

The actions of the Union Army and the men occupying the state governments and Freedman's organizations in the South led to a reaction: a new organization that seemed a great deal like the KGC and the Carbonari. One of their articles of membership, for instance, was, "Any member divulging, or causing to be divulged, any of the foregoing obligations shall meet the fearful penalty and traitors doom, which is Death!"

This new organization did *look* different since they wore hoods. It was the Ku Klux Klan, or KKK.

History says that it was formed by five men, which is more often than not the number we see in the formation of many secret groups, including the Illuminati, several communist organizations, and the KGC. KKK members referred to themselves as "sons of light," a hint of Illuminism.

The KKK also referred to their organization as the invisible circle. They were named after *klukos*, the Greek word from which we get our word *circle*. This hearkened back to the Knights of the Golden Circle, but we must not forget that Weishaupt also referred to his Illuminati as a circle, as did the Illuminist Bonneville and Babeuf of their organizations.

Evidence indicates that the KKK was the KGC revived under the leadership of Gen. Nathan Bedford Forrest, who had worked with the KGC during the war. The organization proliferated too fast for it not to be based on an existing organization. They claimed 500,000 members by 1868, when Forrest lost control and ordered it abandoned.

The KKK used a variation of the letter cipher of the one used by the KGC. They also relied on the old signs and traditions of the Know-Nothings and the KGC. For instance, the secret members within the Know-Nothings grasped the lapel of one's coat with their thumb and forefinger to identify one another in greeting.

The leaders of the KKK were Gen. John T. Morgan in Alabama, former Governor Zebulon Vance in North Carolina, and John B. Gordon in Georgia. All three became U.S. senators after the war. It is interesting that in the last half of the war, Vance was involved in thwarting the draft and other means needed to man the Confederate Army, yet became a leader of the KKK to fight Northern occupation. Yet another secret society leader that conveniently changed his stance as it fit the current agenda.

Gen. Morgan was an expansionist and served six terms as senator.

The most interesting individual who started the KKK in his state and was the head of it there was Albert Pike, the Masonic occultist and a man who rose to be at least a partner of, but probably the head of, the international Carbonari over Mazzini. For years this was common knowledge, but recently these facts have been denied and expunged from several sources.

General George Meade, commander of the 3rd Military District of Georgia/Alabama/Florida, issued an order to suppress the KKK in April 1866. The *New York Herald* lauded the order and also called for him to do the same to the secret Loyal Leagues of Negroes, which were an extension of the Union Leagues. Many felt the Loyal Leagues were fueling the KKK reaction, and both had to stop.

The KKK revived again just before World War I. By the 1920s, it claimed four million members, holding a gigantic parade in Washington in 1928. Several notable politicians were members at one time or another: Harry Truman, Sen. Harry Byrd, Justice Hugo Black, and several Republican U.S. senators and governors. The KKK gradually became more radical politically, and just before World War II it secretly united with the Nazi Bund in joint agenda and actions. It remains so today, with KKK leaders and neo-Nazi leaders often working in cooperation with each other. However, one cannot tell much difference between them and the communists who infiltrated both — all with a smattering of government informants keeping an eye on them.

The modern KKK and Nazi groups appear to be more of an attempt to keep the specter of militant extremism alive, to act as an example for the liberal media to point to as a danger to freedom and tar-brush conservative organizations, because the very small units of KKK and Nazis are given more publicity than any real danger warrants.

The only influence that white supremacist groups have today is to serve as an example to provide an excuse for onerous social legislation. The numbers of members are insignificant. Rallies and meetings rarely draw more than a few. If it is in the scores, it is because people come from all over the country to attend. The media and counter-demonstrators usually outnumber the extremists.

Only the government knows how many of these members are actually on the government payroll as investigators. Too many times these "investigators" actually promote violence by these groups that fits a political agenda, by providing an excuse for new legislation or simply a reason for the government agencies to exist. It gives legitimacy to the idea that domestic terrorism is "right-wing," even though Nazi means national *socialist*.

The only thing right about it is that it is on the right side of the Left — which is where the term came from. It never was used early on as meaning the right of the whole political scale, only the socialist scale.

This erroneous association is accomplished by having these extremists agree with some conservative or constitutional position, and then tar-brush by their actions all who may agree on that one issue, such as the Second Amendment. It is not unusual for true constitutionalists to be called extremist, Nazi, KKK, or even communist by the mainstream media, using the small, insignificant extremist organizations as the example.

This author was in a hotel in Geneva, Switzerland, in the 1980s and watched a television program which purported to document the American Nazi movement. A ridiculous statement in the documentary said that 70% of Americans supported the American Nazis. Preposterous to us, but as long as they could show four or five idiots prancing around a rural tavern in Nazi SS uniforms, it might look plausible to gullible people or those who have never even been to the United States.

The same technique applies for an American audience. Due to any audience's ignorance of the facts, they can be convinced by visual means of how many people have turned out for a demonstration, by close up shots or angles that project the idea of great numbers, or vice versa. If the media can *fill the screen* with a few Nazis, it can have the appearance of quite a number.

If the media wishes to project the idea of small numbers, they video or photograph a periphery area off to the side of some event where the people are small in number, when a swing of the camera would show the main event is attended by a large number. It is the reverse of filling the screen with a few. A few are shown, but from a distance so that they do not fill the screen. This is quite common with the rallies of constitutionally oriented political candidates' events, and gives a distorted view to the television viewer as to the real strength of conservative organizations.

If the media is for a candidate or movement, they show only the moderate people at an event. If they oppose the candidate or movement, they find the most offensive or outlandish people in the audience and capture their image for the news with the idea that these are representative of the typical attendee.

This author was involved in a case in the late 1960s where a government informant joined a group he was involved with and attempted to radicalize them. When he could not persuade them and it was decided by all that he should leave, he moved on to greener pastures and performed a sting operation on people less moral. He got them to form a bank robbery team to gain money for the "cause," and they all ultimately served ten to twenty years in prison — and the government got its headlines aimed at illustrating "patriots" as the extremists.

This was needed since the media was, due to the overwhelming number of terrorist acts, filled with stories of the domestic terror of Leftist anti-war and so-called civil rights extremists' violence. A balance was needed to offset the growing public pressure to punish these Leftist terrorist groups.

Those who experienced these shenanigans by "liberals" in the media and government to convince the public that "right wingers" were the problem were quite concerned when the Obama administration issued guidelines to watch for potential terrorists during his first term. The report said that potential terrorists could be veterans returning from Iran and Afghanistan, pro-life activists, and strict constitutionalists. Mention of Leftist activists was sparse.

Seminars are given to local police all over the country to try to give them the impression that domestic terrorism emanates from the above sources. They throw in brief mention of radical Muslims to claim that they are fair and balanced. These seminars are usually run by the Southern Poverty Law Center, or their materials are used. The SPLC is a heavily financed tax-deductible foundation that has as its main concern trying to convince the world that the main threat to freedom is from the right, not the left. Their financial portfolio is always in the hundreds of millions of dollars.

There were other organizations besides the KKK that fought for the restoration of Southern government during the Reconstruction. One was the Red Shirts, commanded by Wade Hampton, which was virtually a revolution that swept Reconstruction out of South Carolina by force. The use of red shirts was specifically inspired by Garibaldi's use of the red shirt.

Daniel Henry Chamberlain, a member of the Order, was a Union officer who became state attorney general and then governor of South Carolina spanning the years from 1868 to 1876.

The war moved state sovereignty into limbo and increasingly democracy and nationalism became the prevailing thought, although both had been a steadily encroaching idea within the American political debate for some years. There were, from time to time, attempts to re-establish what had regrettably become known as states rights (in and of itself a self-defeating term, rather than the term state sovereignty). Not until the mid-20th century were organized *grassroots* efforts made to restore the balance between the sovereign states and the federal government.

In the aftermath of the war nationalism grew until it almost became supreme. John W. Burgess, in his *Political Science and Comparative Constitutional Law*, 1890, said, "It is no longer proper to call them states at all. It is in fact only a title of honor, without any corresponding substance."

Note that his definition of a state corresponded to a state being a sovereign entity, not simply a part of a larger whole.

A growing "federalism" took more and more control away from the states over the next century. By the time of Nixon's administration, he openly attempted to eliminate the states entirely through his "New Federalism" plan and substitute in their place ten regions, which the federal government still uses today to break down federal responsibility geographically around the country. One does not know how far this would have progressed if he had not been forced to resign over the Watergate scandal.

War took its toll on the general morality and economic picture, just as it did as a result of the War for Independence. Over the next ten years approximately 50,000 businesses failed, initially due to the manipulation of the currency.

The issuance of the famous Greenback produced 50% inflation. The process robbed the citizens of the North of 50% of the value of everything they owned since everything they owned was based on the monetary system in use. It was a hidden tax to conduct the war and build the bureaucracy.

It was worse in the South. There the inflation rate had been over 90%. After Appomattox the Confederate dollar was worth one cent. It took nearly a century for the South the recover economically from this devastating misuse of the government printing presses and the manner in which money was raised from the people turning in precious metals in return for a promise never kept.

What prevented normal recovery in the South was government interference and corruption. The military took over the courthouses and in many instances demanded the citizens pay taxes back to 1861. Since most were not in a position to do so due to the economic collapse, property was confiscated. This created a "fire sale" for unscrupulous Northerners to come in and buy up property at depressed foreclosure prices. A great deal of land and estates changed hands. Not all the money found its way into the government, and much remained in the pockets of the military officers in charge.

The term "carpetbaggers" came into use to define these opportunists. The cheap form of baggage in those days was made out of a heavy fabric used to make carpets, and these types of opportunists made use of this form of baggage. All manner of men from the North seeking to make a "killing" threw a few clothes into a carpetbag and descended on the South. People of means had baggage made out of leather.

One of the problems in 45 counties across the South was the destruction during the war of the courthouses containing the records for the legal relationships and ownership of land in the communities. This raised havoc in establishing title to property in order to retain ownership, and some lost their property as a result.

The economy was devastated to the point that rail lines were in disrepair — if they existed — with many of them destroyed by Northern and Southern forces, each of them wanting to deprive the other of their use during the war. The difference in rail gauges was still a problem; water transportation was disrupted due to the destruction of paddle boats, two-fifths of the livestock of the South had been destroyed, farm implements had been reduced by an amazing percentage, etc.

While President Johnson rejected Carl Schurz's plan to reorganize the South, nonetheless the attack on the old social order went forward. Karl Marx lauded Reconstruction, and may have coined the use of the term to begin with as it relates to the Southern occupation by the Union Army, since he used the term before it was commonly referred to by that name. The process was what Marx laid out in the *Manifesto*: the destruction of the old social order.

It was to be a reconstruction of society, not reconstruction of damaged infrastructure or cities.

The states were required to ratify the 14th Amendment *before* they were allowed back into the Union. In 1866, the United States government removed the Southern states from the union. They had not allowed them to secede, and the official position of the North was that they were only states in rebellion, yet they declared them non-states after the war. They were required to perform as a state — ratify the 14th — *while no longer recognized as an official part of the Union.*

In other words, in order to re-join the union, they had to ratify the 14th. If they did not, they could not rejoin the union, which means they were in a condition the North would not recognize officially in 1861, and were being placed in that situation by the very government that said they could not leave the union! In this condition of *not being recognized as a state, they could not officially or constitutionally ratify the amendment*, but the Radical Congress counted it as ratified.

Eleven states ratified the amendment after military rule was imposed. Most of these states rejected the amendment before they were ruled by the five military districts. The Union states of New Jersey, Ohio, and Oregon tried to withdraw their ratification. The reason that New Jersey did so was, they said, because that specific states were unlawfully denied representation in the House and Senate at the time. Only one state rejection was allowed to stand: Maryland's.

This does not make the amendment good or bad, just the ratifying process illegal. In any normal court of law, the amendment would have been null and void.

Over the next century all of the states moved to ratify the amendment, one at a time. "Political correctness" drove this initiative.

Interestingly, one of the most prominent organizations defending home schooling has used the 14th Amendment — originally an illegal amendment — for the basis of its arguments in court. In the process, the idea that the state may have de facto control over the education of children rather than the complete right and freedom of the parents to educate their children as they deem fit has been maintained. Yes, the parents may proceed to educate their children, but only if they register and/or follow state-mandated requirements and regulations. So-called home school victories are faux victories if the state still maintains the "right" to regulate and keep track of home schoolers.

It would be the same as saying that you have the right to keep and bear arms, you just have to register them!

Another problem that existed was that the Radicals wanted to bring back the states as something other than republics, which was mandated by the Constitution. This was an ongoing problem for the subversives to get around, and ultimately the states were restored as nominal republics. They could not be restored completely as republics (nor the rest of the states) since the very term means a sovereign state, not a subordinate unit of a larger government. It was supposed to be a union, not a national government.

Anti-slavery did not die out as a movement right away due to the pressure to pass amendments to the Constitution and the activities of the KKK, as well as the fact that slavery was still in existence in Union areas. This did not change until the ratification of the amendment that freed the slaves.

Then too, the condition of the Negro in the South was terrible. This was the result of either the local governments treating them as "independent" slaves as far as their employment and land tenancy was concerned, or freeing the slaves with no means of support or employment. Saying that people are free with no job, no land, no food, no livestock, etc. is all well and good, but how do they subsist? Many didn't.

The *National Anti-Slavery Standard* stayed in print, edited by A. M. Powell. After the war it opened its columns to the communist First International, finally endorsing the organization in the early 1870s. The plight of the Negro would still be used to move the communist agenda forward. This was the case well into the 20th century; it was revitalized under the Lyndon Johnson administration, and again under the Obama administration and Attorney General Eric Holder.

The rejection of Carl Schurz' plan for land reform in the South by Andrew Johnson prompted a speech by Schurz wherein he attacked Johnson in a manner that would land him in jail by Homeland Security if given today. The speech was applauded when Schurz talked about hanging the Southern leaders and said,

"If there is any man who ought to hang for supporting these principles, it is Andrew Johnson."

Yet in 1868, Carl Schurz was elected temporary chairman of the Republican Party's national convention, and he delivered the keynote address. He seconded the nomination for vice president of Benjamin Wade, the man who would have been president if all of the assassinations during Lincoln's assassination had been carried out. Schurz did not support Grant initially, and later would become a leader of the Liberal Republican Party formed primarily in opposition to Grant's re-election.

Grant referred to Schurz as an infidel and an atheist. To others he was considered a social Darwinist. One could say the same about Marx. While Grant may have considered Schurz as described, he at the same time appointed men to positions who created criminal and political corruption in their offices and who held the same beliefs. Perhaps the worst for the long-term effect on the country was Justice Morrison Remick "Mott" Waite, seventh chief justice of the United States.

Waite was a member of the Order and had helped organize the Republican Party in Ohio. His decision in the *Munn vs. Illinois* case argued that states had the right to regulate private enterprise as to the pricing and fees they charged.

In his dissent to the court's decision, Justice Stephen Johnson Field said this:

> If this be sound law, if there be no protection, either in the principles upon which our republican government is founded, or in the prohibitions of the Constitution against such invasion of private rights, all property and all business in the State are held at the mercy of a majority of its legislature.

It was a giant step toward any state government controlling the economic system within their state, and perhaps beyond if the business affected the economy of any other state — this on top of the federal monetary policy and the beginnings of the banking system which came about during the Civil War.

Federal economic interference based on this decision would be the next logical step. It came during the administration of FDR in the National Recovery Act (NRA), but was found unconstitutional under the then current court. Since then, slowly but surely, the federal government has continued to find ways to get around the decision. The NRA used the infamous Blue Eagle as its logo, which can still be seen on old movie credits from the 1930s shown on television.

For this and other reasons, FDR called for the expansion of the number of Supreme Court justices (which was not passed by the Congress) so that he could pack the court with men who had a more "liberal" view of the Constitution. Even so, FDR was able to appoint men who supported his socialist schemes over time as men retired.

The full dissent of Justice Field is a lesson in property rights and common sense. The decision and Field's dissent can be seen online.

Another of Grant's appointees was Ebenezer Hoar as attorney general. Hoar was at a meeting with John Brown, Emerson, Thoreau, et al. to help raise financial and other aid for Brown. Hoar was for the paper money system and had Grant nominate men to the courts to support the unconstitutional issuing of paper money.

The idea of American empire promoted before the Civil War did not end with the war. Grant wanted to annex Santo Domingo.

Sen. Sumner, chairman of the Senate Committee on Foreign Relations, wanted England to pay for not only the direct losses of the war, but also for the indirect ones arising from Britain's prolonging the Civil War for two years as a result of England's foreign policy at the time. The sum would exceed two billion dollars, and it was widely assumed that the only way England could pay would be to cede Canada to the United States.

The radical wing, including Schurz, pushed for this initiative. Empire isn't evil, just who runs it, it would seem.

Today, there are few people that know of the general feeling toward Britain regarding its position during the war and how many, if not most Northerners believed that initially England played a role in the Civil War on the side of the South. One reason was simply that some of the famous battle ships built for the Southern Navy were built in Britain.

The opposition to Grant by the more openly radical Republicans, such as Schurz, served to give a moderate look to the existing mainstream party under Grant, which was needed due to the actions and appointments listed above, though these were by no means the only illustrations.

The passage of the National Banking Act of 1863, which remained in force after the war, gave monetary power to bankers, both domestic and foreign.

Sen. John Sherman and Rep. Samuel Hooper led the fight to use the gold standard as the basis for the continuation of the Greenback. The bankers of Europe had gold, but the metal most found in the United States was silver. So the exclusive use of gold as our standard started to give an edge to the European bankers. The Constitution *called for the use of both metals*, not paper. Sherman was to become the secretary of the Treasury under President Hayes.

There was a movement to completely de-monetize silver that was promoted on both sides of the Atlantic, and many radicals were involved. This would have placed the United States at a disadvantage relative to the use of our wealth on the world stage. This may seem to be a contradiction to the idea of the United States being used to help build a New World Order except for one thing: silver is the poor man's currency. It would have deprived the average citizen the advantage of having an intrinsic metal at his disposal, free from the banking system controlled by the Conspiracy.

It was fine for the governments and international bankers to have gold at their disposal, but as for the common man being able to be independent financially, well that was simply rhetoric. They can be taxed, but not allowed to accumulate independent wealth that will allow them individual self-sufficiency apart from the system.

The Constitution established our currency as gold and silver. This was to be used by all citizens. Since the policies put in place during and subsequent to the Civil War, the Constitution has been ignored and Americans have been deprived of the use of gold and silver, pushing them increasingly into being wards of the state.

Due to the inflation of our money since the end of the Civil War and increasingly under the Federal Reserve, most Americans are unaware of the power of silver coinage utilized in a free market. Gold has always been a problem for the poor. It is usually out of reach of their economic status. Silver, on the other hand, can be broken down into more usable denominations. For instance, just after the war, it was not unusual to be able to rent a room at a hotel for 20 cents.

Just as a very real illustration of inflation and the changes that result there from, in preparing this manuscript, the cent sign could not be used in the illustration above because it no longer appears on the keyboard as it did when this author was a young man. It has been phased out due to the rarity of its use — due to inflation. It is true that the cent sign can be accessed with the Insert function, but it used to be a standard key.

The movement by the Radicals to install and retain changes in the federal government led to a large increase in government employees. In 1860 the federal government employed 37,000 people, and the vast majority worked for the U.S. Postal Service. By the end of Reconstruction the employment doubled due to the growth of government other than the Post Office. After this time, federal employment would continue to grow far out of proportion to private- sector job growth.

16

POSTWAR LEFTISTS

The communist First International was formed in London in 1864. It was called "The International Workingmen's Association" (IWA), and its purpose was to unite all the different organizations of revolutionary tendencies in Europe: Marxists, working-class leaders, anarchists, Mazzini disciples, Owenites, etc., to bring a more centralized focus to them. A few workingmen's organizations in America allied themselves. The members initially called each other *citizen* rather than *comrade*, reminiscent of the French Revolution.

As is usual, these people could not get along, with each one vying to be the leader. Finally, Marx became its overt leader and then dissolved the group because the anarchists were trying to take over. The goal was to use anarchism as a tool, not to allow it to succeed. And, the personalities could not get along. It was one of the last times the Carbonari and the communists were united at their core leadership *organizationally*. Even so, at the top, the puppeteer still remained in control of both.

This may seem strange at first glance until you use the example of a family of children that simply cannot get along. They will fight each other and won't talk to one another, but when it comes to the family pulling together against an outsider, they do. And, if they don't, father will make sure.

Morris Hillquit, the communist historian, said, "The first strictly Marxian organization of strength and influence on American soil" was the Allegemeiner Deutscher Arbeiter Verein. In 1869 this organization was admitted to the National Labor Union as Labor Union No. 5 of New York, and the following year it joined the IWA as Section 1, New York. The German communists were just as active after the war as before.

Over the next several years, the number of communist sections grew in New York, Chicago, San Francisco, Newark, New Orleans, Springfield, Washington, and Brooklyn. John Murray Spear, a Universalist minister, was the founder of the San Francisco section. Spear was also a leader in the spiritualist movement, as well as a friend of William Lloyd Garrison and Theodore Parker.

Spear was an activist at one time in New England with Bronson Alcott, Lydia Maria Child, Dorothea Dix, Longfellow, and Douglass. He was a leader there in the New England Non-Resistance Society and Anti-Slavery Society. He helped found free-love communities and helped lead the Equal Rights Party of Woodhull.

The first American radicals to join the IWA had a great deal of experience in the movement. The oldest men, such as John Commerford and Gilbert Vale, had worked alongside Thomas Paine. Commerford was also active in the Brotherhood of the Union and the Garibaldi Wide Awakes.

Timothy Messer-Kruse expresses the lineage of the Americans in the IWA this way:

Before the eventual seating of the trinity of Marx, Engels, and Lenin, theirs was a pantheistic faith: the statuary in their temple began with Tom Paine, Fourier, Owen, Swedenborg, and John

Brown and ended with Brisbane, Kellogg, Proudhon, and, of course, Karl Marx.
— *The Yankee International*

Even before all of this, Communist Clubs of militant atheists were formed among the Germans in New York, Chicago, and Cincinnati in the late 1850s. Their first political outlet, or issue, was anti-slavery.

By 1870, several communist organizations had merged to form a provisional central committee of the International in the U.S. under Friedrich Adolph Sorge, a German 48er and friend of Marx and Engels, as corresponding secretary. In one year they reported over 30 sections having a combined membership of several thousands.

The success of the communist movement in America before, during, and for years after the Civil War was so great that it was decided, and Marx agreed, to move the headquarters of the communist movement to the United States. It was moved from London to New York in 1872 under the general management of Sorge. Yet neither Marx nor Engels had any plans to move here himself, which demonstrates one of two things, either, these gentlemen could wield control by and through the organization no matter how far removed they were physically, or they really were not at the pinnacle of the Conspiracy, only serving the orders of the secret inner party.

By all indications, the Insiders within the Conspiracy began to move their entire center of operations to the United States from London; prior to that the Conspiracy's epicenter was Paris, and before that, Germany. By this we mean the entire conspiratorial apparatus, not just the communist wing.

Elite organizations began to be formed in the late 1800s in New York, and by the conclusion of World War I it was obvious that the Conspiracy could not operate without the leadership in New York, regardless of the movement or its geographical "headquarters." It was rare that a country became communist, national socialist, or socialist after 1900 without the help from American Insiders. Volumes have been written about this problem, particularly after World War II, and it will not take long for an interested party to seek out and read such books. Most were written prior to 1970.

Relative to New York becoming the epicenter, the Council on Foreign Relations had its initial membership in New York. They added non-resident membership as part of their structure, combining it all in the early 1970s. Then in the early 2010s, they opened an office in Washington, D.C.

Initially most IWA members were of foreign extraction, but one which was not was Section 12 of New York City, led by the sisters Victoria Woodhull and Tennessee Claflin. They propagated female suffrage and sexual freedom — a situation with which they had no problem. Section 1, a German unit, demanded their expulsion in 1872. Section 12 then held a convention and changed its name to the Equal Rights Party, and nominated Woodhull and Frederick Douglass as the presidential and vice presidential candidates.

Douglass is honored today in American schools as a great civil rights leader of the 19th century. It is not mentioned that he was always in the company of communists and terrorists.

Woodhull published a magazine called the *Humanitarian* for five years. While many histories look back at the suffrage movement and treat their leaders, such as Anthony and Stanton, as moderates, these two nonetheless worked with Woodhull and Rachel Foster-Avery for years.

Rachel Foster-Avery was a socialist activist and helped in the publication of Frederick Engels' American edition of *The Condition of the Working Class in England*, and served as secretary of the National Woman Suffrage Association.

By the middle of 1876, the International was declared dead. It was put to death so that it wouldn't be taken over by non-Marxist leaders, not because it was a waning movement. They could not have the gullible communist or anarchist rabble take over what was started by the still-secret League of Just Men conspiracy.

Much of the problem was due to personalities. When criminally minded people get together, they cannot trust one another and each wants to be "The Leader." This was intolerable to Marx and his minions, more and importantly, to those behind Marx.

Let us point out again that certain men have no ability to run anything. The Napoleons, Stalins, Hitlers, and Obamas of the world are placed in leadership based on their ability to front for the Conspiracy and their ruthlessness once they start to accumulate power. Marx was no different. He could not manage a family, had no control over his ability to manage money, and in general was a basket case when it came to any kind of fiscal or societal responsibility. To honestly believe that he was really the leader of a vast movement is too much of a stretch.

After the dissolution, the Marxists got back together and formed the Working Men's Party, the same name used by the Owenites in 1829. Edward Everett had supported the earlier effort by the Owenites. After studying at Göttingen University in Germany in the early 1800s, he had gone on to be the governor of Massachusetts, U.S. ambassador to England, president of Harvard, and secretary of war under Taylor. He delivered the main address the day of the famous Gettysburg Address of Lincoln. He had run for vice-president on the Constitutional Union Party ticket with Bell in 1860.

This last example shows that while the communist movement became Marxism, there was already a movement that existed which operated at a visible, but higher level within American society that came about during the early years after 1800. But before that, American circles of Illuminati had already ingratiated themselves into even greater roles in politics, religion, and industry. The street-level communist movement was simply a manifestation of all the work that had come before and *would be used to play off against the elite wing* to provide the excuse for more government.

The problem that good people have in dealing with conspirators is that they are dealing with criminals. Good people operate in the open and morally. The conspirators and those who want power do not. This places moral people at a disadvantage, since they must always operate morally and ethically while the conspirators use any and all means to move their agenda forward, with the ends justifying the means.

The problem conspirators deal with is they also have to deal with criminals — there is "no honor amongst thieves." They will always fragment due to the ambitions of those involved, each wanting to be the leader, unless as in totalitarian communist states, the power of the inner party is enforced through the state, not allowing dissent unless it is for the purpose of drawing out dissidents into the open to crush them before they get too strong, or to deflect a growing discontent.

Drawing them out into the open helps identify those they need to eliminate from effective opposition, either by killing them, infiltrating them, outmaneuvering them, or simply smearing them. This then is coordinated by the secret society within the larger movement, such as the League of Just Men.

This technique was used several times by the Soviet Union in its satellite countries. They would allow dissent to boil up prematurely, even help it do so, in order to crush it before it got out of hand. In many cases they actually supplied the leadership in order to control the outcome, just as we have explained that the best thing a conspiracy can do is to create their own opposition. Probably, the most notable case of this was in Poland, with the so-called solidarity movement. Any student of international socialism knows that *solidarity* is a socialist term and many organs of socialist groups have had that title. This author witnessed this in Vienna when visiting the socialist headquarters there, as only one instance.

The organization of the IWA would have had about 50 American sections had it not been for the exclusionary policy of Frederich Sorge that matched his biases. Several groups and individuals did not apply for membership even though they supported communism, since they did not want to come under his organizational discipline. Sorge remained in the labor movement in the United States for the rest of his life as a communist.

His grand-nephew was the famous Soviet communist spy from Germany who helped turn Japanese ambitions in the Pacific toward attacking the United States rather than Russia in the late 1930s and early 1940s. The group he led was named the Sorge Spy Ring, and several books have been written about this affair. This spy was finally executed by Japanese authorities during World War II even though Japan had a nonaggression pact with communist Russia all during the war. The USSR violated that pact after the atomic bombs had been dropped so they could pick up the pieces in Asia based on American, British, and Nationalist Chinese lives and treasure.

From the late 1860s through the late 1870s, several socialist parties, organizations, and labor unions were formed in the U.S., all with their roots in the general communist movement.

Through the younger participants, such as Peter J. McGuire, Leander Thompson, Hugh McGregor, John McMakin, John Elliott and Theodore Banks, the IWA contributed to the development of socialism and the labor movement into the 20th century.

McGregor was a Scot and a veteran of Garibaldi's campaigns in Italy. He would become a future leader of the American Federation of Labor after being a clerk, and running the AFL office in the absence of the president, Samuel Gompers. Gompers sent him to Paris in the 1880s with a letter from the AFL declining to join in an international effort to unite the union movement because the socialists and the Marxists could not get together. It was also felt at the time that there was a need to unite all of the union movement in America before joining in an international effort. That would change in the 20th century.

There was even an initiative to make the union labor movement appear Christian. The Boston Congregationalist Rev. Jesse Henry Jones, who advocated socialism, formed the Christian Labor Union in 1872.

The Labor Department of the federal government came about as a direct result of the work of the aforementioned socialist leaders. The National Labor Union in convention in 1867 called for the establishment of such a department. This was picked up by the Industrial Congress, later called the Industrial Brotherhood, and finally by the Knights of Labor.

In the process, the Congress held hearings on the matter, using the testimony of such individuals as Hugh McGregor, to ultimately create the department.

In their early years Marx and Engels had considered moving to America. In his youth, before Marx co-wrote the *Manifesto*, he had petitioned the head of the government in Trier, his birthplace, for an Emigration Certificate to move to the U.S., Texas specifically.

This is entirely contrary to the idea that people have that the center of communism is/was Moscow. Dr. Bella Dodd, former member of the Communist Party USA Central Committee, found this out when she was told to ask three American businessmen who lived at the Waldorf Towers for answers to emergency needs of the CPUSA just after World War II.

Many revolutionaries and ex-revolutionaries looked to the United States as a refuge or a base from which to further their brand of the internationalist movement. Even the older brother of Napoleon, Joseph, acquired 150,000 acres in New York as a refuge for Napoleon should he escape his exile. The acquisition had to be approved by an act of the New York Assembly to enable him to hold real estate. An act was passed in New Jersey for the same purpose in 1817.

Two of Napoleon's brothers lived in America for a time. And Charles Joseph Bonaparte, Napoleon's grand-nephew, served in Theodore Roosevelt's Cabinet as secretary of the Navy. A year later, as attorney general, he founded the Federal Bureau of Investigation. He was active as a leader in the Civil Service Reform League and the National Municipal League, which into the 20th century promoted urban government consolidation into huge metropolitan governments, sometimes called Metro Government.

All of these revolutionaries who came to America assimilated into American life and influenced the future course of American politics, the above example being only one.

By the time Lenin was ready to go into Russia and take over that country with the help of German Intelligence during World War I, the importance of American communists in the struggle had reached a point where Lenin wrote in 1916 and acknowledged their help: "It can make easier the conditions under which its principal and most faithful ally, the European and American proletariat, would enter upon the decisive struggle."

Several volumes have been written about the help of American financiers and American agents that put up the funds and went into Russia to help Lenin establish the Bolshevik government. It is a truism that without the help of American conspirators, primarily, Russia could not have sustained a communist government — at least not for several more years. These volumes may be accessed online, but here again, be careful since some of them tend to exaggerate or sell a form of racial bias. The truth is bad enough. A place to start is with Mr. Armand Hammer.

At the same time, a contingent of American Army troops was sent to Russia, ostensibly in opposition to the Bolshevik government. This provided a cloak for the real agenda. No one would believe that Americans were actually helping Lenin if we had troops stationed in Russia. These troops operated primarily along the Trans-Siberian Railroad.

The modern equivalent is the War on Terror. Our troops are fighting terrorists while a portion of our intelligence community is creating more terrorist organizations in league with other governments. This can be proven to the reader by starting an extensive online search for the origins of al-Qaeda and ISIS.

Again, there is no evidence that the foreign service of the United States purged itself of communists from the days of Franklin Pierce. One can only imagine the ability of communist agents within the staff of this agency to have built up over the last 160 years a dedicated core of operatives that have remained the shadow authority within the state based on civil service.

Union Leagues

There was an organization established that would support much of the program of the communists, but within a higher caste of American society: the Union League.

The Union League of New York was originally called the National League. This name, however, spoke too candidly of its aims and the name was changed to Union, which was used very well as a semantics tool during the war. The aim was a national government, but using the term "union" made it seem a goal of simply keeping the states *united* rather than the real goal of building nationalism with the elimination of state authority.

The New York League was the most prominent and contained many who were either already very influential or would become important.

In many ways the Union Leagues were the expansionist counterpart of the Knights of the Golden Circle sans a secret membership. They started out with an image of a benevolent organization, with a motive to use the façade of benevolence to further radical Republican politics in the South, and in the North, "a club which should be devoted to the social organization of sentiments of loyalty to the Union."

Note the use of the term, "devoted to the social organization," again, a subtle reference to the changing of the social structure of America.

In some areas, and the farther west they were organized, they tended to become paramilitary or militia referred to as "home guards" or "loyal legions."

Most history books on the subject claim the Union Leagues were first organized in Philadelphia in 1862, and they were known as circles of freedmen. They were to combat disloyalty and win support for the Lincoln administration. They followed the Union army into the South, provided teachers for the Negro schools, and advocated Negro suffrage. They then dedicated themselves to building a dominant Republican Party in the South.

Their general aims were said to be: to strengthen love and respect for the Union, to discourage whatever tends to give undue prominence to local interests, and to urge upon the public attention schemes for national advancement. The leaders had more in mind than preserving the Union.

Charles G. Came, the Order, wrote an essay on Legal Nominations for the Philadelphia Union League. Came was known for his works on political organization.

Charles Goepp, nee C. Cöpp, wrote essays on political organizations for the Philadelphia Union League as well as a tract on Kossuth. Later he wrote proposals for changes in the New York State constitution for the New York Republican Party.

Regardless of the histories of the Union League stating that they started in Philadelphia, Union Leagues already existed in several states using that name or some variant. Union Clubs existed at St. Louis in January 1861 and formed in Kentucky, Maryland and Ohio. More secretive Union Leagues existed across Tennessee, using the trappings of secret societies at the time because it was a Southern state.

The New York League mailed a confidential "call" to a select group of New Yorkers to build up a group of rich young men. No one seems to know who drew up the list and mailed out the call. Into their membership came Parke Godwin, George Bancroft, Horace Greeley, George Gibbs (a former student at Round Hill), Franklin Delano (the granduncle of Franklin Delano Roosevelt) and Richard M. Hunt, the architect of the building on the Yale campus for Scroll and Key, the sister organization to Skull and Bones.

The New York League's membership was selective; one could not just ask to join and pay dues. You had to be vetted and some very notable men could not join, including Theodore Roosevelt until many years after he applied. J. P. Morgan and John D. Rockefeller were not denied.

One of their renowned members was Thomas Nast, the political cartoonist that history credits with bringing down Tammany Hall. While Nast's campaign against Tammany led to a diminishing of Tammany's power, the organization did not dissolve until well into the middle of the 20th century, contrary to the idea portrayed by the stories of the era.

The Union League repudiated Lincoln's soft peace platform, joined the Radicals in demanding that Rebel property be confiscated, and proposed that the conquered South be considered a prize of war.

This should not be surprising when you consider Joshua K. Ingalls of the National Reform Association and Brotherhood of the Union, who said years later that the Brotherhood "was absorbed during the war by the Union League." This was true perhaps for the moment and in certain locales, but the Brotherhood continued on for several years. What really happened was that they had interlocking membership.

In addition to those mentioned above, the New York Union League and Loyal League attracted other men whose politics fit the Illuminist goals: Peter Cooper, Friedrich Kapp, William Oland Bourne, and Robert M. Poer. It was not unusual for Sen. John Parker Hale to be in attendance at their functions.

Some years before, Sen. Hale was feted at a banquet in his honor by the Free Democratic League. He had no problem with the platform being decorated with the "French Red Republican flag" of the Union Socialiste along with the American flag. The red flag bore a triangle inscribed "Union Socialiste" around which was placed "Liberté, Egalité, Fraternité."

The Free Democrats included feminist Antoinette Brown, Frederick Douglass, and radical Democrat Sanford E. Church. Sen. Henry Wilson attended their functions, and the group contained members of the Brotherhood of the Union.

Union Leagues still exist in New York, Philadelphia, and Chicago, projecting a more liberal elitism. The New York unit founded the Metropolitan Museum of Art and built the pedestal of the Statue of Liberty and Grant's Tomb. The pedestal was designed by the same architect who designed the Scroll and Key Building at Yale, Richard Morris Hunt, who for a time worked with Olmsted on Central Park.

The Union Leagues had their roots in the Wide Awake movement and the Democrats looked upon them as the modern Jacobins, with Francis Lieber writing pamphlets for the N.Y. Union League.

Born in Berlin, Germany, Lieber had a heavy influence on Lincoln. He was arrested in Berlin as a "liberal" and then persecuted in Jena as a member of the Turnverein, specifically the Turnerschaft. In other words, he was active in the second-generation organizations of the Illuminati.

He became a confidant of Charles Follen, nee Karl Follen. He took part in the Greek revolution and returned home, but was again imprisoned. He fled to England, and then to the U.S. in 1827. He was active in academic circles, teaching at a number of colleges and tutoring.

He wrote the first systematic treatise on political science that appeared in the U.S. It was a more scientific method and was a decided reaction against individualism. This, along with German immigrants and others, inserted a nationalistic and Teutonic missionary aspect into American political thought.

At an inaugural address as a professor at Columbia, he delivered the speech "Individualism; and Socialism, or Communism." He was the professor of history and political science and always had nationalism undergird his philosophy. He was adept at ingratiating himself into any company. After the war he identified with the radical Republicans.

Lieber set the standards for the code of warfare, starting with the Lieber Code, written at Lincoln's request, which set the model for the Union Army in occupied areas, leading ultimately to the Geneva Convention. While the code was written and issued, it was not always followed; however, it served as a cover for the government when accused of cruel and corrupt use of the troops in occupied territory. In other words, there may have been problems by overzealous commanders but they were not in step with the code issued by the federal government, as they looked the other way.

In 1865, Lieber was appointed superintendent of the bureau in Washington for the collection, arrangement, and preservation of the records of the Confederate government. It reminds one of the employment that the character Winston had in the novel *1984*, where certain information detrimental to the Inner Party would go down the memory hole. It is anyone's guess how much of the archives was preserved for posterity and how many papers were destroyed that could have been embarrassing to the Washington government or American revolutionaries. *To the victor go the myths and monuments*.

Many of the papers held by Southerners which would have revealed the Conspiracy, both in the South and the North, were destroyed or simply disappeared through a variety of circumstances, particularly those which contained information on the organization led by the Confederate Secret Service that had the mission of attempting to capture and/or assassinate key Northern leaders, including Lincoln.

Many of the Confederate records went with the generals who left the country for parts of Brazil and other Latin American destinations.

The literature that was disseminated by the Union Leagues generally told stories of "Southern outrages," to rile people up and recruit them into helping the Union Leagues and their political agenda. The New York League disseminated 70,000 such tracts. The club of Philadelphia bested that, and over an eight year span circulated 4,500,000 pamphlets with 144 different titles.

While much of this propaganda was used to support the war and the radical agenda after the war, it was also used to defame those who opposed the war. In the case of Clement Vallandigham, the League disseminated lies about the congressman's involvement in acts of terror and treason to lay down the base of support for his deportation from the country.

Not to be outdone by the masculine leagues, a women's National Loyal League was formed in New York in 1863 by Elizabeth Stanton, Susan B. Anthony, Martha Coffin Wright, Amy Post, Lucy Stone, Angelina Grimke Weld, et al. In addition to supporting the Union, they worked for an amendment to abolish slavery.

The Union Leagues, as they started to recruit Negroes into membership in the South, soon altered their neo-social aspects to become secret lodges with elaborate and outrageous ceremonies, oaths, pledges, passwords, etc. There was an initiation with an altar that contained a Bible, an American flag, a small anvil, and a shuttle or sickle — emblems of industry.

They cooperated with the Freedman Aid Societies, the Department of Negro Affairs and finally the Freedmen's Bureau to win votes for the Republicans. The methods used were no different than today, using a combination of welfare and government authority. History has proven over and over again that a large number of people will vote for what they perceive as a free lunch. Gradually, the Leagues became more of a Negro organization in the South.

In New Orleans, the first attempt to work with the Negro citizens by the government was assisted by Thomas J. Durant and Paschal B. Randolph, the Rosicrucian leader. There is no doubt that well-meaning people were involved, but the history of such initiatives included many socialists and secret society leaders attempting to radicalize as many freedmen as possible.

In Indiana, Gov. Oliver P. Morton took steps during the war to organize Union Leagues into military companies. He supplied Leagues that had organized "legions" with arms from the state armory. This was done to offset the KGC and similar groups in Indiana.

The Union Leagues gave rise to the war party that nominated Fremont for president in 1864, the Radical Republicans, and later supported the impeachment of Johnson. In 1881, the first member of the Union League became president, Chester A. Arthur. His father was a close friend of Gerrit Smith, and Chester was an active abolitionist as well. He was immediately involved in the Republican Party, campaigning for Fremont in 1856. The next member elected was Theodore Roosevelt.

The Union Leagues spread rapidly and for two years controlled the political situation in almost all Southern states, until supplanted by the largely Negro militia.

Near the close of the war, the Freedmen's Bureau was established as a branch of the War Department, with the communist Robert Dale Owen as secretary and de facto executive officer. This came about as a result of Stanton naming him to the original Inquiry Commission of the Bureau.

There were a large number of Northern ministers who were employed by the Freedmen's Bureau, who in many instances took over the property of Southern churches, especially those of the Methodist and Baptist persuasions.

These churches were then used to liberalize the Christian population. Even today, the Southern Baptists have a conservative reputation but from time to time employ ministers who got their start in the Left.

One current leader is a member of the Council on Foreign Relations. Recently, certain of their leadership started to move their membership toward a more liberal view of homosexuality.

While the Union Leagues were initially composed of whites, the Negroes' counterpart was the Freedmen's Bureau. It exercised a strong hand in economic and social affairs in the South and dabbled in politics, but was not as successful as the Union League. The superintendent of the freedmen schools was John Watson Alvord, who was a trustee of the Freedman's Savings and Trust Company. He had been an agent for the Anti-Slavery Society under Garrison in the 1830s.

President Johnson vetoed the new Freedmen's Bureau Bill that financed the organization and placed freedmen into positions of responsibility in the South, but his veto was overridden.

There was also the Freedman's Relief Association. Though it was supposedly to help the freed slaves, it had an agenda that was different than most realized, since the president of the organization was Francis George Shaw, who was a Garrisonian abolitionist and who served for a time as treasurer of the American Union of Associations, the group which produced nearly 50 communist communes across the U.S.

It becomes obvious by the appointment of such men as Owen, Alvord, and Shaw that the intent of the Freedman organizations was more than helping the freed slaves of the South. It was ACORN in spades, not simply an indirect attempt at organizing communities into socialist voting blocs as in the 1990s, but a direct, government program to build socialism in the South.[63]

The Union League of New York came about primarily due to those who were also involved in the leadership of the U.S. Sanitary Commission, which was founded to provide medical and charitable aid to the Union Army and elements of the civilian population. It was to be the forerunner of socialized medicine.

The New York organization was involved in raising money for the commission and Clara Barton's Red Cross.

The commission's executive secretary was Frederick Law Olmsted, graduate of Yale, engineer, and architect. For a brief time during the war, he was its president. It was he who supervised the construction of Central Park in New York. He was prominent in the arts in New York and served as the head of the Department of Public Parks there in 1872. He became a leading expert on parks in general and also designed the grounds of the U.S. Capitol. He had ties to Greeley and was a Fourierist. While on a visit to Europe, he visited with Karl Marx in his home in London.

The Sanitary Commission had as an overriding purpose to bring about nationalistic feelings, and through those a national, as opposed to a federal, government. The Union League's goals were similar: To promote national devotion as opposed to a state or region; To strengthen the love and respect of the Union; To discourage whatever tends to give undue prominence to local interests; To urge upon public attention schemes of national advancement.

The Sanitary Commission's chief promoter and first president was Henry Whitney Bellows, who was a Unitarian minister of the Emerson school. He wanted a hard reconstruction of the South. On the Easter Sunday after the assassination of Lincoln, he called for vengeance, not leniency, toward the South and said that Lincoln was taken by God, his work over, like Christ.

A later president of the New York Union League was Chauncey Mitchell Depew, member of the Order and prominent New York politician. He canvassed the state for Fremont in 1856 and Lincoln in 1860,

---

63 ACORN was a community action organization designed to enlist votes and activities for ultra-liberal causes, and was largely financed by government grants. Several units and workers for ACORN were charged with voter fraud in their registration drives. By and large, ACORN, under that name, ceased to exist after massive public exposure in the 2010s, but the personnel connected to it continued on under different names and façades.

became prominent in the railroad business by managing Cornelius Vanderbilt's interests, and was an orator at the unveiling of the Statue of Liberty.

He was not the only member of the Order involved. Charles Janeway Stille was on the executive committee of the Sanitary Commission during the war.

The Union Leagues in many ways had the political outlook of the Young Americans, but without the overt radical bent toward socialism. However, they tended toward government solutions to problems and their members certainly contained socialist leaders. They became cheerleaders for American interventionism around the globe, particularly during the Spanish American War.

We hope that by now the reader understands that one does not have to actually be a member of a communist or socialist party to actively work for the goals of what we call communism.

In fact, too many people think that communism is a violent movement. In reality, it only becomes violent within the general population when enough power is accumulated, either by the size and influence of its members and/or when it gains sufficient control of or influence in government. It may participate in occasional terrorist acts, but not widespread terrorism until the above conditions are met, enabling them to create a reaction in the population and take advantage of that reaction with the growth of government.

This fact is not understood among Americans today, who as a result react to such acts of terrorism as beheadings in exactly the manner those who control the "beheaders" want them to. Too often the media say that these terrorists did not understand the reaction that the beheadings would produce in the American people — wanting to bomb terrorists and send in the troops. Those behind the terrorism do understand. The reaction always leads to a situation that furthers the involvement of the United States in schemes leading to the New World Order, something taking the shape of military coalitions, which expand into permanent foreign entanglements.[64]

Do the bombing and war by NATO kill the terrorists and result in collateral damage? Of course, but then the terrorists are only ignorant minions. As we stated earlier, the leaders of the Carbonari laughed at their underlings because they were willing to die for the plans of the leadership. We are sure that the terrorist leaders do as well.

After all, does anyone see the terrorist leaders strapping explosives to their chests? It is the dummies at the bottom of the scale that do that.

On the other side of the ledger, does anyone believe that *everyone* in the American government respects the people they supposedly serve?

Only by understanding the entire agenda of the Illuminist initiatives can one begin to get his head around how a diversity of organizations and personages, seemingly unrelated, can move irrepressibly toward a common yet hidden goal. Also, only by looking at the *interlocking* personnel can one begin to get an idea of the depth of coordination between seemingly unrelated issues and groups and how they tie together into this common purpose.

The only way to defeat such a force is to form a large enough organization with leadership that understands the above and aims its agenda at the defeat of strategic pieces of the evil agenda in order to crack its foundation — and to be organized in such a fashion to move its members at the same time in the same

---

64 Beheadings of people by so-called Muslims is not new. The communist revolutionaries in Algeria in the 1950s posed as Muslims, and the minions at the bottom were Muslims. But the leaders were communists, just as the leaders of modern Iran after the Shah were trained communists calling themselves Islamic clerics. The communists used the terror tactic of beheadings on a large scale to intimidate the Muslim population in French Algeria to side with the revolution against France. It led to the installation of the communist Ben Bella as the leader of Algeria. The reader is invited to search the web for communism in Muslim countries, then expand the search with the information he will find. Extend the lines to the eventual outcome if they should succeed in continuing to fool the American people about "Muslim terrorism."

direction under local, full-time staff leadership. The organization also needs to expose the interlocking leadership of the seemingly divergent groups — in other words, expose the people involved, as only by exposing the people involved will the entire scheme be thwarted. Without such exposure, the same people will keep coming back again and again.

The Illuminist agenda is a mosaic, composed of many issues that of necessity must move concurrently. If you aim at the key issues — those which the rest of the agenda *must* depend on — and defeat them at that level, you stifle the progress of the overall agenda. Plus, if you expose their personnel, they tend to be less aggressive. They may squeal and rail against those that expose them, but exposure makes them paranoid and more cautious, slowing down their activities if nothing else.

In the process of exposing them, you will be called "conspiracy theorists," paranoid, fear mongers, and worse by those in their sphere. It is always wise to note who uses these terms.

Had you known in your education about the people presented so far and their motivation, your study of history would have been far different, as would your understanding of the direction our country has taken over the past two centuries.

After the war, in the midst of the deterioration of public morality that always happens due to a long war, there was a proliferation of organizations that openly challenged Christianity and traditional religion. The net effect of such organizations helped delay the recovery that would have taken place by the Christian community in pulling things back together.

Spiritualism After the War

After the war, the spiritualist leaders formed the American Association of Spiritualists in 1868. In 1871, they elected the communist leader Victoria Woodhull its president. While the membership numbers are not known, it is estimated that they had a first-level influence on at least 600,000 people through their meeting places and nearly 30 periodicals.

They also engaged in education by opening a large number of Children's Progressive Lyceums. The association officially engaged in women's suffrage, world peace, temperance, and industrial education.

Many volumes on spiritualism document certain aspects of the movement but pointedly leave out others. This leads a researcher to believe that the omission or revision of facts by the use of semantics on the scale it has been done has to be deliberate to hide facts that would reveal what was happening then, and what is really going on today.

For instance, one volume on the history of American spiritualism states that Warren Chase was a leader in the movement, but refers to his involvement in the communist commune in Ripon as participating in a "communitarian" experiment. Likewise, there is no reference to Victoria Woodhull as the head of the American Association of Spiritualists — not even the organization — only listing the National Association of Spiritualists that was formed later in the 1890s. Mentioning Woodhull would have shown the communist influence in the entire movement. So by only reading this particular book, one would not have a true perspective on what the spiritualist movement was all about. They engaged in the two-pronged goal of the Illuminati: world government and getting rid of God.

The same problem of research exists on the Internet concerning the spiritualist organizations just after the Civil War. The record is nearly wiped clean relative to communist involvement in spiritualism.

Those who get involved in spiritualism usually get immersed in the socialist/communist agenda, whether they realize it or not at first. In the 1960s, the Seattle office of the Communist Party's *People's World* newspaper was right next door to the office of the spiritualists in an old multi-story office building.

The spiritualist office did not have a sign on the door, only a blank frosted door window. The communists did have a sign. Coincidences of this nature abound, and the experienced researcher into communism can readily see that communism is promoted just as much in spiritualist bookstores as spiritualism — only under a different label.

The audacity of the writings of spiritualists would astound modern eyes. In 1875 Samuel Watson started the *American Spiritual Magazine* which included the stories of mediums who were able to conjure up the likes of George and Martha Washington. This publication lives on today in one's ability to buy it in book form online.

Gradually, the movement flourished and then morphed into several subcultures, including Satanism, Swedenborgianism, the theosophical movement, and what would be known today as the New Age movement. These various movements are today more widespread than the average American realizes, and he sees their symbols and logos in public often without realizing what they are or their significance.

The Free Religious Association (FRA) was established in Boston in 1867 by Robert Dale Owen, Francis E. Abbot, Rev. Cyrus Augustus Bartol, Rev. Octavius Brooks Frothingham (their first president) and other atheists. Their journal was *The Index,* published in Boston. It combined Theodore Parker's religious philosophy with social Darwinism. Parker felt that God would create a soul larger and greater than Jesus. Frothingham represented the radical wing of the Unitarian Church and was a leader in the movement to inject rationalist ideas in theology and he rejected any church. He was for a time the art critic for the *New York Tribune.*

When Thomas Paine died, Frothingham eulogized him. He wrote of the downfall of Christianity, but it may take 1,000 years for anyone to notice. Rev. John W. Chadwick, another Unitarian, also eulogized Paine.

Let us interject something we hope the reader is noticing: the anti-God movement has often been promoted by so-called Christian ministers, men who had an agenda and wormed their way into the Christian world to subvert it. With the clear examples we have documented throughout this book, why is it so hard to believe that so-called conservatives who are on the other side have wormed their way into the respect of innocent conservatives?

The FRA came out of the National Conference of Unitarian Churches after they objected to Christian language in the statement of principles. They were the most radical of the Unitarians. Although the Unitarian leadership agreed with Parker, and while the FRA agreed with almost all of what the Unitarians were doing, the FRA members were "purist" in their disbelief. This is yet another example of people not getting along and forming new radical groups, with the benefit of making another organization look moderate. For many years, the Unitarian organization tried to woo them back as part of the parent movement.

Key members of the FRA not mentioned above were Lydia Maria Child, Thomas W. Higginson, David Wasson, John Weiss, Ralph Waldo Emerson, and Amos B. Alcott.

The same year, 1867, the Radical Club was formed. This was an initiative to continue to influence the arts and letters, publishing, etc., similar to the German Union and was an outgrowth of the Free Religious Association. It started in the home of Rev. and Mrs. John T. Sargent and included Emerson, Higginson, Frothingham, Phillips, Longfellow O. W. Holmes, Julia Ward Howe, Henry James, Rev. W. H. Channing, Rev. Dr. Hedge, Rev. Dr. Bartol, Bronson Alcott, Elizabeth Peabody, James Freeman Clarke, Louisa Chandler Moulton of *The New York Tribune*, and John Weiss.

Weiss believed in rationalism and was a Unitarian clergyman, an abolitionist, and a Transcendentalist. Emerson withdrew when the discussion of the club became public. Too much exposure hurts conspiracy. Their first meeting hosted 30 people, their last 200, twenty or so years later. It was the core of the

Transcendentalist movement prominent before the war. Contributors to the club attempted to set the tone for all manner of issues, such as education, science, literature, and so forth. Carl Schurz was known to attend its functions. Toward the end, as members got older and left this Earth, the group would host memorial meetings for their departed, such as Charles Sumner.

When the communist Sumner died, his Senate seat was filled by the legislature with William B. Washburn, a member of the Order.

While their meetings may seem small, it was their influence in the arts that counted, especially when coordinated into a single idea which they promoted. They were all leaders in their own right, and this extended their influence far beyond their numbers. Working in concert they had a great and lasting influence on the humanities, particularly when there was no counterpart working to offset their influence.

The Theosophical Society was formed in New York in 1875. The famous Annie Besant became part of this organization. She became increasingly radical in her socialism as she grew older. Part of their aim was a Universal Brotherhood, or new world order. The society was founded by Helena Blavatsky, the Satanist; Henry Steel Olcott; William Quan Judge; and over a dozen more. Its influence went far beyond its numbers as well. It has established organizations around the world and gone through a number of schisms. It was a guiding force behind what became the Indian National Congress that has ruled India off and on for decades.

In 1876, the American Secular Union and Freethought Federation was formed. Its purpose was to eliminate Christianity from the United States, eliminate Bible reading in the schools, abolish judicial oaths, and just about anything you can imagine eliminating Christianity from public life and view. Its leading light was Robert Green Ingersoll, abolitionist and promoter of Charles Darwin. Ingersoll's friendships, extended from Walt Whitman to Andrew Carnegie and to Mark Twain.

By the 21st century, many of these organizations' goals had been reached. In 2010, the Secular Student Alliance had 200 college campus chapters and 50 high school chapters, with a growing push to form more at the preparatory level. They were organized to spread atheism and organize activities on campus, such as celebrating Darwin's birthday. The organization projects an image of youth, but the leaders are white-headed old "secular" activists.

Keep in mind that each campus unit has to have a faculty advisor. These advisors are what drive the agenda and keep the organization alive year after year, since the students leave and something or someone has to be the catalyst for their longevity. Now, extrapolate this atheism into the "normal" teaching by these advisors in their classes, expand this across several campus organizations, and you get an idea of the problem with education today.

No student organization can exist for long without faculty leadership to give it impetus year after year. After all, the student leadership graduates and moves on.

The Society of Ethical Culture, under Dr. Karl Adler, was also formed in 1876, in New York. It was a "church" for freethinkers and non-Christians. Dr. Adler delivered one of the eulogies at Carl Schurz' funeral.

There was an American committee that wanted to revise the New Testament and circulate a weaker version of the Scripture. One of the members was Ezra Abbot, professor of New Testament criticism and interpretation at Harvard Divinity and a Unitarian.

The year 1876 was a busy one for forming new atheistic organizations. The National Liberal League was founded by Frances E. Abbott of the Free Religious Association, T. B. Wakeman, and Elizur Wright, who were the key luminaries. Abbott would eventually commit suicide after coming to the idea that Christianity based on Christ was no longer tenable.

Wright had co-founded the American Anti-Slavery Society in 1833 and was its national secretary. He began as a Congregationalist and evolved into atheism. The surface agenda isn't always the true agenda.

Perhaps the best known of the National Liberal League founders to modern Americans was the vice president, Robert Green Ingersoll. Known for his militant atheism, he was forced to resign but came back as its president after they renamed the league the American Secular Union.

The league had several chapters all over the Midwest and back into New York. It was not unusual for the leaders to be former clergy.

Ingersoll in the late 1870s offered an award of $1,000 in gold for anyone who could prove that Thomas Paine recanted his rejection of Christ, since the rumor was that he had. He published a long list of individuals who saw Paine in the last fortnight of his life who apparently discussed the issue with Paine and said that he had not. If true, it is strange that so many would have brought up the issue at Paine's bedside. Some were clergy, some friends, some neighbors.

It is also strange that someone was taking notes as to who visited Paine the last days of his life.

Ingersoll offered the same reward regarding Voltaire, but had no documentation of the last days of Voltaire.

The spiritualist D. M. Bennett established *The Truth Seeker*, which by the late 1870s had 50,000 subscribers. The publication continues today.

As we have said, the reader must now realize that much of the activity of with early Illuminism and communism involved elements of the clergy. This remains a serious problem in modern America, particularly in the area of community activism that leads innocent citizens into programs that promote socialism, especially in the areas of helping the poor, promoting peace, and enlisting more and more people into government programs. These start in the liberal and social gospel churches.

The media plays a role in this since they give publicity to and elevate the more liberal of the clergy, and rarely give any notice to traditional Christian or Jewish leaders on a national scale unless to channel the religious into false solutions led by seemingly conservative religious leaders. It would take another book to document the "ex" communists of the 1960s and 1970s who are religious leaders today promoted by *Time* and other mainstream media.

Politics as Usual

Gen. Ulysses S. Grant became president in 1869. His secretary of war was Alphonso Taft, co-founder of the Order, who also served as attorney general.

Grant's administration was a combination of heavy-handedness and corruption, receiving less and less support among the people.

As a result, a new party was formed within Republicanism — the Liberal Republican Party — which nominated Horace Greeley for the presidency in 1872. Carl Schurz was the primary manipulator in Greeley's nomination. The Party's main platform was to defeat Grant and support civil service reform, but it made the Grant administration look moderate by comparison.

The main figures within the Liberal Republican Party were Greeley, Schurz, Charles Sumner, W. C. Bryant, Charles Francis Adams, and, interestingly, Vallandigham, who during the war was supposedly the enemy of these gentlemen as one of the leading Copperheads in the North. Vallandigham died shortly after the party's formation. Former Grant Cabinet officers Ebenezer Hoar and Jacob Cox were involved as well.

Charles Francis Adams served as our ambassador to England and it was he who, at Lincoln's request and in his name, wrote to Karl Marx thanking him for his and the IWA's support during the Civil War.

At this time the radical element had working control over all political parties. The Radicals still had effective control over the Republicans, while the Liberal Republicans and the Democrats nominated an open socialist as their candidate. There was something for everyone, but it was all controlled at the top. No matter whom you chose, you lost. The situation has not changed in the last 150 years.

While there was great concern over Grant's presidency, the net result of the parties opposing Grant was to split the votes in such a manner as to re-elect him. This is a common tactic played out not only nationally, but quite frequently in state races, particularly for Congress.

Today, if a liberal Republican runs for re-election and is in trouble, suddenly four or five conservative candidates come along to split the vote sufficiently to get the liberal through the primary. This happens so frequently that it cannot be an accident.

Vote splitting has long been a tactic used by the Conspiracy to get their men through the elective process. The close observer will see that some of these conservatives simply appear out of the blue, with no real backing or experience. Some are completely unknown among conservative activists — no one has ever heard of them. The tactic works well also if there is no serving Republican, and it is obvious that the voters will no longer abide an obviously liberal Democrat incumbent. The "right" Republican must be elected, and splitting the ticket will be engineered.

This author has *often* seen individuals appear out of the blue calling themselves conservatives and running in primaries to split the vote. Once the election is over, they disappear once again from public view, never working to solve the problems they supposedly wanted to solve by running for office. In some cases, in order to re-elect the incumbent Democrat, the primary winner has then to run a very poor campaign and be defeated. They too then disappear from the limelight.

The lesson for activists is: Never support leadership you do not know that has not been tested.

In Grant's first year in office he nominated Stanton to the Supreme Court, but Stanton died four days after his confirmation by the Senate, before he could take the oath of office.

Earlier in the year, the National Labor Union (NLU) split off a short-lived political party called the National Labor Reform Party. Its policies were in general militant and pro-Marxist. The NLU's leading lights were William Sylvis, a member of the First International, and Andrew Cameron of the Chicago *Workingman's Advocate*. Cameron was sent to the First International as the U.S. delegate in 1868. However, even with the very close linkage to the International, both organizationally and with those involved, the NLU never officially joined with it.

The NLU had delegates from over sixty organizations at its founding convention and served as a cover for the other political parties' radicalism by being even more radical.

Sylvis had been a leader in the formation of the Iron Molder Union, which the members tried to make into a secret society. Sylvis stopped that; it cost him the presidency at the time and instead he was made the treasurer. During the war he finally was elected president of this 3,500-member union.

There had been some early success at the local level for the movement, including running Wendell Phillips as a candidate for governor in Massachusetts. Benjamin Butler was also associated with the NLU. The NLU promoted the idea of inflation as a remedy for the plight of the farmer since the farmer had to sell his produce at low prices.

It was not unusual for political movements after the war to push for inflation. Since the people were kept ignorant of what it produced in the long run, they saw it as a remedy for bad times. The communist leaders, however, knew what the results would be and how it would destabilize the economy so they could take advantage of the ensuing problems by enlisting more people into their movement.

The Reform Party nominated David Davis as its candidate for the presidency. Davis had been one of the three campaign managers for Lincoln's election at the Republican Party convention in 1860. He was appointed to the Supreme Court by Lincoln. When he could not secure the nomination of the Liberal Republican Party after being nominated by the Reformers, he withdrew in favor of Greeley. Davis was an ancestor of George Bush.

The party, like the NLU, was for the abolition of the national banking system, for federal authority over interest rates, and for the conversion of government bonds to Greenbacks, placing the economic system into the hands of the state, all in the name of fighting the bankers. Government bonds had been issued during the Civil War to raise money for the conflict. Some of these bonds, but not all, specified repayment in gold. This is why the party wanted conversion into Greenbacks, to prevent the payment in gold.

There was no grassroots organization of any strength in opposition to either the position of the NLU or the retention of the national banking system. The choice was one or the other — you lose.

The parent NLU was upset by Davis' nomination and called on Charles O'Connor, a former Tammany Democrat from New York, to be their candidate, and that caused the collapse of the entire party.

When William Sylvis was elected as president of the National Labor Union, it represented at least 43 local trade unions and several other labor initiatives. At the time Sylvis was active in the communist First International and wanted to move the NLU into becoming a political party. In 1990, the State of Pennsylvania honored him with an historical marker at Indiana University of Pennsylvania at Indiana, Pennsylvania.

By 1873, the NLU dissolved into the Knights of Labor. The Knights of Labor was formed in 1869 by Uriah S. Stephens in Philadelphia as a secret order. Their symbol was an equilateral triangle within a circle.

They were prominent in the violence in the 1870s that was spawned by organized labor. One of the men who became quite notable within the organization was Theodore Frederick Cumo. He was active in the First International with Marx and Engels, and had been exiled from Saxony, Austria, Italy, Belgium, *and* Spain for his communist activities. He was welcomed into the United States with open arms in 1872 when he became involved as a journalist.

In his recollections, he recalled marching in May Day celebrations in Europe singing *La Marseillaise*. In the United States, he remembered the first May Day celebration under the auspices of the New York Central Labor Union and the Knights of Labor, when 50,000 people marched in the streets.

Within a few years, the International Labor Union was formed by the likes of Sorgé and others who were either internationalists or land reformers at a minimum — communist, or willing to work with communists. Abolitionists such as Garrison, Phillips, Gerrit Smith, Sumner, and Karl Heinzen joined the Eight-hour day movement, which was a major issue within the ILU. They were joined by leaders who promoted spiritualism. It was a petri dish of nearly all the radical movements of the day.

Reconstruction Wanes

The election between Republican Rutherford Hayes and Democrat Samuel Tilden closed the chapter on Reconstruction. It was a hotly contested affair. It finally ended up in the hands of an electoral commission that was composed of 15 members: five from the House of Representatives, five from the Senate, and five from the Supreme Court. It would have split at seven each for the Republicans and Democrats, with the more independent David Davis on the court as the man who would break any tie. At least that was the thought.

Davis had become known as a moderate in his decisions on the court. The Democrats felt that he was a man who could see that Tilden was elected, and as a result they voted for him in the Illinois State Legislature, appointing him to the U.S. Senate to attempt to sway his vote on the electoral commission. Davis, however, immediately resigned from the court to take his seat in the Senate, which meant that the weight on the commission went to the Republicans.

One of the chief investigators for the election to decide who had won was Francis Channing Barlow, who received a great deal of his childhood education at Brook Farm. At the beginning of the Civil War, he was an attorney for the *New York Tribune* under Greeley. He would become one of the founders of the American Bar Association. The main founder of the ABA was Simeon Eren Baldwin, the Order, who became governor of Connecticut.

Hayes won by one electoral vote. No one seems to know who actually won the election — not then, not now. The voting was too full of fraud to be certain. There seemed little question that Tilden received the majority of the popular vote, but it was the electoral votes that counted.

But a deal had been made in the process to stop Reconstruction and withdraw all federal troops from the South, and Alphonso Taft, as attorney general, engineered the backroom deal that gave the election to Hayes.

Carl Schurz became secretary of the interior under Hayes, and was part of the inner circle with more influence than other members of the Cabinet. It was under Schurz that the reservation program became the means to make the American Indian dependent on the state and instigated the low manner of totally dependent living for the Indian population for many decades.

The final degradation of the Indian was accomplished by benevolence rather than force, although the relocation of the Nez Perce under Chief Joseph and the Northern Cheyenne was anything but a happy time for these tribes. The Indian becoming a ward of the state should serve as an example to all of the danger of anyone coming under a government welfare system.

What the Indians became for a century — before they started to break out of it — was the result of reservation socialism. In many cases life became easier materially, but it robbed them of their soul. No responsibility always has a debilitating effect on people. There were exceptions, of course, with most of these exceptions usually having occurred off reservation. This author's family was one such case.

As secretary of the interior, Schurz had Hayes appoint Frederick Douglass as marshal of Washington, D.C. By 1881, Schurz was the editor of the *New York Evening Post* with E. L. Godwin under the ownership of Henry Villard, a German who changed his name and married the daughter of William L. Garrison. Two of Villard's uncles were leaders in the German revolution of 1848. After Reconstruction, in the mid-1880s, he returned to Germany, and then returned to the U.S. as an agent of the Deutsche Bank.

Villard serves as another example of the radical-turned-capitalist who then constantly hired socialists. He was a friend of Lincoln. His son, Oswald Garrison Villard, purchased the left leaning magazine *The Nation* and served as its editor until 1933. With the communist W.E.B. DuBois and others, he was a founder of the NAACP.

Over the years, Schurz worked with men who would go on to have great influence on the promotion of communism, such as Andrew Carnegie and Jacob Schiff. Carnegie in later years would buy no fewer than 18 British newspapers and run them in the interest of the radicals in England, according to *Appleton's Cyclopaedia of American Biography* published in 1886. Schiff would later give millions for the Bolshevik revolution in Russia — billions in today's money.

Schurz was active in the National Civil Service Reform League, becoming its president by 1893. The league played a major role in codifying civil service. Teddy Roosevelt was a member of the league. After being the Republican president, he became openly a Progressive, the moniker used by the more establishment-based socialists. His speeches became more and more openly socialist without ever using the term. He too believed in American empire building. In reality, his policies were nothing more than the complete Young America agenda refined.

Most Americans think that the party Roosevelt ran on in 1912 was the Bull Moose Party, but that was only its nickname. The party's real name was the Progressive Party, and it temporarily divided the Republican Party. The split of the socialists in the GOP into the Progressive Party made the remainder of the Republican Party look conservative in comparison. The Republicans were thought to represent the conservatives thereafter, even though they regularly nominated liberals for president (except for Harding and Coolidge).

The Republican Party never fared well in the South — it was nearly non-existent — until the 1960s due to the dislike of the radicals before, during, and after the Civil War. This Solid South was then used to build socialism within the Democrat Party by supporting far too much of what that party desired, because they literally hated the Republicans due to the Civil War. It took over one hundred years for this to begin to change and allow the election of Republicans in the South.

Nor did the *establishment* of the Republican Party ever move into the conservative or constitutionalist camp. From time to time the rhetoric was conservative if it was needed to keep the rank-and-file Republicans happy, but the control at the top of the party never deviated from its Radical origins. They did become more sophisticated in promoting socialism, however, selling it as either patriotism or compromise.

After the war, the initiatives to take Cuba continued. There were literally a hundred filibuster initiatives and all of them, Cuban — and American — centered, worked for the inclusion of Cuba into the U.S. This continued to be the case until the Spanish-American War, when the policy was abandoned. In its place was substituted a policy of control rather than the more difficult policy of ownership and all that came with it. In poorer countries, this would have meant a drain on America resources rather than an exploitation of certain spheres of the countries.

Control is more important than ownership, and is less of a burden on the controlling entity. And, the owners believe that they possess private property or, in the case of a country, independence.

After World War I, and increasingly under the FDR administration, the foreign entanglements we engaged in started to enmesh America in internationalism (which was finally codified in 1945 with our membership in the United Nations). This served to enhance the anti-Yankee feeling that led to the growth of communism around the world in opposition to American interference and, in many cases, occupation. Modern Americans have no idea of how U.S. interference and military occupation began and how many times American armed forces occupied Latin American countries and others between World Wars I and II.

Since the middle of World War II, we have been engaged in a full-scale campaign to enmesh our people, government, and economy by foreign entanglements into the New World Order. Other than strict constitutionalists, the blame for this is across the entire spectrum of politicians of all political parties.

No one who was not in favor of this initiative has been elected president since the end of World War II. You might mull over the men elected, and if you think that there was an exception, you should look more closely. The beginning of the idea of the North American Union was originally proposed by Ronald Reagan, for instance. During his candidacy in 1979, he proposed the North American Accord, which has proven to have been the first in a series of steps toward the North American Union through the presidencies of those who came after.

The two conditions of control and foreign entanglements led to the growth of the term "Yankee Imperialism" used by communist cadres. These conditions were used again in the Muslim countries in the late 20th and early 21st centuries, and led to an exponential growth of terrorism by communist Muslims in retaliation.[65]

Our foreign policy for years was to send radicals as our agents to other countries. It segued into aligning ourselves with other countries once these countries were themselves under the spell of socialists and/or social reformers. This then would cause the conservative population in these countries to become anti-American.

So in other words, our American foreign policy turned either the liberal or the conservative peoples against us, depending on the situation in the foreign country at the time.

Most conservatives cannot see past the anti-American feelings that spring up in other countries, which in turn create an angry reaction in Americans. Due to the ignorance of the American people as a result of the establishment media, they cannot fathom why anyone should be mad at Americans. These foreigners, at first, were not mad at Americans, they were mad at the American government. Then they got mad at Americans because we did not take care of the problems with our government interfering in other countries' affairs. Americans fail to realize that we can serve as an example without interference in foreign affairs, especially when the affairs are run by American socialists.

The media withholds from Americans the machinations of our own State Department, in league with such organizations as the Council on Foreign Relations, in the internal affairs of other countries, which always leads to the imposition of some form of socialism in those countries, sometimes even radical Islam. This interference is sold as the helpful hand of the American people, when in reality it is the Conspiracy using the name of the American people.

And, to be fair, the involvement of the State Department is couched in the use of front groups indirectly financed by State so that the American people cannot see the involvement. This is what happened in Egypt in 2013 that brought about the election that temporarily propelled the Muslim Brotherhood into power. Three American organizations indirectly funded by the State Department and led by members of the Council on Foreign Relations helped create the conditions for the Muslim Brotherhood to come to power.

Later, once the military threw out President Morsi, a Muslim Brotherhood leader, the leaders of these organizations, such as Sen. John McCain, a longtime member of the CFR, demanded that "democracy" be restored. They never said to restore the Muslim Brotherhood to power, but that would have been the net result.

The reaction among Americans to anti-American feelings in other countries serves the Conspiracy's goal for the foreign policy of America by getting Americans to support the moves of our State Department through emotional involvement, rather than the common sense of our first presidents. It serves as one example of why George Washington and other Founders, even Thomas Jefferson later, warned us against foreign entanglements.

Americans just cannot believe that people in their own government are complicit in building international socialism. They can see the moves toward socialism at home, but are blind to the same condition being implemented overseas.

It is all relatively simple: If the federal government is moving America toward socialism domestically, why would anyone believe that the same people would have a foreign policy of freedom and "democra-

---

65 For a comprehensive but easy-reading background of the dangers of modern foreign entanglements, read *International Merger by Foreign Entanglements*, 2014, by this author, from ShopJBS.org.

cy"? If the federal government is moving to eliminate God from every aspect of public life at home, what makes anyone think that they would be moving to protect Christians and Jews abroad?

During the George W. Bush administration, a photograph was taken in the Oval Office of all the eighteen living secretaries of state and defense. All were members of the Council on Foreign Relations except Bush, whose father had been a director of the CFR. The organization stands for a world government under a state-controlled economy; in a word; socialism. These have been the people in charge of our foreign policy and the troops sent to enforce it.

Let us use an example to bring the idea of intervention home. If I get along with my family, that is well and good. If, however, I hear that over a block or two there is a family that does not get along, is it my job to go over and occupy their house until they agree to stop quarreling? Is it my job to gather the local residents of the homes on that block to meet in the street and hash out a solution to their marital problems and hold them to that settlement by coercion or force?

We all understand these things at a personal level, but cannot seem to understand them on an international scale.

As a free people, we cannot give any more power to the government than what we hold as individuals. If we cannot take from one to give to another, we cannot delegate the power for government to do it either. It is called stealing, no matter what the motivation or high-sounding reason for this "charity."

The same applies to our foreign policy, and our Founders did not believe in going around the world to seek out countries to fight if they did not attack us and our citizens. John Quincy Adams said as secretary of state on July 4, 1821, during a major foreign policy speech, that America was a haven for freedom and an example to the world. Yes, the United States knew there were countries that existed outside of the definition of freedom,

But she does not go abroad, in search of monsters to destroy.

Since World War II, we have fought almost every monster in the world, and engaged in foreign entanglements that have hidden from the American people their detriment to our independence and economy.

The practice of sending the worst sort of political radicals and members of secret societies as our representatives continued after the Civil War. These men represented the U.S. government, but not necessarily the American people. Many examples have already been given but one which was to become an institution in the embassies of Europe was Eugene Schuyler, the Order, who first was consul in Moscow in 1867 and then in charge of several legations until 1884, mostly in Central Europe. Schuyler was a contributor to the magazine *The Nation* most of his life.

The Marxist Louis Blenker was appointed our man in Nantes, France. Alexander Asboth, who had served with Kossuth in 1848, was our man in Argentina and Uruguay, and Daniel Sickles was made our minister to Spain — again a slap in the face of Spain since it was Sickles who was very active in the writing of the Ostend Manifesto, and his involvement with George Sanders and the revolutionaries in England was well known. James Russell Lowell was named our ambassador to the Spanish mission in Madrid by President Hayes, then transferred to the Court of St. James in 1880.

After serving as secretary of war and then attorney general under Grant, co-founder of the Order Alphonso Taft was appointed U.S. minister to Austria and then Russia. He was a candidate for governor of Ohio, but his dissenting opinion on the use of the Bible in schools cost him the nomination in 1875.

Schurz, after supporting a movement to annex Canada to the United States, became active in the anti-imperialism movement, another typical switch. He and other men *who at one time supported U.S. expansion* formed a league funded by Andrew Carnegie against imperialism, another example of controlling both sides of an issue. Schurz grew so close to Carnegie that Carnegie was a pall bearer at Schurz' funeral.

Out of this movement came the modern Carnegie Endowment for International Peace. A comprehensive study of this organization will tell any observer that it has been more of a war organization to promote international socialism than a peace organization — all in the name of the American people and peace. It is your typical elitist organization cooperating with the initiatives and membership of the Council on Foreign Relations.

Schurz became a celebrity in Germany as well as in the United States, visiting with Bismarck at least three times. Schurz' 70th birthday was celebrated in Berlin as well as in New York.

Hayes' secretary of state was William Maxwell Evarts, member of the Order. In 1881, he went to Paris as a delegate from the U.S. to an international monetary conference. They had made the banking system over during the Civil War and had made paper "money" the medium of exchange; it was time to start the steps toward an international system that would have its effect on American banking. These steps would ultimately lead to such entities as the International Monetary Fund and the World Bank.

The American socialist and spiritualist influence on other countries sometimes led to sea changes in those countries. Ralph Waldo Emerson and his brother, William, had an indirect influence throughout the entire liberal party of England, primarily through Unitarian contacts.

Thomas Davidson started a group in England called the Fellowship of the New Life. According to a prominent early member, its foundational beliefs were based on the influence of Henry Thoreau and Ralph Waldo Emerson.

Out of this organization came the Fabian Society and the Labour Party in England. The Fabian Society went on to have a tremendous influence in communizing and socializing governments around the world, including not only Great Britain, but India and Pakistan. Annie Besant was among the leading members of this organization.

Likewise, the Indian National Congress party was founded out of the Theosophical Society founded in America. Indeed, Annie Besant was the head of the Indian organization for several years in the early 20th century.

What we see here is the influence of prominent American spiritualists and socialists on English and Indian politics. These are but the tip of the iceberg. The tables were beginning to turn from English influence on America to American influence on Britain.

The detective agency of Pinkerton became powerful as a result of the war. By 1880, his detective force numbered approximately 30,000 and was larger than the U.S. Army. They became instrumental in breaking up unions. This would seem to be contradictory, unless you are aware of the motivation of producing conditions and crises for more government intervention and control. Then too, not all corporations are equal — some were owned by the socialists who got rich and powerful in the Conspiracy.

It is all well and good for socialist businessmen to support unions until they mess with their own pocketbooks. Unions are for the other guy to lose his business and thereby destroy the socialist's competition.

Socialists always advocate unions until they come to total power, at which time they either bring them under complete government control or suppress them.

Before the Civil War unions and feminism started their rise, but after the war, with the influence of the communist movement, they both became important on the American scene.

The New England "reformers" led by Julia W. Howe, Thomas Higginson, and Henry Ward Beecher formed the American Woman Suffrage Association, with Beecher as president, in 1869. (It is always nice to have a man at the helm of a women's organization, particularly one who has such a propensity for women!) Beecher was a Christian evolutionist who finally said that reading Spencer "made me a citizen of the world." He became a political ally of the socialist Thomas Higginson.

The New York "reformers" formed the National Women Suffrage Association, all staffed by women: Elizabeth Stanton, Susan B. Anthony, and Paula Wright Davis. The association attracted large numbers of revolutionary women, including Mathilde Anneke, the estranged wife of Friederich Anneke, who worked closely with Stanton and Anthony. Stanton was a cousin of Gerrit Smith.

Frau Anneke was not new to the feminist movement. She and her husband were involved in revolutionary newspapers, with her starting *Die Frauen Zeitung*, a feminist newspaper in 1848. The same year she rode with her husband in a revolutionary cavalry brigade in Germany, and after fleeing to Wisconsin she restarted *Die Frauen Zeitung,* which upset many of the German immigrant males. She founded a German-language school in Milwaukee, and in 1869 helped found the Wisconsin Woman Suffrage Association.

One of the publications of the feminist movement was *The Revolution*, with Stanton, Anthony, and Parker Pillsbury as co-editors. *The Revolution* gave good notice of the First International. Stanton and Anthony were very close until the advent of the People's Party, when Stanton helped the communist Victoria Woodhull become the nominee. Anthony at that time split away from Stanton. It had more to do with personalities than politics.

Woodhull would die in 1927 a wealthy widow in England, another communist who seemed to rise higher in economic status than those she professed to want to make equal in an egalitarian society.

Susan B. Anthony is looked upon today by conservative Republicans as a leading light in the feminist movement and most have not looked into her background, or would not recognize the significance of her involvement if they did; if you have read this far you know how much history has been distorted. In the 1850s she managed her family farm, and frequent visitors there were Frederick Douglass, William Garrison, and Wendell Phillips. She was active in the American Anti-Slavery Society. Henry Brewster Stanton converted her to the suffragette movement. When she married Stanton, she had the word "obey" omitted from her marriage ceremony. Some historical biographies state she was never married.

She was also actively involved in the temperance movement, as many of the New England socialists were. On the surface, it looked as if the cause was to ban "liquor" from the public scene. They finally achieved their goal, and the infamous Prohibition period was the result.

At first Anthony was heavily involved in the abolition movement and became prominent in teachers' associations. She once stated,

> Out of the doctrine of original sin grew the crimes and miseries of asceticism, celibacy and witchcraft; women becoming the victim of all these delusions.
> — *2,000 Years of Disbelief: Famous People with the Courage to Doubt*

There are worse quotes regarding Christianity that were spoken by Anthony, so bad in fact that the reader would be hard-pressed to believe them. The above was chosen simply to show her opinion of religion in regard to feminism. There are several books which contain quotes of this nature by Anthony.

She was part of the Free Religious Association, as were Robert Dale Owen and Parker Pillsbury, who worked with Stanton on *The Revolution*. Pillsbury had been an emissary to England for the American Anti-

Slavery Society. Pillsbury was a contributor to the Free Thinker's magazine. The association combined Theodore Parker's religious philosophy with social Darwinism.

One has to wonder why so many Republicans who profess to be conservatives hearken back to Ripon and people such as Anthony in their zeal to look like traditional Americans. While the rank-and-file Republican may plead ignorance, it is doubtful that the leaders do not understand what they are doing. The pro-life movement also embraces the image of Anthony, which may provide a clue as to why they have failed to achieve their goals, especially with the numbers of people that are involved.

The first woman to have her image on an American coin was Susan B. Anthony, on a minted dollar. Now that you know more of her background, you might get a sense that the leadership in Republican circles is not what it seems on the surface.

A subtle result of the temperance movement was that, for the first time, the Constitution was to be used not to control the federal government, but to control individuals and businesses. The political atmosphere of 1912 led to several fundamental changes in our system: the Federal Reserve, the IRS, direct election of U.S. senators — and Prohibition.

Since Prohibition came about by means of a federal amendment and the subsequent regulations, to put teeth into it required *federal* police enforcement as opposed to our traditional local police controlled by local citizens.

Prohibition played a large role in promoting the idea of federal law enforcement as opposed to local and/or state police agencies, and the rise of federal interference into local law enforcement has steadily increased ever since. Hollywood and television played a role in programming Americans into thinking that federal police and marshals were something to be encouraged until about the year 2000, at which time the message became mixed for different audiences.

The War on Terrorism has done this as well. During the so-called Red Scare Era in the early years of the 20th century, when communists were engaged in bomb scares or actually bombing local authorities and buildings, the situation was curtailed without the general violation of the Bill of Rights except in very rare instances. Today, for example in Boston in 2013, curfews are imposed, the Internet closed down, telephone cell towers rendered inoperative, and searches rendered door to door in violation of the Fourth Amendment — all in the name of catching terrorists — and the people applaud.

When will people understand that warrantless searches from house to house will breed more terrorism in angry reaction to them? It does not matter whether it is in a foreign country or your local neighborhood — it builds terrorism, not eliminates it. There will always be an element that will react into violence over time to violations of their liberty — regardless of the reason. This then will lead to more violations, and the process escalates.

The temperance movement started a century before the amendment was passed that started the process of federal law enforcement. The whole idea of federal law over the individual and the imposition of morality at the federal rather than state or local level found fertile ground in temperance.

Temperance was promoted as a Christian movement, but far too many of its leaders were socialists and anti-Christians even while calling themselves Christian, and in general they programmed the movement into what it became. An example was La Roy Sunderland, prominent in both the temperance and anti-slavery movements. He quit as a Methodist minister and opposed Christianity for 40 years before his death in 1885.

In the name of morality, these leaders were successful in propagating the idea that changing the very nature of the Constitution from limiting government to limiting the individual could be a good thing. It took them 120 years to impose Prohibition, and while it was later rescinded, the ideas stuck of interfering in morality and the enforcement of law by the federal government rather than by the local governments and local police.

The founders of the Prohibition Party included Alvan Bovay. He became the first chairman of the Wisconsin Central Committee of the Prohibition Party after serving as a Wisconsin State Assemblyman. He was also a founder of Ripon College.

As his reason for his involvement in Prohibition, Bovay stated that the Republican Party had run its course from its original mission and that it was time to form another party.

The Prohibition Party is the third oldest political party still in existence. It enjoyed widespread support in the early years, but never achieved much political success with candidates running on its ticket. Part of the problem for this party was the lack of support from other organizations for their candidates. This included the Women's Christian Temperance Union, which was run by the lesbian Frances Willard.

In their desire to curtail one error, conservatives promote another when they seek a national solution. If you have a national law, you need a national policing agency to enforce it. In the end you will have a national police force, which will be far worse than the evil intended to be eliminated.

All law is the legislating of morality, but whose morality? Any laws that need to be passed for a social agenda must not go beyond a state law, or the consequences of a national system will give power to people who will misuse it. The communist leaders know that; Christian Republicans do not, and advocate many laws and amendments that would in the long run give inordinate power to Washington, D.C.

In addition, as stated, the Constitution is intended to limit government, not give it more power. Also, the 9th and 10th Amendments specify that all powers not delegated to the federal government by the states are retained by the states or the people. The power to federally regulate morality was not delegated.

Do not misunderstand — public morality and decency are necessary for a free state. But allowing the national government to start down this path will ultimately mean morality is what the national government says it is; if the government itself is not moral, then what? It is best retained at the local or state levels.

Government socialists used Prohibition to initiate far more government controls than simply banning liquor, such as the content and regulation of food items, which they have only expanded on since.

This was done in the name of eliminating alcohol from all items sold over the counter regardless of their use, such as cough medicine, tonics, etc. At first, several manufacturers made a great deal of money selling some product that contained alcohol that could substitute for the products sold in saloons. As a result in some cases, the federal regulations forced manufacturers to use dangerous forms of alcohol as a substitute, which injured many people. Likewise, people started to look to other substitutes for alcohol such as narcotics, tobacco, hashish, and marijuana. These crutches grew into large problems during Prohibition.

Once Prohibition was repealed the problem of dangerous forms of alcohol cleared up, but government intrusion into the regulation of consumables remained — and so did the substitutes for alcohol.

Many issues had as an underlying tenet the abolition of private property. The movements such as suffrage and slavery attacked property by using what seemingly were benevolent causes. The idea was to move the American system a small step away from private property as a right, or as a basis for our republican representation with the requirement of property ownership in order to vote.

Suffrage was a means to codify voting in *persons* rather than *property ownership* which was the original basis for voting. Anti-slavery attacked the idea of property by making the point that man cannot be property, which any responsible person would agree with, but then attacked property ownership in general. The latter led too many people into opposing abolition. If anti-slavery organizations had not been so entrenched in the socialist idea, it is more than likely that abolition would have occurred sooner and without bloodshed.

But then, the whole idea was to change the social order, not to solve the problems within the social order to make it better.

When slavery became an issue, it intensified into a conflict between nationalism and state sovereignty. As it worsened, the compromise theory of divided sovereignty was replaced by extremists pushing the dogma of state sovereignty on one hand and national supremacy on the other.

As mentioned earlier, the Sanitary Commission came on the American scene during the Civil War. Some of the people involved also became involved in the Red Cross. The Red Cross we know today is not the same organization as after the war. There were competing units vying for official recognition by Congress, and thereby the acknowledgement of the International Red Cross in Switzerland.

Clara Barton was the head of the unit that won recognition. She was the daughter of an abolitionist mother and a Universalist Mason father. She wore her father's Masonic badge during the war.

For a time she appeared as a speaker for women's rights with Stanton, Anthony, Stone, and Julie Ward Howe. She had been won to the cause of abolition and women's rights by Frances Gage. Later she devoted herself to the Red Cross almost exclusively, and late in life became interested in spiritualism.

Gage was involved in temperance, abolition, and women's rights. She was a Universalist, but abandoned even this religious view to become something less. A famous quote of hers was: "There came time when Universalists refused to go with me as an abolitionist, an advocate for the rights of women, for earnest temperance pleaders. Then it came to me that Christ's death as an atonement for sinners was not truth, but he had died for what he believed to be truth."

Barton was close to Benjamin Butler and Sen. Henry Wilson, who visited her almost daily when she worked as a clerk in Washington before the war. Wilson was her ally throughout her quest for recognition as the head of the official Red Cross. There were widespread rumors of a sex life with Wilson and others. When Wilson died, she had a nervous breakdown. She went into the sanitarium in Dansville, New York, run by new-age thinker Dr. James Jackson.

When it came to the competition for recognition of her Red Cross, she conducted a smear campaign against all of her competition.

A unit organized under the American Red Cross later served as a cover for American involvement in helping to solidify Lenin's Bolshevik government in Russia.[66]

---

66 A good summary of this affair is contained in the book *The Creature from Jekyll Island*. The only weakness in the narrative is apologetic language for the organization being used. There is ample evidence of the hierarchy of the organization having been controlled by members of the Order.

Johann Pestolazzi. Illuminati whose educational theories came to permeate American education.

Andrew Jackson. President. Conspirator with Aaron Burr. Transferred Second U.S. Bank funds to friends' banks.

Alvan E. Bovay. Young America leader. Associate of Horace Greeley. Founder of the modern Republican Party.

Alan Pinkerton. Detective. Chartist leader in Britain. Worked with John Brown. The force behind the Wide Awake Republicans.

Alfonso Taft, co-founder of Skull and Bones. Secretary of War and Attorney General under President Grant.

DeWitt Clinton. Governor of New York. Member of the Columbian Illuminati.

Susan B. Anthony. Co-editor, The Revolution. Anti-Christian. Worked with the American communist leader Victoria Woodhull.

Frederich Ludwig Jahn. Founder of the Turnverein a key influence on German-American immigrants in the 1850s.

Rev. Thomas Wentworth Higginson. Served as a link between several terrorist, socialist, and atheist organizations.

17

Post Mortem

What we have seen has been the changing of the American representative Republic through reform, subversion, and the major catalysts of war and crises. The primary instrument of the changes has been the progeny or direct lineage of the Illuminati influence through the proliferation of organizations they spawned. The organizations worked together through interlocking leadership.

Whether they still exist as the Illuminati today is open to speculation since no reliable proof one way or the other exists. This was effected by their ability to change their name and image at will, and we have seen that this was a tactic they realized they would need to do early in their formation to hide their organization. Solid evidence did exist into the 1820s, long after the history books say the Illuminati had ceased to function. Circumstantial evidence has never ceased to exist based on the same goals of the succeeding lineage of leadership leading directly back to the Illuminati.

They can never hide their agenda, since in order to fulfill their program much of it has to be out in the open, working throughout the various issues they use to impel the agenda forward. The agenda of the Illuminati still exists, propelled by several movements. It is obvious that a central coordination exists, since there are too many organizations and countries having the same goals and ends, working toward a common purpose, to be functioning independently.

They cannot all arrive at the same place, at the same time, with the same goal in mind for it to be accidental, as Lincoln pointed out with his famous analogy of different people building a house.

Some believe that it is the Socialist International, but we have seen that socialist organizations have only been a part of the total array of groups and individuals at play, including seemingly anti-socialist capitalists.

There has to be some central coordination, since the far-flung aspects that all come together at the same time and place to effect the same outcome indicate this as a reality. And, what comes together remains the goal of the Illuminati: one world government, world court, statism regardless of its label, and the elimination of religion, particularly any based on a Judeo-Christian concept.

Mirabeau called for the conspiratorial organization to dive deep and then resurface later under a new image and a new name if they were exposed.

From Weishaupt and Voltaire, we see the German Illuminist influence on German education, and this pool of educators had a tremendous influence on American students studying abroad, who in turn directly or indirectly influenced other students in America; these this included Everett, Emerson, Bancroft, Mann, and many, many more. In fact, a German education was highly desired if you meant to be at the top of your profession.

Even before this came the French revolutionaries with their Illuminated Jacobin Clubs, forming the Democratic Societies in America that quickly evolved into the Republican-Democrat Party.

The attack on religion came through the Illuminist influence, with the help of Thomas Paine and his cohorts.

German organizations that were a direct result of the Illuminati came to America through Frederich Jahn, Karl Follen, and William Russell — but by no means were they the only people involved.

The communist influence in the United States came from Illuminist influence through Gracchus Babeuf and Nicholas Bonneville, and through individuals such as Joel Barlow, Charles Dana, and many immigrants.

The idea of empire-building came through the leaders of Young America. This influence was likewise part of the effect of the Illuminati through the lineage of the Carbonari.

We have shown that the numbers in leadership did not involve multi-thousands, rather it was an inner core, and that regardless of the organizations they spawned, they tended to be the same people. In other words, the organizational leadership tended to be interlocking, with the same people in leadership over and over again. It remains so today. This was and is the evidence of a coordinated design.

From city to city, state to state, and nationally, any study of the Illuminati goals put forward will show that it is the same people in their community doing so while they try to appear unrelated to one another. If one picks up literature of one organization, then another and another, the same basic core people will appear as officers or sponsors of these organizations. Some local groups will even have the same address as the contact point. It is easier today, however, to hide the latter since the Internet provides the opportunity to look different from website to website — even if these websites are built and operated by the same webmasters. There is also the fact that Illuminist thinking has permeated so much within academic circles that there is not often much need to have organizational control, only intellectual control.

During the period that this writer was involved in investigating Marxist organizations in a major metropolitan area, there was an instance where five organizations, all with the outward appearance of independence, shared the same office and receptionist/secretary. Each had a different P.O. Box and telephone number. They each had an issue they were involved in: peace, civil rights, socialism, schools, etc. They also shared the same basic lists of sponsors, with minor fluctuations, and rotated the leadership in such a manner to make it look as if they were independent and unconnected.

It looked as if one person would be the chairman of this group, another would be president of the other, and so on, revolving the leadership on paper but all having interlocking leadership and membership. The media never seemed to notice — but then some of the media was involved in the process.

They do not always need to have direct control over someone or organization. It can be done by controlling a person's education.

If people are educated to think a certain way, there is no need to have strings attached in order to control what they will do as a result of that education. This is the point behind educating the youth to act as wards of the state rather than as individuals who can think logically for themselves.

Ultimately the Conspiracy moved forward the basic strategy of producing a Civil War within the United States as a major catalyst to change the American system of government and instigate the breakdown of the American Judeo-Christian base — regardless of the issues they used to to organize and influence as many people as possible, such as abolition, human rights, temperance, suffrage, etc.

These movements likewise had the common goal of a world government, sold under the banner of several initiatives to enlist the American people to achieve it.

All of this subversion had an underpinning of being anti-God, particularly anti-Christian. It later evolved into anti-Semitism among some branches, while being pro-Jewish in others.

Over the years, not only were statues raised in honor of some of the people who had the subversion of our system as their goal, but schools, ships, and even cities were named after them, sometimes the movements themselves. It is hard to find a state which does not have a city named after Lafayette, using his name or some derivative of it, for example.

The chamber of the House of Representatives has two large portraits on either side of the speaker's platform. On the left, where the House Democrats sit, is George Washington. On the right is Lafayette, as he appeared during his last sojourn in the United States. Most visitors do not recognize the portrait of the person on the right, the side where the Republicans are seated. Of those who do know who he is, no one seems to ask why a foreigner is prominently displayed there, let alone this particular non-citizen.

Yes, he helped us during the War for Independence, but are there not Americans that would better serve in that place of honor? What about Steuben? A case could be made that he did more for our colonial army overall than any other foreigner. Lafayette was a dashing leader, but Steuben made the Continental Army into a real army.

There are several towns called Young America and New Harmony, and there is even a Greeley, Colorado. The latter was named by Nathan C. Meeker, who was the agricultural editor at the *New York Tribune*. He had organized Union Colony in 1869 as a semi-cooperative, and in 1870 changed its name to Greeley.

It took over ten years after the official end of the Civil War before the violence was to subside. Even then, many of the combatants never could return to pre-war civilized life, and such criminals as the James gang, the Dalton brothers, and the Hatfields and McCoys settled their differences by the gun rather than by civilized means. These are the more famous, but by no means the only examples.

By 1876, the nation was close to civil war again. The usual problems of so-called grassroots militias sprang up, though not to the pre-war level, and corruption was widespread, with evidence of voter fraud ultimately throwing the election to Rutherford Hayes. By this time, people were getting tired of the openly Radical influence from Washington, but they had no organization with which to combat it. It all played out within the major political parties, which were themselves a problem. All the major organizations were controlled by the radicals or under their influence, directly or indirectly.

The sessions in Congress were so volatile that some congressmen waved pistols while in session.

The fear of the discontent in the South was such that President Grant ordered Gen. William T. Sherman to deploy his troops there to ensure a peaceful tabulation of votes. Considering whom he sent, a peaceful tabulation really meant no one could be allowed to object to how the Radicals wanted the vote tallied. Besides, the radical element controlled all parties at the top.

It is interesting that history as we are taught concentrates on the battles of the Civil War rather than the politics, particularly the international politics. People all over the southeastern part of the country dress in period uniforms and re-enact the battle scenes. Why the southeast? Because that is where the battles were (except Gettysburg). The battles were in the South due to the invasion by the North.

Instead of enacting the battles, they should weep over the fact that the American people were manipulated into the war — and for the reasons that they were — not glorify something that was used to forever change our system of government and society.

If these people would spend the same amount of time and money working to preserve the Constitution and the independence of the American people, they would perform a wonderful service to their fellow citizens and their children.

If people studied the politics and the effects of the conspiratorial organizations on our country that led to at least one million people dying probably more, they would better understand what is going on today. The mere fact that people do not know that at least one million people died — soldiers, sailors, and civilians — says a great deal about how history is presented.

Richmond was leveled by cannon. Atlanta was burned, and several other cities were destroyed, including Charleston and Columbia. Vicksburg and countless other Southern cities were decimated, yet we hear nothing of civilian casualties or deprivation leading to their demise. After all, when people lose everything, how do they survive? Some didn't.

Again, this ignorance is due to the concentration on the battles rather than the whole mess we call the Civil War. In the battles, we lost well over half a million men. Many scholars today now say that the official figures for military casualties were too low by twenty percent, that as many as 800,000 may have actually perished.

We never hear about the civilians — and particularly the slaves — whose lives were lost.

Think about it for a moment. The Union Army went through the South and liberated the slaves, forcing them off the property of the former owners, with no means of support. It is a testament to the honesty and integrity of the black Americans that they did not pillage and rob everyone and everything in order to survive. And many of them did not survive.

Many of the freed slaves were immediately conscripted into the Union Army. The North had the draft; once the slaves were "free" they were "eligible" for the draft, and this was done immediately. Evidence as to the freedmen *who already were free* within the South being drafted is little to none. Also, records of deaths due to "service" were not well kept, with the "service" being battle, hard labor use in all black battalions, sickness, etc.

There were organizations which sprang up to give aid and comfort to such folk, both black and white, but the job was too large, and many of these organizations had an agenda, just as we see in some so-called charitable foundations and community-action organizations today.

We can quantify the shipping that was destroyed, but not the human life on board American vessels ravaged from the seas. They were not military sailors, but merchant seamen, whalers, and passengers. There have been a great many studies made of casualties, but most do not even seem to take into consideration that there were any casualties among naval military personnel, let alone civilian sailors and passengers.

In fact, most people whom this author has talked to do not even know that there was a naval component to the war. That is how deficient the education system has been about the bloodiest conflict we have ever had.

The white Southern population suffered after the war as well, by being displaced from their land and businesses or by being killed. The number of the civilians is never calculated in the losses due to the war. To tally these losses would mean that this part of history would have to be discussed; by discussing it, part of the hidden history would likely be exposed.

In some quarters, as law and order broke down, looting and mishandling of civilians by Union troops and marauding bands of outlaws led to confrontations. Some people fought back. Some died as a result. How long after the war should the war be blamed for the ensuing violence? It took years for the violence directly attributable to the war to subside. How many deaths occurred during this period?

Our educational system is so lacking that this author has never found a single American who knows that at least 10 million people died in Europe at the hands of those in authority immediately after the cessation of World War II. In France alone over 100,000 were falsely accused of being Nazi collaborators and killed. They actually fought the German occupation, but did not cooperate with the communist wing of the French resistance and so could not be allowed to influence post-war French politics. Similar events took place in Poland, Italy, Yugoslavia, and elsewhere, with communist cadres trying to eliminate any opposition to their attempts to establish local or national communist goverments.

Many of these incidences have been personally related to the author by individuals who lived through such experiences. However, there are many books and articles that document these facts.

James Forrestal, who became the first secretary of defense, raised the money to prevent the takeover of Italy by the communists immediately after World War II. He experienced a paradigm shift that made him realize that the mistakes being made by the American Foreign Service could not be mistakes if they were made 100% of the time. He said that you would think that at least one incidence would work in our favor instead of for the communists.

His efforts to make some sense of American policy cost him his life. His death was made to look like suicide, but circumstantial evidence makes it seem more like murder.

Forrestal was a member of the Council on Foreign Relations and an internationalist, but came back around because he was an American at heart.

There are many examples of Northern men in authority who wanted to wipe out Southern society. The only way this could be done, ultimately, was to eliminate the Southern population, or at least the middle class and wealthy. There were men in the Union Army, such as Adam Badeau, who advocated this "punishment" on the South.

Badeau was an aide to Gen. Sherman, and then joined Gen. Grant's staff during the war as his military secretary. He was with Grant at Appomattox. He was made a colonel, and on retirement was brevetted a general. He wrote that the Southern people would have to be "annihilated." It is difficult to believe that, with an attitude like this among the staff of the military leaders, the treatment of Southern civilians was not harsher.

This is not to say that the harsh treatment was universal, only that we have to bring the overall treatment into perspective since the harsh aspects have been left out of our school texts.

Hollywood in its early days used to depict some of the harsh treatment Southern civilians received from Union troops. A famous Shirley Temple flick had this theme, although moderated. *Gone With the Wind* is another example. It was still close enough to the war for people alive to remember, as not all had passed on. Even in the youth of this author, a few veterans of the Civil War still attended memorial celebrations and were placed in positions of honor at events.

Resisters to looting did not always fare well, and food and material goods were taken. If the Southerner was lucky enough to hide any livestock, he would be hard pressed to feed them if Union troops had confiscated the fodder.

Although many Union troops behaved well, some were incredibly cruel.

After the war, Badeau joined the sort of radicals that had become the norm as our ambassadors, with his appointment to service in London and Havana. During 1877-1878, he accompanied Grant on his world tour.

These actions, coupled with the debasement of currency by the Confederacy and the war bonds imposed upon the Southern states by the federal government to pay for the war, created an economic condition within Southern society from which it took a hundred years to recover.

From the beginning of the war to the end, both the North and the South adopted many of the same policies, some of which ran contrary to why the war was supposedly started in the first place.

Supposedly the North was opposed to slavery and the South supported it. The political reality was that neither side was totally for or against it. Not all of the areas that constituted the Union had laws against it. The South was trapped in the system and there seemed no easy way out, particularly under the political conditions that prevailed.

The North soon adopted a policy of bringing in Negroes as troops, but treated them as second-class citizens *within the army*. By the end of the war the South was adopting the same policy; however, while Negroes served with some white units in the South, in the North they were totally segregated. In addition, the South did not conscript Negroes, but the North did as they moved into and through the South, forcing freedmen to serve in the Union Army.

With few exceptions, northern politicians looked upon the Negro race as unequal, and most wanted them shipped to Africa or Central America, including Lincoln. After the war, the radicals saw them as votes and installed many of them into positions of power beyond their immediate capabilities as a whole. This led to a voting bloc, but also was a source of continual resentment and agitation the Radicals could exploit.

If ex-slaves had the wisdom to immediately vote upon being freed, then it belies the myth of the Southerner keeping them in total ignorance as part of the argument against slavery. Think about it. You do not need irrational arguments to be against slavery. It is wrong based on principle, no matter how well educated the slave may or may not be.

In Rome, slave owners sometimes bought or educated their slaves to serve in some industrial or intellectual capacity. Also, they trained and educated some to be the overseers of their slaves and managers of agriculture. This is well documented. Yet we have the opinion that in the South such things did not happen.

Propaganda such as *Uncle Tom's Cabin* portrayed the average slave as being deprived of everything, including education. In some areas this was the law, but not all over the South. Even when it was against the law, slaves were being educated. It is obvious that anyone makes a better worker if he understands more than simple menial tasks.

A businessman understands that an employee becomes more valuable as he gains experience, education, and training. The same applied to a slave and, pardon the analogy, but for even the simple idea of re-sale value, this would be an incentive to a slave master.

Even so, history is rife with stories of Southern legislatures immediately after the war with Negro legislators and their excesses — if you know where to look. These men were elevated well beyond their capabilities and individual responsibility levels, and for a time ruined the government while voting the way the occupying army wanted them to "vote."

Peace organizations continued to operate even though many of them found the rationale to justify war in this case. They did not change much from their support of socialist ideas among their leadership. In some cases, they were financed by men who had something more in mind than peace as the average American would define it. The *Bond of Peace*, the organ of the Universal Peace Society, for instance, was very sympathetic to the First International.

The Universal Peace Society evolved after a short time into the Universal Peace Union. Their annual meetings only drew 60 or so the first year, but by the 1880s the attendance was nearly 10,000.

The North started to print money rather than pay in specie by the end of 1861. The South did likewise. The South went even further than the North producing a nearly worthless currency through inflation.

There have been four gold confiscations by government in our history. Two occurred during the runaway inflation caused by the paper currency known as the "Continental," since it was issued by the Continental Congress. It was so worthless that the saying "Not worth a Continental" lasted in the American lexicon for two centuries. One gold confiscation occurred in 1933 under Franklin Roosevelt, and one occurred under the Confederacy.

At the end of the war, the Southern states were made to pay war reparations and take out loans to survive. This author was riding in a car to an event one evening when one of the passengers in the car stated that his state had finally paid off their war bonds. I foolishly asked, "From World War II?" He replied no, saying, "From the Civil War."

At that moment in time it had been one hundred years.

That was the spark that led to my interest in the events surrounding the most calamitous episode this country has ever experienced. Why did I not know about this? What else did I not know? I began my quest for American history.

The North moved against state sovereignty immediately at the onset of secession. The Confederate States of America (CSA) did likewise but experienced more resistance. In the South, it led many states to consider secession from the Confederacy and going their own way. Some feel that had the Southern states been more cohesive in cooperation with the Confederate Army, the war could have lasted long enough to perhaps effect a settlement rather than a Southern defeat. There were too many instances of non-cooperation between the Southern states and the Confederate government. We did not begin to touch on the width of the cleavage between the states within the Confederate States of America and how many even considered secession from the Confederacy due to the actions of the CSA, since our focus has been on the Northern aspects of conspiracy.

There are those who have documented the Southern wing of the Conspiracy since the days of the Civil War itself. We have left this work to others. As we have stated more than once, it was the Northern wing of the Conspiracy that ultimately had more influence on America for decades after the war. New York has been the epicenter for a long time.

The lack of a cohesive and united military strategy, with the Confederate Army on one hand and several state armies on the other, meant that the South could not develop the strategy and tactics that would have benefited the overall resistance to Northern armies. This problem was manifested in not only combat per se, but supply, intelligence, and manpower.

The strategy associated with conspiratorial organizations was two-fold: to work to destroy the unity of the United States simply as a catalyst to use war to destroy the freedom of the American people as protected by the Constitution, leading to a nationalist government, and then to use the might of a re-united America to subdue the world into a New World Order. Along the way, the constitutional underpinnings of liberty had to be purged from the American understanding. Otherwise the scheme to produce a world government by the use of American might and troops would not be tolerated by the American people.

While some wanted an exclusively American-led empire, the plan of the Insiders was to use three countries — Russia, China, and the United States — after it became obvious that America and her great experiment in liberty were not soon to be thwarted by the Illuminist minions in our fledgling years, and that America would ultimately loom large on the world's stage.

The Illuminati had to take over the United States and destroy the great experiment of liberty in order to fulfill their aims. They tried at first by the Jacobin movement, but essentially failed. How were they to succeed?

Keep in mind that no nation or combination of nations existed that could be used to fight the U.S. on equal terms on our soil. In order to create the onerous edicts, military law, taxation, and all that the war spawned to alter society, and to prepare the way for the Conspiracy to rule, the conflict had to be on American soil. To have a war that could be used to alter our society meant the need for a civil war.

Disunion was voiced from the first, at the formation of the country, reaching a crescendo in 1861. Once the Civil War started and the radicals were in control, the rhetoric shifted to support for the Union in the North. Then the master plan, to use a compliant citizenry and an American empire to subvert the planet, became a distinct possibility and it came time to do all they could to maintain the base by preserving the union — but only after a prolonged war to subvert American society, the system of government, and the morality of the nation to enable the few to establish their nearly absolute control.

How do we know that this was the strategy? Simply by looking at the organizations and leaders who brought on the conflict with their words and actions, in connection with the overall goals of the Conspiracy, both inside and outside of government — and the results.

While the disunionists in the North became ardent unionists once the war started, prominent disunionists in the South became obstructionists who led to the disorganization of Southern resistance; many then joined the Radicals as soon as the battles ceased.

The battle over Southern conscription was intense between the Confederacy and the states. North Carolina, Georgia, Alabama, Mississippi, and Texas all organized their own state armies as a means of interfering with the draft, and kept their men under their control. It was the deciding factor in many losing battles and campaigns.

The attitude held by the likes of Gov. Joseph Emerson Brown helped lose the war. If his Georgia state troops had formed an integral part of the Confederate Army before Sherman was able to enter the state, Sherman would never have been able to march to the sea. There have been many studies attempting to prove that there were other reasons for the success of Sherman.

War almost broke out ten years earlier than it did. If it had, the South would have been able to sustain its independence. Much of the advantage the North had in industrial might, railroads, population, etc. did not exist before 1860. The massive immigration that occurred in this period had not yet begun to reach the levels that it did, which more than tipped the scales of population between the North and South. The population had not yet been prepared by the Conspiracy to elect the number of radicals that came to power in 1860, nor had an effective political party yet been conceived and formed to facilitate the split and war. This was done four years later.

The southern aristocrats were portrayed before the war as being aloof, only interested in horses and mint juleps, in order to inspire hatred for the South as exploiters of slaves. The Northern aristocrats were portrayed after the war as "robber barons," in order to inspire hatred for "capitalists" as exploiters of everyone. The net result was a socialist mind-set against free enterprise, whether agrarian or industrially based.

Interestingly, the robber baron capitalists were primarily those who were themselves socialists or who helped the Conspiracy. So much for the downtrodden.

Slavery was slowly disappearing long before the war. The importation of slaves had become illegal. Without the agitation of the militant abolitionists, emancipation would have been more rapid. Men of culture all over were freeing their slaves, albeit mostly through their wills. In 1850, due to abolition efforts, 1 in 8 blacks were free: 434,495 free compared to 3,204,313 enslaved. In three slave states alone there were 160,000 freedmen, some of whom owned slaves themselves. Of all the states, Mississippi was the worst for freedmen due to restrictive laws against blacks. Less than a thousand freedmen lived there, primarily because of these strict laws.

The image of the cruel slave master who whipped his slaves and set the dogs on them as a universal condition defies logic. It was not that unusual for the overseer to be one of the slaves. Think about it — and this is no apology for slavery, which is abhorrent — in those days a slave was capital. A slave cannot work or be viable for resale if beaten, whipped, or chewed up by dogs.

Did such things happen? Of course. Were they the norm? No. But it made great propaganda — just enough truth to whip up the sentiments of those who desired justice without recognizing what the polarization was doing to the country. The consequences of the solutions offered could be used by those who wanted to change the entire system, not just slavery, and those changes could be used to enslave all.

This is not an exaggeration. Regulations and laws have been imposed on the American people that control what they may or may not do with their land, their homes, and their businesses; what they can buy and what they cannot; and the education of their children by proclaiming that the children are wards of the state, not the parents, even if they are "allowed" to home school. Punitive taxes are designed to limit the consumer. The "right of eminent domain" is a masterful means of the use of semantics: there is no right by government, but we have been programmed to use this term as if there is.

There were laws that worked both ways regarding the treatment of slaves, some that protected certain rights and many that limited them. The latter laws came about due to a few conspiracies that led to slave revolts, with some evidence of outside influence from both the French and English. Consequently, some of the laws passed at the state level were against teaching slaves to read and forbade freedom of assembly by blacks without white supervision, including Sunday services. With each new revolt, more strident laws were passed. Prior to slave revolts — none of which succeeded — the slaves were allowed wide-ranging freedom of movement and education. Here again, the action is in the reaction.

Even with the strident laws in some areas, whites continued to educate slaves — particularly in order to facilitate their ability to perform more than menial tasks — and to instruct them in Scripture. The Christian outreach that was performed before the war has had a residual effect on the black population ever since.

One wishes that the English method for ending slavery had been emulated. But the people were not allowed to think in such terms due to the agitation that was stirred up by radicals on both sides of the issue.

The effort of John Brown at Harper's Ferry was to be the first step in a massive slave revolt. There were people who felt that the agitation had been sufficient to effect this outcome. They were wrong. First, no one informed the slaves that a revolt was planned. Second, the Negro people were not docile, but neither were they stupid enough to serve as cannon fodder for the conspirators. And third, in some areas the slaves were better off than people realized, then and now.

The efforts of John Brown from beginning to end had all the earmarks of an enterprise to create a reaction, not to actually accomplish what the publicly stated goals were.

In more and more cases the Southern people were doing what they could to make the slaves equal in education and morality, in spite of the laws in some areas. The classic case is the famous Confederate General Stonewall Jackson. Study what he did before the war for the Negro population and you begin to realize that he could not have been the warrior he was just to preserve slavery. His motivation was far different.

Likewise, the mass of Confederate soldiers who never owned a slave would never have served and died so that wealthy white Southern plantation owners could own slaves. Nor would the Negroes that served in the Confederate Army have done so.

The blame for slavery rests just as much with the North as it does the South. The money from the slave market was initially made in the North. It was Yankee ships that ran the slave trafficking from Africa to America. Foreign governments looked down equally upon the South, for using slaves, and the North, for trafficking in them.

Had there been a reasonable and responsible organization to promote the end of slavery instead of using the condition to inflame *white* people, slavery would have ended as it did with the English, peacefully and without rancor.

It would not have been long before slavery would have ended on its own. While one does not want to condone slavery or prolong it, in a few years with the advancement of machinery, the realization that free labor works better than slave labor and is more productive, the lands producing labor-intensive crops would have worn out, if not, the continued invention of farm machinery would have lessened the reliance on slave labor, so with all of these things and more, slavery would have been a losing proposition. The North would have out produced the South in agricultural products with the use of machinery and demonstrated the futility of continuing the use of slavery as a viable economy.

Industry would have grown in the South much more quickly, and the entire country would have become even more of a superpower than she did.

There is more than one type of slavery. If you doubt that, then think of the fact that in a communist country all are slaves. How have their economies operated without outside capital flowing in? Slavery does not work as a modern economic system in the long run any more than communism does unless stimulated by outside capital.

Another image that is projected in history is that the South is anti-black and anti-Semitic, and the North is more fair to all. However, during the period up to and including the Civil War, there were many Jews in the Confederacy in the local, state, and Confederate governments. The most notable was Judah Benjamin, who held three different Cabinet posts in the Confederacy. He was only one individual who held important positions in the governments of the South. The South contracted for a loan from the Jewish-owned banking house in Europe, Erlanger, and those who invested in the loan had to take the loss due to the Southern defeat.

Contrast this with the North, where there was only one member of the Jewish faith outside of the military in the federal government, and he was a low-level functionary. Gen. Grant was so anti-Semitic that he ordered Jews expelled from Southern territory under his command. Lincoln rescinded the order a month later, but only after the Jews had been moved out and their property confiscated.

Sherman and Butler were also notorious anti-Semites, as were other Union generals. The War Department was run by anti-Semites such as Stanton and Watson. *There was no Northern politician who debated against the order of Grant to expel the Jews from his military territory when it came before the Congress.*

John Slidell, another Confederate official, had a close relationship with Belmont and had met with Salomon de Rothschild in Paris just before the war broke out as part of a delegation from the South. His daughter married Frederic Emile d'Erlanger.

Many thousands of those of the Jewish faith fought for the Confederacy, believing the North and particularly Lincoln to be a dictator. The onerous edicts of Grant and others reinforced this belief. An exclusively Jewish regiment was raised for the Confederacy.

Members of the Jewish faith also held positions in Southern society and were not unknown within many of the Masonic orders, especially around Charleston, South Carolina. This was not true in the North.

If the conspiracy leadership was Jewish, one would have thought the South would have won.

Slavery is never justified and is abhorrent to the true Christian and Jew. One wishes that it could have been eliminated without the high cost of life, both black and white, and without the huge step toward socialism and destruction of the social order that was the Civil War.

After the war, many radical leaders remained in power, gaining a more respectable reputation as they mellowed somewhat. Some of the population grew more used to their goals and rhetoric as even more radical organizations were formed — the growth of the communist movement in the streets and the violence of the unions made earlier radicals seem moderate.

In addition, there was no organization formed to fight the radicals on a broad agenda and promote the Constitution. There was a small group of Northern officers who formed to promote the return to the Constitution, but in the face of the overwhelming size of the Grand Army of the Republic, they had little influence.

The writing of history and the entire idea of the American system of government came under the purview of the Northern intelligentsia. There were many reasons for this, including the fact that the South didn't even have the paper to print books at first to tell their side of the story. The minions of the public school organizations moved into the South, ruling the formation of new schools and reorganizing the old. They decided on the books that would be used.

Until recently, the history of the Civil War was set by the Northern authors, represented by the likes of Emerson and the web of literary clubs founded by his coterie. The entire publishing industry came under the purview of organizations and individuals who were part of the problem then, such as the American Historical Association and various state historical associations.

Today, more and more histories are being written by Southerners in magazines and books concerning this tragic chapter of our history. Far too much of it is still focusing on the battles and not the politics. Of the political books there are, too many are biased against the North without realizing that their own leaders were just as much to blame. Some are beginning to see the broader picture of a conspiracy, but limit it to simply Marxism, without seeing that Marxism was and is only a finger on a larger hand and that Marx was still a relatively minor player up to and during the war period.

The original edition of The *Communist Manifesto* in 1848 did not have Marx's or Engels' name on it. They were not that important in the general scheme of things at the time. They wrote it on the orders of the League of Just Men. It was the leadership of this secret society that was more important and hidden from view. If you study the life of Marx, you come to realize that he could not have been the leader of anything. He was a puppet, just like Hitler and Obama. All were too incompetent and had no experience to rise to the pinnacles they did and lead. In fact, you could say they ruined what they ostensibly led.

This does not mean that they were not intelligent. It means that they lacked the ability to run effective organizations on their own without direction and mentoring.

In the case of the two latter men, both were renowned for their oratory. They were the mouthpieces of the Conspiracy, set up to do a job. This author believes that there was a design to their actions and subsequent decisions, which he will for the time being withhold from the reader.

Any real study of Hitler would immediately tell the student that he was either grossly incompetent or deliberately destructive of the fiber, industry, and military strength of Germany. Any one of approximately ten decisions that he made either cost them the war or hastened the end of it. And, these were decisions that flew in the face of his *known* advisors.

It must likewise be obvious that the policies of Obama have been destructive of the fiber, economy, industry, and military strength of the United States. Was it incompetence or, as some have concluded, deliberate?

Interestingly, neither Hitler nor Obama was actually born in the country he helped ruin. While Marx was not a leader of a country, he nonetheless became the ostensive leader of an international movement, and was for all practical purposes a man without a country.

Today, the idea of secession is thought to be illegal. Civilization cannot exist unless contracts are honored, and this is true whether one is talking about business or government. However, what is the recourse if one or more parties do not adhere to a contract? What are the remaining parties to do?

Are we to say that if one party violates a contract, and there is no recourse by another party, that the contract continues on being misused? If that be the case, it is a contractual form of slavery, locked in forever.

In the union, the states entered into the compact with each other voluntarily. Are we to say that the states cannot, therefore, withdraw from the contract voluntarily? It is the same philosophy as one vote, one time — forever, as done in communist countries.

The states formed the federal government, not the other way around. There is no legal philosophy that says that a union cannot be broken upon the violation of the contract, regardless of the structure of the agreement.

Equally, no one should deny anyone, person or government, the right to choose. If so, liberty cannot exist. Granted, the choice may require great consequences, but that is the responsibility of the parties involved.

The benefit of declaring this right is to be able to apply pressure on any centralized government to behave in a manner so that no part of it wants to secede. If they know you can go your own way if you do not like what the government is doing, maybe they will act in a manner more consistent with the will of the governed — and the terms of the original contract.

The tragedy is that secession has been forever linked in future students' minds with the idea of defending slavery or some other "extremist" condition.

No American wants to see our country split or torn apart — heaven forbid — but the spirit of liberty must be understood at all levels.

If the "contract" of the people and states with the federal government, the Constitution, is no longer followed by the federal government and there appears to be no remedy, what then? The answer is in the next chapter. Patriotism is a fine thing unless it is in support of a government that has become totalitarian.

Let us not forget that secession was how this Republic was founded. We seceded from Great Britain, pure and simple. You may state that it was a founding principle.[67]

There grew in our country the idea that once some aspect of government was passed into law or implemented, there was no reversal. One vote, one time. This has also been applied relative to amendments to the Constitution (with the exception of Prohibition). From this has come the argument that once a state has submitted a call for a constitutional convention, they cannot change their mind; the call will stand and be counted toward the convention.

There is no principle or law in business, personal relations, government, or any other sphere of human endeavor that states that people cannot change their minds and act accordingly. To do so may have consequences and responsibilities that go along with the decision, but to deny this is to deny liberty.

The appointment of socialists into government after the war became normal. The appointment of Carl Schurz as secretary of the interior under Hayes was not an isolated incident. And, it was not unusual to see the leaders of our nation have socialists in their family or be socialists themselves. John Humphrey Noyes, the socialist leader, for example was first cousin to President Hayes.

Members of the Order became increasingly prominent in the federal government, and the son of the co-founder Alfonso Taft was elected to the presidency. He would not be the last member of the Order

---

67 If a government is totally corrupt or out of control, amending the contract will not suffice to bring that government into compliance. A radical change, revolution, or secession must take place. Consider this in relationship to a constitutional convention or conference of the states if the government that is a "runaway" government is allowed to remain in place. We do not advocate the above radical solutions, but bring them up to point out the futility of an amendment or two to remedy the problem. Without widespread support for constitutional government among the people, there will not be a remedy that works, either in the short or long term.

to hold that office. Two presidents, the Bushes, won election posing as the opposite of what they were: Bonesmen. Both, but particularly George H. W. Bush, advocated publicly, over and over again, the establishment of the New World Order. YouTube is replete with examples of this fact.

And, George H. W. Bush served for a time on the board of directors of the Council on Foreign Relations, before he was president. It was only one of the reasons many conservatives were less than enthusiastic about the Reagan candidacy. What would have been the future of American government had Bush become president as the result of a John Hinckley bullet, and the open march toward a New World Order pushed by Bush come seven years earlier?

Stuff happens. We believe that Reagan got the message, for if he had had any idea of implementing what he had promised to do in the election, he changed his mind. The American people still got the rhetoric, but his CFR-laden Cabinet got the action. It was under Reagan that the federal debt started to climb radically, for instance, contrary to the image.

After the war, the American government continued its policy of appointing radicals as our representatives to foreign countries, instituting policies that directly led to these countries becoming our enemies and/or socialist.

Radicals in government and throughout the political system led to the election debacle of 1912 and the subsequent changes in government. such as Prohibition, the Federal Reserve System, the income tax, and the direct election of U.S. senators, whereby they became the representatives of the population of the states rather than the state legislatures. In this manner, they became just another representative of the people rather than the state government, eliminating the check and balance within the Congress.

The number of votes for the socialist candidate in 1912 was the equivalent of over three million votes today. This was not even the entire socialist vote when you consider the Progressive Party votes and those for Wilson; there was a tremendous socialist bent in the population.

The subsequent changes led to the gradual lessening of resistance to the federal government and of working to maintain state-sovereignty influence in the Senate. Worse, they led to the lack of balanced federal budgets, since the controls by the states on federal spending were eliminated by both the direct election of senators and the income tax, which filled the coffers of the federal government so it would not have to dun the states to make up any shortfall in the federal budget, as was originally done before the 17th Amendment.

Most conservatives do not link Prohibition to the forces of socialism and the changes that came into government due to its implementation: national policing, federal regulation of consumables (including content), etc. The government imposed regulations that went far beyond what most people think of as alcoholic beverages, including anything which contained alcohol, such as cough medicine. Most have never studied the full ramifications of how government changed and started to interfere in the people's food supply as a result of Prohibition. This also set the stage for government control over the individual, as opposed to the people's control over the government by means of the Constitution.

This control began just after 1900 when some condiments and food stuffs had a short shelf-life, contained harmful material, or were shoddily prepared. Major companies, while having all of the appearances of supporting government regulation in the name of product safety, also benefited from the regulations as smaller companies were put out of business because they could not immediately comply with the letter of the regulations, or afford to since their margins were too small. As a result, many brands disappeared from the store shelves, never to return.

Did the regulations do some good? Yes, but capped off by Prohibition, along with the good came a permanent federal policing structure.

The use of the courts by the consumers of products that harm people is the correct method to rectify any harm. Preventative measures in any sphere of human activity lead to the loss of liberty. Crime prevention; disease prevention that demands inoculations, examinations, and testing; water additives, and myriad government edicts, all done in the name of the public good, lead ultimately to a draconian system no matter what the benevolent reason was in the beginning. It is mommycide smothering by a maternal government.

The Turner organizations remained radical, but by the time of the mid-1870s, what they stood for had become more mainstream, as the leaders had become older and more moderate in their habits. Some, because they were engaged in gymnastics, became the basis for several of the circuses that started to tour the country, gradually evolving through consolidation into larger and more famous enterprises. Other Turners, such as in Milwaukee, opened restaurants and remained low key, utilizing their organizational skills, and helped elect a long line of socialist city governments, state legislators, and members of Congress, the most famous being Victor Berger. By the 20th century 172 Turner groups still existed, with a membership of 31,000.

The aftermath of the war brought on the phenomenal growth of what we call today the Marxist movement. All socialist groups claim their origin in Marx. They morphed into politics, labor, education, and just about every facet of society. The movement produced a level of violence in the late 19th century and the first decades of the 20th century not seen since the days of the Jacobins. This violence subsided for a time, but resurfaced in the 1960s in the anti-war and civil rights movements and came from the same root.

Labor unrest alone accounted for arsons, beatings, murders, riots, etc. on both sides. From the Upper Midwest out across to the Pacific, the International Workers of the World, or "Wobblies," created a war zone in several industries, particularly lumber and railroads. Many of the 20th century's American communist leaders cut their teeth in the IWW.

The early 20th century in the Pacific Northwest was marked by street battles between the communists and authorities, and in one instance house to house combat between the communists and the American Legion. There was even an attempt to blow up the mayor of Seattle with a bomb sent through the mail. The city of Everett, where the Boeing 747 and 787 would be built decades later, was occupied for a time by the communists, and they were strong enough to repel attempts to take the city back for several days. This history has disappeared from the minds of the local citizens since those who lived through it are long gone and "history" doesn't mention it.

Public education as we know it today proliferated across the country after the war, controlled increasingly by state government. Based on the infiltration already accomplished at the major universities and colleges by freethinkers, socialists, and the Order before the Civil War, school teachers were educated to teach their charges socialist ideals, slowly at first in some areas, openly in others. With each succeeding generation teachers were "dumbed down" due to their education as teachers in colleges dominated by the Order or socialists, so that their students learned less and less about how early Americans produced the United States Republic and specifically why.

The concentration was in the colleges, since they produced the teachers that fanned out across the entire country. Once indoctrinated, it was hard for most to regain common sense, although many did and worked to bring sound education to their charges. However, it was a losing battle without a sound organization to counter the socialist-led education associations.

Most teachers did not realize that they were producing the thinking processes among their charges for the acceptance of more radical ideas when preparatory students went on to college. It was not so much the facts being taught as it was the method of thinking that was being inculcated, with logic, constitutional law, and Judeo-Christian philosophy gradually disappearing from the curricula.

Teachers themselves became victims in this process, not realizing that the education colleges were molding change-agents rather than intellectual educators.

Lincoln said it well regarding this strategy of using education as a tool for change: "The philosophy of the school room in one generation will be the philosophy of the government in the next."

The modern school is the product of two centuries of work by the enemies of our system. At first it was coordinated on a national scale by the Conspiracy through a variety of means, higher education and publishing primarily, but local controls still existed which blocked a completely nationally controlled system.

We now have a national Department of Education, which has been long advocated by the communists and part of their platform. A "recent" example is the book by William Z. Foster, *Toward Soviet America*, published in 1932, wherein he called for the establishment of a federal Department of Education. Foster was the head of the Communist Party USA at the time.

Since the department's inception, prayer and the Judeo-Christian God have been removed from the classroom. Since our system of government takes an acknowledgment of the existence of God and that our rights come from Him, it can no longer be taught in its original intent. In its place has come internationalism in the form of the United Nations, and the UN now controls a great deal of what is taught through UNESCO. This fact is not well known to the parents or the teachers, since it flows subtly through the books from the textbook publishing companies.

New programs come along every decade to convince parents and teachers that the latest change will solve the problems of school dropouts, poor test scores, etc. In every case it makes the problem worse because the parents and teachers do not understand the root of the problem they are trying to solve, and they have little or no control over the process since it is now controlled out of Washington, D.C., and the umbilical cord is money. These federal programs are tied into UNESCO, whether it is Race to the Top, School-to-Work, Outcome-based Education, No Child Left Behind, Common Core, or any other new name.

Recently, we have seen test-based education as the basis for money from the federal government. In this system, teachers and administrators have been caught changing test scores to qualify for the funds. An article about Atlanta, Georgia educators being found guilty of such practices in April 2015, said that these conditions may be happening in 40 states.

If this is the case, it is not just the taxpayers who are being cheated, it is the students themselves.

By 1875, William Torrey Harris was the president of the National Education Association (NEA). He was a member of the Missouri Hegelians, a founder of the Philosophical Society of St. Louis, and an active member of the Concord School of Philosophy, and in 1880 was the representative of the U.S. Bureau of Education at the International Congress of Education in Brussels. Yes, they started to internationalize the education process even then, and in the process would ultimately create internationalism in the students rather than a love of our own system, and how and why it was superior to any other.

Go to any website of an educational organization or union and you will find that they are more concerned about Americans fitting into an international system than anything else. Indeed, a book needs to be written documenting the international ties of the American teachers unions and Department of Education to international associations and the United Nations, and the influence on American curricula as a result.

The NEA was originally attacked in the Catholic press for trying to establish a huge, centralized, government monopoly of education. One of the first things that the NEA advocated was the dropping of Greek as an entry requirement into colleges. The dropping of Greek is interesting in that it is the basic language of the New Testament. One fluent in Greek can read the Bible's New Testament in its original language, rather someone else's translation. It is also the language of the Greek philosophers. Again, one would not need another's translation.

In both cases, translations can serve the purpose of the translator, particularly if they have an agenda. A person reading Greek can read the original on his own. One who cannot has to read the translation of another who has the ability to have it published. Granted, it is possible to alter the original Greek in publishing; this can catch up to the forger if the educated are fluent in the original language, but not if they are ignorant of it.

By the mid-20th century, educational subversion had become so bad that the majority of the school teachers in New York City were members of the socialist/communist-controlled teachers union. While not to that level in the rest of the country, the dumbing-down process by their capture of school text publishing and teachers colleges was so complete that God and the original intent doctrine of the Constitution disappeared out of the schools.

It is little wonder that in 2013, the voters of the City of New York elected as mayor an open socialist who had worked with communist revolutionaries in Central America. Before that Mayor Bloomberg got them to quit drinking sodas in excess of 16 ounces, so they drank the Kool-Aid of open socialism, with the subsequent problems that came of the city government siding with radical elements.

While education was sinking in the city, the state teachers union of New York still had responsible teachers in their midst and from time to time resisted the dumbing-down process, when it was blatant and too much of a large step to be ignored, such as Common Core.

Parents have never realized the level of socialism that has been taught in the schools. With each passing generation it has become worse, with parents either not paying attention to what is going on, or not wanting to make a "federal case" of it because it only goes a little further than what it was when they were students. Then, just how many parents actually read their children's school books? Do you?

The process is so prevalent that private and home school curricula are also subjected to its influence. Most parents who home school their children were educated in the public schools and therefore have no compass when it comes to history or classic liberal arts to be able to tell when something is false, and even within this venue history is deficient.

The situation this author has witnessed with his own eyes and experience would shock the average parent. In some schools in metropolitan areas, the teachers openly teaching Marx and other socialist theories are the norm. It is all done in the name of a well-rounded education, but Frederick Hayek is unknown. Even graduating economics majors in college have never heard of Hayek, Henry Hazlitt, Ludwig von Mises, or the Austrian School of Economics, which teach classic economics. Commenting on them means that the student may want to look into them, so they are not mentioned, keeping the student in a state of ignorance.

One method for you to see for yourself how education has changed is to look for 19th-century school textbooks in antique stores and compare them with the texts of today. It is not unusual to find English and grammar primers of the 1850s that taught first graders what we would consider high school English today.

In fact, most would have put to shame the *McGuffey Readers* that became standardized texts in the latter half of the 1800s. McGuffey's were the first attempt to nationalize the curricula by promoting their universal use in all the schools, due to their reasonably well-done outlines and ability to flow from one class to the next in content and increasing skill through the primary and secondary grades. Yet today the situation is so bad that *McGuffey* seems great in comparison.

The deterioration of reading and English skills is indicated by a university study released in 2015 that stated that students entering college today have a seventh-grade level of reading proficiency. Texting has become the new low.

The name Berkeley has become synonymous with college radicalism due to the campus of the University of California, Berkeley. The Berkeleys of America are rampant, and by no means is this a modern problem; it has been going on for some time with less fanfare. The University of Wisconsin, Madison, has a reputation for radicalism in its teaching. It was established in 1848, and when Carl Schurz came to America he was a trustee (from 1858 to 1859), as were other radicals. Members of the Order were active in the 19th century establishing universities and gaining the presidency of many of the now-prominent institutions.

The evolution of such institutions as Harvard and Yale is typical of how once great Christian-centered colleges became centers of Hegelian and Transcendentalist thought. These changes began very shortly after our country was founded.

Even Jefferson got into the act, by his advocacy of a national system of education which would have at some point separated out the laboring class from the learned, forever setting students on the paths to two classes of people, similar to the foundations of education today called Common Core. By this we mean only the separation of the classification of education the student received, not necessarily the level of competence.

The process of instilling Hegelian and Transcendental thought has been replicated over and over again in the institutions of higher learning across our country. It is rare that the communities which harbor institutions of higher learning are not the most liberal in mores and politics due to the influence of the institutions on the communities.

This situation also manifested itself in the publishing of histories and textbooks. One need look no further than the index of almost every history book and ask why the following subjects are not even mentioned, or if they are, why only in passing: Young America; the pre-war Knights of the Golden Circle; German revolutionaries in the Union and their influence on the election of 1860; the origins of the two Republican Parties; the communist influence in the formation of the union labor movement; the deaths of civilians in the South; the confiscation of property, not only in the North but especially in the South; the foundations of what became the Federal Reserve and the Income Tax; control over agriculture and mining, and how this is based on the blueprint of *The Communist Manifesto*, etc., etc., etc.

This list does not include the importance of certain foreign and domestic radicals in American political and intellectual life. You will find references to these radicals in some texts, but as heroes who fought for equality. Even when this author went to school it was a common theme that communism isn't bad; it is just misguided people who misuse Marx's theories that make it bad, was the argument.

The facts behind all the above has gone down a memory hole as told by George Orwell in his famous novel *1984*. It has not been a physical department of government as depicted in the book, but a systematic coordination of the centers of intellectual thought and publishing by the minions of the Master Conspiracy over decades and decades, slowly removing and changing history as we know it.

The most effective way to destroy people is to deny and obliterate their own understanding of their history.

— George Orwell

Liberty cannot be preserved without a general knowledge among the people.

— John Adams

An example of how a member of the Order could serve as a "Winston" working at the memory hole is Henry Stevens. This is how one man could have a great influence on the preservation of documents and books — or not. He was the purchasing agent for the Smithsonian and Library of Congress, and was instrumental in securing Americana for the libraries of New York and Providence, Rhode Island. He also spent nearly 40 years in London as a collector of Americana for the British Museum and other libraries back home.

Today, the real possibility of a "Memory Hole" exists in the Internet should the government or even a single private entity gain control of it.

Other arms of the world conspiracy were manifested in the ethnic warfare that embroiled Europe, as well as in the United States, with the Irish immigrants' organization known as the Molly Maguires, for example. The Irish unrest leading to the Young Ireland movement and all the way to the modern IRA has been an unbroken chain from the Illuminati. It is easier to document this statement about the radical Irish than almost any other movement. The problems the Irish have suffered for two centuries is the result — on both sides of the conflict.

The financial world was slowly consolidated into a national banking system then into bigger and bigger banks. The result was the ability of certain bankers to manipulate the economy for their own gain. Then in the name of the misuse of the banks by the "bankers," the recommendation of a federal reserve to control the bankers came about and was adopted in 1914. The Federal Reserve is *The Communist Manifesto's* step five for communizing a country. Since that time, steady control over and then the liquidation of more and more small banks have occurred, with the calamity of 2008 being only one step in the process of consolidating the banking industry for control of the entire American economy by a very few.

The next step is international control through foreign entanglements such as so-called free trade pacts, which always call for regulation and merger of regulations of the agreeing parties. Free trade agreements are in reality mergers between the countries of their economies, regulations, and institutions.

The 16th and 17th Amendments changed our system of government more than people today realize.

Ask yourself how the federal government financed its budgets for over 100 years before the income tax. If you do not know the answer to that question, ask yourself why you do not know. Here again, it is a matter of a lack of education. If you knew the answer, you would realize that in order to put our federal budget and economy in order, the 16th and 17th Amendments would have to be repealed — no new amendment(s) would be required.

The way it used to work was that the federal government would draw up a budget; it had to flow from the House of Representatives to the Senate. The senators represented the state legislatures. If the tariffs and other resources to tax did not meet the budget requirements, the federal government sent a bill to each of the state legislatures to send them the necessary funds to meet the budget based on the population of the states. You can imagine that a senator who did not watch out for the finances of his state at the federal level soon found himself with another job.

Today's system is a result of the 17th Amendment, the Federal Reserve, and the income tax, the latter two part of *The Communist Manifesto*. The solution to our financial problems is to repeal, not add amendments to the Constitution. If the states once again had to finance the federal government, rather than receiving as much as half of their state budgets from the federal government, the situation would change immediately. It would reverse the state governments from eating at the trough to filling the trough, with a decided difference in attitude about spending and budgets.

Unless the American people are educated to understand the principles of the Constitution, more changes will come, not only destroying the economy as a means of producing massive changes all across the board, but destroying the economic independence of people, forcing their reliance on government. This will, more importantly, curtail the ability of good people to organize, to have the time to organize, and to have the money to finance it — *unless enough people start to get to work now* and join together in a time-proven organization to stop what is happening.

This is a clue as to what has to be done: The first step on the road to recovery is the education of the people, especially the opinion molders in a community.

The Constitution was amended to facilitate step two of *The Communist Manifesto,* the graduated income tax. Prior to this amendment it was unconstitutional for the federal government to directly tax the citizen. Our Founders understood that with taxation comes control. A federal tax would have a direct national control over the individual, and they framed the Constitution in such a manner to prevent it.

The use of the IRS to control, harass, and investigate Tea Parties, voter monitoring groups, and constitutionally-minded organizations during the Obama administration was an example of where our Founders knew such a system would ultimately lead. They wrote the Constitution to prevent that, but it was amended in ignorance to produce the federal income tax and the Internal Revenue Service as its enforcement arm; ignorance on the part of the people, that is, but not those who promoted it.

Again, what is needed is not simply education, but understanding — an understanding of the ramifications and the inherent nature of some aspects of the original Constitution without the 16th and 17th Amendments. Facts are one thing, but understanding how they fit into the general scheme of things is equally important.

As we have already mentioned, the universal rise of the public schools, the final step in *The Communist Manifesto*, came after the war. The communists want only government education so that children's education and thought processes can be controlled. Independent schools are diverse. Government schools are not, no matter how hard they try to project the image of diversity and tolerance. Tolerance in the schools means tolerance for just about everything but God and constitutional thinking. At the minimum, a government school is not going to teach something that runs counter to what government wants, nor are unionized teachers.

Having a public school locally is one thing. To consolidate into massive community schools, then the state, federal, and finally internationally is a serious problem: The larger the institutional base, the more opportunity for corruption, in all its forms. We remind you again of Lord Acton's dictum: Power corrupts. Other than mentioning it, we have barely touched on the goal of the Conspiracy for international standards and control over education. Such standards and control are already a large part of American education.

With such international control, curricula will not teach the wisdom of the Founders of the United States, but will substitute a glorification of internationalism and the New World Order.

After the war, the small school came under the rapidly increasing control of local districts, then the state, and finally the federal government through the Department of Education, called for in 1932 by the American communist leader William Z. Foster.

In addition, after the war the states used mandatory attendance laws for children to attend public schools to bring into law the idea that children were wards of the state. These laws effectively destroyed the principle that the parents were responsible for the upbringing of their own children. The problems with this attitude would require another book.

Most parents who have allowed their children to be educated by the state and so have not come in conflict with these laws have never experienced the heavy hand of statist punishment. Parents who have wanted to educate their children outside of the public system or a system sanctioned by the state have experienced cases where their children have been taken away from them, placed in foster homes, and worse. While no one wants to see child abuse, in the name of such a condition many states have passed laws and regulations that go well beyond simple means to see that child abuse is punished.

In the 1930s, the authorities in some states even used sterilization to make sure poor people or those they deemed mentally deficient could not have children. If you doubt this, go online; if you search hard enough you will see that these numbered in the tens of thousands and no one thought anything of it. And, by the way, Hitler used to write letters thanking the Americans engaged in such activity for leading the way. Again, all of this you can verify with an online search.

Allowing the states to have power over parenting is a very dangerous proposition. Any misuse of parental rights can be punished by existing felony laws; there is no need for other laws.

Beginning in the 1970s, a growing movement has forced the states to acquiesce to such things as home schooling. However, most states simply tolerate it for the time being; they have not relinquished their power, nor have they affirmed rights of the parents free from the state.

Saying that it is okay for parents to educate their children as long as they register with the state or school district, is the same as saying you can have gun ownership as long as you register your gun.

There are those who have gained a reputation among conservatives for establishing this "privilege." It is an example of where parents have not noticed the basic principles involved as long as the state has allowed them to continue to educate their children through home schooling. It would be interesting to study what other causes these people have been involved in and how their efforts will lead conservatives into false solutions.

Many leaders besides Lincoln have expressed the fact that what is taught in the government-controlled schools will shape the world to come — at least in their own countries. Some have expressed it as the schools, some as themselves or their party shaping the future by first shaping the children. Certainly this was the case with the Nazis and communist governments.

The motto of the National Education Association says it all: Great Public Schools for Every Child. In other words, every child in a public school.

By the end of a decade after the Civil War, the groundwork had been laid for the control of most major industries in the United States for years to come. The industrial leaders overlapped into other areas as well, such as financing. Some of the men behind these industries employed members of the Order as their top personnel and managers:

Industry	Leader	Affiliation
U.S. Steel	J.P. Morgan/A. Carnegie	The Order
Oil	Rockefeller	The Order
Meat Packing	Gustavus Swift	
Tobacco	James Duke	
Coal	Henry Clay Frick	
Grain processing	James Pillsbury	The Order
Merchandising	Ward and Roebuck	

The reader should not be shocked to read what the former head of the Communist Party USA, Earl

Browder, said in his 1942 book, *Victory — and after*:

> Thomas Jefferson was denounced as a communist and red by the Federalists, before and after his elevation to the Presidency, and it was no answer at all to point out that there was no Communist Party.
>
> Andrew Jackson was denounced as a communist and red and he had to fight through the issues of his day on their merits despite the fact there was then no Communist Party in the United States.
>
> Abraham Lincoln was denounced as a communist and a red by the slave power and by the Northern Copperheads. In his time there were American Communists, as well as an international Communist organization, but Lincoln did not ask them to commit suicide. Instead, he commissioned their American leaders as officers in the Union Army, and expressed his gratitude to the international Communist organization (the First International) for its help to the Union cause in Europe.

Such rhetoric if said by any constitutionalist would be condemned as the rantings of an extremist. While communists are extremists, they do understand the background of their own movement better than anyone else. There is little question that Jefferson was involved in the movement before turning around after his election to the presidency, becoming almost a Federalist in his actions and outlook. Jackson was involved from early on in his life and remained so his entire life. Lincoln changed this country from a federation to a national government and moved the country halfway from what it was toward the implementation of *The Communist Manifesto*.

Browder was simply stating the obvious, which all true students of history should understand.

And that is the object of this tome: to provide history that has been suppressed for over a century with the goal of understanding how to restore our constitutional republic.

You cannot return home if you do not know where you started from. If you do not know what we were, the system and the nuances within it, how would you know how to restore the fundamental system laid down to protect our liberty?

> *To be ignorant of what occurred before you were born is to remain always a child.*
>
> — Cicero

Early on, socialist reporters and editors fed false information to their readers. Today the newspapers and media have become purveyors of opinion or philosophy in addition to false information. This change over time came as a result of journalism schools teaching how to humanize stories rather than simply report the facts and operate within journalistic ethics. The Conspiracy does not have to directly control the news since they have programmed how journalists think by their education. Added to this is knowing on which side one's bread is buttered, which means knowing what the publisher wants as a slant on the news.

This does not mean that the media did not or has continued to have people who are on the Left, consciously subverting our country, system of government, and society. There are those who understand what they are doing. From the days of the Jacobins up to today this is true.

Notable communist leaders of the 19th century had sons who became prominent in the media. Albert Brisbane's son, Arthur, worked for Pulitzer until hired away by William Randolph Hearst to run the *New York Journal*. He became a close friend of Hearst and has been referred to as a socialist who drifted into the profit system. We have seen that before; he may have enjoyed making a profit, but the idea of government control through a system of socialism remained. His column, according to *Time* magazine, was read by 20 million people.

Albert Brisbane's grandson was named public editor of the *New York Times* in June 2010.

Since the inception of our country there has been a systematic, organized movement to destroy our Republic. The most effective tool they have used besides war is the capture of the education of American youth and the dumbing down of American society. They have deprived the average American of vital information, history, logic, and a moral compass. It has been done with patient gradualism, so the parents have not been overly concerned about what was being taught because it never seemed to be that outrageous at any given time (with few exceptions).

In other words, as the populace has been dumbed down, the next step is only a salami-slice from the last step. This has even fooled average teachers, believing they are teaching the students what they need to know when in fact many haven't a clue. If you are a teacher, do not get mad at the messenger, look for yourself and start to inject sound education into your classrooms.

John Adams said that education was a two-step process of teaching what a student needs to make a living and teaching them how to live at the same time.

In the beginning of this work, we related the fact that what became the education system in America was influenced by men who studied in Germany and were heavily influenced by Prussian education. Rev. Charles Brooks of Boston, a Unitarian minister, wrote some remarks about education and other factors in Europe. These were placed into a publication, "Remarks on Europe, Relating to Education, Peace and Labor; and Their Reference to The United States," in 1843. Remarking about Prussia he said:

> A maxim among them seems to be this; whatever we would have in the State we must first introduce into the school-room. Thus, by providing self-government for every mind, they hope to save the expenses of an armed police, while they render the people industrious, peaceful and happy.

While he expressed that the Prussians wanted to control their people through education, he pointed out that the education in France was not based on morality, and as a result the people were not moral.

He then went on to say:

> Look at the difference between our country and the old world. A republican is an intelligent, virtuous, self-governing man, who has learned the art of choosing rulers and making laws. This trade of politics was commenced by him at ten or twelve years of age, and when arrived at twenty-one, he had gone through a quiet but powerful system of training, which, while it had inspired him with the love of liberty, had also taught him the supreme value of order and justice. He therefore came prepared for the exercise of his civil rights. There is not such education for the masses in Europe.

Yet there were and are those whose wish to teach in the Prussian manner outlined above: "whatever we would have in the State we must first introduce into the school-room."

Rev. Brooks goes on to point out the miserable percentage of illiterates in Europe and says, " … and in the last census it was ascertained that our Connecticut contained but one adult who could neither read nor write!"

Yet after all of this, he worked to install public education based on the Prussian system!

This was before public schools as we now know them. Today, in some parts of the country, as many as one-third of those who start school never graduate from high school, and American education is anywhere from 19th to 25th behind the rest of the world, depending on the subject.

Computers have made the problem worse by disguising the ignorance. As a small example, clerks at the counter of any store are no longer proficient in making change. They just hand you what the computer tells them. If you make any out-of-the-ordinary moves to pay in cash, it can throw them into confusion.

And, nowhere is true history taught, neither in the United States nor around the world.

Something is vitally wrong, and it is not for lack of money.

18

THE FUTURE,
WHERE DO WE GO FROM HERE?

The reader of this volume may by now be feeling that the situation is hopeless, that the problem has embedded itself too deeply into American politics and society, and he would be wrong.

The solution is found in the problem: a lack of education and with it understanding.

Americans can think, and they can think correctly if they have the proper background and facts. And, truth is a wonderful thing. It doesn't cost nearly as much time, effort, and money as a lie to disseminate. A lie costs many, many millions to disseminate. A few dollars' worth of material telling the truth can destroy a lie. Enough distribution, in the area of a few thousands of dollars, will create a ripple of truth out among the population in rapid order if it is connected to a nationally coordinated campaign, especially if it is aimed at those who run the local communities.

George Washington said, "Truth will ultimately prevail where there is pains taken to bring it to light."

John Adams stated that the revolution came about due to the education of the American people, that *this* was the true revolution. In a letter to H. Niles on February 13, 1818 he penned:

> But what do we mean by the American Revolution? Do we mean the American war? The Revolution was effected before the war commenced. The Revolution was in the minds and hearts of the people; a change in their religious sentiments, of their duties and obligations.... This radical change in the principles, opinion, sentiments, and affections of the people was the real American Revolution.

It can be done again. All it will take is for enough patriotic people of good character and religious ideals to make it happen.

George Washington said, "Liberty, when it begins to take root, is a plant of rapid growth."

This is the hard part: Planting liberty requires getting involved — in other words, work and especially organization. Too many individualists believe they can be more successful "on the outside" of an organization under attack due to the influence of the Conspiracy. There was never a more effective neutralizer than when the Conspiracy planted this thought in the minds of their opposition. Remember, *the Conspiracy will never allow a comfort zone for those who actually are hurting their agenda and exposing their minions.*

If you are successful in thwarting the agenda of the Conspiracy then expect to be attacked, often from quarters that will surprise you.

Another thing to remember is that you cannot usually see the weaknesses of the Conspiracy and their program. Often, when they are hurting the most, they will do all they can to make it appear as if there is no stopping their success. Many victories have come about in the face of massive campaigns designed to demoralize the opposition to the Conspiracy's agenda, when that opposition simply kept pressing on.

We have tried to give you a background of how we got to the point where we are in our country by outlining the movement to destroy the Constitution and God in our country from its onset. It probably has been difficult for some to read, losing heroes and accepting history you were never taught.

The solution for our country is equally difficult due to not just the lack of education of the people, but its misapplication. Without a moral compass and the ability to think logically, let alone having sufficient facts, the people will fall for any systematic propaganda disseminated through the media. That is why you see the tactic of the use of the smear by the media to keep people away from participating in organizations that oppose our march into socialism, particularly the only organization that can educate, involve, and nationally organize enough people to defeat the socialist conspiracy.

Never in the history of man had there ever been a permanent organization formed to enlist individualists into a permanent organization in opposition against collectivism. There had been some temporary ones for a single issue or in opposing a tyrant, but nothing permanent and nothing that was organized to build the movement on an education-action platform. Once the issue was gone or the tyrant defeated — or vice versa — what organizations may have existed died, if indeed you could call them *organizations* rather than *associations*.

The only attempt to form such an organization prior to 1958 was in the heyday of the Jacobins in early America, and it fell flat before it got started.

The collectivists organize. That is their basic philosophy: group together. Individualists, on the other hand, want to be left alone and rarely group together, even for self-preservation.

In the campaign to win back our country from the influence of the Conspiracy, the first element must be a systematic education of the American people, especially the opinion molders in the community, to serve as the base for uniting them against what the socialist minions are doing to our country and people. This education must do three things at the same time: 1) Teach sound principles and the liberal arts upon which the Constitution is based, reinforcing the layers of strength and morality in the American people, 2) point out the best method for returning to the original intent of the Constitution, then 3) enlist people into that method via a concerted action program.

People must realize that we are fighting people more than issues. People conceive, plan, organize and finance the problems we see in regard to attacking the Constitution and God. Expose them, and it goes a long way in diminishing the capabilities of our domestic enemies to achieve success.

If they are not *exposed*, they will return again and again to subvert our Americanist system and moral base.

Let us make a point that we have neglected so far: *There are no initiatives in the political realm that do not involve planning and gathering together a group of people to implement these plans.* If it is for evil, it is a conspiracy. Anyone involved in politics, and more so if in a leadership position, knows that small, confidential groups are the norm. The individuals in these groups then fan out and make things happen among the larger political movement. It's that simple.

To the average person such an initiative to educate Americans would seem to be insurmountable; however, it can be easier than even most experienced people would believe.

Only five percent run a community. Reach these people, and the community begins to change. Just reaching three percent, in other words 60% of the opinion molders, will do the job. Looking at it this way makes the task much easier.

The Building of Americanism

In 1958, a concerned citizen with a great deal of business and political experience, a student of history and of what made organizations successes or failures, formed an organization based on that study to promote Americanism and fight collectivism. His name was Robert Welch, and the organization became The John Birch Society, named in honor of Capt. John Birch who was a missionary to China and then a U.S. Army Air Corps intelligence officer who was killed by the Chinese communists less than two weeks after the end of World War II.

Robert Welch knew that he was going to have to form an organization that could do the above — educate Americans while exposing the Conspiracy — but at the same time would need to be protected as much as possible from destruction by the very enemies he knew would try to destroy the Society from within and without.

And he was correct in his foresight. Within a very short time, the Conspiracy took note that a new organization was in existence, giving leadership to the entire conservative movement that it had never experienced before. They knew something was going on because they started to meet coordinated opposition on a national scale — opposition the Conspiracy had never encountered before outside of small local areas or national personalities with no organization to back them up.

Since the Conspiracy was adept at organization and concerted action and familiar with the results of such effort, they recognized in 1959 that something was afoot by what they saw taking shape in the political atmosphere of America in opposition to what they were doing.

People who have experience investigating communist infiltration and tactics can tell at a glance where the impetus comes from for a leftist movement and who the leaders are, because they have studied them. It is the same with the conspirators; they can see the hand of The John Birch Society due to the timing; identical rhetoric, slogans, and phrases; methodology; leaders; and the intellectual arguments all across the country at the same time, while others are oblivious to either the communist or the Bircher.

It did not take them long to see that the coordinating factor was The John Birch Society. They decided at once that this force had to be met head on.

At the meeting in 1960 of the "81 Communist and Workers' Parties" from around the world in convention in Moscow, the communist leadership said that the only thing standing in their way for global victory was the growing anti-communist movement in America. The word went out that this movement had to be stopped. The John Birch Society took the brunt of this attack, according to the congressional testimony of Edward Hunter, the U.S. Army expert on what became known as brainwashing of our POW's during the Korean War. The initial assault was orchestrated from the official organ of the West Coast Communist Party, *People's World*, which subsequently became the official national organ of the party.

From the opening salvo against the JBS in this communist newspaper, within two weeks the establishment media picked up the attack and launched a smear campaign against the JBS that still has some residual negativity over 50 years later among the people who were politically aware at the time.

It was amazing how many people had a negative feeling about the JBS but could not articulate why — all they knew was that it was bad, not knowing how they had been influenced to believe so.

The attacks were similar, but far more intense, to those that were levied against Tea Party activists in the 2010s. Veterans who were members of the JBS took their oath of office as members of the military to defend the Constitution from all enemies, foreign and domestic, seriously. Everyone knows the foreign enemies, but only the JBS identified the domestic enemies; therefore, they received the bulk of attacks leveled against constitutionalists.

The communists and the Insiders were successful in preventing their own defeat by stopping enough people from enlisting in the JBS to ensure a conservative victory, but were not successful in making the JBS go away. In the ensuing years the JBS has suffered defeats, but at the same time has sustained many victories, most of them out of the sight of the average citizen; in other words, often the people were not even aware there was an issue, much less the involvement of the JBS in that issue.

Since the JBS studies where the Insider agenda is the weakest, or where an agenda is the most vital to their success, the JBS attacks there. This may often not be a public issue, and the activity takes place behind the scenes in political arenas hidden from the public by the mass media. Also, because the JBS does not spend money touting its successes and would rather spend it on solving the problems, there is a dearth of publicity as to just how effective the JBS is.

This is contrary to most organizations, which spend a goodly amount of time and money advertising themselves, sometimes even taking credit for JBS victories (since the JBS does not spend time and money bragging and therefore people are unaware of the Society's involvement).

Probably the most famous case in which the JBS was the primary *organization* was the impeachment of President Clinton. The impeachment process was blunted in Congress, however, by removing the original charges of bribery and treason. The movement became something they could not stop, so they deflected its effectiveness by altering the charge to lying. However, there was ample evidence of treason and bribery relative to the Chinese communists and President Clinton's involvement.

Clinton was impeached by the House of Representatives. He was not, however, found guilty by the Senate.

Hillary Clinton knew who was behind it when she referred to the "vast right-wing conspiracy" behind her husband's problems. She did not want to give publicity to the JBS, so she referenced the situation in the manner that she did.

Most of the people who participated in the impeachment process did not know the JBS was the primary organization because much of the work was done through an ad hoc committee formed by the JBS. However, publications such as the *Washington Post* newspaper did, and accordingly gave credit to the JBS.

While this may have been the most famous issue involving of the JBS, it by no means was their only success. Literally scores of issues and campaigns have been successfully implemented, albeit outside of the public view, since the national media has a habit of only reporting on those things they deem important, which usually means something they want to indoctrinate the people on so they can move the agenda forward.

The most notable success of the JBS among conservatives was the massive campaign that stopped the North American Union in its tracks under George W. Bush. The North American Union's official name was the Security and Prosperity Partnership, and its aim was the merger of the three North American countries of Canada, Mexico, and the United States. Millions of dollars and a herculean effort coordinated by the JBS staff led to literally millions of contacts educating the opinion molders around the country, leading over 25 state legislatures to consider resolutions against the North American Union (NAU).

There were others involved, but the bulk of what was done, about 90%, was accomplished by members of the JBS.

None other than the leader of this initiative for the Council on Foreign Relations wrote before he died that it was the JBS and Eagle Forum that had stopped the Security and Prosperity Partnership. The bulk of the physical effort was carried out by the JBS, and millions of pieces of literature and a special edition of their magazine, *The New American,* were disseminated to opinion molders.

Under Obama, the Conspiracy again started to move the initiative forward, a salami slice at a time, under a new façade, the North American Leadership Initiative.

A case can be made that the JBS over the years through their coordinated activities have set back the timetable of the Conspiracy for consolidating their New World Order by a minimum of forty years. To document this would take another four or five chapters. One can go online to the JBS website, JBS.org, where there are listed many of the victories of the Society.

There are sufficient layers of moral and political strength that still exist among the American people, and some of these layers are growing. Much of this is due to the approximately one billion — with a "B"— pieces of literature, books, reprints, magazines, congressional and legislative voting records, etc. disseminated by members of the JBS for over 50 years.

This does not count the millions of people who have seen JBS videos posted on the Internet at www.JBS.org, embedded in other websites, or shown in public and private events (and the millions who viewed filmstrips and movies prior to video and the Internet). Most of the JBS videos online that have been posted by others have been cropped so as to not show the JBS symbol on the screen, to hide the involvement of the JBS. This is mostly to make it appear that others are responsible for the work, and to have the viewer contact them rather than the JBS.

One of the affiliates of the JBS, American Opinion Foundation, as of this writing, has reached well over 10,000,000 views of our videos. This is a conservative estimate. Most of these videos are on the Constitution. How much overlap between the two entities and their video viewings is unknown. However, the two programs tend to approach a similar, but not unified grouping of people.

The JBS goes about its business in local areas by organizing local, neighborhood chapters. Its structure is designed to withstand the attacks by outside influences, whether they come from any element of the Conspiracy, racists, or simply those who wish to use the JBS for purposes other than its mission. Its altruistic members serve in volunteer positions of leadership, although the JBS has a fulltime staff that serves all over the country to coordinate JBS activities and organizational growth.

The success of the JBS is such that the attacks against it continue, and they rise in intensity from time to time when an important issue is on the table. The opposition do all they can to negate JBS influence and try to turn people away from involving themselves in the organization, thereby preventing the JBS from having the necessary strength to defeat the Insiders completely. Some of these attacks come from organizations and individuals who have the appearance or reputation of being conservative.

Indeed, when certain seemingly conservative groups support an initiative that The John Birch Society does not support, they spend a good deal of time trying to negate the influence of the JBS entirely, not just allowing the argument to stand or fall on its merits. In some cases, the attacks are aimed more at the JBS than would seem necessary if indeed coming from conservatives.

There is an initiative within the general conservative movement to split it up, to create discouragement and disillusion to negate its success. Working together, conservatives will always win. Split apart, they are readily defeated. In other words, it is a divide and conquer tactic.

The attacks against the JBS tend to linger, and it takes time and good will to repair the coalitions of conservatives working together.

For those who have been involved for years in the fight to save America, the JBS likes to ask, "Where have we been wrong in the nearly 60 years of our activity?" In hindsight, after the rhetoric has been turned off, and the emotions have subsided, the answer has been never.

This does not mean that there has never been public disagreement amongst members and leaders of the Society. The organization is, after all, composed of individualists. Sometimes a public pronouncement by a leader of the Society is used as the official position of the JBS when it may or may not be true and may only be the opinion of the member, not the organization.

One such case involved the official position of the Society against an Article V convention in 2015. It was made to appear, by certain conservatives, that the JBS had changed its opinion from that of the founder of the Society, Mr. Welch, and a former chairman of the board, Rep. Lawrence McDonald, who were supposedly for an Article V convention.

The entire affair would take a couple of pages to explain. Rather than do that, it is enough to realize that the JBS stopped supporting the Liberty Amendment because we could not get its author to stop playing with fire by advocating forcing the Congress to move forward by threatening them with an Article V convention. The amendment was sound; the methodology of getting it adopted was dangerous.

Lawrence McDonald never endorsed a convention, he merely reported that it was one of the methods advocated by the Liberty Amendment committee. He tried to implement the ratification by submitting a bill before Congress, and his address in favor of the amendment was taken out of context. In other words, he was trying to get the amendment ratified the traditional way through Congress, not by a "Con-Con."

Americans can do well by contacting the JBS and learning how they can become involved — or not — at www.jbs.org.

While the country can be saved, we must say that what has been documented herein is only the tip of the iceberg. To write about it all would take three volumes just for the period of 1776-1876. And, we have not even begun to document the financial aspects of control by the Conspiracy.

We would like to say in regard to the latter, that stories of the power of the Rothschilds and others in the very early years are generally myth. Their power and influence did not become an earth-shaking influence until many years after the formation of the Illuminati and they were not involved in the foundation of the Illuminati.

The money power was produced by the Conspiracy, not the other way around.

We have wanted to show that the changes made in our country, in the body politic, education, religion, and other areas, have not come about as a result of "history" or the natural deterioration of civilization, but have by a coordinated attack on Americanism: our Judeo-Christian heritage, the Declaration of Independence, and the Constitution in its original intent.

In some areas, it has been difficult to show the coordination and/or the main personalities and the control they exert. The record disappeared too long ago and it is very difficult to reconstruct the history from the information that is left. We wish, for instance, that the records of the Lodge of the Nine Sisters and other Illuminist groups had not been confiscated by the Gestapo. Who knows what information would have been available about early American involvement? All we know is that Americans were involved, but not to what extent.

We have mentioned other instances of the disappearance of the record surrounding the Lincoln assassination, Harper's Ferry, the Confederate Secret Service, the private records of Aaron Burr, etc., and these are just a few of the *documented* disappearances of evidence. Who knows what records of conspiratorial events have never made the light of day enough to know that they once ever existed?

What we are witnessing is the result of a coordinated effort through the years to subvert America. It is subversion from within, since no power or combination of powers could subdue our country as long as our people are free, the Constitution is intact, Americanism is taught, and we only allow a limited number of people to immigrate into our country each year. Massive immigration can destroy the previous caveats by overwhelming numbers of people who simply do not understand our system.

Remember, it is the government that sets the standards for educating immigrants to qualify for citizenship. These standards today, while teaching minutia about our government, do not teach basic constitutional law. For example they teach that our country is a democracy rather than a republic, never stating the difference between the two.

There are many volumes the reader can read. We have not documented, other than a sketch or two, the tremendous march toward the control of education of our children by the socialist conspiracy and the part played by Horace Mann. Others have done this well and there is no need to replicate their work. Some of the best information on this subject has been done by Samuel Blumenfeld.

We also have not documented the systematic attack on American religious denominations, since that would take a full volume and probably be misconstrued as an attack on these denominations, some of which were born in this country. Some started out radical but evolved into more mainstream sects. In some cases, they started out radical and the other sects caught up to them.

In this regard, we have not shown the influence on American religion by the so-called Burnt-over District of New York and the birth of religions in that area. Some were sound, some were taken off course by unscrupulous leaders, and some had a great influence on the neutralization of Northern Christians to fight the Conspiracy that existed right before their eyes. This neutralization continues into modern times, has spread heavily into the South, and has become entrenched as "gospel."

The true Gospel tells the reader to oppose evil and the consequences of not doing so. Any doctrine that states not to oppose evil, or is a de facto influence not to, springs from a source not of God. It has been the anti-God movement using Christians to send themselves to concentration camps. In Germany and Russia, it was both Christians and Jews who sold out their co-religionists.

People cannot understand how the German Jews could have been fooled. "Why did they not resist while there was time?" is a popular question. Christians in America have and are being fooled by drinking the same well-water the Germans were fooled by. The only reason it has taken longer for this water to brainwash the American people is the layers of strength and liberty within the American people and culture.

Look around you — the overt signs of government being against the practices of Christians and Jews are rising. When will it be too late?: When too many Americans do nothing.

We have shown that the American foreign policy and military came under the influence of conspirators and militant socialists descended directly from the Illuminist influence and its second and third generation organizations. The infiltration by such individuals and organizations was attempted under the first two federal administrations, began to exert its influence increasingly during and after the third administration, and then rose to nearly total influence from Pierce through Lincoln.

It continued after the Civil War. There is no reason to believe that our State or Defense Departments are not totally controlled by their progeny today. One has not heard of any purge of such individuals at any time since. Our actions as a country leading us into, and then the conduct of all wars since the Civil War, indicate that this is the case. All wars since that time have had an agenda quite different from the simple defeat of the enemy. However this is not taught in school. Just as is the case with the Civil War.

When it comes to purging our government of subversives, any attempt to rid our government of communists, for instance, is met with concerted opposition. Anyone attempting to do so is vilified by the media, government officials, academia, non-government agencies, and non-profits. The most serious attempt in the 20th century was by Sen. Joseph McCarthy; his vilification destroyed his life, and continues even after his death. The attacks against him became so intense that his name is still used to denote any attempts to expose any socialist agenda or person: McCarthyism.

One of the most common misunderstandings regarding the activities of McCarthy is that he had something to do with the so-called Blacklist of Hollywood. He was concerned about the Departments of State and the Army, and was a U.S. senator. It was the House of Representatives that was concerned about subversion in Hollywood and in other layers of society.

Did McCarthy make mistakes? Yes, but not those he was accused of making. There was an organization that had a substantial reward for anyone who could prove that McCarthy ever falsely accused a person of being a communist. No one ever stepped forward to claim the reward.

Otto Otepka, a deputy director of the Office of Security of the State Department, also tried to rid known communists from State by furnishing information to the U.S. Senate. His longstanding exemplary career was destroyed within the State Department as a result.

In the Defense Department, the anti-communists that got in the way were drummed out or neutralized, such as Patton, Walker, and MacArthur. Pro-communists, or generals that had no problem working with communists, were elevated, some so quickly through the ranks as to make one's head swim. It is rare that the Joint Chiefs of Staff did/do not contain members of the Council on Foreign Relations.[68]

This government that is attempting to eliminate God from public life in America is the same government that is supposedly trying to save us from the militant Muslim. The results, however, are more militant Muslim governments and the elimination of all Christianity and Judaism from those Muslim countries where we have interfered either militarily or diplomatically. Both the State and Defense Departments are involved in this process. Look to the results for original intent, particularly if they are always the same regardless of the excuse used for our involvement.

Achieving the same results over and over again is not a sign of mistakes, it is a sign of intent.

It is simply an extension of the ultimate goal of eliminating Christianity and Judaism, though not an obvious one. Indeed, the Christian community, out of patriotism and the feelings generated against Islam, supports the very process by which Christianity is being wiped out in the Middle East, the cradle of Christianity: intervention by war and foreign entanglements.

Literally millions of Christians and Jews have been murdered and/or displaced and exiled as a result of our foreign policy run by members of the Council on Foreign Relations in Muslim countries — countries wherein these sects resided for two millennia.

One of the mainstays in the Conspiracy's tactics is to assume the leadership of their own opposition. The JBS was structured to prevent any successful implementation of that tactic within the organization. No other organization can say this. The JBS has not been successful in preventing partial infiltration and the subsequent damage, but these attempts have always been localized and brief.

The JBS likewise has not been successful in preventing the formation of ersatz organizations that have the appearance of opposition to the Conspiracy or its issues. These groups have then either deflected the necessary strength from being consolidated into one concerted action program, or promoted a false solution. Thus, many groups exist that knowingly or unknowingly detract Americans from effective opposition.[69]

---

68 The best documentation for this process remains *The Politician*, by Robert Welch. If and when you read it, and it is highly recommended that you do, remember that a great deal that was not included in the book came to light after its publication.

69 These organizations and personalities tend to be well funded from unknown sources, whereas the JBS is funded by its membership and nearly all of the monies with the exception of less than one percent, come from that body. Since this is the case, the membership has leverage on the future leadership and direction of the JBS — it is, in that sense, self-policing against future divergence from JBS principles and goals.

One clue of such a condition is the lack of JBS leaders appearing on national media by so-called conservative national talk-show hosts. In fact, JBS spokesmen have been asked on, then cancelled at the last moment to substitute more establishment conservatives in their place. The viewer is none the wiser. By this method, people who have very little organizational following are promoted among conservative audiences. This leads people to believe that the JBS doesn't even exist or is ineffective when the opposite is the case — out of sight, out of mind.

Some of these so-called conservative organizations are nothing more than an office with very few employees. Some do not even have a membership; they are only mailing lists. A visit to their office, and then a visit to the JBS complex comprised of three substantial buildings, should immediately tell the visitor which one is the viable organization.

The reader should also ask himself why some uber conservative talk-show hosts have been able to make it big in the commercial market that eschews conservatism. Why do they represent conservatism, and how did they raise the money and get the sponsorship and/or the blessing of the major media moguls?

This is a question never asked by conservatives who believe the mass media to be controlled by left-leaning owners and managers.

Talk is cheap, in the sense of actively doing something effective. *Talk or texting is not **doing** something.*

The Civil War could not change our people sufficiently to bring permanent tyranny to our country; the layers of strength among our people were too broad and deep. These layers of strength needed to be eroded first: religion, morality (both personal and civic), responsibility (both personal and organizational), a love for and understanding of the Constitution, the classic liberal arts education that led to its adoption, etc.

It took a long time to erode these layers of strength, but a reversal began to take place once the JBS started its program and these layers have been growing back; however, they have not yet resulted in replacing socialists in government or abolishing unconstitutional government because it is difficult to stay ahead of the deficient education in the schools and seminaries, as well as the tremendous increase in immigration, all of which affect millions.

The centers of power that have grown have been controlled by the Conspiracy's minions as well. It has been well documented that certain American financiers, industrialists, and politicians have played key roles in installing dictators and bringing about wars abroad that our country then has to fight. They did it with the Civil War, and have been doing it ever since around the world.

It is not well known that our Federal Reserve (or those connected with it) helped finance the build-up of the German and Japanese war machines in the 1930s. Likewise prominent Americans helped bring dictators to power in other countries, and/or helped them build up their military capabilities. This was true of Lenin, Hitler, Mao, Ho Chi Minh, Saddam — the list goes on and continues today.

Conservatives have a hard time understanding that sometimes their heroes can be involved in the Conspiracy and serve as a means to spread the New World Order under the banner of conservatism. This problem is centered primarily among those referred to as neo-conservatives. Neoconservatives generally have the strategy of the Young America wing of the Conspiracy. To understand the latter, one should do a comprehensive study of the Dulles brothers and Bush family before and after World War II, along with their influence within the Republican Party.

Today organizations abound that promote the agenda of the Conspiracy, especially their New World Order. It is rare that a member of the Council on Foreign Relations is not the head of our State Department or Defense Department, along with their assistants and general staff. Since most Americans have a warm feeling for our fighting men, they cannot imagine that some of their generals and admirals serving in the

Joint Chiefs of Staff may have a different agenda than the soldier, sailor, and American people.

For instance, the former commander of the coalition forces in Afghanistan, an America general, was a member of the CFR and in retirement continued to influence government policy through a foreign policy group founded and dominated by members of the CFR. In addition, two other American commanders in Afghanistan were shown to be corrupt and resigned their positions in disgrace.

This has happened in the lifetime of you the reader, yet did you ever see these facts presented to you in such a manner in your media?

The battle for the hearts and minds of the American people is not a battle we can shrink from. Defeat by the enemies we fight is unthinkable.

Retreating from the courage to get involved makes cowards of men and can only lead to the enslavement of our children, perhaps for hundreds of years. What we do here and now as Americans will determine what will happen to the rest of the world. It is not a stretch to say that with the fall of liberty in the United States, a new Dark Age will descend upon the entire planet.

We have to educate our children in our true history and work to restore our heritage to its rightful place in American life.

We have no illusions that this volume will gain widespread circulation, if for no other reason than it advocates a solution, not simply relating information. People love to read about the problem — few do anything about it, and they do not want to be disturbed in their reading.

What about you? What will you tell your children and grandchildren if we lose to a militant socialist machine?

The Conspiracy does not care what you know, only what you do about what you know.

APPENDIX ONE:

The Ten Essentials Reading/Viewing list

The Communist Manifesto, Karl Marx and Frederick Engels. Only by reading and comprehending what they are trying to do will one understand the dangers around him and his community. The *Manifesto* must be read extending the lines of many of its statements and goals. The real picture of what they mean to establish is there, but hidden within its over-worded sentences. Take the time to think about the passages and what they really portend. Sun Tzu in his *Art of War* told us to know our enemy — what better way than to read the *Manifesto*?*

The Creature From Jekyll Island, G. Edward Griffin. This best-seller is a fascinating and comprehensive look at the formation of the Federal Reserve System. Yes, there was a secret meeting to establish the Fed; this book tells who was there, who they represented, and how they were able to con the American people into support for the system.*

Dollars and $ense, John F. McManus. This John Birch Society DVD is an excellent, simple, entertaining, and common-sense analysis of economics enabling you to discuss the subject after one viewing.*

None Dare Call It Conspiracy, Gary Allen and Larry Abraham, Concord Press. Circulated in the millions in the 1970s, this small volume helped people understand the politics of the day and how a small number of people were able to influence an entire nation. The lessons it teaches are still valid today. Out of print but available online.

Overview of America, John F. McManus. This John Birch Society DVD is an excellent breakdown of the American system and how it differs from all others. Viewed and enjoyed by millions, and recommended for people of all walks of life and education.*

The Politician, Robert Welch, Belmont Publishing Company, 1964. This book documents the influences that elevated Dwight David Eisenhower from a Lt. Colonel in the U.S. Army to the leader of all Allied forces in Europe during World War II within a very short period of time. The information is valuable in order to see and understand the influences that are at play today in our military.*

Shadows of Power, James Perloff, American Opinion Press. Documents the power center of the Council on Foreign Relations and its influence on the American body politic in support of the New World Order today. Includes a membership list.*

NEA: Trojan Horse in American Education, Samuel Blumenfeld. A comprehensive look at the history of American public education, the organizations and people who started it all.*

The Whole of Their Lives, Benjamin Gitlow. The story of a former member of the Central Committee of the Communist Party USA and editor of the Communist Party newspaper *The Worker*, and why he left the movement and the tactics the party uses.

Proofs of a Conspiracy, John Robison. The first contemporary look at the Illuminati during its known existence. Robison was an English Mason warning others about the infiltration by the Illuminati, including the Grand Orient of Continental Europe. There are those who claim that Robison was actually shown the Order's mission personally by Weishaupt in an attempt to enlist him in propagating the Order in England. Robison did not like what he saw and thus wrote the book against the Illuminati. Widely circulated at the time among Masons who were fearful of the Order.

Robison was held in such high esteem in America that he was elected a member of the Philosophical Society in Philadelphia. In England, his book led to the passage in 1799 of the secret societies law. He was honored by degrees from the University of Edinburgh and the University of Glasgow, and held memberships in several prestigious academies and societies from America to Russia.

He was not, in other words, someone who was known as a paranoid conspiracy theorist, as modern historians tend to promote.*

*May be ordered through ShopJBS.org. All other volumes may be found through Amazon.com or a similar source.

APPENDIX TWO:

System of Government

Our system of government essentially was and is a republic: the rule of law. This system limits the government rather than the people, and uses the government to protect the God-given rights of the people as long as it is strictly adhered to as codified in a Constitution.

This is the opposite of a democracy, wherein the majority rule without restraint.

Our Constitution mandates that every state government be a republic. You will not find the word democracy in the Constitution or in any of the fifty state constitutions.

Some governments call themselves a republic only to mask what they really are. It is a distortion of the rule of law. This false doctrine does not diminish the need to have a true republican system of government.

No individual or minority can be safe in a democracy. You must have the rule of law or the government will be unrestrained in its rule over the people, in the name of the people.

Karl Marx and Frederick Engels understood this, and that is why they wanted to "win the battle of democracy" as the first step toward a dictatorship of the proletariat — in reality the dictatorship of the party leadership, who have organized the masses to vote the way the revolution desires until the communists have consolidated control, and then a dictatorship, over all people.

Democracy will implode when the people realize that they can vote to take something from one group and give it to themselves in the form of taxes and benefits, land and public domain, perceived superior status over inferiors, etc., if the government is not constrained.

In the extreme, democracy will eliminate the minority who are different than the majority in religion or race. At the minimum, democracy will be used by the majority to prevent the minority having any success at the ballot box by placing "legal" roadblocks in their way. (Only white folk can vote, as an example.)

You have seen that there were, and are, those who wish to change our system into an unbridled democracy on the road to a socialist and ungodly system. They used, and use, any and all situations that create an emotional response and/or a crisis to effect changes which are untenable to freedom and liberty.

Let us briefly examine the arguments that were used to change our government from what it was in the beginning to what it became after the Civil War.

1. The idea that the states had no sovereignty was totally the opposite of the situation as it was during the War for Independence.
    a. The colonies were under the Crown but totally independent from one another, and they formed the United States. The federation did not form the states.
    b. Once the Constitution was presented, state ratifying conventions approved the new Law. No one asked the Constitutional Convention to present a totally new system to them, only to amend the Articles of Confederation; nonetheless, the wisdom of the men who crafted it was recognized and it was ratified, albeit under the new rule of three-fourths rather than needing a unanimous vote as called for under the Articles of Confederation *which the states were still bound by until the ratification of the new Constitution.*
    c. If the states were not sovereign, then why ask them to ratify the Constitution and not simply im-

pose it upon them? Just as an individual should not be asked to vote away his liberty, the states were not asked to give up their sovereignty by ratifying the Constitution.
   d. If there is no sovereignty residing in the states, then why:
      i. The provision in the federal Constitution that the states ratify amendments to the federal document?
      ii Have the Senate, which was supposed to represent the state legislatures, in the federal legislature — although ruptured by the 17th amendment?
   e. The very idea of a centralized government was abhorrent to the Founders of our country. They had just conducted an exhausting war against such an entity — why produce another in its place? We were to be a federation, a confederacy of sovereign states.
   f. The Constitution affirms and mandates that each state shall be a republic. It is impossible to have a republic without having sovereignty, otherwise the term means nothing.
   g. If it is true that the people formed the new state governments later admitted to these United States, then the rights of the people and the responsibility to provide justice and the protection of those rights flows up from the people, through the local and state governments, not down from a central government.
2. While slavery was and is abhorrent, to oppose it while denying the foregoing leads to the eventual slavery of all, not just the minority. Every step away from the free system which our forefathers bequeathed to us is a step backward toward what the rest of the world had and toward tyranny. Without America leading the way and setting the example, the world would not have the degree of freedom that exists for many people today, particularly in Europe. The American system was new, an experiment that has led to the greatest country on earth.
3. A spirit of cooperation is necessary in any union. Except for the fanatics, most Southerners knew slavery would ultimately end. The economics of the situation demanded it, in addition to the moral aspect. Before the issue became an emotional one, many states debated its continuance.
   a. The states concerned about *state sovereignty* had a majority in the Senate. While the republican system lasted, they had a good chance of maintaining enough votes to stop the federal encroachments advocated by the Radicals.
   b. The state sovereignty issue was also a great concern among the people of all sections, and the activity within the Democrat Party and the Copperheads in what remained of the federation during the Civil War bears this out.
   c. It was becoming increasingly obvious that the agrarian system based on slavery was regressive compared to the industrialization of the North with free labor. The South continuing forward independently as a separate country would have stifled the growth of the economy of the South if it had maintained the status quo economically.
   d. Only by mutual cooperation between the states could America grow and move forward as a giant among nations.
4. The problem with the state sovereignty issue in those days, as well as today, was that it was tied to an emotional issue. Emotions ran high and while some men tried to solve the problems amicably, they were hit by fanatics on both sides and they became nothing more than dead skunks in the middle of the road.
   a. The impetus for a peaceful settlement had been circumvented by abolitionist extremists when they deliberately and effectively put the colonization theory for all practical purposes out of business. The plan for colonization may not have worked, but the point is that the Radicals on both sides did not want anything to work.

> > i. They did not want any plan to work to eliminate slavery peacefully, otherwise they would have adopted a goal of supporting some plan based on what the English had done to eliminate slavery. Interestingly, the British socialists involved in helping American abolition apparently were not interested in having the U.S. replicate the British example.
> > ii. Both the abolitionists and extreme slavery advocates hated the republican system.
> > iv. They became nationalists as the first step toward a world government. They used the issue of slavery to put the focus on emotion and away from reason. They put the focus on national sovereignty and away from any state sovereignty as a right.
>
> b. The goal of centralized control on the road toward world government was also true of the fanatic slavery advocates.
> c. There were and are certain responsibilities delegated to the union. These responsibilities cannot simply be pulled back from the federal government to the state or group of states if a viable confederacy is to be maintained.

To secede from the union, either as a state or a group of states, simply meant being run over sooner or later by the remainder. There is no way that a group of seceded states would have been a stronger group than the remainder left in the federal union. This situation was even compounded within the Confederacy with the actions of many of the Southern state governments against Confederate laws.

Last, but not least, there is the simple fact of breach of contract. No one can be held to a contract if the opposing party has engaged in a breach of contract. If this were to be otherwise, no contract would be safe. It is dishonest.

Civilizations cannot hold together if contracts are not honored, particularly the contract referred to as the Constitution, with the people and their local, state, and federal governments. If a government breaches its constitution, what then? Are people, or any local government that represents the people, to stand by and idly allow the continuation of the breach? Heaven forbid. One would hope at the minimum that enough people would get involved to ensure that whatever or whoever would be brought back into fulfillment of the contract and/or punished in the process.

Once this contractual agreement is violated over and over — and generally it can only be violated by government — the whole fabric of a country begins to unravel.

The danger of allowing oneself to become too emotionally involved could well mean that false solutions can overwhelm common sense. This will always be a problem for individualists relative to maintaining a free society, especially if there is a body of people who will use conspiracy to gain their objectives.

Happily, slavery does not exist today in the form that it did prior to the Civil War. One wishes that the abolition could have happened without the violence and changes that were made in our government, which will continue to haunt us until we restore the system that our Founders gave us.

BIBLIOGRAPHY

Aaron Burr, by Samuel H. Wandell and Meade Minningerode, Volume One, G. P. Putnam's Sons, New York and London, The Knickbocker Press, 1925

The Abolitionist Legacy, by James M. McPherson, The Princeton University Press, Princeton, NJ, 1975

The Abolitionists, The Growth of a Dissenting Minority, by Milton L. Dillon, Northern Illinois University Press, DeKalb, 1974

Abraham Among the Yankees, Abraham Lincoln's 1848 Visit to Massachusetts, by William F. Hanna, Taunton, MA, The Old Colony Historical Society, 1983

Abraham Lincoln, by Carl Sandburg, Volume I — VI, Charles Scribner's Sons, New York, 1939

Abraham Lincoln, 1809-1858, by Albert J. Beveridge, 2 vols., Houghton Mifflin, Boston, 1928

Abraham Lincoln and the Fifth Column, by George Fort Milton, The Vanguard Press, NY, 1942

Abraham Lincoln and the Second American Revolution, by James M. McPherson, Oxford University Press, New York, Oxford, 1960

The Adams Family, by James Truslow Adams, The Literary Guild, New York, 1930

Academic American History, The Gilded Age, The War Between Capital and Labor, www.academicamerica.com

The Advocate of Peace, (1837-1845), Published by the World Affairs Institute.

Affairs of the Late Insurrectionary States, 2nd Session, 42nd Congress, South Carolina, Volume 2.

Against the Current, The Life of Karl Heinzen, (1809 — 80), by Carl Wittke, University of Chicago Press, Chicago, Illinois, 1945

The Age of the Democratic Revolution, A Political History of Europe and America, 1760 — 1800, In two volumes, "The Challenge," and "The Struggle," by R. R. Palmer, Princeton University Press, Princeton, New Jersey, 1959

The Age of Hate: Andrew Johnson and the Radicals, By George Fort Milton, Coward — McCann, Inc., New York, 1930

The Agrarian Crusade, by Solon J. Buck, New Haven: Yale University Press, 1920

Albert Gallatin, American Statesmen Series, by John Austin Stevens, Houghton, Mifflin and Co., Boston, 1888

Alexander Hamilton, by Henry Cabot Lodge, Houghton Mifflin Company, Boston and New York, 1882 and 1910

A Life of Clement L. Vallandigham, by His Brother, Rev. James Laird Vallandigham, Baltimore: Turnbull Brothers, 1872

Ambivalent Conspirators, John Brown, The Secret Six, and a Theory of Slave Violence, by Jeffery Rossbach, University of Pennsylvania Press, Philadelphia, 1982

America & the British Left, From Bright to Bevan, by Henry Pelling, London, Brown and Company, Boston, 1953

America And French Culture, 1750 — 1848, by Howard Mumford Jones, The University of North Carolina Press, Chapel Hill, 1927

American Historical Review, Vol.12, No. 3, (April 1907), "The Sharpes Rifle Episode in Kansas History," by W. H. Isely

The American Review: A Whig Journal Devoted to Politics And Literature, New Series, Vol. IV — Whole Vol. X, New York: Published at 118 Nassau Street, 1849

America's Secret Establishment, Anthony Sutton, Library House Press, Billings, MT, 1986

American Antiquarian Society Proceedings, "John C. Calhoun and the Secession Movement of 1850," by Henry V. Ames, New series, XXVIII, 1918

American Aurora, A Democratic-Republican Returns, The Suppressed History of Our Nation's Beginnings and the Heroic Newspaper that tried to Report it, by Richard N. Rosenfeld, St. Martins Press, New York, 1997

The American Bookseller's Complete Reference Tradelist, etc., Compiled by Alexander V. Blake, Published by Simeon Ide, Claremont, New Hampshire, 1847

The American Catholic Quarterly Review, Volume XIII, From January to October, 1888, Philadelphia, Hardy & Mahony, Publishers and Proprietors, 1888

The American College & University, A History, by Frederick Rudolph, Alfred A. Knopf, New York, 1862

The American Conflict, A History of The Great Rebellion in the United States of America, etc., 1860-'64, by Horace Greeley, Published by O. D. Case & Company, Hartford, Volume I, 1864; *1864-'65*, Volume II, 1866

The American Counterrevolution: A Retreat from Liberty, 1783 — 1800, by Larry E. Tise, Stackpole Books, Mechanicsburg, PA, 1998

American Experience Series, "Telegrams From the Dead," Ellen Burnstyn, narrator, WGBH Boston Production, 1994

American Historical Review,
    XXXII, 1926, "Young America," by Merle Curti
    XLVII, 1941, "The Knights of the Golden Circle: The Career of George Bickley," by Ollinger Crenshaw

American History Illustrated,
    Volume XXII, No. 10, February 1988, Page 42, "Mr. Garrison and the Mob," by Robert Elliott MacDougall
    Volume XXIII, No. 1, March 1988, page 21, "Louisa May Alcott," by William T. Anderson; Page 30, "Concord's Man for the Twenty-First Century"; Page 38, "Concord's Literary Heritage."
    Volume XXIII, No. 2, April 1988, "History Bookshelf."
    Volume XXIII, No. 3, May 1988, Page 38, "The Proving Ground," by Peter F. Stevens

Volume XXIII, No. 7, November 1988, Page 37, "A Few Appropriate Remarks," by Harold Holzer; Page 28, "Master Fraud of the Century — The Disputed Election of 1876," by Roy Morris, Jr.; Page 34, "'Boss' Tweed: Colossus of Corruption?", by Joseph Gustaitus; Page 50, "Clara Barton"
Volume XXIII, No. 10, February 1988, Page 15, "El Presidente Gringo," by Roger Bruns and Bryan Kennedy
Volume XXIV, No. 3, May 1989, Page 5, "Mailbox — Filling Walker's War Chest"
Volume XXIV, November/December 1989, "Clara Barton, Founder of the American Red Cross," by Cathleen Schurr, pages 50 — 64 Mailbox, Page 16
American Labor Leaders, by Charles A. Madison, Harper and Brothers Publishers, NY, 1950
"The American Movement," by Eugene V. Debs, *The Appeal to Reason*, 1908
American Paradox: the conflict of thoughts and action, by Merle Curti, Rutgers University Press, New Brunswick, NJ, 1956
American Political Parties, Their Natural History by Wilfred E. Binkley, Alfred A. Knopf, NY, 1962
American Progress or The Greatest Events of the Greatest Century, by Hon. R. M. Devens, Published by Hugh Heron, Chicago, 1886
The American Quarterly Church Review, and Ecclesiastical Register, Vol. XV 1863-64, New York, N.S. Richardson, London, Trübner & Co., 1864
American Statesman: Andrew Jackson, As a Public Man, By William Graham Sumner, Boston, Houghton, Mifflin and Co., NY, 1892
American Statesmen, and Patriots of the United States, no author, no date, 188(?), Hurst and Company, Publishers, New York
The Americans, A Social History of the United States, 1587 — 1914, by J. C. Fiernas, G. P. Putnam's Sons, New York, 1969
America's Utopian Experiments, Communal Havens from Long-Wave Crises, by Brian J. L. Berry, Dartmouth College, Published By the University Press of New England, Hanover and London, 1992
An Authentic Exposition of the "K.G.C." "Knights of the Golden Circle;" OR a History of Secession From 1834 to 1861, By a Member of the Order, Indianapolis, IND. 1861
Anthony Burns: The Defeat and Triumph of a Fugitive Slave, by Virginia Hamilton, Alfred A. Knopf, New York, 1988
Andrew Jackson, As a Public Man, American Statesmen series, by William Graham Sumner, Houghton, Mifflin and Company, Boston, 1892
Antimasonry, The Crusade and the Party, by Lorman Ratner, Prentice — Hall Inc., New Jersey, 1969
Antislavery, by Dwight Lowell Damond, Ann Arbor: University of Michigan Press, 1961
The Antislavery Appeal, American Abolitionism After 1830, by Ronald G. Walters, The Johns Hopkins University Press, Baltimore & London, 1976
The Anti-slavery Society Convention, 1840, by Benjamin Robert Hayden
The Anti-Slavery Crusade, by Jesse Macy, Yale University Press, 1919, Chronicles of America Series, Volume 28
An Appeal To The Public on the Controversy Respecting the Revolution in Harvard College, by J. Morse, DD, Charleston, 1814, Printed for the Author
Appleton's Cyclopedia of America Biography, edited by James Grant Wilson and John Fiske, NY, D. Appleton and Co., 1887, Volumes I — VI
The Armies of the Streets, The New York City Draft Riots of 1863, by Adrian Cook, University Press of Kentucky, 1974
The Assassination of Abraham Lincoln, by Osborn H. Oldroyd, Published by the author, Washington, D.C., 1901
Assassination and History of the Conspiracy, by J. R. Hawley, J.R. Hawley & Co., New York and Cincinnati, 1865
Assassination of Lincoln, A History of the Great Conspiracy, by T. M. Harris, 1890.
August Belmont: A Political Biography, by Irving Katz, Columbia University Press, New York 1968
Autobiography of Andrew Carnegie, Houghton Mifflin Company, Boston and New York, The Riverside Press Cambridge, 1920
Autobiography of Brook Farm, edited by Henry W. Sams, Prentice-Hall, Inc. Englewood Cliffs, New Jersey, 1958
Back to the Republic: The Golden Mean: the Standard Form of Government, by Harry F. Atwood, Laird & Lee, Inc. Publishers, Chicago, 1918
Banks and Politics in America, from the Revolution to the Civil War, by Bray Hammond, Princeton University Press, Princeton, 1957
Barricades: The War of the Streets in Revolutionary Paris, 1830 — 1848, By Jill Harsin, Palgrave, New York, 2002
Battle Cry of Freedom, The Civil War Era, by James M. McPherson, Oxford University Press, New York, Oxford, 1988
Beecher, Hibben, 1927
The Beechers, by Milton Ruyoff, Harper and Row, Publishers, NY, 1981
A Biographical Dictionary of Free Thinkers of All Ages and Nations, by J.M. Wheeler, London: Progressive Publishing Company, 1889, Printed and Published by G. W. Foote
The Biographical Encyclopedia of Kentucky of the Dead and Living Men of the Nineteenth Century, "George Nicholas Sanders," by William M. Corry, J. M. Armstrong & Co., Cincinnati, 1878
The biography of the principle American military and naval heroes, Vol. I, by Thomas Wilson, Published by John Low, New York, 1821
A biography of the State of Maine from the earliest period to 1891, Joseph Williamson, Maine Historical Society, Volume II, The Thurston Print, Portland, 1896
The Black Flag of Anarchy, Antistatism In The United States, by Corinne Jacker, Charles Scribner's Sons, NY, 1968
Blockade Runners of the Confederacy, by Hamilton Cochran, The Bobbs-Merrill Company, Inc., Indianapolis, New York, 1958
Bohemian Brigade, Civil War Newsmen in Action, by Louis M. Starr, Alfred A. Knopf, New York, 1954
The Book of Rosicruciae, by R. Swinburne Clymer, M.D., Supreme Grand Master, The Philosophical Publishing Company, "Beverly Hall," Quakertown, Phila., 1947
The Bowery Boys: Stout Corner Radicals And The Politics of Rebellion, by Peter Adams, Praeger Publishers, Westport CT, 2005
The Boys of '61: Or, Four Years of Fighting, by Charles Carleton Coffin, Boston: Published by Estes and Lauriat, 1883
British and American Abolitionists, An Episode In Transatlantic Understanding, by Clare Taylor, Edinburgh University Press, 1974

BIBLIOGRAPHY

British Chartists in America, 1839-1900, by Ray Boston, Manchester University Press, Rowman & Littlefield, Inc., Totowa, New Jersey, 1971
The Brotherhood, The Secret World of the Freemasons, by Stephan Knight, Dorset Press, 1984
Bushwackers of the Border, by Patrick Brophy, Vernon County Historical Society, Nevada, MO, 1980
The Business of Enlightenment, by Robert Darnton, The Belknap Press of Harvard University Press, Cambridge, 1979
California Legislature, 1953, Eleventh Report, Senate Investigating Committee on Education, Communism and the Illuminati, Published by the State of California
California's Utopian Colonies, by Robert V. Hine, University of California Press, Berkeley, 1983
Campaigner, March 1980, "The Treachery of Thomas Jefferson," by Donald Phau, Pages 4 — 32. Information from this source must be verified prior to use, but it does contain clues of what to look for.
Carl Schurz, by Hans L. Trefousse, University of Tennessee Press, Knoxville, 1982
Carl Schurz, Tremendous Dutchman and True American, by Lewis W. Tusken, The Winchester Academy Press, 1983
The Case Against Socialism, A Handbook for Speakers and Candidates, with a Prefatory Letter by The Right Hon. A. J. Balfour, New York, The Macmillan Company, London: George Allen & Sons, 1908
The Catholic Church and the Knights of Labor, by Henry A. Brown, The Catholic University of America Press, Washington, D.C.. 1949
The Celebrated Case of Fitz John Porter, by Otto Eisenschiml, The Bobbs — Merrill Co., Inc., 1950
Eighteenth Century Studies, Vol. 20, No. 3 (Spring 1987),"Cercle Social, the Girondists and the French Revolution" by Gary Kates, The Johns Hopkins University Press
Changing of the Guard, by David S. Broder, Simon and Schuster, NY, 1980
Charles W. Quantrell, by John P. Burch, Vega, Texas, 1923, published by the author.
Chartism and the Chartists, by David Jones, St. Martin's Press, NY, 1975
The Chartists, by Dorothy Thompson, Pantheon Books, NY. 1984
Choosing Terror: Virtue, Friendship. And Authenticity in the French Revolution, by Marisa Linton, Oxford University Press, 2013
Christianity and American Freemasonry, by William J. Whalen, The Bruce Publishing Company, Milwaukee, 1958
Chronicle of the Union League of Philadelphia, 1862 to 1902, Wm. Fell & Co., Philadelphia, 1902
Citizen of the World, Essays on Thomas Paine, Edited by Ian Dyke, Christopher Helm, London, 1987
The Civil War, The American Iliad as told by Those Who Lived It, Volume I. by Otto Eisenschiml and Ralph Newman, Grosset & Dunlap, Inc., New York, 1956, Volume II, *The Picture Chronicle, etc.*, by Ralph Newman and E. B. Long, Grosset & Dunlap, Inc., New York, 1956
Civil War Albums, by Tom Robotham, Brompton Books Corp., Greenwich, CT 1992
The Civil War and Reconstruction, by J. G. Randall, D. C. Heath and Co., Boston, 1937
Civil War History, A Journal of the Middle Period, John T. Hubbell, Editor, Published by the Kent State University Press, Vol. XXIV, September 1978, No. III
The Civil War in the American West, by Alvin M. Josephy, Jr., Alfred A. Knopf, New York, 1991
The Civil War In Missouri, 1861 — 1865, Civil War Centennial Commission of Missouri, Dr. Bert E. Maybee, Chm.
The Civil War in the United States, by Marx and Engels, International Publishers, New World Paperback edition, 1937
Civil War Times Illustrated,
    Volume XXVI, No. 10, February 1988, Page 42, "Our Constitution," by Jeffery Wert
    Volume XXVI, No. 12, April 1988, "A Legend of the South: 'Stonewall' Jackson, Life of a Confederate Hero," by Mark Grimsley
    Volume XXVII, No. 3, May 1988, "The One-Armed Devil," by Richard Pindell
    Volume XXVII, No. 7, November 1988, Page 37, "Abraham Lincoln's Few Words"
    Volume XXVIII, No. 3, Page 13, "Stonewall Jackson," by Mark Grimsley
    Volume XXVIII, No. 5, Page 29, "Rumors of War," by Kenneth Paul Czech; Page 40, "The Message of Julia Ward Howe," by Peggy Robbins
    Volume XXVIII, No. 6, November/December 1989, Page 10, "Island Haven For A Struggling Confederacy"; Page 34, "The Real JEB Stuart"
    Volume XXIX, No. 2, May/June 1990, "He Would Steal?", page 46, by Richard Pindell
    January/February, 1991, Page 37, "The Vice President Resides In Georgia," by Richard Pindell
The Civil War Years, by Robert E. Denney, Sterling Publishing Company, New York, 1992
Collected Works of Abraham Lincoln, Volume 3, University of Michigan Digital Library Production series, Ann Arbor, MI, 2001
Collections of the Illinois State Historical Library, Volume III, Lincoln Series, Vol. I, The Lincoln-Douglas Debates of 1853, Published by the Trustees of the Illinois State Historical Library, Springfield, Illinois, 1908
Colonel of the Black Regiment, the Life of Thomas Wentworth Higginson, by Howard N. Meyer, Norton Publishing, New York, 1967
Colonel Grenfell's Wars, the Life of a Soldier of Fortune, by Stephen Z. Starr, Louisiana State University Press, Baton Rouge, 1971
Come Retribution, The Confederate Secret Service and the Assassination of Lincoln, by William A. Tidwell, University Press of Mississippi, Jackson, 1988
Commander Vanderbilt, An Epic of the Steam Age, by Wheaton J. Lane, Alfred A. Knopf, NY, 1942
Commonwealth College Fortnightly, May Day 1935, Page Two and Three.
The Commonwealth of Missouri, A Centennial Record, Edited by C. R. Barns, Bryan, Brand & Co., Publishers, St. Louis, 1877
Communism and Socialism in Their History and Theory, by Theodore D. Woolsey, Charles Scribner's Sons, New York, 1880 and 1894 editions.
Communism: From Marx's "Manifesto" to 20th Century Reality, by James D. Forman, Franklin Watts, New York and London, 1972
Communist and Co-operative Colonies, by Charles Gide, Thomas Y. Cronwell Company, Publishers, New York, 1928 at Bath, Great Britain

The Communistic Societies of the United States; From Person Visit and Observation, by Charles Nordhoff, Hillary House Publishers, Ltd., NY, 1875 and 1960

A Compilation of the Messages And Papers of the Presidents, 1789 — 1902, by James D. Richardson, Published by the Bureau of National Literature and Art, 1905, Volumes I — X, *Supplements One* and *Two*, 1906

A Compendous History of New England, by Jedidiah Morse, DD, and Elijah Parish, DD, Published at Newberryport by Thomas & Wipple, 1809

The Comprehensive History of the Southern Rebellion and the War for the Union, by Orville J. Victor, James D. Torrey, Publishers, New York, 1862

Confederate Agent, A Discovery In History, by James D. Horan, Crown Publishers, Inc. NY, 1954

The Confederate Cherokees, John Drew's Regiment of Mounted Rifles, by W. Craig Gaines, Louisiana State University Press, Baton Rouge and London, 1989

Confederate Operations In Canada and New York, by John W. Headley, The Neale Publishing Company, New York and Washington, 1906

The Congregational Quarterly, Volume XX — New Series, Vol. X, Editor and proprietor Rev. Christopher Cushing, D.D., Boston: Congregational House, 1878, Alfred Mudge & Son, Printers, Boston

Coningsby: Or The New Generation, by Benjamin Disraeli, Elibron Classics, New York, 1844 and 2005

Conquest and Conscience: the 1840's, by Robert Sobel, Thomas Y. Crowell Company, New York, 1971

The Copperheads in the Middle West, by Frank L. Klement, University of Chicago Press, 1960

Conspiracy Theories & Secret Societies For Dummies, by Christopher Hodapp and Alice von Kannon, Wiley Publishing, Inc., Hobokan, NJ 2008

The Constitutional and Political History of the United States, by Dr. H. von Holst, Volume V, 1854-1856, Callaghan and Company, Chicago, 1885

A Covenant with Death, The Constitution, Law, and Equality in the Civil War Era, by Phillip S. Paludan, University of Illinois Press, Urbana, Chicago, London, 1975

Crooked Paths, by Peter Clecak, Harper and Row, NY. 1977

The Crown of Mexico, Maximilian and His Empress Carlota, by Joan Haslip, Holt, Rinehart and Winston, New York, etc., 1971

The Crusade Against Slavery, 1830 — 1860, by Louis Filler, Harper and Row, Publishers, New York, Evanston and London, 1960

Czars and Presidents, The Story of a Forgotten Friendship, by Alexander Tarsaidze´, McDowell, Obolensky Inc., New York, 1958

Dark Lanterns, Secret Political Societies, Conspiracies, and Treason Trials in the Civil War, by Frank L. Klement, Louisiana State University Press, Baton Rouge, 1984

The Day Lincoln Was Shot, by Jim Bishop, Harper and Brothers, New York, 1955

Death to Traitors, The Story of General Lafayette C. Baker, Lincoln's Forgotten Secret Service Chief, by Jacob Mogelever, Doubleday & Company, Inc., Garden City, New York, 1960

The Decline of the American Republic, And How to Rebuild It, John T. Flynn, The Devin — Adair Company, New York, 1955

The Democratic Speakers Handbook: Containing everything necessary for the defense of the National Democracy in the coming Presidential Campaign, and for the assault on the Radical Enemies of the Country and its Constitution, complied by Matthew Carey, Jr., Miami Printing and Publishing Company, Cincinnati, 1868

Democracy In America, by Alexis De Tocqueville, In Two Volumes, Arlington House, New Rochelle, New York, No date of publication, "Classics of Conservatism" boxed series.

The Description of American Democracy, by Roy Franklin Nichols, The Free Press, NY, 1948

Details of An Unpaid Claim On France for 24,000,000 Francs, Guaranteed by the Parole of Napoleon III, by Robert A. Parrish, Jr., Philadelphia: 1869 Demonstrates the anti-Semitic and anti-Catholic views within those who partially understood the conspiracy in the North in those years.

Diary of Gideon Welles, Secretary of the Navy Under Lincoln and Johnson, Forgotten Books, 1911

Dictionary of American Biography, Schribner's Sons, Volumes VII, XVI, XIX

Dictionary of American History, Charles Scribner's Sons, NY, 1951, Volumes I — IV.

A Dictionary of Secret and Other Societies, compiled by Arthur Preuss, B. Herder Books Co., St. Louis, MO, 1924

Diderot, by Arthur M. Wilson, Oxford University Press, New York, 1972

Duel, Alexander Hamilton, Aaron Burr and the Future of America, by Thomas Fleming, Basic Books, New York, 1999

DuPont, The Autobiography of an American Enterprise, E. I. DuPont De Nemours & Company, Distributed by Charles Scribner's Sons, New York, 1952

The Early Years of the Saturday Club, 1855 — 1870, by Edward Waldo Emerson, Boston and New York, Houghton Mifflin Co., 1918

Eberhard Weis Montgelas, Erster Band Zwischen Revolution und Reform, 1759-1799, by Verlag C. H. Beck, Pera-Druck Matthais KG, Germany

1848, The making of a Revolution, by Georges Duveau, Harvard University Press, Cambridge, 1984

1848, The Romantic and Democratic Revolutions in Europe, by Jean Sigmann, Harper Brothers, Publishers, New York, 1953

1848-1876, The Yankee International, Marxism and the American Reform Tradition, by Timothy Messer-Kruse, the University of South Carolina Press, 1998

The 1899 Hague Peace Conference: 'The Parliament of Man, the Federation of the World,' by Arthur Eyffinger, Kluwer Law International, Martinus Nijhoff Publishers, 1999

The Element Encyclopedia of Secret Societies, by John Michael Greer, Harper Element, London, 2006

Elements of Geography, By Jedidiah Morse DD, Printed at Boston, by I. Thomas & E. T. Andrews, December 1795

Elements of Socialism, A Text Book, by John Spargo and George Louis Arner, PhD, The Macmillian Company, New York, 1912

BIBLIOGRAPHY

Emancipating Slaves, Enslaving Free Men: A History of the American Civil War, By Jeffrey Rogers Hummel, Open Court, Chicago and LaSalle, Illinois, 1996

Empire for Liberty, The Genesis and Growth of the United States of America, by Dumas Malone and Basil Ranch, Appleton — Century — Crafts, Inc., NY, Volume I, 1960

Empire of the Columbia, by Dorothy C. Johansen and Charles M. Gates, Harper & Brothers, Publishers, New York, 1957

Encyclopedia of African American History, 1619-1895, Paul Finkelman, Editor in Chief, Oxford University Press, Oxford and New York, 2006

Encyclopedia of the Age of Political Revolutions and New Ideologies, 1760-1815, edited by Gregory Tremont-Barnes, Greenwood Press, Westport, CT, 2007

The Encyclopedia of American Intelligence and Espionage, From The Revolutionary War to the Present, by G. J. A. O'Toole, Facts On File, New York, Oxford, 1988

Encyclopedia of American History, edited by Richard B. Morris, Harper and Brothers, Publishers, New York, 1953

Encyclopedia of American History, by Morris and Commager, Harper and Row, 1970

Encyclopedia Britannica, The Werner Co., Akron, OH, Volume XII, 1904

An Encyclopedia of Freemasonry, by Albert G. Mackey, M.D., 33°, et al, in two Volumes, Published by The Masonic History Company, Chicago, New York, London, 1921, original copyright 1813.

An Encyclopedia of Occultism, by Lewis Spence, University Books, New Hyde Park, New York, 1960

Encyclopedia of Occultism & Parapsychology, In Three Volumes, edited by Leslie Shephard, Gale Research Co., Detroit, MI, property of the Boston Library.

Encyclopedia of Occultism & Parapsychology, Fourth Edition, Volume I, A-L, edited by J. Gordon Melton

The Encyclopedia of Social Reform, Edited by William Dwight Porter Bliss, Funk & Wagnalls Company, New York and London, 1897

Encyclopedia of Transcendentalism, by Tiffany K. Wayne, Facts on File, Inc., New York, 2006

Encyclopedia of U. S. Labor and working-class history, Vol. 1, by Eric Arneson, Taylor & Francis Group, New York, New York, 2007

English Radicals and the American Revolution, Colin Bonwick, University of North Carolina Press, Chapel Hill, 1977

The Enlightenment: An Interpretation, The Rise of Modern Paganism, by Peter Gay, W. W. Norton & Company, New York, London, 1966

The Establishment of the Establishment, by T. Herodotus, Lance Books, Oklahoma City, 1975

Europe in the Nineteenth Century (1789 — 1914), by A.J. Grant and Horace Temperley, Longmans, Green and Co., London, New York, Toronto, 1931

Europe In Revolt, by Reneˊ Kraus, The Macmillan Company, New York, 1942

Europe Looks at the Civil War, edited by Belle Becker Sideman and Lillian Friedman, The Orion Press, New York, 1960

The European Magazine and London Review, published by the Philological Society of London, Vol. 29, From January to June 1796, London, 1796

The Eve of Conflict, Stephen A. Douglas and the Needless War, by George Fort Milton, Houghton Mifflin and Co., Boston and New York, 1934

Exhibiting the Present Danger & Consequent Duties of the Citizens of the United States of America, Jedidiah Morse, DD, Charleston, Printed by Samuel Etheridge, 1799

The Expansionist Movement in Texas, 1836 — 1850, by William Campbell Binkley, Berkley, 1925

The Expositors of Individualist Anarchism in America, 1827-1908, by James J. Martin, Adrian Allen Assoc., DeKalb, IL, 1953

The Expression of the Emotions in Man and Animals, by Charles Darwin, D. Appleton and Company, New York, 1873

Family Encyclopedia of American History, The Reader's Digest Association, Inc., Pleasantville, New York, 1975

Fanny Kemble's America, by John Anthony Scott, Thomas Y. Crowell Co., NY, 1973

Fateful Lightning: A New History of the Civil War and Reconstruction, by Allen C. Guelzo, Oxford University Press, 2012

FDR: His Personal Papers, Duell, Sloan and Pierce, New York, 1950

The Federalist Era, 1789 — 1801, by John C. Miller, Harper and Row Publishers, NY, 1960

The Fiery Epoch, 1830 — 1877, by Charles Willis Thompson, The Bobbs-Merrill Company, Indianapolis, 1931

The Filibuster, The Career of William Walker, by Lawrence Greene, The Bobbs-Merrill Company, Indianapolis, New York, 1937

Filibusters and Financiers: The Story of William Walker and His Associates, By William O Scroggs, PhD, The Macmillan Company, New York, 1916

Fifty Million Brothers, A Panorama of American Lodges and Clubs, by Charles W. Ferguson, Farrar and Rinehart, Inc., 1937

Fifty Years of Party Warfare (1789 — 1837), by William O. Lynch, The Bobbs — Merrill Co., Indianapolis, 1931

Fire In The Minds of Men, Origins of the Revolutionary Faith, by James H. Billington, Basic Books, Inc., Publishers, NY, 1980

Fitz-Greene Halleck, An Early Knickerbocker Wit and Poet, by Nelson Frederick Adams, Yale University Press, New Haven, London, 1930

Fleshing Out Skull and Bones: Investigations into America's Most Powerful Secret Society, edited by Kris Millegan, Trine Day, Waterville, OR 2011

For Liberty and Glory: Washington, Lafayette, and Their Revolutions, by James R. Gaines, W. W. Norton & Company, Inc., New York, 2007

Foreigners in the Confederacy, by Ella Lonn, Peter Smith, Gloucester, Mass, 1965

Forging a Majority, The Formation of the Republican Party in Pittsburgh, 1848 — 1860, by Michael Fitzgibbon Holt, University of Pittsburgh Press, 1990

Founding of the First International, A Documentary Record, International Publishers, New York, 1937

Franklin, The Apostle of Modern Times, by Bernard Faÿ, Little, Brown and Company, Boston, MCMXXIX

The Fraternitatis Rosae Crucis, by R. Swinburne Clymer, The Philosophical Publishing Co., Beverly Hall, Quakertown, Pa, 1929

Free Soil, The Election of 1848, by Joseph G. Rayback, The University Press of Kentucky, 1970
The Free Soilers, Third Party Politics, 1848 — 54, by Frederick J. Blue, University of Illinois Press, Urbana, etc., 1973
Freedom, by William Safire, Avon Books, NY, 1987
Freemasonry. Its Pretensions Exposed in Faithful Extracts of Its standard Authors, etc., By a Master Mason, Henry Dana Ward, New York, 1828, Harvard Collection.
Freemasonry In American Culture and Society, By Bobby J. Demott, University Press of America, Inc., 1986
Freemasonry in American History, by Allen E. Roberts, Macoy Publishing and Masonic Supply Co., Inc., Richmond, VA, 1985
The French and American Revolutions Compared, by Friedrich Gentz, (1800), Translated by John Quincy Adams, Reprinted by St. Thomas Press, Houston, Texas, 1975
The French Revolution, by Nesta H. Webster, Christian Book Club of America, Hawthorne, California, 1969, First published 1910.
The French Revolution: A History in Three Parts, by Thomas Carlyle, New York: G. P. Putnam's Sons, London: Methuen and Company, 1902, A New Edition by C.R.L. Fletcher, M.A., Oxford
Friedrich Engels: His Contributions to Political Theory, by Fritz Nova, Philosophical Library, NY, 1967
The Founding of the First International, International Publishers, 1937
From Colonial Times to the Founding of the American Federation of Labor, International Publishers, 1947
A Full Exposition of the Clintonian Faction and the Society of the Columbian Illuminati, by John Wood, Pennington & Gould, Newark, 1802
Garibaldi, The Man and the Nation, by Paul Frischauer, Claude Kendall & Willoughby Sharp Publishers, NY, 1935
A General History of Free-Masonry in Europe, Translated and Compiled from the Masonic Histories of Emmanuel Rebold, M.D., by J. Fletcher Brennan, American Masonic Publishing Association, Cincinnati, 1868
General Sterling Price, And the Civil War in the West, by Albert Castel, Louisiana State University Press, Baton Rouge and London, 1968
George Bancroft, The Intellectual as Democrat, by Lillian Handlin, Harper & Row, Publishers, New York, 1945
George Washington Freemason, by William Moseley Brown, P.G.M., Garrett & Massie, Inc., 1952
The Germans of Charleston, Richmond and New Orleans During the Civil War Period, 1850 — 1870, by Andrea Mehrländer, Walter de Gruyter GmbH & Co., Berlin and New York, 2011
German Diasporic Experiences, Mathias Schulze, *et al*, editors, Waterloo Centre for German Studies and Wifred Laurier University Press, Canada, 2008
The German Museum, Or Monthly Repository of the Literature of Germany, the North and the Continent in general, Vol. 1 for the Year 1800, London, Printed for C. Geisweiler and the Proprietors.
The Germans in the American Civil War, by Wilhelm Kaufmann, Translated by Steven Rowan, R. Oldenbourg, Munch, 1911, John Kallmann Publishers, Carlisle, PA, 1999
Germans in the Making of America, by Frederick Franklin Schrader, The Stratford Co., Publishers, Boston, Massachusetts, 1924
The Global Ramifications of the French Revolution, edited by Joseph Klaits and Michael H. Haltzel, Published by The Press Syndicate of the University of Cambridge, Cambridge, 1994
god.com: a deity for the new millennium, by John A. Henderson, M.D., Copyrighted by the same, 2002
The Gospel Visitant, etc., Vol. 1., Superintended by Thomas Jones, Hosea Ballou, Abner Kneeland, Edward Turner, Printed by William S. & Henry Spear, Charleston, 1812
The Granger Movement, A Study of Agricultural Organization and Its Political, Economic, and Social Manifestations, 1870 — 1880, by Solon Justus Buck, University of Nebraska Press, Lincoln, 1913
Gray Raiders of the Sea: How Eight Confederate Warships Destroyed the Union's High Seas Commerce, by Chester G. Hearn, Louisiana State University Press, Baton Rouge and London, 1992
The Great Conspiracy: Its Origin and History, by John A. Logan, NY, A. R. Hart and Co., Publishers, 1886
The Great Conspiracy and England's Neutrality, by John Jay, an Address on the 86th Anniversary of American Independence, Roe Lockwood & son, New York, 1861
The Growth of the American Republic, by Samuel Eliot Morison and Henry Steele Commager, Volume I, Oxford University Press, NY, 1930 — 1950
The Growth of American Thought, by Merle Curti, Harper Brothers, NY, 1943, 1951
The Handbook of Texas, by Walter Scott Webb, Editor-in Chief, The Texas State Historical Association, Austin, 1952, Volumes I and II
Handbook of the United States of America and Guide to Immigration, Compiled by L. P. Brockett, M.D., Published by Gaylord Watson, New York, 1885
Harper's Encyclopedia of United States History: From 458 A.D. to 1902, Volume 9, Benson John Lossing, LL.D., Harper & Brothers Publishers, New York, London, 1907
Harper's School Geography, Harper & Brothers, New York, 1880
Harriet Beecher Stowe: A Spiritual Life, by Nancy Koester, Wm. B. Eerdmans Publishing Co., Grand Rapids, Michigan, Cambridge U.K., 2014
The Hebrew Gospel and the Development of the Synoptic Tradition, by James R. Edwards, Wm. B. Eerdmans Publishing Co., Grand Rapids, MI; Cambridge, UK, 2009
The Hell-Fire Clubs: A History of Anti-Morality, by Geoffry Ashe, Sutton Publishing, (England), 1974
Henry Ward Beecher, An American Portrait, by Paxton Hibben, The Press of the Reader's Club, NY, 1927
The Hidden Civil War, The Story of the Copperheads, by Wood Gray, The Viking Press, NY, 1942
The Hidden Face of the Civil War, by Otto Eisenschiml, The Bobbs — Merrill Co. Inc., Indianapolis, New York, 1961
The Hidden Lincoln, From the Letters and Papers of William H. Herndon, by Emanuel Hertz, The Viking Press, New York, 1938, First edition,

no. 77 of 150 copies, signed by the author.
Historic Hillsdale College, Pioneer In Higher Education, 1844 — 1900, by Arlan K. Gilbert, Hillsdale College Press, 1991
Historic Turner Restaurant, Menu, Milwaukee, Wisconsin, 1997
History of the American Civil War, by John William Draper, M.D., LL.D., Harper & Brothers, Publishers, New York, 1868, Volume II
History of American Conspiracies, A Record of Treason, Insurrection, Rebellion, &c. in the United States of America From 1760 to 1860, by Orville J. Victor, James D. Torrey, Publisher, New York 1863
A History of American Life, Volume VII, "The Irrepressible Conflict," by Arthur Charles Cole, Macmillan Co., 1934
A History of American Political Theories, by Charles Edward Merriam, PhD, New York, Russell and Russell, 1903
History of American Socialisms, by John Humphrey Noyes, Hillary House Publishers, Ltd., New York, 1870, 1961
The History of the American Working Class, by Anthony Bimba, International Publishers, New York, 1927
The History and battlefields of the Civil War, by John Bowen, The Wellfleet Press, Secaucus, New Jersey, 1991
History of Bigotry In The United States, by Gustavus Myers, Random House, NY, 1943
The History of the city of Newark, New Jersey, Volume II, by Frank John Urquhart, Lewis Historical Publishing Company, New York and Chicago, 1913
The History of the Civil War in America: Comprising a Full and Impartial Account of the Origins and Progress of the Rebellion, etc., by John S. C. Abbott, Published by Gurdon Bill, Springfield, Mass., Volume I, 1863
A History of Civil, Political and Military of the Southern Rebellion, by Orville J. Victor, J. D. Torrey Publisher, New York, Volume II, 1861
History of the Commune of 1871, Translated from the French of Lissagaray, by Eleanor Marx Aveling, Second Edition, New York, International Publishing Co., 1898
History of the Communist Party of the United States, by William Z. Foster, Greenwood Press, Publishers, New York, 1968
The History and Evolution of Freemasonry, by Delmar Duane Darrah 33°, P.R.C. Publications, 1954
A History of Freemasonry Its Antiquities, Symbols, Constitutions, Customs, ETC., Volume IV, John C. Yorston and Co., Publishers, New York, Cincinnati, and Chicago, 1889
History of the Girondists, by Alphonse De Lamartine, In Three Volumes, Volume I, Harper Brothers, New York, 1854
History of the Great Rebellion, Etc., by Thomas P. Kettell, Two Volumes — Volume I, New York, N. C. Miller, 25 Park Row, Publisher of Subscription Books, H. H. Bancroft and Co., San Francisco, Cal., 1863, Entered in Congress 1862
History of the Great Rebellion, by Thomas P. Kettell, L. Stebbins, Hartford, Conn., 1865
A History of the Kansas Crusade, Its Friends and Its Foes, by Eli Thayer, Harper and Brothers, NY, 1889
History of the Labor movement in the United States, Vol.1, *From Colonial Times to the Founding of the American Federation of Labor*, by Philip Sheldon Foner, International Publishers, New York,1947
The History of Labour In The United States, by John R. Commons, et al, Vol. I, The Macmillan Company, New York, 1918
A History of Missouri, Volume II, 1820 to 1860; Volume III, 1860 to 1880, by Perry McCandless, University of Missouri Press, 1972
A History of the Nineteen Century Year by Year, by Edwin Emerson, Jr., In Three Volumes, P. F. Collier and Son, New York, 1900
History of Political Thought, by Raymond G. Gettell, The Century Co., NY 1924
History of the Public School Society of the City of New York, by William Oland Bourne, Wm. Wood & Co., New York, 1870
A History of the Republican National Conventions from 1856 to 1908, by John Tweedy, Published by John Tweedy, Danbury, CN, 1910
The History of Ripon Wisconsin, by Samuel M. Pedrick, edited by George H. Miller, Ripon Historical Society, Ripon, 1964
History of the Rise and Fall of the Slave Power In America, by Henry Wilson, Volume II, Boston: James S. Osgood and Co., 1874
History of the Rise and Fall of the Slave Power In America, by Henry Wilson, Volumes I — III, Boston and New York, Houghton, Mifflin and Co., 1877
A History of Royal Arch Masonry, Issued Under Authority of the General Grand Chapter Royal Arch Masons, 1956, In Three Volumes, Everett R. Turnbull and Ray V. Denslow, 1956
The History of the Seal of the United States, Washington, D.C., Department of State, 1909
A History of Secret Societies, by Arkon Daraul, A Citadel Press Book, Secaucus, NJ, 1961 and 1994
History of Socialism, by Harry W. Laidler, Thomas Y. Crowell, Co., NY, 1968
A History of Socialism, by Thomas Kirkup, Adam and Charles Black, London, 1906
History of Socialism in the United States, by Morris Hillquit, Funk and Wagnalls Co., NY, 1903
A History of the Southern Confederacy, by Clement Eaton, Macmillan Co., NY, 1954
History of The Supreme Council 33°, 1801 — 1861, by Ray Baker Harris, 33°, James D. Carter, 33°, The Supreme Council 33°, Washington, D.C., 1964
History of the Thirty-Ninth Congress of the United States, by William H. Barnes, A.M., Negro University Press, New York, 1969, Originally published 1868.
History of the Three Internationals, The World Socialist and Communist Movements from 1848 to the Present, by William Z. Foster, International Publishers, New York, 1955
A History of the Union League Club of New York City, by Will Irwin, Earl Chapin May, Joseph Hotchkiss, Dodd, Mead and Co., NY 1952
History of the United States, by John Clark Ridpath, A.M, L.L.D., Volume IV, The Review of Reviews Co., NY, 1874, 1911
History of the United States of America During the Great Rebellion, by Edward McPherson, Philip & Solomon, Washington, D.C., 1865
History of the United States, From The Earliest Period to the Administration of President Johnson, by J. A. Spencer, D.D., Volume 2 and 3, NY, Johnson, Fry and Co., 1866
"A History of the Village of Barton," (Wisconsin), by Richard H. Dressel, from an unfinished manuscript, 1996, concerning the Village of

Young America
History of Western Political Thought, by R. S. Chaurasia, Atlantic Publishing and Distributors, New Delhi, India, 2001
The History of Wisconsin, Volume II, The Civil War Era, 1848 — 1873, by Richard N. Current, State Historical Society of Wisconsin, Madison, 1976
History of Work Cooperation in America, by John Curl, Published on the Internet, 1980.
History of the World, by John Clark Ridpath, LL.D., The Jones Brothers Publishing Co., Cincinnati, O., 1911
Home Front Heroes: A Biographical Dictionary of Americans During Wartime, edited by Benjamin F. Shearer, Greenwood Press, Westport, Connecticut, 2007
Horace Greeley: Champion of American Freedom, by Robert Chadwell Williams, Ney York University Press, New York and London, 2006
Horace Greeley, Printer, Editor, Crusader, by Henry Luther Stoddard, G. P. Putnam's Sons, New York, 1946
Horace Greely, Voice of the People, by William Harlan Hale, Harper & Brothers, New York, 1950
Horace Greeley and other Pioneers of American Socialism, by Charles Sotheran, The Humboldt Publishing Co., New York, 1892
The House of Morgan, An American Banking Dynasty, and the Rise of Modern Finance, by Ron Chernow, Atlantic Monthly Press, New York, 1990
House Undivided, The Story of freemasonry and the Civil War, by Allen E. Roberts, Macoy Publishing And Masonic Supply Co., NY, 1961
How To Make A Revolution Without Firing A Shot: Thoughts On The Brissot-Chastellux Polemic (1786-1788), By Doina Pasca Harsanyi, Oxford University Press, 2008
The Idea of a Southern Nation, Southern Nationalists and Southern Nationalism, 1830 — 1860, by John McCardell, W. W. Norton & Company, New York, London, 1979
Ideology and International Relations in the Modern World, By Alan Cassels, Routledge, London, New York, 1996
Illuminati Manifesto of World Revolution (1792), De l ésprit des religions, by Nicholas Bonneville, Translated and Introduced by Marco di Luchetti, Esq., 2011
The Impending Crises, 1848 — 1861, by David M. Potter, Harper & Row, Publishers, 1976
The Impeachment Trial of Andrew Johnson, by Michael Les Benedict, W. W. Norton & Company, Inc., New York, 1973
In An Age of Revolution, by Cyril Garbett, Archbishop of York, Hodder Stoughton, London, 1952
In the Shadow of Lincoln's Death, by Otto Eisenschiml, Wilfred Funk, Inc., New York, 1940
Incredible Carnegie: The Life of Andrew Carnegie (1835-1919), by John K. Winkler, The Vanguard press, New York, 1931
Indiana Magazine of History, "The History of the Know Nothing Party in Indiana," by Carl Fremont Brand, XVIII, 1922
Information for Kansas Immigrants, by Thomas H. Webb, secretary, Northwest Emigrant Aid Co., Boston, Printed by Alfred Mudge and Son, 1856
The Insanity File, The Case of Mary Todd Lincoln, by Mark E. Neely, Jr., and R. Gerald McMurtry, Southern Illinois University Press, Carbondale and Edwardsville, 1986
Inside Paris: During The Siege, by An Oxford Graduate, MacMillan and Co., London, 1871
The International Encyclopedia of Secret Societies & Fraternal Orders, by Alan Axelrod, Facts On File, Inc., New York, 1997
The Invention of the American Political Parties, by Roy F. Nichols, The Macmillan Co., NY, 1967
The Invisible Empire, The Story of the Ku Klux Klan, 1866 — 1871, no publishers name or copyright.
Invisible Siege, The Journal of Louis E. Chittenden, April 15, 1861 — July 14, 1861, American Exchange Press, San Diego, California, 1969
Iowa Masonic Library, March 1926, Number 3, "John Quincy Adams: Anti-Masonic Letter Writer," by Erik McKinley Eriksson, Ph.D., Pages 87 — 94.
The Irish Brigade, by Paul Jones, Robert B. Luce, Inc., Washington — New York, 1969
Is Public Education Necessary?, by Samuel L. Blumenfeld, The Paradigm Co., Boise, Idaho, 1985
James Madison: A Biography, by Ralph Louis Ketcham, University of Virginia Press, 1971 and 1990
James Shepherd Pike, Republicanism and the American Negro, 1850 — 1882, by Robert Franklin Durden, Duke University Press, Durham, NC, 1957
Jefferson, The Forgotten Man, by Samuel B. Pettengill, America's Future, Inc., New York, 1938
The Jefferson Conspiracies, A President's Role in the Assassination of Meriwether Lewis, by David Leon Chandler, William Morrow and Company, Inc., New York, 1994
Jefferson's Bible, The Life and Morals of Jesus of Nazareth, by Thomas Jefferson, American Book Distributors, Grove City, PA, 1996
John Adams, by Page Smith, Volumes I and II, Doubleday & Company, Inc., Garden City, New York, 1962
John Brown, 1800-1859, A biography Fifty Years After, by Oswald Garrison Villard, Houghton Mifflin Company, Boston and New York, 1910
John Brown, Abolitionist, by David S. Reynolds, Alfred A. Knopf, New York, 2005
John Brown And His Men, by Richard J. Hinton, Funk & Wagnalls Company, New York and London, 1894
John Brown and the Legend of Fifty-Six, by James C. Malin, Haskell House Publishers, Inc., NY, 1971, Volume II
John C. Calhoun, Sectionalist, 1840 — 1850, by Charles M. Wiltse, The Bobbs-Merrill Company, Inc., Indianapolis, New York, 1951
John Charles Fremont: Character as Destiny, by Andrew Rolle, University of Oklahoma Press, Norman and London, 1991
John D. Rockefeller, His Career, by Silas Hubbard, New York, Published by the author, 1904
John O'Sullivan and His Times, by Robert D. Sampson, Kent State University Press, Kent, OH 2003
"John Quincy Adams: Anti-Masonic Letter Writer," by Erik McKinley Eriksson, PhD, *Iowa Masonic Library*, Number 3, Mrch1926
Joining The Club: A History of Jews and Yale, by Dan A. Oren, Yale University Press, New Haven and London, 1985
Journal and Proceedings of the Convention of the Border States, Frankfort KY, Printed at the Yeoman's Office, Jno. B. Major, State Printer, 1861

BIBLIOGRAPHY

Journal of Southern History,
   May 1955, Vol. XXI, No. 2, "Pierre Soulé: southern Expansionist and Promoter," by J. Preston Moore, pp.203-223
   February 1957, Vol. XXIII, No.1, "Blueprint for Radical Reconstruction," by John G. Sprout
   November 1979, Vol. 45, No. 4, "Thomas J. Durant, Utopian Socialism, and the Failure of Presidential Reconstruction in Louisiana," by Joseph G. Tregle, Jr.
Joshua Leavitt, Evangelical Abolitionist, by Hugh Davis, Louisiana State University Press, Baton Rouge and London, 1990
Judah Benjamin, The Jewish Confederate, by Eli N. Evans, The Free Press, NY, 1988
The Justices of the U. S. Supreme Court, by Friedman Israel, Chelsea House, Volume II, 1969
Kansas And Nebraska, by Edward E. Hale, Boston, Phillips, Sampson and Co., NY, 1854
Karl Marx: Racist, by Nathaniel Weyl, Arlington House, New Rochelle, New York, 1979
"K.G.C.: Address to citizens of Southern States by Order of the Convention of K.G.C. held at Raleigh, N.C., May 7 — 11, 1860."
"The KGC In Texas, 1860 — 1861," by Roy Sylvan Dunn, *The Southwestern Historical Quarterly*, Volume LXX, No. 4, April 1967
Klandestine: The Untold Story of Delmar Dennis and his role in the FBI's war against the Ku Klux Klan, by William H. McIlhany II, Arlington House, New Rochelle, 1975
"Knights of the Golden Circle," research papers, housed in the Texas Room, Old Houston Library, misc. dates
Knights of the Golden Circle: Secret Empire, Southern Secession, Civil War, by David C. Keehn, Louisiana State University Press, 2013
The Ku Klux Klan, America's Recurring Nightmare, by Fred J. Cook, Julian Messner, NY, 1980
Labor History, "Ira Steward and the Anti-Slavery Origins of American Eight-Hour Theory," by David Roediger, 2001
Lafayette, by W. E. Woodward, Farrar and Rinehart, Inc. New York, Toronto, 1938
Lafayette and the Liberal Ideal, 1814 — 1824, Politics and Conspiracy in an Age of Reaction, by Sylvia Neely, Southern Illinois University Press, Carbondale and Edwardsville, 1991
The Land They Fought For, The Story of the South as the Confederacy, 1832 — 1865, by Clifford Dowdey, Doubleday & Company, Inc., Garden City, N. Y., 1955
The League to Enforce Peace, American Branch, William Howard Taft, President, Printed by the League to enforce Peace, New York, 1915
Lectures on the Rational System of Society, etc., by Robert Owen, Published by the Home Colonization Society, London, 1841
Lee, The Last Years, by Charles Bracelen Flood, Houghton Mifflin Company, Boston, 1981
Letter, Beverly Hall Corporation, Quakertown, Pa., February 9, 1998, concerning Abraham Lincoln's membership in the Rosicrucian's, from Dr. Gerald E. Poesnecker, President, a Rosicrucian center.
Letters of Fyodor Michailovitch Dostoevsky to his Family and Friends, Translated by E. C. Mayne, Horizon Press, New York, 1961
Letters of Henry Adams, (1858 — 1891), edited by Worthington Chauncey Ford, Houghton Mifflin Company, Boston and New York, 1930
Letters of James Russell *Lowell*, edited by Charles Eliot Norton, Vol. II, Part 1, Harper and Brothers, New York, 1894
The Life of Andrew Carnegie, by Burton J. Hendrick, Harper and Row, NY, 1932
Life And Campaigns of General T. J. (Stonewall) Jackson, by R. L. Dabney, Sprinkle Publications, Harrisonburg, Virginia, 1977 of an 1865 edition
The Life of Horace Greeley, The Editor of the New York Tribune, by J. Parton, Published by Mason Brothers, New York, 1855
The Life of James Abram Garfield, by J. M. Bundy, A. S. Barnes & Co., New York, 1881
The Life of Jedidiah Morse, D.D., by William B. Sprague, D.D., LL.D, Anson D. F. Randolph and Co., NY, Copyright 1874 by Richard C. Morse
The Life of John Jay: With Selections from His Correspondence and Miscellaneous Papers, Volume II, by William Jay, J. & J. Harper, New York, 1833
The Life and Letters of John Hay, by William Roscoe Thayer, Volumes I & II, Houghton Mifflin Company, Boston and New York, 1908
Life and Public Service of Charles Sumner, by C. Edwards Lester, United States Publishing Company, New York, 1874
The Life and Times of Aaron Burr, by J. Parton, Mason Brothers, New York, 1858
The Life and Times of Noah Webster, An American Patriot, by Harlow Giles Unger, Published by John Wiley and Sons, New York, 1998
The Life of Robespierre, quite old, author and publisher unknown, first pages torn from the volume.
The Life of Timothy Pickering, by Charles W. Upham, Vol. III, Little, Brown, And Company, Boston, 1873
The Life And Speeches of Henry Clay, Volume I, Greeley & McElrath, Tribune Buildings, New York, 1843
The Life, Speeches, and Public Service of James A. Garfield, by Russell H. Conwell, George Stinson & Company, Portland, ME., 1881
The Life and Ventures of the Original John Jacob Astor, by Elizabeth L. Gebhard, Brayn Printing Company, Hudson, N. Y., 1915
The Life of Thomas Paine, Published by Calvin Blanchard, New York, 1860
The Life And Works of Thomas Paine, Volume I, by William M. Van der Weyde, New Rochelle, NY, Thomas Paine National Historical Association, 1925
Lifeline of the Confederacy, Blockade Runnings During the Civil War, by Stephen R. Wise, University of South Carolina Press, 1988
Lightening Over the Treasury Building, by John R. Elsom, Meador Publishing Co., Boston, 1941
Limits of Dissent, Clement L. Vallandigham & The Civil War, by Frank L. Klement, The University Press of Kentucky, Lexington, 1970
Lincoln, by Emil Ludwig, Translated from the German by Eden and Cedar Paul, Grosset & Dunlap, New York, 1929
Lincoln, A Psycho-Biography, by L. Pierce Clark, Charles Scribner's Sons, New York, London, 1933
Lincoln and The Emperors, by A. R. Tyrner-Tyrnauer, Harcourt, Brace and World, Inc., NY, 1962
Lincoln and Greeley, by Harlan Hoyt Horner, The University of Illinois Press, 1953
Lincoln and the Radicals, by T. Harry Williams, University of Wisconsin Press, Madison, 1965
Lincoln and the Russians, The story of Russian-American diplomatic relations during the Civil War, by Albert A. Woldman, The World Publishing Company, Cleveland and New York, 1952

The Lincoln Conspiracy, by David Balsiger & Charles E. Sellier, Jr., Schick Sunn Classic Books, Louisiana, 1977
Lincoln's Foreign Legion, The 39th New York Infantry, The Garibaldi Guard, by Michael Bacarella, White Mane Publishing Company, Inc., Shippensburg, PA, 1996
Lincoln's Gadfly, Adam Gurowski, by LeRoy H. Fischer, University of Oklahoma Press, Norman, 1964, by a grant from the Ford Foundation
Lincoln's Herndon, by David Donald, Alfred A. Knopf, New York, 1948
The Lincoln Legion, The Story of Its Founder and Forerunners, by Rev. Louis Albert Banks, D.D., The Mershon Company, New York, 1903
The Lincoln Murder Conspiracies, by William Hanchett, University of Illinois Press, Urbana and Chicago, 1983
The Lincoln Nobody Knows, The Mysterious Man Who Ran the Civil War, by Webb Garrison, Rutledge Hill Press, Nashville, Tennessee, 1993
Lincoln Über Alles: Dictatorship Comes to America, by John Avery Emison, Pelican Publishing Company, Gretna, LA, 2009
Lincoln Unmasked: What You're Not Supposed to Know About Dishonest Abe, by Thomas J. DiLorenzo, Crown Forum, New York, 2006
"Lincoln's offer of a command to Garibaldi," *The Century Illustrated Monthly Magazine,* by Harry Nelson Gay, November 1907, The Century Company, New York
Lincoln's War Cabinet, by Burton J. Hendrick, Little, Brown and Company, Boston, 1946
The Lost Cause, by Edward A. Polland, E. B. Treat and Co., NY, 1867
The Lost Cause, The Confederate Exodus to Mexico, by Andrew F. Rolle, University of Oklahoma Press, Norman, 1965
Lost Keys of Freemasonry, by Manly P. Hall, 33°, K.T., Macoy Publishing and Masonic Supply Company, Inc., Richmond, Virginia, 1976
Lost Men of American History, by Stewart H. Holbrook, The MacMillian Company, New York, 1948
Louisiana History, "Some Determinants of Know Nothing Electoral Strength in the South, 1856," by James H. Broussard, VII, 1966
Lyman Turnbull, Conservative Radical, by Mark M. Krug, A. S. Barnes and Company, Inc., New York, 1965
Makers of the Red Revolution, by Olivia Cooledge, Houghton Mifflin Co., Boston, 1963
The Making of the English Working Class, by E. P. Thompson, Penguin Books, London, 1963 & 1980
Making Sense of the Molly Maguires, by Kevin Kenny, Oxford University Press, 1998
The Man Who Elected Lincoln, by Jay Monaghan, The Bobbs — Merrill Co., Inc., Indianapolis — New York, 1956
The Man Who Killed Lincoln, by Philip Van Doren Stern, The Literary Guild of America, Inc., New York, 1939
Manifest Destiny, A Study of Nationalist Expansion in American History, by Albert K. Weinberg, The Johns Hopkins Press, 1935
Manifest Destiny And The Imperialism Question, edited by Charles L. Sanborn, John Wiley and Sons, Inc., NY, 1944
Manifest Destiny And Mission In American History, by Frederick Merk, Alfred A. Knopf, NY, 1963 and 1970
Manual of the Constitution of the United States, by Israel Ward Andrews, American Book Company, Cincinnati, 1887, Revised to 1892
The March of Socialism, by J. Alvarez Del Vayo, Translated by Joseph M. Bernstein, Hilland Wang, NY 1974
Martyrdom In Missouri: A History of Religious Proscription, The Seizure of Churches, And The Persecution of Ministers of the Gospel, In the State of Missouri During the Late Civil War, etc., by Rev. W. M. Leftwich, DD, St. Louis, Southwestern Book and Publishing Co., 1870
Marxian Socialism In The United States, by Daniel Bell, Cornell University Press, Ithaca and London, 1952
Marx's General: The Revolutionary Life of Friedrich Engels, by Tristam Hunt, Henry Holt and Company, LLC, New York, New York, 2009
Mary Lincoln, Biography of a Marriage, by Ruth Painter Randall, Little, Brown and Company, Boston, 1953
The Masonic Magician: The Life and death of Count Cagliostro and His Egyptian Rite, by Philippa Faulks and Robert L.D. Cooper, Watkins Publishing, London, 2008
Masonry Defined, A Liberal Masonic Education, Compiled from the Writings of Dr. Albert G. Mackey, 33°, et al, Masonic Supply Co., Memphis, Tenn., 1929
Masons Who Helped Shape Our Nation, by Henry C. Clausen 33°, Sovereign Grand Commander, 1976
Massachusetts Anti-Slavery Society, *11th Annual Report,* S. E. Sewall, Auditor, Boston, January 25, 1843
McClellan's War, by Ethan S. Rafuse, Indiana University Press, Bloomington, IN, 2005
Means and Ends in American Abolitionism, Garrison and His Critics on Strategy and Tactics, 1834 — 1850, by Arleen S. Kraditor, Elephant Paperbacks, 1967, 1989
Melting Pot Soldiers, by William L. Burton, Iowa State University Press, Ames, 1988
Memoir of the Life of Richard Henry Lee, and His Correspondence, etc ... and of the Events of the American Revolution, by His Grandson Richard H. Lee, Volume II, H. C. Carey and I. Lea, Philadelphia, 1825
Memoirs of a Nobody: The Missouri Years of an Austrian Radical, 1849-1866, Translated and Edited by Steven Rowan, Missouri Historical Society Press, St. Louis, 1997
Memoirs Illustrating the History of Jacobinism, by A. Barruel, Real-View-Books, Published by the American Council on Economics and Society, 1995, originally printed 1798
Memoirs of Aaron Burr, Matthew L. Davis (Matthew Livingston), 1836 and 2005, Project Gutenberg
Men Against the State: The Expositors of Individualist Anarchism in America, 1827-1908, by James J. Martin, Ralph Myles Publisher, Inc., Colorado Springs, 1970
Men of Peace, by Bradford Smith, J. B. Lippincott Co., Philadelphia and New York, 1964
Men of Wealth, The Story of Twelve Significant Fortunes from the Renaissance to the Present Day, by John T. Flynn, Simon and Schuster, New York, 1941
Mesmerism and the end of the Enlightenment in France, by Robert Darnton, Harvard University Press, 1968
Milwaukee Journal Sentinel,
    May 19, 1996, "Clinton — Kohl Meeting In Milwaukee," page 14A.
    August 31, 1997, "A Woman's Place is in the Museum," by Carol Greensburg, page L1

BIBLIOGRAPHY

Minutes of the Commissioners for detecting and defeating Conspiracies in the State of New York, Volume I: 1778 — 1779, Volume II: 1780 — 1781, Published by the State of New York, Albany, 1909
The Mithraic Mysteries, Restored and Modernized, by Kenneth Sylvan Gutherie, 1925, Plantonist Press, Yonkers, NY, 1967
Modern American Spiritualism: A Twenty Year Record, etc. by Emma Hardinge, New York, Published by the author, 1870
Modern History, From the Coming of Christ, etc., to 1867, by Peter Fredet, D.D., Baltimore, Published by John Murphy and Co., 1879
Modern American spiritualism, by Emma Hardinge Britten, published by the author, The New-York Printing Company, New York, MDCCLXX (1870)
Moreau de St. Mèry's American Journey, 1793-1798, Translated by Kenneth & Anna M. Roberts, Doubleday & Company, Inc., Garden City, New York, 1947
The Movement For Peace Without Victory During The Civil War, by Elbert J. Benton, Cleveland, Ohio, 1918
Mozart and Masonry, by Paul Nettl, Dorset Press, New York, 1957
Murdering Mr. Lincoln: The New Detection of the 19th Century's Most Famous Crime, by Charles Higham, New Millennium Press, Beverly Hills, 2004
My Life, by Leon Trotsky, Charles Schribner's Sons, New York, 1930
Mystic Americanism or The Spiritual Heritage of America Revealed, Edited by, Dr. Paul P. Ricchio, Published by Philosophical Publishing Co., Beverly Hall, Quakertown, Pennsylvania, USA, 1975
Myths After Lincoln, by Lloyd Lewis, Introduction by Carl Sandburg, Harcourt, Brace and Co., 1929
Napoleon's Sorcerers: The Sophisians, by Darius A. Spieth, Rosemont Publishing and Printing Corp., 2007
National Carl Schurz Association Records, December 2002, The Historical Society of Pennsylvania, Philadelphia, PA
The National Cyclopedia of American Biography, James T. White and Co., NY, 1898 — 1967, I — XXV, A — K
NEA: The First Hundred Years, The Building of the Teaching Profession, by Edgar B. Wesley, Harper & Brothers Publishers, New York, 1957
A Neglected Factor in the Anti-Slavery Triumph in Iowa in 1854, by F. I. Herriott, Year Book of the German — American Historical Society of Illinois, 1918
The New American,
    Volume 5, No.6, March 13, 1989, Page 31, "Forces That Shaped America," by Warren L. McFerran
    Volume 5, No. 9, April 24, 1989, Page 23, "The Regulatory State," by Warren L. McFerran
    Volume 5, No. 14, July 3, 1989, Page 21, "Stoking the Fire," by William F. Jasper
A New Encyclopedia of Freemasonry, by Arthur Edward Waite, Combined Edition, Wings Books, New York, Avenal, New Jersey, 1970
New England And The Bavarian Illuminati, by Vernon Stauffer, 1918, The Invisible College Press, Arlington, VA, 2005
The New England Emigrant Aid Company, by Eli Thayer, Published by Franklin P. Rice, Worcester, MA, 1887
The New Freedom, by Woodrow Wilson, Prentice Hall, Inc., Englewood Cliffs, New Jersey, 1961, Original copyright 1913
New Frontiers, by Henry Wallace, Raynel & Hitchcock, New York, 1934
The New Harmony Movement, by George B. Lockwood, D. Appleton And Co., New York, 1905
New York Historical Quarterly, "Seward and the Know Nothings," by Thomas J. Curran, LI, 1967
New York Tribune, September 2, 1854, Page 1
New World Order, The Ancient Plan of Secret Societies, by William T. Still, Huntington House Publishers, Lafayette, LA, 1990
The New York Times, October 26, 1853.
New World Utopias, by Paul Kagan, Penguin Books, 1975
"The 1996 — 1997 Ripon Guide," Ripon Community Publications, 1996
No Compromise!, The Story of the Fanatics Who Paved the Way to the Civil War, by Arnold Whitridge, Farrar, Straus and Cudahy, NY, 1960
Noah Webster, The Life and Times of an American Patriot, by Harlow Giles Unger, John Wiley and sons, NY, 1998
Noted Guerrillas, Or, The Warfare of the Border, by John N. Edwards, St. Louis, MO, Bryan, Brand and Co., 1877
Novus Ordo Seclorum, The Intellectual Origins of the Constitution, by Forrest McDonald, University Press of Kansas, Lawrence, 1985
The Occult, A History, by Colin Wilson, Random House, NY, 1971. The author viewed an edition signed by Alistair Crowley's grandson using 666 below the signature. Part of the Amber Unicorn Bookstore collection.
Occult Theocracy, by Lady Queenborough (Elizabeth Starr Miller), Volume I, Christian Book Club of America, Los Angeles, 1933
Old Gentlemen's Convention, The Washington Peace Conference of 1861, by Robert Gay Gunderson, Greenwood Press, Publishers, Westport, Connecticut, 1961
The Old Guard, A Monthly Journal, Devoted to the Principles of 1776 and 1787, Vol. I, 1863, C. Chauncey Burr & Co., New York
On America and the Civil War, by Karl Marx, McGraw — Hill Book Co., 1972
On the Duty of Civil Disobedience, Henry Thoreau, 1849
On the First International, by Karl Marx, The Karl Marx Library, Volume III, edited by Saul K. Padover, McGraw — Hill Book Co., NY, 1973
Oneida Community, by Constance Noyes Robertson, Syracuse University Press, 1970
Ordeal of the Union, Fruits of Manifest Destiny, 1847 — 1852, Volume I, by Allan Nevins, Charles Scribner's Sons, New York, London, 1947
Ordeal of the Union: A House Dividing, 1852 — 1857, Volume II, by Allan Nevins, Charles Scribner's Sons, New York, London, 1947
Orestes Brownson, Sign of Contradiction, by R.A. Herrera, ISI Books, Wilmington, DE, 1999
The Origins of Socialism, by George Lichtheim, Frederick A. Praeger, Publishers, New York, Washington, 1969
Other Powers, The Age of Suffrage, Spiritualism, and the Scandalous Victoria Woodhull, by Barbara Goldsmith, Harper Perennial, New York, 1998
Our Naval War With France, by Gardner W. Allen, Houghton Mifflin Company, Boston and New York, 1909
The Paper: The Life and Death of the New York Herald Tribune, by Richard Kluger, Alfred A. Knopf, NY, 1986

The Papers of Andrew Johnson, Volume III, 1858 — 1860, edited by Leroy P. Graf and Ralph W. Haskins, The University of Tennessee Press, Knoxville, 1972

The Papers of Henry Clay: Candidate, Compromiser, Whig, March 5,1829-December 31, 1836, Volume 8, by Henry Clay, edited by Robert Seager II, University Press of Kentucky, Lexington, KY, 1984

Parade Magazine, March 8, 1998, "The Woman Who Set America on its Ear," by Barbara Goldsmith, Pages 14 — 16.

The Pariah Files: 25 Dark Secrets You're Not supposed to Know, by Philip l. Rife, iUniverse, Inc., Lincoln, NE, 2003

Parisian Masonry, the Lodge of the Nine Sisters, & the French Enlightenment, by R. William Weisberger, 32°.

The Patriarchal Order, or, True Brotherhood; etc., by J. Shoebridge Williams, Longley Brothers, Cincinnati, 1855

The Peabody Sisters of Salem, by Louis Hall Tharp, Little, Brown, and Co., Boston, 1950

The Peaceable Revolution, by Betty Schechter, Houghton Mifflin Company, Boston, 1963

The Pennsylvania magazine of History and Biography, January 1976, "The Philadelphia *Aurora*, The New England Illuminati, and the Election of 1800," by Alan V. Briceland

Perfectibilists, The 18th Century Bavarian Order of the Illuminati, by Terry Melanson, Trine Day LLC, Walterville, Oregon, 2009

"The Philadelphia Aurora, the New England Illuminati, and the Election of 1800," by Alan V. Briceland, *The Pennsylvania Magazine of History and Biography,* January, 1976, page 3-36.

Pictorial History of the Civil War in the United States of America, by Benson J. Lossing, Volumes I — III, George W. Childs, Publisher, Philadelphia, 1866

The Pinkerton's, A Detective Dynasty, Richard Wilmer Rowan, Little, Brown, and Co., Boston, 1931

A Plea with Christians for the Cause of Peace, by Rev. George C. Beckwith, Samuel J. May Anti-Slavery Collection, American Peace Society.

The Political Conspiracies Preceding the Rebellion or The True Stories of Sumter and Pikens, by Thomas M. Anderson, G. P. Putman's Sons, New York, 1882

Political Discussions, 1856 — 1886, by James G. Blaine, Norwich, Conn., The Henry Bill Publishing Co., 1887

The Political Evolution of the Mexican People, by Justo Sierra, University of Texas Press, Austin & London, 1969

Political History of the United States, by J. P. Gordy, Ph.D., Volume I, Henry Holt and Company, New York, 1904

Political Power and the Press, by William J. Small, W. W. Norton and Co., Inc., NY, 1972

Political Science Quarterly, "Horace Greeley and the Working Class Origins of the Republican Party," by John R. Commons, XXIV, 1909

Political and Social Growth of the American People, 1492 — 1865, by Homer Carey Hockett, The Maximillian Company, New York, 1949

The Politicos, 1865 — 1896, by Matthew Josephson, Harcourt, Brace and Company, New York, 1938

Politics and Opinions in the Nineteenth Century, by John Bowle, Oxford University Press, New York, 1954

Powder Keg, Northern Opposition to the Antislavery Movement, 1831-1840, by Lorman Ratner, Basic Books, Inc., Publishers, New York, 1968

The Premises and Significance of Abraham Lincoln's Letter to Theodore Canisius, by F. I. Heriott, Reprinted from Deutsch-Amerikanische Geschichtsbätter, (Yearbook of the German-American Historical Society of Illinois), 1915

Preparing For Power, America's Elite Boarding Schools, by Peter W. Cookson, Jr., and Caroline Hodges Persell, Basic Books, Inc., NY 1985

Present Dangers, Jedidiah Morse, DD, 1799, Boston Library archives.

President James Buchanan, A Biography, by Philip Shriver Klein, Pennsylvania State University Press, University Pk, PA, 1962

"President Lincoln and the Illinois Radical Republicans," by Arthur C. Cole, *The Mississippi Valley Historical Review*, Vol. 4, No. 4, March 1918, Organization of American Historians.

Presidents of the Manifest Destiny, by Wallace Patterson and Sam Patrick, Los Angeles Times, 1972

A proletarian revolt: A history of the Paris commune of 1871, By George B. Benham, International Publishing Company, San Francisco, 1898.

Proofs of a Conspiracy, by John Robison, A. M., Western Islands, Boston, 1967 of a 1798 edition

The Public Good, Philanthropy and Welfare in the Civil War Era, by Robert H. Bremner, Alfred A. Knopf, New York, 1980

The Public Men of the Revolution, by Hon. William Sullivan, Philadelphia, Carey and Hart, 1847

Public Men of Today, by P. C. Headley, Hartford: S. S. Scranton & Company, 1882

Pulitzer, by W. A. Swanberg, Charles Scribner's Sons, New York, 1967

Quotations of George Washington, Applewood Books, Bedford, MA, 2003

Race and Manifest Destiny, The Origins of American Radical Anglo-Saxonism, by Reginald Horseman, Howard University Press, Cambridge, 1981

The Radical Republicans, Lincoln's Vanguard for Racial Justice, by Hans L. Trefousse, Alfred A. Knopf, NY, 1969

Radical Republicans and Reconstruction, 1861 — 1870, edited by Harold M. Hyman, The Bobbs-Merrill Company, Inc., New York, 1967

Radical Spirits, Spiritualism and Women's Rights in Nineteenth-Century America, by Ann Deborah Braude, Indiana University Press, Bloomington, IN, 1989

Radicalism In America, by Sidney Lens, Thomas Y. Crowell Co., NY 1966

Ralph Bunche: An American Life, by Brian Urquhart, W. W. Norton & Company, 1993

Raralette: The Rosicrucian's Story, by Pashel Beverly Randolph and R. Swinburne Clymer, 1939, Kessinger Publishing Company ed. 2005

Realism And Nationalism, 1851 — 1871, by Robert C. Binkley, Harper and Row, NY, 1941

Reconstructing the Union, Theory and Policy during the Civil War, by Herman Belz, Cornell University Press, Ithaca, New York, 1969

Reconstruction, The Ending of the Civil War, by Avery Craven, Holt, Rinehart and Winston, Inc., 1969

The Records of the Universal Peace Union, [1846-1866], 1867-1923, 1938, Swarthmore College Peace Collection, Swarthmore, Pennsylvania, 2005

The Red 48'ers, Karl Marx and Frederick Engels, by Oscar J. Hammen, *Charles Scribner's Sons, NY, 1969*

Bibliography

Red Mexico, by Captain Francis McCullagh, Brentano's Ltd., London, 1928

Red Republicans and Lincoln's Marxists, Marxism in the Civil War, by Walter D. Kennedy and Al Benson, Jr., iUniverse, Inc., New York, Lincoln, Shanghai, 2007

Reflections on the Revolution in France, by Edmund Burke, Arlington House, no date of publication, Classics of Conservatism boxed series.

Refugees of Revolution, The German Forty-Eighters in America, by Carl Wittke, University of Pennsylvania Press, Philadelphia, 1952

Register of the Military Order of the Loyal Legion of the United States, Published under the Auspices of the Commandry of the State of Massachusetts, Boston, January 1, 1906

Religion In America, or, an account of The Origin, Relation to the State, and Present Condition of the Evangelical Churches in the United States, by Robert Baird, NY, Harper Bros., Publishers, MDCCCLVI (1856)

A Religious History of the American People, by Sydney E. Ahlstrom, Yale University Press, 1972

The Reluctant Spiritualist: The Life of Maggie Fox, by Nancy Rubin Stuart, 2005

The Remarkable Life of John Murray Spear, Agitator for The Spirit Land, by John Benedict Buescher, University of Notre Dame Press, Notre Dame, Indiana, 2006

Remarks On Europe, Relating to Education, Peace and Labor; And Their Reference to the United States, Rev. Charles Brooks, C. S. Francis and Company, New York, 1846

Reminiscences of an octogenarian in the fields of industrial and social reform, by Joshua King Ingalls, M. L. Holbrook & Co., New York, 1897

Reminiscences of Levi Coffin, the Reputed President of the Underground Railroad, by Levi Coffin, Cincinnati, 1876

Reports of the Trials of Colonel Aaron Burr, for Treason, etc., In Two Volumes, Volume II, Published by Hopkins and Earle, Philadelphia, 1808

The Republican Party, Its History, Principles, and Policies, edited by Hon. John D. Long, Winter & Co., Publishers, Springfield, Mass., 1888

The Republicans: A History of Their Party, by Malcom Moos, Random House, NY, 1956

Requiem for Marx, edited by Yuri N. Maltser, Ludwig von Mises Institute, Auburn University, Alabama, 1993

The Restoration Quarterly, Vol. 9, No. 3, 1966, "Christian Connexion and Unitarian Relations 1800 — 1844", by Thomas H. Olbricht, Abilene Christian University

The Return of Lafayette, 1824 — 1825, by Marian Klamkin, Charles Scribner's Sons, New York, 1975

Reveille In Washington: 1800 — 1865, by Margaret Leech, Harper and Brothers, New York and London, 1941

The Revolutionary Internationalists, 1864 — 1943, edited by Milorad M. Drachkovitch, Hoover Institution on War, Revolution, and Peace, Stanford University Press, Palo Alto, 1966

Revolutionary Radicalism, Its History, Purpose and Tactics, Report of the Joint Legislative Committee Investigating Seditious Activities, Filed April 24, 1920, In the Senate of the State of New York, Part I, Volume I, Albany, J. B. Lyon Co., Printers, 1920

Revolutionary Writers, Literature and Authority in the New Republic, 1725-1810, by Emory Elliott, Oxford University Press, New York, Oxford, 1982

The Ripon Guide, 1996-97, Published by The Ripon Commonwealth Press, May, 1996, Ripon Community Publications, Ripon, WI

The Rise and Fall of the Paris Commune In 1871, by W. Pembroke Fetridge, Harper and Brothers Publishers, New York, 1871

The Rise of the American Nation, 1789 — 1824, by Francis Franklin, International Publishers, New York, 1943

The Rise of the House of Rothschild, by Count Egon Caesar Corti, Western Islands, Belmont, Massachusetts, 1972 of a 1928 edition.

The Road to Disunion, Secessionists at Bay, 1776 — 1854, Volume I, by William W. Froehling, Oxford University Press, New York, Oxford, 1990

The Robber Barons, The Great American Capitalists, 1861 — 1901, by Matthew Josephson, Harcourt, Brace and Company, New York, 1934

Robert Dale Owen, by Richard William Leopold, Octagon Books, New York, 1969

Robert Owen and the Owenites in Britain and America: The Quest for the New Moral World, by John Harrison, Routledge and Kegan Paul Ltd, London, 1969

Rockefeller, :Internationalist," The Man Who Misrules the World, by Emanuel M. Josephson, Chedney Press, 1952

The Roots of American Loyalty, by Merle Curti, Columbia University Press, NY, Morningside Heights, 1946

The Rose Cross and the Age of Reason, by Christopher McIntosh, Published by State University of New York Press, Albany, 2011

Rosicrucian Enlightenment, by Frances A. Yates, Barnes and Noble Books, NY, 1972

The Rosicrucian Fraternity In America, by Dr. R. Swineburne Clymer, Published by the Rosicrucian Foundation, 1935

Rosicrucian Questions and Answers, with Complete History of the Rosicrucian Order, by H. Spencer Lewis, PhD, F.R.C., Supreme Grand Lodge of AMORC, San Jose, CA 1929

The Rosicrucians — Their Teachings, by R. Swineburne Clymer, The Philosophical Publishing Co., 1941

Rousseau and Revolution, Will and Ariel Durant, Simon and Schuster, New York, 1967, *The Story of Civilization: Part X*.

Sable Arm, Black Troops in the Union Army, 1861-1865, by Dudley Taylor Cornish, University of Kansas Press, 1956, 1987

The Samuel Gompers Papers: The Early Years of the American Federation of Labor, 1887-90, By Samuel Gompers and edited by Stuart B. Kaufman, 1987, University of Illinois

Samuel Gridley Howe, Social Reformer, 1801 — 1876, by Harold Schwartz, Harvard University Press, Cambridge, 1956

San Francisco Chronicle, June 5, 1998, "150 Years Ago Today, S.F. Bay's Entrance Became Golden Gate," Page A20

The Sanders Odyssey: Study of A Nineteenth Century Insider, by Randall Haines, unpublished manuscript, 1973.

The Scots Magazine or, General Repository of Literature, History, and Politics, For the Year MDCCXCVI, Vol. 58, Printed by Alex. Chapman and Company, 1796

Scribner's Magazine, "Gen. Sam Houston and Secession," by Charles A. Culbertson, XXXIX, 1906

Secession Movement In Middle Atlantic States, by William C. Wright, Farleigh Dickinson University Press, Rutherford, Madison, Teaneck, 1973

The Secession Movement in Virginia, 1847 — 1861, by Henry T. Shanks, Garrett and Massie, Publishers, Richmond, 1934
Secret Ritual and Manhood in Victorian America, by Mark C. Carnes, Yale University Press, New Haven & London, 1989
Secret And Sacred, The Diaries of James Henry Hammond, a Southern Slaveholder, ed. By Carol Bleser, Oxford University Press, New York — Oxford, 1988
The Secret Service of the Confederate States In Europe, by James D. Bulloch, Volumes I and II, Richard Bentley And Son, London, 1883
The Secret Service of the Confederate States in Europe, or How the Confederate Cruisers Were Equipped, by James D. Bulloch, Volume I, Thomas Yoseloff, New York, London, 1959
Secret Service, the Field, the Dungeon, and the Escape, by Albert D. Richardson, American Publishing Company, Hartford, Conn, 1865
The Secret Six, John Brown and the Abolitionist Movement, by Otto J. Scott, Times Books, NY 1979
The Secret Six, The True Tale of the Men Who Conspired with John Brown, by Edward J. Renehan, Jr., Crown Publishers, Inc., New York, 1995
Secret Societies, ed. by Norman MacKenzie, Holt, Rinehart and Winston, New York and London, 1967
The Secret Societies of All Ages and Countries, by Charles William Heckethorn, In Two Volumes, London, 1896, University Books, reprinted 1965
Secret Societies and Subversive Movements, by Nesta Webster, Christian Book Club of America, Hawthorne, California, 1967, first printed 1924
Secret Societies: Illuminati, Freemasons and the French Revolution, by Una Birch, edited, enlarged and introduced by James Wasserman, Ibis Press, Lake Worth, Florida, 2007, originally published in 1911
Secret Societies, Yesterday and Today, by Arkon Daraul, Frederick Muller, London, 1961
A Secret Society History of the Civil War, by Mark A. Lause, University of Illinois Press, 2011
A Sermon, delivered at Charleston, July 23, 1812 (on the consequence of a Declaration of War with Great Britain), by Jedidiah Morse, DD, Pastor of the Congregational Church in Charleston, Charleston, Printed by Samuel Etheridge, Jun'r, 1812
A Sermon to the Grand Lodge of Free Masons, Jedidiah Morse, 1798
SEVENTEEN EIGHTY NINE: An Unfinished Manuscript which explores the early history of THE COMMUNIST CONSPIRACY, American Opinion Preview Series, Belmont, M.A., 1968
Sexuality, Magic And Perversion, by Frances King, The Citadel Press, Secaucus, New Jersey, 1972
The Shadow of Lincoln's Death, by Otto Eisenschiml, Wilfred Funk, Inc., New York, 1940
A Short History of the United States, 1492-1920, by John Spencer Bassett, PhD, The MacMillan Company, New York, 1923
The Shut-door and the Sanctuary: Historical and Theological Problems, by Wesley Ringer, Southern Conference of Seventh-day Adventists, April 6, 1982
Sickles the Incredible, by W. A. Swanberg, Charles Scribner's and Sons, NY 1956
Silver & Gold Report, P. O. Box 510, Bethal, CT 06801, promo 1989
"Sigismund Kaufmann, Abolitionist: How A German 48'er became a Brooklyn political leader," by I. B. Bailin, *Jewish Currents* magazine, July-August, 1961
Six Frigates: The Epic History of the Founding of the U.S. Navy, by Ian W. Toll, Norton, New York and London, 2006/2008
Sketches and reminiscences of the Radical club of Chestnut Street, edited by Mary Elizabeth Fiske Sargent, Mrs. John T. Sargent, James R. Osgood and Company, Boston, 1880
The Slave Power Conspiracy and the Paranoid Style, by David Brian Davis, Louisiana State University Press, Baton Rouge and London, 1969
Smithsonian, July 1989, "Radical and Chic, a duke who courted revolt and doom," by Robert Wernick, pages 66 — 73
June 1996, "Smithsonian Perspectives," by A. Michael Heyman, Page 14
So I Killed Lincoln, John Wilkes Booth, by Charles J. Bauer, Vantage Press, New York, etc., 1976
Social Ideas of the Northern Evangelists, 1826-1860, by Charles C. Cole, Jr., Octagon Books, A Division of Farrar, Straus and Giroux, New York, 1977
Socialism, Promise or Menace, by Morris Hillquit, and John A. Ryan, The Macmillan Company, New York, 1914
Socialism In America, by Albert Fried, Doubleday and Co., Garden City, New York 1970
The Socialist Network, by Nesta Webster, London, 1926
The Socialist Tradition, Moses to Lenin, by Alexander Gray, Harper Torchbooks, New York Evanston, and London, 1946
Sociology: The Reconstruction of Society*, Government, and Property, etc.*, By Lewis Masquerier, Published by the Author, New York, 1877
Society and Thought in Early America, by Harvey Wish, David McKay Company, Inc., New York, 1950
Some Recollections of our Antislavery Conflict, by Samuel J. May, Arno Press and the New York Times, NY, 1968
Sons of Garibaldi in Blue and Gray: Italians in the American Civil War, by Frank W. Alduino and David J. Coles, Cambria Press, Youngstown, New York 2007
South Atlantic Quarterly,
XXVII, 1928, "George Sanders, American Patriot of the Fifties," by Merle Curti
South of Appomattox, by Nash K. Burger, and John K. Bettersworth, Harcourt, Brace and Company, New York, 1959
Southern History of the War, Volume I, The First Year of the War, by Edward A. Pollard, Books for Libraries Press, Freeport, NY, 1862 — 1863, Reprinted 1969
Southern History of the Civil War, by Edward A. Pollard, Two Volumes in One, The Fairfax Press, 1977, originally printed 1866
Southern Sketches, Number 9, First Series, "State Socialism in the Confederate States of America," by Louise B. Hill, The Historical Publishing Co., Inc., Charlottesville, Virginia, 1936
Southwestern Historical Quarterly, "The Knights of the Golden Circle: A Filibustering Fantasy," by C. A. Bridges, XLIV, 1941

Bibliography

Sovereignty and an Empty Purse, Banks and Politics in the Civil War, by Bray Hammond, Princeton University Press, Princeton, NJ, 1970
Speech of Mr. Sprague on The Removal Of The Deposits Delivered in the Senate of the United States, January 1834, Printed by Gales and Seaton, 1834
Speeches and Writings 1832-1858, edited by Roy P. Basler, Abraham Lincoln Association, Rutgers University Press, 1953
Spies for the Blue and Gray, by Harnett T. Kane, Hanover House, Garden City, NY, 1954
The Spirits of '76, A Catholic Inquiry, by Donald J. D'Elia, Christendom Publications, Front Royal, Virginia, 1983
Spiritualism in Antebellum America, by Bret E. Carroll, Indiana University Press, Bloomington & Indianapolis, 1997
The Spurious Rites of Memphis and Misraim, by Albert Pike, 33° and William L. Cummings, 33°
The Spy of the Rebellion, by Allen Pinkerton, New York, G. W. Carleton & Co., Publishers, 1883, Published 1886
St. Louis Public Schools, Twenty-First Annual Report of the Board of Directors for the Year Ending August 1, 1875. St. Louis, Globe-Democrat Job Printing Co., 1876
Stanton: The Life and Times of Lincoln's Secretary of War, by Benjamin P. Thomas and Harold M. Hyman, NY, 1962
Stanton, Lincoln's Secretary of War, by Fletcher Pratt, W. W. Norton & Company, Inc., New York, 1953
The State and Freedom of Contract, edited by Harry N. Scheiber, Stanford University Press, Stanford, CA, 1998
The State Makers, by Bill and Sue Severn, G. P. Putnam's Sons, NY, 1963
Statesmen of the Lost Cause, by Barton J. Hendrick, The Literary Guild of America, Inc., NY, 1939
Stephen A. Douglas, by Robert W. Johannsen, Oxford University Press, New York, 1973
Storm Over the Land, by Carl Sandburg, Harcourt, Brace and Co., NY, 1939
The Story of the Political Philosophers, by George Catlin, Tudor Publishing Co., New York, 1939
The Strange Disappearance of William Morgan, by Thomas A. Knight, Published by the Author, At Brecksville, Ohio, Eastern Distributors: The Macoy Publishing and Masonic Supply Company, New York City, 1932
Studies In Revolution, Edward Hallett Carr, London, Macmillan and Co., Ltd., 1950
The Suppressed Truth About the Assassination of Abraham Lincoln, by Burke McCarthy, date and publisher unknown, printed in Taiwan
Symbolism of Freemasonry or Mystic Masonry, by J. D. Buck, M.D., F.T.S.S.R., 32°, Chas. T. Powner Co., 1925, Kegan Publishing Co.
Table of the Brethern who Compose the Provincial French Lodge, Printed by Willett and O'Conner, Norfolk, In the Epoch of John 5798 (1798)
Tammany Hall, by M. R. Werner, Doubleday, Doran & Company, Inc., Barden City, New York, 1931
Territorial Record, Volume I, No. 1, January 1988, Published October 1987, Pollack Pines, CA 95726, "The Knights of the Golden Circle," by J. K. Richards
The Texas Rangers, A Century of Frontier Defense, by Walter Prescott Webb, Houghton Mifflin Co., Boston — New York, 1935
Thaddeus Stevens, by Samuel W. McCall, Houghton, Mifflin and Co., Boston, 1899
Thaddeus Stevens, A Being Darkly Wise and Rudely Great, by Ralph Korngold, Harcourt, Brace and Co., NY, 1955
Thaddeus Stevens, Scourge of the South, by Fawn M. Brodie, W.W. Norton and Co., NY, 1959
A Theological Dictionary, etc., by Charles Buck, Two Volumes in One, Fifth American Edition, Printed for W. W. Woodward, Philadelphia, 1818
The Theosophical Enlightenment, by Joscelyn Godwin, State University of New York Press, 1994
A Thesis Presented to the Faculty of the Department of History, East Carolina University, by Kimberly Lane Eslinger, August 2005 on the USS Commodore
This One Mad Act, The Unknown Story of John Wilkes Booth and His Family, by His Granddaughter Izola Forrester, Hales, Cushman & Flint, Boston, 1937
Thomas Jefferson, A Life, by Willard Sterne Randall, Harper Perennial, New York, 1993
Thomas Paine, Apostle of Freedom, by Jack Frchtman, Jr., Four Walls Eight Windows, New York, London, 1994
Thomas Starr King, Eminent Californian, Civil War Statesman, Unitarian Minister, by Robert Monzingo, The Boxwood Press, Pacific Grove, CA, 1991
The Three Faces of Charles H. Vail, by Dan McKanan, Collegium/UU History & Heritage Convocation, October 2010
The Times of the Rebellion In The West, by Henry Howe, Howe's Subscription Book Concern, Cincinnati, 1867
To Covet Honor, A Biography of Alexander Hamilton, by Holmes Alexander, Western Islands, Belmont, Massachusetts, 1977
Toward a Patriarchal Republic, The Secession of Georgia, by Michael P. Johnson, Louisiana State University Press, Baton Rouge and London, 1977
Toward a Soviet America, by William Z. Foster, International Publishers, New York, 1932
The Tragic Era, The Revolution After Lincoln, by Claude G. Bowers, The Literary Guild of America, Cambridge, 1929
Transactions of the Supreme Council 33° for the Southern Jurisdiction of the United States of America, October 1905, Charleston
Transcendentalism as a Social Movement, 1830 — 1850, Anna C. Rose, New Haven: Yale University Press, 1981
Transcendentalism In New England, by Octavius Brooks Frothingham, Gloucester, Massachusetts, 1876, 1965 ed.
The Transcendentalists: An Anthology, by Perry Miller, Harvard University Press, Cambridge, 1950
The Trial of Theodore Parker for the "Misdemeanor" of a Speech in Faneuil Hall against Kidnapping, etc., Allen and Farnham Printers, Cambridge, for the author, 1855
The Trial of Mary Todd Lincoln, by James A. Rhodes and Dean Janchius, The Bobbs-Merrill Company, Inc., Indianapolis, New York, 1959
A True History of the Assassination of Lincoln And of the Conspiracy of 1865, by Louis J. Weichmann, Alfred A. Knopf, Inc. New York, 1975
The True History of the Civil War, by Guy Carleton Lee, J. B. Lippincott Company, Philadelphia & London, 1903
The Trust, The Private and Powerful Family Behind The New York Times, by Susan E. Tifft and Alex S. Jones, Little, Brown and Company, Boston, New York, London, 1999

Truth Seeker, The Journal of Independent Thought, Volume 125, 1998, Worlds Oldest Freethought Publication, Since 1873

Der Turner Soldat; A Turner Soldier in the Civil War; Germany to Antietam, by C. Eugene Miller, Forrest F. Steinlage, Calmer Publications, Louisville, Kentucky, 1988

Twenty Days, by Dorothy Meserve Kunhardt and Philip B. Kunhardt, Jr., Harper and Row, Publishers, New York, 1965

2,000 Years of Disbelief: Famous People with the Courage to Doubt, by James A. Haught, Prometheas Books, New York, 1996

Uncommon Americans, by Don C. Seitz, The Bobbs — Merrill Co., Indianapolis, 1925

An Unfinished Revolution: Karl Marx and Abraham Lincoln, by Robin Blackburn, Verso, London and New York, 2011

The Union Cause In St. Louis In 1861, "An Historical Sketch," by Robert J. Rombauer, St. Louis Municipal Centennial Year, 1909, Press of Nixon — Jone Prtg Co., St. Louis

The United States of America, Volumes I and II, by David Saville Muzzey, PhD, Ginn and Co., 1924

The United States Sanitary Commission, "A Sketch of Its Purposes and Its Work, Compiled from Documents and Private Papers", Little Brown and Company, Boston, 1863

The Unlocked Book, A Memoir of John Wilkes Booth, by his sister Asia Booth Clarke, Arno Press, New York Times Co., New York, 1977

The Un-Marxian Socialist, A Study of Proudhon, by Henri De Lubac, Sheed & Ward, New York, 1948

Until Victory, Horace Mann and Mary Peabody, by Louise Hall Tharp, Little, Brown and Company, Boston, 1953

Utopian Alternatives, Fourierism in Nineteenth Century America, by Carl J. Guarneri, Cornell University Press, Ithaca and London, 1991

Victory — and after, by Earl Browder, International Publishers, 1942

Vindication of Thomas Paine, by Robert Green Ingersoll, Bank of Wisdom, Louisville, Kentucky, 1877

Walker, The True Story of the First American Invasion of Nicaragua, by Rudy Warlitzer, Harper and Row, Publishers, 1963 and 1987

The War Between The States, America's Uncivil War, by John J. Dwyer, Bluebonnet Press, Denton, Texas, 2005

War of the Rebellion, A Compilation of the Official Records of the Union and Confederate Armies, Government Printing Office, Washington, 1880, Series I, Volume I.

Was Secession Taught at West Point?, Military Order of the Loyal Legion of the United States, Brevet Lieut-Colonel James W. Latta, 1909

Washington, The Man and the Mason, by Charles Callahan, 1913

Washington In Germantown, by Charles Francis Jenkins, Philadelphia, William J. Campbell, 1905, Canterbury Press, Philadelphia

Washington University Studies, "South Carolina and the South on the Eve of Secession, 1852 to 1860," by Chauncey Samuel Boucher, Humanistic Series, VI, 1919

The Web of Conspiracy, The Complete Story of the Men Who Murdered Abraham Lincoln, by Theodore Roscoe, Prentice-Hall, Inc., Englewood Cliffs, N.J., 1959

Wendell Phillips: The Agitator, by Carlos Martyn, Funk & Wagnalls Company, New York, London, Toronto, 1890

The Whiskey Rebellion, Frontier Epilogue to the American Revolution, by Thomas P. Slaughter, Oxford University Press, New York, Oxford, 1986

Who Was Who in American Politics, by Dan and Inez Morris, Hawthorne Books, Inc., New York, 1974

Who Was Who in the Civil War, by Stewart Sifakis, Facts On File Publications, New York, Oxford, 1988

Why The Civil War?, by Otto Eisenschiml, The Bobbs — Merrill Co., Inc., Indianapolis — New York, 1958

Why Was Lincoln Murdered?, by Otto Eisenschiml, Halcyon House, New York, 1937

William Lloyd Garrison and the Challenge of Emancipation, by James Brewer Stewart, Harlan Davidson, Inc., Arlington Heights, Illinois, 1992

William Woods Holden, Firebrand of North Carolina Politics, by William C. Harris, Louisiana State University Press, Baton Rouge and London, 1987

The Wind from America, 1778 — 1781, by Claude Manceron, Alfred A. Knopf, New York, 1978

The Wisconsin Story: The Building of a Vanguard State, by H. Russell Austin, Published by The Milwaukee Journal, 1948

Woodrow Wilson's Right Hand, The Life of Colonel Edward M. House, by Godfrey Hodgson, Yale University Press, New Haven and London, 2006

A World Without Jews, Karl Marx, Philosophical Library, New York, 1959

Workers And Allies: Female Participation in the American Trade Union Movement, 1824 — 1976, by Judith O'Sullivan and Rosemary Gullick, Published for the Smithsonian Institution Traveling Exhibition Service, Smithsonian Institute Press, Washington, D.C., 1975

Works of Fisher Ames, As Published by Seth Ames, Edited and Enlarged by W.B. Allen, Volumes I & II, Liberty Fund, Indianapolis, 1983

The Works of Ralph Waldo Emerson: Lectures and biographical sketches, Houghton Mifflin and Co., Boston, New York

World Revolution, by Nesta Webster, London, Constable and Co., Ltd, 1921

Writings of John Quincy Adams, by Worthington Chauncey Ford, Vol. I, Macmillan, 1913

The Writings of Thomas Jefferson, Volume XVI, The Thomas Jefferson Memorial Association, 1905

www.phoenixmasonry.org/10,000_famous_freemasons

Yankee Communes, Another American Way, by Flo Morse, Harcourt, Brace, Jovanovich, Inc. NY, 1971

The Yankee International: Marxism and the American Reform Tradition, 1848 — 1876, by Timothy Messer-Kruse, University of North Carolina Press, 1998

Yankee Reporters, 1861 — 65, by Emmet Crozier, Oxford University Press, New York, 1956

Yankees First, Germans Second, "Barton/Young America," author and date unknown.

Year of Decision, 1846, by Bernard DeVoto, Little, Brown and Company, Boston, 1943

Young America, by Donald Scott Harter, The LTD press, The University of Wisconsin, Madison, WI, 1972

Young America, The Flowering of Democracy in New York City, by Edward L. Widmer, Oxford University Press, New York, 1999

Bibliography

Young America: Land, Labor, and the Republican community, by Mark A Lause, University of Illinois Press, Urbana and Chicago, 2005
The Young America Movement and the Transformation of the Democratic Party, 1828 — 1861, by Yonatan Eyal, Cambridge University Press, 2007
Young Folks' History of the Civil War, by Mrs. C. Emma Cheney, Published by Estes and Lauriat, Boston, 1884
A Youth's History of the Great Civil War in the United States, From 1861 to 1865, by R. G. Horton, Van Evrie, Horton & Co., 1866

Index

Abbot, Ezra, 409
Abbot, Francis E., 408
ACLU, 72
ACORN, 254, 405
Adams, Charles Francis, 410
Adams, John, xxxiii, xli, 4, 22, 30, 60, 72-74, 77, 79, 82, 84, 89, 94, 95, 112, 177, 196, 209, 222, 274, 329, 416, 440, 444, 447, 468, 470, 478
Adams, John, miniseries, 89
Adams, John Quincy, xxxiii, xli, 30, 82, 112, 196, 209, 222, 416, 468, 470, 478
Adams, William, 268, 373
Adet, Pierre Auguste, 97
Adirondack Club, 151
Adler, Dr. Karl, 409
Aerial America, 159
Affordable Care Act, xlii, 58, 138, 376
Agassiz, Louis, 151, 259
Age of Reason, xxxvi, xxxvii, 2, 150, 232, 342, 475
Agenda, ix, xi, xiii, xiv, xix, xxvi, xxvii, 4, 9-11, 27, 32, 39, 46, 60, 73, 86, 89, 116, 120, 121, 127, 131, 136, 139, 145, 151-155, 160, 177-179, 183, 186, 188, 200, 205, 209, 215, 219, 225, 231, 235, 236, 238, 240, 243, 247, 250, 254, 258, 259, 262, 266, 271, 273, 274, 277, 278, 280, 286, 295, 296, 301, 309, 317, 328, 335, 338, 350, 355, 361, 364, 373, 390, 391, 394, 399, 401, 404-410, 414, 420, 423, 426, 433, 438, 447, 448, 450, 453-456
Alcott, Amos Bronson, 127, 198, 199
Alcott, Louise May, 209
Alien and Sedition Acts, 31, 79, 80, 82, 83, 85, 88, 112, 195, 241, 309
Alinsky, Saul, 254
Allegemeiner Deutscher Arbeiter Verein, 397
Allen, Benjamin, 369
Allen, Major E. J., 354
Allen, Ethan, 14, 16, 17, 180
Allen, Gary, 145, 457
Allen, Henry W., 328
Allen, John, 144, 239
Allen, William, 269
Al-Qaeda, 401
Alta Vendita, 125, 126, 216
Alvord, John Watson, 405
American Anti-Slavery Society, 49, 141, 188, 191, 268, 272, 303, 410, 418, 474
American and Foreign Anti-Slavery Society, 191
American Association of Spiritualists, 407
American Bar Association, 138, 413
American Brotherhood, 144, 237, 415
American Civil Liberties Union (ACLU), 72
American Colonization Society, 104, 257, 258, 274
American Committee, 28, 29, 141, 192, 271, 294, 350, 409
American Democratic Clubs, 61
American Federation of Labor, 400, 468, 469, 475
American Fröbel Union, 200
American Friends Service Committee, 350
American Geographical Society, 50
American Historical Association, 27, 50, 321, 378, 433
American Labor Reform League, 144
American Legion, 21, 436
American party, 237, 238, 242, 280, 301, 397
American Peace Society, 157, 208, 209, 269, 270, 272, 474
American Phalanx, 223, 225, 239
American Philosophical Society, 68, 70, 91, 93
American Polish Committee, 294
American Red Cross, 421, 464
American Secular Union and Freethought Federation, 409
American Spiritualist, 202, 204, 234, 407, 417
American Spiritual Magazine, 408
American Temperance Society, 293
American Union of Associations, 37, 143, 160, 161, 197, 220, 235, 238, 240, 405
American Woman Suffrage Association, 294, 418
American Workers League, 351
Ames, Adelbert, 389
Anarchism, 209, 212, 214, 220, 397, 467, 472
Anderson, Thomas M., xxii, 474
Anderson, Robert, xxii
Andrew, Edward, 351
Andrew, John A., 192, 274, 302, 347
Andrews, Stephen Pearl, 144
Anneke, Friederich, 165, 418
Anneke, Mathilde, 418
Anthony, Susan B., 220, 300, 404, 418, 419, 422
Anti-Masonic, 114, 210-212, 470
Anti-Masonic Party, 114, 211, 212
Anti-Masonic Review, 212
Anti-Masonry, 210
Anti-slave Trade Act, 257
Anti-Slavery Convention, 267, 268, 272, 275, 310, 464
Anti-Slavery Society, 49, 141, 157, 188, 191, 192, 209, 250, 268, 271, 272, 274, 293, 303, 310, 321, 344, 397, 405, 410, 418, 464, 472, 474
Arbiter-Vereine, 345
Arbeiterbund, 142, 164, 220
Arcesilaus, 7
Arnold, Benedict, xxxvii
Arthur, Chester A., 404
Articles of Confederation, 50, 57, 71, 75, 102, 459
Asboth, Alexander, 416
Ashley, James Monroe, 172
Ashmun, George, 222, 246
Asiatic Brethren, 23, 42, 43
Associated Gymnastic Unions of North America, 245
Association of All Classes of All Nations, 155
Astor, John Jacob, 35, 47, 49, 69, 109, 112, 296, 471
Ataturk, 129
Athens, xxxiv, 9, 81
Atlanta, 338, 426, 437
Atlantic, xxiv, 12, 48, 64, 97, 119, 151, 156, 157, 192, 279, 304, 396, 470, 475, 476
Atlantic Club, 48, 151
Atlantic Journal, 157
The Atlantic Monthly, 192
Atomic absorption spectrophotometer, 381
Atwood, Harry, 76, 464
Atzerodt, 381
Atzlan, 117
Aurora, 67, 79, 93, 98, 101, 463, 474
Ayers, Bill, 232
Ba'ath Party, xii
Babeuf, Gracchus, 5, 35, 239, 424
Bache, Alexander Dallas, 159
Bacon, Leonard, 294
Bacon, Samuel, 258
Badeau, Adam, 427
Baha'i, xxviii
Bailey, Gamaliel, 238
Baird, Robert, 195, 196, 475
Baker, Joseph B., 136
Baker, Lafayette, 360, 361, 381, 466
Baldwin, Simeon Eren, 413
Ballou, Adin, 121, 209, 269
Band of Virtue, 341
Banks, Nathaniel, 221, 228, 237, 238, 243, 350, 352
Banks, Theodore, 400
Barker, Joseph, 189
Barlow, Francis Channing, 413
Barlow, Joel, 36, 37, 84, 112, 424
Barmby, Goodwyn, 164, 207
Barnes, Joseph K., 49
Barry, William, 28
Barruel, Abbe, xxxii, 6, 8, 9
Bartol, Cyrus Augustus, 408
Bayard, James A., 112
The Beacon, 249
Beauregard, Pierre, 248, 284, 312
Beck, Charles, 47, 49
Beckley, John, 88
Beecher, Henry Ward, xxxiv, 144, 158, 203, 242, 291, 296, 300, 303, 373, 417, 468
Beecher, Lyman, 203, 291
Bell, John, 140, 228, 246
Bellows, Henry Whitney, 47, 49, 373, 405

Belmont, August, 28, 132, 135, 136, 219, 221, 230, 244, 247, 248, 369, 464
Bennett, James Gordon, 48, 135, 238
Benson, Ezra Taft, 232
Benjamin, Judah P., 227
Bennett, James Gordon, 48, 135, 238
Beveridge, Albert J, 378, 463
Bible Society, 131, 209, 274
Bickley, George, 281, 463
Biddle, Nicholas, 116, 212, 222
Biden, Joseph, xxviii
Bigelow, 203
Bigler, John, 225
Bilderberg, xxvii
Billington, James H., 18, 467
Bird, Francis W., 242, 275
Bird Club, 48, 276, 297
Bismarck, Otto, 34, 227, 350
Black, Hugo, 391
Black Knights, 341
Black Panthers, 69, 78, 188
Black Shirts, 125
Blaine, James G., 242, 262, 313, 474
Blair, Austin, 243
Blair, Eric Arthur, 56
Blair, Francis Preston, 238, 249
Blair, Montgomery, 165, 300, 357
Blanc, Louis, xxxiii, 4, 24, 124, 130, 133, 141, 347
Blanchard, Jonathon, 212
Blanqui, Louis Auguste, 5, 24, 46, 130
Blanshard, Joshua P., 269
Blavatsky, Helena, 124, 203, 409
Bleeding Kansas, 290, 298
Blenker, Louis, 242, 416
Blennerhassett, Harman, 102
Bloor, Ella Reeve, 198
The Blue Book, 254
Blumenfeld, Samuel, 453, 457, 470
Bode, Christian, 6, 7, 31
Boeing, 436
Bohemian Club, 198
Bollman, Justus Erich, 101, 102, 127
Bonaparte, Charles Joseph, 400
Bonaparte, Joseph, 222, 400
Bond of Peace, 428
Bonneville, Benjamin, 5, 35, 36
Bonneville, Nicholas, 5, 7, 24, 31, 36, 70, 239, 424, 470
Booth, John Wilkes, 140, 175, 296, 353, 361, 377-379, 476-478
Booth, Junius Brutus, 379
Booth, Sherman W., 241
Börnstein, Heinrich, xxvi, 238, 349
Boston Chronicle, 67, 98
Boston Independent Chronicle, 67
Boston Liberator, 358
Boston Post, 202
Boston Public Library, 47, 279, 331
Boston Traveler, 287, 297

Bourne, William Oland, 402, 469
Bovay, Alvan E., 218, 221, 422
Bowdoin College, 269
Bowman, James F., 198
Brackenridge, 63
Brisbane, Albert, 38, 48, 141, 143, 144, 149, 192, 198, 220, 239, 244, 283, 294, 350, 443, 444
Brissot, Jacques-Pierre, 62
British Colony of Republicans, 141
Britten, Emma Hardinge, 203, 473
Brooks, Charles, 444, 475
Brooks, Preston, 153, 262
Brotherhood of Death, 26
Brotherhood of Life, 226
Brotherhood of the Union, xxii, 16, 130, 141, 142, 183, 220, 281, 287, 293, 306, 308, 345, 397, 402, 403
Brown, Albert Gallatin, 309
Brown, James, 222, 470
Brown, John, xxxi, 27, 104, 105, 141, 142, 191, 192, 199, 250, 252, 271, 274-277, 287, 288, 290-297, 299, 302, 305, 313, 315, 351, 352, 379, 381, 388, 395, 422, 431, 463, 470, 476
Brown, Joseph Emerson, 281, 338, 430
Brown, Mary, 300
Brownson, Orestes Augustus, xxvi, 143, 198
Bryant, William Cullen, 37, 49, 122, 201, 219, 222, 239
BU - Brotherhood of the Union, 141
Buchanan, James, 133, 135, 221, 228, 230, 474
Buck, Charles, 6, 477
Buckley, William F., 217, 254, 255
Bull Moose Party, 252, 414
Bunch, Robert, 380
Buonarroti, Fillipo Michele, 126
Bureau of Mines, 374
Burgess, John W, 392
Burlingame, Anson, 324
Burnside, Gen., 358
Burschenschaften, 341, 343, 344
Bush, George, xxviii, 27, 412, 416, 435, 450
Bush, Prescott, 27
Butler, Benjamin, 125, 136, 170, 218, 221, 303, 304, 321, 373, 382, 389, 411, 421
Byrd, Harry, 391
Cabet, Etienne, xxxiii
Cagliostro, 23, 31, 97, 472
Calhoun, John, 135, 203, 463, 470
Capone, Al, ix, 361
Came, Charles G., 402
Cameron, Andrew, 411
Campbell, Lewis Davis, 173
Canadian Alliance Society, 122
Carbonari, xxxiii, 5, 8, 10, 15, 36, 38, 46, 83, 85, 117, 122-131, 133, 135, 140, 141, 156, 163, 164, 209, 215-223, 226, 229, 230, 274, 280, 282, 287, 288, 290, 293, 307, 320, 324, 339, 341, 347, 349, 350, 362, 385, 387, 390, 397, 406, 424
Cardinal Franzelin, xxvi
Carlton, James, 180
Carlyle, Thomas, 203, 468
Carnegie Endowment, 270, 271, 417
Carnegie, Andrew, xxxi, xxxiii, 409, 413, 417, 464, 470, 471
Carpenter, Philo, 250
Cass, Lewis, 134, 225
Castro, xxviii, 1, 232, 282, 298
Castro Colony, 282
Catherine the Great, 65, 346
Catholic Church, 9, 25, 29, 30, 125, 174, 237, 285, 328, 465
Catholicism, xxvi, 126, 208, 382
Catholics, xxvi, 9, 191, 237, 276, 385
Central American League, 225, 231
Central Democratic Committee, 231, 311
Central Illinois Railroad, 246, 321, 352
Central Park, 122, 201, 403, 405
Central States, xxiii, 223, 283, 329, 365
Centuries, xvi, 9, 12, 20, 33, 87, 88, 114, 133, 176, 178, 209, 212, 223, 259, 280, 407, 415, 428, 437, 440
Century America, 8, 232, 272, 273, 331, 478
Cercle Social, xxviii, 5, 23, 24, 29, 31, 34-36, 44, 62, 164, 206, 465
Ceresco, 143, 235, 236, 295
Chaffey Company, 361
Chamberlain, Daniel Henry, 392
Chandler, David Leon, 105, 470
Chandler, John, 228, 236, 350
Channing, William E., xxxiii, 150, 197, 208
Channing, William H., 150
Channing, William M., 202
Chardon Street Convention, 272
Chartism, xxxiii, 465
Chartist, xxxi, xxxiii, xxxiv, 37, 118, 144, 180, 188-190, 206, 220, 250, 268, 272, 293, 303, 352, 354, 422
Chase, Salmon, 238, 243, 250, 278, 350
Chase, Warren, 235, 236, 407
Chatham House, xv, 181
Chauvenet, William, 50
Cheever, 294
Chicago Times, 365
Chicago Tribune, 239, 287, 294, 296, 297, 384
Chicago Union, 352
Child, Lydia Maria, 397, 408
Children of God, 266
Children's Progressive Lyceums, 407
Chile, 296
Chillicothe Ohio Gazette, 103
Chilton, Samuel, 300
Choate, Rufus, 159
Christian Citizen, 209
Christian Constitutional Society, 184
Christian Faith, 91, 132, 207

INDEX

Christian Labor Union, 400
Christian Socialism, 143, 154, 197, 199, 209, 400
Christian Socialists, 197, 419
Christian Union, 143, 208, 400, 420
Church League of America, 206
Churchill, Winston, 2, 271
Cicero, iii, 443
Cincinnati, 144, 293, 301, 307, 342, 355, 398, 464, 466, 468-470, 472, 474, 475, 477
Circle of Free Brothers, 36
Circle of Honor, 289
Citizen of the World, 71, 210, 220, 223, 418, 465
Claflin, Tennessee, xxxi, 201, 226, 398
Claflin Weekly, 226
Clark, George Rogers, 65, 90
Clarke, Asia Booth, 382, 478
Clay, Henry, xxxiii, 102, 104, 112-114, 257, 442, 471, 474
Clinton, DeWitt, 38, 46, 114, 185, 202, 212, 222, 251, 332, 422
Clinton, George, 37, 66, 68, 72, 95, 114, 185, 202
Clinton, Hillary, 181, 450
Clinton, Bill, 242
Cloots, 35
Club Blanqui, 217
Cluss, Adolf, 159
Cluseret, Gustave-Paul, 130, 165, 244
Clymer, George, 14, 15, 17
CNN, 80, 189
Cobbett, William, 37
Cochrane, 186, 314
Codding, Ichabod, 245
Cogswell, Dr. J. G., 46
Colby, William, 202
Colfax, Schuyler, 373
Collectivists, xv, xix, 31, 334, 448
Colonization, xx, 102, 104, 188, 257-259, 266, 274, 328, 460, 471
Colonization Society, 102, 104, 257, 258, 274, 471
Columbia, 135, 167, 208, 228, 403, 426, 464, 467, 475
Columbia University, 135, 464, 475
Columbian Illuminati, 202, 249, 422, 468
Columbian Order, 183
Columbian Star, 284
Columbus, 21, 183, 201, 210, 243
Come-outers, 273, 309
Commercial Institute, 27
Common Core, xxi, 59, 155, 193, 204, 205, 437-439
Common Sense, xliii, 18, 29, 30, 34, 83, 132, 395, 415, 436, 461
Commonwealth of Nations, 192
La Commune Revolutionnaire, 24
Communes, xxxiii, 37, 38, 98, 143, 149, 150, 154-156, 160, 161, 200, 226, 235, 236, 239, 405, 478
Communism, in passim
Communist, in passim
Communist Church, 189, 206, 207, 262
Communist Clubs, 398
Communist First International, 49, 161, 202, 214, 351, 394, 397, 412, 443
Communist League, xxxiii, 4, 36, 46, 159, 163, 164, 167, 170, 206, 226, 267, 346
Communist Manifesto, xxxiii, xxxiv, xl, 4, 75, 76, 121, 144, 163, 164, 176, 177, 226, 278, 357, 373, 433, 439-441, 443, 457
Communist Party USA Central Committee, 400, 457
Comuneros, 132, 173
Concord School of Philosophy, 437
Concordists, 341
The Condition of the Working Class in England, 398
Condorcet, Marquis de, 31, 127
Confederate Congress, 28, 361, 432
Confederate Constitutional Convention, 57
Conference of Peace, 132, 466, 473
Congregational, 466, 476
Congress of Nations, 208, 209, 218, 219
Conklin, J. B., 201
Connecticut National Guard, 27
Connecticut State Legislature, 27
Conscription Act, 338
Considerant, Victor, 38, 283
Conspiracy Against All, xx, 12, 34
Conspiracy of Equals, 35, 36
Constitution Union Party, 140
Constitutional Convention, 41, 57-59, 70, 71, 73, 89, 93, 102, 172, 177, 213, 311, 316, 338, 434, 459
Constitutional Party, 235, 246, 285, 399
Constitutional Societies, 63, 339
Constitutional Union Party, 246, 399
Continental, xxii, xl, xli, 12, 89, 117, 141, 142, 145, 425, 428, 457
Continental Congress, xl, 89, 428
Continental Union - Brotherhood of the Union, xxii, 141
Convention of Associations, 198, 220, 235
Conway, Martin, 294
Cooper, Gary, 263
Cooper, James Fenimore, 192, 203
Cooper, Peter, 46, 402
Cooper, Thomas, 195
Copperheads, 338, 375, 410, 443, 460, 466, 468
Corbett, Thomas P. "Boston", 377
Cornell, 26, 27, 472, 474, 478
Corps de Belgique, 289
Coste, Felix, 349
Council of Three, 14-17
Court of St. James, 133, 182, 230, 416
Cousin, Victor, 134, 197
Cox, Jacob Dolson, 283
Craig, Sir James Henry, 110
Crescent, 219, 224
The Crescent City, 219
Crittenden, Parker, 224
Crockett, Davy, 333
Croxton, John Thomas, 389
Cult of Empire, 53
Cumo, Theodore Frederick, 412
Cupples, Dr. George, 282
Curtis, George William, 198
Cushing, Caleb, 165, 221, 230
Custer, George Armstrong, 41
Czar, xxiv, xxv, 145, 204
Daily Evening Traveller, 131
D'Alembert, 2, 9
Dallas, Alexander James, 70
Dallas, George M., 159, 228
Dana, Charles A., 9, 198
Danton, 54
Darrah, Delmar Duane, 18, 469
Darwin, Charles, 291, 409, 467
Darwinism, 225, 341, 408, 419
Das Kapital, 200
Declaration of Mental Independence, 156
Deism, 32, 120, 318
Deitzler, George W., 295
Democracy, xxv, xxvi, xxx, xxxii, xxxvi, 44, 56, 61, 71, 73-77, 110, 130, 132, 151, 163, 176-178, 190, 198, 202, 209, 221, 223, 240, 243, 244, 333, 392, 415, 453, 459, 466, 478
Democratic Clubs, 61, 65-67, 69, 75, 77, 95, 106, 423
Democratic Party, 112, 218, 230, 311, 322, 337, 369, 479
Democratic Review, 10, 136, 193, 218, 219, 221, 230
Democratic Societies of America, 106
Democratic Speaker's Handbook, 276
Department of Agriculture, 297, 374
Department of Education, xxxix, 147, 204, 437, 441
Department of Homeland Security, 80, 384
Department of Negro Affairs, 404
Department of Ohio, 354
Department of Public Parks, 405
Depew, Chauncey Mitchell, 405
Descartes, 197
Deutsche Bank, 413
Deutsche Turnkunst, 49
Devoy, John, 229
Devyr, Thomas Ainange, 189
Dewey, John, 27, 46
Dial, xxxv, 193, 198, 304
Dickinson, Daniel S., 228
Dictionary of American History, xxv, 32, 466
Diderot, 2, 3, 197, 466
Die Revolution, 128, 351

Dietsch, A., 341
Dinsmore, Silas, 111
Disraeli, Benjamin, xxvi, 466
Disunion, 86, 111, 127, 157, 171, 193, 201, 262, 271, 274-277, 283, 294, 295, 298, 303, 309-312, 322, 337, 429, 475
Disunion Convention, 157, 275-277, 294, 298, 310
Dix, Maj. Gen. John, 358
Dodd, Dr. Bella, xxxv, 145, 334, 400
Dominican Republic, 258
Dohrn, Bernardine, 232
Dorr Rebellion, 177, 220
Douai, Adolph, 200
Douglas, Stephen A., 132, 140, 221, 246, 467, 477
Douglass, Frederick, 190, 287, 288, 293, 300, 398, 403, 413, 418
Dowd, F. B., 17
Druid, 206
DuBois, W. E. B., 413
Duc d'Orléans, 217
Duke, Basil, 282
Duke, James, 442
Dulles, John Foster, 138, 232, 355
Duncan, Secretary Arne, 200
Dumont, Etienne, 31
Dupont, Charles I., 222, 466
Dupont de Nemours, 32, 127, 466
Dwight, John S., 197
Dwight, Theodore, 141
Dwight, Timothy, xxxvii, 28, 29, 51
Dwight's Journal of Music, 197
Dyer, Doctor, 250
Eastern Star, 20
Eaton, Gen., 103
Eckert, Thomas T., 382
Economist, 364
Edinburgh, 92, 458, 464
Edmonds, John W., 203
Education, ix, xi, xiii, xvi, xix, xxii, xxiii, xxix, xxxix, xl, xlii, 3, 27, 29, 30, 40, 45, 46, 50, 51, 59, 69, 78, 127, 133, 146, 147, 151, 154-158, 169, 186, 192, 199, 200, 203, 204, 206-208, 213, 235, 238, 244, 260-262, 264, 278, 298, 300, 307, 349, 360, 374, 389, 394, 407, 409, 413, 422-424, 426, 428, 431, 436-445, 447, 448, 452, 453, 455, 457, 465, 469, 470, 472, 475
Eight-Hour Day, 412
Eisenhower, Dwight David, 138, 355, 457
Eldridge, S. W., 294
Electoral College, 60, 74, 85, 88, 90, 101, 106, 112, 116, 353
Electoral Commission, 412, 413
Electrol Palatinate, 130
Elliott, John, 400
Ellsworth, Elmer, 248
Emancipation League, 192

Emancipation Proclamation, 192, 201, 304, 362-364
Emancipation Society, 303
Emerson, Edward Waldo, 47, 48, 52, 151, 466
Emerson, Ralph Waldo, 10, 47-49, 52, 120, 121, 134, 143, 150, 151, 197, 206, 208, 218, 221, 272, 287, 300, 408, 417, 478
Emigrant Aid Societies, 291
Emigrant Aid Society, 287, 291, 294, 297
Emile, Frederic, 432
Emmanuel, Victor, 217, 352
Emperor Maximilian, 173, 227, 327
Encyclopedists, 9, 10
English Royal Institute of International Affairs, 216
Equal Rights Party, 122, 288, 397, 398
Erlanger, Baron Emile, 248, 327
Erskine, Dr., 92
Eustis, Gov. William, 222
Evans, George H., 141, 150, 186, 218, 236
Evarts, William M., 243
Everett, Edward, 28, 46-48, 52, 140, 279, 295, 350, 351, 399
Evening Post, 37, 152, 201, 203, 239, 240, 287, 297, 349, 413
Eye of Horace, 249
Eye of Horus, 248, 352
F. H. C. Society, 30
Fabian Society, 417
Fabrication, 3
Failure of Free Society, 261
Faneuil Hall, 274, 477
Farewell Address, 20, 74, 87, 92, 139, 183
Farmers-General, 127
Farragut, Admiral David, xxv
Fauchet, Abbe Claude, 31
Fauchet, Jean, 97
FBI, xxxv, xliii, 301, 302, 383, 471
FDR, 137, 330, 331, 395, 414, 467
Feder, Johann, xxxiv
Federal Bureau of Investigation, 401
Federalist, xxii, 38, 65, 74, 86, 88, 106, 443, 467
Fenian, 189, 191, 229, 244
Fenian Ram, 229
Ferrari, Giuseppe, xxiv
Fessenden, Samuel, 309
Field, Stephen Johnson, 395
Fifth Column, 34, 82, 285, 463
Fifty-four Forty, 112
Filibuster, 136, 223, 226-228, 242, 253, 281, 282, 284, 414, 467
Fillmore, Millard, 192, 211, 238, 242, 346
Findley, 63, 95
First Church of Theophilanthropy, 32
First Communist International, 49, 161, 202, 214, 351, 394, 397, 412, 443
First Kansas Colored Regiment, 297
Fitz-Hugh, George, 261

Florence, Thomas Birch, 144
Florida, xxiv, 64, 101, 104, 111, 112, 180, 252, 312, 325, 330, 390, 476
Flynn, John T., 45, 384, 466, 472
Follen, Charles (Karl), 403
Forbes, Hugh, 140, 144, 287, 292, 302, 349
Forbes, John Murray, 49, 300
Ford, 18, 120, 471, 472, 478
Ford Foundation, 472
Foreign Affairs, 139, 208, 228, 308, 325, 327, 415
Foreign Anti-Slavery Society, 191, 268
Foresti, Elentario Felice, 135
Forrest, Nathan Bedford, 390
Forsyth, John, 227
Foss, Andrew T., 131, 275
Foster, Stephen S., 274
Foster, William Z., 21, 437, 441, 469, 477
Foster-Avery, Rachel, 398
Fourier, Charles, 29, 37, 239
Fourierism, 49, 199, 208, 239, 478
Fowler, Postmaster Isaac V., 186
FRA - Free Religious Association, 408
Francis, Convers, 206
Francis, Dr. J. W., 203
Franco, Gen., 34
Franklin, Benjamin, 3, 5, 14, 15, 17, 32, 37, 57, 79, 91, 93, 144, 159, 187, 221, 257, 264, 271, 379
Fraternitas, 30
Frederick William II, 12
Free Democrat, 241
Free Love League, 220
Free Religious Association, 408, 409, 418
Free Soil, 142, 191, 192, 220, 468
Free Soil Party, 142, 191
Freedman, 390, 404, 405
Freedman Aid Societies, 404
Freedman Relief Association, 405
Freer, L. C., 250
Freethought Federation, 409
Fremont, John C., xxxiv, 224
French Society of Patriots of America, 67
Freneau, Philip, 66, 67
Friends of France, 68
Friends of the Blacks, 62, 187
Friends of Truth, 24, 34, 84
Fröbel, Friedrich, 50, 200
Frond, Victor, 230
Frothingham, Octavius Brooks, 408, 477
Fruitlands, 199
Fry, William, 351
Fugitive Slave Act, 241, 296
Fuller, Margaret, 150, 197, 198
Gabriel Over the White House, 294
Gadsden Treaty, 224
Galena and Chicago Railroad, 352
Gallatin, Albert, 38, 63, 69, 71, 111, 112, 156, 159, 223, 309, 463
Gallo-American Society, 25, 38, 62

INDEX

Garfield, James, 49, 471
Garibaldi, 123, 124, 126, 129, 130, 132, 133, 140-142, 210, 244, 290, 292, 304, 323, 324, 349, 352, 385, 392, 397, 400, 468, 472, 476
Garrison, Cornelius K., 223, 226
Garrison, George Thompson, 188, 304
Garrison, Wendell Phillips, 275, 304, 310, 418
Garrison, William Lloyd, xxxiv, xxxix, 187, 188, 191, 197, 209, 262, 268, 269, 272, 275, 303, 306, 397, 478
Garrisonians, 188, 190, 274
Geisenheimer, Sigmund, 43
Genet, Edmond Charles, 64
Geneva Convention, 167, 403
Gentz, Friedrich, xli, 196, 468
George William Curtis, 198
Georgia Senate, 262
Georgia State Legislature, 327
German Commune of Young America, 233
German Confederation, 13, 34, 123, 165, 227, 264
The German Museum, 7, 468
German Revolutionary League, 136
German School of American Unitarianism, 204, 279
German Tribune, 299, 300
German Union, 13, 35, 47, 48, 92, 151, 165, 167, 245, 345, 408, 439
Gestapo, xl, 8, 20, 41, 93, 452
Gettell, Raymond G., 116, 469
Gettysburg, 28, 52, 198, 305, 313, 337, 399, 425
Gettysburg Address of Lincoln, 399
Gibbs, George, 47, 402
Gibson, Mel, 181
Giddings, Joshua R., 242, 243
Giles, Edward, 143, 235
Gilman, Daniel Coit, 27, 51
Girard College, 116, 159
Girard, Stephen, 116
Girod, Jean Francois, 222
Girondist, 29, 202
Gitlow, Benjamin, 145, 334, 370, 457
Glasgow Democratic Club, 250, 352
Goddard, Paulette, 263
Godwin, Edwin L., 240
Godwin, Parke, 37, 143, 198, 235, 239, 277, 402
Goethe, 17, 46
Göpp, C., 136
Gorbachev, xxviii
Gordon, John B., 390
Gotha, 12, 31
Göttingen, xxxiv, 12, 46, 47, 49, 52, 102, 126, 200, 205, 224, 279, 399
Graham, Lindsey, 190
Gramscian, 7, 93, 279
Grand Lodge of Freemasons, 21

Grand Orient, 10, 18, 21-23, 25, 32, 64, 91, 127, 130, 211, 457
Grant, Ulysses S., 27, 389, 410
Grays, 278
Greeley, Horace, xxix, xxxi, 36, 48, 76, 102, 121, 143, 150, 161, 198, 203, 204, 211, 216, 219-221, 234-236, 238-240, 243, 249, 287, 295, 296, 302, 319, 333, 337, 386, 402, 410, 422, 463, 470, 471, 474
Green, Joseph, 52, 279
Green Peace, 294
Greenback, 144, 168, 250, 303, 335, 338, 374, 393, 396
Greenback Party, 168, 303, 335
Greene, William Bradford, 144, 213
Greenwood, John, 183
Grey, Sir Edward, 326
Griswold, Hiram, 300
Griswold, Rev. Dr. Rufus Wilmot, 203
The Group, x, xii, xix, xxvi, 9, 12, 19, 25, 44, 49, 77, 87, 95, 112, 114, 125, 126, 145, 154, 161, 167, 191, 192, 202, 207, 216, 217, 219, 225, 228, 229, 236, 237, 249, 271, 274, 276, 281, 285, 286, 289, 295, 300, 330, 331, 341, 342, 350, 372, 387, 397, 400, 403, 405, 409, 417, 424, 433, 448, 456, 459, 461
Guaranty Trust Company, 331
Guiteau, Charles, 154
Gurowski, Adam, 10, 250, 297, 350, 472
Gwin, William, 365
The Hague Peace Conference, 50, 466
Haldeman, Richard Jacobs, 230
Hale, Edward Everett, 295
Hale, John P., 228, 320, 353
Hall, Gus, 128
Hammer, Armand, 401
Hammond, James Henry, 261, 476
Hampton, Wade, 392
Hancock, John, xx
Hannegan, Edward, 135, 228
Harbinger, 37, 193, 198
Harding, President, 414
Harmony, xxxiii, 23, 57, 91, 143, 144, 150, 154-157, 159, 171, 353, 425, 473
Harney, George Julian, xxxiv
Harriman, 331
Harris, B. G., 377
Harris, Thomas Lake, 226
Harris, William Torrey, 437
Harrison, Burton Norvell, 228, 258
Harrison, William, 212, 242
Harte, Bret, 197, 198
Hartford Convention, 309, 337
Harvard Divinity, 92, 200, 220, 409
Harvard University, 52, 344, 465, 466, 472, 475, 477
Harvey, Louis P., 346
Hawkes, Dr., 203
Hawthorne, Nathaniel, 47-49, 143, 150, 198,

200, 218, 219, 221, 230, 355
Hay, John, 236, 350, 471
Hayek, Frederick, 438
Hayes, Rutherford, 154, 170, 247, 412, 425
Hearst, William Randolph, 443
Healey, John, 17
Heaven, 113, 128, 155, 197, 199, 261, 434, 461
Hecker, Friederich Karl Franz, 342, 344
Hedge, Frederic Henry, 198, 200, 206
Hedge Club, 200
Hegel, Georg Wilhelm Frederick, 26
Hegelian, xxxiv, 26, 29, 35, 45, 46, 136, 167, 279, 439
Heinzen, Karl, 136, 412, 463
Hell Fire, 32, 379
Helper, Hinton, 276
Henningsen, Charles Frederick, 225, 231
Henrick, Burton J., xxxiii
Henry, John, xxxiii, 48, 49, 110, 112, 197, 198, 239, 257, 287, 328
Henry, Patrick, 83, 98
Herbart, Johann Friedrich, 50
Herndon, William H., 198, 316, 318, 468
Heroes of America, 339
Hertz, Emanuel, 378, 468
Herzen, Alexander, 29, 144
Heywood, Ezra, 220
Higginson, Thomas W., 408, 417
High Court of Nations, 208
Hillard, George Stillman, 47, 49
Hillquit, Morris, 397, 469, 476
Himmler, xxix
Hines, Thomas H., 365
Hinton, Richard J., 293, 297, 470
Hiss, Alger, 24, 271
The History And Evolution of Freemasonry, 18, 469
Hitchcock, Ethan allen, 14, 16, 17
Hitler, Adolf, x, 123, 262, 341, 346
Hoar, Ebenezer, 287, 395, 410
Hoar, Samuel, 262
Höckerig, Johann, 164
Holcombe, 380
Holder, Eric, 307, 394
Holland, J. G., 305
Holmes, Oliver Wendell, 28, 48, 192, 193, 269, 304
The Holy Family, xxviii
Holy Spirit, 91, 232
Homeland Security, xxvi, 80, 353, 384, 394
Homestead Act, 150, 251, 308, 340, 374
Hooper, Samuel, 396
Hoover, J. Edgar, xliii
Hopedale Community, 209
Horus, 248, 249, 352
Hosmer, E. M., 275
Hotel de Ville, 192
House, Edward Mandell, 182, 326, 330, 331
Houston, George, 249

485

Houston, John W., 311
Houston, Sam, 281, 475
Hovey, A. P., 155
Howe, Julia Ward, 197, 294, 300, 408, 417, 465
Howe, Samuel G., 274, 295
Hoyt, George Henry, 300
Hugo, Victor, 141, 203, 231
Hull's Crucible, 202
Humanidad Lodge, 14, 17
Humanitas, 30
Hunt, Richard M., 402
Hunters' Lodge, 122
Hussein, Saddam, xii, 189
Illinois Central Railroad, 246, 321, 352
Illinois Legislature, 176, 319, 363, 413
Illustrated Sunday Herald, 2
Impeachment Papers of Andrew Johnson, 170
Impending Crises, 276, 470
Imperial Council, 204
Income Tax, 31, 168, 250, 360, 374, 435, 439-441
Independent Order of Odd Fellows, 206
Indian National Congress, 409, 417
Indiana Legislative Assembly, 157
Indiana State Legislature, 157
Indiana University, 381, 412, 472, 474, 475, 477
Indiana University of Pennsylvania, 412
Ingersoll, Robert Green, 409, 410, 478
Ingolstadt University, 10, 18, 91
Inner Party, xii, xxiv, xxix, 1, 34, 35, 56, 77, 336, 398, 399, 403
Innis, Judge Harry, 102
Inquiry Commission, 192, 404
Internal Revenue Act, 360
International Congress of Education, 437
International Democratic Association, xxxiv
International Labor Union, 412
International Legion, 130
International Monetary Fund, 417
International Peace, 269-271, 417, 428
International Red Cross, 421
International Republican Institute, 96, 218
International Workers, 25, 436
International Workingmen, 234, 397
Irish Liberator, 268
Irish People, 189
Irish Republican Brotherhood, 229
Iron Molder Union, 411
IWA - International Workingmen's Association, 397
Jackson, Andrew, 37, 90, 101, 104, 111-114, 122, 135, 157, 185, 187, 199, 202, 204, 212, 222, 238, 251, 268, 330, 331, 356, 422, 443, 464
Jackson, Dr. James, 421
Jackson, Stonewall, 431, 465, 471
Jacksonian Democrats, 100, 333

Jacobin Clubs, 13, 61, 62, 65, 72, 75, 106, 180, 423
Jahn, Frederick Ludwig, 47, 49, 340, 422
James, Henry, 49, 86, 110, 112, 143, 198, 261, 272, 373, 408, 442, 469, 474, 476
Jay, John, xxiii, 62, 92, 95, 96, 187, 257, 320, 321, 468, 471
Jay, William, 259, 471
Jefferson Bible, xxxvii, 87, 470
Jefferson States Rights Resolutions, 102
Jefferson, Thomas, xv, xxi, xxxvii, 3, 30, 60, 63, 68, 70, 84, 97, 100, 103, 127, 244, 330, 415, 443, 465, 470, 477, 478
Jeffersonian, 87, 100, 333
Jesus Christ, 2, 131, 150
Jew, 207, 432
John Birch Society, 8, 30, 45, 77, 119, 128, 146, 176, 184, 191, 232, 240, 254, 255, 280, 449, 451, 457
Johnson, Andrew, 169, 170, 175, 211, 370, 394, 395, 463, 470, 474
Johnson, Charles F., 50
Johnson, Manning, 128
Johnston, Gen, 375, 376
Joseph, Franz, 327
Jones, Howard Mumford, 6, 463
Jones, Jesse Henry, 400
Journal de Amis, 25
Journal of Commerce, 358
Journal of Music, 197
Juarez, Benito, 173, 174
Judaism, 42, 113, 158, 454
Judd, Norman B., 243
Judenloge, 43
Judeo-Christian, xi, xiii, xxxii, xxxvi, xxxix, 71, 72, 113, 118, 158, 423, 424, 436, 437, 452
Judge, William Quan, 409
Kagi, John H., 297
Kaiser, Charles, 293
Kansas Aid Committee, 294
Kansas Aid Society, 287, 294, 297
Kansas Historical Society, 291
Kansas Legion, 295
Kansas Legislature, 377
Kansas Regulars, 295
Kapp, Friedrich, 247, 314, 402
Kaufmann, Sigismund, 476
Kearny, Philip, 47, 49
Kennedy, John F., 280, 369
Kennedy, John Pendleton, 283
Kennedy, Joseph, 370
Kentucky Legislature, 85, 104
Kentucky Resolutions, 84, 85, 106, 133
Keyworth, Kate, 228
KGC - Knights of the Golden Circle, 217, 281
Kindergarten, 200
King Charles X, 135
King George, xx, 187, 246

King, Martin Luther, 267, 301, 383
King, Prescott, 246, 350
King, Preston, 238, 376
King, Rufus, 242, 385
King of Prussia, 2, 44
Kingdom of Heaven, 197
Kinkel, Gottfried, 346
Kissinger, Henry, xxviii, 119
Knights of Columbus, 21, 210
Knights of Labor, 144, 400, 412, 465
Knights of the Silver Star, 219
Knights of the True Faith, 284
Know Nothings, 473
Knox, Gen., 65
Kriege, Hermann, 149, 221
Kristol, Irving, 216, 254
Ku Klux Klan, 124, 390, 470, 471
La Cosa Nostra, 53, 304
La Falange Americana, 223, 225
La Grange Kentucky, 365
Labour Party, 417
Ladd, William, 208
Laden, Osama bin, xxvi, 80
Lafitte, Jean, 111, 187
Lamon, Ward Hill, 353, 356
Land Grant College Act, 374
Land Reform, 35, 142, 168, 169, 218, 236, 257, 308, 394
Lane, James H., 376
Lane, Joseph, 365
Lang, Dr. M., 341
Langes, Marquis de Savalette de, 23, 31
La Réunion, 283
Latham, Milton Slocum, 365
Lawrence, Amos A., 295, 300
Law, George, 47, 219, 221, 223, 225, 237, 366
Le Socialiste, 226
League of Democracy, 130
League of Freedom, 241
League of the Just, xxxiii, 4, 36, 46, 163, 164, 170, 207, 233, 399, 433
League of Men, 138, 207, 320, 341, 399, 433
League of Nations, 132, 137, 138, 271
League of Outlaws, 4, 163, 164
League of United Southerners, 281
League of Universal Brotherhood, 209
League of Youth, 341
Lebensborn, xxix
Lechevalier, Jules, 141
Leclerc, xxviii
Ledru-Rollin, Andre, 129, 140
Lee, Arthur, 94
Lee, Edwin E., 384
Lee, Henry, xxx, 66, 67, 472
Lee, Richard Henry, xxx, 472
Lee, Robert E., 276, 284, 340, 357, 365
Leftwich, W. M., 195, 472
Legendre, 25
Leggett, William, 122, 218, 221, 222

INDEX

Legion of Honor, 49, 244
Legislature of Massachusetts, 105
Lehrbach, Graf (Count), 31
Lenin, xi, 10, 61, 118, 125, 174, 214, 244, 371, 397, 401, 421, 455, 476
Lenin Bolshevik, 401, 421
Les Amis Réunis, 7, 31
Leslie's Weekly, 247
Lewis and Clark, 96, 104, 105, 109, 117, 180
Lewis, Meriwether, 20, 90, 96, 104, 105, 470
Liberal Club, 190
Liberal Republican Party, 201, 337, 395, 410, 412
Liberation Theology, 285
The Liberator, 187, 192, 262, 268, 271, 306, 332, 358
Liberia, 102, 257
Liberty Party, 190, 191, 250, 274
Leib, Michael, 101
Lieber, Francis, 227, 262, 403
Lincoln, Abraham, xiv, 16, 102, 140, 222, 246, 261, 262, 285, 296, 319, 369, 378, 443, 463-465, 471, 474, 477, 478
Lincoln, Levi, 222
Lincoln, Mary Todd, 377, 470, 477
Lincoln, Robert T., 378
Lincoln, Willie, 202
Lippard, George, 14, 16, 17, 141, 142, 281, 287, 306
Litvinenko, Alexander, xxvi, 371
Livingston, Chancellor, 95
Livingston, Edward, 114
Livingston, Robert L., 222
Lloyd, James, 222
Logan, John A., 169, 468
Lodge of Les Amis Réunis, 7, 31
The Log Cabin, 242, 243
Longfellow, Henry Wadsworth, 48, 197, 198
Lopez, Narciso, 219, 223
Lord of the Mountain, 128
Louis XVI, 61, 127
Love, Alfred H., 269
Lovejoy, Elijah, 152, 153, 250
Lovejoy, Owen, 242, 249
Lowell, James Russell, 28, 143, 192, 198, 272, 390, 416, 471
Loyal Leagues, 296, 391, 404
Loyal Leagues of Negroes, 391
Lucifer, 3, 124, 202, 203, 207
Luciferian, 207
Lyman, Chester Smith, 151
Maclure, William, 155
MacVeagh, Franklin, 27
Madame Blavatsky, 129, 203
Madison, James, xxx, 4, 19, 63, 74, 79, 95, 110, 177, 470
Madison State Journal, 346
Mafia, x, 53, 125, 263, 304, 383
Magruder, John, 328
Mandela, Nelson, xxvii, 267

Manifest Destiny, xii, 136, 201, 223, 231, 232, 253, 472-474
Mann, Horace, 46, 143, 156, 157, 192, 200, 453, 478
Manny, John H., 166
Marat, xxxvii, 62
Marck, Dr., 203
Marseillaise, 61, 134, 211, 296, 339, 412
Marshall, John, 86, 95, 106, 177
Martin, Luther, 102, 267, 301, 383
Mason, James M., 242
Mason, John Y., 135, 221, 230
Masonic University, 365
Masquerier, Lewis, 144, 218, 221, 476
Massachusetts Abolition Society, 266
Massachusetts Anti-Slavery Society, 157, 310, 472
Massachusetts Constitutional Convention, 213
Massachusetts Labor Party, 304
Massachusetts Peace Society, 198, 208, 269
Massey, Gerald, 203
Matamoros, 326
Mather, Frederick Ellsworth, 170, 331
Maury, Matthew Fontaine, 328
Maximilian, Emperor, 173, 227, 327
May, Samuel J., 157, 275, 474, 476
May Day, 22, 412, 465
Mazzei, Philip, 68
Mazzini, 5, 17, 29, 121, 122, 124, 126, 129, 130, 133, 134, 140, 141, 163, 165, 191, 192, 198, 201, 207, 217-219, 221, 231, 293, 304, 320, 344, 346-350, 390, 397
McCain, John, 96, 190, 218, 415
McCarthy, Joseph, xxi, 370, 453
McCarthyism, 454
McCook, Robert L., 167
McCormick, Cyrus H., 166
McDonnell, J. P., 229
McGregor, Hugh, 400
McGuire, Peter J., 400
McKaye, James, 192
McKeon, District Attorney John, 186
McKinley, William, 253
McMakin, John, 400
McManus, John F., 255, 457
McMaster's History, xxxvii
McVeigh, Timothy, 307, 383
Meade, George Gordon, 28, 305
Meagher, Thomas Francis, 229
Mechanics Mutual Protection Association, 220
Meeker, Nathan C., 425
Meiners, Christoph, 205
Mesmer, 23, 91
Mesmerism, 62, 71, 91, 224, 274, 472
Methodist, 172, 189, 266, 318, 404, 419
Methodist New Connection, 189
Metro Government, 401
Metropolitan Museum of Art, 403

Mexican, 173-175, 224, 226-228, 253, 283, 286, 310, 351, 366, 474
Mexican War, 226, 227, 283, 310, 351
Michaux, André, 90
Mierostawski, Ludwik Adam, 130
Mifflin, 70, 463, 464, 466, 467, 469-474, 477, 478
Mill, John Stuart, 303
Milner, Lord, 216
Mirabeau, xvi, 5-8, 10, 22, 31, 62, 67, 70, 93, 127, 163, 164, 276, 423
Miramón, 285
Missouri Hegelians, 437
Missouri Red Leg Scouts, 300
Mithraism, 53
Molly Maguires, 440, 472
Monroe, James, xxxiii, 95, 139, 172, 177
Monroe Doctrine, 253
Montgelas, Maximillian Josef, 13
Mooney, William, 183
Morals, xxx, xxxix, xli, 124, 194, 196, 470
Morgan, Charles, 223, 226
Morgan, J. P., xxxiv, 47, 331, 402, 442
Morgan, John T., 390
Morgan, William, 210, 477
Mormons, 284
Morris, Robert, 89, 127
Morrow, William, 105, 470
Morse, Jedidiah, 21, 22, 25, 92, 196, 466, 467, 471, 474, 476
Morse, Robert, 20
Morse, Samuel, 29, 309, 467
Mosby, John Singleton, 247, 382
Moses, Franklin J., 390
Mott, Lucretia, 268, 300
Moultrie, William, 65
Müller, M. L. B., 341
Mudd, Dr., 381
Munn vs. Illinois, 395
Murat, Prince Lucien, 20
Muslim, xiii, 42, 80, 96, 128, 129, 189, 190, 215, 292, 307, 354, 406, 415, 454
Muslim Brotherhood, 80, 189, 190, 415
Mussolini, Benito, 20, 46, 174
Mutual Instruction, 208
Mutual Protection Society, 220, 289
Muzzey, David Saville, xxv, 50, 303, 478
Mysteries of History, 12
NAACP, 69, 413
Napoleon I, 6, 193
Napoleon, Louis, 350
Napoleonic, 42, 43
Nashville Convention, 309
Nast, Thomas, 402
The Nation, xv, xxv, xxvii, xxx, xl, xliii, 31, 33, 55, 73-77, 79, 106, 123, 124, 141, 156, 176, 177, 190, 194, 196, 201, 204, 205, 223, 232, 240, 244, 257, 271, 275, 285, 312, 315, 330, 351, 387, 413, 416, 425, 430, 434, 457, 463, 468, 470, 475

487

National Anti-Slavery Standard, 394
National Association of Spiritualists, 407
National Bank, xxv, 66, 69, 89, 112, 115, 319
National Bank of New York, 112
National Banking Act, 250, 374, 396
National Chamber of Commerce, 27
National Civil Service Reform League, 401, 413
National Conference of Unitarian Churches, 47, 49, 408
National Convention of Associationists, 197
National Convention of Associations, 198, 220, 235
National Democratic Convention, 369
National Detective Police, 360, 361
National Education Association, 437, 442
National Gazette, 66, 67
National Hotel, 231
National Industrial Congress, 141, 142, 164, 233
National Labor Union, 265, 303, 397, 400, 411, 412
National Labor Reform Party, 411
National Labor Relations Board, 265
National Labor Union, 265, 303, 397, 400, 411, 412
National Lawyers Guild, 188
National League, 47, 50, 66, 164, 191, 401, 404, 405, 409, 410, 413
National Loyal League, 404
National Recovery Act, 395
National Reform Association, 141, 149, 150, 164, 220, 233, 236, 240, 402
National Reform League, 401, 413
National Reform Movement, 189, 220, 308
National Review, 203, 217
National Rifle Association, 191, 211
National Socialism, 204, 342
National Union Party, 243
National Women Suffrage Association, 418
Nationalism, 32, 33, 114, 123, 126, 127, 164, 194, 220, 223, 332, 333, 392, 401, 403, 421, 470, 474
Natural Selection, 158, 203
Naval Academy, 50
Necker, 127
Nell, William C., 197
Neoconservatism, 216, 253, 254
Neo-Radicals, 215
Neue Rheinische Zeitung, 238
Neuf Soeurs, 32
Neutrality Act, 136, 225
Neutrality Law, 219
Nevada State Constitution, 309, 360
New Age Movement, 207, 408
New Church, 32, 199, 204, 409
New Democracy, 132, 202, 221, 478
New Departure, 337
New Eden, 199, 471

New England Anti-Slavery Society, 188, 209, 397
New England Emigrant Aid Society, 291
New England Labor Reform League, 144, 220
New England Non-resistance Society, 209, 397
New England Workingmen, 220
New Federalism, 393
New Harmony Gazette, 155
New Harmony Philanthropic Lodge of Masons, 156
New Jerusalem, 199
New Lanard, 155
New Life, 37, 226, 417, 463, 469-471, 473, 477
New Nation, 156, 177, 190, 240, 244
New Orleans Crescent, 224
The New Orleans Journal, 170
The New Rome, xxiv
New Testament, 2, 29, 197, 409, 437
New York Abolition Society, 187
New York Argus, 67, 98
New York Assembly, 202, 219, 331, 400
New York Central American League, 225
New York Central Labor Union, 412
New York Democratic Party, 311
New York Democrats, 238
New York Evening Post, 37, 201, 239, 240, 287, 297, 413
New York Governor George Clinton, 68
New York Herald, 48, 134, 135, 140, 229, 238, 249, 299, 300, 391, 473
New York Journal, 164, 266, 358, 443
New York League, 37, 47, 50, 135, 201, 225, 401, 402, 404, 405, 469, 471
New York Mining and Stock Exchange, 365
New York Morning News, 223
New York Times, 45, 232, 287, 297, 324, 339, 381, 444, 471, 473, 476-478
New York Tribune, xxix, 48, 141, 161, 189, 190, 197, 198, 203, 219, 234, 238, 239, 275, 277, 287, 288, 294, 297, 299, 300, 351, 408, 413, 425, 471, 473
New York World, 66, 234, 358, 365, 383, 398, 470, 471, 473, 478
New Yorker, 243
Newton, 197
Niles, H., 447
Nine Sisters Lodge, 20, 32, 62, 70, 93, 452, 474
Nixon Administration, 119, 393
North American Community, 156, 285
North American Gymnastic Union, 345
North American Phalanx, 239
North, John W., 243
North Star, 190
Northwest Republic, 186, 365
Noyes, John Humphrey, 143, 144, 154, 199, 209, 434, 469

NRA - National Reform Association, 150, 220
Nullification, 82, 196, 309, 311, 332
Obama, xxxviii, xxxix, 1, 40, 62, 83, 96, 146, 156, 178, 194, 200, 232, 244, 267, 286, 341, 359, 361, 364, 392, 394, 433, 441, 451
O'Connell, Daniel, 268
O'Connor, Charles, 412
Ohio Hegelian, 167
Oklahoma City, 307, 383, 467
O'Laughlen, Michael, 380
Olcott, Henry Steel, 203, 409
Oliphant, Lawrence, 226
Olmsted, Frederick Law, 295, 405
Olshauser, Theodore, 349
On The Origin of Species, 158
Oneida, 143, 150, 154, 473
Oneida Colony, 150
The Order, xvii, xix, xxiii, xxvii, xxx, xxxii, xxxvi, xl, xli, xliii, 2, 3, 6, 8, 9, 12, 13, 17, 18, 20-23, 26-28, 30-33, 35, 39-41, 44, 46, 50, 51, 56-58, 64, 66, 75, 79, 80, 84, 91-93, 96, 97, 110, 113, 115, 117-119, 121, 122, 124, 125, 128, 129, 132, 138, 140-142, 144-146, 150, 151, 154-156, 163, 164, 166, 168-170, 175, 177, 183, 187, 193-195, 200, 203, 205, 206, 209, 212, 215, 216, 219, 220, 227, 228, 230, 237, 242, 243, 245, 247, 250, 252, 255, 258, 262, 265, 266, 268, 270-273, 278, 282, 284, 291, 292, 296, 297, 303, 304, 306, 308, 311, 313, 317, 319, 321, 331-333, 336, 342, 344, 348, 354, 358, 361, 363, 364, 366, 371-375, 379, 383, 385, 389, 391-396, 399, 402, 405, 406, 409-411, 413, 414, 416, 417, 420, 421, 429, 430, 432, 434-436, 439-442, 444, 447, 451, 455, 457, 464, 471, 473-475, 478
Order of American Knights, 289
Order of the Lone Star, 227, 284
Order of United Americans, 237
Orsini, Cesare, 211
Orsini, Felice, 133, 211
Orwell, George, iii, xiii, xxiv, 1, 35, 56, 439
Ostend Manifesto, 134-136, 228, 230, 323, 416
Osterhaus, Peter, 135
O'Sullivan, John, 10, 46, 218, 221, 223, 230, 470
Oswald, Lee Harvey, 388
Owen, Allen Ferdinand, 228
Owen, Robert, xxxi, xxxiii, 98, 122, 143, 150, 154, 155, 157, 159, 160, 173, 189, 192, 197, 198, 200, 201, 203, 204, 207, 218, 220, 222, 230, 231, 234, 238, 249, 304, 404, 408, 418, 471, 475
Owen, Robert Dale, 122, 143, 157, 159, 160, 173, 192, 198, 200, 222, 230, 231, 234,

404, 408, 418, 475
Owenite, 49, 122, 144, 155, 156, 208
Pacific Railway Act, 374
Pacific Republic, 365, 366
Paine, Thomas, xxxvii, 2, 5, 6, 14, 15, 17, 30, 68, 72, 144, 183, 185-187, 189, 195, 202, 204, 220, 303, 308, 318, 379, 397, 408, 410, 423, 465, 471, 477, 478
Paladin, 227
Palmer, Elihu, 32, 37, 202, 249
Palmerston, Lord, 131, 132
Panama Canal, 223, 366
Papal, 328, 385
Paris Carbonari Society, xxxiii
Paris Commune, 5, 46, 140, 141, 244, 283, 345, 474, 475
Paris Moniteur, 68
Parties, xix, xxxv, xxxviii, xl, 9, 21, 38, 44, 73, 74, 76, 88, 100, 104, 112, 114, 116, 120, 121, 137, 140, 153, 184, 187, 190, 211, 215, 235-237, 240, 245, 250, 264, 280, 308, 313, 320, 334, 383, 384, 386, 400, 411, 414, 425, 433, 434, 439-441, 449, 464, 470
Pastor, Dr. Robert, 156
Patriot Act, 80, 283, 384
Patterson, Leonard, 128
Peabody, Elizabeth, 143, 157, 199, 200, 408
Peebles, James Martin, 203
Pennsylvania Abolition Society, 257
Perfectionism, 154
Perkins, John Jr., 28
Perot, Ross, 184
Perry, Commodore, 135, 248
Pestalozzi, Johann Heinrich, 46
Peters, Richard, 222
Phelps, Dr. James R., 17
Philadelphes, 24, 25, 164
Philadelphia Academy of Natural Sciences, 155
Philadelphia Society, 25, 65, 194, 202, 458, 473
Philalèthes, 24
Philanthropist, 63, 249
Philip Dru, Administrator, 182, 294
Phillips, William A., 201, 293, 294
Philosophical Society of New York, 185
Philosophical Society of St. Louis, 437
Pickens, Francis, 230
Pickett, John Thomas, 227, 228
Pierce, Franklin, xxiv, 132, 221, 229, 401
Pierce, Henry L., 276
Pierpont, John, xxxiv, 272
Pike, Albert, 17, 18, 124, 132, 140, 207, 237, 390, 477
Pike, James, 351, 470
Pillsbury, James, 442
Pillsbury, Parker, 418
Pinkerton, Alan, 287, 300, 352, 422
Pintard, John, 37, 183

Pittsburgh Commonwealth, 103
Poe, Edgar Allen, 219
Poer, Robert M., 402
Political Register, xxxiii
The Politician, xxvi, 15, 79, 102, 106, 157, 251, 288, 405, 432, 454, 457
Polk, James K., 50, 132, 221
Pope, xxvi, 130, 210, 324, 328
Popov, Admiral Andrei Alexandrovich, xxiv
Pösche, Theodor, xxiv
Post, Amy, 404
Powell, A. M., 394
Prati, Gioacchino, 341
Preetorius, Emil, 349
Present, xvi, xxi, xxvii, xxviii, xxx, xxxii, xliii, 22, 49, 55, 57, 65, 90, 92, 93, 98, 150, 167, 174, 202, 240, 280, 304, 310, 311, 356, 359, 369, 386, 459, 467, 469, 472, 474, 475
The Present Age, 202
Preservation of Favoured Races, 158
Price, Sterling, 63, 328, 468
Priestly, Joseph, 63, 196
Prince of Light, 124, 207
Principles of Communism, 222
The Principles of Spiritualism, 203
PROCLAMATION, 101, 187, 192, 201, 304, 320, 321, 362-364
Progressive Party, 252, 253, 414, 435
Prohibition Convention, 172, 304
Prolaterierbund, 351
Protestant, 63, 237, 301
Protocols of the Elders of Zion, 43
Proudhonian Club, 198
Proudhon, xxiv, 134, 144, 168, 177, 203, 213, 220, 398, 478
Pulitzer, Joseph, 48, 346
Purchase Street Church, 206
Putman's, 474
Quincy, xxxiii, xli, 30, 82, 112, 196, 209, 222, 272, 273, 416, 468, 470, 478
Quitman, John A., 223, 226
Quoting, xxi, xxxv, xli, 62, 193, 276
Radical Club, 48, 151, 408, 476
Radical Patriots, 77
Radical Republican, 49, 70, 169, 172, 192, 229, 236, 238, 243, 251, 303, 357, 373, 376, 401
Raffin, Constantine Samuel, 157
Rage, 24, 203, 305
Randolph, Edmund, 70, 102, 177, 223, 224
Randolph, John, 103, 104, 177, 257
Randolph, Dr. Paschal Beverly, 17
Rathbone, Henry, 376
Reading Societies, 12, 13, 48, 151, 276
Reconstruction Act, 389
Red Cross, 405, 421, 464
Red Flag of Socialism, 344
Red Shirts, 244, 290, 392
Redpath, James, 275, 297, 300

Reese Committee, 270
Reform Party, 184, 411, 412
Reichstag fire, 55
Reign of Terror, xii, 33, 36, 56, 60, 61, 68, 103
Rep, 156, 160, 170, 228, 287, 396, 452
Repealers of Ireland, 220
Republican Associationists of France, 220
Republican Clubs, 241
Republican, in passim
Republics, 76, 119, 283, 312, 365, 394
The Revolution, xxviii, xxx, xxxiii, xl, xli, 2, 6, 8, 12, 23, 24, 27, 30, 32-38, 42, 50, 60-63, 66-69, 72, 76, 93-95, 99, 100, 117, 118, 127, 128, 134, 135, 140, 149, 160, 161, 163, 164, 167, 173, 174, 181, 183, 186, 187, 192-196, 198, 202, 217, 220, 224-226, 231, 238, 239, 249, 251, 274, 275, 277, 278, 285, 294, 295, 297, 299, 300, 303, 323, 325, 333, 340, 344, 346-348, 350, 351, 354, 371, 397, 403, 406, 413, 418, 422, 447, 459, 463-468, 470, 472, 474-478
Revolutionsfest, 149
Reynolds, James, 67
Reynolds, Maria, 65, 67
Rhett, Robert Barnwell, 281, 309
Rhodes, Cecil, xv, 157, 216
Rhodes Scholarships, 157
Rice, William H., 185
Richmond Enquirer, 225
Richmond Examiner, 67, 98
Riggs National Bank, xxv
Right, xiv, xxi, xxiii, xxxv, xxxvii, 39, 40, 44, 45, 63, 71, 82, 114, 133, 137, 153, 159, 169, 174, 176, 191, 194, 197, 204, 232, 242, 251, 260, 262, 263, 269, 275, 279, 290, 298, 306-308, 310, 318, 320, 324, 345, 352, 357, 358, 360, 361, 363, 364, 378, 386, 387, 391, 392, 394, 395, 407, 409, 411, 420, 425, 431, 434, 453, 461, 465, 478
Rights, xii, xxi, xxvii, xxxvii, xxxix, xl, 3, 30, 35, 39, 71-73, 78-80, 83, 84, 97, 102, 103, 106, 107, 113, 114, 116, 117, 122, 128, 138, 150, 152, 158, 160, 165, 171, 176, 177, 183, 188, 193, 216, 218, 229, 232, 237, 257, 259, 260, 265-267, 271-273, 283, 284, 286, 288-290, 301, 302, 307, 308, 314, 315, 317, 319, 329, 332, 334, 338, 355, 356, 360, 373, 377, 386, 387, 389, 392, 395, 397, 398, 419, 421, 424, 431, 436, 437, 442, 444, 459, 460, 474
The Rights of Man, 30, 71, 183, 308
Ripley, George, 9, 49, 143, 150, 197, 206, 235, 239, 272
Ripon Society, 241, 243, 469
Robespierre, Maximilien, xii, 231
Robinson, Charles, 276, 290, 295

Robinson, William S., 276
Robison, John, 12, 13, 457, 474
Rock Island, 352
Rockefeller, David, xxxiv
Rockefeller, John D., 166, 402, 470
Rockefeller Foundation, 271
Rockwell, Norman, 152, 350
Roebuck, 442
Roehm, Ernst, 54
Roger, xiv, 72, 330, 356, 464
Roger Williams Bank, 330
Rome, xxiv, xl, 33, 51, 54, 136, 193, 239, 320, 359, 383, 385, 386, 428
Romney, George, 254
Roosevelt, Franklin Delano, 1, 330, 331, 402
Roosevelt, Theodore, 28, 137, 401, 402, 404
Rothschild, Salomon Mayer von, 43
Round Hill School, 46, 47, 52
Round Table, 181
Rousseau, Jean-Jacques, 36
Roux, xxviii
Royal Arch Masons, 202, 469
Royal Institute of International Affairs, xv, 181, 216
Ruby, Jack, 388
Rucker, E. G., 352
Ruffin, Edmund, 281
Ruge, Arnold, 136
Rush, Dr. Benjamin, 87, 187
Rush, Richard, 134, 159
Russell, Jonathan, 112
Russell, Lord, 326
Russell, William, 26, 198, 287, 288, 291, 424
Russia, xxiv, xxvi, xxix, 21, 34, 50, 54, 59, 65, 78, 80, 81, 96, 104, 111, 119, 120, 132, 138, 173, 179, 182, 183, 185, 213, 232, 294, 307, 341, 346, 350, 366, 371, 384, 400, 401, 413, 416, 421, 429, 453, 458
Rychman, Lewis, 221
Sage, Henry W., 203
Saint-Just, Antoine, 56, 61
Salomon, Edward S., 346
San Francisco Committee of Vigilance, 366
Sanborn, Frank B., 276
Sanders, George, 133, 136, 140, 186, 216, 217, 219, 221, 229-231, 237, 247, 280, 288, 323, 332, 339, 379, 380, 386, 416, 464, 476
Sandinistas, 224
Santo Domingo, 136, 395
Sargent, John T., 408, 476
Satanism, 32, 124, 408
Santa Anna, 228
Saturday Club, 47, 48, 151, 259, 466
The Saturday Evening Post, 152, 349
Scaliger, Charles, 53
Schaff, Philip, 29
Schiff, Jacob, 413

Schleiermacher, Friedrich, 49, 197
Schuster, Theodor, 164
Schuyler, Eugene, 416
Scott, Gen., 351, 361
Scott, Orange, 266
Scottish Rite Masonry, 140
Scroll and Key, 28, 89, 402, 403
Secret Committee of United Friends, 18
Secular Student Alliance, 409
Sedition Acts, 31, 79, 80, 82, 83, 85, 88, 112, 195, 241, 309
Seeger, Pete, 296
Seiler, Sebastian, 170
Senate Foreign Relations Committee, 192, 211, 234, 258, 395
Seward, William H., 211, 212, 228, 242, 243, 287, 302
Seymour, Horatio, 358
Sharp's-rifle Christians, 294
Shay's Rebellion, 337
Sheridan, Gen., 173, 244, 328
Sherman, John, 396
Sherman, William Tecumseh, 167, 305
Shields, James, 203
Show, Judy, xi
Sickles, Daniel E., 136, 221, 230, 389
Siegburg, 347
Sigel, Franz, 135, 242
Single Tax Movement, 199
Skidmore, Thomas, 186, 202, 218, 221, 308
Skull and Bones, 26-28, 50, 89, 170, 228, 242, 255, 271, 288, 291, 321, 402, 422, 467
Slidell, John, 227, 327, 432
Smith, Caleb B., 243
Smith, Gerrit, xxxi, 190, 218, 221, 234, 274, 287, 293, 294, 296, 297, 303, 347, 386, 404, 412, 418
Smith, Timothy L., 232
Smith College 208
Smithsonian, 18, 27, 157-160, 234, 351, 440, 476, 478
Smithsonian Committee, 159
Social Circle, 36
Social Democrats, 121, 122
Social Reform Association, 149, 164, 233
Socialism, in passim
Socialist Gymnastic Union, 245
Socialist Labor Party, 144, 168, 200
Socialist Party, xxiv, 27, 28, 78, 81, 121, 144, 156, 168, 189, 200, 241, 252, 265, 267, 297, 322, 406, 435
Socialist Turnverein, 344
Socialist Workers, 78, 265, 371
Society of Cincinnatus, 67
Society of Ethical Culture, 409
Society of Free Men, 238
Society of Friends, 24, 62, 84, 187, 272
Society of the Friends of Truth, 24, 84
Sons of Liberty, 289

Sorge, Friedrich Adolph, 144, 398
Sorge Spy Ring, 400
Sotheran, Charles, 76, 236, 346, 470
Soulé, Pierre, 135, 226, 228, 230, 284, 471
South Africa, xxvii, 136, 257, 267
Southern Bivouac, 282
Southern Confederate Congress, 361
Southern Constitutional Convention, 338
Southern Emigration Society, 231
Southern Peace Conference, 314
Southern Rights Clubs, 284
Southern Secret Service, 382
The Southern Times, 261, 354
Spartan Band, 220
Spear, John Murray, 144, 397, 475
Speed, Joshua, 296
Spencer, Herbert, 303
Spencer, J. A., 97, 469
Spittler, Ludwig Timotheus, xxxiv, 205
Spooner, Lysander, 144, 296
Spooner, Thomas, 238
Sprague, Sen. Peleg, 115
Sprigg, Gov. Samuel, 222
Spring, xxx, 245, 275, 326, 348, 354, 415, 465
Springfield, 17, 248, 272, 296, 305, 318, 324, 377, 397, 465, 469, 475
Springfield Library Association, 296
Springfield Republican, 272, 305
SS, xxix, 204, 391
The St. Louis Democrat, 287, 294
St. Tammany, 183, 229
Stalinist, 371
Stallo, John Bernhard, 167
Standard Oil, 166
Stanton, Darwin, 202
Stanton, Edwin, xxxiii, 165, 169, 192, 276, 350
Stanton, Elizabeth, 144, 197, 198, 404, 418
Stanton, Henry B., 188
The Star, 20, 56, 190, 219, 225, 227, 230, 237, 284, 307, 313
Star Chamber, 307
The Star Spangled Banner, 230, 237
Starr, W., 241
State Sovereignty, 50, 71, 75, 84-86, 102, 114, 176, 252, 309, 312, 317, 333, 360, 392, 421, 429, 460, 461
States Rights Resolutions, 84, 102, 106
Statue of Liberty, 403, 406
Stearns, George L., 276, 295
Stein, Ben, 158
Stephen, xiv, 115, 116, 132, 133, 135, 140, 144, 190, 221, 231, 244, 246, 274, 275, 303, 395, 465, 467, 471, 477
Stephens, Alexander H., 281
Stephens, James, 229
Stephens, Uriah S., 412
Stevens, Aaron Dwight, 300
Stevens, Ambrose, 380

INDEX

Stevens, John Austin, 71, 72, 463
Stevens, Thaddeus, 160, 172, 173, 211, 242, 477
Stille, Charles Janeway, 406
Stockton, John Potter, 172
Stone, Charles, 357
Stone, Lucy, 404
Stone, William M., 243
Stowe, Harriet Beecher, 291, 355, 468
Strauss, David Friederich, 197
Strong, Caleb, 309
Sturge, Joseph, 268, 272
Subterranean, 220, 345
Suffrage, 160, 177, 178, 184, 220, 236, 259, 261, 268, 294, 389, 398, 402, 407, 418, 420, 424, 473
Suffrage Association, 220, 294, 398, 407, 418
Sullivan, John L., 230
Sumner, William Graham, 113, 464
Sumner, Charles, 28, 47, 49, 151, 153, 192, 211, 234, 238, 244, 274, 287, 300, 302, 350, 409, 410, 471
Sumter, xxii, xxiv, 248, 300, 304, 312-314, 317, 357, 474
Supreme Star Spangled Banner, 237
Surratt, Anna, 376
Surratt, John, 328, 380, 384
Surratt, Mary E., 376
Sutherland, La Roy, 266
Swartwout, Samuel, 101, 185
Swedenborg, Emanuel, 199
Swedenborgian, xxxiii, 16, 17, 199, 202, 226
Sylvis, William, 411, 412
Taft, Alphonso, 26, 27, 156, 242, 321, 354, 410, 413, 416
Taft, William Howard, 27, 271, 471
Talleyrand, 6
Tallmadge, 203
Tammany, 37, 135, 136, 144, 150, 183-186, 220-222, 225, 229, 314, 402, 412, 477
Tappan, David, 92
Tappan, Lewis, 190, 275
Taussig, James, 349
Taylor, Stewart, 300
Taylor, Zachary, 229
Temperance, xii, 209, 262, 293, 407, 418-421, 424
Templar, 46, 379
The Temple of Reason, 249
Temple School, 199
Ten Commandments, xxvi, 58
Texas Medical Association, 283
Thacher, Thomas Anthony, 44
Thayer, Eli, 295, 469, 473
The New American, xxix, 50, 54, 59, 119, 137, 191, 208, 225, 237, 238, 244, 288, 307, 310, 351, 370, 383, 384, 409, 417, 450, 451, 457, 460, 463, 466-468, 470, 473, 475

The Patriot, xvi, 69, 80, 122, 181, 183, 215, 283, 341, 384, 473, 476
Theistical Society, 202, 249
Theodor, Karl, 8
Theodore D. Weld, 304
Theological Dictionary, 6, 477
Theophilanthropy, 32
Theosophical Society, 31, 203, 409, 417
Thomas, Norman, 121
Thompson, George, 187, 188, 268, 303, 304
Thompson, Jacob, 186, 365
Thompson, Leander, 400
Thompson, William A., 37
Thoreau, Henry D., 38, 218
Thousand Year Reich, 341
Thuggees, 128
Thule Society, 41
Ticknor, George, 46, 47, 279
Tilden, Samuel, 219, 412
Tilton, Theodore, 226, 314
Tocqueville, Alexis de, xxx, 141, 209, 466
Todd, J., 294
Toombs, Robert, 281, 312, 327, 338
Totenbund, 26, 341
Toward a Soviet America, 21, 477
Tower of Babel, 19, 35, 44
Trade Center, 383
Trafalgar, 95, 180
Treaty of Ghent, 111, 112
Trent Affair, 319, 320
Trilateral Commission, 21
Triumph of Reason, 202
Trotsky, Leon, 8, 126, 370, 473
Trotskyite, 216, 254
True Faith, xxviii, 131, 284
Truman, Harry, 211, 391
Trumbull, Lyman, 236
Tugendbund, 49, 340, 341, 343
Turners, 27, 170, 245, 251, 284, 340-345, 436
Tuscaloosa, xxiv
Twain, Mark, ix, xxiii, 300, 409
Tweedy, Edward, 143, 235
U-Boats, 325
U. S. Bank, 69, 70, 89, 102, 107, 112, 115, 116, 159, 212, 329, 330, 350, 422
U. S. Bureau of Education, 437
U. S. Communist Party, xxxv, 21, 128, 145, 198, 288
U. S. Constitutional Convention, 102
U. S. Geological Survey, 155, 159
U. S. National Museum, 159
U. S. Sanitary Commission, 47, 49, 159, 405
Underground Railroad, 190, 199, 250, 352, 475
Union League, 37, 47, 50, 135, 201, 220, 271, 322, 401-405, 410, 465, 469
Union Reform League, 220
Union Theological Seminary, 29, 373
Unitarians, 121, 204, 408

United Ancient Order of Druids, 206
The United Friends, 31
United Irishmen, 229, 268
The United States Magazine, 10
Universal Brotherhood, 3, 70, 203, 209, 409
Universal Community of Society of Rational Religionists, 155
Universal Confederation of the Friends of Truth, 24, 34
Universal Peace Society, 209, 428
Universal Peace Union, 209, 269, 428, 474
Universal Reform, 202, 272
Universal Republic of United Mankind, 136
University of Berlin, 26, 340, 350
University of California, 27, 439, 465
University of Göttingen, xxxiv, 47, 52
University of Ingolstadt, 18, 91
University of South Carolina, 195, 466, 471
University of Virginia, 195, 470
University of Wisconsin, 346, 348, 439, 471, 478
Universology, 190
Vale, Gilbert, 220, 397
Vallandigham, Clement L., 166, 289, 463, 471
Van Buren, Martin, 49
Vance, Zebulon, 281, 338, 390
Van Ness, William, 183
Vanderbilt, Cornelius, xxxi, 201, 223, 226, 234, 296, 386, 406
Vatican Zouave, 328
Veda, 197
Venceremos Brigade, 232
Vendee, 25
Vergennes, 127
Vigilance Committee, 241, 366
Villard, Henry, 48, 240, 413
Villard, Oswald Garrison, 413, 470
Volney, 84
von Baader, 31
von Fellenberg, Philip Emanuel, 46
von Ickstatt, Johann Adam Baron, 18
von Weber, Max, 135
Wade, Benjamin, 172, 211, 236, 258, 357, 372, 395
Waite, Morrison R., 395
Waite, William S., 218, 221
Waldorf Towers, xxxv, 400
Walker, Isaac P., 218, 221
Walker, Robert John, 332
Walker, William, 136, 221, 223, 231, 467
Walsh, Mike, 220, 345
Warren, Dr. J. C., 150
Warren, Josiah, 144, 190, 299
Washington, George, xv, xvi, xx, 19, 61, 64-66, 68, 70, 85, 92, 93, 97, 98, 102, 114, 139, 140, 223, 373, 408, 415, 425, 447, 468, 474
Washington, Martha, 408
Washington National Era, 287, 297

491

Washington Peace Conference, 311, 314, 473
Wasson, David, 408
Watson, John, 385, 405
Watson, Peter H., 166
Watson, Samuel, 408
Wayland, Francis, 270
Webb, Thomas Smith, 202
Webster, Daniel, 177, 274
Webster, Nesta, 42, 468, 476, 478
Webster, Noah, 69, 471, 473
Webster, Timothy, 250
Weed, Thurlow, 211, 212, 242, 243
Wehrmacht, 167, 341, 346
Weishaupt, Adam, xxxii, 10, 13, 35, 52, 54, 69, 91, 126
Weiss, John, 408
Weitling, Wilhelm (William), 164
Welch, Robert, 76, 146, 232, 254, 449, 454, 457
Weld, Angelina Grimke, 404
Weld, Theodore D., 304
Weller, John, 225
Wells, Gideon, 375
Westliche Post, 346, 349
Wetmore, William, 198
Weydemeyer, Joseph, 141, 167, 345, 351
Wheeling, 136
Whig Party, 102, 140, 161, 211, 222, 237, 243, 245
Whiskey Rebellion, 62-64, 67, 69, 70, 72, 91, 95, 97, 102, 478
White, Andrew Dickson, 26, 50, 51, 258
White, Horace, 239
Whitman, E. B., 294
Whitman, Walt, 47, 48, 122, 132, 142, 197, 198, 203, 218, 221, 350, 409
Whitney, 47, 49, 331, 373, 405
Whittier, John Greenleaf, 48, 198
Wide Awakes, 249-251, 276, 397
Wildey, Thomas, 206
Wilkes, John, 140, 175, 296, 353, 361, 377-379, 476-478
Wilkinson, James, 90, 97, 104
Willey, Waitman T., 172
Williams, David, 32
Williams, T. Harry, 355, 471
Williamson, Isaac H., 222
Willich, August, 167, 346
Willis, 203, 467
Wilson, Henry, 276, 287, 294, 302, 403, 421, 469
Wilson, Woodrow, xxxv, 473, 478
Windt, John, 218, 221
Winston, 2, 56, 271, 403, 440, 466, 474, 476
Winthrop, Robert C., 223
Wirt, William, 159, 211
Wobblies, 436
Woerner, J. Gabriel, 299
Wolf's Head, 28, 171

Wood, Fernando, 186, 365, 386
Wood, John, 202, 468
Wood, S. H., 294
Woodhull, Victoria, xxxi, 144, 201, 226, 234, 288, 398, 407, 418, 422, 473
Woodruff, Jacob, 240
The Word, xi, xxii, 29, 35, 44, 66, 73, 84, 113, 118, 125, 132, 144, 145, 155, 156, 171, 174, 176, 184, 200, 216, 220, 240, 279, 286, 292, 313, 316, 322, 333, 336, 342, 364, 370, 386, 390, 416, 418, 449, 459
Workingman's Advocate, 150, 220, 411
World Affairs, 208, 463
World Anti-Slavery Convention, 267, 272, 275
World Bank, 54, 417
World Congress of Phalanxes, 37
World Court, 49, 132, 192, 208, 326, 423
World Court of Justice, 132
World War I, xxiv, 55, 80, 81, 109, 119, 120, 129, 175, 181, 183, 253, 270, 271, 391, 398, 401, 414, 429
World War II, xxxv, xxxviii, xl, 4, 17, 34, 41, 80, 81, 93, 99, 137, 138, 145, 167, 178, 181, 183, 204, 271, 334, 336, 346, 354, 375, 383, 391, 398, 400, 414, 416, 426, 427, 429, 449, 455, 457
A World Without Jews, 342, 478
Wren, John V., 284
Wright, Edward H., 380
Wright, Elizur, 191, 276, 409
Wright, Fanny, 127, 186, 200, 222
Wright, Henry C., 269, 272
Wright, Martha Coffin, 404
Wundt, Karl, 50
Wundt, Wilhelm, 50
YA - Young America, 123, 186, 215
Yale, xxxvii, 26-28, 89, 92, 113, 151, 152, 203, 210, 230, 255, 321, 331, 402, 403, 405, 439, 463, 464, 467, 470, 475-478
Yancey, William Lowndes, 309
Yankee Imperialism, 137
Yates, Joseph C., 222
YMCA, 373
Young, Mr., 378
Young America Pioneer Club, 225
Young America, 10, 37, 114, 123, 129, 132, 133, 136, 141, 149, 150, 168, 174, 186, 191, 215-218, 220, 221, 223, 225-227, 229, 233, 236, 240, 242, 246, 247, 251, 252, 281, 287, 288, 366, 414, 422, 424, 425, 439, 455, 463, 470, 478, 479
Young England, xxvi
Young Europe, 123, 127, 129, 203, 217, 228, 287, 323
Young Germany, 129
Young, Horace G., 378
Young Ireland, 129, 229, 268, 440
Young Italy, 126, 129, 304

Young Poland, 130
Young Turks, 129
Zwack, 31
Zawahiri, xxvi, 80
Zion's Watchman, 266
Zionism, 2, 342
Zouaves, 248